Lecture Notes in Computer Science   7319

Commenced Publication in 1973
Founding and Former Series Editors:
Gerhard Goos, Juris Hartmanis, and Jan van Leeuwen

Judy Kay   Paul Lukowicz   Hideyuki Tokuda
Patrick Olivier   Antonio Krüger (Eds.)

Pervasive Computing

10th International Conference, Pervasive 2012
Newcastle, UK, June 18-22, 2012
Proceedings

 Springer

Volume Editors

Judy Kay
University of Sydney, NSW, Australia
E-mail: judy.kay@sydney.edu.au

Paul Lukowicz
DFKI GmbH, Kaiserslautern, Germany
E-mail: paul.lukowicz@uni-passau.de

Hideyuki Tokuda
Keio University, Fujisawa, Kanagawa, Japan
E-mail: hxt@sfc.keio.ac.jp

Patrick Olivier
Newcastle University, UK
E-mail: patrick.olivier@newcastle.ac.uk

Antonio Krüger
DFKI GmbH, Saarbrücken, Germany
E-mail: krueger@dfki.de

ISSN 0302-9743   e-ISSN 1611-3349
ISBN 978-3-642-31204-5   e-ISBN 978-3-642-31205-2
DOI 10.1007/978-3-642-31205-2
Springer Heidelberg Dordrecht London New York

Library of Congress Control Number: 2012939512

CR Subject Classification (1998): C.2, I.6.3, K.4.1, K.4.2, J.2, J.3

LNCS Sublibrary: SL 3 – Information Systems and Application, incl. Internet/Web and HCI

Typesetting: Camera-ready by author, data conversion by Scientific Publishing Services, Chennai, India

Printed on acid-free paper

Springer is part of Springer Science+Business Media (www.springer.com)

Preface

Welcome to the proceedings of the 10th International Conference on Pervasive Computing (Pervasive 2012) held in Newcastle, UK. Before coming to Newcastle, the conference made a long journey around the globe: starting in Europe (Zurich, Linz, Munich, Dublin), traveling to Canada (Toronto), Australia (Sydney), Japan (Nara), Finland (Helsinki), followed by the USA (San Francisco) last year. This annual conference is the premier forum for researchers to present their latest results in all areas related to the architecture, design, implementation, application and evaluation of pervasive computing. Pervasive 2012 included a highly selective program for technical papers, accompanied by late-breaking result posters, videos, demonstrations, workshops, a doctoral colloquium and other events.

We received a total of 138 high-quality submissions, from which we accepted 28 papers (a healthy 20% acceptance rate). This year we chose to accept both full papers (up to 18 pages) and shorter "notes" (up to 8 pages). We are pleased to say we received 110 full papers and 28 notes, accepting 25 (25%) and 3 (11%), respectively. Pervasive is a truly international and interdisciplinary conference attracting work from over 500 individual authors from over 28 countries, and from a wide rage of disciplines, academic and industrial organizations.

A rigorous and comprehensive process for selecting papers was undertaken by 34 Program Committee members, from the most prestigious universities and research labs in Europe, North America and Asia/Oceania. The committee was supported by 354 external reviewers chosen by the committee on the basis of their domain knowledge and relevance to pervasive computing. We ran a three-phase double-blind process and all papers were reviewed by two Program Committee members and two or more eternal reviewers. This resulted in 628 total reviews. We had 4.5 reviews per paper on average, no less than four and as many as nine. All papers were discussed electronically prior to the Program Committee meeting.

The Program Committee meeting was held at a conference room of the Palo Alto Research Center Inc. in Palo Alto, USA. Over one and half days we discussed 76 papers selected on the basis of review score, controversy, or at the request of any Program Committee member. Additional readers were solicited during the meeting to assist with the most controversial cases. We thank PARC, in particular Kurt Partridge, for their generous support and assistance in hosting the TPC meeting.

This event would not be possible without the help of many people: Workshop Chairs Fahim Kawsar and Thomas Ploetz, Video Chairs Michael Schmitz and Jin Nakazawa, Demo Chairs Andreas Bulling and Daniel Jackson, Poster

Chairs Shinichi Konomi and Paul Dunphy, Doctoral Consortium Chairs Elaine
M. Huang and Aaron Quigley, Media Chairs Nick Taylor and Alexander De Luca,
Production Chair Tom Bartindale, the Media and Production Chairs worked
John Shearer and Stephen Lindsay.

Finally, we would like to thank all of the authors who submitted their papers
to the conference, and the conference participants who took part in active discussions. We are grateful for the efforts of the Program Committee members in
reviewing papers, and the Steering Committee of Pervasive for their guidance in
making Pervasive successful. The Media and Production Chairs worked hard to
coordinate the conference. We thank all of them for their tremendous efforts to
make Pervasive 2012 successful.

June 2012   Judy Kay
                                                        Paul Lukowicz
                                                         Hide Tokuda
                                                       Patrick Olivier
                                                      Antonio Krüger

Organization

Conference Committee

General Chairs

Patrick Olivier   Newcastle University, UK
Antonio Krüger   DFKI/Saarland University, Germany

Program Chairs

Judy Kay   University of Sydney, Australia
Paul Lukowicz   University of Passau, Germany
Hide Tokuda   Keio University, Japan

Workshops

Fahim Kawsar   Bell Labs, Belgium
Thomas Ploetz   Newcastle University, UK

Videos

Michael Schmitz   DFKI/Saarland University, Germany
Jin Nakazawa   Keio University, Japan

Demos

Andreas Bulling   University of Cambridge/ Lancaster University, UK
Daniel Jackson   Newcastle University, UK

Posters

Shin'ichi Konomi   University of Tokyo, Japan
Paul Dunphy   Newcastle University, UK

Doctoral Consortium

Elaine M. Huang   University of Zurich, Switzerland
Aaron Quigley   University of St. Andrews, UK

Media

Nick Taylor   Newcastle University, UK
Alexander De Luca   University of Munich, Germany

Production

Tom Bartindale   Newcastle University, UK

Social

John Shearer	Newcastle University, UK
Stephen Lindsay	Newcastle University, UK

Program Committee

Gregory Abowd	Georgia Institute of Technology, USA
Daniel Avrahami	Intel Labs Seattle, USA
Tico Ballagas	Nokia Research Center, USA
Frank Bentley	Motorola Mobility, USA
Andreas Bulling	University of Cambridge/Lancaster University, UK
Hao-Hua Chu	National Taiwan University, Taiwan
Naranker Dulay	Imperial College London, UK
Silvia Giordano	SUPSI, Switzerland
Jens Grossklags	Pennsylvania State University, USA
Mike Hazas	Lancaster University, UK
Jesse Hoey	University of Waterloo, Canada
Elaine M. Huang	University of Zurich, Switzerland
Judy Kay	University of Sydney, Australia
Minkyong Kim	IBM T.J. Watson Research Center, USA
Shin'ichi Konomi	University of Tokyo, Japan
Gerd Kortuem	The Open University, UK
John Krumm	Microsoft Research, USA
Nic Lane	Microsoft Research, USA
Kuhn Lukas	Qualcomm, USA
Paul Lukowicz	University of Passau/DFKI Kaiserslautern, Germany
Lena Mamykina	Columbia University, USA
Tom Martin	Virginia Tech, USA
Florian Michahelles	ETH Zurich, Switzerland
Mirco Musolesi	University of Birmingham, UK
Jin Nakazawa	Keio University, Japan
Nobuhiko Nishio	Ritsumeikan University, Japan
Bashar Nuseibeh	Lero/The Open University, UK
Kurt Partridge	PARC, USA
Shwetak Patel	University of Washington, USA
Trevor Pering	Intel, USA
Daniela Rosner	UC Berkeley, USA
Chris Schmandt	MIT, USA
Ichiro Siio	Ochanomizu University, Japan
Hide Tokuda	Keio University, Japan

Steering Committee

James Landay	University of Washington, USA
Xing Xie	Microsoft Research, China
Jeffrey Hightower	Google, USA
Elaine M. Huang	University of Zurich, Switzerland
Jakob Bardram	IT University of Copenhagen, Denmark
Marc Langheinrich	Università della Svizzera Italiana, Switzerland
Patrik Floreen	Helsinki Institute for Information Technology, Finland
Antonio Krüger	Saarland University, Germany
Sunny Consolvo	Amazon, USA
Hans Gellersen	Lancaster University, UK
A.J. Brush	Microsoft Research, USA
Hide Tokuda	Keio University, Japan
Joe McCarthy	University of Washington, USA
James Scott	Microsoft Research, UK
Adrian Friday	Lancaster University, UK
Aaron Quigley	University of St. Andrews, UK
Gregory Abowd	Georgia Tech, USA
Thomas Strang	University of Innsbruck/German Aerospace Center, Germany
Anthony LaMarca	Intel, USA
Khai Truong	University of Toronto, Canada

Reviewers

Nova Ahmed	A.J. Brush	Anthony Collins
Florian Alt	Martin Brynskov	Scott Counts
Glen Anderson	Leah Buechley	Henriette Cramer
Ismail Arai	Ingrid Burbey	Piergiorgio Cremonese
Yutaka Arakawa	Dan Chalmers	Fabiano Dalpiaz
Rosa Arriaga	Keng-hao Chang	Sheep Dalton
Matthias Baldauf	David Chen	Mathieu D'aquin
Arosha Bandara	Nicholas Chen	Scott Davidoff
Vladimir Barash	Yihua Chen	Alexander De Luca
Jakob Bardram	Yu-han Chen	Yves-Alexandre De
Christian Beckel	Marshini Chetty	Montjoye
Alastair Beresford	Sonia Chiasson	Rogério De Paula
James Biagioni	Alvin Chin	Marco de Sa
Igor Bilogrevic	Eun Kyoung Choe	Graham Dean
Jon Bird	Tanzeem Choudhury	Anind Dey
Staffan Björk	David Chu	Li Ding
Ulf Blanke	Gabe Cohn	Changyu Dong
Frank Bridges	Andrea Colaco	Steven Dow

Serge Egelman
Jesus Favela
Martin Flintham
Stefan Föll
Anna Förster
Adrian Friday
Jon Froehlich
Kaori Fujinami
Dario Gallucci
Raghu Ganti
Daniel Gatica-Perez
Fosca Giannotti
Nan-Wei Gong
Matthew Goodwin
Paul Grace
Keith Green
Ben Greenstein
Tovi Grossman
Marco Gruteser
Marek Grzes
Sidhant Gupta
Nils Hammerla
John Hansen
Bjoern Hartmann
William Hazlewood
Jennifer Healey
Ted Herman
Klaus Herrmann
Jeffrey Hightower
Baik Hoh
Juan Pablo Hourcade
Gary Hsieh
Shamsi Iqbal
Masaki Ito
Daisuke Iwai
Giulio Jacucci
Xiaofan Jiang
Mark Jones
Mikkel Baun Kærgaard
Yasuaki Kakehi
Michelle Karg
Stephan Karpischek
Fahim Kawsar
Jofish Kaye
Konstantinos Kazakos

Matthew Keally
Julie Kientz
Donnie Kim
Songkuk Kim
Yongdae Kim
Younghun Kim
Matthias Kirchner
Ben Kirman
Vassilis Kostakos
Christian Kray
Shonali Krishnaswamy
Tsvi Kuflik
Bob Kummerfeld
Kai Kunze
Brano Kveton
Ted Tsung-Te Lai
Anthony LaMarca
Marc Langheinrich
Eric Larson
Lucian Leahu
Jinwon Lee
Ilias Leontiadis
Jonathan Lester
Bill Lewis
Ming M. Li
Robert Likamwa
Janne Lindqvist
Per Ljung
Claire Loock
Hong Lu
Mika Luimula
Paul Lukowicz
Emil Lupu
Qin Lv
Kent Lyons
Takuya Maekawa
Apostolos Malatras
Marco Mamei
Clara Mancini
Stefan Mandl
Winter Mason
Joe McCarthy
Scott McCrickard
David McDonald
Stephen Mckenna

Yevgeniy Medynskiy
Emiliano Miluzzo
Kazuhiro Minami
Takashi Miyaki
Iqbal Mohomed
Ed Morris
Leonardo Mostarda
Haris Mouratidis
Jörg Müller
Mor Naaman
Shishir Nagaraja
Tatsuo Nakajima
Yasuto Nakanishi
Vidya Narayanan
David Nguyen
Haruo Noma
Petteri Nurmi
Lora Oehlberg
Takeshi Okadome
Eamonn O'Neill
Kazushige Ouchi
Wei Pan
Michela Papandrea
Joseph Paradiso
Andrea Parker
Nirmal Patel
Fabio Paternò
Sameer Patil
Don Patterson
Eric Paulos
Matthai Philipose
Santi Phithakkitnukoon
Fabio Pianese
James Pierce
Irena Pletikosa Cvijikj
Thomas Ploetz
Pascal Poupart
Blaine Price
Bob Price
Alessandro Puiatti
Daniele Quercia
Mashfiqui Rabbi
Carlos Ramos
Andrew Rice
Jukka Riekki

Daniel Romero
Mario Romero
Barbara Rosario
Shankar Sadasivam
Alireza Sahami
Alanson Sample
Tomas Sanchez Lopez
Anthony Sarah
Anne Kathrin Schaar
Bernt Schiele
Albrecht Schmidt
Eve Schooler
James Scott
Peter Scupelli
David A. Shamma
Daniel Siewiorek
Morris Sloman
Caleb Southern

Chris Speed
John Stankovic
Martin Strohbach
Yasuyuki Sumi
Babak Taati
Leila Takayama
Bruce Thomas
Keerthi Thomas
Edison Thomaz
Hong-Linh Truong
Khai Truong
Joe Tullio
Janet van der Linden
Tim van Kasteren
Kristof Van Laerhoven
Salvatore Vanini
Jo Vermeulen
Ian Wakeman

Mark Weal
Jules White
Kamin Whitehouse
Lauren Wilcox
Amanda Williams
Jacob Wobbrock
Allison Woodruff
Nicole Yankelovich
Svetlana Yarosh
Takuro Yonezawa
Chuang-wen You
Chen Yu
Tae-jung Yun
Bin Zan
Pei Zhang
Meiyuan Zhao
Yu Zheng

Sponsors

Microsoft Research
Nokia
Culture Lab

Intel
Qualcomm
Computing Community Consortium

Table of Contents

HCI

Development Tools and Devices

Indoor Location and Positioning

Social Computing and Games

Privacy

Public Displays and Services

Personalized Driving Behavior Monitoring and Analysis for Emerging Hybrid Vehicles

Kun Li[1], Man Lu[1], Fenglong Lu[1],
Qin Lv[2], Li Shang[1], and Dragan Maksimovic[1]

[1] Department of Electrical, Computer, and Energy Engineering
[2] Department of Computer Science
University of Colorado Boulder, CO 80309 USA
{kun.li,man.lu,fenglong.lu,qin.lv,li.shang,maksimov}@colorado.edu

Abstract. Emerging electric-drive vehicles, such as hybrid electric vehicles (HEVs) and plug-in HEVs (PHEVs), hold the potential for substantial reduction of fuel consumption and greenhouse gas emissions.
User driving behavior, which varies from person to person, can significantly affect (P)HEV operation and the corresponding energy and environmental impacts. Although some studies exist that investigate vehicle
performance under different driving behaviors, either directed by vehicle
manufacturers or via on-board diagnostic (OBD) devices, they are typically vehicle-specific and require extra device/effort. Moreover, there is
no or very limited feedback to an individual driver regarding how his/her
personalized driving behavior affects (P)HEV performance.
    This paper presents a personalized driving behavior monitoring and
analysis system for emerging hybrid vehicles. Our design is *fully automated and non-intrusive*. We propose *phone-based multi-modality sensing* that captures precise driver–vehicle information through de-noise,
calibration, synchronization, and disorientation compensation. We also
provide *quantitative driver-specific (P)HEV analysis* through operation
mode classification, energy use and fuel use modeling. The proposed
system has been deployed and evaluated with real-world user studies.
System evaluation demonstrates highly-accurate (0.88-0.996 correlation
and low error) driving behavior sensing, mode classification, energy use
and fuel use modeling.

1   Introduction

Energy use for transportation represents a pressing challenge, due to the heavy
and growing reliance on petroleum and the environmental impacts of emissions from fossil fuel combustion. Recent studies have shown that *transportation
electrification*, such as (P)HEVs, holds the potential to significantly reduce greenhouse gas emissions and the ever-growing dependence on oil [22]. (P)HEVs integrate an internal combustion engine (ICE) powered by gasoline with an electric
motor powered by the battery system. Active market penetration of HEVs, such
as Toyota Prius and Ford Escape, has been observed in recent years. Automobile

J. Kay et al. (Eds.): Pervasive 2012, LNCS 7319, pp. 1–19, 2012.

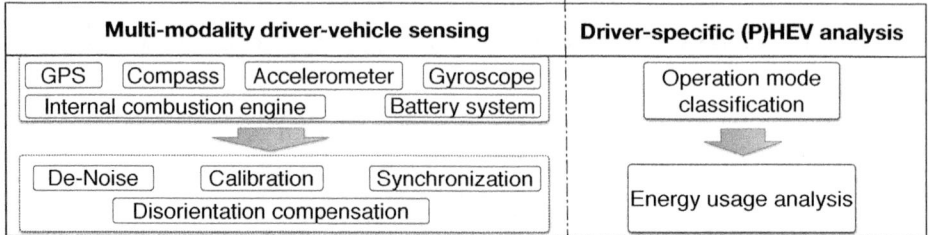

Multi-modality driver-vehicle sensing	Driver-specific (P)HEV analysis
GPS Compass Accelerometer Gyroscope Internal combustion engine Battery system	Operation mode classification
De-Noise Calibration Synchronization Disorientation compensation	Energy usage analysis

Fig. 1. Personalized driving behavior monitoring and analysis for emerging (P)HEVs

manufacturers are poised to introduce new models of PHEVs and their market penetration is expected to increase rapidly in the coming years.

Advancing (P)HEV technology and promoting its market adoption require *comprehensive and quantitative investigations of how user-specific driving behavior affects run-time (P)HEV operation, which in turn determines the energy and environmental impacts of (P)HEVs*. To date, little is known regarding the relationships between user-specific driving behavior and (P)HEV performance. Previous studies on vehicle fuel economy and emissions were typically tested or modeled over a limited number of driving cycles designed to represent "typical" driving profiles [3]. These standard cycles ignore the diverse driving behaviors among users, which strongly influence vehicle fuel consumption and emissions [17]. Furthermore, previous studies have focused on conventional gasoline vehicles, which work very differently than emerging (P)HEVs [7].

Automobile manufacturers have recently started to consider user-specific driving behavior. Toyota, for example, conducted a "world's first large scale" user study with around 100 PHEVs in September 2007, which aimed to understand how the new technology performs under real-world user driving behaviors [2]. While such manufacturer conducted user studies can be well organized and detailed data can be easily collected, they are limited in that: (1) Little feedback is provided to individual drivers, even with dashboard display. MPG (miles per gallon) alone can be misleading for (P)HEVs. It is not clear how specific driving behavior translates to (P)HEV energy and environmental impacts. (2) Building personalized analysis software directly into the vehicles would require support and adoption by automobile manufacturers, and such systems would be vehicle-specific and significantly limited in ubiquity.

Feedback of vehicle performance is also possible through the on-board diagnostic (OBD-II) interface. Still, the format of vehicular sensor readings differ by manufacturer and vehicle, and the readings do not translate directly to (P)HEV energy and environmental impacts. In addition, this approach requires special hardware like OBD scanner and extra effort from user to connect and pair the device each time, which limit its applicability to the general public.

In this work, our goal is to bridge this information gap through *a personalized driving behavior monitoring and analysis system* (Figure 1). The system is designed to be *fully automated and non-intrusive*. It is based on smartphones, which are widely available nowadays. A user only needs to download the phone application and have it running during a trip, and personalized quantitative reports will be generated given his/her specific driving behavior. Such simplicity and functionality make it attractive for most drivers. Even drivers who do not currently own a (P)HEV could use this application to predict the energy and environmental impacts if they switch to (P)HEVs. Moreover, the aggregated data from a large number of drivers can be invaluable for vehicle manufacturers and researchers as they keep improving the design of (P)HEVs.

A number of sensing capabilities are available in modern smartphones, making it possible for personalized driving behavior monitoring and analysis. However, signals obtained from individual sensors suffer from a number of intrinsic and contextual issues: (1) *noise, drift*, and *mis-synchronization* of multi-modality driver–vehicle data; (2) substantial *disorientation* of vehicle movement sensing at the start of and during each driving trip; and (3) complex (P)HEV *operation mechanisms* and driver-dependent vehicle performance.

To address these issues, we propose innovative techniques that "fuse" together multiple types of sensor readings to enhance signal quality and driver–vehicle sensing, as well as techniques that classify driver-specific operation modes and analyze the corresponding energy and environmental impacts. Our work makes the following contributions:

(1) **Multi-modality driver–vehicle sensing.** We propose fully-automated, phone-based sensing techniques that effectively correct the noise, drift, mis-synchronization in multiple types of sensor data, as well as compensating initial/dynamic phone–vehicle disorientation using wavelet-based analysis.

(2) **Driver-specific (P)HEV analysis.** We propose operation mode classification, run-time energy use and fuel–CO_2 emission modeling, to map specific driving behavior to (P)HEV energy and environmental impacts; and

(3) **Real-world deployment and user driving studies.** System evaluation demonstrates high correlation for vehicle sensing (0.88-0.96), energy use and fuel use modeling (0.918, 0.996), operation mode classification (89.9%, 87.8% accuracy).

The rest of the paper is organized as follows. Section 2 presents the problem formulation and design overview. Section 3 and Section 4 describe in detail multi-modality driver-vehicle sensing and driver-specific (P)HEV analysis. Section 5 describes system deployment and user studies. Section 6 evaluates the proposed system. Section 7 discusses related work. Section 8 concludes.

2 Problem Formulation and Design Overview

HEVs and PHEVs are the emerging solutions for transportation electrification. HEVs feature a gasoline internal combustion engine (ICE) and an electric motor equipped with a battery system for harnessing and storing run-time braking energy. PHEVs have an additional electrical plug to directly recharge the battery system from the electrical grid. The energy and environmental impacts of (P)HEVs are primarily determined by (P)HEV operation, which in turn is

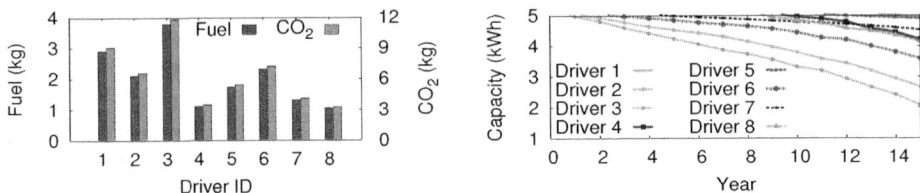

Fig. 2. Heterogeneous fuel use, CO_2 emissions, and battery system long-term capacity degradation based on eight different users' daily commute driving profiles

heavily affected by user-specific run-time driving behavior, such as speed, acceleration, and road condition, etc. Figure 2 shows the fuel use, CO_2 emissions, and battery system long-term capacity degradation based on eight different users' daily commute driving profiles. Among the eight drivers, over $3\times$ variation is observed in terms of fuel use and CO_2 emissions for battery system, and based on the system-level battery model developed by Li et al. [16], over $9\times$ long-term capacity variation can be expected.

A comprehensive and quantitative sensing and analysis system is thus essential for advancing (P)HEV technology and promoting its market adoption by individual drivers. We propose a personalized multi-modality sensing and analysis system that effectively captures and fuses the following signals: (1) **user-specific driving behavior**, including speed, acceleration, road and traffic conditions; and (2) **(P)HEV operation profile**, including fuel use, battery system charge/discharge current and voltage.

Accurate characterization and quantification of the relationships between user-specific driving behavior and (P)HEV energy and environmental impacts require fine-grained, time-stamped, robust sensor readings during users' driving trips, as well as accurate modeling of (P)HEV internal operation mechanisms. We propose a two-staged process, as illustrated in Figure 1.

1. Multi-modality driver–vehicle sensing: The first stage captures and enhances the quality of multiple types of sensor data using novel de-noise, calibration, and synchronization techniques. It then automatically identifies potential phone–vehicle disorientation and compensates the corresponding sensor readings at run-time for accurate vehicle movement sensing.

2. Driver-specific (P)HEV analysis: In the second stage, we propose to first map users' driving behaviors to the corresponding (P)HEV operation modes via an effective mode classifier. Then, leveraging battery system modeling and fuel–CO_2 emission modeling, we quantitatively analyze the energy and environmental impacts of (P)HEVs under specific user driving behavior.

3   Multi-modality Driver–Vehicle Sensing

Using multiple types of sensors that are readily available on mobile phones, we propose techniques to obtain high-quality sensor data for both user driving behavior and vehicle movement. The challenge is to achieve personalized, accurate,

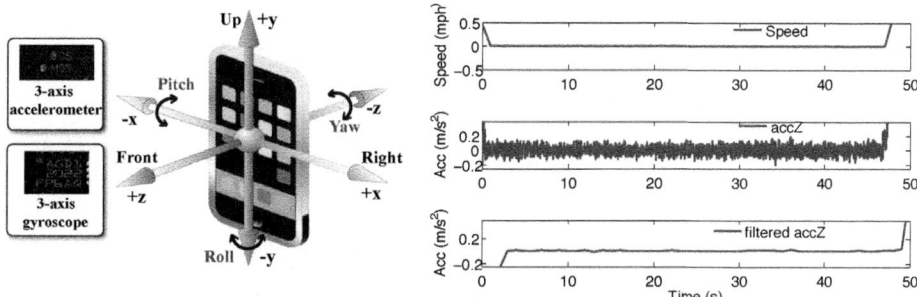

Fig. 3. Linear & angular acceleration sensing using accelerometer and gyroscope

Fig. 4. Acceleration noise when vehicle is stationary; de-noise via low-pass filtering

and run-time data acquisition with minimum inconvenience and obstruction to individual drivers. Specifically, we allow the phone to be unrestricted in the vehicle (i.e., not mounted in a fixed position), yet still effectively identify and remove noises and inconsistencies in multiple types of sensor data, as well as compensating for potential phone-vehicle disorientation.

3.1   User Driving Behavior Sensing

A user's specific driving behavior can be represented by his/her driving trips with regard to speed, acceleration, slope, and turning at individual time points. Specifically, **speed** is directly reported by GPS; **slope** of the road can be calculated from altitude reported by GPS; **acceleration** is reported by accelerometer but requires further compensation by gyroscope; and **vehicle turning** information is derived from gyroscope readings and calibrated by digital compass. As illustrated in Figure 3, accelerometer and gyroscope can be used to sense linear and angular acceleration. By combining the readings of both sensors, detailed information about the device's six-axis movement in space can be derived.

Noise of sensor is a major technical barrier to precise sensing. There are two primary kinds of noise sources. One is *intrinsic* high frequency noise due to the combined effects of thermally dependent electrical and mechanical noise [21]. The other is *contextual* noise caused by vehicle vibration during a trip, whose frequency usually peaks at around 3-5Hz. For example (Figure 4), acceleration readings ranging from -0.2 to $0.2 m/s^2$ are reported even when the vehicle is stationary (speed $= 0$). A low-pass filter with 2Hz cutoff frequency is applied to improve the signal to noise ratio. The noise characteristics of gyroscope are more complex, which we address later in this section.

Another source of error in motion sensing is the *drift* of sensor. In particular, calculating the angular position using gyroscope requires integration of noisy angle change rate readings, which accumulates over time and results in large drift. Such drift can be potentially compensated by periodically resetting the gyroscope to the known directional source: gravity, which is collected whenever

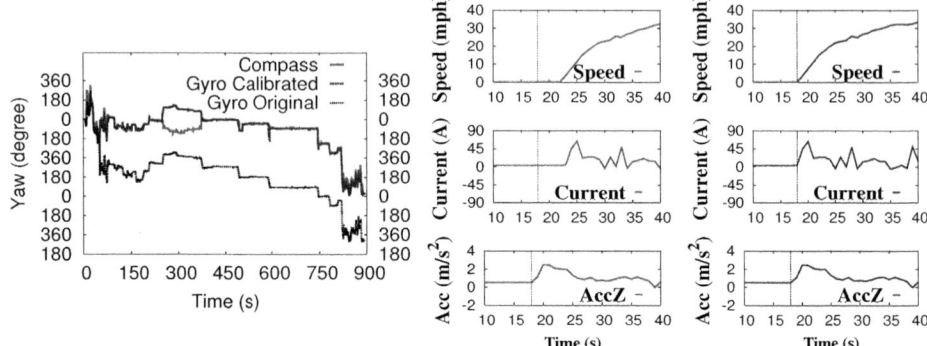

Fig. 5. Degree of drift: Digital compass vs. gyroscope (original and calibrated)

Fig. 6. Unsynchronized (left) vs. synchronized (right) signals

the phone is determined to be stationary, e.g., when the vehicle is stopped for traffic light. The acceleration vector of gravity is parallel to the Yaw-axis of the reference coordinate system, which requires special calibration with the digital compass. Figure 5 shows an experiment in which the phone was returned to the original position after 14 minutes of driving. We can see that digital compass has much less drift than gyroscope. In our system, the gyroscope value is calibrated whenever the compass reading is steady for a period of time.

Using OBD devices, information regarding the (P)HEV operations can also be collected, including speed, steering, battery system charge/discharge and fuel use. Such information is used as ground truth in our evaluations. One major challenge lies in appropriate *synchronization* of multi-modality data from three different data sources: mobile phone, internal combustion engine, and battery system. As demonstrated in Figure 6, when the vehicle speeds up from stationary status, both current and acceleration should change to non-zero values at the same time, but they did not in the raw monitored data. We propose to synchronize the multi-modality data streams by maximizing the correlation between each data stream and the reference data stream:

$$\text{corr}(A, B) = \frac{E[(A - \mu_A)(B - \mu_B)]}{\sigma_A \sigma_B} \tag{1}$$

We select acceleration as the reference stream since its noise can be effectively removed and is more precise than others. We also exploit stops (based on speed and acceleration to segment each trip into several sub-trips and apply synchronization to each sub-trip.

3.2   Vehicle Movement Sensing

Although it is possible to obtain vehicle movement information by mounting a phone in a fixed position before each trip, it is cumbersome and inconvenient for users. Our solution allows the phone to be unrestricted in the vehicle. This leads to potential phone–vehicle disorientation. Let (X, Y, Z) be the vehicle's

Fig. 7. Frame of reference orientation of vehicle (blue) and phone (red). Left: oriented; Middle: initial disorientation; Right: dynamic disorientation.

Cartesian frame of reference, and (x, y, z) be the phone's frame of reference. As illustrated in Figure 7, these two frames of reference should be well-oriented in the ideal case. However, the phone may be placed anywhere in the vehicle (e.g., driver's pocket) at trip start (*initial disorientation*), and may shift around during a driving trip (*dynamic disorientation*). Such disorientation can be substantial and highly dynamic, as shown in Figure 8.

Initial Disorientation Compensation. The phone's (x, y, z) axes are disoriented with respect to the vehicle's (X, Y, Z) axes. Leveraging the automatic attitude initialization method originally proposed by Mohan et al. [20], the rotation matrix needs to be calculated and applied to x, y, and z in sequence in order to transform arbitrary orientation of (x, y, z) to (X, Y, Z). According to the definition of Euler Angle [1], any orientation of the accelerometer can be represented by a pre-rotation ϕ of Y, followed by a tilt θ of Z, and then a post-rotation α of Y. Thus, the rotation matrices associated with these three rotation angles are:

$$R_\phi = \begin{bmatrix} \cos\phi & 0 & -\sin\phi \\ 0 & 1 & 0 \\ \sin\phi & 0 & \cos\phi \end{bmatrix}, R_\theta = \begin{bmatrix} \cos\theta & \sin\theta & 0 \\ -\sin\theta & \cos\theta & 0 \\ 0 & 0 & 1 \end{bmatrix}, R_\alpha = \begin{bmatrix} \cos\alpha & 0 & -\sin\alpha \\ 0 & 1 & 0 \\ \sin\alpha & 0 & \cos\alpha \end{bmatrix} \quad (2)$$

ϕ and θ can be calculated by applying the rotation matrix to the accelerometer reading $[a_x, a_y, a_z]^T$ when the vehicle is stationary, i.e., gravity $[0, 1, 0]^T$:

$$\begin{bmatrix} 0 \\ 1 \\ 0 \end{bmatrix} = R_\theta * R_\phi * \begin{bmatrix} a_x \\ a_y \\ a_z \end{bmatrix} = \begin{bmatrix} \cos\theta & \sin\theta & 0 \\ -\sin\theta & \cos\theta & 0 \\ 0 & 0 & 1 \end{bmatrix} * \begin{bmatrix} \cos\phi & 0 & -\sin\phi \\ 0 & 1 & 0 \\ \sin\phi & 0 & \cos\phi \end{bmatrix} * \begin{bmatrix} a_x \\ a_y \\ a_z \end{bmatrix} \quad (3)$$

Thus, $\theta = \cos^{-1}(a_y), \phi = \tan^{-1}(a_z/z_x)$.

Next, we need to estimate the post-rotation α of Y. When a trip starts, the vehicle goes from stationary to acceleration, producing a force in a known direction. Suppose that after rotation of ϕ and θ, the acceleration vector $[a_x, a_y, a_z]^T$ changes to $[a'_z, a'_y, a'_z]^T$, reflecting the force produced. While in the vehicle's coordinate system, only a_Z has a significant value and a_X should be 0. So the summation vector of a_x and a_z is exactly a_Z, and we get $\alpha = \tan^{-1}(a'_x/a'_z)$. In the end, we get a rotation matrix $R = R_\alpha * R_\theta * R_\phi$, which can transform accelerometer readings of the mobile phone to the vehicle's true accelerations. Note that this approach also works when car starts on a non-flat surface.

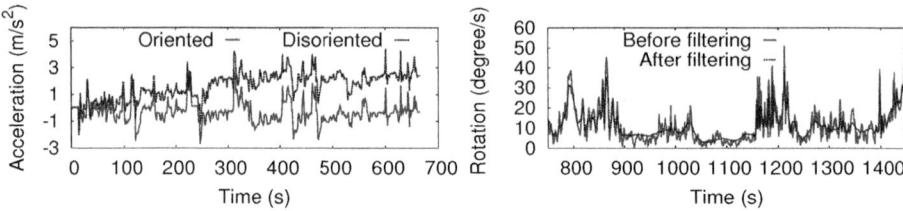

Fig. 8. Error of dynamic disorientation   **Fig. 9.** Gyroscope de-noise using wavelets

Dynamic Disorientation Compensation. Dynamic disorientation is highly unpredictable and may occur at anytime during a trip. If not detected and corrected in real time, it introduces significant error to the sensing value, as illustrated in Figure 8. Thus, it needs to be compensated before the measured acceleration values can be used. We propose a wavelet-based technique, which analyzes the rotation information received from the gyroscope in order to separate true vehicle movement from contextual noise. This technique is based on multi-resolution analysis [26], by which a given time-series signal can be decomposed into multiple wavelet levels, each corresponding to a specific frequency range.

One important observation is that *vehicle movements and phone movements have different characteristics and tend to occur in different time–frequency domains*, e.g., vehicle changing lane vs. phone moving in driver's pocket. Wavelets are particularly suitable for such joint time–frequency analysis.

Wavelet-Based Gyroscope Noise Filtering. The gyroscope signal has unique noise characteristics. True rotation can appear in both high frequency and low frequency, and signal noise cannot be removed via simple low/high-pass filtering. We leverage a wavelet-based de-noise method [23] to improve the signal quality from gyroscope. Let $s(n) = f(n) + \sigma e(n)$ be the raw gyroscope signal, where n is the index of equally-spaced time points, $f(n)$ is the true signal and $e(n)$ models the noise. We assume $e(n)$ is a Gaussian white noise and the noise level σ equals to 1. We make the following observations: (i) Signal from gyroscope should be mostly smooth, with a few abrupt changes caused by vehicle turning or phone's sudden movement. Therefore, it should have only a few non-zero wavelet coefficients. (ii) A white noise signal is reflected by the coefficients at all levels. Also, a Gaussian noise after orthogonal wavelet transform still preserves the Gaussian property. Thus, noise can be estimated by removing the correlated signal at each level. Thus, for each level of decomposed signal, we select a threshold (0.2506 based on our experiments) and ignore high-frequency coefficients whose absolute values are lower than the threshold. We then reconstruct the signal using all remaining coefficients. As we can see in Figure 9, the gyroscope signal becomes much smoother after wavelet-based de-noise.

Wavelet-Based Movement Analysis. Figure 10 schematically depicts the wavelet-based procedure that is applied to the rotation rate signal acquired from gyroscope, which is the combination of three-dimensional signals $s_{total} = \sqrt{s_{pitch}^2 + s_{roll}^2 + s_{yaw}^2}$. After DWT decomposition using the db6 wavelet

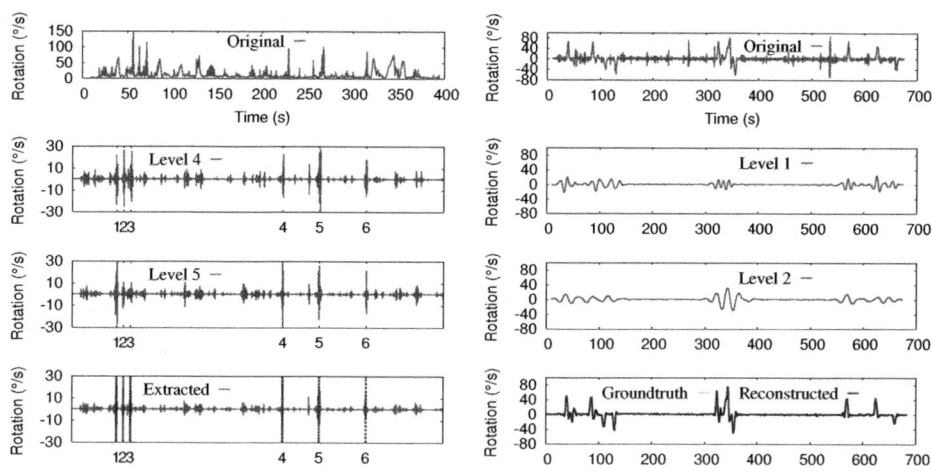

Fig. 10. Wavelet-based detection of phone movement (Left) and vehicle turning (Right)

function, the energy content of each level is calculated and plotted against the observed movements. As shown in Figure 10, attitude change of the phone caused by vehicle movement and phone movement are well-separated after the decomposition – the former by higher-level wavelet coefficients (low frequency domain) and the latter by lower-level wavelet coefficients (high frequency domain). In the left figure, level 4 and 5 coefficients are selected as they correlated well with true phone movements relative to vehicle (blue vertical lines). In the right figure, level 1 and 2 coefficients are selected as they correlated well with true vehicle turning events.

4 Driver-Specific (P)HEV Analysis

Given the multi-modality driver-vehicle data that our sensing system collects, our goal is to analyze, quantitatively, how user-specific driving behavior affects (P)HEV operation, which in turn results in different energy use and environmental impacts. This has been a challenging problem due to the high complexity of (P)HEVs. Leveraging the multi-modality sensing data, we propose an analysis approach that consists of three key components: (1) **Operation mode classification** characterizes the key (P)HEV operation modes and maps user-specific driving behavior to corresponding operation mode; (2) **Energy profile analysis** identifies and quantifies the underlying relationship between (P)HEV electricity and fuel use and different operation modes; and (3) **Fuel–CO$_2$ emission analysis** characterizes the relationship between fuel use and greenhouse gas emissions.

4.1 (P)HEV Operation Mode Classification

First, we investigate the relationship between user driving behavior and (P)HEV operation. Modeling (P)HEV energy use is a difficult task. On one hand, users' driving behaviors are diverse and vary by road and traffic conditions. On the

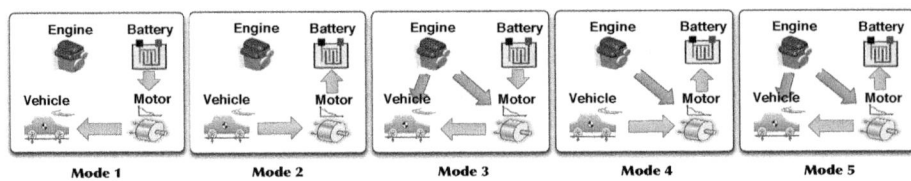

Fig. 11. Categorization of (P)HEV operation modes under different driving scenarios

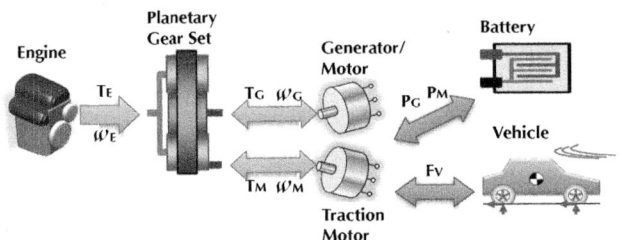

Fig. 12. (P)HEV energy profile analysis. Engine and battery system work together to balance the power demand of the vehicle.

other hand, under different conditions, a (P)HEV may be powered by either battery or fuel, or both, each of which is a complex process. To address these issues, we have identified five operation modes for the Toyota Prius control system, based on the operation animation displayed on dashboard. The modes are illustrated in Figure 11. **Mode 1**: Only the battery system is used to drive the vehicle. It occurs primarily during city driving with low speed. **Mode 2**: Extra energy (e.g., breaking) is harnessed by the vehicle to charge the battery system. It happens when the vehicle is decelerating. **Mode 3**: Both the ICE and battery system are providing energy to drive the vehicle. It happens when the vehicle is driving at high speed and needs massive amount of energy to sustain the movement. **Mode 4**: ICE is charging the battery system. It occurs when the energy generated by ICE exceeds the need to maintain the vehicle movement. **Mode 5**: ICE is both charging the battery system and powering the vehicle. It typically occurs when the battery's SOC (state of charge) is very low while the vehicle has high energy demand.

Based on our analysis of real-world user driving data, we choose to use speed, acceleration, acceleration change, and altitude as the input for (P)HEV operation mode classification. We then construct a decision tree using the CART method [5]. The output of the model is the working status of the engine (on or off) and the battery system (charging or discharging).

4.2 (P)HEV Energy Profile Analysis

Based on the different operation modes, we develop an analytical (P)HEV model specifically for Toyota Prius in MATLAB. Prius adopts series-parallel structure in its drive-train, where the engine, generator/motor and traction motor are coupled together through the planetary gear set to provide the demanded traction power. The driving power requirement is distributed between the Motor and ICE depending on the different modes and user-specific driving behavior. This

Fig. 13. Sensing devices (OBD and personal mobile phones) deployed in (P)HEVs for real-time monitoring. OBD data are only used as ground truth in system evaluation.

Table 1. Types of Data Collected in Multi-modality Driver–Vehicle Sensing

Category		Types of Data	Frequency (Hz)	Category		Types of Data	Frequency (Hz)
Vehicle	battery system	temperature	10	User	trip information	elevation	1
		current	125			GPS location	1
		voltage	125				
		state-of-charge/health	10				
	gasoline engine	air intake	3-4		driving behavior	speed	1
		engine RPM	3-4			acceleration	50
	other	speed	3-4			rotation rate	50
		steering	3-4			heading	1

procedure is illustrated in Figure 12. Mathematically, **battery energy use** can be expressed as [13]:

$$- \Delta SOC = \frac{T_G \omega_G \Delta t}{\eta_G(T_G, \omega_G)} + \frac{T_M \omega_M \Delta t}{\eta_M(T_M, \omega_M)} \tag{4}$$

where ΔSOC is the change of SOC, which is the integration of the exchanged energy between motors and battery system. η_G and η_M are the efficiency of generator/motor and traction motor respectively. They are functions of (T_G, ω_G) and (T_M, ω_M) respectively, where T represents output torque and ω represents angular speed. And **fuel consumption** can be calculated by:

$$fuel = \frac{T_E \times \omega_E \times \Delta t}{m \times \eta_E(T_E, \omega_E)} \tag{5}$$

where m is the unit energy generated by ICE, η_E is the efficiency of the ICE and is determined by T_E and ω_E.

4.3   Fuel–CO$_2$ Emission Analysis

To determine the amount of CO_2 emissions from fuel consumption, we consider the chemical reaction model that assumes predominantly complete combustion of the gasoline to carbon dioxide. With current motor vehicle emission control technology, this assumption has no more than 1% error. The chemical reaction and stoichiometry is shown below([12]):

$$C_8H_{18} + 12.5O_2 + 46.4N_2 \rightarrow 8CO_2 + 9H_2O + 46.4N_2 \tag{6}$$

Using this model, we determine the ratio of the mass of CO_2 emissions to the mass of air input: 0.208 gram of CO_2/gram of air. Since the vehicle run-time

Table 2. Comparison of Different Participants' Driving Trips

Driver ID	1	2	3	4	5	6	7	8
Total time (s)	43,176	26,218	22,188	37,498	44,615	103,608	4,702	10,057
Total distance (mile)	366.4	177.8	166.5	322.4	185.6	537.1	40.5	112.0
Total days	14	9	5	27	11	25	3	10
Total trips	26	22	18	37	43	35	5	10
Time per day (s)	3,084	2,913	4,438	1,388	4,056	4,144	1,567	1,006
Distance per day (mile)	26.2	19.8	33.3	11.9	16.9	21.5	13.5	11.2

fuel consumption can be accurately measured by monitoring its air intake rate (gram/s). The proposed model provides efficient and accurate estimation of vehicle CO_2 run-time emissions.

5   System Deployment and User Studies

The proposed personalized driving behavior monitoring and analysis system has been implemented and deployed for real-world user driving studies. In this section, we describe the details of system deployment and user studies. The data collected in our user studies are then used for system evaluation and driver-specific (P)HEV analysis in Section 6.

5.1   System Deployment

Our sensing system is designed as an application on personal smartphones. It collects, stores, and transmits personalized vehicle and user driving data, and supports user interaction and presentation of analysis results. As shown in Table 1, our sensing system supports real-time collection of comprehensive vehicle and user driving data that are relevant to energy use and environmental impact. For ground truth collection, the OBD cables we use are OBDLink Scan Tool, which supports the OBD-II specification and WiFi communication (with Baud rates 9600 up to 2M). For the personal mobile devices, we use two iPhone 4 smartphones for each trip, one mounted and one unmounted. The smartphones communicate with the OBD devices and computer server via WiFi. Figure 13 shows the OBD and personal mobile phone sensing devices deployed in (P)HEVs for real-time monitoring.

In total, we have deployed the sensing system on ten different vehicles. Two of them are PHEVs, one Ford Escape and one Toyota Prius, both using customized plug-in battery system developed by a clean-energy transportation company. The PHEV battery system consists of over 1000 Li-ion battery units, organized into over 100 modules, with an overall 5.2 KWh energy storage capacity. The other eight cars are owned by the participants. Four of the vehicles are regular HEVs (Toyota Prius), and the other four are conventional gasoline-powered vehicles.

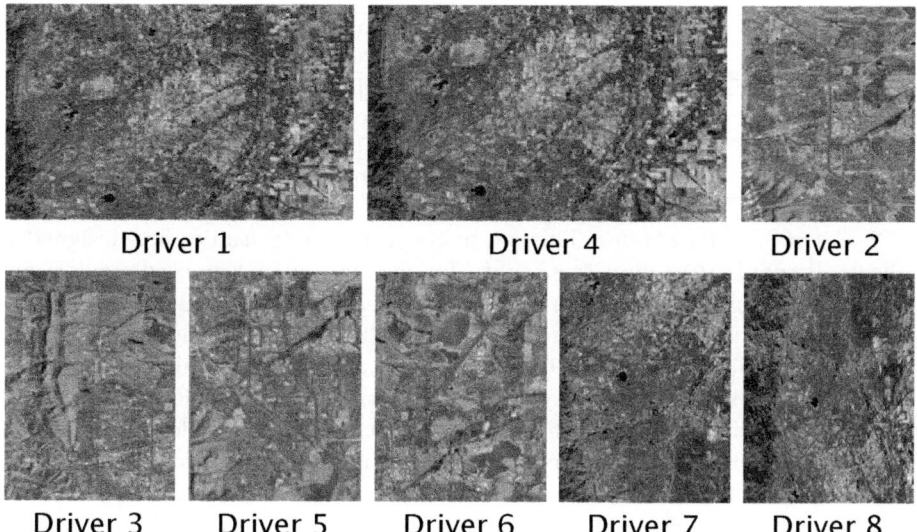

Fig. 14. Heterogeneous routes driven by the eight participants in the macro-driving user studies

5.2   User Studies

Over a period of one year, we have conducted a series of user studies using the deployed sensing systems. Our goal is to: (1) demonstrate the feasibility and correctness of the sensing system we have developed; (2) collect real-world user driving data and (P)HEV operation information at run-time; and (3) analyze quantitatively how user-specific driving behavior affects (P)HEV energy and environmental impacts. Besides user studies for prototyping and debugging purposes, we have conducted the following user studies:

(1) *Macro-driving studies*: In this set of studies, 8 different participants have been asked to drive their own vehicles (with the deployed sensing systems) according to their daily driving needs. Sensing data are collected and stored locally on the mobile devices whenever a user drives, and the data are uploaded to the server machine when WiFi connection is available. Over 150 trips have been recorded in this set of studies. Table 2 summarizes the key characteristics of the eight participants' daily driving trips, which vary in both time and distance. Figure 14 shows the routes taken by our eight drivers in their regular driving activities. These routes vary significantly from driver to driver. For instance, driver 4 traveled more on freeway, while drive 5 spent most of his driving time on city roads. These trips cover diverse weather and road conditions, such as temperatures from -7°F to 71°F, city vs. highway driving, sunny vs. rainy vs. snowy weather, and driving time throughout the day. The participants also drive differently and have different impact on vehicle, which can be seen in Figure 2 (e.g., driver 3 vs. driver 5).

Position	Seat	Pocket Upper	Pocket Lower	Bag	Mounted (reference)
MAE-before (m/s^2)	5.19	9.99	9.57	8.10	0.14
Corr-before	0.08	0.12	0.16	0.28	0.97
MAE-after (m/s^2)	0.26	0.46	0.22	0.17	0.14
Corr-after	0.88	0.80	0.92	0.96	0.97

Table 3. Accuracy of Acceleration Sensing with Different Phone Positions. Results shown are MAE and correlation values before and after sensor data correction.

(2) *Micro-driving studies*: This set of controlled user studies are designed to collect all required ground truth data for evaluation of proposed models and investigate specific factors of users' driving behavior and vehicle operation. 4 different participants have been asked to drive the PHEVs under different road and traffic conditions. Over 20 trips have been conducted in this set of studies.

Our real-world system deployment and user studies have demonstrated the feasibility and effectiveness of the multi-modality driving–vehicle sensing system we have developed. The comprehensive user driving and vehicle operation data we have gathered are then used in the following section for detailed system evaluation and driver-specific (P)HEV analysis. The data provide valuable insights into users' driving behaviors, as run-time acceleration, speed, and slope are critical factors in determining the power demands of the hybrid vehicle components.

6   System Evaluations and Analysis Results

In this section, we evaluate the proposed personalized driving behavior monitoring and analysis system for emerging hybrid vehicles. Using the real-world user-driving data we have gathered from the deployed systems, we would like to answer the following questions:

1. Does our system achieve high accuracy for driver–vehicle sensing?
2. Does our system achieve high accuracy with regard to operation mode classification, (P)HEV modeling of battery system use and fuel use?

6.1   Sensing System Validation

We have demonstrated in Section 3 that individual sensor readings can be effectively processed to enhance quality. Here, we focus on evaluating the "end results", i.e., vehicle movement in terms of acceleration and speed, whose accuracy are crucial in (P)HEV analysis. In particular, obtaining the correct vehicle acceleration information requires complex processing of accelerometer, gyroscope, and digital compass readings, as well as disorientation compensation.

In our experiments, we consider four different ways of positioning a phone in the vehicle: (1) *Seat*: Phone lays flat on the passenger seat. (2) *Pocket Upper*: Phone is in the driver's jacket pocket. (3) *Pocket Lower*: Phone is in the driver's pant pocket. (4) *Bag*: Phone is in a bag on the passenger seat. We use the *mounted* position as our reference, where the phone is securely mounted to the front of the windshield. We use **mean absolute error (MAE)** and **cross-correlation coefficient** (Equation 1) to measure the accuracy of the corrected sensor readings. Given two series A and B each with n values a_i and b_i ($i = 1, \ldots, n$), we define

$$MAE = \frac{1}{n} \sum_{i=1}^{n} |a_i - b_i| \qquad (7)$$

Table 3 shows the accuracy of acceleration readings before and after correction, using the mounted phone reading as reference. Note that even under exactly the same context, there are still differences between samples from different sensors. The acceleration readings between two mounted phones have an MAE of $0.14 m/s^2$ and correlation of 0.97. We can also see that our corrected acceleration readings effectively improve the vehicle acceleration sensing accuracy over the raw readings, under all four typical positions, e.g., 0.28 vs. 0.96 correlation and 8.10 vs. 0.17 MAE, before and after correction, when phone is placed in a bag on the passenger seat. As shown in Figure 15, the corrected acceleration readings match well with the ground truth.

Figure 16 also shows that the GPS speed readings match very well with the OBD (ground truth) speed readings (0.99 correlation).

6.2 Analysis Model Validation

We first evaluate the accuracy of the operation mode classifier we have developed, which maps user driving behavior to the corresponding (P)HEV operations mode. The ground truth is generated from the engine RPM and electrical current reported by OBD device. We use k rounds of 0.632 bootstrapping [6], a widely used approach, to generate k pairs of training and testing data sets. For each pair, about 63.2% of the instances are in the training set and the remaining instances are in the testing set. Let M_i be the classifier obtained using the i-th round training set, $\zeta(M_i)_{test}$ and $\zeta(M_i)_{train}$ be the accuracy of M_i on the i-th round testing set and training set, respectively, the expected accuracy of our operation mode classifier is

$$\zeta(M) = \sum_{i=1}^{k}(0.632 * \zeta(M_i)_{test} + 0.368 * \zeta(M_i)_{train}) \qquad (8)$$

Using $k = 10$ rounds and real-world user driving data, the expected classification accuracy is 89.9% for engine status and 87.8% for battery status.

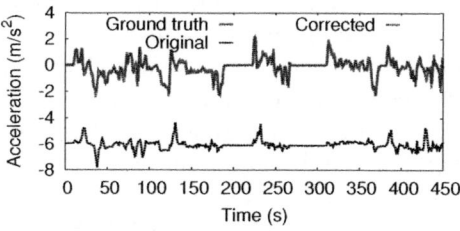

Fig. 15. Accuracy of acceleration sensing

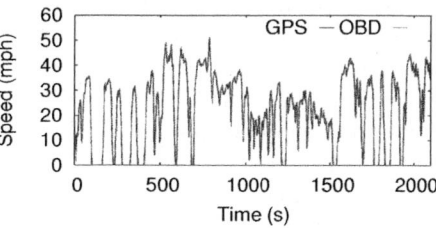

Fig. 16. Accuracy of speed sensing

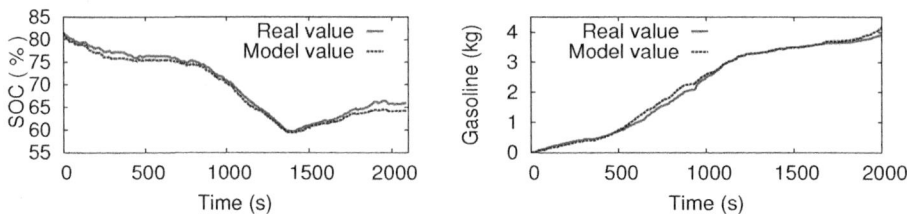

Fig. 17. Accuracy of (P)HEV run-time energy use and fuel use modeling

Figure 17 shows the modeling results for run-time battery use (left) and fuel use (right), respectively. Battery energy use is reported as SOC (%) over time, and fuel use is based on gasoline (kg). Both figures show that the values predicted by the models match well with the real (measured) values. The battery use model achieved 0.41% MAE and 0.918 correlation; while the fuel use model also achieved a very low MAE of 0.07 kg and a high correlation of 0.996.

6.3   Discussions

Vehicle systems are highly complex, and a large number of factors come into play, with varying impacts on fuel efficiency, battery system run-time performance and long-term aging. Although it is difficult to model all factors in a complex vehicle system, our solution does provide good approximation of vehicle performance in real-world driving scenarios, thus bridging the information gap between driver and vehicle. Here, we further discuss other related factors and limitations of the proposed solution.

For fuel consumption, the ground truth is derived from air flow mass reported by the OBD device, using formula proposed in (http://www.lightner.net/lightner/bruce/Lightner-183.pdf). This approach works very well in a modern automobile, which is accurate to within a few percent. Although some factors are not explicitly modeled in our system, our evaluation data set does contain diverse weather and road conditions, and the high accuracy of our system would be generalizable in many scenarios. As our future work, we plan to conduct larger-scale user driving studies and incorporate explicit modeling of other related factors such as temperature, humidity, road conditions, etc.

Although the speed information reported by GPS is accurate (i.e., highly consistent with the speed reported by OBD, as validated in our studies), the altitude information from GPS may suffer from significant noises and can impact our results to some extent. Our evaluation data set contains substantial altitude variations, and our system achieves high accuracy. We are therefore confident that the proposed system can be deployed in almost all physical settings. Nevertheless, places with large altitude variations may benefit from more accurate GPS reporting and better algorithm to reduce the noise in altitude sensing data.

We have evaluated the proposed system with four different phone positions in a vehicle (seat, pocket upper, pocket lower, and bag), which should capture most driving scenarios. Still, other phone positions may be possible and may affect the accuracy of our system. In addition, due to the lower quality sensors used in mobile phones, other types of noises may arise and may not be effectively removed by our current solution.

Our battery system model is constructed based on the type of PHEVs developed by Toyota. The specific vehicle design is orthogonal to our solution and adaptation to different PHEVs can be achieved through vehicle-specific driving studies and data-based parameter tuning. We expect the overall trend of fuel consumption and battery system use to stay the same for the same type of driving behavior.

7   Related Work

Our work focuses on personalized driving behavior monitoring and analysis for emerge hybrid vehicles. It draws upon research works in several related areas, which we summarize in this section.

Mobile Sensing System for Vehicles. Sensing systems that utilize mobile platform and other devices such as GPS, accelerometer, and OBD device, have been developed for monitoring road and traffic conditions [24], commute time, WiFi deployment, and automotive diagnostics [11], or finding the optimal route in terms of lowest fuel consumption [9]. These systems require purchasing extra devices, which limits user adoption. Privacy of driving trips has also been studied [14]. Several techniques have been proposed to classify a wide variety of human movements and activities using mobile device [15]. However, previous works typically require stable sensor placement for data collection, e.g., mounting the phone in a fixed place. Such requirement is intrusive and inconvenient for users. During a driving trip, the phone may move relative to the vehicle (e.g., sliding or user picking up a phone call). Such abnormal movements make statistical models inadequate and affect the quality of monitored data [19]. This may be addressed by taking extraneous activities into consideration [18]. However, these methods are not suitable for detecting transient movements of phone relative to vehicle, nor can they dynamically compensate for the error. Our work differs from these systems in that we focus on the energy and environmental impacts of user-specific driving behavior on emerging electric-drive vehicles. Moreover, our proposed sensing techniques and analysis system make it possible to separate transient phone/vehicle movements at run-time and use the mobile platform to automatically fulfill all functionalities, thus eliminating the inconvenience of user intervention and extra OBD devices.

Driving Cycle Analysis. Driving cycle analysis for performance assessment of conventional vehicles has drawn significant attention in the past [25]. Due to the challenge of collecting real-world trip data, standard driving cycles have been developed to describe various driving modes in different regions, such as UDDS, HFEDS, US06, etc. These driving cycles are used in previous research to simulate real-world conditions for vehicle performance analysis [8]. Recently, driving cycle analysis studies began to consider hybrid vehicle technologies [10].

For instance, standard driving cycles are used to investigate different power train configurations [8]. A few works have used speed information in real-world trips to investigate (P)HEV battery performance [4]. We take a systematic approach to identify the corresponding operation mode under specific driving behavior, model (P)HEV battery system use and fuel–CO_2 emissions, therefore enabling personalized, comprehensive, and quantitative analysis of (P)HEV performance and environmental impacts.

8   Conclusions

We have developed a personalized driving behavior monitoring and analysis system for emerging hybrid vehicles. We propose techniques for multi-modality drive–vehicle sensing, including de-noise, drift calibration, synchronization, and wavelet-based disorientation compensation for precise vehicle movement sensing. In addition, via operation mode classification, (P)HEV battery system modeling and fuel-CO_2 emissions modeling, our system enables comprehensive and quantitative analysis of (P)HEV energy environmental impacts under user-specific driving behavior. Real-world system deployment and user driving studies demonstrate the feasibility and high accuracy of the proposed system, with 0.88–0.996 correlation values.

Acknowledgements. This work was supported in part by the National Science Foundation award CNS–0910995. We thank our shepherd, Hao-Hua Chu, and the anonymous reviewers for constructive comments.

References

1. Euler angles, http://en.wikipedia.org/wiki/Euler_angles
2. Toyota edf, http://www.edfenergy.com/media-centre/press-news/
   edf-energy-and-toyota-launch-uk-trials-of-plug-in-hybrid-vehicle.shtml
3. Development of speed correction cycles. Tech. rep., US EPA Assessment and Modeling Division, NVFEL (1997), EPA report no. M6.5PD.001 (1997)
4. Adornato, B., Patil, R., Filipi, Z., Baraket, Z., Gordon, T.: Characterizing naturalistic driving patterns for plug-in hybrid electric vehicle analysis. In: IEEE VPPC (2009)
5. Breiman, L., Friedman, J., Olshen, R., Stone, C.: Classification and Regression Trees. CRC Press (1984)
6. Davison, A.C., Hinkley, D.: Bootstrap Methods and their Application, Cambridge (2006)
7. Ehsani, M., Gao, Y., Emadi, A.: Modern Electric, Hybrid Electric, and Fuel Cell Vehicles: Fundamentals, Theory, and Design. CRC Press (2009)
8. Ganji, B., Kouzani, A.Z., Trinh, H.M.: Drive Cycle Analysis of the Performance of Hybrid Electric Vehicles. In: Li, K., Fei, M., Jia, L., Irwin, G.W. (eds.) LSMS 2010 and ICSEE 2010, Part I . LNCS, vol. 6328, pp. 434–444. Springer, Heidelberg (2010)
9. Ganti, R.K., Pham, N., Ahmadi, H., Nangia, S., Abdelzaher, T.F.: GreenGPS: a participatory sensing fuel-efficient maps application. In: MobiSys 2010 (2010)

10. Huang, X., Tan, Y., He, X.: An intelligent multi-feature statistical approach for discrimination of driving conditions of hybrid electric vehicle. In: IJCNN 2009 (2009)
11. Hull, B., Bychkovsky, V., Zhang, Y., Chen, K., Goraczko, M., Miu, A., Shih, E., Balakrishnan, H., Madden, S.: CarTel: a distributed mobile sensor computing system. In: SenSys 2006, pp. 125–138 (2006)
12. Harte, J.: Consider a Spherical Cow. University Science Books (1988)
13. Jonasson, K.: Analysing hybrid drive system topologies. Licentiate thesis (2002)
14. Krumm, J.: Realistic Driving Trips For Location Privacy. In: Tokuda, H., Beigl, M., Friday, A., Brush, A.J.B., Tobe, Y. (eds.) Pervasive 2009. LNCS, vol. 5538, pp. 25–41. Springer, Heidelberg (2009)
15. Lane, N., Miluzzo, E., Lu, H., Peebles, D., Choudhury, T., Campbell, A.: A survey of mobile phone sensing. IEEE Communications Magazine 48(9), 140–150 (2010)
16. Li, K., Wu, J., Jiang, Y., Hassan, Z., Lv, Q., Shang, L., Maksimovic, D.: Large-scale battery system modeling and analysis for emerging electric-drive vehicles. In: ISLPED 2010, pp. 277–282 (2010)
17. Lin, J., Niemeier, D.A.: Regional driving characteristics, regional driving cycles. Transportation Research Part D 8, 361–381 (2003)
18. Lu, H., Yang, J., Liu, Z., Lane, N.D., Choudhury, T., Campbell, A.T.: The jigsaw continuous sensing engine for mobile phone applications. In: SenSys 2010 (2010)
19. Miluzzo, E., Papandrea, M., Lane, N., Lu, H., Campbell, A.T.: Pocket, bag, hand, etc. - automatically detecting phone context through discovery. In: PhoneSense 2010 (2010)
20. Mohan, P., Padmanabhan, V.N., Ramjee, R.: Nericell: rich monitoring of road and traffic conditions using mobile smartphones. In: SenSys 2008, pp. 323–336 (2008)
21. Mohd-Yasin, F., Nagel, D.J., Ong, D.S., Korman, C.E., Chuah, H.T.: Low frequency noise measurement and analysis of capacitive micro-accelerometers: Temperature effect. Japanese Journal of Applied Physics 47(6), 5270–5273 (2008)
22. Samaras, C., Meisterling, K.: Life cycle assessment of greenhouse gas emissions from plug-in hybrid vehicles: Implications for policy. Environ. Sci. Technol. 42 (2008)
23. Sardy, S., Tseng, P., Bruce, A.: Robust wavelet denoising. IEEE Transactions on Signal Processing 49(6), 1146–1152 (2001)
24. Thiagarajan, A., Ravindranath, L., LaCurts, K., Madden, S., Balakrishnan, H., Toledo, S., Eriksson, J.: VTrack: accurate, energy-aware road traffic delay estimation using mobile phones. In: SenSys 2009, pp. 85–98 (2009)
25. Tong, H.Y., Hung, W.T., Chun-shun, C.: On-road motor vehicle emissions and fuel consumption in urban driving conditions. Joural of the Air and Waste Management Association 50, 543–554 (2000)
26. Torrence, C., Compo, G.P.: A practical guide to wavelet analysis. Bulletin of the American Meteorological Society 79, 61–78 (1998)

Mimic Sensors: Battery-Shaped Sensor Node for Detecting Electrical Events of Handheld Devices

Takuya Maekawa[1], Yasue Kishino[2], Yutaka Yanagisawa[2], and Yasushi Sakurai[2]

[1] Graduate School of Information Science and Technology
Osaka University
takuya.maekawa@acm.org
[2] NTT Communication Science Laboratories
surname.name@lab.ntt.co.jp

Abstract. In this paper we propose and implement a battery-shaped sensor node that can monitor the use of an electrical device into which it is inserted by sensing the electrical current passing through the device. We live surrounded by large numbers of electrical devices and frequently use them in our daily lives, and so we can estimate high-level daily activities by recognizing their use. Therefore, many ubiquitous and wearable sensing studies have attempted to recognize the use of electrical devices by attaching sensor nodes to the devices directly or by attaching multiple sensors to a user. With our node, we can easily monitor the use of an electrical device simply by inserting the node into the battery case of the device. We also propose a method that automatically identifies into which electrical device the sensor node is inserted and recognizes electrical events related to the device by analyzing the current sensor data. We evaluated our method by using sensor data obtained from three real houses and achieved very high identification and recognition accuracies.

Keywords: Sensors, Electrical devices, Battery.

1 Introduction

Daily activity recognition is one of the most important tasks in pervasive computing applications because it has a wide range of uses in, for example, supporting the care of the elderly, lifelogging, and home automation [1,2]. Many studies have employed body-worn accelerometers to recognize human activities [3,4,5]. While the wearable sensing approach can sense users' activities in both indoor and outdoor environments, wearing sensor devices on parts of the body may place a large burden on the user's daily life. Many other studies have focused on sensors that monitor indoor environments, and have tried to recognize activities based on dense ubiquitous sensors such as RFID tags and switch sensors installed in the environments [6,7,8]. While the approach does not require the user to wear sensors, the costs involved in deploying and maintaining ubiquitous sensors are huge. Also, sensor nodes attached to many daily objects can detract from the

J. Kay et al. (Eds.): Pervasive 2012, LNCS 7319, pp. 20–38, 2012.

aesthetics of artifacts in the home [9]. In addition, many activity recognition studies that employ machine learning techniques require the end-user to prepare labeled training data herself in her daily life environment.

As outlined above, many existing activity recognition approaches place different kinds of large burdens on users. We summarize the users' costs below.

- **Cost of deployment:** A user has to install many sensor nodes in her daily environment when she uses ubiquitous sensors. In some cases, the user should manually associate a sensor node with the daily object to which the sensor is attached. Before the deployment phase, no sensor node knows to which daily object it is attached.

- **Cost of maintenance:** In many cases, a user must regularly replace the battery in a sensor node. The user must also replace broken sensor nodes.

- **Cost related to long-term daily use:** A user must wear multiple sensor nodes in her daily life and/or use daily objects to which sensor nodes are attached. The sensor nodes can also detract from the aesthetics of the home.

- **Cost related to supervised machine learning:** Many ubiquitous sensing approaches and some wearable sensing approaches require labeled training data created in an end user's environment.

On the other hand, recently, many studies in the pervasive computing research field have attempted to monitor the usage of home electrical devices. Because we live surrounded by large numbers of electrical devices, and frequently use them when we perform daily activities, we can estimate high-level daily activities by recognizing the use of these devices. In addition, due to the growing interest in energy conservation, many studies have tried to monitor the energy consumed by electrical devices. Ubiquitous and wearable sensing approaches have been employed to detect the use of electrical devices. However, many existing approaches place large burdens on users as mentioned above. In this paper, we define a new sensing framework called the *mimic sensor framework* that does not impose large burdens on users. A sensor node designed based on the mimic sensor framework works unobtrusively by mimicking objects and plugs with standardized forms. An example sensor node based on the mimic sensor framework has the shape of objects with standardized forms such as an AA battery and an SD memory card and provides the functions of the original object, e.g., discharge and data storage functions. Because a user can use the sensor node in the same way as the original object, she can easily install the sensor node simply by inserting it into the battery case or SD card slot of an electrical device that she wants to monitor. The sensor node senses phenomena related to the electrical device and wirelessly sends the sensor data to a host computer. As described above, because a sensor node designed based on the mimic sensor framework has the shape of an object that exists in a user's ordinary daily life and the user can employ the node in the same way as the original object, we can monitor the user's daily life transparently.

In this paper, we implement a prototype battery-shaped sensor node as an example mimic sensor. The prototype node includes a battery and provides a current discharge function in the same way as conventional batteries. The node also monitors (senses) an electrical current that flows through the node when the node is inserted into an electrical device and then sends the sensor data to a host computer. We analyze the sensor data and recognize electrical events related to the electrical device. With a digital camera, for example, by analyzing the data we can recognize when the user turns it on and when she takes a picture. In addition, to eliminate the cost related to the association of sensor nodes, we try to automatically identify into which electrical device the sensor node is inserted by analyzing the sensor data.

In the rest of this paper, we first introduce work related to detecting the use of electrical devices, and then describe our definition of the mimic sensor framework. After that, we describe the design and implementation of our prototype battery-shaped sensor node. We also propose a machine learning-based method that identifies which electrical device a battery-shaped sensor node is in and that recognizes electrical events related to the device. The contributions of this paper are that we propose and develop a new battery-shaped sensor node, and propose a device identification and event recognition method by analyzing its data. We also evaluate our method by using sensor data obtained from three real houses.

2   Related Work

As mentioned in section 1, various ubiquitous and wearable sensing approaches have been proposed for recognizing human activities. Many ubiquitous sensing approaches employ a large number of small sensors such as switch sensors, RFID tags, and accelerometers attached to daily objects [8,6,10]. By using ubiquitous sensors, we can detect the use of electrical devices in addition to the use of daily objects. A system proposed in [11] employs ubiquitous sensor nodes equipped with magnetic sensors or light sensors attached to each electrical device to detect its use. Although the ubiquitous sensing approach can achieve fine-grained measurements of daily lives, its deployment and maintenance costs, e.g., battery replacement costs, are very high. Several studies have employed small numbers of sensor devices that monitor home infrastructures to detect the use of electricity, water, or gas in home environments [12,13,14]. In particular, the systems proposed in [14,15] recognize the use of electrical devices by monitoring noise on home electrical systems. The systems focus on stationary electrical devices connected to home electrical systems via electric plugs. On the other hand, the battery-shaped sensor nodes proposed here are designed for use with portable electrical devices that are not connected to home electrical systems. The studies that come closest to our concept involve sensor nodes shaped like a power strip [16,17]. The power strip sensor node has electrical outlets and supplies electrical devices connected to the outlets with electrical power. The sensor node also monitors electrical current drawn from each outlet. Because a user can employ the sensor node in the same way as a normal power strip, her daily activities can be monitored transparently. We consider the sensor node to be one example of a mimic sensor. As another similar example, we can assume a sensor node shaped like a USB hub. The sensor node has USB ports and monitors the use of electrical devices that are connected to the node such as I/O and data storage devices. Here, we consider that the above approaches and our approach are complementary rather than competing techniques because the above approaches can recognize the use of stationary electrical devices that run without batteries.

Most wearable sensing approaches use multiple sensor nodes attached to the wearer's body [4,18,19]. Although these approaches can recognize the wearer's activities in outdoor environments, they impose the burden of the need to wear several sensors during daily life. The system proposed in [20] recognizes the use of portable electrical devices held by a user by employing several magnetic sensors attached to her hands. The system captures magnetic fields emitted by magnetic components such as coils and permanent magnets in portable electrical devices and identifies which electrical device the user is using.

3   Mimic Sensor Framework

As mentioned in section 1, a sensor node designed based on the mimic sensor framework has a standardized form or a plug with a standardized form, which means that the sensor node can be connected to another device or a socket. The sensor node basically receives electrical power via the connection. The sensor node also senses data related to the device or socket to which the node is connected. We consider that sensing the electrical current that flows through the node via the connection may be useful and effective for detecting electrical events related to the device. Note that the sensor node can include other sensors such as an accelerometer and a temperature sensor. This permits us to capture additional information related to the device usage. Examples of sensor nodes based on the mimic sensor framework include an AA battery-shaped sensor node, an SD card-shaped sensor node, a flash memory card-shaped sensor node, a light bulb-shaped sensor node, a fluorescent light-shaped sensor node, a power strap-shaped sensor node, and a USB hub-shaped sensor node. The sensor nodes provide the functions of the original objects that they are mimicking. Therefore, the user can employ the sensor node in the same way as the original object.

In section 1, we mentioned four kinds of burdens placed on users. Here we explain how the mimic sensor approach reduces these burdens.

- **Cost of deployment:** Some studies employ such ubiquitous sensors as RFID tags, infrared sensors, and switch sensors [6,21,7]. However, deploying such sensors requires the user to have specialized knowledge. On the other hand, because the user can use mimic sensor nodes in the same way as the original objects, she does not require specialized knowledge.
- **Cost of maintenance:** Because mimic sensor nodes basically receive electrical power from other devices or sockets to which they are connected, a user need not replace their batteries. Note that the user must recharge/replace the battery included in a battery-shaped sensor node when it runs out. However, this is also the case even if the user employs a regular battery in place of the node. Therefore, the battery-shaped sensor node does not impose any additional burdens

related to battery replacement. Note that when the sensor node does not have a power-saving architecture, the battery replacement interval is shortened.

- **Cost related to long-term daily use:** Because such ubiquitous sensors as RFID tags and switch sensors are usually attached to daily objects, they detract from the aesthetics of those objects. On the other hand, a user can use mimic sensor nodes exactly as she uses the original objects and so her life remains unchanged by sensor installation. Moreover, since such sensor nodes as battery-shaped sensor nodes and SD card-shaped sensor nodes are inserted into electrical devices, the user is not aware of them.

- **Cost related to supervised machine learning:** Many ubiquitous sensing approaches require labeled training data obtained in each user's environment to recognize activities in that environment. However, such data is very costly to prepare. We assume that we sense the amount of electrical current that flows through a mimic sensor node when the node is connected to a device. We consider that the flow characteristics are device-dependent and so users can share training data obtained from the device. Assume that a battery-shaped sensor node is inserted into a CD player in a house, and the player plays music. Sensor data (time-series current values) obtained from the player may have a characteristic frequency and the same model CD player in another house may also have the same characteristic frequency. Therefore, end users need not prepare training data in their houses.

4   Prototype Battery-Shaped Sensor Node

We design and implement a prototype battery-shaped sensor node as an example mimic sensor node. We then undertake an investigation to determine whether we can successfully identify into which electrical device the node is inserted and recognize electrical events related to the device by analyzing the electrical current data obtained from the sensor node. Although many portable electrical devices are now driven by internal rechargeable batteries, the market for primary cells is large and still growing. (about $16 billion in 2010) Also, rechargeable AA and AAA batteries (secondary cells) are widely used in our daily lives. Now, we are living surrounded by many electrical devices that are driven by D, C, AA, and AAA batteries. Moreover, due to the unreliable power supply caused by earthquake related accidents at nuclear power plants in Japan, battery-powered devices have been attracting attention. Also, several countries are reconsidering or have decided to decommission nuclear power plants, and so the value of batteries, which are very stable power sources, will increase. In addition, we can add extra value to conventional batteries by incorporating sensors.

4.1   Design

As mentioned in section 3, a battery-shaped sensor node designed based on the mimic sensor framework will be equipped with an electrical discharge function. That is, the sensor node will include a battery. Also, the sensor node measures an electrical current passing through the node just like an ammeter. In addition,

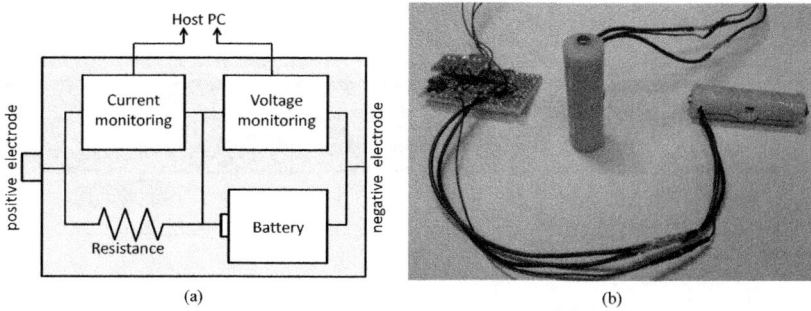

Fig. 1. (a) Schematic of our prototype sensor node. (b) Our prototype battery-shaped sensor nodes and a sensor board.

the sensor node measures the voltage of the battery included in the node. We explain later why we also measure the voltage. Fig. 1 (a) is a schematic of our prototype battery-shaped sensor node. The sensor node includes a battery and a resistance. The node measures a current passing through the resistance. The node also measures the voltage of the included battery. The sensor node samples the current and voltage data at about 1000 Hz. Because the sensor node is a prototype, the node sends the sensor data to a host PC via cables and a sensor board. Fig. 1 (b) shows prototype AA battery-shaped sensor nodes and the sensor board. Because the node is a prototype, we simply incorporate a AAA or N battery in the node. We have also developed D and C battery-shaped sensor nodes. We use the prototype node to measure actual sensor data from various electrical devices and to investigate our device identification and event recognition method introduced in section 5.

4.2 Sensor Data

The prototype sensor node measures an electrical current passing through the node. Fig. 2 shows several sets of example time-series sensor data obtained when we insert the node into various electrical devices and then operate the devices. The upper graph in Fig. 2 (a) shows time-series sensor data obtained from an electric toothbrush. The x-axis indicates time and the y-axis indicates the current sensor data value (mA). Just after the toothbrush was turned on, we observed an inrush of current. Then, we can find the characteristic frequency while the toothbrush was running, which was caused by the motor incorporated in the toothbrush. The lower graph in Fig. 2 (a) shows a frequency spectrogram computed from the time-series sensor data. We can see narrow peaks, which can be discriminative features, caused by the characteristic frequency. The upper graph in Fig. 2 (b) shows time-series sensor data obtained from a flashlight. When the flashlight was turned on, we also observed an inrush of current. Then, the sensor data values become static. The lower graph in Fig. 2 (b) shows a frequency spectrogram. While the flashlight was lit, there was no peak in the spectrogram because the sensor data values were static. We consider that the sensor data

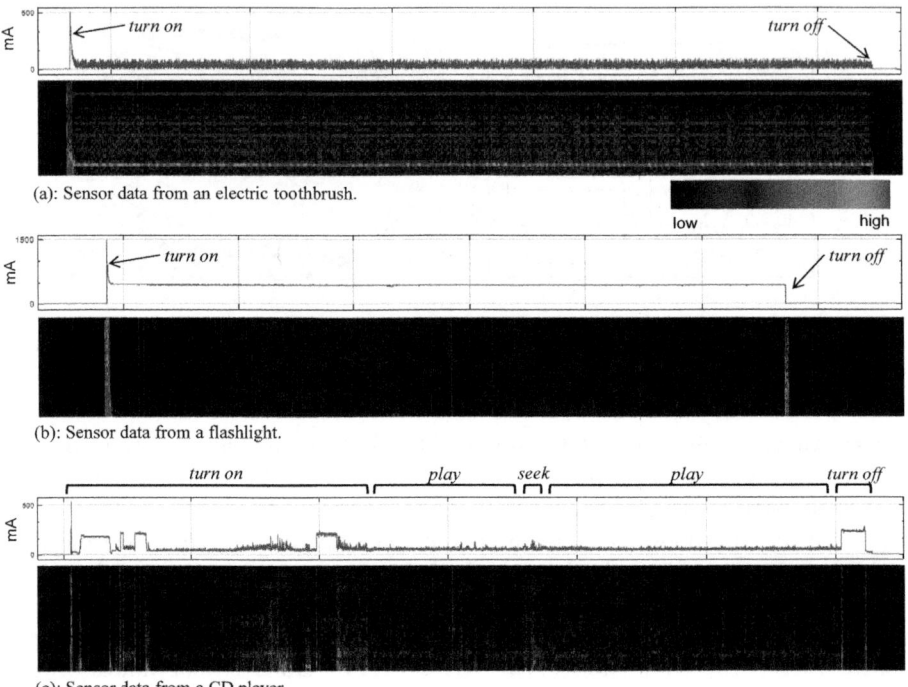

(a): Sensor data from an electric toothbrush.

(b): Sensor data from a flashlight.

(c): Sensor data from a CD player.

Fig. 2. Example current sensor data. The upper graphs show original time-series current data. The lower graphs show frequency spectrograms.

values obtained when the flashlight is lit can be simply used as a characteristic attribute of the flashlight. The upper graph in Fig. 2 (c) shows time-series sensor data obtained from a CD player. The graph also shows electrical events such as 'turn on,' 'play,' 'seek,' and 'turn off' related to the CD player. Unlike the toothbrush and flashlight, it took several seconds for the CD player to start operating. Then, the CD player started to play music. When a user selected the FF or RW button, we observed a noise corresponding to seeking the next/previous track. It also took several seconds for the player to stop operating. The lower graph in Fig. 2 (c) shows a frequency spectrogram. As shown in these graphs, the sensor data from the CD player were time varying, and so we should model temporal changes in the sensor data to recognize electrical events related to the CD player.

Some portable electrical devices such as electric toothbrushes, electric shavers, handheld cleaners, and electric screwdrivers include motors. The rotation of the motors is impeded by various objects and phenomena. For example, motors in certain electrical devices are affected by the gravity of the earth, and so the way that the motor rotation changes may depend slightly on their posture in relation to the direction of the gravitational force. That is, the current sensor data of several electrical devices with motors will change depending on device posture. The upper graph in Fig. 3 shows time-series sensor data obtained from an electric toothbrush. Also, the lower graph in Fig. 3 shows the corresponding frequency

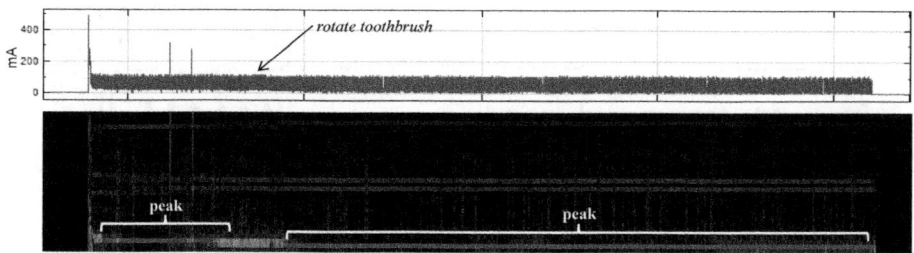

Fig. 3. Sensor data obtained from a toothbrush. We changed the posture of the toothbrush once while the toothbrush was running.

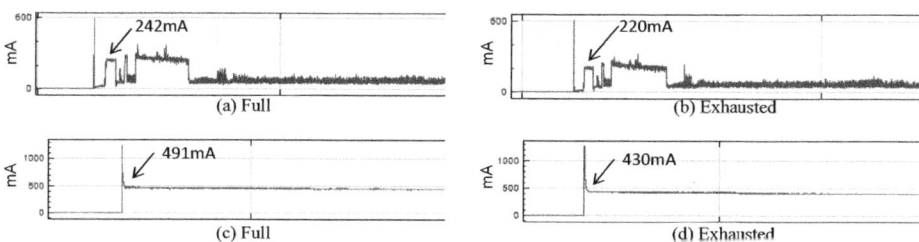

Fig. 4. Sensor data obtained from a CD player (a, b) and a flashlight (c, d) when we used fully charged batteries or exhausted batteries

spectrogram. We rotated the toothbrush 90 degrees while it was running to change its posture. In the spectrogram, we find that the peak frequency changed slightly when we rotated the toothbrush. This was caused by the gravity of the earth (and the posture change of the toothbrush). That is, when we recognize electrical events related to motors with machine learning approaches, we should collect training sensor data of such devices under various conditions, e.g., by changing the postures of the devices as in actual use.

Here, we focus on battery-powered electrical devices. With use, the voltage of the battery decreases and this affects the electrical current passing through the device (and our sensor node). Fig. 4 shows current sensor data obtained from a CD player and a flashlight, both of which employ two AA batteries. The graph in Fig. 4 (a) shows sensor data obtained from the CD player when we used two fully charged batteries with a total voltage of 3.097 V. By contrast, the graph in Fig. 4 (b) shows sensor data obtained from the CD player when we used two exhausted batteries with a total voltage of 2.689 V. Although the two time-series sequences are similar, the sensor data values in Fig. 4 (b) are slightly smaller than those in Fig. 4 (a) even though we used the same CD player. For example, the current values just after the player was switched on, as indicated by the arrows in Fig. 4 (a) and (b), were about 242 and 220 mA, respectively, and they were slightly different. Also, the graph in Fig. 4 (c) shows sensor data obtained from the flashlight when we used two fully charged batteries with a total voltage of 3.161 V. On the other hand, the graph in Fig. 4 (d) shows sensor

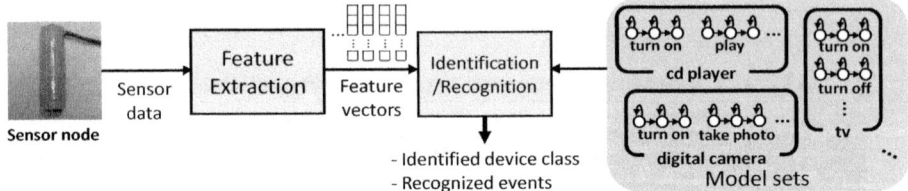

Fig. 5. Architecture of our identification/recognition method

data obtained from the flashlight when we used two exhausted batteries whose total voltage was 2.654 V. The current values while the flashlight was lit in Fig. 4 (c) and (d) were about 491 and 430 mA, respectively. As above, the current sensor data values change depending on the voltage values of the batteries. We need to cope with this problem when we identify electrical devices by employing machine learning approaches. There are two solutions to the problem. The first is to collect training sensor data from an electrical device by using batteries with various voltage values. The second is to compute a feature specific to the device and independent of battery voltage.

5   Our Method

By analyzing sensor data obtained from our sensor node, we try to identify in which electrical device the sensor node is inserted and recognize electrical events related to the device. Fig. 5 shows the architecture of our identification/recognition method. We first extract features from sensor data obtained from a sensor node. Then, we identify the electrical device and recognize electrical events by employing the extracted feature vectors. To achieve device identification and event recognition, we compare the vectors with a model set prepared for each type (product model) of electrical device constructed by employing a hidden Markov model (HMM). We describe our method in detail below.

5.1   Feature Extraction

We assume time-series current data, and so we compute a feature vector for each sliding time window. We extract features based on the FFT components of 64 sample time windows. As mentioned in section 4.2, the FFT components and simple current values can be distinguishable features. Therefore, we use the computed FFT component values and the mean in each window as features. In addition to these features, we use the variance and energy, which can capture the intensity of sensor data changes, computed in each window as features. The energy feature is calculated by summing the magnitudes of squared discrete FFT components. For normalization, the sum was divided by the window length. Note that the DC component of the FFT is excluded from this summation.

In section 4.2, we mentioned that the current sensor data change depending on the battery voltage. To cope with this problem, we simply take account of the electrical resistance of the electrical device. The relationship between the voltage of a battery V, the current passing through the battery I, and the resistance of the device R when a certain electrical event occurs is described as $V = IR$. Because $R = V/I$ depends only on the device (electrical event), we use R as a feature. Our sensor node can measure both current and voltage, and so we can compute R. Note that because R reaches an infinite value when I is zero, we actually use $1/R$ as a feature. We describe how well this approach works by using the examples shown in Fig. 4. We first focus on the CD player sensor data in Fig. 4 (a) and (b). The current values indicated by the arrows in Fig. 4 (a) and (b) are about 242 and 220 mA, respectively (10.0% difference). On the other hand, the computed $1/R$ values in Fig. 4 (a) and (b) are 0.0782 and 0.0819, respectively (4.6% difference). With the flashlight, the current values obtained while the flashlight was lit shown in Fig. 4 (c) and (d) were about 491 and 430 mA, respectively (14.2% difference). On the other hand, the computed $1/R$ values in Fig. 4 (c) and (d) are 0.155 and 0.160, respectively (3.2% difference). It may be very difficult to reduce the error (difference) to zero because of the effects of many phenomena such as the voltage difference between the battery in our node and other batteries in the same device, the conversion characteristics of the regulator IC in electrical devices, and the ambient temperature. However, we consider that, simply by employing $1/R$, we can reduce the effect of the different battery voltages. Note that with an electrical device that can include n batteries connected in series, the value of I/V computed from the voltage and current values sensed by a sensor node in the device actually corresponds to n/R. This is because our sensor node can measure the voltage value of just the battery included in the node. As above, we extract a total of 36 features (32+1+1+1+1) from each window.

5.2   Hybrid Identification/Recognition Method with HMMs

A feature vector sequence is extracted from sensor data obtained from a sensor node. The task is to identify in which electrical device the node is inserted and recognize electrical events related to the device. As shown in Fig. 5, our method identifies the device and simultaneously recognizes electrical events by comparing the sequence with model sets of electrical devices prepared in advance. We train the model sets by using labeled training data collected in advance. A model set is prepared for each type of electrical device and consists of left-to-right HMMs prepared for each electrical event. The HMMs allow us to capture the temporal regularity of events.

We explain our identification/recognition method in detail. We focus on a model set and recognize a feature vector sequence obtained from a node by using the model set. That is, we assume that the node is inserted into the electrical device related to the model set, and then recognize the sequence by using the HMMs in the model set. For the recognition, we simply use the Viterbi algorithm to find the most probable state sequence in/across the HMMs [22] and to compute the likelihood (score) of the state sequence. From the state sequence, we can know into which HMM (electrical event class) a feature vector at time t is classified. Here, because the model set (electrical device) includes multiple HMMs (electrical events), we assume state transitions across the HMMs. That is, we take account of a state transition from the last state of an arbitrary HMM to the first state of another HMM. With a CD player model set, for example, it corresponds to a state transition from a 'play' HMM to a 'turn off' HMM (and to all other HMMs in the model set). By taking the above state transition into account, we can represent transitions of electrical events. Here, we can specify state transitions among HMMs by using a handcrafted grammar. With a digital camera model set, for example, we can specify that an 'on' event (power ON state) must occur just after a 'turn on' event. We construct such a grammar for each model set (electrical device product) and investigate its effect in the next section.

We mentioned that the Viterbi algorithm outputs the most probable state sequence and its score when we recognize the feature vector sequence obtained from the node with a model set. So, we compute the most probable state sequence and its score when we recognize the feature vector sequence with each model set, and we decide that the node should be inserted into an electrical device (model set) corresponding to the highest score. As above, we can identify into which electrical device the node is inserted and recognize electrical events related to the device at the same time.

6   Evaluation

6.1   Data Set

For the evaluation, we prepared the many portable electrical devices listed in Table 1. We selected these devices from those frequently found in appliance and online stores. Table 1 also shows electrical events related to each device. Each device includes an 'off' event that means the power OFF state. In addition, it takes several seconds for devices such as TVs, CD players, and digital cameras to start. Such devices include 'turn on' events. On the other hand, it takes a very short time for such devices as flashlights and toothbrushes to start. We do not consider that such devices include 'turn on' events because it is very difficult to annotate such short events. We also ignored events (functions) where the electrical current values remain unchanged. For example, the 'zoom' functions of the digital cameras and digital camcorder used in our experiment did not induce any change in the current values from those of 'on' events (power ON state), and so we regard 'zoom' events to be included in 'on' events. This may be because the regulator IC in the device could provide sufficient current required for the event, and so the current that the batteries supplied to the regulator did not change. In addition, with electrical devices with a large number of functions, we focus only on the main events (functions).

We obtained training data in our experimental environment by using the devices listed in Table 1. We inserted one sensor node into an electrical device to collect data. As mentioned in section 4.2, we collected training data by changing the postures of the devices as if in actual use. We also changed the battery voltages of the node. We used each device about 30 times in total. We collected test data in real three houses (houses A, B, and C). In section 4.2 we showed that sensor data are affected by changes in the posture of electrical devices,

Table 1. Electrical devices used in our experiment and their electrical events

device	events	device	events
digital camera 1	on, turn on, turn off, take photo, focus, off	cd player 1	turn on, turn off, play, seek, off
digital camera 2	on, turn on, turn off, take photo, focus, off	cd player 2	turn on, turn off, play, seek, off
digital camcorder	on, turn on, turn off, take video, off	tv 1	turn on, turn off, show, off
vacuum 1	vacuum, off	tv 2	turn on, show, off
vacuum 2	vacuum, off	lantern	light, off
video game	on, off	flashlight 1	light, off
shaver 1	shave, off	flashlight 2	light, off
shaver 2	shave, off	cassette player 1	ff/rw, play, off
shaver 3	shave, off	cassette player 2	ff/rw, play, off
screwdriver 1	ff/rw, light, off	dvd player	turn on, play, off
screwdriver 2	ff/rw, off	soldering iron	on, off
toothbrush 1	brush, off	mill	coarse, fine, off
toothbrush 2	brush, off	toy 1 (ship)	go ahead, off
toothbrush 3	brush, off	toy 2 (car)	go forwards, go backwards, off

and so we tested the use of devices by different participants. We gave several different electrical devices to a participant in each house (House A: 10 devices, house B: 10 devices, house C: 8 devices. See Tables 3, 4, and 5.) and asked the participant to use the devices equipped with our nodes. We collect sensor data by using a semi-naturalistic collection protocol [4] that permits greater variability in participant behavior than laboratory data. In the protocol, each participant took part in a session that included the use of electrical devices in a random sequence following instructions on a worksheet. The participants were relatively free as regards how they used each device because the instructions on the worksheet were not very strict, e.g., "play music freely with a CD player" and 'watch an arbitrary TV channel(s).' Because our prototype devices were connected to a host PC via cables, they were used in the same room in each house. However, we asked the participants to employ the devices as in actual use. Note that, as regards the soldering iron, the participant simply turned it on and did not solder anything. Each participant completed a total of ten sessions. (A and B: 10 devices×10 sessions, C: 8 devices×10 sessions) Each session lasted about ten minutes. We used fully charged batteries in the first house, and then used the same partly used batteries in the next house. Note that, when a battery became very weak, we replaced it with new one. We observed the participants by using video cameras to enable us to annotate the obtained data.

6.2 Evaluation Methodology

We constructed a model set by using training data obtained in our experimental environment, and evaluated the performance of our method by using test data obtained in the participants' houses. That is, we assumed that end users did not prepare training data in their houses. To investigate the effectiveness of our approach, we tested the following eight methods.

- **HMM:** This method models electrical events with HMMs as mentioned in section 5.2. This method does not use $1/R$ as a feature. Also, this method assumes that the transition probabilities across HMMs are all identical.
- **HMM(grammar):** This method models electrical events with HMMs. This method does not use $1/R$ as a feature. Also, this method employs a handcrafted grammar prepared for each device when computing transitions among HMMs. We provide some grammar examples written in extended BNF. The grammar for flashlights is described as ('off' {'light' 'off'}). With this grammar 'off' and 'light' events are defined as being alternately repeated. The grammar for a digital camera is described as ({'off' 'turn on' 'on' {'take photo'|'focus'|'on'} 'turn off' } 'off'). With this grammar the definition is that 'off,' 'turn on,' and 'on' events occur sequentially and then 'take photo,' 'focus,' and 'on' events are repeated alternately before the 'turn off' and 'off' events occur. More specifically, for example, the transition probabilities from the last state of the 'turn on' HMM to the first states of other HMMs except for the 'on' HMM are defined as zero. By contrast, the transition probability to the 'on' HMM is one. Also, the transition probabilities from the last state of the 'take photo' HMM to 'focus,' 'on,' and 'turn off' are identical $(1/3)$. By contrast, the transition probabilities to the other HMMs are zero.
- **SVM:** This method uses the SVM in place of the HMM. We construct a classifier for device identification that classifies each feature vector into an electrical device class. We classify feature vectors obtained from a sensor node and then we identify the device class of the node by using the majority voting of the feature vector classification results. Note that when we construct the classifier, we ignore feature vectors whose current mean values are zero, which corresponds to 'off' events, because 'off' events are included in all device classes. We also construct a classifier for event recognition for each electrical device product. The classifier classifies each feature vector into an electrical event class. Unlike HMM-based methods, this method cannot model the temporal regularity of electrical events. This method also does not use $1/R$ as a feature.
- **Tree:** This method uses a decision tree in place of the SVM in the above SVM method. This method does not use $1/R$ as a feature.
- **HMM-R:** This method uses $1/R$ as a feature. Also, this method assumes that the transition probabilities across HMMs are all identical.
- **HMM-R(grammar):** This method uses $1/R$ as a feature. This method also employs handcrafted grammar.
- **SVM-R:** This method uses $1/R$ as a feature. This method also uses the SVM in place of the HMM.
- **Tree-R:** This method uses $1/R$ as a feature. This method also uses the decision tree in place of the HMM.

6.3   Results

Device Identification. Fig. 6 shows the transitions of device identification accuracies when we increase the number of test sessions used to identify devices. When the number of sessions (#sessions) is three, for example, we identify devices by using only the sensor data obtained in each house in the first three

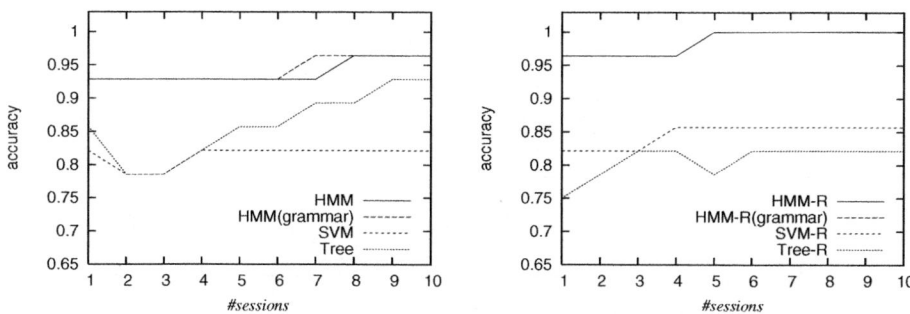

Fig. 6. Transitions of device identification accuracies when we increase #sessions that are used to identify devices

Table 2. Event recognition accuracies (average F-measure) in each house

	House A	House B	House C	AVG.
HMM	0.795	0.807	0.839	0.814
HMM(grammar)	0.861	0.822	0.853	0.845
SVM	0.823	0.834	0.837	0.831
Tree	0.834	0.773	**0.908**	0.839
HMM-R	0.816	0.809	0.843	0.823
HMM-R(grammar)	**0.872**	**0.865**	0.875	**0.871**
SVM-R	0.821	0.828	0.839	0.829
Tree-R	0.822	0.779	0.889	0.830

sessions. Because we prepared model sets of 28 electrical devices, the random guess ratio is only 3.6% ($1/28 = 0.036$). However, the HMM and HMM(grammar) methods achieved 96.4% accuracies when #sessions was ten. These methods greatly outperformed SVM and Tree, which cannot capture the temporal regularity of electrical events. The HMM-R and HMM-R(grammar) methods achieved 100% accuracies when #sessions was larger than four. (The transitions of these methods were completely identical in the right graph in Fig. 6.) By using the $1/R$ feature, we could identify devices perfectly. These methods also greatly outperformed SVM-R and Tree-R. That is, we confirmed the importance of capturing the temporal regularity of electrical events and taking the electrical resistances of electrical devices into account. Basically, a larger #sessions exhibited greater identification accuracy because we could use sufficient quantities of sensor data and capture the discriminative features of the sensor data. However, the HMM-R and HMM-R(grammar) methods achieved 96.4% accuracies even when #sessions was one. These results indicate that even if a battery sensor node is removed from an electrical device and then inserted into another device, these methods can soon identify the new device.

Event Recognition. To evaluate the event recognition performance, we assumed that the device identification results were all correct, and then calculated

Table 3. Event recognition accuracies in house A

		HMM			HMM-R			HMM-R(grammar)		
		precision	recall	F-measure	precision	recall	F-measure	precision	recall	F-measure
digital camera 2	on	0.874	0.671	0.759	0.895	0.716	0.796	0.887	0.726	0.799
	turn on	0.473	0.561	0.513	0.493	0.593	0.538	0.978	0.714	0.826
	turn off	0.316	0.391	0.349	0.335	0.396	0.363	1	0.941	0.97
	take photo	0.356	0.408	0.38	0.377	0.415	0.395	0.518	0.776	0.622
	focus	0.362	0.694	0.476	0.378	0.694	0.489	0.44	0.898	0.591
	off	0.975	0.975	0.975	0.975	0.975	0.975	0.975	0.975	0.975
vacuum 2	vacuum	0.993	0.996	0.994	0.993	0.996	0.994	0.993	0.996	0.994
	off	0.988	0.977	0.982	0.988	0.977	0.982	0.988	0.977	0.982
video game	on	1	0.939	0.968	1	0.983	0.992	1	0.983	0.992
	off	0.83	1	0.907	0.947	1	0.973	0.947	1	0.973
shaver 1	shaving	1	0.987	0.994	1	0.986	0.993	1	0.986	0.993
	off	0.925	1	0.961	0.919	1	0.958	0.919	1	0.958
screwdriver 1	ff/rw	0.997	0.982	0.99	1	0.982	0.991	1	0.982	0.991
	light	0.988	0.995	0.992	0.987	0.995	0.991	0.987	0.995	0.991
	off	0.976	0.979	0.977	0.976	0.979	0.977	0.976	0.979	0.977
toothbrush 1	brush	1	0.994	0.997	1	0.994	0.997	1	0.994	0.997
	off	0.972	1	0.986	0.976	1	0.988	0.976	1	0.988
cd player 1	turn on	0.484	0.51	0.497	0.515	0.579	0.545	1	0.569	0.726
	turn off	0.287	0.566	0.381	0.482	0.762	0.59	0.621	0.979	0.76
	play	0.961	0.65	0.775	0.956	0.686	0.799	0.946	0.898	0.922
	seek	0.047	0.66	0.088	0.06	0.681	0.11	0.075	0.936	0.139
	off	0.995	0.996	0.995	0.995	0.999	0.997	0.991	1	0.995
tv 1	turn on	0.73	0.514	0.603	0.731	0.651	0.689	0.75	0.982	0.851
	turn off	0.309	0.488	0.379	0.336	0.382	0.357	0.917	0.089	0.163
	show	1	0.987	0.994	1	0.994	0.997	0.999	0.999	0.999
	off	0.795	1	0.886	0.866	1	0.928	0.918	1	0.957
lantern	light	0.999	0.994	0.997	0.999	0.994	0.997	0.999	0.994	0.997
	off	0.97	0.997	0.983	0.97	0.997	0.983	0.97	0.997	0.983
cassette player 2	ff/rw	0.936	0.945	0.94	0.938	0.985	0.961	0.938	0.985	0.961
	play	0.962	0.947	0.954	0.991	0.947	0.968	0.991	0.947	0.968
	off	0.976	1	0.988	0.976	1	0.988	0.976	1	0.988
AVG.		0.790	0.832	0.795	0.808	0.850	0.816	0.893	0.913	0.872

the precision, recall, and F-measure based on the results for the estimated event class at each time slice. Also, the precision, recall, and F-measure were computed by using all test data (all ten sessions) obtained in each house. Table 2 shows the event recognition accuracies of the three houses for each recognition method. The HMM results were poorer than those of SVM and Tree, which are the discriminative models. This may be because the classification performance of the discriminative techniques, which find the discriminant boundaries of the classes, is often superior to that of generative models such as the HMM. On the other hand, HMM(grammar) outperformed HMM, SVM, and Tree. As described in detail later, the method was good at recognizing events of electrical devices that produced confusing sensor data patterns by using the handcrafted grammar. HMM-R(grammar), which uses both the grammar and the $1/R$ feature, achieved the highest accuracy.

Tables 3, 4, and 5 show the detailed event recognition accuracies obtained in each house. Because most electrical devices have only two electrical events, the event recognition accuracies were high in each house. We first focused on the HMM and HMM-R methods. By using the $1/R$ feature, we could slightly improve the accuracies of almost all the events. We then focused on the HMM-R and HMM-R(grammar) methods. By using the grammar, we could greatly improve the accuracies of the highly functional devices, namely CD players, TVs, DVD players, digital cameras, and a digital camcorder, which have many electrical event classes. The average improvement as regards F-measure was 0.122. As shown in Fig. 2 (c), 'turn on' and 'turn off' events of these devices have complex time-series sensor data. Therefore, the recognition accuracies with the HMM-R

Table 4. Event recognition accuracies in house B

		HMM			HMM-R			HMM-R(grammar)		
		precision	recall	F-measure	precision	recall	F-measure	precision	recall	F-measure
digital camcorder	on	0.902	0.994	0.946	0.886	0.976	0.929	0.884	0.976	0.928
	turn on	0.663	0.757	0.707	0.676	0.77	0.72	1	0.747	0.855
	turn off	0.278	0.252	0.264	0.282	0.256	0.268	0.659	0.966	0.784
	take video	0.965	0.649	0.776	0.906	0.611	0.73	0.907	0.703	0.792
	off	0.979	0.998	0.988	0.979	1	0.989	0.976	1	0.988
shaver 2	shave	1	0.994	0.997	0.997	0.994	0.995	0.997	0.994	0.995
	off	0.984	1	0.992	0.984	0.992	0.988	0.984	0.992	0.988
screw-driver 2	ff/rw	1	0.982	0.991	1	0.982	0.991	1	0.982	0.991
	off	0.972	1	0.986	0.972	1	0.986	0.972	1	0.986
tooth-brush 2	brush	1	0.992	0.996	1	0.992	0.996	1	0.992	0.996
	off	0.983	1	0.991	0.983	1	0.991	0.983	1	0.991
cd player 2	turn on	0.838	0.392	0.534	0.93	0.422	0.581	0.987	0.487	0.652
	turn off	0.387	0.765	0.514	0.506	0.824	0.627	0.674	0.948	0.788
	play	0.924	0.945	0.935	0.916	0.967	0.941	0.915	0.969	0.941
	seek	0.018	1	0.035	0.019	1	0.037	0.02	1	0.04
	off	0.995	0.982	0.989	0.996	0.995	0.996	0.986	0.995	0.99
flash-light 1	light	1	0.99	0.995	1	0.99	0.995	1	0.99	0.995
	off	0.975	1	0.987	0.975	1	0.987	0.975	1	0.987
flash-light 2	light	1	0.986	0.993	1	0.987	0.994	1	0.987	0.994
	off	0.973	1	0.986	0.976	1	0.988	0.976	1	0.988
cassette player 1	ff/rw	0.94	0.239	0.381	0.543	0.038	0.071	0.543	0.038	0.071
	play	0.551	0.908	0.686	0.492	0.912	0.639	0.492	0.912	0.639
	off	0.798	0.976	0.878	0.822	0.998	0.901	0.822	0.998	0.901
dvd player	turn on	0.7	0.742	0.721	0.788	0.785	0.787	0.998	0.992	0.995
	play	0.392	0.343	0.366	0.56	0.564	0.562	0.984	0.996	0.99
	off	0.989	0.989	0.989	0.989	0.989	0.989	0.989	0.989	0.989
soldering iron	on	0.994	0.992	0.993	0.994	0.992	0.993	0.994	0.992	0.993
	off	0.982	0.986	0.984	0.982	0.986	0.984	0.982	0.986	0.984
AVG.		0.828	0.852	0.807	0.827	0.858	0.809	0.882	0.915	0.865

Table 5. Event recognition accuracies in house C

		HMM			HMM-R			HMM-R(grammar)		
		precision	recall	F-measure	precision	recall	F-measure	precision	recall	F-measure
digital camera 1	on	0.63	0.929	0.751	0.636	0.956	0.764	0.629	0.956	0.759
	turn on	0.556	0.599	0.577	0.675	0.574	0.621	1	0.669	0.801
	turn off	0.611	0.374	0.464	0.702	0.586	0.639	0.995	0.747	0.854
	take photo	0.658	0.554	0.602	0.667	0.577	0.618	0.803	0.869	0.835
	focus	0.397	0.818	0.535	0.382	0.788	0.515	0.311	0.848	0.455
	off	0.984	0.992	0.988	0.968	0.992	0.98	0.976	1	0.988
vacuum 1	vacuum	0.998	0.993	0.996	0.998	0.993	0.996	0.998	0.993	0.996
	off	0.981	0.995	0.988	0.981	0.995	0.988	0.981	0.995	0.988
shaver 3	shave	1	0.994	0.997	1	0.994	0.997	1	0.994	0.997
	off	0.987	1	0.993	0.987	1	0.993	0.987	1	0.993
tooth-brush 3	brush	0.998	0.989	0.994	0.998	0.989	0.994	0.998	0.989	0.994
	off	0.974	0.996	0.985	0.974	0.996	0.985	0.974	0.996	0.985
tv 2	turn on	0.716	0.536	0.613	0.751	0.53	0.621	0.892	0.484	0.627
	show	0.886	0.92	0.903	0.881	0.95	0.914	0.875	0.976	0.922
	off	0.578	0.965	0.723	0.525	0.625	0.571	0.552	0.98	0.706
mill	coarse	1	0.955	0.977	1	0.963	0.981	1	0.963	0.981
	off	0.977	1	0.988	0.977	1	0.988	0.977	1	0.988
toy 1	go ahead	1	0.994	0.997	1	0.995	0.997	1	0.995	0.997
	off	0.971	1	0.985	0.977	1	0.988	0.977	1	0.988
toy 2	go forwards	0.684	0.849	0.757	0.67	0.858	0.752	0.67	0.858	0.752
	go backwards	0.801	0.563	0.661	0.812	0.563	0.665	0.812	0.563	0.665
	off	0.949	1	0.974	0.975	1	0.987	0.975	1	0.987
	AVG.	0.833	0.864	0.839	0.843	0.860	0.843	0.881	0.903	0.875

method related to these events were poor. The average as regards F-measure was 0.571. We could greatly improve the accuracies by incorporating such grammar as 'turn on' event follows 'off' event and 'off' event follows 'turn off' event. The average improvement was 0.248.

Finally, we describe the electrical events that HMM-R(grammar) could not recognize with high accuracy. The accuracies as regards the 'seek' events for the two CD players in houses A and B were very poor. This may be because we could not prepare sufficient quantities of training data (feature vectors) about the events. As shown in Fig. 2 (c), the time length of 'seek' is very short. The accuracy as regards the 'turn off' event of tv 1 in house A was poor. The event was mistakenly confused with an 'off' event because the current value approaches zero during a 'turn off' event. Also, the accuracy as regards the 'ff/rw' event of cassette player 1 in house B was poor. Because the player was light in weight, we collected training data by holding it in the hand. However, the participant placed the player on a table and operated it. (We did not collect training data when the player was placed on a table.) As mentioned in section 4.2, the motor rotation is affected by the posture of the motor. The HMMs of the player trained with our training data could not capture the use of the player in house B.

7 Conclusion

In this paper, we proposed and implemented a prototype battery-shaped sensor node for monitoring the use of electrical devices. We also proposed a device identification and electrical event recognition method by analyzing the sensor data. With the method, we can automatically identify into which electrical device the sensor node has been inserted and recognize electrical events related to the device. In addition, we achieved very high identification and recognition accuracies by using sensor data obtained from three real houses. As a part of our future work, we plan to develop other types of sensor nodes based on the mimic sensor framework to capture a broader range of real world activities. We also plan to develop wireless battery-shaped sensor nodes and conduct long-term experiments using them. We consider that there are two problems as regards developping wireless sensor nodes. The first problem relates to the size of the sensor and wireless transmission components. However, our sensing architecture is very simple as shown in Fig. 1 (a). Also, recently, a CPU has become available that includes a wireless transmission component the length of whose side is less than the diameter of an AA battery. Moreover, an SD card that includes a CPU and a WiFi AP component is already on the market (e.g., Eye-Fi[1]). The second problem relates to the energy consumption of the node. We can greatly reduce the energy consumption by stopping the node from transmitting sensor data while the current sensor data value is zero, i.e., OFF state. Also, as shown in Figs. 2 and 3, many electrical devices continually produce similar sensor data patterns. The node should be designed to transmit sensor data only when they are very different from those of the latest sample.

References

1. Mynatt, E., Rowan, J., Craighill, S., Jacobs, A.: Digital family portraits: Supporting peace of mind for extended family members. In: CHI 2001, pp. 333–340 (2001)
2. Maekawa, T., Yanagisawa, Y., Kishino, Y., Kamei, K., Sakurai, Y., Okadome, T.: Object-blog system for environment-generated content. IEEE Pervasive Computing 7(4), 20–27 (2008)

---

[1] http://eye.fi/

3. Lukowicz, P., Junker, H., Stäger, M., von Büren, T., Tröster, G.: WearNET: A Distributed Multi-sensor System for Context Aware Wearables. In: Borriello, G., Holmquist, L.E. (eds.) UbiComp 2002. LNCS, vol. 2498, pp. 361–370. Springer, Heidelberg (2002)

4. Bao, L., Intille, S.S.: Activity Recognition from User-Annotated Acceleration Data. In: Ferscha, A., Mattern, F. (eds.) PERVASIVE 2004. LNCS, vol. 3001, pp. 1–17. Springer, Heidelberg (2004)

5. Maekawa, T., Watanabe, S.: Unsupervised activity recognition with user's physical characteristics data. In: Int'l Symp. on Wearable Computers, pp. 89–96 (2011)

6. Philipose, M., Fishkin, K., Perkowitz, M.: Inferring activities from interactions with objects. IEEE Pervasive Computing 3(4), 50–57 (2004)

7. Tapia, E.M., Intille, S.S., Larson, K.: Portable Wireless Sensors for Object Usage Sensing in the Home: Challenges and Practicalities. In: Schiele, B., Dey, A.K., Gellersen, H., de Ruyter, B., Tscheligi, M., Wichert, R., Aarts, E., Buchmann, A. (eds.) AmI 2007. LNCS, vol. 4794, pp. 19–37. Springer, Heidelberg (2007)

8. van Kasteren, T., Noulas, A., Englebienne, G., Kröse, B.: Accurate activity recognition in a home setting. In: Ubicomp 2008, pp. 1–9 (2008)

9. Beckmann, C., Consolvo, S., LaMarca, A.: Some Assembly Required: Supporting End-User Sensor Installation in Domestic Ubiquitous Computing Environments. In: Davies, N., Mynatt, E.D., Siio, I. (eds.) UbiComp 2004. LNCS, vol. 3205, pp. 107–124. Springer, Heidelberg (2004)

10. Tapia, E.M., Intille, S.S., Larson, K.: Activity Recognition in the Home Using Simple and Ubiquitous Sensors. In: Ferscha, A., Mattern, F. (eds.) PERVASIVE 2004. LNCS, vol. 3001, pp. 158–175. Springer, Heidelberg (2004)

11. Kim, Y., Schmid, T., Charbiwala, Z., Srivastava, M.: ViridiScope: design and implementation of a fine grained power monitoring system for homes. In: Ubicomp 2009, pp. 245–254 (2009)

12. Cohn, G., Gupta, S., Froehlich, J., Larson, E., Patel, S.N.: GasSense: Appliance-Level, Single-Point Sensing of Gas Activity in the Home. In: Floréen, P., Krüger, A., Spasojevic, M. (eds.) Pervasive 2010. LNCS, vol. 6030, pp. 265–282. Springer, Heidelberg (2010)

13. Froehlich, J., Larson, E., Campbell, T., Haggerty, C., Fogarty, J., Patel, S.: Hydrosense: Infrastructure-mediated single-point sensing of whole-home water activity. In: Ubicomp 2009, pp. 235–244 (2009)

14. Patel, S.N., Robertson, T., Kientz, J.A., Reynolds, M.S., Abowd, G.D.: At the Flick of a Switch: Detecting and Classifying Unique Electrical Events on the Residential Power Line (Nominated for the Best Paper Award). In: Krumm, J., Abowd, G.D., Seneviratne, A., Strang, T. (eds.) UbiComp 2007. LNCS, vol. 4717, pp. 271–288. Springer, Heidelberg (2007)

15. Gupta, S., Reynolds, M., Patel, S.: ElectriSense: Single-point sensing using EMI for electrical event detection and classification in the home. In: Ubicomp 2010, pp. 139–148 (2010)

16. Lifton, J., Feldmeier, M., Ono, Y., Lewis, C., Paradiso, J.: A platform for ubiquitous sensor deployment in occupational and domestic environments. In: IPSN 2007, pp. 119–127 (2007)

17. Jiang, X., Dawson-Haggerty, S., Dutta, P., Culler, D.: Design and implementation of a high-fidelity ac metering network. In: IPSN 2009, pp. 253–264 (2009)

18. Ravi, N., Dandekar, N., Mysore, P., Littman, M.: Activity recognition from accelerometer data. In: IAAI 2005, vol. 20, pp. 1541–1546 (2005)

19. Maekawa, T., Yanagisawa, Y., Kishino, Y., Ishiguro, K., Kamei, K., Sakurai, Y., Okadome, T.: Object-Based Activity Recognition with Heterogeneous Sensors on Wrist. In: Floréen, P., Krüger, A., Spasojevic, M. (eds.) Pervasive 2010. LNCS, vol. 6030, pp. 246–264. Springer, Heidelberg (2010)
20. Maekawa, T., Kishino, Y., Sakurai, Y., Suyama, T.: Recognizing the Use of Portable Electrical Devices with Hand-Worn Magnetic Sensors. In: Lyons, K., Hightower, J., Huang, E.M. (eds.) Pervasive 2011. LNCS, vol. 6696, pp. 276–293. Springer, Heidelberg (2011)
21. Logan, B., Healey, J., Philipose, M., Tapia, E.M., Intille, S.S.: A Long-Term Evaluation of Sensing Modalities for Activity Recognition. In: Krumm, J., Abowd, G.D., Seneviratne, A., Strang, T. (eds.) UbiComp 2007. LNCS, vol. 4717, pp. 483–500. Springer, Heidelberg (2007)
22. Rabiner, L.: A tutorial on hidden Markov models and selected applications in speech recognition. Proceedings of the IEEE 77(2), 257–286 (1989)

Leveraging Children's Behavioral Distribution and Singularities in New Interactive Environments: Study in Kindergarten Field Trips

Inseok Hwang[1], Hyukjae Jang[1], Taiwoo Park[1], Aram Choi[1], Youngki Lee[1],
Chanyou Hwang[1], Yanggui Choi[2], Lama Nachman[3], and Junehwa Song[1]

[1] Korea Advanced Institute of Science and Technology, Daejeon, Republic of Korea
{inseok,hjjang,twpark,archoi,youngki,
cyhwang,junesong}@nclab.kaist.ac.kr
[2] Yerang Kindergarten, Daejeon, Republic of Korea
yanggui.choi@gmail.com
[3] Intel Corporation, Santa Clara, California USA
lama.nachman@intel.com

Abstract. The behavior observations on young children in new, first-in-the-life environments have significant implications. We can often uniquely observe a child's unforeseen interaction with the environment and peer-children. It would be not only a piece of discovery but a beginning of an open quest worth exploring. Out-of-classroom activities like kindergarten's field trips are perfect opportunities, but those are quite different from regular classroom activities where the teachers' conventional observation methods are hardly practical. This paper proposes a novel approach to extend the teachers' awareness on the children's field trip behaviors by means of mobile and sensor technology. We adopt the notion of behavioral distribution and singularities. We estimate the children's representative behavioral state in a given context, and study the effect of focusing on the behaviors which are unlikely in this context. We discuss our 14-month collaborative study and various qualitative benefits through multiple deployments on actual kindergarten field trips.

Keywords: Behavior, distribution, singularity, children, kindergarten, field trip, smartphone, sensor.

1   Introduction

Careful observations on children's behaviors, such as play, interactions, and class activities, give many implications of their social status [4], skills [21], development [26], and assessments [23]. Behavior observations are particularly important in young ages as their linguistic skills are in early stage. Pervasive technologies have assisted the human experts to be more observant on and aware of children's behaviors in terms of clinical needs [9, 15], collaborative learning [19], etc. Kindergartens[1] are good

---

[1] Kindergartens in Korean communities are institutions for children who are not old enough to attend elementary schools, typically 4~6 years old.

J. Kay et al. (Eds.): Pervasive 2012, LNCS 7319, pp. 39–56, 2012.
© Springer-Verlag Berlin Heidelberg 2012

examples around us where the teachers conduct extensive observation on their children's behaviors every day, and make use of it on the way they teach, interact with, and take care of each child.

We newly explore the behavior observations of young children in out-of-classroom activities, such as field trip events, by means of pervasive technologies. Our empirical study in a kindergarten supports that the children's behaviors in field trips imply great significance; their behaviors in first-in-the-life environments are often unforeseen, uniquely observable and hardly reproduced in classroom routines. In spite of the importance, behavior observations are hardly possible in field trip situations. A new, out-of-routine environment with full of cognitive stimuli and feeling of freedom is an excellent condition to excite young children and even make them careless. Unfamiliar environments make the children more dependent on adults. The teachers should watch over the children in a bird's-eye-view, devoting their full efforts to protect them against potential incidents and taking care of their basic needs. The teachers cannot afford consistent attention to each child and make timely recording, and a lot of unique, situation-specific behaviors are hardly observed and not persistently retained.

In this paper, we leverage the collective behavioral features of children monitored by wearable sensing platforms, offering the teachers the behavioral clues of the children which were hardly noticeable in the field but potentially significant. Those clues may serve as motives where the teachers would like to review the situation around those moments and might find important implications. For example, in an outdoor hiking, a pair of girls spends minutes at a dandelion while the rest are randomly playing around. At that time, the teacher cannot pay much attention on those girls as her priority is to prevent the actively playing children from injuries. After they come back, she gets a report about those two girls' distinctive behaviors. She gets intrigued, and reviews the video taken around this moment. Then she engages conversation with the girls about what they liked, using their own fun to help developing rich expression and sharing experiences. The teacher further postulates theories of those girls' interests or sympathy on botanical themes, devising personalized contents in regard to them. Our idea of monitoring the children's field trip behaviors gained much interest from both teachers and parents for opening new possibilities of multi-dimensional, persistent benefits obtainable from field trips which might be anecdotal otherwise.

The major challenges in monitoring the field trip behaviors lie in the vast contextual- and population-diversity; there are so many different field trip venues, different themes and activities within, and even different children groups. We can hardly classify all the behaviors which might exist. Determining the significance of a behavior would be an open question depending on the context and applicable disciplines.

In this light, we propose the notions of the children's *behavioral distribution* and *singularities*. Our rationale is that we may find contextual implications from statistical representations of many children's behaviors in a shared situation. Then we hypothesize that the *singularities*, which we define as behaviors that are unlikely in the distribution but do appear, might be likely the points which the teachers find context-specific significance from, but could not notice within the middle of field trips.

We report our empirical study on monitoring the singularities by mobile and sensor technologies. It includes our 14-month studies in a local kindergarten, the collaborative re-design of the children's backpacks into mobile sensing platforms, and the deployment on five different field trips with 9~12 children each. We thoughtfully built a teacher-friendly reporting system, allowing them to conveniently review the singularities suggested. We discuss our observations and advantages from extensive use cases. The teachers often discovered unforeseen behaviors and social relation of a child. They combined those discoveries with their knowledge and built rich theories. They also brought persuasive effects to the children and even recommended the field trip venue a direction to facilitate better experiences in future events.

The major contributions of this study are as follows. First, we delivered the design considerations and field practices to leverage pervasive technologies for behavioral monitoring in field trips. Second, we evaluated our designs by deploying it on multiple field trip events and delivered their rich benefits, especially in terms of extending the teachers' awareness on children's field trip behaviors.

2   Related Works

Monitoring and Archiving Children's Behaviors. The motivations for monitoring children's behaviors are from various clinical, developmental, parental, and educational needs. A large body of researches designed self-stimulatory behavior monitoring of autistic children [9, 15], and elaborated the design principles with functional behavior assessment from longitudinal studies [8]. We focus on the probabilistic notions in a group of general children's behaviors, rather than clinically specific behaviors. Mobile technologies have enabled advanced organization of interesting moments for parental needs [14], presenting an instant capture and organization of their children's interesting moments. We share the notion of finding the moments of interest, but we study a large and dynamic population where a teacher can hardly find individually interesting moment on-the-fly. Playful Toothbrush [1] takes a gaming approach to promote good tooth brushing habits. We later discuss persuasive effects as well, but as a possible implication depending on the teacher's interpretation. Children's physical activity intensities in a classroom are aggregated and compared [12] for possible correlations with their tempers. We address the issues in out-of-classroom activities and rich behavioral features within. We then discuss the qualitative benefits extending field trips from anecdotal events toward better integration with childhood education.

Out-of-Class Learning Activity and Pervasive Technology. The learning experience of children during field trips implies condensed educational values. Empirical studies show that content-related experiences in field trips are engraved in one's persistent memory, recallable even in adulthood with little decline [7], and yield better acquisition of knowledge than simply learning in the classroom [17]. Advances in pervasive technology have enriched students' field trips by digitally augmenting the environment or interactions within. Ambient Wood [24] and Tangible Flags [2] enrich the children's experience by integrating a specifically crafted technology and site-specific contents in existing natural environments. We address a different problem space, postulating that even today's field trips retain considerable potential to better understand the children's behaviors within. We study how technologies bring their behaviors to the foreground of the teachers' awareness, expecting the teachers initiate educative methods in regard to this new discovery. We put effort into the monitoring transparency not to disturb the children's natural behaviors, as well as site-independent technology, envisioning a part of general support for many field trips.

Applying Technology in Educational Settings for Children. The ubiquity of mobile devices and interactive contents is enabling many creative applications in educational settings. It was advised that use of technologies in schools should be under holistic consideration of benefits, risks, policies, etc. [3]. A large scale study provided guidance for deploying technologies in existing settings with pre-structured education [22]. Their efforts greatly affected our design process. We carefully collaborated with the kindergarten not to impede their existing practices. We examined the privacy and safety matters with many stakeholders. Extensive studies in the interaction design and children also enlightened us to better understand children's developmental nature and participatory roles [11]. Although our primary users are the teachers rather than the children, the children joined as testers and informant [5]. We have been advised to find appropriate monitoring modality and attain gradual integration of technology.

Leveraging Collective Characteristics in Population. Large-scale studies on human activities explored correlations between digital traces and human attributes [18, 20]. The similarities within population were incorporated for better personally tuned classification [16]. The symmetries of group activities with interactive tabletops delivered implications of collaboration [19]. These works shed light on characterizing the notion of group in children; the kindergarten is a community with strong similarity in attributes of ages, developments, education, and shared daily activities for up to 8 hours a day. However, we do not correlate a certain behavioral characteristics with a specific attribute. The rapidly changing nature of young children would make it difficult to develop a model with consistent fidelity. Notably, a design guideline for a today's child would be no longer appropriate after months [11]. Instead, we test more general notion of behavioral singularity as the teacher-perceived significance.

3   Motivations and Implications of Behavioral Observation

We discuss significant implications in behavior observation, the challenges and motivation found from our 14-month collaboration with a private kindergarten in the city of Daejeon, South Korea. We regularly discussed with the teachers on a weekly basis, and participated in 11 field trips.

3.1   The Implications and Challenges in Today's Behavioral Observation

We found that observing the children's behaviors is one of the integral, everyday tasks of kindergarten teachers in the classrooms. The teachers arrange notebooks or laptops always available in the classrooms to retain observations as many as possible. To demonstrate the implications in behavior observations, we quote a daily observation log on a child. *"We did 'walking along the thin beams of constellation-shapes.' Ahyun did very good in balancing her body. (...) I encouraged her in praise of her performance. Hearing that, she got apparently more active. She wanted to try more constellations. I saw her performance also gave others confidence, making them try boldly. (...)"* [2] This may seem like a simple episode about 'Ahyun', but it has many implications. (1) It records a new discovery. Previously, this teacher has known for a long time that Ahyun is mostly of little confidence. It explains the importance of her today's performance. (2) It records a lesson that encouraging Ahyun affected the performance of everyone. The teacher retains this lesson and shares it effectively with her fellow teachers in monthly meetings. (3) When switching the teacher in charge, this log is transferred to the newly coming teacher who knows little about Ahyun.

However, when they get out of their classrooms and go to a field, the teachers are required to change their priorities; they have to be protectors and caregivers far more than educators. In brief, they cannot afford to pay consistent and sufficient attention to individual children nor make prompt note-taking. The key attributions are:

- The stimulatory environment often makes children careless, unpredictable, or self-oriented. The sources of stimuli are diverse, e.g., little animals or robots. Many empirical evidences support the attribution. T1 (Teacher #1) stated, *"They just get out of the line and rush to something. It happens in a blink of an eye."* T5 recalled, *"[a child] touched a rose and got pricked his finger. He didn't know about the thorns."* T3 stated, *"When [a child] got immersed in something, he didn't respond to my instruction. (...) Even he couldn't notice we are moving out. (...) I count heads every a few minutes."* The literature explains the relevant natures of young children, that preschoolers concentrate on one aspect at a time and neglect others, without much anticipating what will happen by they are doing [11].
- The unfamiliar environment renders children more dependent on adults. There are well-established developmental milestones expected from a child at a given age [23], like changing clothes and walking up steps. However, being in a new environment makes it difficult for children to do what they used to. T4 states, *"My children are potty-trained, but they have no idea where the toilets are. I find them toilets so many times even during a single field trip. (...) Even there is no small toilet available, so I personally assist them."* T3 states, *"Thirst is a common problem. Fountains are often unavailable, or installed too high for a child to drink alone."*

3.2   Potential Benefits of Extended Behavior Observation in the Field

Although the teachers hardly conduct behavior observations in today's field trips, we discussed what potential benefits would be obtainable if the teachers somehow get to know more about the children's behaviors. We videotaped 7 field trips and reviewed together with the teachers. Actually they do videotape their field trips sometimes, but they do not use it for reviewing the children's behaviors. They attempted it a few times years ago, but discarded it as it was too inefficient.

---

[2] All quotes from the teachers' writing and statements are translated from Korean language.

The teachers and we could discover a large number of small but unique behaviors in each field trip situation. Notably, the following example discusses that a discovery is not only a piece of knowledge but also an origin where rich benefits may emerge. We observed a boy trying to operate a miniature maglev train at Science Quest Park. This place is about half size of a football ground, exhibiting scientific gadgets and interactive tabletops. We found this boy stayed here for over five minutes. T5 stated it was unusually long at his age, stating, "*I'm surprised I couldn't notice this. (…) I passed by him twice to check everybody is doing well. (…) I don't recall such an impressive concentration of him.*" We do not jump to a premature conclusion why he stayed so long. More important lesson is that finding the distinctive behavior is a beginning of an open question worth exploring. The teachers stated that they would need to make conversation with him, to better understand the context and the child. Watching the video together would improve the effectiveness of conversation and the proficiency in his expression. T5 stated that such interaction initiates a natural, self-motivated reminiscence on him, stimulating his memory and making a strong imprint. It helps him keeping this memory for a long time which might be volatile otherwise.

The more important benefit can be found in the literature, that such a process can train him to use long-term memory [11]. Furthermore, noting that he was trying to figure out how to run the train by tapping different permutations of the console buttons, knowing this behavior may help teachers identify a need for scaffolding [25]; a little help from the teacher would enable him to complete a work, which otherwise might remain incomplete on his own. We do not discuss the real-time intervention, but the teachers appreciated it as advices for planning a new activity.

4   Behavioral Singularity: Intuition and Rationale

Due to the individual and contextual diversities and the rapid development of young children, it may not be able to classify all the behaviors observable from the children in the field; even it might not be a closed set. In addition, the significance of a given behavior would be very context-dependent; e.g. the previous maglev example might be interpreted into a distinctive concentration, or into not mingling with other friends. Hence we do not intend to classify or recognize specific behaviors. Alternatively, we leverage the existing conventions of how the teachers watch over the children in the field, like a bird's-eye view. Section 3 discussed that many small, individual behaviors are less paid attention to, and not imprinted on the teacher's memory.

In this light, we postulate that the teacher keeps track of a "blurred" awareness on what the children have been doing in overall. We aim to enrich their awareness by pervasive technology, but do it "selectively" in terms of the behaviors' significance. We must consider that the teachers' resources are highly limited. Not to mention they are extremely busy in the field, it is nontrivial to spare a chunk of time from their existing, densely structured kindergarten workload. Fine chronicles of every single child would be little different from a full video review which was discarded already.

We propose the notion of *behavioral singularity* as an estimate of potential significance. It is defined as the behaviors which are expected less occurring or unlikely with respect to the common behaviors in a given situation. To represent the situation on which we determine a singularity, we adopt the notion of *behavioral distribution*. It is basically analogous to a probability distribution modeling the children's behaviors, used to determine the likelihood of an observed behavior. The rationale behind these notions is that the teacher may retain good awareness of overall behaviors which have been occurring commonly and frequently. Regarding the example of two girls and a dandelion in Section 1, the teacher recalls the overall impression around that time like *"they were actively playing with each other"* and *"they were catching others, and rolling on the grass."* It means that, those girls' behaviors, squatting still in front of a dandelion together, were not one of commonly occurring behaviors.

We do not assert that the notion of singularity may estimate all possible behavioral significances. A child's frequently repeated behaviors would yield high probability, and hence may not be determined as a singularity. However, teachers might find a significant implication from the repetition. We address that frequent behaviors can be easily perceived by the teacher, not necessarily with pervasive technology support.

5   Design Considerations and Prototyping

This section discusses our design considerations and prototypes to test our implication of behavioral singularities. We designed (1) wearable mobile sensing system to transparently monitor behavior features, (2) computational methods to evaluate singularities from the features, and (3) teacher-friendly system to report the singularities.

5.1   Mobile Sensing System for Children's Behaviors in the Field

We designed a mobile sensing system that continuously monitors the physical features of a child's behaviors. We used the off-the-shelf smartphones, Google Nexus One (Android 2.2), to develop our prototype sensing platforms.

Our major considerations were the comfort, safety, and privacy. In overall, the entire study was conducted with voluntary children under the teachers' and the parents' consent. The comfort is very important as our targets are 4~5 years old. An adult may easily carry a smartphone feeling little discomfort, but a child of much smaller body would not. We focused on their backpacks, which they wear for the most time in the field. The average weight of a backpack was 1.3 kg including items like a drink and fruits. Our sensing platform added 0.15 kg, or 11.5% extra weight to the backpack. Figure 1 shows our re-designed backpacks; a smartphone and a sensor mote (discussed below) are securely integrated in SenseCam-like configuration [10]. We communicated carefully with the children wearing these backpacks, looking for any sign of discomfort. Fortunately they liked it, and envied those wearing our backpacks.

We discussed with the parents for children's privacy and safety, explaining the data that can be monitored. Regarding the radio power, we confirmed it far below the government regulation and the international guideline [13]. We also considered third-party privacy of the visitors to the venue, in case of unintentional photographing. It was resolved as our kindergarten usually conducted field trips by reserving the sites for dedicated use. One exception was the mountain-hiking, a naturally open space. But we believe it reduces some concerns as photographing in a public mountain with the presence of passersby is little minded in Korean culture.

Fig. 1. Re-designed backpacks (left), Children wearing the backpacks (Right)

We used multiple sensing modalities available in the smartphone, including accelerometers, compasses, and cameras. The accelerometer and the compass collect the child's activity intensity and body orientation, respectively, at 20 Hz. The camera takes pictures at 1 frame for every 4 sec which may show what is in front of the child. We additionally employed TinyOS-compatible motes with 802.15.4 radio stack, to estimate inter-child proximity at 2 Hz from the radio signal features like RSSI (Radio Signal Strength Indicator). The smartphone was unable to do it as its Bluetooth scan took more than 10 sec at a time, too sparse to track the children's dynamic relocation.

Note that we attempted to introduce a cap with a small camera installed to obtain better coherence to the child's sight. It was declined because wearing a cap was not welcomed by children, as it was not a part of their regular clothing in field trips.

5.2   Evaluating Singularities from Behavioral Distribution

Figure 2 illustrates the overall flow to evaluate the feature-specific singularities from each feature dataset. For each feature type at a time interval, we estimate a distribution well-describing the overall behaviors of the majority of children. Then we determine a singularity, i.e., a child whose behavior features show large disparities with respect to this distribution. As a result, we obtain feature-specific singularity sets, S_O, S_A, S_P, and S_D, each containing singularities of body orientation, activity intensities, peer proximities, and image differentials, respectively. Those are combined and prioritized before being reported to the teachers.

We demonstrate the details by taking an example with a real 'compass' dataset illustrated in Figure 3; the children were listening to the curator's explanation in front of an artwork. The raw data are time-stamped samples of the smartphone's compass heading ranging from 0 ~ 359 ° . Figure 3 shows a cylindrical visualization of a part of those samples monitored from $n = 9$ children for 500 sec. When many children's body orientations remained toward the curator, we can confirm it by their mean compass trajectory (the thick solid line) which is highly concentrated and stable. During this time, the video showed that Child #1 had been looking at a wall-mounted screen aside from the curator for more than 1 minute. The following procedure evaluates Child #1 as a singularity in terms of his body orientation, which is accordant with the flow shown in Figure 2. **Step 1:** Let C_k denote the histogram of Child #k's compass

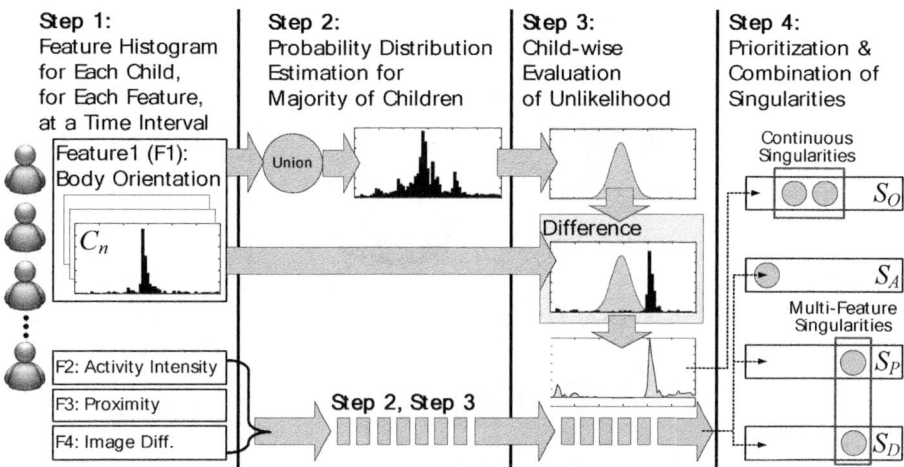

Fig. 2. Overall flow to estimate the behavioral distributions from the children's sensor features, evaluate the singularities, prioritize and combine the singularities

samples collected for a time interval $T_0 = [t_0, t_1)$, where $t_1 = t_0 + w$, w is the window size. (We use 60 sec.) **Step 2:** We estimate the distribution describing the union of the most children's histograms, $C = C_1 \cup \ldots \cup C_n$. We simply hypothesize it is from a normal distribution[3] N. We used Lilliefors test as we did not hypothesize particular values of mean and variance of N. If the hypothesis is rejected, we discard the current iteration and move on to T_1. If accepted, we presume N to be the behavioral distribution for T_0 in terms of body orientations. **Step 3:** We evaluate the per-child unlikeliness of his/her histogram, C_k, with respect to the majority of children's distribution, N. We adopt Kullback-Leibler divergence:

$$D_{KL}(P||Q) = \sum_i P(i) \log \frac{P(i)}{Q(i)}, \text{ where } P\text{: observation, } Q\text{: model.}$$

We use C_k and N for P and Q, respectively. $D_{KL}(P \| Q)$ equals 0 if and only if $P(i) = Q(i)$ for all i, and $D_{KL}(P \| Q) > 0$ otherwise. Its property is accordant with our notion as it puts stronger emphases on larger positive disparities of $P(i)$ over $Q(i)$, i.e., at some part of the sample space, we have more observations than those expected by the probabilistic model. In this example, we obtained the highest D_{KL} for $P = C_1$. Therefore we say child #1 showed a singular behavior around T_0 in terms of his body orientation in an extent of D_{KL}, and add a tuple (child #1, T_0, D_{KL}) to S_O. **Step 4:** We have shown the detailed procedure to evaluate singularities in terms of body orientations. The singularities in terms of other features are evaluated by the step 1 through 3 in similar manners, and we present additional feature-specific explanations below. After obtaining the singularities in each feature set, namely S_O, S_A, S_P, and S_D for the entire field trip duration, those are combined across time and features. If a child is found at the same T from more than one feature set, those are combined and re-weighted

---

[3]   As a heuristic, we try to find a normal distribution well-accepted to the largest number of samples, at least 60% or more.

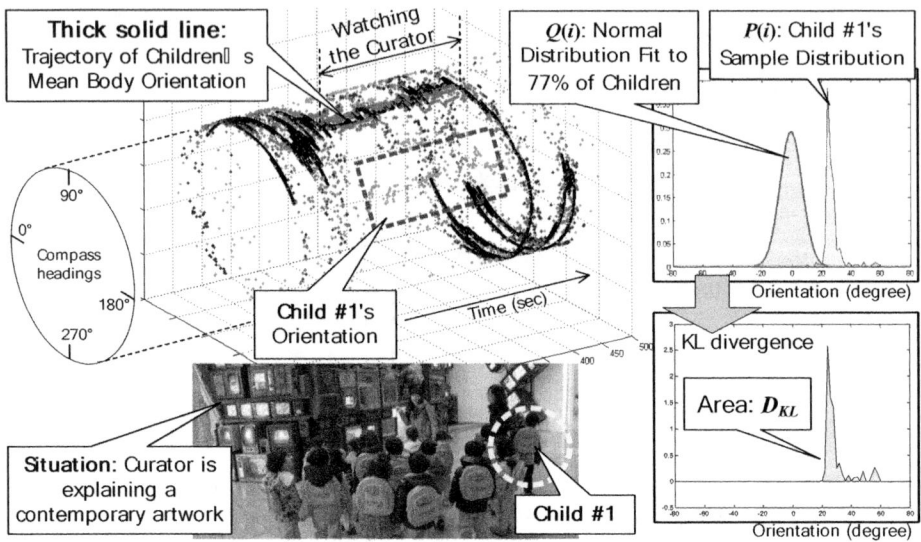

Fig. 3. Evaluating a singularity from the distribution of body orientation (The distribution is re-centered to 0 ° from the actual sample mean of 102.4 ° for presentation purpose)

(denoted as multi-feature singularities in Figure 2). If a child is found consecutively from T_t and T_{t+1}, they are merged as well (denoted as continuous singularities in Figure 2). For entire duration $[T_0, T_{end}]$, all singularities are prioritized based on their weights, D_{KL}, and top-k singularities are reported to the teachers. As k decides the number of singularities suggested to the teachers, selecting an appropriate k depends on their affordable time and perceived fidelity. The following sections discuss it.

The singularities in terms of the activity intensities and the proximities between the children are denoted as S_A and S_P, respectively. We evaluate the activity intensity features with the AC part from the energy frequency spectrum of each child's accelerometer samples. We test if the activity intensities are from an exponential distribution, as we often observed that those were heavily biased toward the low energy spectrum. The rest of procedures to evaluate singularities are analogous to the case of compass. The typical singularities in terms of activity intensities, S_A, are children either being very calm or showing excessive physical activities relative to the majority children. The two girls at a dandelion in Section 1 is an example of this kind.

For the proximity, we make the proximity dataset P_{ij} for $_NC_2$ pairs of children. The elements of P_{ij} are essentially the RSSI values measured between the child i and j. The procedures in Figure 2 are conducted by comparing each pair of children, rather than each single child, to the estimated distribution of all $_NC_2$ pairs of children. Typical examples of the singularities in terms of proximity, S_P, are pairs of children who have been mostly very close to each other or very distant, and sometimes a child moving around under relatively dense and stationary situations.

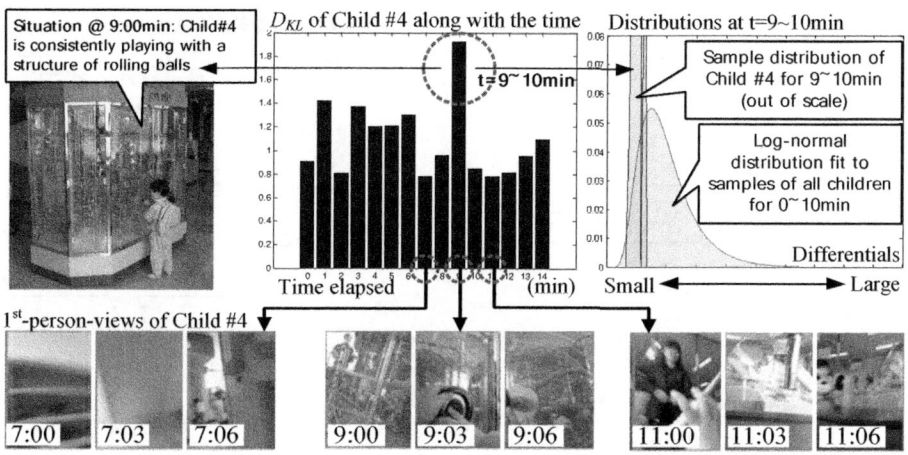

Fig. 4. Evaluating a singularity from the distribution of camera differential features

In addition, we studied an experimental feature, 'image differentials', which are the differentials between the histograms of temporally adjacent images from the phone camera. Image differentials might be an estimate of how often a child changes her interaction targets, especially in settings with many choices of interactive attractions. The place with the maglev in Section 3.2 is such a case where the children freely choose a target, make interactions with their choices, move to another, and begin playing with new ones. We observed that the accelerometers or compass features would not give much discrimination as the children's orientations are mostly random and many attractions involve physical activities. However, the image differentials construct an interesting distribution, mostly from log-normal families. Figure 4 is such an example. The situation is that child #4 entered a hall at $t = 7$ min. At "rolling balls down through a complex structure", he made quite a longer interaction than many other children, around $t = 9$ min. Then he left and played with other attractions but not as long as the previous one. The D_{KL} values are evaluated for per-child histogram of image differential values and the log-normal distribution approximating those of all children. Figure 4 shows his consistent interaction was evaluated as a singularity. It shows his D_{KL} values for $t = 0 \sim 14$ min, showing the peak for $t = 9 \sim 10$ min. At the right, we can see more details at this moment. It shows the log-normal distribution estimated from all the children, overlapped with the child #4's sample distribution. Note that we extended the time window for the overall distribution. It is a heuristic for image differentials to find stable distributions. The set S_D often includes a child whose interaction targets are either very consistent or very frequently changing. But S_D also includes a child who has been standing still, taking a rest, or running around. Hence we do not attribute S_D to interaction consistency; it is subject to teacher's validation.

5.3   Design of Teacher-Reporting System

We designed a system for teachers to conveniently review the suggested singularities. The first consideration is that the monitoring should be not only transparent to the

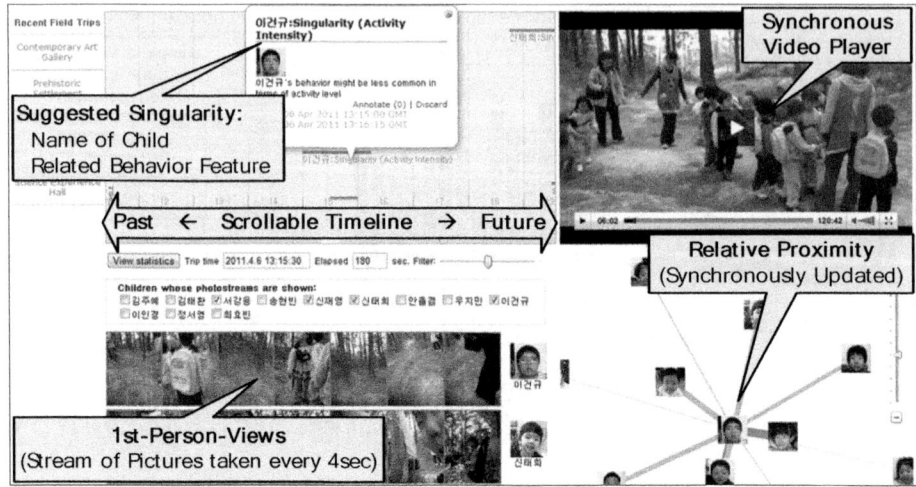

Fig. 5. A screenshot of the web-based teacher-reporting system

children but also unobtrusive to the teachers' duties. In the middle of a field trip, they were hesitant about diverting their attention from the children to mobile devices to see non-safety-critical information. Further discussions led us to a teacher-friendly design philosophy, "retrospect". The second consideration is their limited affordable time. The teachers had different preferences in time availability, like after the children went home, when they take a nap, or even at the teachers' home for thorough reviews. The design needed to be flexible to meet their time and location preferences.

Figure 5 shows our prototype reporting system. It is an interactive web application providing "top-*k*" singularities and the associated videos recorded by an auxiliary teacher or an undergraduate assistant majoring in child education. Once a field trip completed, the monitored features are uploaded and the singularities are prioritized. We built it on the web to enable flexible access. The system shows first top 10 singularities, but gives the teacher an option to see more. On average, the teachers could afford an hour to review one field trip, and reviewed 10~20 singularities per hour.

6   Deployment and Evaluation Study

We deployed our mobile monitoring platforms in five different field trips as shown in Figure 6, with 4~5-year-old 9~12 children (3~4 girls). In total, 16 children participated in at least one trip. Each trip lasted 1.5~2 hours, not counting the transportations to/from the venues. All deployments were under parental consents and supervised by 1~2 teachers. Each field trip report was reviewed by the teacher who led the trip. The evaluation consists of two phases. (1) We collected their subjective validation of singularities suggested by the reporting system. (2) More importantly, we deliver various qualitative observations through free-format interviews with those teachers.

Fig. 6. Five field trip destinations for deployment and evaluation study

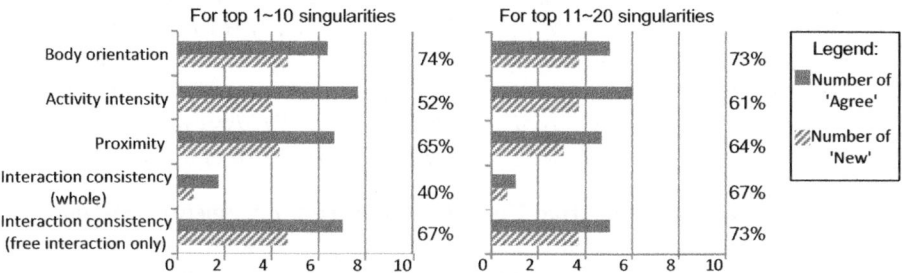

Fig. 7. Subjective validation for 1st and 2nd ten singularities from each feature set. The percentages are the ratios of 'new' out of the 'agreed' singularities.

The subjective validation results are summarized in Figure 7. They validated each singularity by referencing the video and the 1st-person-views shown in the reporting system. The teachers checked it "agree" if they agreed that the child showed less common behavior in terms of the feature type around 1 minute window at the time of singularity. For each agreed one, she checked it "new" if she had not seen this behavior in the field, or she saw it but did not remember it until reviewing the singularity. We report the effect of increasing k by showing the 1st and 2nd ten singularities from each set. Note that we used the term 'interaction consistency' even though we did not attribute the singularities from image differentials to it. It was for the teachers' convenience, as 'image differentials' are not an observable behavior they can validate through the video. In overall, we can see that the smaller number of 'agree' for larger k. However, 'new-to-agree' percentages are not necessarily lower for larger k. The explanation may be that, the singularities become less clear for a larger k, but such a singularity might be likely unnoticed by the teachers in the field. We note the relatively low new-to-agree percentage for the top 1~10 singularities of activity intensity. The major reason for 'not new' was that, the teachers were already aware of the suggested singular child whose activity was a lot higher than other children. We briefly discuss this issue in Section 7. For interaction consistency, we report two result sets: the whole results (upper) and those only from the situations where the children freely choose their interaction targets (lower). Those two sets' largely different results are not surprising as 'interaction consistency' is mostly defined in the latter situations. The lower results show that, if the situation is well fit, the image differentials exhibit good estimations on the singularities in terms of interaction consistencies.

6.1   Qualitative Observations

We present an extensive set of observations, including immediate findings like discoveries and recalls, as well as long-term ones like facilitating interactions with the children or class activities. We broadly categorize the observations below.

Unveiling the Social Dynamics Depending on the Settings and Contexts. The teachers discussed the implications regarding the children's unexpected social interactions. The teachers related some unique interactions to children's polymorphic nature depending on different settings. For example, T5 stated, *"(in Science Quest Park) It helped me find many times that [C3 (Child 3)] and [C15] stayed so close in Science Quest Park. (…) It was quite unexpected to me. I've known [C3] is quite independent and likes playing in her own way."* T5 reasoned later, saying C15 is a 1-year-younger boy than C3, *"I guess [C3] played as if she were an elder sister to [C15]. (…) Actually [C3] had visited that place several times but [C15] visited at the first time."*

Reconstructing the Contextual Understanding from Fragmented Memories. Interestingly, reporting a singularity could often bring back some pieces of fragmented, faint memories to the teachers. Then the teachers easily interconnected the fragments and got some larger, contextual understanding. T5 stated, referring to Science Quest Park, *"I found that, [C9] played so long with the Moon Buggy simulator. Instantly, I recalled a moment there, [C9] mumbled a few words like 'zero gravity' and 'dust'. (…) Now I understand what it was all about. (…) It's amazing! Many children just have fun with the simulator but he found a piece of science!"* We could see that such a small mumbling itself was insignificant to the teacher at that moment in their field trip, and the memory became already blurry since they came back. It would probably have passed out if the teacher did not find some relevant context from the report.

Bringing Reflection and Self-motivation to the Children. Although our direct user group is the teachers, we found many cases that potential benefits were mediated to the children through the teachers. When a teacher found some behavior of a child, the teacher often used it as a part of means to initiate self-motivation and reflection to the child. T5 stated, *"(At National Science Museum,) I found that [C7] was interacting with a rocket launcher for a long time."* It is a button-triggered air-propelled rocket launcher. T5 told us what happened. *"At the museum, I told him 'let's move on to the next hall', but he did not want to leave. (…) Even I tried to lead him by the hand."* When T5 found again this C7's behavior, she recalled his stubborn behavior and devised a strategy to smoothly persuade C7. *"We just gently watched the video together. (…) I was certain that he felt something. (…) He recalled what he did. (…) He was a lot different. If I had just talked to him as usual, he might have taken it just a nag."*

In Unity There Is New Significance. We found that the teachers combined multiple, simultaneous singularities and built new, larger understanding not delivered by individual singularities. Importantly, an insignificant singularity on its own often contributed to some significance by being combined with another. In the hiking, C1 and C5 were frequently suggested as singularities in terms of their activity intensities and close proximities. T9 stated, *"(from the video) I could see they were running the trails together, far ahead of other friends. (...) [C5]'s high activity was not surprising to me. I know him well for more than a year. But [C1] was unexpected. (...) I believe, on that day, mingling with [C5] somehow changed [C1] to be a lot more active."*

Motives of Making Suggestions to the Field Trip Venue. Some singularities motivated the teachers to make a suggestion to the venue for children's better experiences. T9 stated, *"(In Prehistoric Settlement,) I got a report about [C5]'s orientation. (...) The curator was giving a presentation about the settlement. Everyone was sitting and mostly looking at the curator. (...) [C5] was sitting toward his right for a few minutes."* By carefully watching the video and the C5's first-person view, *"I think a computer screen at that corner attracted his attention."* T9 emphasized it would not be appropriate to just tell C5 not to. Instead, T9 made suggestions to the office of the settlement to revise their item placements and shorten their presentation. She added that they would mostly welcome such comments as it is a place designed for children, and we should not blame C5 for something caused by badly designed environment.

7   Discussion, Implications, and Limitations

We discuss the implication, potential extensibility, and the limitations of this study.

The teachers were enthusiastic in bringing new ideas regarding our system. One idea is a tool for parental feedback. They state that kindergarten-driven field trips comprise a large part of children's out-of-routine events in many dual-income families. However, today's parental feedbacks about field trips are lack of rich information. Many parents know little more than the destination, some pictures, and the child's own crude expression. To this end, however, the reporting system needs to be re-designed to fit the parental needs. As the notion of behavioral singularity has implication on other children's characteristics, the disclosure of information about a child to other parents needs to be resolved. Another idea is that the technology-aided reminiscence would extend young children's thoughts and widen their often self-oriented views. T6 suggested a potential use for experience sharing among the children, right after a field trip when they retain vivid memory. T6 discussed, *"For a child, comparing what I did with others would be a lot powerful to widen the child's sight. (...) She might realize many other fun and methods she didn't know so far."*

The singularities we suggested are not *all* informative to the teachers. For example, a boy was suggested as a singularity in terms of his activity intensity, as he kept moving around while his classmates mostly stayed still in front of an exhibit. However, it was not newly informative; the teacher has already seen this particular behavior. Subsequent discussion led us to postulate that it might be trivial for the teachers to isolate a few highly dynamic behaviors out of many calm children. Interestingly, the opposites, noticing a calm child out of mostly dynamic children, are nontrivial even if our system evaluates similar disparity metrics in both cases. This observation would be a topic of further study to incorporate a human cognitive model in evaluating singularities, regarding the isolation of an event from backgrounds with different dynamicity.

It should be discussed that our system does not deliver a complete set of singularities. It did miss to suggest some behaviors which the teacher determines eligible as a singular one. For example, there was an exhibit which can be viewed from any direction around it. Although the children stood still around it and paid consistent attention, our system did not suggest the child whose body orientation was diverted from the exhibit. It can be explained that the circular formation of the children around the exhibit resulted in rather evenly distributed body orientations; therefore it failed to satisfy step 2 in Figure 2. This case shows a limitation where the method assuming a centered distribution may not work. We believe that some modern museums installed with infrared beacons on each exhibit and giving a transceiver to each visitor would help resolving the issue. More general solution may require a broader study on characteristic distribution of children's collective behaviors, but it is a concern that embracing more delicate situations might cause a negative effect on the overall fidelity.

From the practices of field trips, we derived the design philosophy of retrospect for the teacher-reporting. But we believe that, in some cases, real-time intervention can be beneficial. An example would be the scaffolding for the child at the maglev in Section 3.2. However, real-time notifications are very context-dependent issues; otherwise it will be highly annoying and disruptive. It would be a non-trivial research question incorporating interaction design for highly compact and unobtrusive information delivery, context awareness to determine the current risk level and required teacher's attention, and machine learning to make it tuned along a series of field trips.

Some issues remain in regard to fully integrating our prototype system on non-experimental settings. The teachers gave advices to further evolve our prototype to be more complete for persistent use as a part of regular field trips. First, our system needs to be more versatile to cover a larger variety of field trip settings. Although our integration of the smartphone with the backpack satisfied the teachers, parents, and children in terms of the transparency and comfort, it is not completely versatile and interruption-free. For example, it was not possible to monitor the children's quarterly physical exercise event. Children also take off backpacks when taking a rest or having snacks. We envision state-of-the-art sensor technology [6] will enable more seamless daily-life monitoring including a larger variety of field trip situations. The battery lifetime of the smartphones also limit the durations of applicable field trips, typically no longer than 2~3 hours. It still covers the majority of field trips that the kindergarten conducts, but a few exceptions exist like a full-day picnic per semester. Second, the situation-dependencies require further studies. We found that, the singularities from different feature sets may imply different teacher-perceived significances depending on the situations, even if those singularities have similar weight values. An extreme example is the interaction consistencies, which showed largely different results depending on whether we narrowed down the situations to free-choice activities or not. A brief idea by the teachers was having a few presets each representing a field trip type, a coarse-grained classification of situations. They conveniently choose one, and it re-weights each feature set of singularities well-fit to the selected field trip type. The further questions would be the classification problem of a large variety of field trips, and the limitation when a single trip consists of various situation types.

8 Conclusion

We explored the collective behavior monitoring on a group of children under shared contextual settings by pervasive technology, and its assistive potentials for human experts in the child education. We proposed a notion of statistical distribution to describe the collective behavioral characteristics, and studied the educational implications in finding the behaviors which are less probable with respect to the distribution. We have received many qualitative results, but also identified that our notions on behavioral distributions and singularities need to incorporate further considerations for complete and smooth deployment. We believe that our proposed notions may open opportunities in different domains of collective human behavior monitoring.

Acknowledgements. Special thanks to Chulhong Min for his valuable efforts in idea development and discussion. This work was supported by the National Research Foundation of Korea grant (No. 2011-0018120) funded by the Korean Government, and the SW Computing R&D Program of KEIT (2011-10041313, UX-oriented Mobile SW Platform) funded by the Ministry of Knowledge Economy of Korea.

References

1. Chang, Y.-C., Lo, J.-L., Huang, C.-J., Hsu, N.-Y., Chu, H.-H., Wang, H.-Y., Chi, P.-Y., Hsieh, Y.-L.: Playful Toothbrush: Ubicomp Technology for Teaching Tooth Brushing to Kindergarten Children. In: CHI 2008, pp. 363–372. ACM, New York (2008)
2. Chipman, G., Druin, A., Beer, D., Fails, J.A., Guha, M.L., Simms, S.: A Case Study of Tangible Flags: A Collaborative Technology to Enhance Field Trips. In: Proc. IDC 2006, pp. 1–8. ACM, New York (2006)
3. Cramer, M., Hayes, G.R.: Acceptable Use of Technology in Schools. Pervasive Computing 9(3), 37–44 (2010)
4. Dodge, K.A.: Behavioral Antecedents of Peer Social Status. Child Development 54(6), 1386–1399 (1983)
5. Druin, A.: The Role of Children in the Design of New Technology. Behavior and Information Technology 21(1), 1–25 (2002)
6. EcoMote, http://www.ecomote.net/
7. Falk, J.H., Dierking, L.D.: School Field Trips: Assessing Their Long-Term Impact. Curator 40(3), 211–218 (1997)
8. Hayes, G.R., Gardere, L.M., Abowd, G.D., Truong, K.N.: CareLog: a Selective Archiving Tool for Behavior Management in Schools. In: CHI 2008, pp. 685–694. ACM (2008)
9. Hayes, G.R., Kientz, J.A., Truong, K.N., White, D.R., Abowd, G.D., Pering, T.: Designing Capture Applications to Support the Education of Children with Autism. In: Davies, N., Mynatt, E.D., Siio, I. (eds.) UbiComp 2004. LNCS, vol. 3205, pp. 161–178. Springer, Heidelberg (2004)

10. Hodges, S., Williams, L., Berry, E., Izadi, S., Srinivasan, J., Butler, A., Smyth, G., Kapur, N., Wood, K.: SenseCam: A Retrospective Memory Aid. In: Dourish, P., Friday, A. (eds.) UbiComp 2006. LNCS, vol. 4206, pp. 177–193. Springer, Heidelberg (2006)
11. Hourcade, J.P.: Interaction Design and Children. Foundations and Trends in HCI 1(4), 277–392 (2007)
12. Hwang, I., Jang, H., Nachman, L., Song, J.: Exploring Inter-child Behavioral Relativity in a Shared Social Environment: A Field Study in a Kindergarten. In: UbiComp 2010, pp. 271–280. ACM, New York (2010)
13. International Commission on Non-Ionizing Radiation Protection. Guidelines for limiting exposure to time-varying electric, magnetic, and electromagnetic fields (up to 300GHz). Health Physics 74(4), 494–522 (1998)
14. Kientz, J.A., Abowd, G.D.: KidCam: Toward an Effective Technology for the Capture of Children's Moments of Interest. In: Tokuda, H., Beigl, M., Friday, A., Brush, A.J.B., Tobe, Y. (eds.) Pervasive 2009. LNCS, vol. 5538, pp. 115–132. Springer, Heidelberg (2009)
15. Kientz, J.A., Hayes, G.R., Westeyn, T.L., Starner, T., Abowd, G.D.: Pervasive computing and autism: Assisting caregivers of children with special needs. IEEE Pervasive Computing 6(1), 28–35 (2007)
16. Lane, N.D., Xu, Y., Lu, H., Hu, S., Choudhury, T., Campbell, A.T., Zhao, F.: Enabling Large-scale Human Activity Inference on Smartphones using Community Similarity Networks (CSN). In: UbiComp 2011, pp. 355–364. ACM, New York (2011)
17. MacKenzie, A.A., White, R.T.: Fieldwork in Geography and Long-Term Memory Structures. American Educational Research Journal 19(4), 623–632 (1982)
18. Madan, A., Cebrian, M., Lazer, D., Pentland, A.: Social Sensing for Epidemological Behavior Change. In: UbiComp 2010, pp. 291–300. ACM, New York (2010)
19. Martinez, R., Kay, J., Wallace, J.R., Yacef, K.: Modelling Symmetry of Activity as an Indicator of Collocated Group Collaboration. In: Konstan, J.A., Conejo, R., Marzo, J.L., Oliver, N. (eds.) UMAP 2011. LNCS, vol. 6787, pp. 207–218. Springer, Heidelberg (2011)
20. Olguin, D.O., Waber, B.N., Kim, T., Mohan, A., Ara, K., Pentland, A.: Sensible Organization: Technology and Methodology for Automatically Measuring Organizational Behavior. IEEE Trans. Systems, Man, and Cybernetics 39(1), 43–55 (2009)
21. Overy, K., Nicolson, R.I., Fawcett, A.J., Clarke, E.F.: Dyslexia and Music: Measuring Musical Timing Skills. Dyslexia 9(1), 18–36 (2003)
22. Poole, E.S., Miller, A.D., Xu, Y., Eiriksdottir, E., Catrambone, R., Mynatt, E.D.: The Place for Ubiquitous Computing in Schools: Lessons Learned from a School-based Intervention for Youth Physical Activity. In: UbiComp 2011, pp. 395–404. ACM, New York (2011)
23. Ramsay, M.C., Reynolds, C.R., Kamphaus, R.W.: Essentials of Behavioral Assessment. John Wiley and Sons, Inc., New York (2002)
24. Rogers, Y., Price, S., Randell, C., Fraser, D.S., Weal, M., Fitzpatrick, G.: Ubi-learning Integrates Indoor and Outdoor Experiences. Communications of the ACM 48(1), 55–59 (2005)
25. Soloway, E., Jackson, S.L., Klein, J., Quintana, C., Reed, J., Spitulnik, J., Stratford, S.J., Studer, S., Eng, J., Scala, N.: Learning Theory in Practice: Case Studies of Learner-centered Design. In: CHI 1996, pp. 189–196. ACM, New York (1996)
26. Squires, J., Nickel, R.E., Eisert, D.: Early Detection of Developmental Problems: Strategies for Monitoring Young Children in the Practice Setting. Developmental and Behavioral Pediatrics 17(6), 420–427 (1996)

Urban Traffic Modelling and Prediction Using Large Scale Taxi GPS Traces

Pablo Samuel Castro[1], Daqing Zhang[1], and Shijian Li[2]

[1] Institut Telecom SudParis, 9, rue Charles Fourier; 91011 Evry Cedex, France
[2] Zhejiang University, Hangzhou, 310027, P.R. China

Abstract. Monitoring, predicting and understanding traffic conditions in a city is an important problem for city planning and environmental monitoring. GPS-equipped taxis can be viewed as pervasive sensors and the large-scale digital traces produced allow us to have a unique view of the underlying dynamics of a city's road network. In this paper, we propose a method to construct a model of traffic density based on large scale taxi traces. This model can be used to predict future traffic conditions and estimate the effect of emissions on the city's air quality. We argue that considering traffic density on its own is insufficient for a deep understanding of the underlying traffic dynamics, and hence propose a novel method for automatically determining the capacity of each road segment. We evaluate our methods on a large scale database of taxi GPS logs and demonstrate their outstanding performance.

1 Introduction

With soaring birth rates and increasing migration into urban areas, road networks are often used well over their intended capacity. This has led many cities to enforce certain measures such as restricting which vehicles can be used based on their licence plate number. There is thus an urgent need to understand, and ideally predict, the traffic dynamics in a city, not only for reducing traffic congestion, but to also address environmental, economic, and societal needs in support of a sustainable future. In the past, this has been done by installing traffic sensors in different areas of the city and extrapolating these readings throughout the city [1,2,3]. This information is usually only informative for the highways where these sensors are installed, and shed little light on the traffic flow in the rest of the city.

The last few years have seen a dramatic increase in the presence of GPS devices in vehicles for localization and/or navigation purposes. Aside from providing the user with location-based services, these devices have the potential of providing researchers with an unprecedented window into the dynamics and mobility of a city's road network. GPS-equipped taxis, in particular, have proven to be an extremely useful data source for uncovering the underlying traffic behaviour of a city. GPS-enabled taxis can be considered as ubiquitous mobile sensors constantly probing a city's rhythm and pulse. So far they have been

J. Kay et al. (Eds.): Pervasive 2012, LNCS 7319, pp. 57–72, 2012.
© Springer-Verlag Berlin Heidelberg 2012

used for automatic map construction [4], detecting hot spots [5,6], urban computing [7,8,9,10], and characterizing passenger finding strategies [11,12,13,14,15], amongst others.

The aspect of the traffic dynamics we concern ourselves with in this paper is traffic flow and congestion, which is crucial for city planning and environmental monitoring. We measure the *flow* of traffic via the densities (*i.e.* the number of vehicles present) at each road, and consider a road segment *congested* when it has become "saturated" as a result of a high density. A deep understanding of the flow and congestion levels can be useful for improved road network design and maintenance, reducing travel times, as well as for analyzing certain side-effects of vehicle use, such as estimating pollution levels in a city [16].

There are two important problems that we address in order to approach a better understanding of traffic flow and congestion. The first is accurate prediction of future traffic conditions. We address this problem by constructing a *model* of the flow of traffic in the city, based on historical observations. The second is a principled mechanism for determining when a road segment is "over-saturated". We address this problem by examining the distribution of GPS readings in a graph plotting density versus speed.

The three main contributions of this paper can be summarized as follows.

- We define a method for constructing a *model* of the traffic flow in a city, based on the historical taxi GPS logs. This model can be used to predict future traffic conditions based on the current state.
- We argue that predicting density levels is not sufficient to obtain a thorough understanding of the traffic dynamics in a city, and present a method for automatically determining the *capacity* of roads. Coupling these computed capacities with the "raw" densities grants us a deeper understanding of the dynamics and congestion levels of a city's road network.
- We evaluate our methods on a large scale database of 5000 taxis logging their GPS information every minute (resulting in over 300 million GPS entries). Our methods are fast and simple to construct, yet they still enjoy a remarkably high degree of accuracy (less than 3% of the error incurred by the baseline considered).

The paper is organized as follows. In section 2 we discuss related work. In section 3 we describe our data set and how the data was prepared for the ensuing work. We present our predictive method along with empirical results in section 4 and our method for computing capacities in section 5. We conclude our work and discuss future avenues of research in section 6.

2   Related Work

In this section we review some of the existing work most closely related to ours. There are a number of works that propose methods for *monitoring* traffic conditions, but not necessarily modelling or predicting traffic conditions. Wen et al. [17] used GPS-equipped taxis to analyze traffic congestion changes around the Olympic games in Beijing; note that this is an ex post facto analysis of traffic conditions. Schäfer et al. [18] used GPS-enabled vehicles to obtain real-time traffic information in a number of European cities. By considering congested roads as those where the velocity is below 10km/hr, the authors demonstrate a visualization of traffic conditions around the city can be used to detect congested and blocked road segments.

Closely related to estimating traffic conditions are obtaining accurate estimates of the travel time between two points in a city. Blandin et al. [19] use kernel methods [20] to obtain a non-linear estimate of travel times on "arterial" roads; the performance of this estimate is then improved through kernel regression. Yuan and Zheng [21] propose constructing a graph whose nodes are *landmarks*. Landmarks are defined as road segments frequently traversed by taxis. They propose a method to adaptively split a day into different time segments, based on the variance and entropy of the travel time between landmarks. This results in an estimate of the distributions of the travel times between landmarks.

The research most relevant to this paper are those which attempt to model and/or predict traffic conditions. Gühnemann et al. [16] use GPS data to construct travel time and speed estimates for each road segment, which are in turn used to estimate emission levels in different parts of the city. Their estimates are obtained by simply averaging over the most recent GPS entries; this is closely related to the historical means baseline we compare our algorithm against. Šingliar and Hauskrecht [1] studied two models for traffic density estimation: conditional autoregressive models and mixture of Gaussian trees. This work was designed to work with a set of traffic sensors placed around the city, and not with GPS-equipped vehicles. The authors assume the Markov property for traffic flows: the state of a road segment in the immediate future is dependent *only* on the state of its immediate neighbours. We adopt a similar assumption in our construction of a model. Lippi et al. [3] use Markov logic networks to perform relational learning for traffic forecasting on multiple simultaneous locations, and at different steps in the future. This work is also designed for dealing with a set of traffic sensors around the city. Su and Yu [2] used a Genetic Algorithm to select the parameters of a SVM, trained to predict short-term traffic conditions. Their method is meant to work with either traffic sensors or GPS-equipped vehicles. However, their empirical evaluation is quite limited and falls short of fully convincing the reader of their method's practicality. Herring et al. [22] use Coupled Hidden Markov Models [23] for estimating traffic conditions on arterial roads. They propose a sophisticated model based on traffic theory which yields good results. Nevertheless, we argue that this type of sophistication is, in a sense, "overkill". We capitalize on the coarse regularity of traffic flow during the week to construct a model which yields very good results, without having to resort to more sophisticated, and computationally expensive, methods. One of the main motivations driving our work is the application of these results in a real-time setting, where computationally expensive proposals are unsuitable. Yuan et al. [24] used both historical patterns and real-time traffic to estimate traffic conditions. However, the predictions they provide are between a set of "landmarks" which is smaller than the size of the road network. Although suitable for many applications (such as optimal route planning), the coarseness of their predictions make them less suited for a detailed understanding of a city's traffic dynamics.

3   Data Preparation

In this section we present the taxi GPS data set that will be used for this paper. The raw data must be prepared in order for it to be suitable for the work discussed in the sequel and we describe this process below.

3.1   Data Set Description

For this work, we make use of a large data set obtained from around 5000 taxis in Hangzhou, China, over a period of a month (February, 2010), at a rate of approximately once per minute (for each taxi), resulting in over 300 million GPS entries. Table 1 lists the fields for each GPS entry, along with a sample entry.

Table 1. Fields for a GPS entry with a sample

Taxi ID	Longitude	Latitude	Speed (km/hr)	Bearing	Occupied flag	Year	Month	Day	Hour	Minute	Second
10429	120.214134	30.212818	70.38	240.00	1	2010	2	7	17	40	46

3.2   Mapping to a Digital Map

The "terrain" of a city is a continuous two-dimensional area (*i.e.* a subset of $\mathbb{R}^2$), which is difficult to work with. It is more practical to decompose the city into separate (usually disjoint) areas, and work with this decomposition. The way the city is decomposed is crucial to the significance of the results obtained, as the methodologies presented later are defined with respect to the way the city is decomposed. A simple and popular decomposition is to split the city's area into a matrix of disjoint grid cells; however, this has the disadvantage that one grid cell can contain more than one road segment, and it can also split road segments in unintuitive positions.

For our purposes, it is much more useful to use a digital map of the city, as this exactly represents the road network navigated by the various taxis, and it allows us to provide traffic models and/or predictions for each road.

Definition 1. *A **digital map** is a graph (V, E) where V is a set of vertices and E is a set of edges. Each edge $e \in E$ has the following fields: two endpoint vertices e_{v_1} and e_{v_2}; length e_{length} and bearing e_{brng}.*[1]

---

[1] Note that the bearing is the direction from e_{v_1} to e_{v_2}; simply subtract this bearing from 360 to obtain the bearing from e_{v_2} to e_{v_1}.

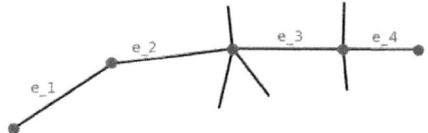

Fig. 1. A street split into various edges

A street can consist of multiple edges, as shown in Figure 1. Note that it is split into segments wherever there is an intersection and/or a change in bearing.

In many cases, a digital map of the city is not readily available. Given the long time span and large number of taxis available in our data set, the city's road network becomes apparent by simply plotting all the GPS entries. In the left panel of Figure 2 we display a sample of the plot obtained from 20 taxis over one month, around the downtown area of Hangzhou. We only plot the pickup and dropoff points, as we found that including full trajectories clutters the plot. A simple (but arduous) option is to "draw" the edges and construct a digital map manually. We split roads into segments at every interesection, as well as anytime the bearing of the road changes considerably. In the right panel of Figure 2 we display the resulting digital map. It consists of 2003 edges and 1585 vertices.

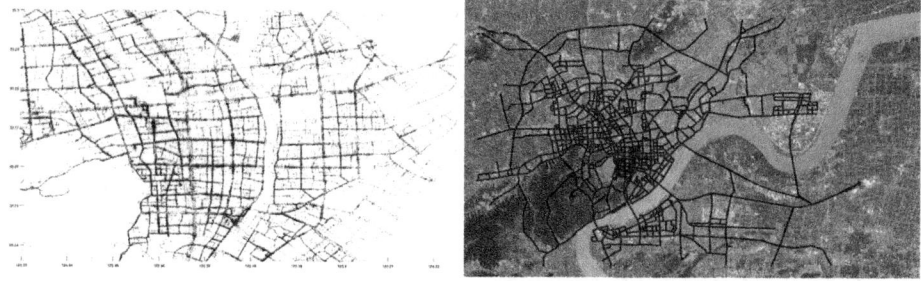

Fig. 2. Left: Traces from 20 taxis over one month. Right: Digital road network drawn over raw traces.

Given a digital map (V, E), one can map each GPS entry to a point on one of the edges from E. Simply mapping to the closest edge may not produce good results, and errors will frequently occur, as shown in the left panel of Figure 3. There are number of approaches to map-matching that take contextual information into consideration such as edit distance [25] and Fréchet distance [26,27]. These approaches map trajectories *globally*, that is, only complete trajectories are considered. This renders these approaches unsuitable for long trajectories, as the computational expense becomes too large. We perform our map-matching on a *local* basis, using contextual information such as distance and orientation (see the right panel of Figure 3). In this example, we are able to avoid mapping (erroneously) to road segment 2 on the left hand side by comparing the orientation of this road segment to the orientation indicated by the GPS logs.

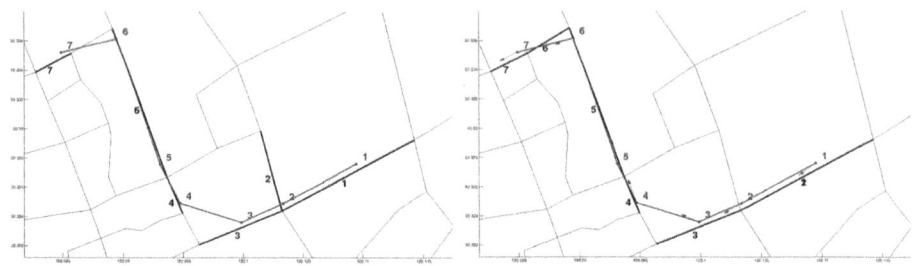

Fig. 3. Mapping trajectories to a digital map, the original trajectory is shown in red, the edge each entry is mapped to is shown in mauve. Left: Mapping each entry to the closest edge; Right: Using bearing information of each GPS entry to improve edge matching.

A GPS entry that has been mapped onto a digital map will result in a new entry, identical except for the latitude and longitude which may be different (so that the point "sits on" the digital map). This new entry is augmented with the fields: *edge* and *orien*. The field *edge* represents what edge $e \in E$ it was mapped to, and *orien* represents what orientation it is following (1 if going from e_{v_1} to e_{v_2} and 2 if going in the other direction).

For the rest of the paper, we will always consider an edge e with an orientation o. For clarity, we will refer to this pair as (e, o) with the following attributes:

$$(e,o)_{v_1} = \begin{cases} e_{v_1} & \text{if } o = 1 \\ e_{v_2} & \text{otherwise} \end{cases}$$

$$(e,o)_{v_2} = \begin{cases} e_{v_2} & \text{if } o = 1 \\ e_{v_1} & \text{otherwise} \end{cases}$$

4   Predictive Model

Now that we have described the data set and the digital map decomposition, we can proceed to describe our predictive model. The main idea is to use the navigational history to model the flow of traffic at different times. We are assuming there is a form of regularity present in the way traffic flows at different times. Although this may seem like a strong assumption, it is justified by the empirical results presented below. Before we describe the predictive model we will describe the way we collect our data and gather the necessary statistics. We will make use of the successors of an edge-orientation pair, defined below.

Definition 2. *The* **successors** *of an edge e with orientation o is defined as the set of consistent adjacent edge-orientation pairs:*

$$succ((e,o)) = \{(e',o') | (e,o)_{v_2} = (e',o')_{v_1}\}$$

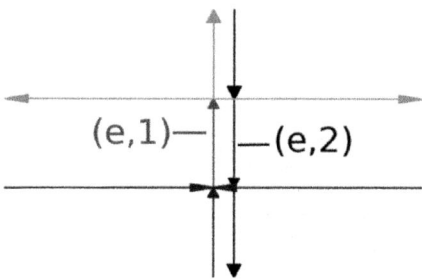

Fig. 4. Successors (in green) and predecessors (in blue) of edge-orientation pair (e, 1) (in red). Note that the vertical arrows represent the two orientations of the same road.

For convenience, we can define the predecessors of a pair (e, o) as

$$pred((e, o)) = \{(e', o')|(e, o) \in succ((e', o'))\}$$

See Figure 4 for clarification.

Since the sampling rate of the GPS devices is once per minute, we will use an initial granularity of one minute, yielding 1440 minutes for each day. For every edge-orientation pair (e, o) and minute m, we maintain the function $moveCounts((e, o), m)((e', o'))$, which is simply the number of times a transition was made from (e, o) to (e', o') in minute m. Note that this function is well-defined even when $(e, o) = (e', o')$, as this simply counts the number of times a taxi *did not* transition to another edge in minute m.

With the above function, we can compute a probabilistic transition matrix for every minute m, as follows:

$$P_m((e, o), (e', o')) = \frac{moveCounts((e, o), m)((e', o'))}{\sum_{(e'', o'')} moveCounts((e, o), m)((e'', o''))}$$

The above formula is simply computing the frequency of the available edge-orientation transitions. Note that, as in Singliar and Hauskrecht [1], we are assuming the Markov property: the state of traffic of an edge-orientation pair in the immediate future is dependent *solely* on the state of its immediate neighbours.

In practice, there is significant variability in the transition distributions between successive minutes, so we propose re-defining this function with a granularity of 15-minute segments, yielding 96 segments per day. Given a 15-minute quarter q, we define the probabilistic transition matrix as follows:

$$P_q((e, o), (e', o')) = \frac{\sum_{m \in q} P_m((e, o), (e', o'))}{15}$$

Henceforth we will only make use of the transition matrix defined over 15-minute quarters, so there will be no risk of ambiguity between P_m and P_q. Note that the size of each matrix P_q is $|E| * 2 \times |E| * 2$ (for our data set this results in a matrix of size 4406×4406).

The purpose of this transition function is to be able to model the flow of traffic in the city. In this paper, we consider traffic as the *density* of taxis. Since we have a large number of taxis continuously driving around the city, we believe they are a good indication of the true vehicular density. We define $D_q((e,o))$ as the number of taxis on (e,o) in 15-minute quarter q. Clearly, the higher the density in a road segment, the higher the level of traffic. Each vector D_q has size $|E| \times 2$.

We can now present our method for predicting the traffic density in the next quarter $q+1$. The main idea is that we predict the next-step densities by *spreading* the current density according to the transition matrix. For instance, the proportion of the current density at (e,o), $D_q((e,o))$, that will "flow" to (e',o') is given by $P_q((e,o),(e',o'))$; similarly the proportion of the current density at (e,o) that will not move is given by $P_q((e,o),(e,o))$. Thus, the predicted density of (e',o') in quarter $q+1$ is computed as follows:

$$\hat{D}_{q+1}((e',o')) = \sum_{(e,o)} D_q((e,o))P_q((e,o),(e',o')) \tag{1}$$

Note that $P_q((e,o),(e',o'))$ will only be positive for $(e,o) \in pred((e',o'))$.

We can compute Equation 1 for all edge-orientation pairs by expressing it as a matrix operation:

$$\hat{D}_{q+1} = P'_q \cdot D_q \tag{2}$$

where P'_q is the transpose of P_q. We may also desire to obtain a prediction for further in the future, which can be easily done by successive applications of the transition matrices. The n-step transition matrix from q is defined as follows.[2]

$$P_q^{(n)} = P_q \cdot P_{q+1} \cdots P_{q+n-1}$$

Obtaining a prediction for n steps in the future is then straightforward:

$$\hat{D}_{q+n} = P_q^{(n)'} \cdot D_q \tag{3}$$

4.1   Empirical Evaluation

In this section we aim to measure the accuracy of our prediction method. Given that traffic congestions and overall vehicular volume is greater during weekdays, we focus on weekdays. The same procedure can of course be applied to weekends; however, a model learned from working and non-working days may not be as accurate, as the traffic patterns differ significantly between the two types of days. We split our month-long data into four work-weeks, yielding 480 15-minute quarters (assuming a five day work-week). We use one of these weeks as the training set, w_I, and another as the testing set, w_T. For a given edge-orientation pair (e,o) and week w, $D_w((e,o))$ is a vector of length 480 containing the densities at (e,o) for each quarter in week w.

---

[2] Note that this must be done module 96, *i.e.* $95 + 2$ should not yield 97, but 1.

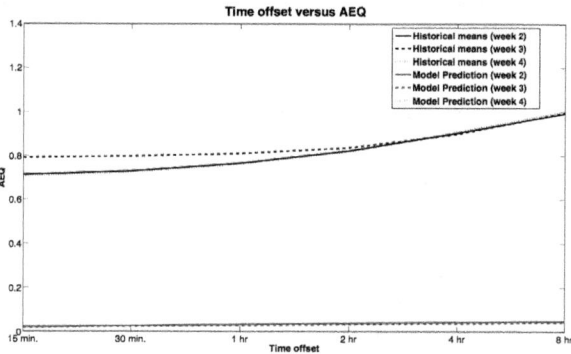

Fig. 5. Time offset versus AEQ

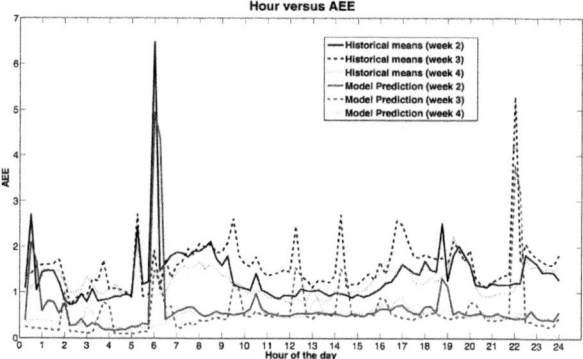

Fig. 6. Hour of the day versus AEE

We use the data from w_I to construct a model, as described in the previous section. Then, given a 15-minute quarter q and a time offset n, we compute $\hat{D}_{q+n}$ as described above. Since there is a fair amount of regularity in the traffic flow during work weeks, a simple way to "predict" traffic would be to use the historical mean of traffic density, given the current 15-minute quarter. We use this as a baseline against which we can compare our algorithm's performance.

We measure the performance of our algorithm and the baseline method using the following measures.

1. Given $\hat{D}_{q+n}$ for all values of q and for a specified offset n, we compute the average error per quarter (AEQ) as follows:

$$AEQ^n(\hat{D}) = \frac{\sum_q \|D_q - \hat{D}_q\|_2}{480} \tag{4}$$

Note that $AEQ(\hat{D})$ is a vector of size $|E| \times 2$, we average over all edges to obtain our final measure:

$$AEQ^n = \frac{\sum_{(e,o)} AEQ^n(\hat{D})((e,o))}{|E| * 2}$$

We plot the results in Figure 5 with varying values of n, where we can clearly see the advantage of using our proposed prediction method over standard means. Indeed, our method incurs less than 3% of the error incurred by the baseline model. From this figure we can also conclude that although there are some regularities in traffic flow from week to week, there is still enough variability to incur a significant error.

2. Given $\hat{D}_{q+n}$ for all values of q and for a specified offset n, we compute the average error per edge (AEE) as follows:

$$AEE^q(\hat{D}) = \frac{\sum_{(e,o)} \|D_q(e) - \hat{D}_q(e)\|_2}{|E| * 2} \tag{5}$$

Because q ranges over a full work week (480 possible values), we average over the 5 working days (resulting in 96 possible values). We plot the results when using an offset of $n = 1$ (i.e. 15 minutes) in Figure 6 for the different weeks. In this graph we can once again see the improved performance of our method, as well as the variability from week to week. We can also observe the same general "shape" present in all the weeks: there is greater error (due to greater complexity resulting from a higher volume of vehicles) during working hours (roughly from 9am to 7pm).

5   Determining Road Capacities

In the last section we demonstrated that we can predict the density at different road segments with sufficient accuracy. However, in the absence of additional information about the road segments, these density predictions may not be very useful, as different road segments get congested with different density levels, depending on their length and width. In this section we propose a novel method for determining the *capacity* of the different road segments, based on the historical density and speed readings.

For each edge-orientation pair (e, o) and minute m we compute $vel((e, o), m)$, defined as the average velocity of all taxis passing by (e, o) in minute m. In the computation of this average velocity we apply some simple filtering schemes, such as ignoring the velocity of taxis that are parked: parked taxis are not navigating the network so are not a proper indication of the average speed through (e, o), and will bring down the computed average velocity.

We can use average velocity as an indication of when a road is congested. Schäfer et al. [18] define a congested road as one where the average velocity is below 10km/hr. In this paper we say a road segment is congested if the velocity of the majority of taxis is below 20km/hr, in a manner that will be made more

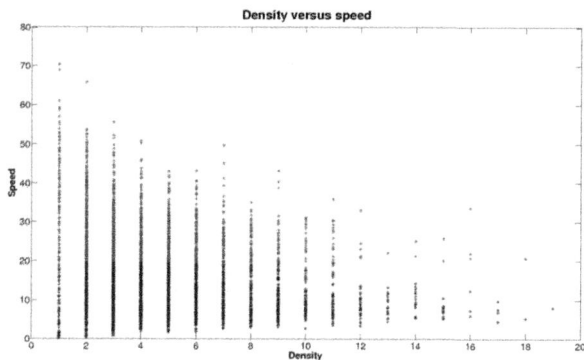

Fig. 7. Density versus speed for one edge-orientation pair

precise below. We choose 20km/hr as our cutoff as this is already quite low, even for residential areas. In Figure 7 we plot density versus average speed for a particular edge-orientation pair; that is, every point in the figure corresponds to one of the 7200 minutes in a week. We colour the points above our 20km/hr limit in red, and those below in blue. We will refer to the red points as the *high* points, and the blue points as the *low* points. As one would expect, the velocity tends to go down as the density goes up. It is inevitable that even with low densities we will have low speed readings, and simply using averages may under estimate the road's true capacity. We compute, for each density level d, the ratio of high points, $high_d$ to low points, low_d:

$$ratio(d) = \frac{|high_d|}{|low_d|}$$

We define the capacity of an edge-orientation pair (e, o), as the density level d, with sufficient data points, whose ratio unambiguously drops below 0.4 (*i.e.* there are at least 250% more low points than high points). A density level d has sufficient data points if $|high_d| + |low_d| > 500$. We say a ratio unambiguously drops below 0.4 at d if $ratio(d-1) > 0.4$ and $ratio(d+1) < 0.4$. The unambiguous drop criterion is meant to exclude outlier "spikes" that may anomalously drop below 0.4 for a single density level. We denote this capacity as $cap((e, o))$. For a pair (e, o), if the ratio never drops below 0.4 or it only drops below 0.4 when there are insufficient points, we say (e, o) does not have a capacity. In Figure 8 we plot density versus ratio as well as the number of points per density for the same edge-orientation pair from Figure 7. The red line in the graph indicates the ratio threshold (0.4) while the green line indicates the capacity determined for this edge-orientation pair.

Unfortunately, we do not have access to "ground-truth" capacities for each road segment, so it is difficult to quantitatively measure the accuracy of our capacity computation method. Nevertheless, by examining weekly traffic patterns for different road segments, we can qualitatively verify that our computed capacities are reasonable. In Figure 9 we display the density over the course of a

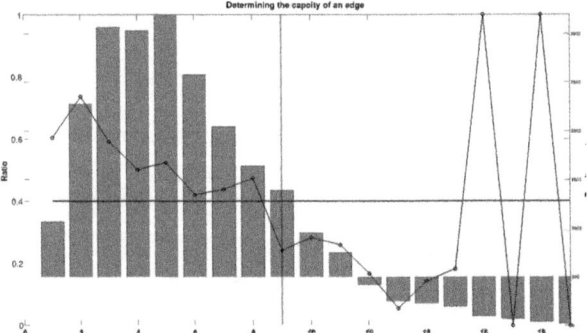

Fig. 8. Density versus ratio (line with left y-axis) and density counts (bar graph with right y-axis) for one edge-orientation pair. The red line is the ratio threshold while the green line is the determined capacity.

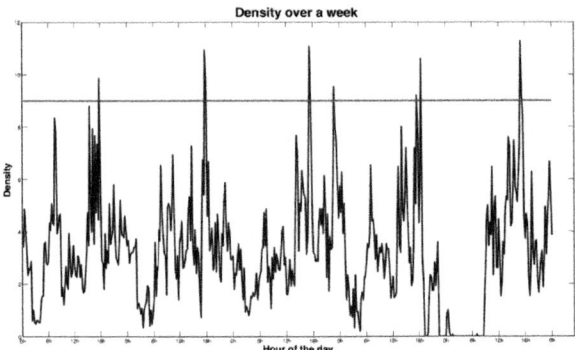

Fig. 9. Density for one edge-orientation over the course of a week, with capacity drawn in red

week for the same edge-orientation pair as in the previous two figures. We can see that this particular edge-orientation pair has density peaks at roughly 6pm every day. It is also intuitively clear that in order to detect these peaks, one would have to set the capacity level somewhere between 8 and 11. Our method sets it at 9, which is within range; however, this value would vary depending on the chosen speed limit (in our case, 20 km/hr) and the ratio threshold (in our case, 0.4). This qualitative verification was performed on a number of different road segments with similar results.

In Figure 10 we display a snapshot of the downtown area during rush hour (10am). On the top panel we display the raw densities at each road segment, where the colours cover the range of densities at the current 15-minute quarter. On the bottom panel we display the density at each road segment divided by its capacity; in other words, the proportion of the capacity of the road segment that has been filled (it may be larger than one if it is filled over its capacity). Because of the small length of the visible road segments, the visualization on

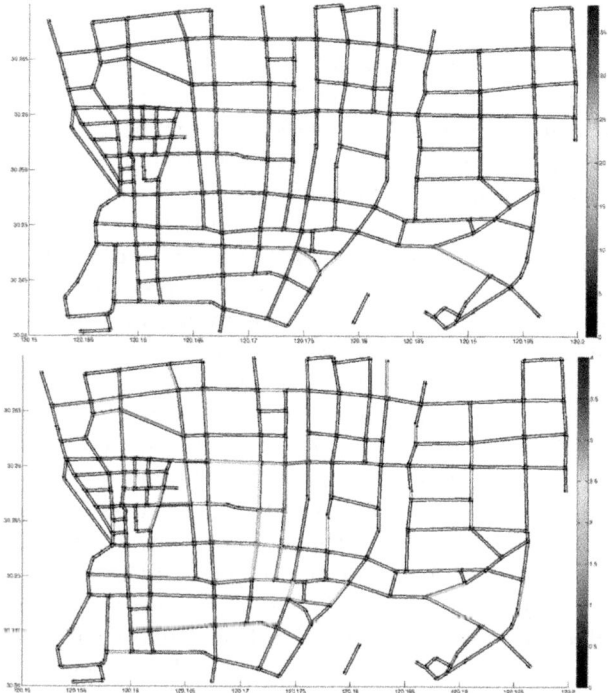

Fig. 10. Density visualization in a part of the downtown at 10am. Top: Absolute densities; Bottom: density divided by road capacity.

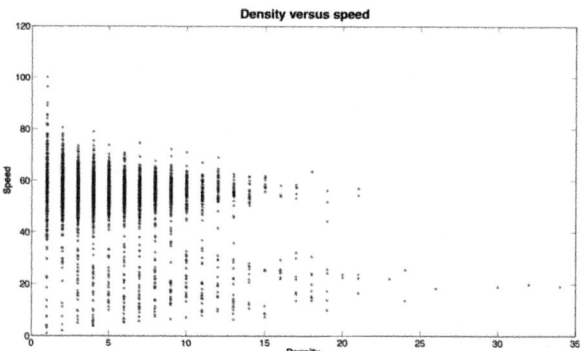

Fig. 11. Density versus speed for a bridge

top conveys very little information about the congestion levels at each of these road segments: relative to larger segments, the absolute density at each of these segments is quite small. On the other hand, when considered with respect to their capacity, we obtain a visualization that is more informative, as on the bottom. If one is interested in monitoring traffic congestion levels in a city, simply observing the absolute densities, as on top, is clearly not sufficient.

6   Conclusion

In this paper we have presented a novel method for modelling the flow of traffic in a large city by means of large scale taxi GPS trajectories. Our method avoids the computational complexity of related works [1,22] while still enjoying remarkable accuracy. The constructed model applies to all visited road segments within a city's road network, which is a finer granularity than solely using hotspots or "landmarks" [24]. Having a finer granularity grants one a more detailed view of the traffic flow; however, road segments that have been infrequently visited will suffer from inaccurate models. Nevertheless, it is precisely those road segments that have a higher visitation frequency that we are most interested in, as these are the road segments that most affect the traffic flow.

We demonstrated that our method is able to provide consistently accurate predictions, even when considering a time frame 16 hours into the future! We proved that this is not simply a consequence of the regularity of traffic densities by comparing against a simple predictor that simply uses the average historical density. It is important to point out that there are two types of regularities discussed in this paper: the first is the aforementioned regularity of traffic densities, which is insufficient for accurate predictions; the second is the regularity of localized navigation decisions. This is the regularity we referred to in the introduction, which allows us to step away from unnecessary sophistication and into a simpler, but comparably accurate, method. We believe the regularity of the second type has less variability, and *results* in the regularity of the first type, which has higher variability.

Our mechanism for automatically determining the capacity of road segments is the first of its kind, and provides a powerful tool for obtaining a deep understanding of the traffic dynamics. Besides its use for automatically determining the capacity of a road segment, the density versus speed plots (as in Figure 7) can provide additional useful information about road segments. For instance, consider Figure 11, which is the plot for one of the bridges in Hangzhou. We can see that there are two "clusters" in this plot, one centered around a speed of 60km/hr, while the other centered around 20km/hr. We believe this behaviour is a result of the presence of bus/taxi lanes in many bridges and highways, which generally have a higher speed than the other lanes. Since our data is coming from taxis, most of the data points fall in the 60km/hr cluster. This suggests that this type of plot can be useful for extracting lane information, which is a problem that has been previously considered [28,29,30].

Although our method provides a means for predicting future traffic conditions, it does not indicate the *correlation* amongst different road segments, and more specifically, the *influence* certain road segments have on other road segments [31]. This information can be extremely useful when planning the closure of certain roads for maintenance, special events, etc. By understanding this influence the road closure schedule can be planned in order to minimize the impact on the city's drivers. We are currently working on this problem, and expect the results presented in this paper to be key elements of this future work.

Acknowledgements. The authors would like to thank Lin Sun, Tiezhen Wang and Xu Qiao for their hard work in constructing the digital map of Hangzhou. The authors would also like to thank Chao Chen for his support throughout this work.

References

1. Šingliar, T., Hauskrecht, M.: Modeling Highway Traffic Volumes. In: Kok, J.N., Koronacki, J., Lopez de Mantaras, R., Matwin, S., Mladenič, D., Skowron, A. (eds.) ECML 2007. LNCS (LNAI), vol. 4701, pp. 732–739. Springer, Heidelberg (2007)
2. Su, H., Yu, S.: Hybrid GA Based Online Support Vector Machine Model for Short-Term Traffic Flow Forecasting. In: Xu, M., Zhan, Y.-W., Cao, J., Liu, Y. (eds.) APPT 2007. LNCS, vol. 4847, pp. 743–752. Springer, Heidelberg (2007)
3. Lippi, M., Bertini, M., Frasconi, P.: Collective Traffic Forecasting. In: Balcázar, J.L., Bonchi, F., Gionis, A., Sebag, M. (eds.) ECML PKDD 2010, Part II. LNCS, vol. 6322, pp. 259–273. Springer, Heidelberg (2010)
4. Lou, Y., Zhang, C., Zheng, Y., Xie, X., Wang, W., Huang, Y.: Map-Matching for Low-Sampling-Rate GPS Trajectories. In: Proceedings of ACM SIGSPATIAL (2009)
5. Chang, H., Tai, Y., Hsu, J.Y.: Context-aware taxi demand hotspots prediction. International Journal of Business Intelligence and Data Mining 5(1), 3–18 (2010)
6. Liu, S., Liu, Y., Ni, L.M., Fan, J., Li, M.: Towards Mobility-based Clustering. In: Proceedings of the 16th ACM SIGKDD International Conference on Knowledge Discovery and Data Mining, KDD 2010 (2010)
7. Hu, J., Cao, W., Luo, J., Yu, X.: Dynamic Modeling of Urban Population Travel Behavior based on Data Fusion of Mobile Phone Positioning Data and FCD. In: 17th International Conference on Geoinformatics (2009)
8. Liu, L., Biderman, A., Ratti, C.: Urban Mobility Landscape: Real Time Monitoring of Urban Mobility Patterns. In: Proceedings of the 11th International Conference on Computers in Urban Planning and Urban Management, CUPUM 2009 (2009)
9. Qi, G., Li, X., Li, S., Pan, G., Wang, Z.: Measuring Social Functions of City Regions from Large-scale Taxi Behaviors. In: PerCom Workshop (2011)
10. Zheng, Y., Liu, Y., Yuan, J., Xie, X.: Urban Computing with Taxicabs. In: Proceedings of the 13th ACM International Conference on Ubiquitous Computing, UBICOMP 2011 (2011)
11. Chang, H., Tai, Y., Chen, H.W., Hsu, J.Y.: iTaxi: Context-Aware Taxi Demand Hotspots Prediction Using Ontology and Data Mining Approaches. In: Proceedings of the 13th Conference on Artificial Intelligence and Applications (TAAI 2008) (2008)
12. Lee, J., Shin, I., Park, G.L.: Analysis of the passenger pick-up pattern for taxi location recommendation. In: Proceedings of the 2008 Fourth International Conference on Networked Computing and Advanced Information Management, vol. 1 (2008)
13. Liu, L., Andris, C., Ratti, C.: Uncovering cabdrivers' behavior patterns from their digital traces. Computers, Environment and Urban Systems 34, 541–548 (2010)

14. Phithakkitnukoon, S., Veloso, M., Bento, C., Biderman, A., Ratti, C.: Taxi-Aware Map: Identifying and Predicting Vacant Taxis in the City. In: de Ruyter, B., Wichert, R., Keyson, D.V., Markopoulos, P., Streitz, N., Divitini, M., Georgantas, N., Mana Gomez, A. (eds.) AmI 2010. LNCS, vol. 6439, pp. 86–95. Springer, Heidelberg (2010)

15. Li, B., Zhang, D., Sun, L., Chen, C., Li, S., Qi, G., Yang, Q.: Hunting or waiting? Discovering passenger-finding strategies from a large-scale real-world taxi dataset. In: PerCom Workshops (2011)

16. Gühnemann, A., Schäfer, R., Thiessenhusen, K.: Monitoring traffic and emissions by floating car data. Institute of transport studies Australia (2004)

17. Wen, H., Hu, Z., Guo, J., Zhu, L., Sun, J.: Operational Analysis on Beijing Road Network during the Olympic Games. Journal of Transportation Systems Engineering and Information Technology 8(6), 32–37 (2008)

18. Schäfer, R.P., Thiessenhusen, K.U., Wagner, P.: A Traffic Information System by Means of Real-Time Floating-Car Data. In: 9th World Congress on Intelligent Transport Systems (2002)

19. Blandin, S., Ghaoui, L.E., Bayen, A.: Kernel regression for travel time estimation via convex optimization. In: Proceedings of the 48th IEEE Conference on Decision and Control (2009)

20. Scholkopf, B., Smola, A.: Learning with kernels. MIT press (2002)

21. Yuan, J., Zheng, Y.: T-Drive: Driving Directions Based on Taxi Trajectories. In: ACM SIGSPATIAL GIS (2010)

22. Herring, R., Hofleitner, A., Abbeel, P., Bayen, A.: Estimating arterial traffic conditions using sparse probe data. In: Proceedings of the 13th International IEEE Conference on Intelligent Transportation Systems (2010)

23. Brand, M.: Coupled hidden markov models for modeling interacting processes. Technical report, The Media Lab, Massachusetts Institute of Technology (1997)

24. Yuan, J., Zheng, Y., Xie, X., Sun, G.: Driving with Knowledge from the Physical World. In: Proceedings of the 17th ACM SIGKDD International Conference on Knowledge Discovery and Data Mining (2011)

25. Yin, H., Wolfson, O.: A Weight-based map matching method in moving objects databases. In: Proceedings of the 16th International Conference on Scientific and Statistical Database Management (2004)

26. Alt, H., Efrat, A., Rote, G., Wenk, C.: Matching planar maps. Journal of Algorithms 49, 262–283 (2003)

27. Brakatsoulas, S., Pfoser, D., Salas, R., Wenk, C.: On map-matching vehicle tracking data. In: Proceedings of the 31st International Conference on Very Large Data Bases (2005)

28. Rogers, S., Langley, P., Wilson, C.: Mining GPS data to augment road models. In: Proceedings of the Fifth ACM SIGKDD International Conference on Knowledge Discovery and Data Mining, KDD 1999, pp. 104–113 (1999)

29. Edelkamp, S., Schrödl, S.: Route planning and map inference with global positioning traces, pp. 128–151. Springer-Verlag New York, Inc., New York (2003)

30. Chen, Y., Krumm, J.: Probabilistic modeling of traffic lanes from GPS traces. In: Proceedings of the 18th ACM SIGSPATIAL International Conference on Advances in Geographic Information Systems (2010)

31. Liu, W., Zheng, Y., Chawla, S., Yuan, J., Xie, X.: Discovering Spatio-Temporal Causal Interactions in Traffic Data Streams. In: Proceedings of the 17th ACM SIGKDD Conference on Knowledge Discovery and Data Mining (2011)

A Unified Framework for Modeling and Predicting Going-Out Behavior

Shoji Tominaga, Masamichi Shimosaka, Rui Fukui, and Tomomasa Sato

Intelligent Cooperative Systems Laboratory, The University of Tokyo,
7-3-1 Hongo, Bunkyo-ku, Tokyo, 113-0033, Japan
{tominaga,simosaka,fukui,tsato}@ics.t.u-tokyo.ac.jp

Abstract. Living in society, to go out is almost inevitable for healthy life. There is increasing attention to it in many fields, including pervasive computing, medical science, etc. There are various factors affecting the daily going-out behavior such as the day of the week, the condition of one's health, and weather. We assume that a person has one's own rhythm or patterns of going out as a result of the factors. In this paper, we propose a non-parametric clustering method to extract one's rhythm of the daily going-out behavior and a prediction method of one's future presence using the extracted models. We collect time histories of going out/coming home (6 subjects, total 827 days). Experimental results show that our method copes with the complexity of patterns and flexibly adapts to unknown observation.

Keywords: Methodology, Activity recognition, Location representation.

1 Introduction

Living in society and interacting with others, going outside one's house is almost inevitable for healthy life. There is increasing attention to this behavior, in many fields of study. For example, Kono et al. [10] show that the frequency of going out during one's period of life preceding old age affects activities of daily living (ADL) of several years later, and Gupta et al. [7] show that grasping going-out behavior of households saves their heating bill. However, Kono et al. used questionnaires about one's going out to collect data in their work. As Krumm and Brush [11] show modeling the rhythm of the behavior outperforms self-reported schedules, we believe that introducing sensor data processing to it enables deeper analyses in many fields such as pervasive computing, medical science, and life log, and the more precise prediction reduces the unnecessary cost of energy.

To predict someone's future behavior elementally needs estimation of someone's state at current time. Most of these researches in pervasive computing can be categorized into two approaches. One employs wearable sensors such as GPS loggers [7,11] and the other installs sensors in the environment [14,16]. When it comes to estimating the state of going out, it can be binarized as "home (inside)" or "away (outside)". Assuming most people go out through the individually same

J. Kay et al. (Eds.): Pervasive 2012, LNCS 7319, pp. 73–90, 2012.

place (i.e. most people go out through the front entrance), sensing the passage of such places should be enough to estimate the state.

Modeling and predicting going out, can be thought as one of the problems to model and predict one's presence or occupancy. Recently, there are increasing studies with probabilistic approaches on this topic in the field of pervasive computing. In these approaches, methods predict the probability of future presence, and so they have some flexibility to unknown observation, even if there are not many training data. Krumm and Brush [11] introduced probabilistic models for going out. The method classifies the going-out data by the day of the week and also predicts one's presence using the pattern of the day. Scott et al. [16] introduced an occupancy prediction algorithm for controlling heating, ventilation, and cooling (HVAC). The algorithm predicts the future presence probability via matching the occupancy data by the current time to the past observation.

There are a lot of factors affecting one's daily going out, such as the day of the week, the condition of one's health, and weather. The behavior is influenced not by only one factor of them, but by the combination with one another. In addition, the number of factors and how they affect it are individually different. However, if we look at a person, there should be one's rhythm or patterns of it. For example, the rhythm of some people definitely differs between working days and holidays. To extract the one's own patterns and model the individually different behavior, prior knowledge cannot be put directory (e.g. the number of patterns). From a statistical point of view, intuitively deciding the number of patterns sometimes causes low performance. Too many patterns cause overfitting, and too few patterns cannot represent the complexity of the data. The more accurate modeling is feasible by estimating the appropriate number of patterns and correctly classifying the data.

There has been a significant amount of prior work in the field of statistics on extracting patterns or rhythm from the sensor data. For example, Farrahi and Gatica-Perez [5] used latent Dirichlet allocation and author-topic model, Ihler et al. [8] used time-varying Poisson processes, and Gill and Hangertner [6] used von-Mises distribution to extract the underlying rhythm. Actually, most of these studies of probabilistic approaches need the number of rhythms or categories a priori. There also exists work using event-mining approaches (e.g. the system of Rashidi and Cook [14]), however, these approaches need large-scale data. The nearest concept to that of ours is done by Shimosaka, et al. [18] with Dirichlet process mixtures (DPM) [2]. We develop this approach from raw data of a sensor as they used, to this abstracted behavior, going out.

In this work, we give three assumptions about daily going-out behavior. 1) It is done in a 24-hour cycle. 2) Each behavior of a day belongs to a certain category. 3) The number of categories is different by each person. These assumptions can also be used to predict the future observation: the target day itself also belongs to one of the categories of the person. You may think some patterns can be shared with other persons, and of course, it is often that going-out patterns of a person are quite similar to those of another. However, thanks to the data-driven approaches, our method eliminates such prior knowledge without performance drawbacks.

Our contribution is summarized as follows: we develop a unified framework for modeling and predicting going-out behavior, coping with the individual tendency. There are two key points in our method. One is that the method mathematically represents this complicated behavior affected by many factors and classifies the data with estimating the number of underlying categories simultaneously. The other is that the method predicts one's future presence from current observation of one day, by estimating to which category the day belongs. Our framework only needs time histories of going out/coming home, and so it is adaptable to many studies or systems in pervasive computing. We collect time histories of total 827 days of 6 subjects to evaluate our method. Experimental results show that our method flexibly copes with the complexity of going out and predicts the future observation with robust performance.

2   Collecting Time Histories of Going Out/Coming Home

We employ two systems to accumulate time histories of going out and coming home: a tracking system and trail cameras. In this section, we show how these systems accumulate the data. As a result, we collect the time history data of 350 days (subject 1) and 239 days (subject 2) with the tracking system, and 31 days (subject 3) and 69 days (subject 4 − 6) with the trail cameras.

2.1   Collecting Time Histories via Tracking System

In the first time histories collection, we employed a human location tracking system [13] with range sensors and installed it into a one-bedroom type apartment for living alone. The size of the apartment is 4.9 meters by 9.5 meters. We installed five laser range finder (LRF) modules (Fig. 1-A), which are combinations of URG-LX04 (Hokuyo Automatic Co., Ltd.) and Armadillo-220 (Atmark Techno Inc.). The LRF modules are arranged at hip-height and located so that most area of the house is covered (the locations of the modules are shown in Fig. 1-B). The tracking system integrates the scan data, detects the resident by background subtraction, and tracks one's position by particle filter. In our work, the system automatically estimates the resident is out, if the system stops tracking at the entrance in more than 10 minutes. An example of trajectories just before the resident go out is shown in Fig. 1-B. Two subjects, both of whom were graduate students in their twenties from our laboratory lived in the house in a different period. Subject 1 lived from Apr. 1, 2009 to Mar. 16, 2010 and subject 2 from Apr. 14, 2010 to Dec. 23, 2010. Total number of days of each subject is 350 and 239, respectively. The original number of days of subject 2 is 255, however, we eliminate 16 days of subject 2 due to unexpected lack of trajectories.

A

B

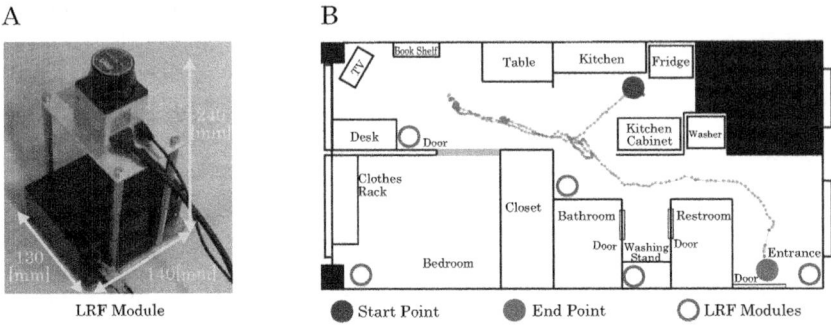

LRF Module   ● Start Point   ● End Point   ○ LRF Modules

Fig. 1. Figure A shows the picture of a LRF module. Figure B shows the layout of the experimental house to calculate trajectories. The red circles in this figure are the position of the modules. The trajectory when the resident was just going out is written as a red line (the blue circle is the start point of it and the green circle is the end point).

A   B

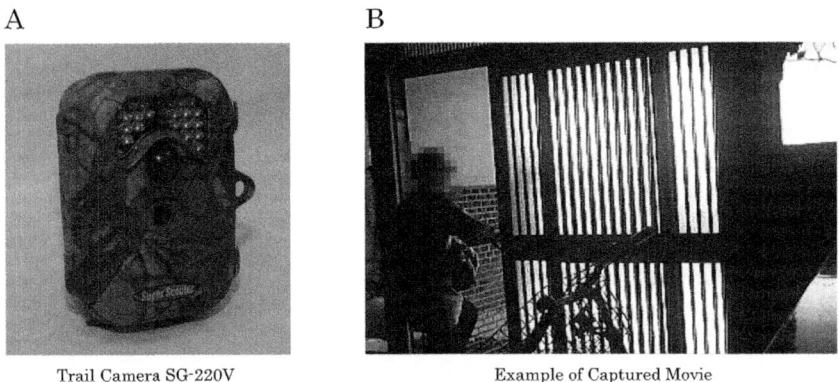

Trail Camera SG-220V   Example of Captured Movie

Fig. 2. Appearance of Trail Camera (Figure A) and Example of Captured Movie (Figure B): The movie was captured just before one of the subjects went out

2.2   Collecting Time Histories via Trail Cameras

In the second time histories collection, we installed trail cameras SG-220V from Shenzhen Siyuan Digital Technology Co., Ltd. (see Fig. 2-A) in the entrance of houses. The camera has passive infrared ray sensors to detect people and records movies when someone passes in front of the camera. Though it is originally used to record behavior of wild animals, it can be also used as a simple security camera. In our work, we recruited 4 volunteers in 3 households, all of whom are elders, with some rewards. We met them, looked at the layout of their houses, and carefully decided where to set up the cameras with simple questionnaires. We also took care about their privacies, so that the camera recorded only the behavior of their entrance passage. A frame example of the captured movies is shown in Fig. 2-B. Since one's going out and coming home were obvious with the recorded movies, we collected time histories manually. As Krumm and Brush [11] did, GPS loggers can substitute for this work. Recording started in Aug. 21, 2011 at the earliest (subject 4 – 6: subject 4 and 5 lived together), not later than Sep. 28, 2011 (subject 3) and we used the data by Oct. 28, 2011.

3   Modeling Going-Out Behavior

3.1   Outline

As described in Section 1, a state of one's going out at some time can be binarized (whether someone is away from home or not). The states is described as random variable $x = \{0, 1\}$ ($0 : home$, $1 : away$) following Bernoulli distribution $p(x|\mu) = \mu^x (1 - \mu)^{1-x}$, where, $\mu = \mu(t)$ ($0 < \mu(t) < 1$) is the time-varying parameter (e.g. if $\mu(t) = 0.9$, the person is out with a probability of 0.9 at the time t). For simplicity, the method discretizes $\mu(t)$, as a sequence $\{\mu_1, ..., \mu_T\}$ with length T. Each content of the sequence corresponds to the probability of going out at the corresponding time.

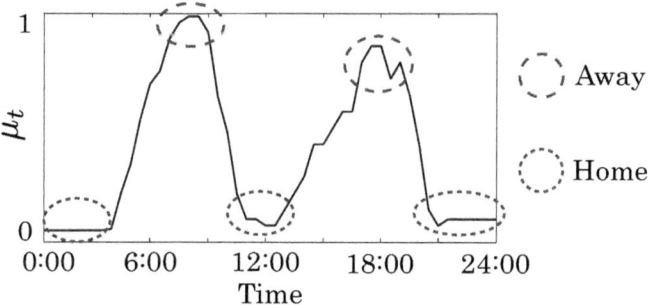

Fig. 3. Description Example of Going out

An example of parameter sequences is shown in Fig. 3. This example indicates that the person is likely to go out around 8 o'clock and 18 o'clock, and stay at home during night and around noon. Each category has its own pattern of parameter sequence.

3.2   Mathematical Description

Let $t = 1, ..., T$ be the time of a day, $n = 1, ..., N$ be the day of each observation, $k = 1, ..., K$ be the ID of the category, and $\boldsymbol{\mu}_k = (\mu_{k,1} \ ... \ \mu_{k,T})^{\mathsf{T}}$ be the parameter sequence of category k. We set the observation data of n-th day $\boldsymbol{x}_n = (x_{n,1} \ ... \ x_{n,T})^{\mathsf{T}}$ ($x_{n,t} = 0 : home$, $x_{n,t} = 1 : away$) by majority decision of each time span of a day (if $T = 24$, $t = 1$ represents the time span from 0

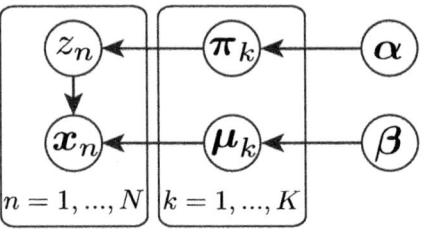

Fig. 4. Graphical Model of Going out

o'clock to 1 o'clock) The likelihood of the parameters for the data is written as
the likelihood product of each time:

$$p(\boldsymbol{x}_n|\boldsymbol{\mu}_k) = \prod_{t=1}^{T} \mu_t^{x_{n,t}} (1 - \mu_{k,t})^{1-x_{n,t}}. \qquad (1)$$

In addition, suppose $\{\mathbf{Z}\}_{n,k} = \{z_{n,k}|z_{n,k} = \{0,1\}, \sum_k z_{n,k} = 1\}$ be the parameters indicating to which category k the data of n-th day belong, z_n is a random variable following multinomial distribution $\mathcal{M}(z_n|\boldsymbol{\pi})$. Then, let $\mathbf{M} = (\boldsymbol{\mu}_1 \cdots \boldsymbol{\mu}_K)$ be parameter sequences of the categories, and the likelihood of the whole parameters are like the equation below:

$$p(\boldsymbol{x}_n|\mathbf{Z}, \mathbf{M}) = \prod_{k=1}^{K} \prod_{t=1}^{T} \left[\mu_{k,t}^{x_{n,t}} (1 - \mu_{k,t})^{1-x_{n,t}} \right]^{z_{n,k}}. \qquad (2)$$

Thanks to the simplicity of the model, it is possible to introduce hierarchical Bayesian representation for avoiding overfitting issues. This representation utilizes prior distributions for flexibility to unknown observations. Specifically, the method uses conjugate prior for each parameter, Dirichlet distribution for $\boldsymbol{\pi}$ and beta distribution for $\mu_{k,t}$:

$$\boldsymbol{\pi} \sim \mathcal{D}(\boldsymbol{\pi}|\alpha) \propto \prod_k \pi_k^{\alpha-1}, \qquad (3)$$

$$\mu_{k,t} \sim \mathcal{B}(\mu_{k,t}|\beta_1, \beta_2) \propto \mu_{k,t}^{\beta_1-1} (1 - \mu_{k,t})^{\beta_2-1}. \qquad (4)$$

Fig. 4 shows the graphical model of the representation. Each arrow represents the dependency between the parameters, for example, parameter $\boldsymbol{\mu}_k$ is generated using hyperparameters $\boldsymbol{\beta}$ (i.e. β_1, and β_2). The method estimates the model, by the posterior distribution of the parameters. For more details about this graphical representation, see Ref. [3].

3.3   Simultaneous Estimation of Parameters and Cluster Number

As we mentioned in Section 1, we cannot give the number of categories a priori. In this work, the method mentioned in Section 3.2 is extended to the simultaneous estimation of the model parameters and the cluster number. To tackle this problem, we employ Dirichlet process mixture (DPM) [2], a framework for Bayesian nonparametrics. DPM describes infinite Dirichlet distribution as a prior of categories. Compared with other methods to estimate the category size such as those introducing information criteria [1,15], DPM parameterizes the category size distribution itself and provides flexible manners to estimate the number of clusters and parameters of each category simultaneously with less calculation cost. To implement DPM, the upper bound of category number K is set as an enough bigger number than that expected (we set $K = 50$). The method estimates the number of them as $k \ll K$.

We use blocked Gibbs sampler [9], variational Bayes (VB) [4], collapsed Gibbs sampler [12] to implement DPM. The VB has an advantage of calculating cost since it provides obvious convergence and reduces the number of cycles, however, the solution of VB is completely affected by the initial state of learning so there exist local optima. In theory, blocked/collapsed sampler never causes the problems if the sampling cycles converge. Compared with each other, the blocked sampler has more chances to reach global optima than the other, and also more risks to diverge. As our prior experiment to evaluate the three, the model by the blocked sampler has the highest likelihood to the observation, and so we actually utilize this method.

The blocked Gibbs sampler for DPM utilizes truncated stick-breaking process [17] to approximate the infinite-dimensional Dirichlet distribution. The process represents beta distribution as a prior of each coefficient of multinomial distribution. In this case, coefficients π_k are represented as:

$$\pi_k = v_k \prod_{i=1}^{k-1}(1 - v_i), \quad v_k \sim \mathcal{B}(v_k|1, \alpha), \tag{5}$$

where, $v_K = 1$ for the maximum number of categories, K. Learning by the blocked sampler consists of two steps. Firstly, the method initializes the parameters. The method samples $\mathbf{Z}$, so that all data are allocated randomly and equally to each category. Lastly, the method iteratively alternate resampling from the posterior distribution (6), and (7):

$$\mathbf{V}, \mathbf{M} \sim p(\mathbf{V}, \mathbf{M}|\mathbf{X}, \mathbf{Z}), \tag{6}$$

$$\mathbf{Z} \sim p(\mathbf{Z}|\mathbf{X}, \mathbf{V}, \mathbf{M}). \tag{7}$$

In our model, the posterior distributions are expanded as:

$$v_k \sim \mathcal{B}(v_k|1 + \sum_n z_{n,k}, \alpha + \sum_{i=k+1}^{K} \sum_n z_{n,i}), \tag{8}$$

$$\mu_{k,t} \sim \mathcal{B}(\mu_{k,t}|\beta_1 + \sum_n x_{n,t}z_{n,k}, \beta_2 + \sum_n (1 - x_{n,t})z_{n,k}), \tag{9}$$

$$z_n \sim \mathcal{M}(z_n|\boldsymbol{\pi}^*), \quad \pi_k^* := \frac{\pi_k p(\boldsymbol{x}_n|\boldsymbol{\mu}_k)}{\sum_k \pi_k p(\boldsymbol{x}_n|\boldsymbol{\mu}_k)}. \tag{10}$$

During the iteration, most of categories have no data allocated, and the data aggregate into some classes. Since there cannot be complete convergence in Gibbs sampling, the number of iteration is set to 100 in our experiment. Finally, parameters of the posterior distribution $v_k \sim \mathcal{B}(v_k|\alpha^\star_{k,1}, \alpha^\star_{k,2})$, $\mu_{k,t} \sim \mathcal{B}(\mu_{k,t}|\beta^\star_{k,t,1}, \beta^\star_{k,t,2})$ are:

$$\begin{cases} \alpha^\star_{k,1} = 1 + \sum_n z_{n,k}. \\ \alpha^\star_{k,2} = \alpha + \sum_{i=k+1}^{K} \sum_n z_{n,i} \end{cases}, \qquad (11)$$

$$\begin{cases} \beta^\star_{k,t,1} = \beta_1 + \sum_n x_{n,t} z_{n,k}. \\ \beta^\star_{k,t,2} = \beta_2 + \sum_n (1 - x_{n,t}) z_{n,k} \end{cases}. \qquad (12)$$

4   Predicting Going-Out Behavior

4.1   Problem Setting and Outline

As we mentioned in Section 1, many practical applications need prediction of future presence (e.g. controlling HVAC). In this section, we show our method of predicting one's future presence utilizing our going-out model (Section 3). We assume that one's observation of a new day should also belong to a category of one's own. The method represents the probabilistic distribution of future observation as a linear sum of a pattern of each category. The coefficient of patterns, sum of which is 1, is proportional to likelihood of each category given the observation by the current time of the target day.

4.2   Calculating Probability of New Observations

Given new observations $x^\star_{1:T} := (x^\star_1 \dots x^\star_T)^\mathsf{T}$ of one day, the approximate parameter likelihood of the posterior distribution (Section 3) is represented as:

$$p(x^\star_{1:T}|\alpha^\star, \beta^\star) = \sum_k \mathbb{E}_\mathbf{V}[\pi_k] p(x^\star_{1:T}|\beta^\star_{k,1:T,1}, \beta^\star_{k,1:T,2}). \qquad (13)$$

There, each term on the right can be expanded into the equation below.

$$\mathbb{E}_\mathbf{V}[\pi_k] = \mathbb{E}[v_k] \prod_{i=1}^{k-1} (1 - \mathbb{E}[v_i]), \ \mathbb{E}[v_k] = \begin{cases} 1 & (k = K) \\ \dfrac{\alpha^\star_{k,1}}{\alpha^\star_{k,1} + \alpha^\star_{k,2}} & \text{(otherwise)} \end{cases}, \qquad (14)$$

$$p(x^\star_{1:T}|\beta^\star_{k,1:T,1}, \beta^\star_{k,1:T,2}) = \prod_{t=1}^{T} \int p(x^\star_t|\mu) \mathcal{B}(\mu|\beta^\star_{k,t,1}, \beta^\star_{k,t,2}) d\mu$$

$$= \prod_{t=1}^{T} \frac{Beta(x^\star_t + \beta^\star_{k,t,1}, 1 - x^\star_t + \beta^\star_{k,t,2})}{Beta(\beta^\star_{k,t,1}, \beta^\star_{k,t,2})}, \qquad (15)$$

where, $Beta(\cdot)$ is beta function $Beta(x, y) = \int_0^1 t^{x-1}(1-t)^{y-1} dt$. Each term of product in (15) follows beta-binomial distribution (the number of trials is fixed to 1 in this case).

4.3 Prediction Algorithm

Given observation data from time $t = 1$ to $t = t_p$ ($< T$), the probability that each category pattern generates the data can be described using the representation of Section 4.2 as $p(\boldsymbol{x}^{\star}_{1:t_p}, z^{\star}_k = 1 | \boldsymbol{\alpha}^{\star}, \boldsymbol{\beta}^{\star}) = \mathbb{E}_{\mathbf{V}}[\pi_k] p(\boldsymbol{x}^{\star}_{1:t_p} | \beta^{\star}_{k,1:t_p,1}, \beta^{\star}_{k,1:t_p,2})$. Let $\gamma_{k,1:t_p}$ be the probability that the target day belongs to category k, and this can be described as:

$$\gamma_{k,1:t_p} := p(z^{\star}_k = 1 | \boldsymbol{x}^{\star}_{1:t_p}) = \frac{p(\boldsymbol{x}^{\star}_{1:t_p}, z^{\star}_k = 1 | \boldsymbol{\alpha}^{\star}, \boldsymbol{\beta}^{\star})}{\sum_c p(\boldsymbol{x}^{\star}_{1:t_p}, z^{\star}_c = 1 | \boldsymbol{\alpha}^{\star}, \boldsymbol{\beta}^{\star})}. \tag{16}$$

The method predicts the presence probability of time t_f ($> t_p$) by a linear sum of category patterns, with coefficient $\gamma_{k,1:t_p}$ as,

$$\begin{aligned} p(x^{\star}_{t_f} = 1 | \boldsymbol{x}^{\star}_{1:t_p}, \boldsymbol{\alpha}^{\star}, \boldsymbol{\beta}^{\star}) &= \sum_k \gamma_{k,1:t_p} p(x^{\star}_{t_f} = 1 | \beta^{\star}_{k,t_f,1}, \beta^{\star}_{k,t_f,2}) \\ &= \sum_k \gamma_{k,1:t_p} \frac{Beta(1 + \beta^{\star}_{k,t_f,1}, \beta^{\star}_{k,t_f,2})}{Beta(\beta^{\star}_{k,t_f,1}, \beta^{\star}_{k,t_f,2})} \\ &= \sum_k \gamma_{k,1:t_p} \frac{\beta^{\star}_{k,t_f,1}}{\beta^{\star}_{k,t_f,1} + \beta^{\star}_{k,t_f,2}}. \end{aligned} \tag{17}$$

For practical applications, the method needs to decide one's future state with the probability. We set the parameter τ ($0 \leq \tau \leq 1$), as a threshold to output prediction. If probability of one's going out exceeds τ, the method predicts the one will be out, otherwise it predicts the one will be at home.

5 Results

5.1 Experiment Setting

The modeling and prediction performance of our method is evaluated with the time histories data collections described in Section 2. To evaluate the modeling method, we use log-likelihood as criteria, and to evaluate the predicting method, we use the classification accuracy of future observation from the past observation. The technical details are in following paragraphs.

For the former method, we see the convergence by the log-likelihood of parameters with all the data of each subject and the flexibility performance by expectation value of log-likelihood leave-one-out cross validation (LOOCV). The log-likelihood of training data shows the adaptation to the complexity of training data. The log-likelihood of LOOCV represents the flexibility to the unknown observation.

For the latter method, we also use LOOCV to predict unknown observations from the other data of the same subject. As more concrete setting, the method predicts the future observation of a day, given the 6, 9, and 12 hours data of the day. The method also predicts the presence by updating each time the method is given the presence of time t. Since the threshold of probability highly depends on applications, we set the threshold τ from 0 to 1 by 0.01 and evaluate the performance by receiver operating characteristic (ROC) curves and the area under the curves (AUC). Each predictive output is evaluated by the state of every minute. For example, suppose that a subject is out in 20 minutes of a time duration t and at home in the rest 10 minutes and the method predicts the one is out, then true positive frames will be 20 and false positive frames will be 10. Note that the performance does not necessarily improve as the observation time of the day progresses, since the applied time of prediction varies from each experiment (e.g. if 6 hours given, the method predicts the rest 18 hours, and if given 12 hours, the method predicts shorter time, 12 hours).

Throughout the experiment, we set the start time of days to 0 o'clock, each time span of a day to 30 minutes (i.e. $T = 48$), the modeling hyper parameters $\alpha = 0.1$ empirically, and $\beta_1 = \beta_2 = 1$ so that prior knowledge about one's home/away presence is eliminated. In this condition, prior of $\mu \sim \mathcal{B}(\mu|\beta_1, \beta_2)$ will be the uniform distribution from 0 to 1.

For comparison to our methods, we implement the presence model of Krumm and Brush [11] (we call this, KB model) for the experiments of both modeling and predicting, and the algorithm for predicting presence by Scott et al. [16] (we call this, Scott's algorithm) for experiment of predicting. In the modeling experiment, we also implement KB mixture model, the mixture model of each pattern of the day of week, the coefficient of which are the ratio of number of days of each pattern to the total number, usually one seventh). Since KB model does not use the current observation of the target day and this might be unfair, we modify KB mixture so as to utilize the current observation. The future distribution is the linear sum of each pattern, and coefficients are proportional to the likelihood of patterns for the given observation. Actually Krumm and Brush also utilize the drive time prediction [7] to improve their performance. In this experiment we do not implement this method since we collect the presence data not by GPS loggers. The Scott algorithm could be affected by how many nearest neighbors are used to estimate future observation, so we set the number k to not only 5 (as Scott et al. used), but also 3, 7 for prediction.

5.2   Modeling Going Out

In this section, we evaluate our modeling method by likelihood to the unknown data. With our implementation, learning the model converges in less than 1 second for each subject.

Table 1 shows log-likelihood expectation values of training data by using all data of each subject and Table 2 shows those during LOOCV of each subject. We examine the performance by separating the subjects into two groups. One is the group of subjects who has long-term data (subject 1 and 2) and the other is that of subjects who has short-term data (subject 3 – 6). With the group of long-term data, our method has high performance in both training data and test data. This suggests that KB model and its mixture, which classify the data by the day of the week, cannot represent the long-term data since seven is not necessarily

Table 1. Log-likelihood Expectation Value for Training Data

Subj.	1	2	3
Proposed	-16.2 ± 5.5	-9.5 ± 5.2	-8.8 ± 4.9
KB	-31.7 ± 5.2	-22.2 ± 12.7	-8.4 ± 5.1
KB mixture	-30.4 ± 4.1	-20.0 ± 9.0	-7.9 ± 5.2

Subj.	4	5	6
Proposed	-9.0 ± 5.2	-5.5 ± 4.3	-10.9 ± 5.3
KB	-7.9 ± 5.1	-4.8 ± 4.4	-13.5 ± 7.7
KB mixture	-8.4 ± 5.5	-5.1 ± 4.7	-13.1 ± 7.1

Table 2. Log-likelihood Expectation Value of LOOCV

Subj.	1	2	3
Proposed	$\mathbf{-18.7 \pm 7.4}$	$\mathbf{-11.1 \pm 7.3}$	-9.8 ± 5.6
KB	-32.7 ± 5.5	-24.5 ± 18.5	-52.7 ± 76.6
KB mixture	-30.6 ± 4.1	-20.2 ± 9.2	-9.1 ± 6.6

Subj.	4	5	6
Proposed	$\mathbf{-9.7 \pm 6.5}$	-6.3 ± 5.6	$\mathbf{-12.7 \pm 7.6}$
KB	-22.8 ± 46.3	-15.9 ± 26.6	-32.4 ± 59.7
KB mixture	-11.0 ± 12.5	-5.5 ± 5.2	-20.4 ± 47.8

enough number of the category. With the group of short-term data, especially in subject 4 and 6, the KB model and its mixture overfit the training data (low likelihood for test data in spite of high likelihood for training data). Even though the compared methods have great gaps of likelihood between training and test data of these subjects, our method flexibly copes with the unknown observation with low gaps. In contrast, with subject 3 and 5, our method has slightly lower LOOCV performance than KB mixture model. The main cause of this result is related with hierarchical Bayes. We set parameter $\beta_1 = \beta_2 = 1$, and this means all category patterns have additional information about one's presence, one home observation and one away observation (i.e. the probability of one's home cannot be 0, even if the person is at home during the all data). In this regard, KB mixture gets higher score in subject 3 and 5. However, the disadvantage of additional information in prior distribution seen in these subjects is trivial, compared with the advantage of flexibility with the data size and appropriateness about categorizing data seen in subject 1, 2, 4, and 6.

Clustered patterns of subject 2 and 6 by our method are shown in Fig. 5. Each graph in the figure represents the going-out pattern of the corresponding category and each value in the graph is the expectation value of posterior distribution (i.e. the probability of being away from home). Patterns of each subject are sorted into descending order by the number of allocated days and patterns with less than 3 days are eliminated. For example, type 8 represents the subject goes out around 10 o'clock and comes home around 20 o'clock. The figure shows that our method can extract peculiar patterns such as type 3 (the subject are out

almost all day) and type 6 (the subject are at home almost all day). The patterns
of subject 2 sum up to be 98 percent of total days (236/239), so it can be said to
the subject that the number of the patterns is 9. The 3 outliers are allocated into
two groups (two days and one day), both of which are the patterns of going-out
twice in different periods of a day. Similarly, the number of patterns of subject
6 is 3. For other subjects 1, 3, 4, and 5, the number is 22, 2, 2, 2, respectively.
The number of patterns has to do with the size of data. Visualization examples
of continuous 140 days of subject 2 and all days of subject 6 are shown in Fig. 6.
Categories in the figure corresponds to those in Fig. 5. Not only our method
automatically classifies the data into appropriate groups, but also it enables us
to analyze long-term going-out data by visualizing each pattern and the sequence
of classification result, for example, from the end of the 2nd week to the start of
the 3rd week, subject 2 might be traveling.

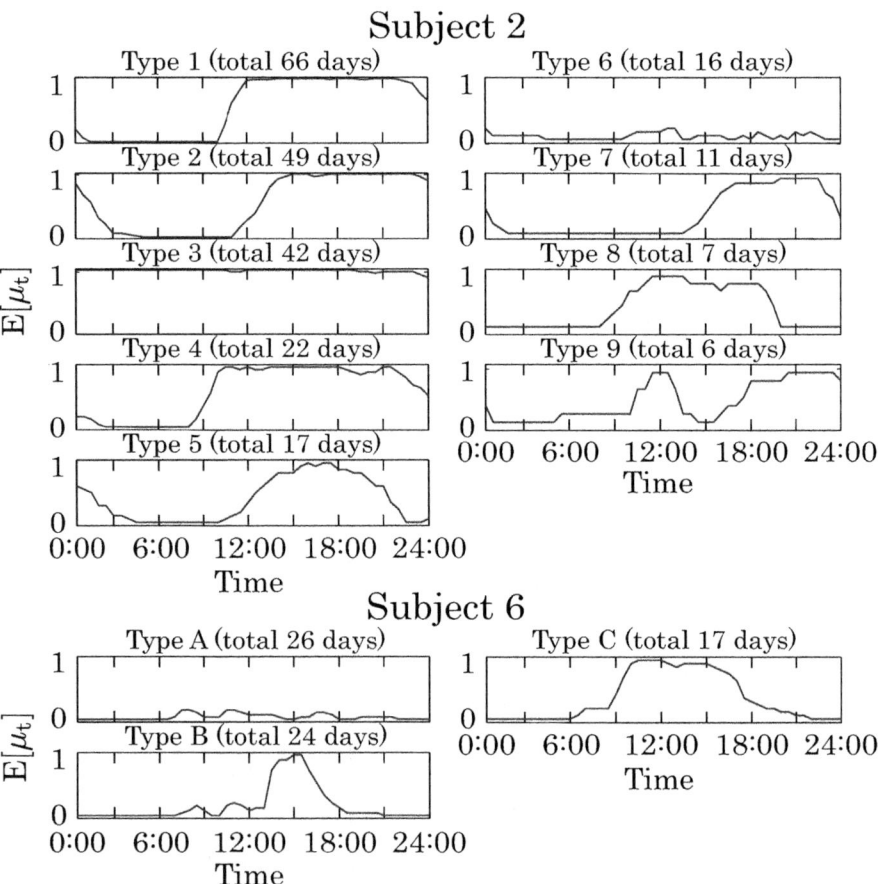

Fig. 5. Examples of Extracted Typical Patterns (Upper: Subj. 2, Lower: Subj. 6):
To emphasize the patterns of the subjects are extracted separately, we use different
representation about categories between each subject.

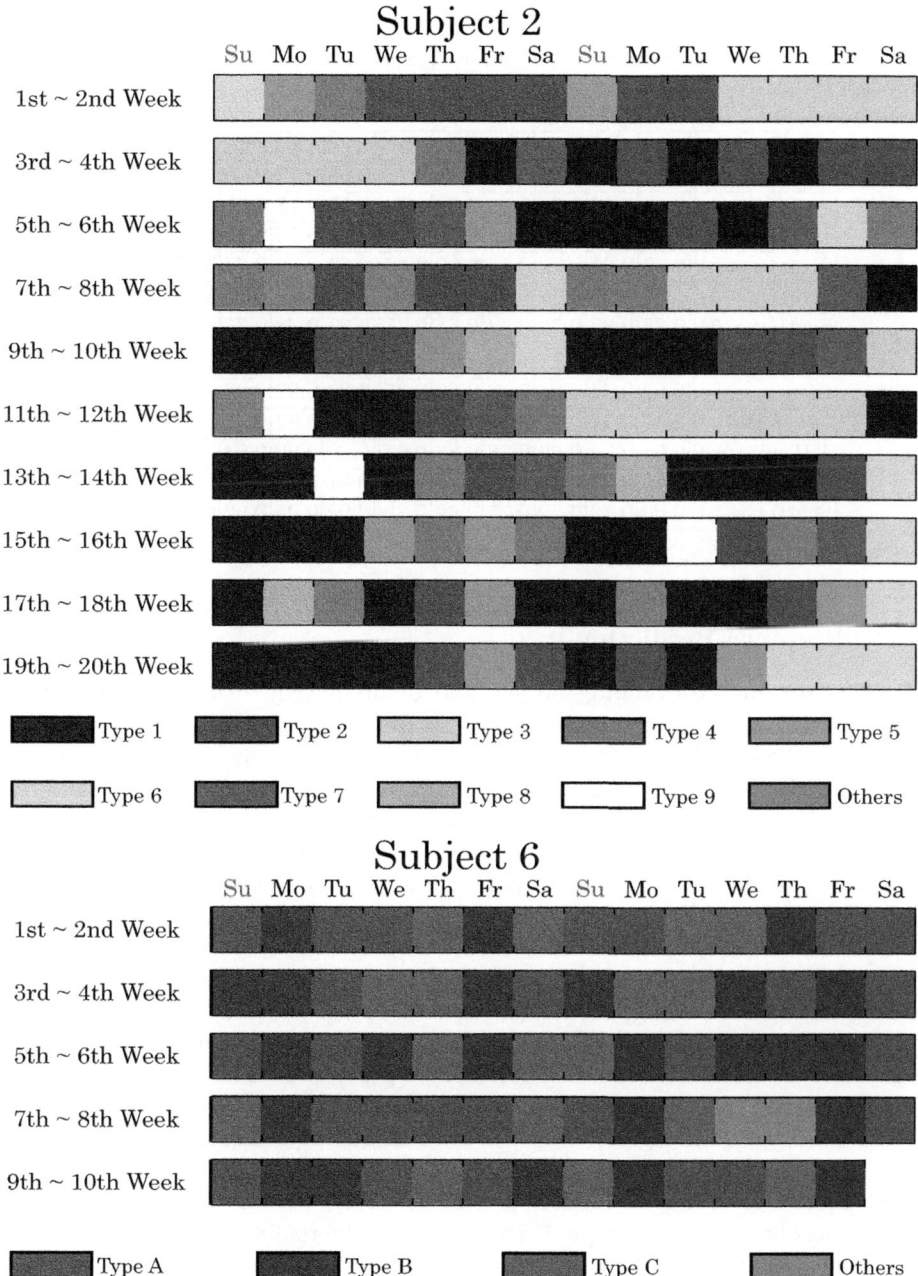

Fig. 6. Examples of Classification Result (Upper: Continuous 140 Days of Subj. 2, Lower: All 69 Days of Subj. 6)

Table 3. Area under the ROC Curves (upper-left: using first 6 hours, upper-right: using first 9 hours, lower-left: using first 12 hours, lower-right: by updating from observation of each time)

Subj.	1	2	3	4	5	6	1	2	3	4	5	6
Proposed	0.68	0.87	0.79	0.78	0.77	0.79	0.63	0.79	0.73	0.76	0.75	0.80
KB	0.60	0.83	0.68	0.73	0.69	0.79	0.55	0.78	0.66	0.73	0.69	0.79
KB mixture	0.62	0.82	0.80	0.78	0.76	0.78	0.56	0.75	0.77	0.76	0.76	0.79
Scott($k = 3$)	0.65	0.81	0.77	0.57	0.52	0.67	0.62	0.76	0.67	0.57	0.52	0.74
Scott($k = 5$)	0.66	0.86	0.77	0.56	0.54	0.76	0.63	0.77	0.74	0.57	0.55	0.76
Scott($k = 7$)	0.67	0.87	0.79	0.54	0.54	0.78	0.63	0.78	0.75	0.59	0.57	0.79
Subj.	1	2	3	4	5	6	1	2	3	4	5	6
Proposed	0.62	0.74	0.84	0.78	0.80	0.85	0.90	0.97	0.93	0.84	0.85	0.91
KB	0.50	0.71	0.71	0.74	0.65	0.82	0.60	0.82	0.72	0.78	0.73	0.83
KB mixture	0.54	0.74	0.86	0.78	0.86	0.84	0.70	0.90	0.94	0.86	0.90	0.88
Scott($k = 3$)	0.60	0.71	0.70	0.55	0.68	0.81	0.91	0.94	0.91	0.79	0.72	0.90
Scott($k = 5$)	0.60	0.72	0.72	0.57	0.69	0.82	0.92	0.95	0.92	0.81	0.72	0.91
Scott($k = 7$)	0.61	0.74	0.79	0.58	0.72	0.84	0.92	0.95	0.92	0.82	0.76	0.91

5.3   Presence Prediction

In this section, we evaluate our method of predicting future presence of new data. Fig. 7 shows the ROC curves with different conditions and subjects by changing the threshold τ from 0 to 1. The frames of true positive, true negative, false positive, and false negative are summed up with two groups by the term of data. One group contains subject 1 and 2 (subjects of long-term data, graphs on the left), and the other contains the rest subjects (subjects of short-term data, graphs on the right). The AUC values with individual subject are shown in Table 3. From the results, our method has stable high performance by all subjects and all conditions. KB or KB mixture is not good at incremental prediction of subjects of long-term data. The main cause of this result is the same as that of the modeling experiment in Section 5.2. That is, KB model cannot handle the complexity of long-term data. Scott algorithm is not good at subject of short-term data, except the incremental prediction. The main cause is that this algorithm relatively needs plenty of past observation for stable prediction since the core of the algorithm is k-nearest neighbor. Compared with KB or KB mixture, our method has an advantage of handling long-term data. Compared with Scott algorithm, our method has an advantage of handling short-term data. It can also be said that our predictive output is the real number (more finer than that of Scott algorithm, which is the rational number), so our method have more flexibility in the trade-off between the true positive and the false positive. It is found that our method does not have the best performance in all subjects and conditions, however, our method achieves the best or nearly the best of all, in all subjects and conditions.

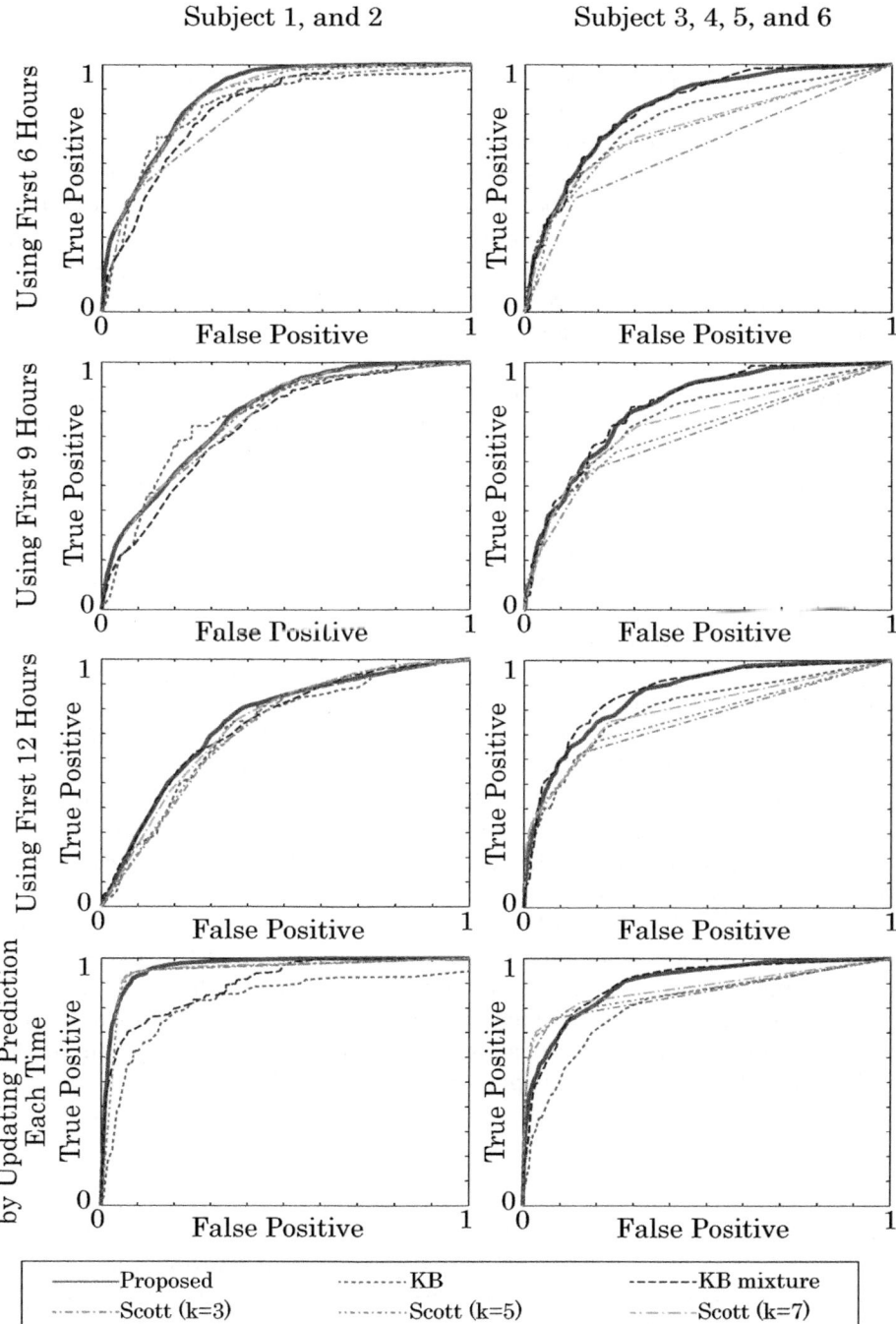

Fig. 7. Receiver Operating Characteristic Curves of Prediction

6   Discussion

We give as little prior knowledge as possible for one's going out to our method. Indeed, there are few parameters in our modeling and predicting method. In our method, there are four parameters α, β_1, β_2, and τ. However, under the precondition that there are no information about one's going out (uniform distribution from 0 to 1 as we did in the whole experiment), the parameters are in effect only α and τ. α is the parameter indicating the degree of category separation. As this parameter grows, our method tends to make more categories. τ is the threshold of prediction, and the proper value differs according to the kinds of applications. Thus, our methods can avoid the troublesome parameter estimation. Experimental results comparing our methods with existing methods suggest modeling going out definitely by the day of the week may cause low performance. There should have relationship between the day of the week and going-out behavior, however, there should also be other unignorable factors affecting the rhythm of the behavior. We believe that even if there is a person whose going-out patterns are entirely decided by the day of the week, our method can classify the date as so. However, we still need the larger data sets of more people to find correspondence between the behavior rhythm and factors such as weather, the day of the week, and social events.

There are two additional advantages of our method in practical use: easiness of updating the model and possibility of making another category. When new data are given, the method updates the parameters by only two steps: assigning the data to the categories with probabilities that each category generates the data (i.e. $\gamma_{k,1:T}$ in Section 4.3), and updating the parameters of the posterior distributions. That is, the method does not need to cluster all the data again. In addition, if the data are too different from the patterns of the categories, our method can make another category and assign the data to it. This can be used to detect the anomaly of one's life.

As we mentioned in Section 1, we regard the problem of modeling and predicting going out, as one of the problems of modeling and predicting one's presence or occupancy (someone is there or not there at that time). Our method can also be used to predict one's occupancy at certain places such as rooms in a house, an office, and a laboratory. In addition, it can be possible that our method represents other behavior of people that can be binarized.

7   Conclusion

In this work, we propose a unified framework for modeling and predicting one's going-out behavior. We assume that it is cyclic and observation of a single day independently belongs to a certain category. Our modeling method estimates the number of categories and assigns the data into the corresponding category simultaneously. Our predicting method outputs the future state of one's going out of a day by estimating the category of the day. We collected the going-out data of 6 subjects and total 827 days by employing a tracking system and trail cameras. Experimental results comparing our methods with existing methods and improved existing methods show that our method achieves the best or nearly the best of all, in all subjects and conditions stably. In addition, since patterns extracted by our framework are easy to understand, the results also show the possibility of helping people analyze the long-term data of one's going out.

As our future work, we will collect the larger dataset of more people, not only for more accurate evaluation of our framework, but also for finding correspondence between going-out behavior rhythm and underlying factors.

Acknowledgement. We desire to express our thanks to Taketoshi Mori and Hiroshi Noguchi for helping us to collect data by a laser range finder tracking system, Masanori Ogihara and Shinya Masuda for negotiation and execution of setting up trail cameras with us, local government officials of Hokuto-shi, Yamanashi prefecture, Japan for permitting us to set up trail cameras into houses, all subjects for giving us data of going out, and all anonymous reviewers for fair review and constructive suggestions.

References

1. Akaike, H.: Information theory and an extension of the maximum likelihood principle. In: Proceedings of the Second International Symposium on Information Theory, pp. 267–281 (1973)
2. Antoniak, C.E.: Mixtures of Dirichlet processes with applications to Bayesian nonparametric problems. The Annals of Statistics 2(6), 1152–1174 (1974)
3. Bishop, C.M.: Pattern Recognition and Machine Learning. Springer (2006)
4. Blei, D.M., Jordan, M.I.: Variational inference for Dirichlet process mixtures. International Society for Bayesian Analysis 1, 121–144 (2006)
5. Farrahi, K., Gatica-Perez, D.: Discovering routines from large-scale human locations using probabilistic topic models. ACM Transactions on Intelligent Systems and Technology 2, 3:1–3:27 (2011)
6. Gill, J., Hangartner, D.: Circular data in political science and how to handle it. Political Analysis 18(3) (2010)
7. Gupta, M., Intille, S.S., Larson, K.: Adding GPS-Control to Traditional Thermostats: An Exploration of Potential Energy Savings and Design Challenges. In: Tokuda, H., Beigl, M., Friday, A., Brush, A.J.B., Tobe, Y. (eds.) Pervasive 2009. LNCS, vol. 5538, pp. 95–114. Springer, Heidelberg (2009)
8. Ihler, A., Hutchins, J., Smyth, P.: Adaptive event detection with time-varying Poisson processes. In: Proceedings of Knowledge Discovery and Data Mining, pp. 207–216 (2006)
9. Ishwaran, H., James, L.F.: Gibbs sampling methods for stick-breaking priors. Journal of the American Statistical Association 96, 161–174 (2001)
10. Kono, A., Kai, I., Sakato, C., Rubenstein, L.Z.: Frequency of going outdoors predicts long-range functional change among ambulatory frail elders living at home. Archives of Gerontology and Geriatrics 45(3), 233–242 (2007)
11. Krumm, J., Brush, A.J.B.: Learning Time-Based Presence Probabilities. In: Lyons, K., Hightower, J., Huang, E.M. (eds.) Pervasive 2011. LNCS, vol. 6696, pp. 79–96. Springer, Heidelberg (2011)

12. Maceachern, S.N.: Estimating normal means with a conjugate style Dirichlet process prior. Communications in Statistics B 23, 727–741 (1994)
13. Noguchi, H., Urushibata, R., Sato, T., Mori, T., Sato, T.: System for Tracking Human Position by Multiple Laser Range Finders Deployed in Existing Home Environment. In: Lee, Y., Bien, Z.Z., Mokhtari, M., Kim, J.T., Park, M., Kim, J., Lee, H., Khalil, I. (eds.) ICOST 2010. LNCS, vol. 6159, pp. 226–229. Springer, Heidelberg (2010)
14. Rashidi, P., Cook, D.J.: Mining sensor streams for discovering human activity patterns over time. In: Proceedings of International Conference on Data Mining, pp. 431–440 (2010)
15. Schwarz, G.: Estimating the dimension of a model. The Annals of Statistics 6(2), 461–464 (1978)
16. Scott, J., Brush, A.J.B., Krumm, J., Meyers, B., Hazas, M., Hodges, S., Villar, N.: PreHeat: controlling home heating using occupancy prediction. In: Proceedings of the International Conference on Ubiquitous Computing, pp. 281–290 (2011)
17. Sethuraman, J.: A constructive definition of Dirichlet priors. Statistica Sinica 4, 639–650 (1994)
18. Shimosaka, M., Ishino, T., Noguchi, H., Sato, T., Mori, T.: Detecting human activity profiles with Dirichlet enhanced inhomogeneous Poisson processes. In: Proceedings of International Conference on Pattern Recognition, pp. 4384–4387 (2010)

The Hidden Image of the City: Sensing Community Well-Being from Urban Mobility

Neal Lathia, Daniele Quercia, and Jon Crowcroft

The Computer Laboratory, University of Cambridge, UK
{neal.lathia,daniele.quercia,jon.crowcroft}@cl.cam.ac.uk

Abstract. A key facet of urban design, planning, and monitoring is measuring communities' well-being. Historically, researchers have established a link between well-being and *visibility* of city neighbourhoods and have measured visibility via quantitative studies with willing participants, a process that is invariably manual and cumbersome. However, the influx of the world's population into urban centres now calls for methods that can easily be implemented, scaled, and analysed. We propose that one such method is offered by pervasive technology: we test whether urban mobility—as measured by public transport fare collection sensors—is a viable proxy for the visibility of a city's communities. We validate this hypothesis by examining the correlation between London urban flow of public transport and census-based indices of the well-being of London's census areas. We find that not only are the two correlated, but a number of insights into the flow between areas of varying social standing can be uncovered with readily available transport data. For example, we find that deprived areas tend to preferentially attract people living in other deprived areas, suggesting a segregation effect.

Keywords: Mobility, Urban Analysis, Sensors, Well-Being.

1   Introduction

An ever-increasing proportion of this globe's 7 billion-strong population is living in or moving into cities; in the United Kingdom, this figure was projected to have already surpassed the 90% mark[1]. In this setting, the ability to design and monitor urban spaces that enable social and economic well-being becomes critical. In the past, urban planners have asserted that the well-being of communities is related to their *visibility* or *imaginability* [1]. The key idea is that the less imaginable a social setting is, the more unnerving experiences within it will be. Sociologists have thus measured urban visibility by asking study participants to draw mental maps of their city [2], the assumption being that urban residents' recall of their city reflects the extent to which different city parts are visible and form a coherent picture in people's minds. More recently, longitudinal studies have been launched (e.g., Understanding Society[2], The Happiness

---

[1] Data from the World Resources Institute, http://www.wri.org
[2] http://www.understandingsociety.org.uk

J. Kay et al. (Eds.): Pervasive 2012, LNCS 7319, pp. 91–98, 2012.
© Springer-Verlag Berlin Heidelberg 2012

Project[3]) to survey participants about the features of their lives that include strong indicators of community well-being. The ongoing studies are being conducted manually and must therefore take great care with continuous sampling of its participants [3]: the inherent labour involved in conducting such enquiries presents a clear challenge that complicates the measurement (and continuous monitoring) of well-being in the cities of the future.

We posit that data from pervasive technology that tracks city residents' movements across a metropolitan area is a valid proxy for urban visibility. To validate this hypothesis, we examine the relation between two independent datasets from the London, England: (1) a month-long sample of public transport mobility data, measured with passive sensors, and (2) publicly available community well-being census data (measured as community social deprivation). In doing so, we find that urban flow correlates with social deprivation. We also uncover facets of flow between communities (Section 4):

- Socially-deprived communities in London tend to be visited more than well-off communities.
- In general, homophily does not hold: residents of an area with a given deprivation do not travel to equally-deprived areas. At first sight this suggests that Londoners do not segregate themselves with like-minded people. However, by separating deprived communities from less deprived ones, we observe a different picture: well-off areas tend to attract people living in areas of varying social deprivation; by contrast, deprived areas tend to preferentially attract people from other deprived areas: social segregation holds only for socially-deprived areas, and not for well-off areas.

More generally, these results suggest that large-scale and real-time monitoring of community well-being is cheaply available via the passive sensors that urban residents pro-actively carry and use for public transport access.

2   Related Work

Smart phones and embedded sensor systems have given researchers unprecedented access to new and rich datasets, recording detailed information about how people live and move through urban areas. In this section, we describe a select number of examples that highlight how new datasets are lending insight into individuals' lives and urban analysis. Embedded sensors have recently been used to measure the spatio-temporal patterns of an entire city's usage of a shared-bicycle scheme [4]. Smart-phones' sensors have been used to augment psychological research [5]; Bluetooth sensors have been used to measure social interactions [6]; GPS sensors have been shown to aide urban planning and design [7,8]. Lastly, this paper uses the same dataset from public transport automated fare collection systems which was previously used to investigate travellers' perceptions and incentives [9]. Raw sensor readings, however, tend to lack qualitative

---

[3] http://www.somervillema.gov/departments/somerstat/report-on-well–being

descriptions of the context of people who are moving about urban spaces: there is a growing awareness that online resources may offer contextually-rich data that is otherwise absent from sensor readings. Recent research includes the use of "check-ins" (where users input their location to their mobile device) [10] and geo-tagged photos [11] to understand the relation between urban space, social events, and mobility.

These new data sources now allow researchers to quantitatively test past assertions made by urban planners, geographers, and social scientists. In 1960, Kevin Lynch published a book titled "The Image of the City" in which he argued that one of the most important conditions for a liveable and enjoyable city is high "imaginability" [1], or the city dwellers' ability to form a coherent representation of the overall structure of the city. Considerable research then went into quantifying imaginability or, more specifically, the recognizability of a city. Milgram did so for New York City [2]. He found that, as expected, the least deprived (i.e., richest) boroughs happen to be the most recognisable ones. More recently, using a nation-wide communication network obtained from telephone data, Eagle *et al.* showed that less-deprived UK neighbourhoods tend to be associated with residents whose social contacts are geographically diverse [12]. Until recently, however, data has not been available to quantify city recognizability at scale: we will use a London's transport dataset, compute two recognizability measures, and correlate them with UK census' community well-being scores.

3   From Mobility to Community Well-Being

To begin with, we describe the data and the methodology that we applied to examine the relation between urban flow and community well-being. Broadly speaking, by analysing a large sample of trips taken with public transport, we infer the communities that different travellers belong to. From this, we derive a *flow matrix* of visit patterns between different communities (i.e., n residents of location i visit location j). This data can then be used to, first, validate our hypothesis by computing its correlation to *IMD* and, second, to investigate the extent that homophily emerges in large-scale travel patterns.

Mobility and Well-Being Datasets. London is the biggest city in the United Kingdom; by most measures, it is also the largest urban area in the European Union. We obtained well-being data from the UK Office for National Statistics[4], as measured (based on national census results) with the Index of Multiple Deprivation (*IMD*). The *IMD* is a composite score derived from the income, employment, education, health, crime, housing, and the environmental quality of each community [13]. We note that the data is normally distributed. Broadly speaking, socially deprived communities have higher *IMD* scores (e.g., Tottenham, Hackney); whilst less deprived the communities have lower scores (e.g., Mayfair, Belgravia). In this work, we assume that a census area represents a community; we choose such a definition because it has been widely used in recent studies of social deprivation (including the related article by Eagle *et al.* [12]).

---

[4] http://data.gov.uk/dataset/index_of_multiple_deprivation_imd_2007

While *IMD* data partitions the city according to spatially bounded communities, the Transport for London (TfL) public transport infrastructure forms a network that binds the city together. The transport system is a vast, multimodal network of underground trains (11 interconnected lines with 270 stations), overground trains (5 lines with 78 stations) and buses (about 8,000 buses serving 19,000 stops) as well as trams, river services, and other specialised services. Moreover, TfL operates an automated fare collection system, which uses RFID-based smart card tickets (called *Oyster cards*); by 2009, this system accounted for approximately 80% of all public transport trips in the city [14]. Detailed information about each trip is captured each time an Oyster card is used to both enter and exit the public transport network; most importantly, it allows for individual travellers' trips to be linked [15].

The Oyster card dataset that we obtained contains every single journey taken using smart cards throughout the 31 days of March 2010. This amounts to roughly 89 million journeys, of which 70 million are tube journeys, with the rest made up of trips taken on National Rail, Overground and other rail systems. Each record details the day, anonymised user id, the origin and destination pair, entry time, and exit time (measured only as accurately as the minute of entry/exit). We took two steps to clean the data. First, we removed any entries containing erroneous or inconsistent data, as well as all bus trips (since we do not know the destination for these trips). Entries were removed if the start time was earlier than the end time or if the origin and destination were the same. We are left with

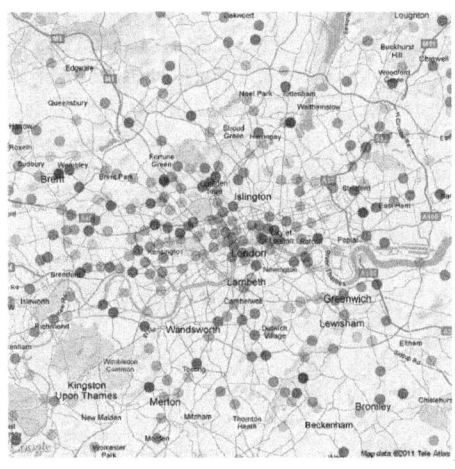

Fig. 1. The geographical distribution of IMD values, mapped using London stations: each circle is a station, darker circles have higher IMD values

96.4% of the original data, amounting to 76, 601, 937 trips by 5.1 million unique users—an average of 2.47 million journeys each day. Lastly, we match stations to census areas by geographical proximity in order to obtain a mapping between stations and *IMD* scores: the resulting geographical layout is shown in Figure 1.

Methodology: We decomposed the process of correlating public transport trips and neighbourhood *IMD* scores into a number of steps:

1. Inferring Travellers' Familiar Locations. This step aims to identify the communities that each traveller is most familiar with. Ideally, we would like to know where each traveller lives; in practice, this data is not available to us. We therefore count the number of entries and exits that travellers have at each station, which allows us to create a ranking of stations for each person. We then pick the top-2 most visited stations by each traveller [16] as their "familiar" locations (which, intuitively, would cover both home and work locations), subject to two conditions. First, the traveller must have had at least 2 trips in the 31 days of our dataset. Second, the inferred locations must also not be major inter-city/international rail stations (e.g., Victoria Station); should both of the top-2 stations fall under this category, the person is dropped from the dataset. Intuitively, this method takes into account typical commuting habits in determining familiar locations [15]; it avoids attributing non-London residents to the communities surrounding intercity train stations *, and also prunes people who do not tend to use public transport from the analysis. Note that, for each remaining person, we may have up to two locations that are deemed as familiar locations.

2. Create User-Visit Matrix. Using each trip by traveller u from origin o to destination d, (u, o, d), we produce a binary matrix C which counts the visits (where a visit is broadly defined as a station entry/exit) of travellers to stations. More formally, each matrix entry $C_{i,j}$ is non-zero if traveller j has visited station i, and i is not (one of) j's familiar locations.

3. Create Community Flow Matrix. Now that we have both home locations (Step 1) and visit frequencies (Step 2), we compute a station-by-station flow matrix F which represents which locations community members visit. Each entry $F_{i,j}$ counts the number of people who live in j and who have visited i. If a particular traveller has two inferred familiar locations (h_1, h_2), we count the provenance of each visit to i as 0.5 from h_1 and 0.5 from h_2. Note that the flow matrix does not take into account the frequency of a user's travel to an area; it just accounts for whether or not she visited it. After this step, we have the data we need: a mapping from stations $\rightarrow$ *IMD* values and a flow matrix of stations $\rightarrow$ stations. We next investigate what this data can reveal by performing two steps:

1. Correlate *IMD* and Flow. The correlation (or the extent that a linear relationship exists) between two vectors of values is computed using the Pearson correlation coefficient. Given a vector X with mean μ_X (e.g., *IMD* values) and Y with mean μ_Y (e.g., flow values), the correlation is defined as the covariance of the two variables divided by the product of the standard deviations. To perform this, we need to condense our flow matrix F into a vector of values, one per station; we define the flow f_i into an area as the sum of the areas that it receives visitors from:

$$f_i = \sum_i F_{i,j} \tag{1}$$

2. Compute Homophily Indices. We also delve further into the flow matrix by computing two different scores that measure the homophily of each community. The first, which we call the *social equaliser* index, measures the extent to which an area attracts people from areas of varying deprivation:

$$H_1(i) = STD \left(\frac{\sum_j F_{i,j} * IMD_j}{\sum_j F_{i,j}} \right) \tag{2}$$

where STD is the standard deviation of the average enclosed in parenthesis. Intuitively, if $H_1(i)$ is high, then area i is a *social equalizer*: it attracts visitors from
areas of varying deprivation (high standard deviation). If it is low, then people
in area i tend to flow between areas with people of similar social deprivation.
The second, which we call the *heterogeneity* index, measures the extent to which
an area attracts people from areas of with similar deprivation:

$$H_2(i) = \frac{\sum_j F_{i,j} \cdot |IMD_j - IMD_i|}{\sum_j F_{i,j}} \qquad (3)$$

If $H_2(i)$ is high, then the area i attracts areas different from itself (*heterogeneous*
pair of areas having different *IMD* scores); if it is low, then area i attracts areas
that are similar to itself. Finally, to examine the relation between community
homophily and social deprivation, we computed the correlations between H_1 and
IMD as well as H_2 and IMD.

4   Results: Correlating Mobility and Well-Being

We study the Pearson product-moment correlation between IMD and metrics of
urban flows. Weak, yet statistically-significant, correlations are found between an
area's deprivation IMD score and the number f_i of areas from which it receives
visits (correlation coefficient $r = 0.21$ with $p < 0.001$), suggesting that the
more deprived the area, the more it tends to be visited. Considering the *social
equaliser* index H_1, we find that it is not correlated with IMD ($r = 0.02$ with
$p < 0.001$). This means that, in general, there is no homophily effect: Londoners
do not tend to visit communities having deprivation scores that are similar to
their own communities'. However, we find that IMD is negatively correlated
with the *heterogeneity* index H_2 ($r = -0.16$ with $p < 0.001$), suggesting that
heterogeneity holds only for well-off areas. These areas tend to attract people
living in areas of varying deprivation. By contrast, Londoners in well off areas do
not tend to visit communities that are deprived. This suggests that segregation
effects are observed only in deprived areas, and that has important implications
in policy making. Finally, to study how the number of visiting areas and the
second (*heterogeneity*) index contribute in explaining the variability of IMD, we
ran a linear regression of the form:

$$IMD_i \sim \alpha + (\beta_1 \times log(H_2(i))) + (\beta_2 \times f_i) \qquad (4)$$

In so doing, we obtain $R^2 = 0.16$, indicating that 16% of the variation in the
IMD is explained only by the two indicators $H_2(i)$) and f_i. Furthermore, the
most important predictor is the *heterogeneity* index ($\beta_1 = -0.51, p < 0.001$)
and the contribution of f_i is significantly reduced and becomes negligible ($\beta_2 =
0.001, p < 0.001$).

5   Limitations and Applications

The results above take the first step into examining how data from pervasive
technology can be used to investigate social mixing and homophily of urban

communities. In this section, we discuss the limitations of our study as well as the theoretical and practical implications of the results we obtained. The public transport data that we have is rife with uncertainty: we do not know the exact home locations of travellers and we had no choice but to drop all bus trips since passengers do not have to use their card when reaching their destination. Our view of the city is also incomplete: we do not have data relating to the penetration of Oyster cards in various communities, which prevents us from knowing the extent that our results are skewed by communities opting for non-public modes of transport (regardless of the reason, e.g., well-off communities using cars). We also do not have data about urban density, in order to normalise against the variability in the number of people who live in different communities. We assume that access to this data would allow us to produce stronger results. Furthermore, we are tied to existing infrastructure: we could only analyse those portions of the city that are covered by the transport network, and the definition of community that we have adopted is in relation to this infrastructure (i.e., each station belongs to one community). We acknowledge that this mapping may not be fully accurate (or indeed capture the entirety of the metropolitan area's communities); a station may sit at the border of two adjacent communities. The results support the emerging research that calls for urban planners [7] and policy makers [9] to leverage mobility data when making and evaluating their decisions. In fact, the lack of coverage limitation of our study may be used alongside *IMD* values to estimate which communities would most benefit from new transport infrastructure. This data may also prove to be invaluable for building tools that monitor the visibility of physical communities, in order to augment longitudinal studies with dynamic and large-scale data.

6   Conclusion

We have used fare collection data to measure how the way people move about cities can be used as an implicit indicator of the visibility of communities. Various fare collection systems are in use in hundreds of other cities throughout the world: repeating this study, as well as discovering novel uses of the data that these systems generate, is a promising area of research. We have three directions of future work. First, we plan on addressing limitations described above by re-examining the relation between home location and travel patterns. We have also measured community visibility from a broad, aggregate view; in practice, the mobility of visitors into a community will be tied to the social events and facilities (work, educational institutions, social venues) in that area. We thus plan to investigate how flows deviate from normal patterns during large-scale events, in order to discover how the dynamics of urban life influence the social well-being of the area. Recent work [17] has also uncovered a relation between *IMD* scores and social media (tweets') sentiment; we plan to enrich the study above by investigating the meeting point of offline physical data and online user-generated content, which increasingly intersect by being geo-located.

Acknowledgements. This research has received funding from the EC FP7 Programme (FP7-SST-2008-RTD-1; grant agreement n. 234239) and from the RCUK through the Horizon Digital Economy Research grant (EP/G065802/1).

References

1. Lynch, K.: The Image of the City. MIT Press, Cambridge (1960)
2. Milgram, S.: The Individual in a Social World, 3rd edn. Pinter and Martin, London (2010)
3. Lynn, P.: Maintaining Cross-Sectional Representativeness in a Longitudinal General Population Survey. Understanding Society Working Paper (June 2011)
4. Froehlich, J., Neumann, J., Oliver, N.: Sensing and Predicting the Pulse of the City through Shared Bicycling. In: 21st IJCAI, Pasadena, California (2009)
5. Rachuri, K., et al.: EmotionSense: A Mobile Phones based Adaptive Platform for Experimental Social Psychology Research. In: ACM UbiComp (2010)
6. Eagle, N., Pentland, S.: Reality Mining: Sensing Complex Social Systems. Pers. Ubiquitous Computing 10, 255–268 (2006)
7. Zheng, Y., Liu, Y., Yuan, J., Xie, X.: Urban Computing with Taxicabs. In: ACM UbiComp (2011)
8. Soto, V., Frias-Martinez, V., Virseda, J., Frias-Martinez, E.: Prediction of Socioeconomic Levels Using Cell Phone Records. In: Konstan, J.A., Conejo, R., Marzo, J.L., Oliver, N. (eds.) UMAP 2011. LNCS, vol. 6787, pp. 377–388. Springer, Heidelberg (2011)
9. Lathia, N., Capra, L.: How Smart is Your Smartcard? Measuring Travel Behaviours, Perceptions, and Incentives. In: ACM UbiComp (2011)
10. Bawa-Cavia, A.: Sensing the Urban: Using Location-Based Social Network Data in Urban Analysis. In: Pervasive PURBA Workshop (2011)
11. Girardin, F., et al.: Digital Footprinting: Uncovering Tourists with User-Generated Content. IEEE Pervasive Computing 7 (2008)
12. Eagle, N., Macy, M., Claxton, R.: Network Diversity and Economic Development. Science 328 (2010)
13. Noble, M., et al.: The English Indices of Deprivation. The Department of Communities and Local Government (March 2008)
14. Weinstein, L.S.: Tfl's contactless ticketing: Oyster and beyond. In: Transport for London, London, UK (September 2009)
15. Lathia, N., Froehlich, J., Capra, L.: Mining Public Transport Usage for Personalised Intelligent Transport Systems. In: IEEE ICDM (2010)
16. Gonzalez, M., Hidalgo, C., Barabasi, A.L.: Understanding Individual Human Mobility Patterns. Nature 453(7196), 779–782 (2008)
17. Quercia, D., Ellis, J., Capra, L., Crowcroft, J.: Tracking "Gross Community Happiness" from Tweets. In: ACM CSCW (2012)

Scalable Mining of Common Routes in Mobile Communication Network Traffic Data

Olof Görnerup

Swedish Institute of Computer Science (SICS), SE-164 29 Kista, Sweden
olofg@sics.se

Abstract. A probabilistic method for inferring common routes from mobile communication network traffic data is presented. Besides providing mobility information, valuable in a multitude of application areas, the method has the dual purpose of enabling efficient coarse-graining as well as anonymisation by mapping individual sequences onto common routes. The approach is to represent spatial trajectories by Cell ID sequences that are grouped into routes using locality-sensitive hashing and graph clustering. The method is demonstrated to be scalable, and to accurately group sequences using an evaluation set of GPS tagged data.

Keywords: Cellular networks, mobility, data mining, location privacy.

1 Introduction

Mobile communication networks have in recent years been recognised as large-scale ubiquitous sensor networks capable of producing massive amounts of valuable mobility data. This data has for instance been used to statistically characterise human mobility [13,24,25], in crisis management [5], for traffic modeling [20], for detecting anomalous events [2,9], to identify common locations [14,17], for mobility prediction [6,26], and to determine low-level properties, such as if a terminal is in motion [15] or mode of transportation [23]. There is also an abundance of work where other types of sensors are used to characterise human mobility, predominantly GPS, such as in [1,3,19,21]. Although GPS data has a higher precision than data acquired from mobile communication networks, the former also has several disadvantages, such as not functioning indoors or underground (e.g. in the subway), or having high energy consumption. The penetration rate of GPS equipped devices is currently also significantly lower than for mobile phones in general.

In this paper a scalable probabilistic method for inferring common routes from sequences of Cell IDs from 2G and 3G networks is presented. Similar sequences are related using locality-sensitive hashing, and grouped using graph clustering. Resulting common routes are constituted by the clusters of Cell ID sequences output by the method. The approach is neither limited to short scale (e.g. Markovian) prediction as it captures long correlations in data, nor is it dependent on GPS trajectories as it operates on network data alone.

J. Kay et al. (Eds.): Pervasive 2012, LNCS 7319, pp. 99–106, 2012.

In a recent related study, Becker et al. have demonstrated that Cell ID handover sequences are stable over routes [4]. Using Cell IDs in concurrence with additional data (e.g. temporal information and cell tower locations), they utilise this to accurately classify sequences with respect to routes given at the outset, although not explicitly addressing scalability. The method presented in this paper, however, infers the routes from data, which is necessary if routes are dynamically changing over time, or not even known (such as during crisis management, where population movements are unforeseen, perhaps on a national scale [5]). Automatically being able to infer common mobility patterns from existing network data is also valuable in several other application areas, such as for facilitating traffic and transport planning, to improve emergency response, or for enabling more accurate empirically grounded epidemic models.

Furthermore, mining mobility patterns has computational advantages. In order to cope with the massive amount of mobility data available the data has to be coarse-grained for viable storage and analysis. The method presented in this paper enables projection of raw Cell ID sequences onto substantially smaller sets of common routes. These projections also result in anonymisation, cf. [10], as information about individual sequences is removed and hence subscribers may "hide in the crowd" [1,12].

2   Methods

Data Set. A mobile communication network consists of cells, where each cell is given by a geographic area covered by a base station. Cells in turn are grouped into location areas. When a terminal moves between location areas, the new location area and the id of the new cell is communicated to the network. Information about cell handovers within a location area, however, is not transmitted to the network. The current Cell ID is also known by the network when the terminal is used, e.g. during a call or when messaging. The network also acquires cell information by occasionally paging the terminal. This is done periodically, but infrequently, such as once per hour. Since each cell is correlated with geographic position, one may use sequences of Cell IDs to represent geographic trajectories. Such a sequence is denoted $S = (c_1, c_2, ..., c_a)$, where c_i is the i:th Cell ID, and a is the length of the sequence.

To enable experiments on empirical data, Cell ID sequences have been collected using terminals that record cell handovers. Handovers within location areas are also acquired. To simulate data as seen by the network, sequences are therefore sparsened by only keeping Cell IDs that occur immediately after a location area change. This corresponds to the "worst case" scenario when a terminal is in idle mode and not being paged.

Relating Sequences. The strategy is to identify common routes by clustering Cell ID sequences under the assumption that two trajectories that share the same route have similar Cell ID sequences. When relating sequences to each other the order of Cell IDs is disregarded and only Cell ID occurrences are considered. The similarity between two sequences S_i and S_j is quantified as the Jaccard index $J_{ij} = |\mathcal{C}_i \cap \mathcal{C}_j|/|\mathcal{C}_i \cup \mathcal{C}_j|$, where $\mathcal{C}_i$ and $\mathcal{C}_j$ are the sets of occurring Cell IDs in S_i and S_j, respectively. $0 \leq J_{ij} \leq 1$, where $J_{ij} = 0$ when S_i and S_j do not share any Cell IDs, and $J_{ij} = 1$ when the two sequences have every Cell ID in common.

Locality-Sensitive Hashing. An exhaustive pairwise comparison of sequences is not feasible due to the potentially huge number of comparisons required. Instead sequences are related using a technique based on the Min-hash [8] and locality-sensitive hashing [16] schemes. Let $h(\cdot)$ be a pseudo-random uniform hash function that maps a Cell ID to a unique integer $i \in \{1, 2, ..., d\}$, where d is the number of distinct cells. Furthermore, let $H(\cdot)$ be a function that maps a Cell ID set to the minimum hash value of the elements in the set: $H(\mathcal{C}) = \min_{c \in \mathcal{C}} h(c)$. Then $H(\cdot)$ has the convenient property that $\text{Prob}[H(\mathcal{C}_i) = H(\mathcal{C}_j)] = J_{ij}$ [8]. This property can be utilised to identify related sequences simply by putting each sequence S_i in a bucket given by $H(\mathcal{C}_i)$. Sequences in the same buckets are then likely to have a high degree of Jaccard similarity. However, this approach results in many false positives, such that buckets contain unrelated sequences. To remedy this, the *two* smallest hash values of a sequence, given by a function $H'(\cdot)$, specify its bucket. That is, $H'(\mathcal{C}) = (H(\mathcal{C}), H(\mathcal{C}'))$, where $\mathcal{C}' = \mathcal{C} \setminus \{c\}$ for element c such that $H(\mathcal{C}) = h(c)$. Then

$$\begin{aligned}
\text{Prob}[H'(\mathcal{C}_i) = H'(\mathcal{C}_j)] = & \\
\text{Prob}[H(\mathcal{C}_i) = H(\mathcal{C}_j)] \cdot \text{Prob}[H(\mathcal{C}'_i) = H(\mathcal{C}'_j)] \approx & \\
\text{Prob}[H(\mathcal{C}_i) = H(\mathcal{C}_j)]^2 = J_{ij}^2, &
\end{aligned} \tag{1}$$

for $|C| \gg 2$, since $h(\cdot)$ is pseudo-random uniform hash function[1]. $H'(\cdot)$, termed a hash signature, drastically reduces the number of false positives, but will also result in numerous false negatives, where similar sequences have different hash signatures. To reduce the number of false negatives the procedure is repeated n times with different hash functions, H'_i, and at each iteration the pairs of sequences that have the same H'_i value are noted.

Graph Clustering. Sequences are related in a graph, where the weight of an edge between two vertices, constituted by sequences, is given by the number of times the corresponding sequences have the same H'_i value. The procedure for building a sequence graph is described in pseudo-code in Algorithm 1. Given the graph, sequences are grouped into common routes using a graph clustering algorithm. There are several such algorithms that can efficiently handle huge networks, c.f. [18]. Here the Louvain method is used [7], which is a good compromise between accuracy and computational complexity. The method hierarchically clusters vertices by iteratively forming higher order clusters that in turn are clustered; see ref. [7] for details.

---

[1] Another approach is to use two different hash functions [8]. This is more accurate, but also less efficient since one has to hash twice.

Algorithm 1. Sequence graph construction. Graph G is initialised to an ordered pair of vertex and edge sets, $(\{S_i\}_{j=1}^m, \mathcal{E})$, where m is the number of sequences, and $\mathcal{E}$ is the set of all possible edges, where each edge has weight 0.

1. Initialise graph G
2. **for** $i = 1$ to n **do**
3.   Clear buckets.
4.   **for all** sequences S_j **do**
5.   Put S_j in bucket $H'_i(\mathcal{C}_j)$
6.   **end for**
7.   **for all** buckets b **do**
8.   **for all** unordered pairs (S, S') such that $S, S' \in b$ and $S \neq S'$ **do**
9.   Increment weight of edge $(S, S') \in \mathcal{E}$ with 1
10.   **end for**
11.   **end for**
12. **end for**

3   Results

Accuracy. A set consisting of 87 GPS tagged sequences, denoted $\mathcal{V}$, is used to evaluate the accuracy of the method. The sequences are taken from three main routes (with 27, 29 and 31 sequences) given by a highway, a smaller road and a railroad. The GPS trajectories of the sequences are shown in Figure 1. Since it is given which route each sequence belongs to, one may compare the correct partition of $\mathcal{V}$ with the partition given by the method. The degree of accuracy is quantified by the Rand index [22], a similarity measure between partitions. This index, denoted r, is the fraction of pairs of elements where both elements are either in the same partition element in both partitions (counting to c_{00}), or where both are *not* in the same partition elements in both partitions (counting to c_{11}). That is,

$$\mathrm{r} = (c_{00} + c_{11}) \binom{m}{2}^{-1} \tag{2}$$

where m is the number of sequences. $\mathrm{r} \in [0, 1]$, where $\mathrm{r} = 1$ when two partitions are identical. As expected the accuracy improves with increasing number of hash signatures since larger n results in a more accurate sequence graph. The choice of n is therefore a trade-off between speed and accuracy, where the latter increases rapidly for small n and then approaches convergence, cf. Figure 2. The method performs well, reaching an accuracy of $\mathrm{r} \approx 0.87$ for a moderate number of hash functions. In other words, sequences are equally related in both partitions (in terms of belonging to the same partition element or not) in approximately 87% of all possible sequence pairs.

Scalability. Since the graph clustering algorithm used is known to be scalable [7], we turn our attention to the scalability of Algorithm 1. The runtime of generating a similarity network is measured for different sequence set sizes. Again the GPS tagged sequences are used, in addition to 503 sequences that approximately start and end in the same areas as the GPS sequences.

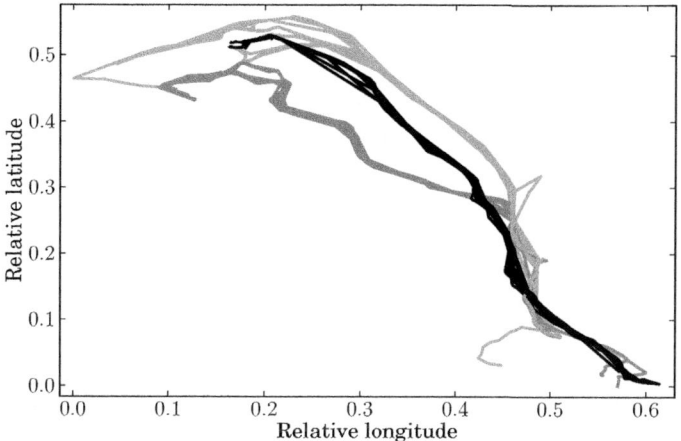

Fig. 1. Evaluation set: 87 GPS trajectories constituting three main routes (coded in black, grey and light grey)

At each of the n iterations the algorithm does one pass through the sequences, where calculating the hash signature of a sequence S_i takes $\mathcal{O}(|\mathcal{C}_i|)$ time, in total $\mathcal{O}(q)$, where $q = \sum_{i=1}^{m} |\mathcal{C}_i|$ for all sequences. The runtime of updating edge weights scales with the number of pairs of sequences that have the same hash signature, which has an expectation value of u. Since there are n iterations, the total runtime of Algorithm 1 is $\mathcal{O}(n(q + u))$. Since $q \gg u$, the runtime is dominated by q at each iteration. This can also be seen in Figure 3, where the runtime scales almost linearly with the number of sequences m for a given number of iterations, implying that $q \sim m$. Note that the number of required iterations n does not grow with increasing m in order to build an accurate similarity network, since the probability that two sequences have the same hash signature at a given iteration is independent of the number of sequences m.

4   Discussion

The method is scalable since one only considers relevant strong sequence similarities that are relatively limited in number compared to all possible sequence relations. Although several hash functions are utilised in order to capture most strong sequence relations, there may still be false negatives due to the stochasticity of the method. However, even though a strong link between two sequences is missed, it is likely that it is indirectly captured in the graph representation, since sequences with a high Jaccard similarity often also share several neighbouring nodes. The reason for this is that the Jaccard distance, denoted and defined as $J_D = 1 - J$, is a proper metric. This results in that the graph clustering algorithm can correctly assign two sequences to the same route, even though the sequences are only implicitly linked.

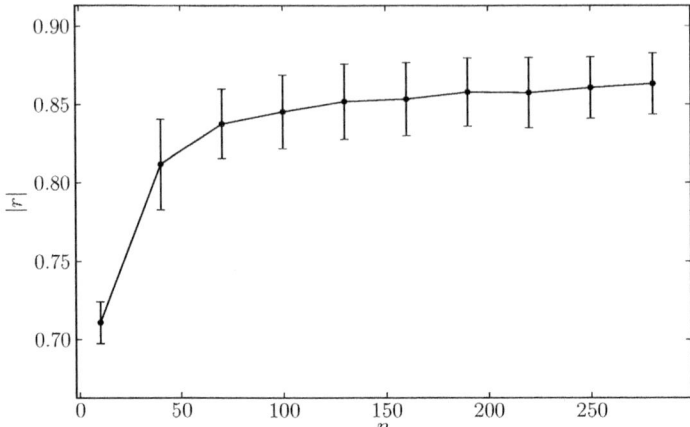

Fig. 2. Mean accuracy for different number of hash signatures, n. Standard deviation displayed by error bars.

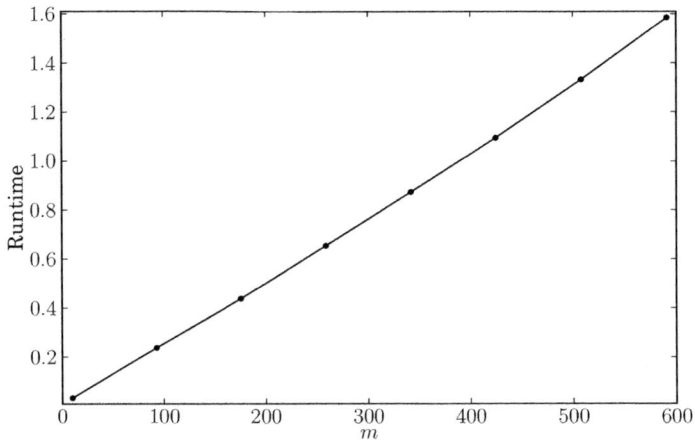

Fig. 3. Runtime in seconds (of a Python implementation run on a laptop) of Algorithm 1 for $n = 200$ and different number of sequences

Although it is demonstrated that the method provides a high degree of accuracy, a few caveats are in place regarding data. Firstly, the method has been evaluated using a dataset collected by the author, coworkers and students – a sample of people that certainly does not represent a cross section of all cell phone users. However, this bias is also an advantage since it enables us to extract a larger evaluation set between a given origin and destination given the limited data available. That is, if the data would be an equally sized uniform sample of Cell ID sequences, very few sequences would be available between a given origin and destination. The second caveat is to note that the method is evaluated on a single set of routes at a given length scale and density of base stations. Further studies are required in order to evaluate the methods performance under other conditions, such as when base stations are more sparsely distributed and trajectories shorter.

Since calculating the hash signatures of sequences can be done independently for each sequence, the method is suitable for parallelisation. One could for instance further speed up calculations by using the MapReduce scheme [11], where the *map* function calculates the hash signatures, and where sequences with identical signatures are aggregated (i.e. put in the same bucket) in the *reduce* step.

5 Conclusions

To summarise, a probabilistic method for grouping Cell ID sequences from mobile communication networks into common routes has been presented. Sequences are related in a graph, where edge weights are given by locality-sensitive hashing. The method has been demonstrated to be scalable, and to accurately group sequences in an evaluation set of GPS tagged sequences. Even though further investigations are required in order to evaluate the methods performance under conditions not captured by the evaluation set, such as for other types of mobility patterns or on other length scales, the results presented here are highly encouraging.

Acknowledgements. The author thanks the participants of the Consider8 project for fruitful discussions, John Krumm and the anonymous reviewers for valuable feedback, and everybody that contributed with the Cell ID data used in this paper. This work was supported by the Swedish Governmental Agency for Innovation Systems (VINNOVA).

References

1. Abul, O., et al.: Never walk alone: Uncertainty for anonymity in moving objects databases. In: ICDE, pp. 376–385. IEEE (2008)
2. Alec, P., et al.: Anomaly detection in a mobile communication network. In: Proceedings of the NAACSOS, pp. 407–422 (2006)
3. Ashbrook, D., Starner, T.: Learning significant locations and predicting user movement with gps. In: ISWC, pp. 101–108 (2002)
4. Becker, R.A., et al.: Route classification using cellular handoff patterns. In: Proceedings of the 13th International Conference on Ubiquitous Computing, UbiComp 2011, pp. 123–132. ACM (2011)
5. Bengtsson, L., et al.: Improved Response to Disasters and Outbreaks by Tracking Population Movements with Mobile Phone Network Data: A Post-Earthquake Geospatial Study in Haiti. PLoS Med 8(8) (2011)
6. Bhattacharya, A., Das, S.: LeZi-update: an information-theoretic approach to track mobile users in PCS networks. In: MobiCom 1999, pp. 1–12 (1999)
7. Blondel, V.D., et al.: Fast unfolding of communities in large networks. Journal of Statistical Mechanics: Theory and Experiment 2008(10) (2008)
8. Broder, A.Z., et al.: Min-wise Independent Permutations. Journal of Computer and System Sciences 60, 327–336 (1998)

9. Candia, J., et al.: Uncovering individual and collective human dynamics from mobile phone records. Journal of Physics A: Mathematical and Theoretical 41(22) (2008)
10. De Mulder, Y., et al.: Identification via location-profiling in GSM networks. In: WPES 2008, pp. 23–32 (2008)
11. Dean, J., Ghemawat, S.: MapReduce: Simplified Data Processing on Large Clusters, pp. 137–150
12. Domingo-Ferrer, J., et al.: Privacy-preserving publication of trajectories using microaggregation. In: SPRINGL 2010, pp. 26–33 (2010)
13. González, M.C., et al.: Understanding individual human mobility patterns. Nature 453(7196), 779–782 (2008)
14. Hightower, J., Consolvo, S., LaMarca, A., Smith, I., Hughes, J.: Learning and Recognizing the Places We Go. In: Beigl, M., Intille, S.S., Rekimoto, J., Tokuda, H. (eds.) UbiComp 2005. LNCS, vol. 3660, pp. 159–176. Springer, Heidelberg (2005)
15. Ian S. et al.: Algorithms for detecting motion of a gsm mobile phone. In: ECSCW 2005 (2005)
16. Indyk, P., Motwani, R.: Approximate nearest neighbors: Towards removing the curse of dimensionality. In: STOC, pp. 604–613 (1998)
17. Laasonen, K., Raento, M., Toivonen, H.: Adaptive On-Device Location Recognition. In: Ferscha, A., Mattern, F. (eds.) PERVASIVE 2004. LNCS, vol. 3001, pp. 287–304. Springer, Heidelberg (2004)
18. Lancichinetti, A., Fortunato, S.: Community Detection Algorithms: A Comparative Analysis. Physical Review E 80(5), 056117+ (2009)
19. Liao, L., et al.: Learning and inferring transportation routines. Artif. Intell. 171, 311–331 (2007)
20. Massey, W., Whitt, W.: A stochastic model to capture space and time dynamics in wireless communication systems. Probability in the Engineering and Informational Sciences 8, 541–569 (1994)
21. Patterson, D.J., Liao, L., Fox, D., Kautz, H.: Inferring High-Level Behavior from Low-Level Sensors. In: Dey, A.K., Schmidt, A., McCarthy, J.F. (eds.) UbiComp 2003. LNCS, vol. 2864, pp. 73–89. Springer, Heidelberg (2003)
22. Rand, W.: Objective Criteria for the Evaluation of Clustering Methods. Journal of the American Statistical Association 66(336), 846–850 (1971)
23. Sohn, T., Varshavsky, A., LaMarca, A., Chen, M.Y., Choudhury, T., Smith, I., Consolvo, S., Hightower, J., Griswold, W.G., de Lara, E.: Mobility Detection Using Everyday GSM Traces. In: Dourish, P., Friday, A. (eds.) UbiComp 2006. LNCS, vol. 4206, pp. 212–224. Springer, Heidelberg (2006)
24. Song, C., et al.: Limits of predictability in human mobility. Science 327(5968), 1018–1021 (2010)
25. Song, C., et al.: Modelling the scaling properties of human mobility. Nature Physics 6(10), 818–823 (2010)
26. Yavas, G., et al.: A data mining approach for location prediction in mobile environments. Data Knowl. Eng. 54, 121–146 (2005)

Accounting for Energy-Reliant Services within Everyday Life at Home

Oliver Bates, Adrian K. Clear, Adrian Friday, Mike Hazas, and Janine Morley

School of Computing and Communications, Lancaster University, UK

Abstract. Researchers in pervasive and ubiquitous computing have produced much work on new sensing technologies for disaggregating domestic resource consumption, and on designs for energy-centric interventions at home. In a departure from this, we employ a service-oriented approach, where we account for not only the amount of resources that specific appliances draw upon, but also how the associated services may be characterised in the context of everyday life. We undertook a formative study in four student flats over a twenty-day period, collecting data using interviews with eleven participants and over two hundred in-home sensors. Following an in-depth description of observations and findings from our study, we argue that our approach provides a more inclusive range of understandings of resources and everyday life than has been shown from energy-centric approaches.

1 Introduction

Prior sustainability-related research in the field of pervasive and ubiquitous computing has most often focused on novel sensing technologies and algorithms (typically aimed at resource disaggregation to the end appliance or tap [5]), or on exploring the conservation potential of technical interventions (e.g. electricity monitors placed in homes). In either case, the area of focus has been on either measuring, or utilising such measures of *energy consumption*. However as Shove points out, "relevant patterns of consumption follow from efforts to provide and sustain what people take to be normal services like those of comfort and cleanliness" [14, p. 198]. Thus, this paper takes an approach departing from prior work in pervasive and ubicomp: to describe energies only alongside the wider context of the *services* in which they are bound up. As background (section 2), we argue that the rationale for this approach is because services are much more relatable to everyday life.

Before proceeding, we should define what we mean by "service". As the above quotation from Shove implies, many services in the home are built up and maintained in the pursuit of comfort and cleanliness. Such services might be heating, lighting or food preparation (cooking). In addition to comfort and cleanliness, we would also add that services (such as those provided by information technology) may support expectations for play and work at home. In any case, *services* are "composite accomplishments generating and sustaining certain conditions and experiences... services have to do with the orchestration of devices, systems,

J. Kay et al. (Eds.): Pervasive 2012, LNCS 7319, pp. 107–124, 2012.

expectations and conventions" [14, p. 165]. Thus, to comprehensively describe a service, we should consider not only the resources (energies) necessary for its upkeep, but also the appliances, infrastructures, social norms and human action, within which the service is bound and reproduced.

The thesis of this paper is that compared to an energy-centric approach, a service-oriented analysis creates a more inclusive, nuanced and well-rounded understanding of the relation of resources to everyday life at home. Such an analysis necessarily relies upon both qualitative and quantitative data, in order to be able to frame the services in the context of their associated practices, expectations, energies, infrastructures and appliances.

Putting the service-oriented analysis to work in a case study, **our primary contribution is to give an account of how three services are composed and maintained in four homes, and the insights relating to resource intensity that arise from this.** Through the exposition of our accounting exercise, a secondary contribution is to consider possible pervasive sensing solutions appropriate for gathering data contributing to understandings of service components. Following a description of our participant flats and accounting methods (section 3), and the characterisations of service in this case study (section 4), we take a step back and identify the advantages of our service-oriented approach and consider possible limitations (section 5).

2   Background

As has been previously discussed [4,11], much of sustainability-related research in ubicomp and HCI has been concerned with estimation and display for consumption feedback approaches. While the 5–15% reductions [3] historically associated with feedback-based interventions are not insignificant, Pierce et al. [10] highlight that very little is known about the changes implicated with these reductions, and how the reductions relate (or not) to particular types of feedback.

Strengers [16] developed the critique that eco-feedback systems are "grounded in a basic assumption that home dwellers lack information" [10, p. 244] which presumably is required if they are understood as "micro-resource managers" [16, p. 2135]. Strengers argues that such assumptions result in problems best characterised by a disconnect between the types and methods of feedback, and "the realities of everyday life." As Strengers poses, solutions might be to offer less data-oriented forms of feedback; target "non-negotiable practices" and changing expectations by making and sharing practical recommendations and knowledge; and encourage debate about what is normal and necessary. To support such goals, researchers and designers need to understand everyday life: "what people do in their homes, how people use energy and water and why" [16, p. 2142].

We would argue that consumption feedback is but one instantiation of *resource-centric* approaches more generally; another class might be demand-side investigations of consumption. Such framings tend to base the focus of enquiry tightly around quantitative measurements of resources such as electricity, natural gas, or water. Many of the above points about consumption feedback apply to resource-centric approaches more broadly: without a framework that factors in people's habits, expectations, and interactions with devices and infrastructure (all part of everyday life) then the resulting understandings are narrow. This reflects wider literatures on energy and consumption studies [13]; part of a process of connecting the development of sensing and interaction to other domains and theoretical approaches [1], which we view as essential to achieve more inclusive accounts of domestic resource-reliance and sustainability.

Moving on, what would a more inclusive framing be? One analytical trick borrowed from sociology is to de-centre the user and consider the activity or practice [18] taking place. Identifying a practice and what shapes it is one way to think about "engag[ing] with social and cultural dynamics" of everyday life. In place of a concept in which people consume energy, we could suggest that practices consume resource-reliant services. A service-oriented analysis, then, may be a suitable way of understanding the quite indirect connections between resource consumption and practice. The concept of services (defined above), encompasses varied components, requiring both a qualitative and quantitative investigative approach. Hybrid qualitative/quantitative methods have been proposed by others looking at sustainability, but from different directions [6,8,15].

Aspects of our study echo those of certain previous formative studies of current practices [12] but with two distinctions: (i) we do not seek to understand human action or attitudes related to energy *per se*, but rather as practices in which energy-reliant services are consumed, and (ii) we gather energy (electricity) data as a quantification of the resources involved. The method we pilot might also be used by researchers to evaluate eco-feedback systems: addressing the lack of knowledge [10] about the nature of any changes they create.

3   Methods

Like Hayes and Cone [9], our target was shared student accommodation on a university campus. We chose to focus on this specific population for two reasons: (1) they are in close proximity to our research building, which meant that it was convenient for us to conduct and monitor the sensor deployment, and make ourselves readily available to our participants; and (2) because of an existing university initiative, we had access to historical energy readings for on-campus flats. Since we are interested in understanding the reasons for resource variations in different homes, the per-flat historical data allowed us to recruit participants in flats whose measured consumption was high-average or low-average, but not extreme. Our participants are undergraduates, many in their final year of study, of mixed gender and subject specialism.

We studied four flats for a duration of twenty days. Each flat was composed of eight individual study bedrooms, two showers, two toilets, and a kitchen, arranged around a central corridor. We used sensors (see below) to monitor the shared areas in all flats, and twenty-two participants agreed to have their personal bedrooms instrumented (3, 8, 5 and 6 bedrooms in each flat). We conducted face-to-face, follow-up interviews with eleven of the participants, and solicited near-time 'mini-accounts' (answers to a small number of short questions posed by SMS or email during the study). We refer to the flats as Green, Blue, Red and Yellow and give participants pseudonyms to preserve their anonymity.

Fine-grained, whole flat electricity readings are logged from OWL brand electricity meters. We use a Plugwise "Circle G" to log power at each socket—four per study bedroom, two in the corridor and nine in the kitchen. Participants were asked to treat the device as they would a normal socket. We noted the mapping from sockets to appliances where possible, although some sockets were connected to multiway adapters and hence may correspond to multiple appliances.

To capture cooking activity we mounted a motion-triggered wildlife trail camera (*the hobcam*) above the cooker (also known as a "stove" or "range"), looking down at the hob (or "burners"). Since the cookers were wired directly into the mains, we were not able to directly measure their energy using Plugwise. The energy for each cooking session is identified by correlating data from the OWL meters with the start and end time of the cooking session. The start and end times are derived from the timestamps on the hobcam images, corrected by visually inspecting each session and making fine adjustments using a time-series plot of the high-frequency (six-secondly) OWL data. The cooking session energy is computed by subtracting the total socket energy, and an *energy baseline* averaged from a 30-minute window either side of the session (to account for unmetered devices) from the whole flat consumption.

We deployed MS13E2 "Hawkeye" motion/light sensors (X10 wireless) in each bedroom, shower, corridor and kitchen. These help to disambiguate active and passive use in study bedrooms, and use of the shared areas. The motion/light sensors are only capable of capturing binary representation (light/dark, and motion/no motion) in each room.

Each flat had its own data logging PC connected to an RFXCOM receiver and a Plugwise "Circle+" node. We use Domotiga,[1] an open source home automation software package to decode the X10 and Plugwise packets.[2] We subtract the load for the data logging PC and Plugwise units from our analysis. In total 129 Plugwise, 42 motion/light sensors and 38 temperature/humidity sensors were used in our deployment across the four flats.

Limitations and Assumptions. We gathered data from a relatively small, very specific set of participants: thirty-one students at a UK university in shared institutional accommodation. As is typical for micro-level studies of a small number of homes, some of our findings will be highly localised to our participants, while other findings may be more generalisable. Regardless, this does not detract from our ability to demonstrate what a service-oriented analysis can expose.

We were not able to measure lighting energy directly, so we assume the following minimal model: at night (between local times for sunset and sunrise) we attribute energy to lighting whenever a sensor reported light in bedrooms. We assumed the light source to be the ceiling light of known power (72 W). We

---

[1] http://domotiga.nl/, accessed 28 February 2012.

[2] Plugwise is closed-source and uses a proprietary protocol partially reverse engineered by the home automation community.

ignore other possible bedroom light sources such as desk lamps. During the day, we assume that only 20% of the bedroom lighting time is due to the ceiling light (although from testimony we know it was common for curtains to be drawn and the ceiling light to be on, during the day). The shower rooms had no windows, so we attribute light (20 W) and fan (35 W) power for the durations that the light sensor reported light, day or night. We further assume that the corridor lights (64 W) are on only when both corridor light sensors activate simultaneously. Toilets were not monitored in our study, so we assume the light (20 W) and extractor fan (35 W) in each toilet are active for two hours per day, which from participant accounts seems conservative.

There were instances where Plugwise sensors failed to report, yet were known to be under constant loads, for example in a Blue bedroom a PC and amplifier (combined 240 W) were left on continuously. In such cases (shown as shaded regions in figures 1 and 2) we were able to reinstate the data by interpolation. We measured the various appliances in a range of operational modes during our follow-up analysis to verify this approach. In any case, none of our findings rely solely on analysis of such reconstituted data.

For unmonitored bedrooms, we estimated the appliance energy based on what we knew about the devices in those rooms, and the reported Plugwise data for monitored rooms with similar sets of appliances (e.g. 4.4 kWh for rooms with a single laptop, and up to 29.0 kWh for those with entertainment systems). The lighting in unmonitored bedrooms is assumed to be in the lower quartile of lighting estimates from similar rooms (4.8–8.7 kWh). We do not use the unmonitored bedrooms' estimated energy in any of our findings; they only appear in two figures, purely for the purposes of visualisation.

We label any remaining unexplained energy between our fine accounting and the OWL flat aggregate as "dark energy". It is additional energy from the unmonitored bedrooms, use of devices not reported by Plugwise, and additional lighting not in our conservative estimates. By far the largest proportion of consumption we monitored in bedrooms is attributable to entertainment, IT and lighting, and we have seen nothing in the sensor data or participant accounts to suspect that anything outside of these contributes significantly to dark energy.

4   Findings

Our service-oriented analysis begins with the resources (figures 1 and 2): in terms of electricity-reliance, the three most significant services are those of entertainment and IT, lighting, and food preparation and storage (i.e. cooking and refrigeration). Although our participants discussed some energy-reliant services that do not fit into these three categories (e.g. grooming or cleaning), we do not include a discussion of these due to their vanishingly small total energy. For each category of service, we will report on its energy attribution, the associated practices, appliances, and expectations. We will then discuss opportunities for making effective changes within the provision of these services, and the potential role of sensing in accounting for that service.

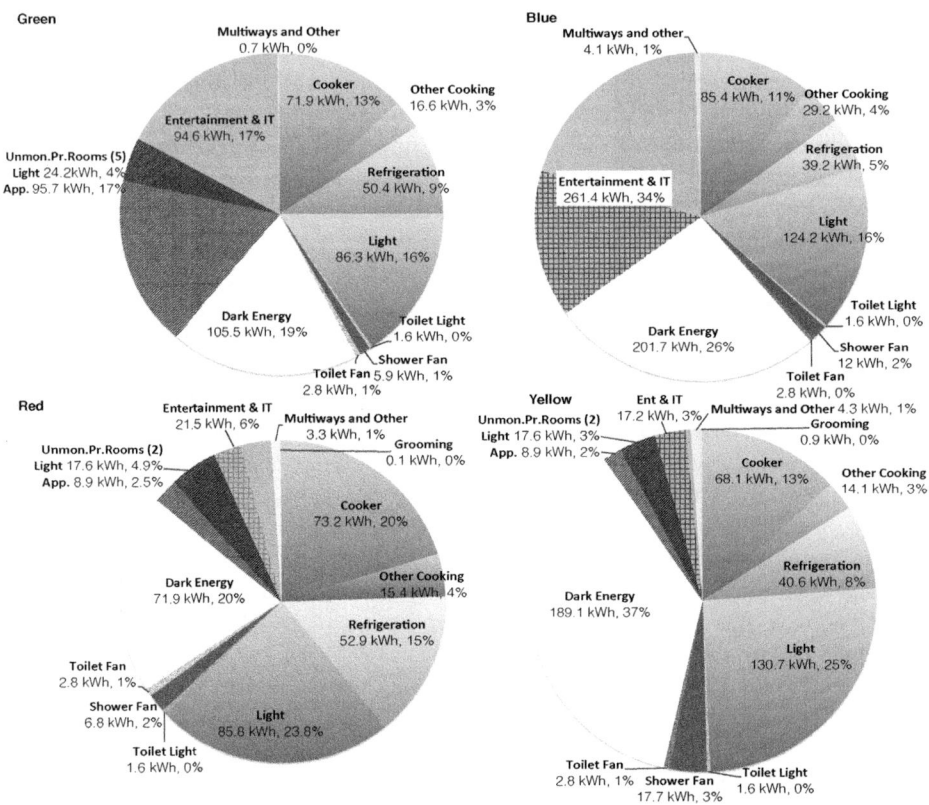

Fig. 1. The relative energy breakdown of the flats over the twenty days. Shaded regions indicate where we have reconstituted data or made minimal assumptions (see section 3).

4.1   Entertainment and IT

We begin our investigation with the most variable of the services we observed: entertainment and IT. This class of service accounts for 3.5%–34% of a flat's total electricity consumption (figure 1)—ranging from 17.2 kWh to 261.4 kWh in absolute terms (figure 2). To analyse how this energy-reliant service is composed, we first look to the device inventory taken in the participant bedrooms. Generally, most participants owned a laptop; two had both a desktop PC and a laptop; and one had a PC only. None of the female participants possessed a PC, and compared to the male participants, they had few other entertainment or IT devices (a printer, a games console, a TV, an iPod dock). Conversely, nine of the twelve male participants had extra audio, video or gaming devices, and five of these possessed more than one of these devices.

Device presence correlates with a room's energy level. For example, none of the PCs, audio, video or gaming devices were identified in Red. Blue, the domicile with the highest entertainment and IT energy, contains two always-on PCs acting as servers, and all four male participants have audio, video and

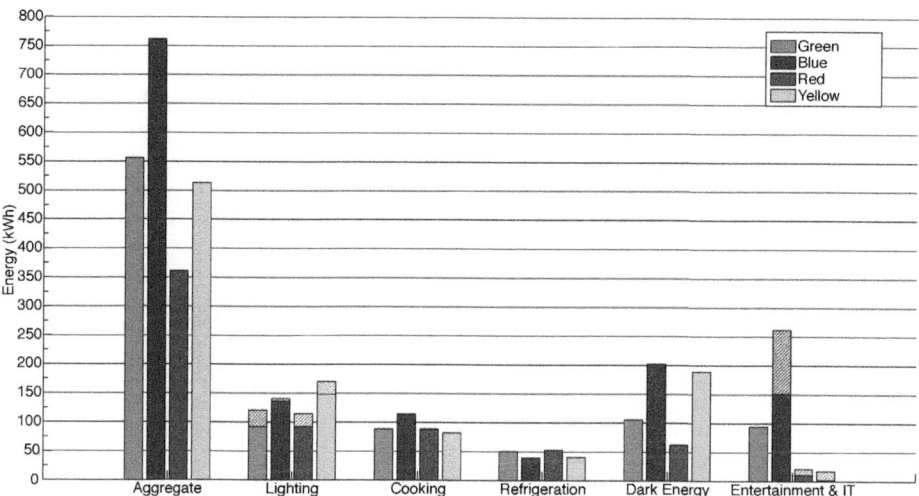

Fig. 2. The absolute energy consumption of the flats. For lighting, shower fans are included, and the upper shaded part of the bars represent our energy assumption for the toilets (light+fan) and unmonitored bedroom lights. For entertainment and IT, the shaded parts represent where we have reconstituted the Plugwise data for appliances in that category.

gaming electronics. In Green, Henry's room accounts for most of the energy in this category (61.8 kWh compared to 18.5 kWh and 6.3 kWh for Callum and Leah, respectively). Henry owns a sizeable collection of IT and peripheral devices. Yet for Yellow, consumption is lower than we would expect given our initial inventory: three of the male participants had some combination of audio, video and gaming devices. It is possible that Plugwise sensors were unplugged or faulty and missed some of this consumption—contributing to dark energy in this category.

Of course, the presence of a device is only an indication of its actual use. The data showed that the duration and frequency of use of PCs and laptops varied: some were characterised by periods of discrete and distinct use, whereas others appeared to be on for the majority of the deployment period. PCs commonly have an array of power management settings, such as *on, off, standby,* and *hibernation.* Laptops are more complex, including an additional *charging* state, which consumes energy, and they have the option to be powered from battery: this makes assumptions about the state of activity of a laptop difficult. For entertainment devices, such as televisions, amplifiers and gaming consoles, the power management functionality is generally less complex (*on, off* and *standby*).

Table 1 details the daily energy consumption of participants' laptops, where it was possible to distinguish them from other devices. This illustrates that the resulting consumption can vary considerably: for example, Miranda's laptop consumed twice the energy of Aaron's. While it is not surprising that the power requirements of various laptops differ [19] (Aaron's consumed up to 65 W to

Table 1. Energy breakdown for nine bedrooms

Participant	Flat	Energy (kWh)		
		Entertainment & IT (Laptop)	Other	Lighting
Aaron	Red	2.64 (2.64)	0.13	8.32
Thomas	Red	9.92 (9.92)	0.26	12.69
Callum	Green	18.45 (4.17)	0.09	9.6
Henry	Green	61.75	0.148	10.97
Leah	Green	6.29	0.3	11.94
Ellie	Blue	2.9 (2.9)	1.39	6.5
Feng	Blue	9.34	0.21	6.74
Miranda	Blue	5.28 (5.28)	0.068	5.33
Rachel	Blue	4.83	0.41	11.28

Miranda's 40 W), we see that patterns of use vary considerably: consistent with previous findings in US homes [2], our participants exhibited variety in using and managing their devices. Miranda's laptop was "on" in a state that draws around 10–15 W for two or three days at a time, whilst Aaron's regularly consumed under 5 W. To understand this difference, we need to turn to the interviews. Miranda reported that her laptop was, in fact, broken: it wouldn't charge. Because of this she leaves it plugged in all the time, and for fear that it won't start up again, she never turns it off; she just closes the lid. Interestingly, Aaron's laptop is also broken but there is one, potentially decisive difference: whilst he leaves it plugged in to the power supply so that it will also be charged if he needs it, Aaron, unlike Miranda, will shut it down *"every time...mainly for battery reasons"*. This suggests that management of the laptop's battery and power states affects consumption but this will vary depending on the type of device, state of disrepair and the person using it.

This also appears to be the case for PCs. For example, we can see clear periods in the power data when Henry's PC was on and off—his PC switch-off is visible around 2 A.M. in figure 3. He reports, *"I'll turn it off properly... I'll turn the switch off at the wall sometimes. I turn my hard drives off at night because the light annoys me when I try to sleep."* Gary, on the other hand, leaves his desktop on all of the time as its used for both work and as a media server, and this is evident in the lack of gaps in his sensor data.

Our participants used their laptops and PCs in a multitude of activities, including listening to music, watching TV and movies, communication, shopping, getting news, and doing work. Whilst some types of activities might be reflected in a particular pattern of use, it seems that hardly any activities are distinguishable from the data alone. For example, Henry uses his PC for work, study and entertainment. The data from Henry's room showed that his "computer" (which was in fact a number of different devices served by two wall sockets) was on for a distinct period of time which, when asked in the interview the next day, matched a time Henry said he was running a test-bed as part of a paid consultancy project. However, Henry also did some work of another of kind—looking up lecture notes for his course—earlier in the day. These two different activities were indistinguishable from the electricity (resource) data alone.

PCs and laptops are often used to carry out multiple simultaneous or overlapping activities. For example, work becomes interspersed with listening to music or social networking. One of Callum's mini-accounts gives an example of such a situation: *"I was browsing the Internet and doing work on my laptop and listening to music using my speakers and amp."* The multi-purpose, multi-tasking nature of these devices presents a challenge in directly attributing electricity consumption data to any one particular activity. Other entertainment devices such as TVs are usually dedicated to the provision of a specific service, making it easier to connect the data traces that they provide to a particular activity.

Perhaps because of their ability to support all sorts of different activities, participants often referred to their laptops in particular as the device that they use most regularly and could not live without. In the case of Miranda, although she acknowledges that her laptop needs to be fixed, she is waiting for a time when she would *"be less devastated without it."*

It appeared that those with especially high entertainment and IT resource-reliance usually possessed a number of devices linked together, including the PC. For example, Henry reports that *"I've got my hard drives, my router, my two monitors, my stereo and my desktop, that's all hooked together."* Quite often, these devices were used simultaneously, as a system, in order to perform an activity like gaming or watching TV. In this case, the energy makes the most sense attributed to the broader service of entertainment, rather than to the individual devices involved in that service.

It was common for the participants to mention watching TV and movies, playing computer games, and listening to music with flatmates and friends. This can be a regular, routine occurrence: *"Everyone's normally in the kitchen about 5 or 6 and everyone watches* Friends *and there's* Scrubs *on at the same time so everybody watches that"* (Henry). Sometimes entertainment events are pre-arranged. For example, Ellie will *"have like movie nights in people's flats"*, whereas other times they are unplanned: *"We spend a lot of time in each others rooms just talking and watching telly"* (Henry).

Participants reported watching TV and movies, and playing computer games, for a break from work, because they were bored or had nothing else to do. For Ellie, whether she watches TV shows or not *"depends like if my friends are doing something."* For Ian it depends on the particular time of the year: *"Well like the next few weeks its gonna be, next term, yeah, there'll be a lot of TV and that because there's nothing to do. No lectures, no group work, just revising, and there's only so much revision you can do."* Henry does not play computer games as frequently as he used to because he is busier than he used to be, but also because he has found other things to do: *"First year I used to play lots of games... because well I had a lot of time and I was probably less mature[...] But now if I'm not doing something I'm doing something else. I'm socialising or I've found other hobbies."* Access also factors into the amount some of the Blue participants watch. Ellie describes how an online service allows her to watch her weekly TV shows and according to Ian, *"It's been a thing this year. We got a free download thing now so we watch a lot."*

Opportunities for Change: Based on this detailed understanding of energy used to support entertainment and IT services, we suggest four potential avenues for reducing it. First, our findings confirm Chetty et al.'s observations, that some gains appear possible by improving the technical efficiency and power management regimes of laptops and PCs [2]. Second, many entertainment and IT devices appear to be left in standby when not in use. This instant availability sometimes seemed useful: some participants would keep documents or web-pages open for quick reference. Third, less time spent actively using entertainment services appears feasible. This already seems to vary at different times of the year and for some participants it appears to be a resort when there is nothing better to do. Fourth, it is most remarkable that consumption in this category was dominated by a small number of participants, who appeared to spend more time gaming, working with IT, and watching TV and movies, typically with linked complexes of specialised devices supporting these pursuits. It is perhaps best to consider these participants as connoisseurs of these services and the technologies that provide them, and perhaps look to working with the wider (sub)culture that shapes these tastes.

Sensing and Accounting: It is feasible to associate electricity consumption values with particular devices (e.g. after [5]). Where those devices are part of a constellation supporting a service, this is the level that would require sensing. Since IT devices have diverse and often simultaneous uses, it will remain difficult to associate computer consumption with particular activities—consequently it may be difficult to understand what the possibilities are for reductions. A crucial first step might be to log the activity of applications on the computer to aid with finer-grained accounting.

4.2   Lighting

Lighting is a service relied upon across indoor life. It accounts for 16%–29% of the total energy consumption (figure 1). The per-bedroom average lighting energy is comparable (table 2), but the lighting energy in communal areas (kitchen, corridor and showers) is significantly more variable. The communal area total was highest in Yellow (84.8 kWh), almost twice that of the lowest, Red (45.6 kWh). Our interview data illustrates a mix of conventions, expectations and actions around turning lights on and off.

Leah always leaves the lights on and acknowledges that *"I do mean it, I am conscious of it though but I don't really do anything about it."* Likewise, Wendy acknowledges that, in her flat *"we have them on all the time constantly"*. She notes that her flat are *"literally terrible, we have all, everything plugged in, all the lights on, run the water for ages [embarrassed laughter]."* Indeed, this account is consistent with table 2. However two participants left lights on for a reason that went beyond simple indifference. Miranda leaves the lights on in the shared corridor *"because I've turned it off before and [pause] people don't know where*

Table 2. A breakdown of the lighting consumption in each flat. The communal areas are homogeneous in layout, light fixtures and sensing, and the associated energy used for lighting can be directly compared. Lighting totals for the monitored bedrooms are shown, alongside the per-bedroom average. This table contains none of our assumed figures for unmonitored bedroom or toilet lights.

Flat	Grand total	Communal area lights				Bedroom total (Average)	Unmonitored rooms
		Kitchen	Corridor	Shower+fan	Total		
Green	92.12	27.31	18.55	13.75	59.61	32.51 (10.83)	5
Blue	136.19	24.95	24.03	18.65	67.63	68.56 (8.57)	0
Red	92.58	19.47	15.56	10.59	45.62	46.96 (9.39)	2
Yellow	148.34	32.06	25.17	27.58	84.81	63.51 (10.59)	2

the switches are in the corridor so if they come and its dark, erm, I get moaned at so I usually leave that on." Ellie was not sure whether the corridor light could be turned off because at her previous university, they had to be left on due to safety regulations.

Most of the participants spoke about turning the lights off, at least in their bedrooms, when they were not in use. For Donna, Henry and Miranda, this was a habitual thing. For example, Miranda switches off the kitchen light when she leaves because "*just growing up, my mum used to say 'switch off and save' and so I just always have, just a habit I got into.*" Before he goes to bed at night, Henry turns off the communal lights in Green because "*otherwise [...] they're just on for no reason.*" Donna, on the other hand, is motivated by climate change issues. When asked if there was an environmental background to her switching the lights off, she replied "*Yeah, I think we should all help to slow down global warming even if we can't stop it.*"

Three of the participants turned the shower room lights off because, otherwise, "*[the noise of the extractor fan] comes through the wall and its really annoying*" (Donna). Jess turned the corridor lights off because the light shone underneath her bedroom door and prevented her from sleeping. For Wendy, and some of the Blue participants, annoyance was sometimes a factor in leaving the lights on: "*I well I don't really like the dark. [...] when I come out of my room its dark and I'm like arrr*" (Wendy).

Opportunities for Change: Each flat contained fifty-eight fluorescent light elements. One clear avenue for saving energy is to replace existing fixtures with lower power alternatives. Though as Wall and Crosbie caution, this is unlikely to be straightforward, due to perceived performance and aesthetic shortcomings [17]. Our study does reveal surprisingly significant energy attributable to lighting, especially in the communal areas at night: one tactic could be to fit motion-triggered lighting, or equip the corridor with a low-power night light.

Sensing and Accounting: It is difficult to attribute lighting consumption to a particular activity and, in fact, it may not even make sense to do so as lighting is a basic requirement for almost any activity outside daylight hours. The important information for accounting is the state of lighting (on/off), occupancy, and outdoor light intensity. However, this utilitarian view may not be sufficient: from testimony it was clear that lighting contributes to perceptions of both security in adjacent rooms and to safety in the corridors at night.

4.3   Cooking and Refrigeration

The domiciles in our study contained two fridges, two freezers and a cooker. Food-related energy was between 20%–39% of the flat total. On average, over half of this comes from energy directly consumed by the cooker, one third as a result of the fridge and freezer, and the rest is other kitchen appliances (i.e. kettles, microwaves, toasters and standalone grills)—cooking and refrigeration are clearly visible in figure 3.

The cookers in the flats had four hobs and a built-in grill and oven, enabling participants to boil, fry, grill and bake foods. We saw that the energy required to prepare a dish is a function of cooking time and technique, and this is closely related to the type of foods being cooked. For example, eggs require little energy to cook because they use a single cooker element for a short period of time, whereas frozen chips require the oven for much longer periods.

We observed different cooking methods in each flat: Red tended to boil foods regularly (36% of the time), whereas Green often fried foods (34% of the time). Our analyses show that the most efficient cooking method (in terms of energy per unit of pre-cooked food weight) is *heating* in a pan on the hob, and this is employed the least (8% of the time). Both *frying* and *boiling* were more frequent (26%)—frying is more efficient than boiling. *Grilling* and *baking* are the most energy intensive, and these were used 19% and 21% of the time, respectively. Some foods were cooked using more than one method, inviting comparison of the time and energy involved: e.g. when sausages were grilled (6.7 kWh/kg average over 7 sessions) they resulted in 5.6 times the energy of when they were fried (1.2 kWh/kg average over 12 cooking sessions). We also saw variability in the energy required to cook the same food using the same method: boiling 100g of pasta used from 0.2 kWh–0.75 kWh (compared across thirteen cooking sessions).

Food preparation as practised by our participants typically relied upon the service of refrigeration, although the energy attributable to refrigeration seems less directly affected by times or durations of use. The very minor variation for refrigeration in figure 2 could be a result of different thermostat settings, frequency of openings, refrigerator model, or states of repair (e.g. faulty door seals).

Opportunities for Change: We observed energy due to lengthy pre-heat times and cooker components left on accidentally after use (in one case lasting five hours and consuming 9.4 kWh). These were most impactful for the oven: in general, the oven and grill are energy-intensive components and changes to their roles in meal preparation could lead to significant reductions. For example, discouraging the use of these components for small quantities of food, and encouraging their use to cook multiple meal portions to share or to store and eat later. We

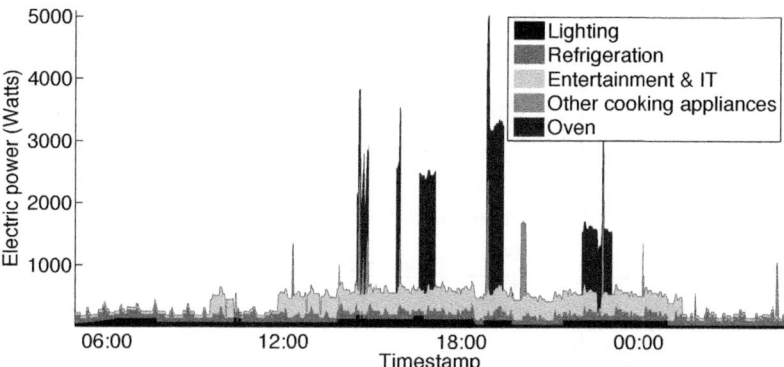

Fig. 3. A time-series representation of Green over the course of a day. Services are stacked on top of each other illustrating the relative proportions of each over time.

did see some evidence of this in our data, but in general participants preferred to be opportunistic with their food. When asked if they had regular or typical meal times, Jess replied *"erm, no not really"* and Polly said simply, *"I don't really have typical [pause] anything!"*. A few of our interviewees, like Miranda, seem to perceive themselves as doing this sort of thing throughout the day: *"I just tend to eat when I'm hungry ...I just don't think about it. I just kind of graze, and I don't plan meals really."* Fridges and freezers may help in efforts to optimise cooking energy through bulk cooking, and their energy is not impacted as dramatically by changes in use. Their presence may not be 'negotiable' but it may be possible to reduce the freezers from two per domicile to one, and the seals and settings should be checked as part of routine maintenance.

Sensing and Accounting: Energy data from the cooker may be best linked with data about the cook's technique—particularly, the settings, timing and cooker components used. Existing cookers should be monitored at the cooker's supply—even this resolution of data will present challenges in attribution (i.e. disaggregating cooker components used simultaneously), and leave gaps in understanding (i.e. identifying cooks and consumers of meals prepared). This is fertile ground for sustainable technological and social intervention [7]. To encourage social meals or increase bulk cooking, however, we should be careful not to neglect the importance of convenience—all eleven interviewees framed their daily cooking activities in terms of this.

5   Reflections on the Service-Oriented Approach

In our service-oriented approach, we have not only quantified the energies associated with entertainment and IT, lighting and food preparation, but also positioned them in their everyday context by providing an account of the actions, routines, infrastructures, devices, systems and expectations associated with those services. In discussing the three service areas, we have highlighted requirements and opportunities for pervasive sensor devices (summarised in table 3) appropriate to service-oriented accounting. For eco-feedback and other researchers striving for deeper and more nuanced understandings of resource and practice at home, we now provide a summary of the advantages and limitations of this service-oriented approach.

Table 3. Sensing considerations for service-oriented accounting

	Entertainment/IT	Lighting	Cooking	Refrigeration
Disaggregation scale	Per device where used independently; per complex where devices used in a system; within-appliance disaggregation to monitor particular states e.g. standby in combination with activity sensing	By light fitting, by room	By cooking devices e.g. microwave; Within-cooker elements e.g. grill, oven, hobs	By appliance
Time granularity	High—power consumption changes rapidly, these devices are actively used	Medium—to reliably capture on and off events at fairly coarse intervals	High (once in use)—to capture effects of cooking techniques & settings	Coarse—possibly only for a staged check
Sensors	Direct per-appliance	Luminance sensors directly on fixtures	Point sensor near or within-cooker; image-based possible but complex	Direct per-appliance
Activity sensing to enhance interpretation	Computer-based use logs to capture time spent actively using applications	Presence (motion); outdoor light intensity	Non-intrusive sensing of control settings	Door opened sensor
Possible framings	Organised around power states and complexes of devices; co-ordinated with particular uses of computers	Organised by room, highlighting consumption and significant unoccupied durations with lights on	Based on consumption of particular cooking sessions, and quantities of food cooked	Door-open durations may be matched up with consumption and amount of food in storage

5.1 Advantages over Resource-Centric Approaches

As Strengers and Pierce have argued, much of sustainability-related research has been concerned with estimation and display for feedback approaches. This has three tendencies: to limit the focus of enquiry to quantitative measurement of resources such as electricity and water; to cast "users" as rational resource managers [16]; and to cast designers as experts who decide what is sustainable and what is not [1]. Complementary to these arguments, we identify advantages that a service-oriented approach has to offer, over resource-centric approaches.

The infiltration of service-reliance across practice is made clear. Creating a comprehensive account of a single service shows how it is put to work in supporting multiple practices. In our study, IT was relied upon for personal and group entertainment, paid work, education and staying in touch with friends.

Lighting supported not only a majority of practices indoors, but also facilitated meaningful feelings such as cosiness or security.

Relevant systems of devices and constellations of services are easier to identify. In a similar way, the approach exposes interactions and dependencies among devices, and among services. Groups of devices (an amplifier, television and computer streaming video) worked together to deliver an entertainment service. The services of cooking and entertainment (watching *Friends*) were together relied upon to create a spontaneous (yet habitual) social event at mealtime.

Resource measurements can be actioned more effectively, taken in the context of everyday life. The relation of service provision to routines and meanings is just as important as the quantification of resources. At times, reliance on service can be very practical (leaving corridor lights on allows one to see when going to the toilet at night) and at other times, the service provision may not have immediate, practical utility but has important meaning (leaving corridor lights on gives a feeling of cosiness when in one's room). An energy-centric account might lead to the conclusion that motion-controlled lights are a solution to reduce lighting, but a service-oriented account could testify that corridor navigation and meaningful cosiness are both best supported by a nightlight. In the end, the problem space of "resource reduction at home" should not simply be one of the consumption of end appliances or taps, but should include the service-reliant practices, social meanings, expectations, and purposes of everyday life.

It facilitates a higher-level reconsideration of how service (and in turn, practice) might be reconfigured in the context of sustainability. Finally, a service-oriented approach more naturally lends itself to questioning the arrangement of everyday life, rather than simply "tweaking things" (resource management, appliance efficiency) within the domicile's existing, highly contingent regime of devices, infrastructures, and expectations. It allows researchers to more readily question the existing bounds of what is considered normal. Given the vast difference in energy observed for entertainment and IT in Blue and Yellow, should desktop computers, amplifiers, and large displays be somehow discouraged in student accommodation? This line of thought rapidly becomes politically-charged, wrapped up with concepts of need, expectation and entitlement. But arguably since practice is continually in flux, then researchers and designers might have as valid a claim as anyone to being active in its reshaping.

5.2   Possible Limitations of a Service-Oriented Analysis

Alongside the advantages, we should consider how a service-oriented approach might constrain understandings of everyday life, resources and sustainability.

Findings are highly localised and specific. Our service-oriented accounting is very much at the "micro" level, and transferability of findings must be approached with care. For example, our characterisation of entertainment and IT might be applicable elsewhere in the UK. Our findings on lighting in the specific context of shared student accommodation may be less widely applicable.

Service externalities are not accounted for. Focusing on service provision within the home tends to sideline or exclude resource and practice outside the home. For example, some of our participant accounts revealed that laptops were charged up and used to provide IT services in places like the library. Or, if we extend beyond energy to ask broader questions about the sustainability of services at home, then issues such as carbon impacts of appliance and infrastructure manufacturing and shipping, or energy generation, may be of concern.

5.3   Other Ways to Account for Services

While we do advocate investigative methods that lend themselves to a service-oriented analysis, we do not mean to mandate the methods used in our case study. We drew important elements such as agency, identity, activity, location and expectation from the discussion of sensor data during interviews with our participants, and the mini-accounts that they supplied. However, there may be other ways to gather such data. Pervasive sensing techniques such as activity recognition or positioning systems might aid in recording types of activity at the kitchen sink, or the use of portable devices around the house. Lifelogging (semi-automated capture of events, with the option for hand annotation) on a mobile phone might capture some of the same elements that our interviews did.

5.4   Specific Items for Future Work

As a final testimony to the merits of a service-oriented analysis, we would like to conclude by returning to some of our findings which exposed important areas for future work in sustainability at home.

Connoisseurs of IT. The high variability between participant bedrooms comes down to the amount of electronic equipment, and the durations for which it is active. We feel that this is a wider issue with entertainment and IT service provision: some homes have many more electronic goods, and those tend to function in groups (a video playback device might rely on a display and an audio amplifier). Why might it be a convention that lights be turned off, but desktop PCs be left on? The ubiquity of home and personal electronics is growing, but this seems to be rooted in rising expectations of the entertainment and IT services supported by those devices. Some of our participants relied upon large displays and personal media servers, on a daily basis. What are possible future alternatives?

Cooking and its relation to other services. In general, provision of different services was heavily intertwined. This was particularly striking with food preparation. We observed lengthy pasta boils and pre– and post-heating of the oven and grill, concurrent with socialising and watching TV in the kitchen, showering, and bedroom-based work and console gaming. Because certain types of cooking lend themselves to waiting periods, where no cooking-related action seems to be required, it appeared that the tendency of our participants was to simply go do something else instead. We would like to understand this interaction of services better in the context of our student participants (who emphasised convenience and flexibility when it came to food preparation), and it would be interesting to see how food preparation interacts with services in other types of household.

6   Conclusion

We have shown what new domicile-specific knowledges and insights may result from moving energy analysis to the level of *services*. In this demonstration, we have quantified the energy relied upon, and described how the service was structured in the context of everyday life (appliances, interactions, time-use, activity, expectation and role in practice). During the process, we have also put forth considerations for service-relevant sensing.

We expect that a service-oriented approach will require significantly more accounting effort than a resource-centric one. We argue that the payoff for this effort is a shifting from simple measures of how much energy is consumed by appliances, to a more inclusive understanding of the bundle of devices, infrastructures, practices, expectations and resources that make up a service. For researchers considering possible design avenues, it can immediately expose where services support single or multiple practices, what devices function in groups (and why), and results in a broader view of the possible reconfigurations of service. In contrast to energy-centric accounting where the design path tends to be one of managing resources more efficiently while maintaining existing expectations and arrangements, a service-oriented approach allows sustainability at home to be cast as a contingent yet still-negotiable interplay between resources, infrastructures and devices, and practices which have purpose and meaning.

Acknowledgements. We would like to thank our anonymous reviewers for their insightful and detailed reviews; Lancaster University, especially Darren Axe and John Mills, for their cooperation and support. We are grateful to EPSRC for funding this work via grants EP/I00033X/1 and EP/G008523/1. Most of all, we are indebted and offer sincere thanks to our study participants.

References

1. Brynjarsdóttir, H., Håkansson, M., Pierce, J., Baumer, E.P., DiSalvo, C., Sengers, P.: Sustainably unpersuaded: How persuasion narrows our vision of sustainability. In: Proc. of CHI (2012)
2. Chetty, M., Brush, A.B., Meyers, B.R., Johns, P.: It's not easy being green: understanding home computer power management. In: Proc. of CHI, pp. 1033–1042 (2009)
3. Darby, S.: The effectiveness of feedback on energy consumption. Tech. rep., Environmental Change Institute, University of Oxford (2006)
4. DiSalvo, C., Sengers, P., Brynjarsdóttir, H.: Mapping the landscape of sustainable HCI. In: Proc. of CHI, pp. 1975–1984 (2010)
5. Froehlich, J., Larson, E., Gupta, S., Cohn, G., Reynolds, M., Patel, S.: Disaggregated end-use energy sensing for the smart grid. IEEE Pervasive Computin 10(1), 28–39 (2011)
6. Gram-Hanssen, K.: Residential heat comfort practices: understanding users. Building Research and Information 38(2) (2010)
7. Green, K., Vergragt, P.: Towards sustainable households: a methodology for developing sustainable technological and social innovations. Futures 34, 381–400 (2002)

8. Hackett, B., Lutzenhiser, L.: Social structures and economic conduct: Interpreting variations in household energy consumption. Sociological Forum 6, 449–470 (1991)
9. Hayes, S.C., Cone, J.D.: Reducing residential electrical energy use: payments, information, and feedback. J. Appl. Behav. Anal. 10(3), 425–435 (1977)
10. Pierce, J., Fan, C., Lomas, D., Marcu, G., Paulos, E.: Some consideration on the (in)effectiveness of residential energy feedback systems. In: Proc. of DIS, pp. 244–247 (2010)
11. Pierce, J., Paulos, E.: Beyond energy monitors: Interaction, energy, and emerging energy systems. In: Proc. of CHI (2012)
12. Pierce, J., Schiano, D.J., Paulos, E.: Home, habits, and energy: Examining domestic interactions and energy consumption. In: Proc. of CHI (2010)
13. Shove, E.: Beyond the ABC: Climate change policy and theories of social change. Environment and Planning A 42(6), 1273–1285 (2010)
14. Shove, E.: Comfort, Cleanliness and Convenience: The Social Organization of Normality, Berg, Oxford, UK (2003)
15. Sonderegger, R.C.: Movers and stayers: The resident's contribution to variation across houses in energy consumption for space heating. Energy and Buildings 1(3), 313–324 (1978)
16. Strengers, Y.A.: Designing eco-feedback systems for everyday life. In: Proc. of CHI, pp. 2135–2144 (2011)
17. Wall, R., Crosbie, T.: Potential for reducing electricity demand for lighting in households: An exploratory socio-technical study. Energy Policy 37(3), 1021–1031 (2009)
18. Warde, A.: Consumption and theories of practice. Journal of Consumer Culture 5(2), 131–153 (2005)
19. Zimmermann, J.P.: End-use metering campaign in 400 households in Sweden. Contract 17-05-2743 for Swedish Energy Agency, Enertech (September 2009)

Smart Blueprints: Automatically Generated Maps of Homes and the Devices Within Them

Jiakang Lu and Kamin Whitehouse

Department of Computer Science, University of Virginia
Charlottesville, VA, USA
{jklu,whitehouse}@cs.virginia.edu

Abstract. Off-the-shelf home automation technology is making it easier than ever for people to convert their own homes into "smart homes". However, manual configuration is tedious and error-prone. In this paper, we present a system that automatically generates a map of the home and the devices within it. It requires no specialized deployment tools, 3D scanners, or localization hardware, and infers the floor plan directly from the smart home sensors themselves, e.g. light and motion sensors. The system can be used to automatically configure home automation systems or to automatically produce an intuitive map-like interface for visualizing sensor data and interacting with controllers. We call this system *Smart Blueprints* because it is automatically customized to the unique configuration of each home. We evaluate this system by deploying in four different houses. Our results indicate that, for three out of the four home deployments, our system can automatically narrow the layout down to 2-4 candidates per home using only one week of collected data.

1 Introduction

Commercial off-the-shelf home automation devices are becoming smaller, more reliable, and less expensive. Furthermore, low-power wireless technology allows these devices to be surface-mounted, which obviates the need for home re-wiring and dramatically reduces installation costs. However, creating a do-it-yourself smart home involves much more than just installing hardware; the application software must also be configured with the *physical context* of each device, including its location within the home and its spatial relationship to other devices. For example, a lighting automation system must know which lights and motion sensors are in the same room in order to turn the lights on when the room is occupied. Home automation devices today, however, are unaware of their context within the home. For example, Figure 1(a) shows a typical home automation tool: it automatically detects all devices in the home network and displays them to the user as a list. The user must note the serial number on each sensor and mentally map each physical device to its virtual representation in software. Then, the physical relationship between devices must be encoded in software as abstract logical rules, e.g. *"Lights #19 and #28 should be controlled by light sensor #5 and motion sensor #15.* This manual configuration process is tedious and error-prone.

In this paper, we present an approach to automatically infer the spatial layout of smart home deployments, including (i) the floor plan of the house and (ii) the location

J. Kay et al. (Eds.): Pervasive 2012, LNCS 7319, pp. 125–142, 2012.
© Springer-Verlag Berlin Heidelberg 2012

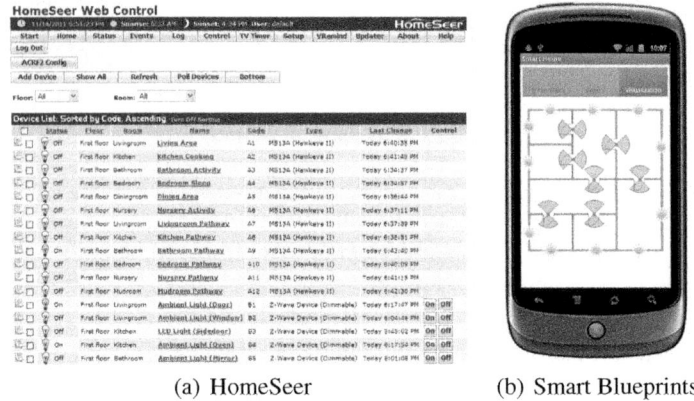

(a) HomeSeer   (b) Smart Blueprints

Fig. 1. A conventional user interface for home automation software shows all available devices in a list, while Smart Blueprints automatically infer the home's floor plan and shows the sensors in their physical context

of the devices within that floor plan. Our approach requires no specialized deployment tools, 3D scanners, or localization hardware; the floor plan is inferred from the smart home sensors themselves, e.g. light and motion sensors. A homeowner can simply snap sensors into place, and the sensors can provide useful functionality with little or no additional configuration effort. For example, home automation systems can automatically configure space heaters to respond to the temperature and motion sensors found to be in the same room. The system can also produce an intuitive map-like interface for visualizing sensor data or interacting with controllers. Figure 1(b) shows an example of this interface, which is more intuitive than the conventional list-based interface in Figure 1(a). We call this system a *Smart Blueprint* because it is automatically customized to the unique layout of each home and that home's devices.

As a case study, this paper considers the sensors that are required for a home energy management system: light sensors on windows, temperature sensors throughout the house, and motion sensors in each room. Armed with only these sensors, the Smart Blueprint system uses a three-step process to infer the floor plan and sensor locations. (1) First, it analyzes sensor data to infer how many rooms are in the house and which devices are in each room, using the insight that motion sensors in the same room tend to be triggered at similar times due to occupant movement. (2) Once the rooms are identified, the system analyzes motion sensor data to infer which rooms are adjacent, and it analyzes light patterns to decide which side of house the windows in the room are more likely to be on, e.g. East or West. This analysis constrains the location of each room with respect to the other rooms. (3) Finally, the system pieces the rooms together like a puzzle to find the floor plan that best explains the sensor data. If multiple floor plans explain the data equally well, the system asks the user to choose between a small number of alternatives.

The sensor data alone is not sufficient to fully constrain the floor plan and sensor lay-out, so we *pair* the devices in strategic ways to create additional constraints. First, we deploy motion sensors in pairs by packaging them into a single physical enclosure that snaps in place behind the door jamb of a doorway with the sensors facing in opposite directions, thereby creating a new constraint that the two sensors must be in different rooms. This constraint helps to separate clusters of sensors that show overlapping activ-ity patterns, such as motion sensors with visibility into neighboring rooms, or sensors in different rooms that are often used at the same time by different people. Next, we pair light sensors with motion sensors so that the light sensors can be associated with a particular room, based on activity patterns. Finally, motion sensors in doorways are paired with magnetometers in order to infer the doorway's cardinal direction.

Our basic approach is to infer constraints on spatial layout based on patterns in the sensor data, strategically using sensor pairing and supplemental sensors as necessary to fully constrain the floor plan and sensor layout. Smart Blueprints do not require any specific set of sensors to operate and the sensors described in this paper are only an ex-ample; the general approach that can be applied to any smart home or home automation system. For example, many devices such as wireless light switches and electronic appli-ances will also have usage patterns that correlate with occupant movement and activity. Furthermore, any device can be paired with a motion sensor to constrain its room loca-tion, a magnetometer to constrain its orientation, or a light sensor to constrain its side of the house. Additional constraints are also possible by pairing with other sensors, or applying other signal processing algorithms. Pairing sensors to create new constraints adds only marginal hardware cost and, as more constraints are added, the floor plan and sensor layout become easier to infer.

To evaluate this approach, we deployed Smart Blueprints in four houses for 1-3 months each. For three of the houses, the system narrows the system layout down to 2-4 candidates after processing only one week of data. Most users should be able to select their own floor plan out of only 2-4 choices. On the fourth house, however, the system did not identify the correct topology because the house had multiple floors and a very modern, open floor plan. We discuss these and other limitations of our system, as well as future techniques to improve it. We also present the performance of our sys-tem using simulated data based on 15 additional floor plans that were downloaded from architecture sites on the Internet. Aside from the Smart Blueprints system itself, the contributions of this work include insights into the computational structure of homes and how sensors can be used to generate and infer topological constraints.

2   Background and Related Work

Many existing technologies can automatically map out the floor plan of a building or localize devices in a building, but to our knowledge the Smart Blueprints system is the first to do both simultaneously without the need for user intervention or specialized deployment tools. For example, optical [1], laser, acoustic, and RF [2] sensors have all been used to find the boundaries of a room, and can be combined with mobile robots [3] or a mobile human [4] to create a complete map of a building. Approximate floor plans can also be generated by tracking personnel movement with in-building tracking systems [5]. However, Smart Blueprints are easier to use because no specialized tools, robots, or in-building tracking systems are required. Furthermore, the notion of using an installation tool or process does not always apply to do-it-yourself deployments that may occur piecemeal over the course of many months or years, as the homeowner adds new functionality. In contrast, the Smart Blueprints system can automatically assimilate new devices into the existing map at any time, with no additional overhead.

An installer could manually configure a smart home deployment using a graphical interface to quickly draw the house floor plan and locate the sensors within that plan. Several such tools already exist that offer visual drag-and-drop interfaces, and some are even designed for cell phone usage to facilitate on-site sketches[1]. However, this approach is no less tedious or error-prone than manually configuring a conventional list of devices: users must still manually create a mapping between the physical world and its virtual representation. Similarly, users could provide basic information about the home such as the number of rooms or the directions of the walls, as initialization information for a Smart Blueprint. We do not preclude this possibility and believe that it will in fact improve results, but it will also introduce new challenges about the confidence of user-supplied information. For example, does a foyer, stairway landing, or hallway count as a room? How many rooms is a great room (a living room, dining room, and kitchen that are not separated by walls)? Similar types of ambiguity exist for the number of floors and the direction of windows or walls. We informally asked several people to indicate how many rooms and floors are in our evaluation homes and received different answers from each. In this paper, we aim to demonstrate that the Smart Blueprints approach is possible even in the absence of any user input.

Smart homes have been an active area of research for several decades, typically involving long-term and highly-engineered sensor installations [6,7]. In contrast, the goal of our work is not to enable new smart home applications, but to facilitate the deployment process for do-it-yourself installations. Several prior projects have addressed configuration challenges for home and building automation systems, but focus on interoperability [8,9], automatic service discovery [10], or the use of modularity [11] and ontologies for seamless integration [12]. All of these solutions are necessary for a zero-configuration smart home system. In this paper, we focus on a different aspect of the configuration issue: identifying the physical context of devices.

A large body of literature has developed formalisms to specify a building floor plans as a constraint satisfaction problem (CSP) so that an architect can review all possible floor plans that satisfy certain physical constraints (e.g. types of rooms, minimum/maximum size, etc.) [13]. The Smart Blueprints system also uses constraints and search algorithms, but generally has much more specific constraints (e.g. doorway #3 has a north-to-south orientation) because it has a different goal: to find a small number of constraints that uniquely specify a single floor plan. Our contribution is not the ability to specify or search through floor plans, but the ability to automatically infer constraints on those floor plans from sensor data.

---

[1] http://www.floorplanner.com/; http://www.smartdraw.com/

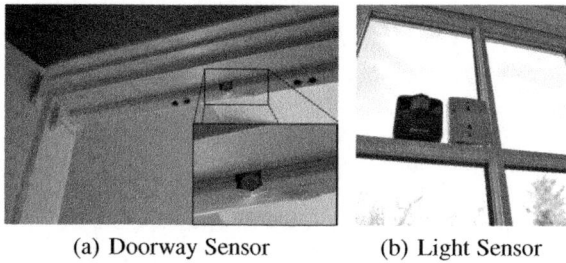

(a) Doorway Sensor   (b) Light Sensor

Fig. 2. We packaged multiple sensors together to detect *structural relationships* between data streams, thereby constraining the floor plan

3 A Case Study: Home Energy Management

The Smart Blueprints system presented in this paper is part of a broader project that aims to reduce the two largest energy consumers in the home: 1) lighting, and 2) heating and cooling. The system performs two types of controls. First, it uses a zoned residential heating and cooling system to control the temperature in each room individually, based on activity detected by motion sensors: when the room is occupied, it is heated or cooled to a comfortable setpoint temperature and, when it is not occupied, the temperature is allowed to float to a more energy-efficient setback temperature. Second, the system uses controllable windows shades to adjust the amount of light and heat admitted into the room. This control component builds on the previous work of the authors in daylight harvesting technology [14], and uses both light and motion sensors: when a room is occupied, the system prioritizes indoor lighting comfort and, when it is not occupied, the system prioritizes solar gain through the window to optimize heating and cooling efficiencies. In order to execute these two control strategies, the system needs at least three types of sensors: a motion sensor in each room, a light sensor on every controllable window, and a temperature sensor in each room. We demonstrate how the Smart Blueprints approach can be applied to this home energy management system by modifying the design and deployment of these sensors. However, the general approach can be applied to other home sensing systems as well.

4 Designing Sensors to Infer Context

The first implementation of our zoning and daylight harvesting systems used conventional motion, temperature, and light sensors that were manually configured with room location and other contextual information. In this paper, however, we take a novel two-pronged approach to sensor design that enables contextual information about a sensor to be inferred. First, we always *pair* multiple sensors together in the same physical enclosure. In this way, the values measured by one sensor serve as contextual information for the others, and vice versa. The pairings define a fixed spatial relationship between what would otherwise be independent data streams. By considering all of these relationships at once, we can then piece together both the local context of each sensor and the greater

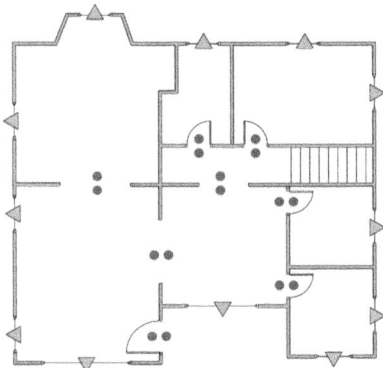

Fig. 3. Two paired motion sensors were installed at each doorway, and a light/motion pair were installed on each window

context of the entire system, i.e. the floor plan. Second, we designed our sensors to be placed at only certain types of moldings and fixtures, specifically in doorways and on windows. The sensors cannot be mounted on any flat surface the way a conventional motion, light, or temperature sensor could be, which add additional constraints on the locations of these sensors.

The doorway sensors are designed to snap in place behind the door jamb for easy installation and architectural camouflage (Figure 2(a)). The device contains two motion sensors, one pointing into each of the neighboring rooms. This physical pairing of motion sensors creates a relationship between the activities in every pair of adjacent rooms. The same enclosure contains a door latch sensor to detect whether the door is open or closed, as shown in the left of Figure 2(a) and can also contain temperature and humidity sensors, and a magnetometer to measure the orientation of the doorway with respect to magnetic north. In our pilot deployment, we built the doorway sensors using Parallax passive infrared (PIR) motion sensors, a standard magnetic reed switch, and the Synapse SNAPpy wireless microcontrollers. Further details about the deployment, power, and wireless properties of the doorway sensors can be found in another paper [15]. Instead of building magnetometers into the enclosure, we used the compass on a smartphone to measure the angle of each doorway.

The window sensors measure both light levels and solar gain caused by each window. The light sensors are placed on the window facing outside and measure the incoming daylight on the vertical glass surface. In our system, we paired these light sensors with motion sensors pointing back into the room. This pairing creates a defined relationship between the light values and the activity in the room that contains that window. The hardware costs only pennies for both light sensors and motion sensors, so this approach should not add substantial financial burden. The pairing can be enforced by putting the two sensors into a single plastic enclosure, although in our pilot deployment we simply deployed two sensors in tandem (Figure 2(b)). We used the X10 passive infrared motion sensors and the U012-12 data loggers designed by Onset, which monitor the environment with the built-in light, temperature, and humidity sensors.

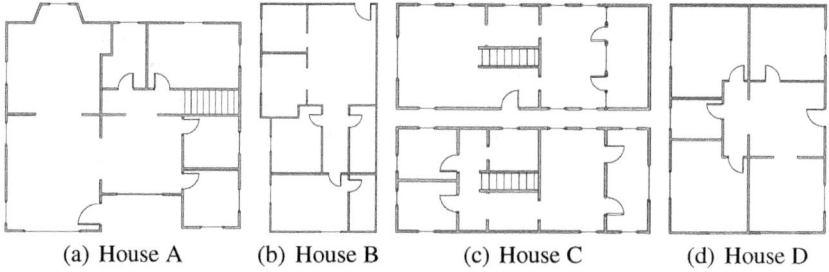

Fig. 4. To evaluate our system, we deployed in four homes with different floor plans

Table 1. We deployed our system in four multi-person homes with a widely varying set of windows, doors, rooms, and floors

House ID	#Residents	#Floors	#Rooms	#Doors	#Windows	Window Orientations	#Months
A	3	1	8	8	12	4	3
B	2	1	7	7	5	2	2
C	2	2	9	15	23	4	1
D	3	1	7	7	4	2	1

We deployed these two types of sensors in four homes of various sizes, including both single-story and multi-story houses, and the durations of the sensor deployments vary from one to three months. We deployed one doorway sensor at the top of doorways that cover all the inner doors, all the inner hallways and all the entryways to the home. We deployed a window sensor on at least one window on each wall of every room. Two homes were detached homes that had windows in all four directions, and two homes were apartments or condominiums that had windows on only two walls. An example of home deployment is shown in Figure 3. The people living in the homes included students, professionals, and homemakers. Scaled diagrams of the actual house floor plans are shown in Figure 4, and the deployment information about these homes is summarized in Table 1.

5   Inferring Rooms and Adjacency

The first step to identify the home's floor plan is to infer the number of rooms in the house, and which rooms are adjacent. For this task, we use the insight that objects in the same room are often used at similar times, and so the number of rooms can be inferred based on the number of clusters of sensors that are temporally correlated. In our pilot study, we use motion sensor data to infer the number of rooms: when people are in a room, multiple sensors in the room should detect motion. This approach faces two challenges. First, motion sensors have visibility through doorways and into multiple rooms. In our deployments, some of the motion sensors could detect activity in up to five rooms. Second, houses with multiple people often have simultaneous activity in more than one room at a time. For these two reasons, the temporal correlation between sensors is a weak indicator of room co-location. In fact, motion sensors in different rooms often had higher correlation than sensors in the same rooms, particularly when they both had high visibility into another highly-frequented room. In prior work, we found that a simple clustering approach was sufficient to identify which devices were in the same room, but this approach assumed only a single motion sensor per room, and could not accurately determine the exact number of rooms [16]. In this paper, we need the exact number of rooms, and we quickly found that a naive clustering approach did not work for any of the four pilot deployments, particularly with more than one motion sensor per room.

To address this problem, we leverage the motion sensor *pairings* on our doorway sensors: any two motion sensors within the same enclosure are guaranteed to be monitoring different rooms. This constraint allows us to ensure that sensor clusterings do not cross room boundaries: any sensor clustering that does is eliminated from consideration. The basic algorithm has five steps. (1) Identify all *simultaneously firing sensors*: those sensors that fire within one second of each other. We call these *firing sets* $S = s_1, s_2, ..., s_K$, where K is the size of the firing set, and $s_i : i < K$ are the sensors in the set. (2) Eliminate any firing set S that contains two paired sensors: if S contains two paired sensors, it might have been caused by multiple people in different parts of the house, or a single person making a doorway crossing. By eliminating firing sets with paired sensors, we increase the likelihood that it was caused by a single person who is safely on the interior of a single room. (3) Calculate the frequency f_S of all remaining firing sets S. (4) Calculate a weight w_S for each firing set S, defined as follows:

$$w_S = \frac{f_S}{\sum_{k=1}^{K} f_{s_k}} \times \frac{f_S}{min_{k=1}^{K} f_{s_k}} \tag{1}$$

The frequency f_S indicates the number of times that a set of sensors fire together. However, this does not necessarily indicate the importance of the set, because some rooms are used more often than others. The weight w_S is designed to normalize the frequency based on the upper bound on the number of times that this set of sensors could possibly have fired together. This upper bound can have two cases. First, the total number of times that any of the sensors fired: $\sum_{k=1}^{K} f_{s_k}$. Second, the number of times that the least frequent sensor fired: $min_{k=1}^{K} f_{s_k}$. We normalize f_S by both of these values to a create a weight w_S that approximates the likelihood that the sensors in the firing set are actually in the same room.

(5) The last step is to merge firing sets into clusters that represent rooms. To initialize, a single cluster is defined as the firing set with the highest weight. We then process the remaining firing sets in a greedy fashion sorted in descending order by weight. Each firing set is merged with a cluster if and only if (a) the merge would not cause the cluster to contain any paired sensors, and (b) the merge would not cause a loop among doorways, which implies any transitive closure of doorways would not contain any paired sensors. Otherwise, the firing set is used to initiate a new cluster. When all firing sets have been processed, the clusters represent individual rooms. Two rooms are defined to be adjacent if the union of their clusters contains two paired sensors.

We apply the technique on our four house deployments, and the percentage of correct room adjacency links detected over 21 days is shown in Figure 5 for Houses A, B, and D. The results show that accuracy fluctuates during the first week but stabilizes

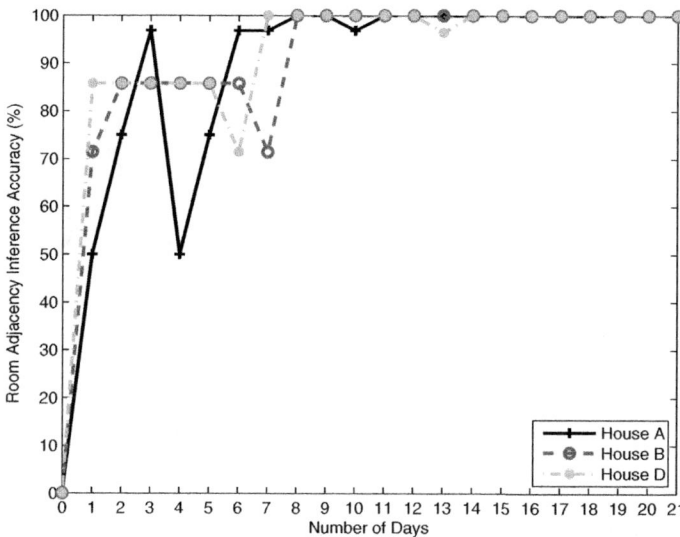

Fig. 5. In homes A, B, and D, the system infers the correct number of rooms and the adjacency of those rooms after collecting motion sensor data for 7-14 days

to the correct number of rooms and room adjacency once it obtains enough data. This means that, for these houses, the system can provide the correct floor plan after a learning period of 1-2 weeks. The sensor clustering for these three houses is illustrated in Figures 7(a), 7(g), and 7(m). Our current algorithm does not work for House C because it has two floors, and the algorithm combines rooms from both floors into a single room. We discuss ways to address this limitation as future work.

6   Inferring Structural Constraints

The number of rooms and their adjacency does not create a fully-specified floor plan, and other structural constraints must also be measured or inferred through other means. In our case study, the application needs a light sensor on every window to manage lighting levels and solar gain. We use these sensors to infer the angle of the windows with respect to true north, based on the patterns of sunlight that are detected throughout the day. In previous work, we noted that light sensors clearly differentiate direct and indirect sunlight, and that direct sunlight occurs at different times of day based on the angle of a window. Therefore, the time of day of the maximum light reading can be used to infer the angle of a window to within a few degrees, when exposed to direct sunlight [17]. Figure 6(a) shows ideal cases in House A for light measurements on windows at different angles. In a home setting, however, the direct sunlight can be consistently blocked by trees or neighboring houses, skewing the angle measurements. We found this to skew some angle estimates enough that windows appeared to be on the wrong wall.

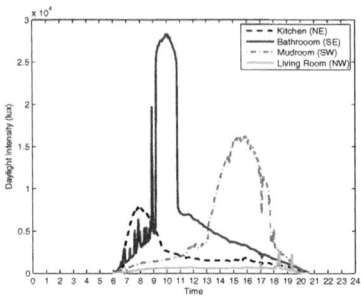
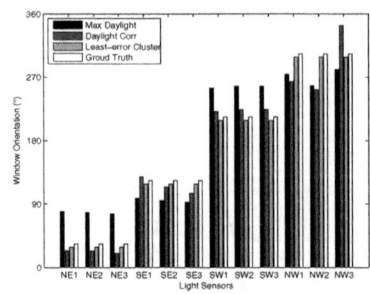

(a) Light Patterns at Different Windows   (b) Window Orientation Accuracy

Fig. 6. Light sensors are needed to manage daylight harvesting and solar gain. We can *also* infer the angle of orientation for each window using patterns in the sunlight data. Our algorithm accurately inferred the angle of all twelve instrumented windows in House A.

In order to overcome this challenge, we use two new techniques. First, we do not simply look at the maximum light reading. Instead, we calculate the expected curve for all possible window orientations, and assign each window the orientation with which its light readings have the highest correlation coefficient. This reduces the impact of partial shade that causes short-term abnormalities in the daily light response curves. Second, we assume that houses are built primarily with right angles, and so the windows point in only four directions. We first use all windows to estimate the angle of orientation of the entire house, and subtract this from the estimated window angles. Then, we cluster the window orientations so as to minimize the difference between the cluster average and the four cardinal directions.

We apply these techniques to light sensors deployed in House A, and the results are shown in Figure 6(b). The naive technique described above (*Max Daylight*) produced 37.1 degrees of error on average, and did not clearly differentiate the SW and NW windows. Using correlation coefficients (*Daylight Corr*) approach improved the absolute error, but did not improve differentiation. Finally, our clustering approach (*Least-error Cluster*) correctly assigned each window to the correct wall, by looking at all windows in aggregate instead of each window individually.

These experiments analyze light sensors on windows, but similar approaches could also be used on the interior of a room: the highest light levels in a room will often be correlated with the side of the house that the room is on. Otherwise, devices in the home can alternatively be equipped with magnetometers. Magnetometers are commonly used as in cell phones, GPS receivers and vehicles to measure orientation with respect to magnetic north. They are small, inexpensive, and low-power devices that can easily be integrated into a sensor package such as our doorway enclosure. In our pilot deployment, we used the magnetometer in an Android cell phone to measure the doorway angle by holding the device up to the wooden doorway trim. This process caused some noise in the angle measurements because the trim is not perfectly straight or the phone is not exactly level. Table 2 lists the measurements of the doorways in House A, which are accurate to within 10-15 degrees. We would expect the same causes of noise to affect values measured by a magnetometer actually embedded into a surface mounted enclosure.

7 Searching the Space of Floor Plans

The goal of our search algorithm is to generate a set of floor plans that are most consistent with the structural constraints that were inferred from our sensors. The input to the search algorithm is a number of rooms R, a $R \times R$ adjacency matrix that indicates the adjacency of rooms, and the angle of orientation for doors and/or windows. The output of the algorithm is a fully-specified topology with (x, y) coordinates for each room.

7.1 Defining the Search Space

First, we define the search space. We illustrate each stage of this search space using Figure 7. In this section, we only discuss Houses A, B and D, where our system is capable of inferring the correct room adjacency. The root of the search tree for each house is the adjacency matrix, which is derived from the sensor clustering performed in a previous step, as illustrated in Figures 7(c), 7(i), and 7(o). The second level of the search tree is the set of all possible doorway assignments, each of which defines a different set of directions for each doorway. Figures 7(d), 7(j), and 7(p) show the correct doorway assignments for each house. For every pair of adjacent rooms, there are four possible orientations for each doorway (North, South, East, and West). Thus, the total number of doorway assignments is 4^D, where D is the number of doorways. For each doorway assignment, the search algorithm explores all possible interior wall assignments. These assignments define whether any pair of rooms is adjacent by an interior wall (but not a doorway). Figures 7(e), 7(k), and 7(q) show the correct doorway assignments for each house. Any pair of two rooms that are not connected by a doorway can possibly be adjacent through an interior wall, and the total number of such room pairs is $n_{pairs} = \frac{R*(R-1)}{2} - D$. Finally, given a set of doorway wall assignments and interior wall assignments, we generate the size of each wall by formulating a linear program that minimizes the length L_i of each wall i subject to the constraints that $L_i \geq 1$ and $L_i = \sum_j L_j : adjacent(L_i, L_j)$. Once the wall sizes are defined, the algorithm tiles the rooms together in sequential fashion to generate the (x, y) coordinates for each room.

Table 2. Clustering magnetometers reduces orientation error to within $\sim 10°$

Doorway	Measured
Dining Room	322
Kitchen	230
Hallway	221
Bathroom	221
Bedroom	225
Mudroom	324
Nursery	327

7.2 Efficiently Searching the Space

The size of this search space is different for each house, but in general it is too large to search exhaustively. The total number of possible topologies is $4^D * \left\{ \sum_{i=1}^{n_{pairs}} 4^n * \binom{n_{pairs}}{i} \right\}$, where D is the number of doorways, n_{pairs} is the number of room pairs that are connected via interior walls, and the number of 4 indicates the four possible directions in which two room can be connected. The maximum value of n_{pairs} is $\frac{R*(R-1)}{2} - D$. The second row in Table 3 titled `total space size` shows the total size of the search space for each of the three houses discussed.

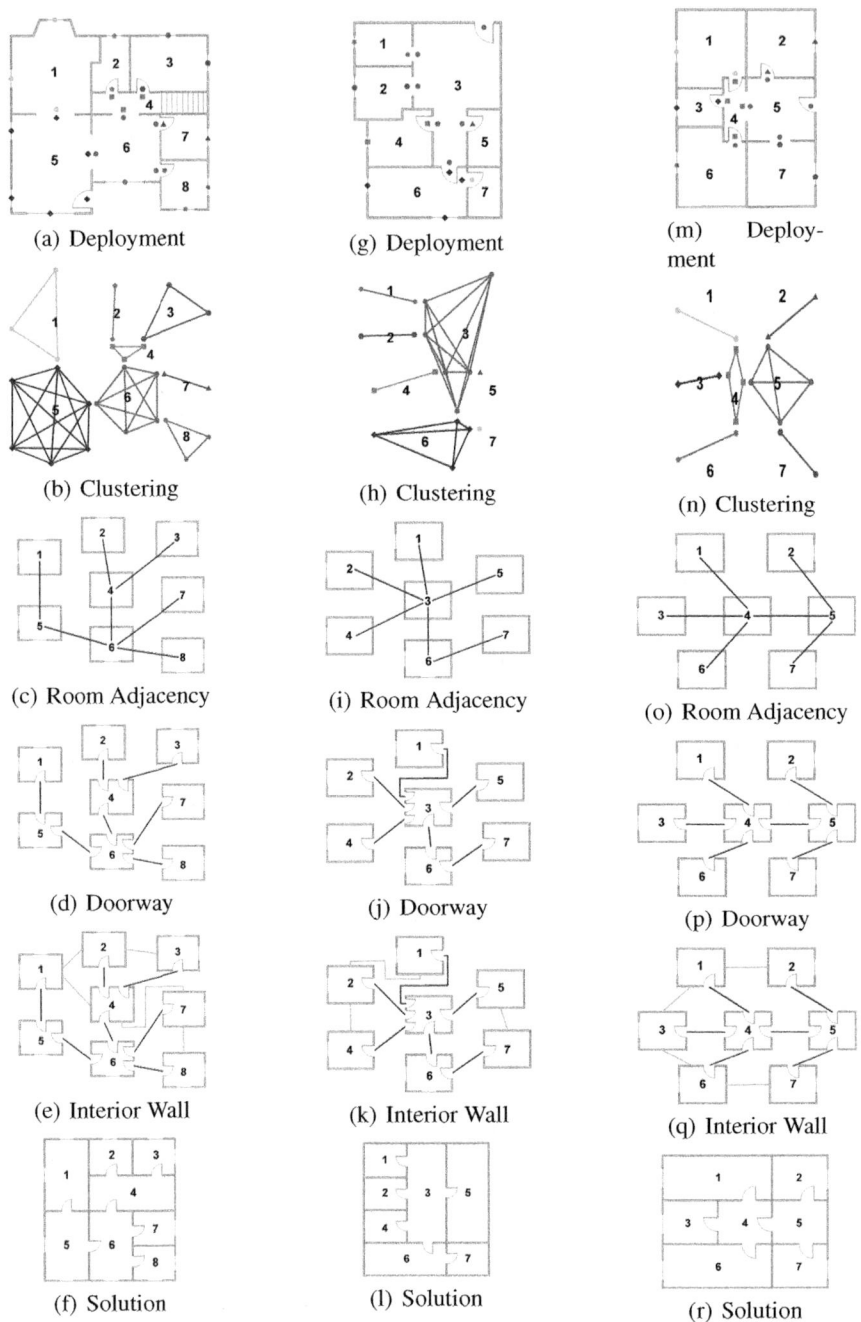

Fig. 7. This figure shows each step of our algorithm (in each row) for all three houses: (1) sensors are clustered together based on similar activity patterns (2) these clusters are converted into rooms and adjacency between rooms (3) doorways are assigned to specific walls (N,S,E,W) (4) interior walls for room pairs are defined to be adjacent (5) spatial layout of the floor plan

In order to more efficiently search this state space, we use three different pruning techniques. First, if the window and/or door orientations are known, we do not explore topologies that are inconsistent with these orientations. In other words, if a doorway is known to be North-South oriented, we do not explore topologies that put the doorway on an Eastern or Western wall of a room. Row 3 in Table 3 shows the size of the search space after constraints on window and doorway orientations are applied. Doorway constraints reduce the search space by two orders of magnitude, window constraints reduce it by five orders of magnitude, and applying both simultaneously reduces it by seven orders of magnitude.

The second and third pruning techniques rely on a non-monotonically increasing score function that we use to assign each node a value. This score function is discussed in the next section. Based on this score function, we use traditional $\alpha - \beta$ pruning: once a leaf node with a low score is found, the search algorithm no longer searches sub-trees where the root of the sub-tree has a higher score. We also use the score function for early termination: when exploring the bottom level of the tree, if the algorithm detects that adding additional interior walls always increases the score of a node, it terminates and backtracks. This pruning technique is based on the observation that the sub-tree is already over constrained. Row 4 indicate that these pruning techniques reduce the number of explored nodes by 7-15 orders of magnitude from the size of the entire search space, dramatically improving search efficiency. Row 4 shows both the number of doorway assignments explored and the number of interior wall assignments explored.

7.3   Choosing the Best Topologies

The pruning techniques described above reduce the number of explored nodes down to the millions or billions. This is computationally tractable, but not acceptable in terms of search accuracy. To be successful, we need to leverage the structural constraints to choose the best out of millions or billions of alternative feasible topologies. To do this, we start with two simple heuristics:

- Minimize the number of doors and neighboring rooms that share a wall with a window.
- Minimize the number of corners of the building.

The first heuristic is based on the observation that most windows are on exterior walls, and it is rare for a room to have a window and an interior door on the same wall, or a window and another adjacent room on the same wall. The second heuristic is based on the observation that most buildings are square, and all squares have four corners. Some houses do have extensions, sheds, or other outcroppings, all of which lead to additional corners. However, the number of corners is typically minimized for cost, real estate efficiency, and heating/cooling efficiency. Therefore, the score of a floor plan increases by one for each corner that it has beyond four. Rows 5 and 6 of Table 3 show that these two cost functions eliminate all but thousands or even tens of floor plan candidates.

Of the remaining candidate floor plans, most can be eliminated because they are self-inconsistent. These inconsistent floor plans are akin to Mobius strips or Escher stairways: due to computational complexity, our search algorithm generates all possible

Table 3. The total size of the floor plan search space is very large (row 2). This space can be reduced using structural information (row 3), cost-based pruning (row 4), score functions (rows 5-6), and filter functions (rows7-12). Door and window orientation helps to different degrees for each house.

	House A			House B		
Total Space Size	6.1×10^{23}			4.9×10^{22}		
House Constraints	Doorways	Windows	Windows +Doorways	Doorways	Windows	Windows +Doorways
	4.8×10^{21}	3.8×10^{17}	2.9×10^{15}	7.6×10^{20}	8.2×10^{16}	1.3×10^{15}
#Doorway	128	420	7	64	1728	12
#Interior Wall	652,668,160	4,615,837,808	60,886,092	71,793,408	2,305,009,408	17,790,744
Constraints Conflicts	56,750,918	269,426	1,856	10,969,360	14,802,389	250,682
#Corners Rooms	4,740,246	13,700	49	1,148,492	733,174	12,090
Room Circles	938,212	4,148	18	74,168	35,562	2,517
Room Sizes	897,310	4,048	18	60,446	32,484	2,146
Overlapped Rooms	163,336	1,148	16	18,615	5,995	513
Room Adjacency	88	7	2	1,076	255	108
Duplicate Floor Plans	76	7	2	588	219	78
Duplicate Shapes	19	7	2	26	12	4

House D		
4.9×10^{22}		
Doorways	Windows	Windows +Doorways
7.6×10^{20}	8.2×10^{16}	1.3×10^{15}
64	3888	64
127,705,728	5,961,165,596	127,705,728
39,119,820	265,569,366	5,678,122
6,489,208	28,248,664	491,038
456,888	2,132,489	27,436
311,628	1,856,657	22,059
81,366	367,957	4,994
176	1,076	11
98	831	11
34	109	3

floor plans without checking global consistency properties, such as multi-room cycles or 2D planarity. Rows 7-12 show the effect of a number of filters that we perform to eliminate this type of floor plan.

- Room Cycles: filter floor plans in which two connected rooms are connected to the opposite walls of a third room. This topology is not feasible in a 2D plane.
- Room Sizes: filter floor plans with for which room sizes cannot be solved by the linear program, due to inconsistent room adjacency.
- Overlapped Rooms: filter floor plans that have overlapping rooms. This topology is not feasible in a 2D plane.
- Room Adjacency: filter cases where two rooms are physically adjacent, but the interior wall assignment indicates that they are not adjacent.
- Duplicate Floor Plans: filter floor plans that are duplicates of others. These plans are underspecified.
- Duplicate Shapes: filter floor plans where the size and location of rooms are identical to others, even if the identities of the rooms are different. Only a single shape can be presented to the user, and the room identities can be expanded in a separate step.

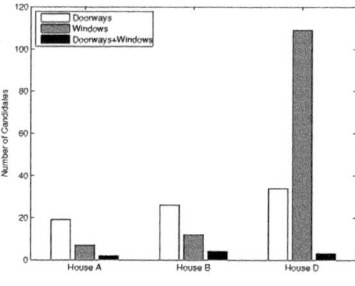
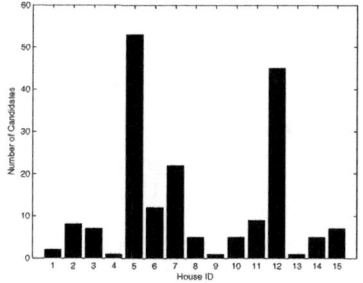

(a) Accuracy of Real Deployments   (b) Accuracy of Downloaded Floor Plans

Fig. 8. Accuracy is the number of candidate floor plans chosen, which determines how easy it is for a user to recognize their own house. (a) Houses A and B are helped more by window orientation and House D by doorway orientation. (b) Most of the 15 topologies downloaded from the Internet have fewer than 10 candidates. All candidate pools include the correct house topology.

After these filters are applied, the remaining candidate floor plans are presented to the user. The user can select the correct floor plan from this pool of candidates.

8 Evaluation

Figure 8(a) shows the number of candidate floor plans that are generated for each of the three houses using a different set of structural constraints: door orientation, window orientation, or both. All candidate pools contain the correct house topology. The combination of doorway and window orientations has the smallest pool of candidates for all the three houses: 2, 4, and 3, respectively. In Houses A and B, we observe that window orientation is more effective than doorway orientation. This matches our analysis in Table 3, where window orientation shows more decrease in topology search space than doorway orientation. However, House D has a different trend where window orientation has the largest pool size, with 109 total candidate floor plans. The explanation for this anomaly is that House D only has windows on two walls, as indicated in Table 1. Thus, window orientation alone is not informative enough to filter the valid but incorrect topologies. In general, houses with more doors and windows will benefit more from information about their orientations.

Due to the difficulty of deploying large-scale sensor systems, our evaluation is limited to only four houses. Although the floor plans of the houses are highly varied, it is difficult to draw statistical conclusions from the results. To increase our sample set size, we collect another 15 house plans that are publicly available online[2]. These floor plans comprise a variety of single-bedroom and multiple-bedroom apartments and houses from various parts of U.S. By analyzing the blueprints, we manually identified room adjacency, doorway orientations, and window orientations in order to evaluate the efficacy of our search heuristics on these topologies. Figure 8(b) indicates the size of candidate

---

[2] http://www.plansourceinc.com/apartmen.htm

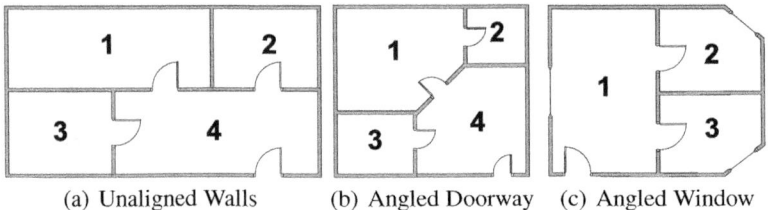

(a) Unaligned Walls   (b) Angled Doorway   (c) Angled Window

Fig. 9. Our system does not yet capture floor plans with non-conventional angles or unaligned walls

pool that our system produced for each house. In two cases, the candidate pool included approximately 50 floor plans. However, the average number of candidates is 12.2, and the candidate pools do contain the correct topology in all 15 test cases. This indicates that our search heuristics are effective for a large range of topologies and can be used to provide a reasonably small set of candidate floor plans to users.

9   Limitations and Future Work

The sensors, data analysis, pruning algorithms, and scoring heuristics that we use in this paper are designed to be generally applicable to a large number of houses. However, they are not applicable to all houses, and the floor plans of many houses will either not be found, or will be found but a large number of other candidates will be given higher rank. House C in our test set is one of these houses. In future work, we believe we can address most if not all of these limitations by extending our algorithms.

Our system performed poorly on the topology shown in Figure 4(c) for two reasons. First, the house has multiple floors, and the stairway sensors covered two floors. This caused the sensor clustering algorithm to group rooms on separate floors as a single room. Furthermore, this house has a very modern and open floor plan, which exacerbates the problem of overlapping sensing ranges that cover multiple rooms. In future work, we will need to address both multiple story buildings as well as open floor plans by developing new sensors and/or analysis algorithms.

Some other floor plans that we currently do not support are illustrated in Figure 9. These include floor plans with unaligned walls, doorways or windows that are angled, and rooms that do not adjoin at 90° angles. Of our four testbeds, two of the houses actually do have unaligned walls and our system generated a reasonable approximation of their floor plans. In future work, we will build on prior work in architecture [13] to specify floor plans using more general formalisms in order to efficiently search over a wider range of topologies.

The evaluation presented in this paper is based on the sensors available to a specific form of home energy management system: light, temperature, and motion sensors. The results are promising, despite the limited spatial constraints that were extracted from these sensors. In current work, we are exploring new ways to extract spatial constraints from these and other sensors. For example, we are exploring whether light sensors can be used to identify room locations based on artificial lighting patterns, and whether light sensors on the interior of a building can identify direction based on indirect sunlight levels. We are also exploring techniques to extract spatial constraints from more complex sensors such as microphones, tracking systems, and water/electrical usage.

10 Conclusions

In this paper, we present the Smart Blueprints system that simplifies the configuration of smart homes by automatically inferring the floor plan of a home and the locations of sensors in the house. This inferred information serves as physical context to better interpret sensors and configure actuators. We evaluate this approach using a combination of motion sensors and light sensors, and present novel inference techniques to infer their physical context within the home. We evaluate the system by deploying in four homes and by analyzing 15 typical floor plans found online. Our results indicate that our system can narrow the floor plan to a small number of candidates: between 2 and 4 for our deployment testbeds. Our approach requires a short period of data collection to automatically infer the floor plan and in our experiments this period ranged from 1 to 2 weeks. During this training period, we expect users to use a basic list-based interface until the graphical interface is ready. As an early stage prototype, our system does have several limitations in terms of the house and floor plans on which it can operate. It could not infer the topology of House C because it failed to generate accurate sensor clusters due to the modern and open floor plan. Similarly, it does not yet address non-conventional angles or alignment. In this paper, we present a proof of concept demonstration and indicate several open questions and new directions of research that could improve these results in the future. We believe the concepts can be extended to other applications, either by using the exact same sensor configurations or by generalizing the principles learned from our pilot study to other types of sensors that are needed for other applications.

Acknowledgements. Special thanks to our reviewers for very helpful feedback. This work is based on work supported by the National Science Foundation under Grants No. 1038271 and 0845761.

References

1. Furukawa, Y., Curless, B., Seitz, S., Szeliski, R.: Reconstructing Building Interiors from Images. In: IEEE 12th International Conference on Computer Vision, pp. 80–87 (2009)
2. Guo, W., Filer, N., Barton, S.: 2D Indoor Mapping and Location-sensing Using an Impulse Radio Network. In: ICU 2005: 2005 IEEE International Conference on Ultra-Wideband, pp. 296–301 (2005)
3. Surmann, H., Nüchter, A., Hertzberg, J.: An autonomous mobile robot with a 3D laser range finder for 3D exploration and digitalization of indoor environments. Robotics and Autonomous Systems 45(3), 181–198 (2003)
4. Schindler, G., Metzger, C., Starner, T.: A Wearable Interface for Topological Mapping and Localization in Indoor Environments. In: Hazas, M., Krumm, J., Strang, T. (eds.) LoCA 2006. LNCS, vol. 3987, pp. 64–73. Springer, Heidelberg (2006)

5. Harle, R., Hopper, A.: Using Personnel Movements for Indoor Autonomous Environment Discovery. In: PerCom 2003: the 1st IEEE International Conference on Pervasive Computing and Communications, pp. 125–132 (2003)
6. Mozer, M.: The Neural Network House: An Environment that Adapts to its Inhabitants. In: Proc. of the AAAI Spring Symposium on Intelligent Environments, pp. 110–114 (1998)
7. Kidd, C., Orr, R., Abowd, G.D., Atkeson, C., Essa, I., MacIntyre, B., Mynatt, E., Starner, T., Newstetter, W.: The Aware Home: A Living Laboratory for Ubiquitous Computing Research. In: Yuan, F., Hartkopf, V. (eds.) CoBuild 1999. LNCS, vol. 1670, pp. 191–198. Springer, Heidelberg (1999)
8. Wolff, S., Larsen, P., Lausdahl, K., Ribeiro, A., Toftegaard, T.: Facilitating Home Automation Through Wireless Protocol Interoperability. In: WPMC 2009: the 12th International Symposium on Wireless Personal Multimedia Communications (2009)
9. Ferrari, G., Medagliani, P., Piazza, S., Martalò, M.: Wireless Sensor Networks: Performance Analysis in Indoor Scenarios. EURASIP Journal on Wireless Communications and Networking 2007(1), 41 (2007)
10. Schor, L., Sommer, P., Wattenhofer, R.: Towards a Zero-configuration Wireless Sensor Network Architecture for Smart Buildings. In: BuildSys 2009: the 1st ACM Workshop on Embedded Sensing Systems for Energy-Efficiency in Buildings, pp. 31–36. ACM (2009)
11. Granzer, W., Kastner, W., Neugschwandtner, G., Praus, F.: A Modular Architecture for Building Automation Systems. In: WFCS 2006: 2006 IEEE International Workshop on Factory Communication Systems, pp. 99–102 (2006)
12. Reinisch, C., Granzer, W., Praus, F., Kastner, W.: Integration of Heterogeneous Building Automation Systems Using Ontologies. In: IECON 2008: the 34th Annual Conference of the IEEE Industrial Electronics Society, pp. 2736–2741. IEEE (2008)
13. Charman, P.: A constraint-based approach for the generation of floor plans. In: Proc. of the 6th International Conference on Tools with Artificial Intelligence, pp. 555–561. IEEE (1994)
14. Lu, J., Whitehouse, K.: SunCast: Fine-grained Prediction of Natural Sunlight Levels for Improved Daylight Harvesting. In: IPSN 2012: the 11th ACM/IEEE Conference on Information Processing in Sensor Networks (April 2012)
15. Hnat, T., Srinivasan, V., Lu, J., Sookoor, T., Dawson, R., Stankovic, J., Whitehouse, K.: The Hitchhiker's Guide to Successful Residential Sensing Deployments. In: SenSys 2011: the 9th ACM Conference on Embedded Networked Sensor Systems, pp. 232–245. ACM (2011)
16. Srinivasan, V., Stankovic, J., Whitehouse, K.: Protecting your Daily In-home Activity Information from a Wireless Snooping Attack. In: UbiComp 2008: the 10th International Conference on Ubiquitous Computing, pp. 202–211. ACM (2008)
17. Lu, J., Birru, D., Whitehouse, K.: Using Simple Light Sensors to Achieve Smart Daylight Harvesting. In: BuildSys 2010: the 2nd ACM Workshop on Embedded Sensing Systems for Energy-Efficiency in Building, pp. 73–78. ACM (2010)

Hacking the Natural Habitat:
An In-the-Wild Study of Smart Homes, Their Development, and the People Who Live in Them

Sarah Mennicken and Elaine M. Huang

Zurich People and Computing Lab, Department of Informatics,
University of Zurich, Zurich, Switzerland
{mennicken,huang}@ifi.uzh.ch

Abstract. Commercial home automation systems are becoming increasingly common, affording the opportunity to study technology-augmented homes in real world contexts. In order to understand how these technologies are being integrated into homes and their effects on inhabitants, we conducted a qualitative study involving smart home professionals who provide such technology, people currently in the process of planning or building smart homes, and people currently living in smart homes. We identified motivations for bringing smart technology into homes, and the phases involved in making a home smart. We also explored the varied roles of the smart home inhabitants that emerged during these phases, and several of the challenges and benefits that arise while living in a smart home. Based on these findings we propose open areas and new directions for smart home research.

Keywords: Home automation, smart homes, domestic technologies.

1 Introduction

Smart and automated home technologies have been an important focus of ubiquitous computing research since the inception of the field. The research community continues to push the boundaries of novel sensing and applications in the home to support various tasks and processes, such as health and wellness, cooking, aging, and communication. In the meantime, commercial systems that support more basic tasks of home automation have been developed, and their adoption and use offer a picture of today's "smart homes" in contrast with the vision represented in most pervasive computing research on smart homes. Although automated home technology has yet to be widely adopted, it is beginning to penetrate beyond an audience of extremely wealthy or extremely technically-savvy homeowners. Furthermore, recent studies by ABI Research indicate the growing ubiquity of home automation, finding that nearly 1.1 million home automation systems will be purchased in North America in 2012[1], and that revenue from such systems will exceed $11.8 billion in 2015[2].

---

[1] http://www.abiresearch.com/press/1555-North+America+to+See+Nearly+1.1+Million+Managed+Home+Automation+ Systems+Shipped+in+2012
[2] http://www.abiresearch.com/press/1633-Home+Automation+Systems+Reve/nue+to+ Approach+$12+Billion+Worldwide+in+2015

J. Kay et al. (Eds.): Pervasive 2012, LNCS 7319, pp. 143–160, 2012.
© Springer-Verlag Berlin Heidelberg 2012

The increased interest in and use of "smart" home automation present a unique opportunity to look at how early adopters of these technologies are integrating them into their homes and lives. An understanding of how home automation is adopted and its impact on people will be valuable in providing insight about how future smart home technology should be designed to fit their needs and expectations. The growing population of people who have opted to instrument their homes with smart home technology provides us with the opportunity to learn about motivations for creating a smart home, the "real-world" process of developing a smart home, and the effects of smart homes on the everyday lives of their inhabitants in a naturalistic, non-experimental, non-laboratory context.

In this paper we report on a qualitative study of three key groups of stakeholders in the current landscape of commercial smart home technology: 1) inhabitants of homes equipped with automation technology, 2) people in the process of planning or building automated homes, and 3) providers of existing commercial solutions for home automation. Our objective was to understand how a smart home currently develops, from the initial idea to instrument the home to the emergent uses of its technology by household members. Our focus was on "smart homes" that made use of either commercial or custom solutions for home automation that are integrated into the home's infrastructure, because such households were reasonably accessible to us, and because we believe these to be some of the important predecessors to the types of innovative home technology on which the research community is focusing.

This work offers several key contributions to the field of pervasive computing, namely the articulation of several stages involved in developing a smart home, challenges that arise in the various stages, and people's motivations for wanting a "smart home", such as the aspiration of modernity, joy of hacking, and experienced benefits that whet one's appetite for more. We also explore the roles that emerge in this process and how each of them influences the development and use of the technology. In addition to these findings, this research poses several other novel contributions, such as providing a holistic understanding of the development of smart homes synthesized from the perspectives of multiple types of stakeholders through naturalistic experiences, and the identification of open areas for new smart home research to support a broader process and variety of roles than have typically been considered.

2   Related Work

Domestic technology and smart homes have been a topic of research for several decades. As such, there is an extensive body of existing research on smart homes and domestic environments which would be too large to cover exhaustively in this paper. We therefore focus our treatment of related work on the specific areas of smart home research that are most directly relevant to the work that we present in this paper.

Research on smart homes has been carried out at various levels of abstraction: Taylor et al. explored the understanding of the general notion of "smart" in this context [29], emphasizing the importance of the actual interaction as an aspect of intelligence. Randall provides a differentiation of several kinds of smart homes that are able to provide smart functionality beyond the accumulation of smart appliances [24]. In this paper we add to the understanding of what the notion of "smart" actually means to people living in smart homes. Crabtree and Rodden highlighted the need to consider specifics of domestic routines [10] by exploring coordination and communication in the home in order to inform design of home technology. In our research we build upon this work by considering such routines within the larger context of the smart home development process.

Other research has been interested in a high-level understanding of people's general intentions regarding ambient intelligence appliances: Allouch and Van Dijk quantitatively investigated prospective users' intentions to get such appliances, based on an acceptance model for anticipated adoption and outcome expectancies [2]. The respondents in their study showed a low degree of intention to adopt those appliances.

One key area of related work has involved the identification of user requirements to provide design guidelines for the domestic environment [11, 25]. For example, Bell and Kaye considered the notion of focusing on the experience of, rather than efficiency with, kitchen technologies [4]. Seminal work by Edwards and Grinter provides an overview about technical, social, and pragmatic challenges that arise in homes equipped with ubiquitous technologies [13]. While this understanding of users' needs might offer hints about the motivations for advanced technology in the home, it does not directly address the concrete reasons for integrating it into one's home in the first place.

Other research has focused on understanding the meaning of space within the home. Elliot et al. highlighted the importance of the diversity of locations in the home [14], and Aipperspach et al. argue that losing heterogeneity of space, technology, and time in the home results in a less fulfilling experience [1].

Some home research has looked specifically at roles within the home in relation to technology. There has been other work in more specific fields on domestic routines and evolving roles of users, such as for example in health applications and Ambient Assisted Living [3, 32], stressing the importance of user-centered and careful integration of (medical) technology in the domestic environment. There has also been work on how people configure their home networks [9] and the different roles householders engage in based on their degree of active involvement [23]. Our work complements some of these findings by considering similar emerging patterns in relation to smart home technology.

Other work has considered people's relationships with home technologies [16], and ways to simplify end-user configuration of ubiquitous home computing technologies [18, 26, 31]. Earlier research on end-user programming in the domestic context explored which appliances are programmed and how [27, 28], to inform better design for end users. More recently, research has been conducted on ways to facilitate the broader adoption of home automation, by providing better means to fit home automation to the inhabitants' needs. Dixon et al. [12] argue for empowering end users by providing home-wide operating system.

In order to study and explore the interaction between people and smart home technology, several universities and research institutions have built smart home laboratories that allow for more ecologically valid, situated installations of home technology. These laboratories have allowed researchers to explore many aspects of home technology, from the challenges of realizing systems to the experience of living with them. Two notable projects amongst others have been the Aware Home [21] and MIT's house_n [19]. These projects provide an interesting complement to our research, as they consider future home technologies in a living laboratory setting that allow for controlled observation. Because home automation technologies have yet to be widely adopted by home owners, few studies have been conducted thus far in technology-equipped, "in the wild" homes. In one example of such a study, Woodruff et al. [33] conducted a home-tour-based study, focusing on a specific user group of Orthodox Jewish families. Brush et al. [5] also conducted a study of automated homes which provided insights about barriers and opportunities for a more general user group of smart home users. In the our study add to this knowledge and expand the scope of research on home automation in-the-wild by considering the broader process involved in planning, building, and living with smart homes.

3   Study Method

We undertook a qualitative study involving three groups of participants to learn about the process of creating "smart homes", beginning in the spring of 2011. Our data was collected in two phases, the first of which focused on smart home professionals, and the second of which focused on inhabitants of smart homes and people in the process of building smart homes. This study design differs from previous studies on "smart homes" in that we strived to extend our understanding to the whole process of making a home "smart" including the planning stage of building or renovating a home. Our study comprised semi-structured interviews with a total of 22 participants (10 inhabitants in 7 households living in smart homes, 5 people in 3 households who were in the process of planning or building smart homes, and 7 professionals) and home tours of six of the inhabitants' homes. All but one of the inhabitant/planned inhabitant interviews were done in person, and all but two took place in the participants' homes. Interviews with smart-home professionals took place over the phone or on Skype (audio only). All interviews were conducted in German (the native language of the participant) except for one that was conducted in English (the common language of the participant and interviewer). All interviews were audio-recorded, and photographs were taken during home tours.

To analyze the data, we used a grounded theory-based affinity analysis [6]. We first transcribed approximately 1200 data items from the interview recordings, and translated them into English to facilitate collaborative data analysis within our international research group. The affinity diagramming process yielded a broad set of findings; this paper relates only a partial subset of these findings, namely those most related to the process of developing a smart home.

4   Participants and Households

Our motivation for studying smart home professionals was to learn how the commercial processes for smart home technology currently work. We wanted to learn whether professionals get feedback from their clients, what kind, and how they integrate it in order to develop new products, which trends they follow, and also to get an initial idea about their clients and the difficulties they face. In the first phase of our data collection we recruited seven professionals (6 male and 1 female, referred to by participant numbers prefixed **P** throughout this paper) from Germany, Switzerland, and Austria by contacting various companies via email. Four were system integrators for distributed bus system solutions, which provide functionality by connecting individually smart components (in this study the KNX[3] standard or proprietary Crestron[4] solutions); their job was to provide consulting for specific distributed bus system solutions and create custom solutions for clients. Two were CEOs of companies providing their own central solutions in which the functionality is handled by a central unit. One professional was employed at a large company which offers components for home automation. They did not receive any incentive beyond the opportunity to be acknowledged in this work. Interviews lasted between one and two hours and were audio recorded.

The second phase of data collection involved interviews with German and Swiss participants who are either current inhabitants of smart homes (*inhabitants*, referred to by participant numbers prefixed **I**) or in the process of planning smart homes (*planners*, prefixed **PL**). We define planners to be people who were in the process of building a home and researching home automation technology to be installed, either on their own or with the assistance of a company providing home automation technology. These interviews focused on the appeal of home automation, participants' understanding of smart homes, and the effects of the technology that they perceive or expect. In the interviews with planners we focused on their experiences with the planning and their expectations of the technology. For inhabitants we focused on the perceived effects of and experiences with the technology. Interviews with planners lasted between 45 and 90 minutes. Interviews in inhabitants' homes (all but I6, who was interviewed over the phone) lasted between two and a half and four hours, including home tours. Participants in this phase were recruited on online forums and social network groups about home building and home automation, and on two system providers' online forums. Additionally, three participants were recruited through references from the professionals interviewed. The participants received gift vouchers of CHF 15 (planners) and CHF 25 (inhabitants). It should be noted that the study participants do not constitute a representative sample of households with smart or automated home technology. In addition to the geographic restrictions of our study, our recruiting method may also place restrictions on the generalizability of our findings. For example, the fact that we recruited smart home inhabitants primarily through online forums may skew our population towards people who rely on and participate in online communities for smart home information and support.

---

[3] http://www.knx.org
[4] http://www.crestron.com

We attempted to recruit participants with a variety of technical expertise. Three of the households had little technical background represented; in the remaining six households the male adult participants had a background in information technology or electrical engineering while the females did not. Our participants came from a variety of occupational backgrounds with a large number coming from tech-related jobs. Occupations included a patent attorney, a banker, two software engineers, a CEO of a software company, two teachers, a tax accountant, a technician for building security, one unspecified part time job, a housewife, an art collector, and a project manager for usability. The participants' living situations are outlined in Table 1. Inhabitants had lived in automated homes for at least three years except for I1 and I6 who had lived in their new flats for six months. I1, I2 and I3 live in their homes together with children. All adult male household members were involved in the programming/configuring in their homes except for I7h, who outsourced or delegated all of the home automation tasks. In all cases, the introduction of automated home technology coincided with a major home renovation or a move into a newly built home, since installing a distributed bus system with independent components requires fundamental renovations unless the home was built with channels for the necessary additional wiring. Most households had a bus system installed in their homes or in combination with a central solution, except for I1, who used only a central solution for his home automation. The visited homes were all owned by the participants, and included two flats, three semi-detached homes, and two larger single-family homes. Because we recruited multiple participants from the same online communities in some cases, we have opted not to associate participants with their occupations as doing so may make them identifiable to other study participants who participate in the same forums. Instead, we provide context about participants' backgrounds when relating their perspectives or experiences as necessary.

Table 1. Participants of the second phase of our study (I(nhabitants), PL(anner), w(ife), h(usband))

Household	Participant (gender, age)	Living situation
I1	I1 (male, early 40s)	Flat, with girlfriend and two kids (15, 17)
I2	I2w (female, late 30s)	Semi-detached home, with two kids (10, 11)
	I2h (male, late 30s)	
I3	I3w (female, 35)	Semi-detached home, with two kids (7, 11)
	I3h (male, 37)	
I4	I4 (male, 51)	Single family home, with girlfriend
I5	I5 (female, 57)	Single family home, with husband
I6	I6 (male, 33)	Flat, with girlfriend
I7	I7w (female, 61)	Semi-detached home
	I7h (male, 61)	
PL1	PL1 (male, 38)	With girlfriend
PL2	PL2w (female, early 40s)	With three kids (5, 7, 9)
	PL2h (male, mid 40s)	
PL3	PL3w (female, late 30s)	
	PL3h (male, early 40s)	

As mentioned earlier, we limited the scope of smart homes to homes that made use of either commercial or custom solutions for home automation that are integrated into the home's infrastructure. All home automation systems included at least automated heating, light, or shades controlled by sensors or time settings. Some households had additional "smart" technologies (such as vacuum-cleaning robots or an independent automatic watering system) independent of the general infrastructure for home control. Every household had advanced climate control and/or feedback. Five households had remote access to some information about the home. Three households had functionalities based on presence detection. Five of the seven households had programmable "scenarios", meaning they were able to assign the execution of several tasks or functions to a dedicated switch or a button on an input panel.

5   The Understandings of "Smart"

Although we approached this study with a particular scope on "smart" homes, we also wanted to understand what our participants considered to be smart, clever, or intelligent about their homes without imposing our definition on them. We asked participants to share their ideas with us, inquiring about what they consider "smart", "clever", or "intelligent" in their homes in general without focusing explicitly on technical aspects of the home. We asked professionals the same question to gain insights into potential mismatches. It should be noted that participants generally did not refer to their homes as "smart homes"; rather, they described certain aspects, features, or functionalities of their homes as smart.

Smart Is What Fits My Routines and Avoids Unnecessary Work. A key theme that emerged was that participants considered "smart" to be that which fits, speeds up, or improves their routines while avoiding unnecessary work (I3h, I4, P7, PL3h). This understanding of "smart" is related to Brush et al.'s finding that one of inhabitants' favorite aspects of home automation is "convenience"[5], our finding does not specifically address home automation technologies but what is considered "smart" in a more general context. This includes also non-technological aspects, such as an appropriate spatial layout of the home (PL3h, PL3w, I3h). I3h: *"The door outside [makes the basement accessible from the garden] so you don't have to walk through the living room with rubber boots on. Absolutely non-technical, but smart in relation to our routines."* Another aspect of "smartness" was that technology, no matter how powerful, needs to fit into everyday life, as expressed by I2w: *"At first I was considering the one that wet-cleans [note: iRobot's Scooba®] because I thought it would be more useful on tile; but it doesn't have a docking station where it can recharge, so I would have to connect it every time, and, well, that's stupid."* In order to support routines in a "smart" fashion, participants felt that a home would need to be equipped with an extensive range of functionalities. They felt a home that was not fully equipped for automation or prepared for future additions of such equipment was restricted in terms of its functionality and potential benefit. (I3h, I6) I3h: *"It doesn't make a lot of sense in home automation to install one part conventionally and another part automated. It always depends on what you want, but a really intelligent or 'smart' home where you can represent scenarios... You really limit the whole house if you don't [fully equip it with the requirements for automation]."*

It's Not Smart If I Can Do It Better. Participants without technical backgrounds or a strong interest in technology reported they did not see a benefit to automation if they could still perform the same task faster or better manually (I1, I2w, I3w, PL3w). Merely being convenient was not sufficient for automation to be considered "smart". E.g., I3w: *"You [addressing her husband] always wanted to [automate] the shades over there, but I felt: 'No, I don't need that,' because I'd argue that I can still do it faster myself."* The stakeholders, including professionals, inhabitants, and planners, all agreed that technology itself is not smart, but applications of technology could be smart. They felt that adding the functionality and mapping functions to the different components was what resulted in instances of intelligence (I3h, I4, PL3w, P4, P6), as stated by P4: *"It actually only becomes smart if you give the thing its function."*

6   Motivations for Home Automation

One of our main goals was to explore people's reasons and motivations for equipping a home with substantial additional technology which requires investment and architectural planning. Our interviews revealed several key factors; households often cited several of them as motivations.

Modern Homes Are Smart Homes. One primary motivation people expressed in our study for getting smart homes was that they felt that a modern home should have the highly advanced technological infrastructure, even when their ideas about such infrastructure were vague. Although people in our study generally did not perceive home automation as having a major impact on their lives, they felt that one ought to consider the latest technology when building a new home (PL1, I5, P3, P7). This was the primary motivation for the two participants who outsourced the installation and programming of their homes, for example I5: *"And we also wanted a modern home; [therefore we wanted one] with technology."* We also discovered a similar attitude among planners, for example PL1, who stated: *"It's nothing you 100% need, but we're in 2011 and normal light switches like those from 40 years ago... it's always the same, nothing new."* This concurs with professionals' impressions of their clients' motivations, e.g, as expressed by P7: *"I never would have thought that they'd want such a solution [home automation], because they haven't even had a real internet connection until now... but it was pretty clear to them: they want a modern house."*

Experiencing Benefits Increases Interest in Upgrades. We found motivation to equip the home was sometimes self-perpetuating among the participants. Just as the act of eating can sometimes stimulate the appetite, participants thought more about what else they might automate, once they felt comfortable and trusted the automated functions in their homes (I1, I2h, I6, PL2, P4, P7). I1: *"At the beginning the control was limited to shutter control and to two lights and then I noticed: actually there are a couple of functions that would be interesting, e.g. that scene control, so that I can express with one single button click: 'I want to watch TV here' and the whole environment adapts itself to it."* Adding technology and functionality in the home seemed to have the effect of feeding the interest in building on such technologies.

Hacking the Home Is a Hobby. Participants with a technical background mentioned a strong general interest in novel technologies and smart-home functionalities. They likened investing time and money in these technologies to investing in any other hobby (PL2h, I1, I2h, I4, I6). As I2h put it: *"Instead of having a model railway I have this home."* Some not only spent money and substantial free time configuring their homes and adding new functionalities, but also engaged in related online communities, shared experiences, participated in interest group meetings, or attended talks on the subject. They mentioned that they enjoy doing things themselves and that their smart home "hobby projects" provide them with a sense of achievement (I1, I3h, I6). I1 said: *"I enjoy doing stuff myself. I prefer that, actually. Not necessarily because of the possibility of saving money, but just to find out: can I do it or can't I?"*

Smart Homes Save Energy. Another reason for investing in advanced building technologies that our participants reported was the desire to save energy (PL1, I3h, I4) I4: *"Saving energy in general is a reason why I decided to invest massively in insulation and so it's actually logical that you do it right and so, you need to think about electricity [consumption]."* Some participants explicitly mentioned the desire to save money and were concerned about whether the investment would pay off (PL2, P5, P7) PL2: *"Energy efficiency is one of our interests and you can discuss if it covers the cost of investment or if you get it back, but on the other hand you invest a lot of money in a home in general."* Although we will not focus on this specific motivation in the analysis presented in this paper, it was mentioned by several participants and will be considered in greater depth in future analyses.

7   Phases of Growing a Smart Home

We derived four key phases of developing a smart home based on our participants' reports of their experiences (see Figure 1) so as to provide a structured framework to present our results. Although we present these phases as a linear sequence, it should also be noted that certain events, such as a software update or addition of a new component (e.g. new sensors) can trigger the return to a previous stage in the cycle.

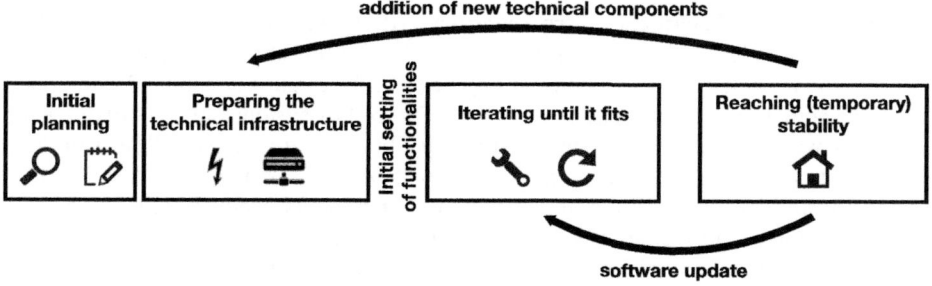

Fig. 1. Different stages of creating a "smart home"

Initial Planning. All inhabitants and planners (except for I2) equipped their homes with automation technologies when either building a new home or performing major renovations. This agrees with previous findings [5], and was confirmed as typical by the professionals we interviewed. In this phase home technology drivers talk to the electrician, and conduct research either online or by talking to professionals. Usually with the assistance of an electrician, architect, or consultant, but in some cases acting alone, they create and iterate upon complex technical installation plans. The duration of this phase varies; professionals stated that some people begin planning the electrical installation and home automation technologies even before purchasing the property, while other participants reported starting with their planning of the automation components just a few weeks before the actual installation in their homes. In some cases the planning phase was limited to the planning of the technical infrastructure for the home, while in other cases it extended to determining the eventual functionality and configuration of the home automation systems. Many participants spent a significant amount of time learning about specifics and the range of available technologies. In one case a participant planned out light, power supplies, and motion sensors along with the positions of the furniture in order to place components optimally and allow for extensive building automation (see Figure 2).

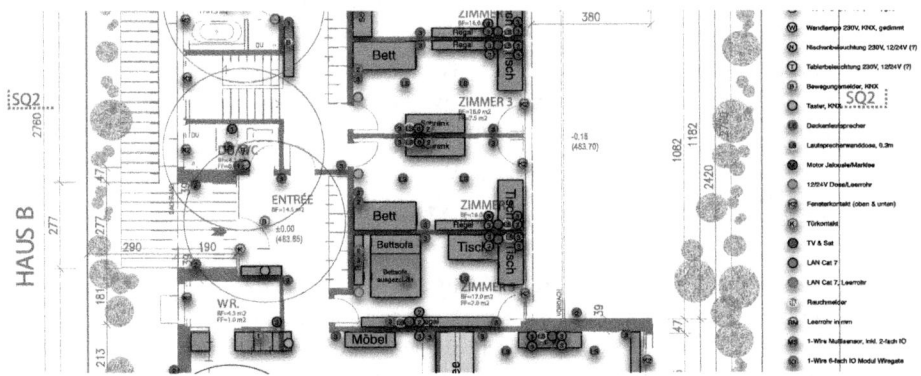

Fig. 2. Participant's document to plan furniture placement, lighting, power sockets, and home automation components. E.g. the circles on the left hand side highlight the areas covered by the motion sensors.

Preparing the Technical Infrastructure. After the needed infrastructure was planned out, electricians or, in the case of two households, inhabitants with a professional background in electrical engineering installed the technical components such as actuators, sensors, switches, and cables for bus systems, etc. As explained by P7, this was not only for reasons of difficulty but also for safety: *"The installation will always be done by electricians. For safety reasons ... it will always be better off with [professionals]."* When the technical components were installed, an initial configuration of the system was done. The duration of this phase depended on the size of the building and complexity of the automation technologies.

Iterating Until It Fits. Following the initial setup was a period of adjustment during which participants learned how the assigned functions fit with their lives and what did not work for them (I2h, I3h, I5, P5). This resulted in iterations of the system configuration. The necessity of iteration has also been reported by Brush et al. [5]. Several participants described this period as frustrating and chaotic, as reported by I3h: *"For me it's like an ongoing construction site. So it's normal that it's nonsense."* This phase often started with frequent changes to the configuration. Changes grew less frequent and as the functions, assignments, and visualizations gradually became better suited to the inhabitants' routines. I1 stated, *"In the beginning, until the shutters worked properly, until the light worked, I actually modified it on a daily basis and adjusted it and tried to get it running. Now that I have the basic functionality [working], the time [between modifications] is getting longer."* The changes became less substantial, indicating a shift from major adjustments to fine tuning, as described by I2h: *"The current visualization is the third version that I created. The first and second ones differed a lot, the second and third not so much."*

Reaching (Temporary) Stability. After the iteration, a period of stability was reached during which the active configuration of functionality stopped (I5, I6, P5). As I6 stated: *"But [the remapping] stopped. From the beginning until I assigned the final setting [...] it was a little chaotic."* This period of stability did not necessarily imply a state of satisfaction with the technology or optimized functionality. Particularly in households with enthusiasts who considered home automation a hobby, this state was temporary because they were still planning new functions or upgrades during these periods. In such cases, the homes soon entered a new cycle of iteration.

8   Roles of Inhabitants

One of the themes that arose repeatedly in our interviews was the variation of roles that household members assumed in relation to their smart homes; these roles appeared to apply to both inhabitants and planners, and reflected how people engaged in the planning, iteration, and use of smart home technology. The roles we describe in the following sections map roughly to the roles introduced by Poole et al. [23] in the home networking context and applied by Brush et al. [5] in the home automation context. We extend upon previous categorizations, deepening the understanding by providing specific characteristics and including the roles in the context of planning a "smart home".

Several participants had a strong technical background, in some cases on account of having done a degree or apprenticeship in a technical field. Such participants engaged actively in the planning phase and assumed primary responsibility for the technology once it was installed. We identified this group of people as **home technology drivers.** They showed a strong interest in equipping their homes with home automation technology and conducted research on the subject in their spare time, acquiring technology for their home and trying it out (I1, I2h, I3h, I4, I6, PL1, PL2h). Three participants engaged in home automation communities by contributing to online forums or attending meetings or talks (I3h, I4, PL2h). They often reported having many ideas for further technology additions to their homes as hobby projects (I1, I3h, I6, PL2h). I1 spoke of needing to manage these ideas, stating *"I have so many whims in my head, so I have to set priorities."* In our study we identified PL1, PL2h, I1, I2h, I3h, I4 and I6 as home technology drivers. They assume technical responsibility for systems while household members turn to them for system support

(I1, I2w, I3w, I4), as described by I2w: *"If something turns on or off or whatever, I simply notify him."*

In two of the households without members with technical backgrounds, some household members still assumed primary responsibility for the technology (I5, I7h, I7w). Although these **home technology responsibles** generally did not engage directly with the technology, they were the ones who were motivated to have the technology installed, and took responsibility for having the technology repaired or adjusted by professionals as needed. In contrast with the role of "assisters" introduced by Poole et al. [23], home technology responsibles in our study did not assist others in their household by taking care of issues or extensions of their home automation.

Most other adult members of the households fell into the category of **passive users**. These participants (PL2w, PL3w, Pl3h, I2w, I3w) did not actively engage in home automation research, planning, configuration, or maintenance, but had some familiarity with the systems and controls through use. They generally left the details of planning and maintenance to the home technology drivers. E.g., PL1 described the decision-making dynamic with his wife regarding the technology planning: *"For those things my wife says: you can decide and then we will see."* In our study several passive users (I2w, I3w, PL2w) were the wives of (male) home technology drivers, though our sample is not large enough to say whether these gender roles generalize to smart-home households in general. Passive users made use of the automation but were generally not interested in adding to its features or actively using it to its full extent, as indicated by I2h and I2w: *Interviewer: "Can you access your home with your phone?" I2w: "Not with mine." I2h: "Yes, you can." I2w: "Yes, but right now I couldn't, because it's not on there." I2h: "Technically you could, but you were never interested in that, in wanting that."* In many cases, however, passive users spend more time at home than the home technology drivers, which made them astute evaluators of the technology (I2w, I3h, I3w, I4). I3w:, *"Technology is mainly his topic. I wait for what he shows me and then I say 'that's good' or 'that's not good.'"*

We did not interview further inhabitants or users directly, but participants referred to other groups of people who were affected by the technology, namely children and guests. Some participants (I1, I2, I3, P2, P7) noted how **children** generally become accustomed to technology easily, as illustrated by an anecdote from I3 in which they talked about how their daughter attempted to turn on the lights by waving her arms while on vacation. I1 talked about how their children were comfortable with the technology and enjoyed playing with the shades using the tablet to control them.

People in our study also expressed the desire to make their homes accessible to **guests** (I1, I2h, I4, I6) but stated that unfamiliar home technology can pose problems for visitors. They pointed out elderly visitors in particular as having potential difficulties with smart technologies: *"If my mother had to start with that [using a touch panel to turn on the light]... well, she can't even remember where she was an hour ago; but she grew up knowing that you have to press [a physical switch]."* As first time users of the technology, guests may be afraid of breaking something in the home, as in the case of I2h: *"In the laundry room [a guest] turned on the [loud vent used for drying clothes] instead of the light and when we got home, we said: 'Why is it running?' and then our guest said he wanted to turn on the light, but he didn't press anything, so he also didn't turn it off again. [He] simply [thought]: I won't touch anything anymore at all."*

9   Discussion

The process of getting and using smart home technology yielded interesting challenges and effects that varied in impact. Especially interesting was the fact that the process of planning, integrating, and iterating upon the technology seemed to have a more notable impact on people's lives than the use of the technology itself once installed and working.

Even Full Automation of Control Is Not a Game Changer. Surprisingly, despite the cost and effort of instrumenting the home with automation technology, participants pointed out very few direct benefits they derived from the technology or major impacts on their lives or practices. Although some inhabitants (I1, I3, I6) replaced existing manual control of light or shades completely either with control via central touch panel or motion sensors, they still described the effects of the technology as small conveniences rather than substantial support for routines or tasks. People perceived it rather as enhancing their comfort level, but also pointed out that the technology was limited in the help it could provide. PL2w explained the distinction: *"You try to make work a little easier with modern technology. But I still have to do my laundry myself. A laundry chute is there; it carries it in one direction, but besides that..."* Other participants, including professionals, believed that technology does not enable new functions, but incrementally improves what one can already do, as stated by P2: *"It's not like you have a rocket engine in the basement or anything like that. It's comparable to what you had before – just a little smarter and cooler."*

The Challenge of Planning for Unfamiliar Technology. It is often difficult to predict what the impact of a new technology will be on one's life or practices; in the case of smart home technology the stakes are particularly high because of the investment involved and the fact that one is not merely purchasing a gadget, but instrumenting one's entire environment. Information about home automation technologies, such as that found on websites, brochures, or manuals, often offers technical details but is less informative about its potential effects on everyday life. At the start of the planning phase, participants reported not understanding potential benefits of technologies (I1, I2h, I3, PL2w) and therefore had difficulties prioritizing those technologies against other needs in the home. Brush et al. found smart home inhabitants "scaling back" installed technologies if they did not provide the expected functionality [5]. We found this pattern as well in our data, but we also found that people were concerned about not being able to anticipate future needs and tried to plan flexible solutions that would allow adding functionality in the future. More specifically, participants without technical backgrounds reported having to rely upon other people's experiences and expertise, and therefore feeling powerless. I5 related a particular incident in which a switchbox installed by electricians proved to be too small, leading to frustration on her part. However, she felt that she could not have prevented the error, as she did not have technical expertise and therefore had to go along with the decisions of the electricians. Passive users seemed to be skeptical about the general use of home automation technology, as highlighted by PL2w's statement: *"It offers many options, but it's really very complex. The question is: do you really need this?"* They relied on other people's experiences regarding the usefulness of a solution (I2w, I2h, I7). I2: *"We learned from* *our neighbor's experience regarding the vacuum cleaner [iRobot's Roomba®], and he said it's an amazing device. And that's why we bought it."* Although they did not participate actively in research or planning, they offered input on other decisions that influenced home automation, especially regarding budget decisions as stated by I3w: *"He came to ask when..." I3h: "...for budget planning." [both start laughing] I3w: "Yes, exactly. But besides that – not at all."* Professionals offered another perspective on the challenges of planning. They reported that customers have difficulties understanding the available technology and options (P1, P2, P4, P5). P2 said: *"It just doesn't make sense to people ... [that] they need power line switches if they [just] want to have access with their smart phone. They don't see the connection."* P7 illustrated this challenge by contrasting smart homes with more familiar technologies: *"The whole issue of home automation is still so remote. For cars, everyone knows what's possible."*

The Challenge of Getting High-Level Expert Advice. Participants also reported frustration over being unable to access authoritative and expert advice for high-level decision-making, despite the existence of experts. Professional system integrators (i.e. home automation experts) typically only provided information on the systems that they offered, and other types of home experts, such as electricians and architects, were rarely able or willing to provide information about home automation technology (PL2w, I2w, I2h, I5, P5, P7). I2: *"That was actually the biggest challenge: from whom do I get information about what I really can do, which elements I can buy or use that have what I want...?"* Participants felt they needed an overview of available products in order to identify their needs and choose the right product or combination of products, as stated by I1: *"There was something that I was looking for, but couldn't find... a website that is comprehensive, including all manufacturers, that is unbiased... that presents the various systems, comparing them, showing their advantages and disadvantages. That would have been genius."*

The Tension between Comfort and Control. Although our participants felt that automation resulted in a gain in comfort for some aspects of the home, they also perceived a loss of control with increased automation. I4 talked about the override functions he had created for the home, and PL2w said she feared becoming "a prisoner of the system." Also I2w expressed frustration with automated functionalities *"It bothers me when it turns on the light ten times and I actually don't need it."* Most home technology drivers (I1, I2h, I3h, I5, PL1) expressed indifference to some of the negative effects or constraints resulting from home automation, as illustrated by I3's statement: *"If that happens once or twice a month [the light turning off unexpectedly], then it's at a relative low priority for the 'construction site' [our home]."* Or I2h: *"I just accept that the shades are down and then I just go to the door to look outside."* The difference in roles and responsibilities in smart homes led to issues of control, such as in one example in which a technology driver (I6h) reconfigured the home in a way that made certain functions unusable to passive users: *"She wanted to turn on the light and then the switch was for the other light because I reassigned it, and then the shutters rolled up on one day, and on another it was a light switch again."*

Experimenting and Testing. Home technology drivers often considered the installation and iterating to be hobby, as illustrated by I4's comment: *"In summer I work outside [in the garden] and in the winter it's the visualization and the device* *automation."* Adult passive users often acted as evaluators (I2w, I3h, I3w, I4, I5) for the drivers' "experiments". *Interviewer: "What turned out to be useless?" I2h: "The motion sensor in the restroom. You [addressing his wife] said: 'No, I don't want that, there needs to be a switch again.' So I added the switch again."* They tended to think about the technology in terms of how it supported their routines and tasks, as exemplified by I3w: *"So when you come home on a winter evening and you've got your hands full of stuff, you open the door but you still have stuff in your hands. So I wanted [the light to turn on automatically] without having to look for the switch."* Technology drivers, in comparison, emphasized the process and implementation. As I1 put it: *"It's not really about [using the technology], but the realization... building this apartment; planning everything, then building it, then making it work. And once everything is done... it's nice to be here, but then new thoughts start: what else could you do?"* Parameterizing, adding new functions, and making it work are perceived as rewarding experiences that provide a sense of achievement, reported explicitly by several of our participants (I1, I4, I6). These findings echo those of previous research that explores the sense of achievement in DIY and repair projects [7, 22].

10   Avenues for Smart Home Research

Our study has uncovered many of the tensions, challenges, and benefits involved in the process of integrating smart home technology into a household. By considering the process in a holistic fashion, we have also identified what we believe to be open areas for smart home research that warrant further exploration.

Design for All Phases. Much research on smart homes has focused on providing configuration tools for smart homes, ranging from complex programming environments to simple visual programming tools. These tools are most applicable after all of the necessary technology has been installed and integrated. However, our research has revealed that people need support not only in deciding how to configure their technology, but also in deciding what technology they will need. This phase of planning for a smart home is critical, but support for it is currently fairly minimal. We believe that there are important opportunities for research to support this phase, in terms of presenting people with information about potential technologies, to inform them about their options and help them to make the best decisions to suit their needs. Similar support might also be valuable in the iteration phase, during which households are trying to optimize installed solutions. Informing inhabitants of the outcome of choices and allowing them to explore options more easily might help to streamline this process, help people to get the most out of the technology, and alleviate the frustrations that people experience with technologies that do not fit well with their lives or that do not work as expected. In architectural planning some dynamic aspects of buildings can be simulated already, such as effects of sunlight or lighting on visual appearances. There are also new ways to plan buildings, such as tools that support building-information modeling[5] and methods to predict building performances in office buildings [15], but usually they are primarily oriented towards experts and not future inhabitants. People in our study considered technologies to be

---

[5] http://usa.autodesk.com/building-information-modeling/

"smart" if they fit their routines and avoid unnecessary work. Thus, early support for the planning process could happen by offering visualizations of current domestic routines, e.g., through collected behavior patterns via sensor data, presenting it to the inhabitants in combination with available automation technology options that can facilitate those routines. While automation experts or consultants are also able to provide support due to their experience with the effects of home automation, we found that our participants had problems getting high-level expert advice.

Supporting Hackers and the Hacking Process. One emerging finding of this study was that the "hacking" of the home was both a primary motivation for installing smart home technology and a perceived major benefit for some household members. Some home technology drivers seemed to want to program the technology as much as they wanted to make use of it. One important direction of smart home research thus far has focused on simplifying the configuration and administration of home technology to make it universally accessible and eliminate the need for "system administrator" knowledge. We agree that this is an important direction to pursue. But our findings also suggest that there may be an important open research direction on providing support to those who want to engage with the technical infrastructure by hacking the home. Providing appropriate tools would not only support the hobby aspect of smart homes but also facilitate experimentation, innovation, and possibly solutions better fitted to the needs of individual households. Although existing products, such as the Arduino[6] prototyping platform and LilyPad[8] support hardware hacking, this avenue of research still presents design challenges in terms of how to support the hacking process specifically within the context of homes. Dixon et al. approach facilitating software prototyping in automated homes by suggesting a common operating system for homes [12] that could help to overcome the problem of sharing source code within the hacking communities across very heterogeneous installations. But as we further identified problems that especially concern other household members, indirect support of the hacking process could include minimizing inconvenience for effected persons, avoiding disruption of their existing routines, and communicating process information to them, e.g., by providing cues about whether the house is currently in a "testing mode" and that it might behave unexpectedly rather than allowing a chance that they might doubt own actions and lose trust in the reactions of their own home.

Exploring Support for Passive Users. Although the passive users in our participant households did not engage directly in the planning or configuration of home automation technology, we found that their needs and practices still had an influence on its design and use. The passive users were asked to give approval for certain decisions and provided feedback towards optimizing the configuration of technologies to suit the household. Although they wanted to give others in the household freedom to "hack", it was apparent that they still had some investment in ensuring that the technologies worked as expected and needed. We therefore feel that there is an important open avenue of research to be explored on how other members of the household can shape and influence the technologies without investing significant time or effort, and possibly while avoiding the need for direct interaction with the system. For example, it may be worthwhile to consider how household members can provide

---

[6] http://www.arduino.cc

feedback to systems or to technology drivers in novel and implicit ways, or perhaps ways to support a more collaborative evolution of the home technology.

By taking a broad approach to studying real-world manifestations of smart home technology, we have uncovered practices and implications that go beyond the interactions of technology enthusiasts with home technology to include a variety of stakeholders and extended process of planning and development. In addition to shedding light on the impacts of these technologies on homes and everyday life, we believe they point to important new areas for the research community to explore.

Acknowledgements. We would like to thank Gunnar Harboe, Christian Remy, Frank Bentley, and Khai Truong for their help on this paper. Thanks to Peter Sperlich for interesting insights. Special thanks to Loxone, nomos system, geSys, myHomeAutomation.de, Zenon Schymiczek, and all other participants for their time and effort.

References

1. Aipperspach, R., Hooker, B., Woodruff, A.: The heterogeneous home. In: Ubicomp (2008)
2. Ben Allouch, S., van Dijk, J.A.G.M., Peters, O.: The Acceptance of Domestic Ambient Intelligence Appliances by Prospective Users. In: Tokuda, H., Beigl, M., Friday, A., Brush, A.J.B., Tobe, Y. (eds.) Pervasive 2009. LNCS, vol. 5538, pp. 77–94. Springer, Heidelberg (2009)
3. Ballegaard, S.A., Bunde-Pedersen, J., Bardram, J.E.: Where to, Roberta?: reflecting on the role of technology in assisted living. In: NordiCHI (2006)
4. Bell, G., Kaye, J.: Designing Technology for Domestic Spaces: A Kitchen Manifesto. Gastronomica 2(2), 46–62 (2002)
5. Bernheim Brush, A.J., Lee, B., Mahajan, R., Agarwal, S., Saroiu, S., Dixon, C.: Home automation in the wild: challenges and opportunities. In: ACM CHI (2011)
6. Beyer, H., Holtzblatt, K.: Contextual Design: Defining Customer-Centered Systems. Morgan Kaufmann Publishers Inc., San Francisco (1997)
7. Buechley, L., Paulos, E., Rosner, D., Williams, A. (eds.): DIY for CHI: Methods, Communities, and Values of Reuse and Customization. Workshop held at ACM CHI (2009)
8. Buechley, L., Eisenberg, M., Catchen, J., Crockett, A.: The LilyPad Arduino: Using Computational Textiles to Investigate Engagement, Aesthetics, and Diversity in Computer Science Education. In: ACM CHI (2008)
9. Chetty, M., Sung, J.-Y., Grinter, R.E.: How Smart Homes Learn: The Evolution of the Networked Home and Household. In: Krumm, J., Abowd, G.D., Seneviratne, A., Strang, T. (eds.) UbiComp 2007. LNCS, vol. 4717, pp. 127–144. Springer, Heidelberg (2007)
10. Crabtree, A., Rodden, T.: Domestic Routines and Design for the Home. In: CSCW (2004)
11. Davidoff, S., Lee, M.K., Yiu, C., Zimmerman, J., Dey, A.K.: Principles of Smart Home Control. In: Dourish, P., Friday, A. (eds.) UbiComp 2006. LNCS, vol. 4206, pp. 19–34. Springer, Heidelberg (2006)
12. Dixon, C., Mahajan, R., Agarwal, S., Brush, A.J., Lee, B., Saroiu, S., Bahl, V.: The home needs an operating system (and an app store). In: HotNets (2010)
13. Edwards, W., Grinter, R.: At Home with Ubiquitous Computing: Seven Challenges. In: Abowd, G.D., Brumitt, B., Shafer, S. (eds.) UbiComp 2001. LNCS, vol. 2201, pp. 256–272. Springer, Heidelberg (2001)

14. Elliot, K., Neustaedter, C., Greenberg, S.: Time, Ownership and Awareness: The Value of Contextual Locations in the Home. In: Beigl, M., Intille, S.S., Rekimoto, J., Tokuda, H. (eds.) UbiComp 2005. LNCS, vol. 3660, pp. 251–268. Springer, Heidelberg (2005)
15. Goldstein, R., Tessier, A., Khan, A.: Customizing the Behavior of Interacting Occupants using Personas. In: SimBuild (2010)
16. Greenberg, S., Neustaedter, C., Elliot, K.: Awareness in the Home: The Nuances of Relationships, Domestic Coordination and Communication. Awareness Systems (2009)
17. Hughes, J.A., O'Brien, J., Rodden, T., Rouncefield, M., Viller, S.: Patterns of Home Life: Informing Design For Domestic Environments. In: Personal and Ubiquitous Computing (2000)
18. Humble, J., Crabtree, A., Hemmings, T., Åkesson, K.-P., Koleva, B., Rodden, T., Hansson, P.: "Playing with the Bits" User-Configuration of Ubiquitous Domestic Environments. In: Dey, A.K., Schmidt, A., McCarthy, J.F. (eds.) UbiComp 2003. LNCS, vol. 2864, pp. 256–263. Springer, Heidelberg (2003)
19. Intille, S.S.: Designing a home of the future. In: Pervasive Comp. (April-June 2002)
20. Kane, S.K., Wobbrock, J.O., Ladner, R.E.: Usable gestures for blind people: Understanding preference and performance. In: ACM CHI (2011)
21. Kientz, J., Patel, S., Jones, B., Price, E., Mynatt, E., Abowd, A.: The Georgia Tech Aware Home. In: ACM CHI Extended Abstracts (2008)
22. Maestri, L., Wakkary, R.: Understanding repair as a creative process of everyday design. In: C&C (2011)
23. Poole, E.S., Chetty, M., Grinter, R.E., Edwards, W.K.: More than meets the eye: transforming the user experience of home network management. In: DIS (2008)
24. Randall, D.: Living Inside a Smart Home: A Case Study. In: Harper, R. (ed.) Insidethe Smart Home. Springer, London (2003)
25. Röcker, C., Janse, M., Portolan, N., Streitz, N.A.: User Requirements for Intelligent Home Environments: A Scenario-Driven Approach and Empirical Cross-Cultural Study. In: ACM sOc-EUSAI 2005 (2005)
26. Rodden, T., Crabtree, A., Hemmings, T., Koleva, B., Humble, J., Åkesson, K.-P., Hansson, P.: Configuring the Ubiquitous Home. In: Proceedings of Designing Cooperative Systems (2004)
27. Rode, J.A., Toye, E.F., Blackwell, A.F.: The domestic economy: a broader unit of analysis for end user programming. In: ACM CHI Extended Abstracts (2005)
28. Rode, J.A., Toye, E.F., Blackwell, A.F.: The fuzzy felt ethnography-understanding the programming patterns of domestic appliances. In: Personal and Ubiquitous Computing (2004)
29. Taylor, A.S., Harper, R., Swan, L., Izadi, S., Sellen, A., Perry, M.: Homes that make us smart. In: Personal and Ubiquitous Computing (2006)
30. Tolmie, P., Pycock, J., Diggins, T., MacLean, A., Karsenty, A.: Towards the Unremarkable Computer: Making Technology at Home in Domestic Routines. In: Harper, R. (ed.) Inside the Smart Home, Springer, London (2003)
31. Truong, K.N., Huang, E.M., Abowd, G.D.: CAMP: A Magnetic Poetry Interface for End-User Programming of Capture Applications for the Home. In: Davies, N., Mynatt, E.D., Siio, I. (eds.) UbiComp 2004. LNCS, vol. 3205, pp. 143–160. Springer, Heidelberg (2004)
32. Wilkowska, W., Ziefle, M.: User diversity as a challenge for the integration of medical technology into future home environments. In: Human-Centred Design of eHealth Technologies (2011)
33. Woodruff, A., Augustin, S., Foucault, B.: Sabbath Day Home Automation: It's Like Mixing Technology and Religion. In: ACM CHI (2007)

The Design of a Segway AR-Tactile Navigation System

Ming Li, Lars Mahnkopf, and Leif Kobbelt

Computer Graphics Group
RWTH Aachen University
Aachen, Germany
http://www.graphics.rwth-aachen.de

Abstract. A Segway is often used to transport a user across mid range distances in urban environments. It has more degrees of freedom than car/bike and is faster than pedestrian. However a navigation system designed for it has not been researched. The existing navigation systems are adapted for car drivers or pedestrians. Using such systems on the Segway can increase the driver's cognitive workload and generate safety risks. In this paper, we present a Segway AR-Tactile navigation system, in which we visualize the route through an Augmented Reality interface displayed by a mobile phone. The turning instructions are presented to the driver via vibro-tactile actuators attached to the handlebar. Multiple vibro-tactile patterns provide navigation instructions. We evaluate the system in real traffic and an artificial environment. Our results show the AR interface reduces users' subjective workload significantly. The vibro-tactile patterns can be perceived correctly and greatly improve the driving performance.

Keywords: Segway, Navigation, Augmented Reality, Vibro-Tactile, Feedback modalities, Real Traffic, Evaluation.

1 Introduction

The Segway Personal Transporter is a two wheeled, self balancing vehicle which can transport the user across mid range distances in urban environments (indoor and outdoor). Due to its mobility and compact size, it is widely used in city touring, airport, security patrol, theme park, gaming, etc. By 2010, it was estimated that 80,000 Segways were in use worldwide [4].

To use the Segway in an unfamiliar terrain, it would be very helpful to have a navigation system to guide the user to the destination, e.g. in a city guide scenario a user drives a Segway in a foreign city. However, the navigation system adapted to the Segway has not been investigated yet. The existing systems are designed for car drivers, pedestrians, and bicycle riders, using visual, auditory or tactile information. The traditional commercial in-vehicle navigation system (TVN) is not suitable for the Segway. Normally the route is presented via a 2D Map View (in orthogonal or perspective view, see Fig. 1(a)) and turn-by-turn audio instructions. When using a navigation system on the Segway, the interactive

J. Kay et al. (Eds.): Pervasive 2012, LNCS 7319, pp. 161–178, 2012.

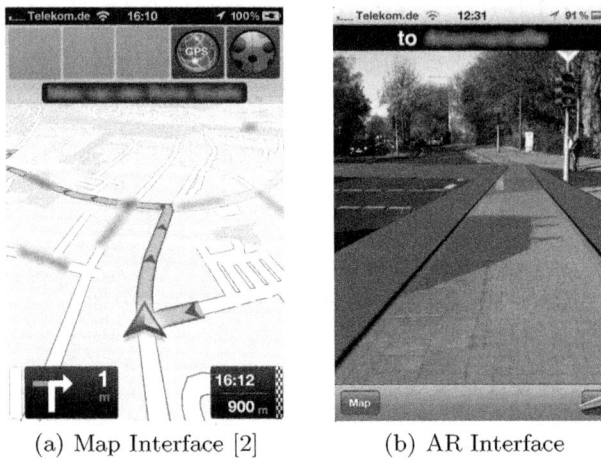

(a) Map Interface [2]   (b) AR Interface

Fig. 1. Navigation Interfaces

task can be classified into primary task (observing traffic and controlling the Segway) and the secondary task (interacting with the navigation information). Unlike car drivers, the listening condition of the Segway drivers is greatly influenced by the surrounding environment. Ambient noise, from wind and traffic, seriously affects the perception of audio instructions. Using a headphone/earplug could improve the auditory perception, but the driver loses the environment awareness which could result in potential accidents and it is prohibited by the law in most countries. The 2D Map View, as an abstract representation of the environment, requires the driver to mentally project the route into the real world, which visually distracts the driver from the primary task and also increases the cognitive workload [16,12]. Therefore the driver has to concentrate visually and auditorily more on the secondary task than the primary task. Since the driver has a limited information processing capacity, that would decrease his/her ability to complete the primary task [19].

In addition, the turning instructions of a navigation system needs to give the driver enough time for perceiving and interpreting. In TVN, the amount of time is customized for vehicles but not for the Segway. For example, if we assume a car moves with 50 km/h, a distance of 50 meters corresponds to 3.6 seconds. Assuming that an audio instruction takes 2 to 3 seconds, a turning instruction in a distance of 50 meters is too late. While for the Segway, since the maximum speed is limited to 20km/h, 50 meters takes about 9 seconds which is still enough for the reaction.

Pedestrian navigation systems are not suitable for the Segway either, because the map resource is collected for walking purpose, e.g. the road network includes staircases, one-way streets and pedestrian zones, where either a Segway can not access or the use of a Segway is forbidden.

Compared to the bicycle, the user experience is different when driving a Segway. It requires less physical effort to drive the Segway and the maximum speed is limited to 20 km/h. Furthermore, the Segway is more agile than the bicycle, e.g. it can rotate 180 degrees in place and it can move backward freely. Due to these differences, the existing research results for bicycle navigation can not be directly applied to the Segway.

In this paper we propose a GPS based Augmented Reality vibro-tactile navigation system for the Segway, which displays the route information in a graphical overlay to the real-world camera input during Segway driving. From the previous researches, the AR View enables drivers to keep high visual attention on the road [12]. Our goal is to investigate whether the same results also apply for the configuration we find on the Segway. We expect the AR view will generate less cognitive complexity than the 2D Map View. In order to further reduce the influence of the navigation task to the primary driving task, we migrate the turning instructions to the tactile channel instead of using the auditory channel, because the vibro-tactile is independent from ambient noise. Multiple turning instructions are encoded in vibro-patterns to deliver direction and distance information. The contribution of the paper is to explore the impact of AR navigation and vibro-tactile turning instructions on users' cognitive workload, preference and driving performance. A TVN is included in our experiment as a baseline for comparison, see Fig. 1(a). We conduct the user study in real traffic in order to get the actual driving experience, e.g. whether the vibration from the bumpy roads and the Segway itself affects the perception of vibro-tactile patterns. We propose two hypotheses.

1. Compared with the 2D-Map navigation interface in TVN, AR interface can reduce users' subjective workload.
2. The vibro-tactile turning instructions can be perceived by drivers clearly, and it improves their driving performance.

To support these hypotheses we design two user studies. The first one is an on-road test-drive to collect users' subjective rating about navigation system variants. The second study is a lane switching test in an artificial environment to measure users' reaction time for controlling the Segway when receiving audio or tactile instructions.

2   Related Work

Jensen et al. [9] presented a study on the impact of different GPS based navigation systems to the car driving behavior and performance. They evaluated the audio, visual and audio-visual output of the navigation in real traffic. Their result showed that using the audio feedback could reduce the amount of eye-glances on the display and improved the driving performance. However, in the scenario of Segway driving, users' perception of the audio feedback is affected by the ambient noise. In our paper, a usability study of the audio feedback for the Segway navigation is done.

Previous work from Medenica et al. [12] indicated that AR navigation introduced less negative impact on car driving than traditional map navigation. In their work, the AR route is displayed on the windshield with a head-up display, which improved the driving safety and reduced the user's reaction time compared to the traditional in-car head-down display. However, the same configuration is not possible for a Segway. How to configure the AR display for the Segway driver and whether users prefer the AR display in this way need to be investigated. Wikitude Drive [3] is the first commercially available AR navigation system, but it is still designed for in-vehicle use and uses audio instructions. We are not aware of any evaluation comparing Wikitude Drive to TVN.

Some researchers proposed vibro-tactile displays for automobile navigation, where vibrators were integrated in the seat to deliver navigation instructions ([7], [6]). The results showed that the tactile navigation can improve the driving performance and reduce the cognitive work load. However such configuration is not practical for a Segway, since the Segway driver has to stand while driving. The contacting location with the Segway are only hands and feet. To exploring other vibro-tactile locations in vehicles, Kern et al. [10] embedded the vibro-tactile feedback into the steering wheel to give navigation instructions. Their results showed that the vibration patterns were ambiguous to users, since the vibration location on the wheel was hard to distinguish. Furthermore, the driver had to hold a certain area of the wheel to receive the tactile feedback, which could be uncomfortable due to different driving habits and situations. Unlike the steering wheel, the Segway driver always holds the grips while driving the Segway, so it is ideal to attach the actuators there. However, the proper vibration patterns, like strength, frequency, duration and users' acceptance, still need to be investigated. Boll et al. [5] introduced a vibro-tactile waist belt for the in-vehicle turn-by-turn navigation to reduce the driver's cognitive load. They presented a series of vibro-tactile patterns for turning instructions, where the number of repetition of discrete pulses corresponded to distance indicators. However, for the Segway driver the counting of pulses introduces extra mental workload which could reduce the driving performance. Additionally since the Segway speed is much slower than an automobile, it is unnecessary to present distance indicators beyond 100 meters (which takes 18 seconds at 20km/h speed).

Pedestrian navigation using tactile feedback for turning instruction has been investigated as well. Pielot et al. [13] proposed a PocketNavigator which encoded turning instructions in vibration patterns. Srikulwong and O'Neill [17] suggested different vibration patterns to represent landmarks on a wearable device. Ross and Blasch [15] presented a shoulder-tapping wearable interface for pedestrian navigation. However, in the Segway scenario the perception of vibro-tactile patterns could be affected by the vibration induced by the bumpy road condition and the engine. The existing configurations and results of the pedestrian vibro-tactile navigation can not be directly applied to the Segway.

Poppinga et al. [14] introduced a tactile display as an orientation aids for the bicycle touring on a touristic island. They integrated two vibration actuators to the handlebars to indicate coarse direction information and announce points of interest. For an open area exploring tour, the cycling is more like leisure and fun. The requirements for the navigation efficiency are much lower than for in-city navigation, where we have dense street networks, environment pressure and traffic rules to obey. The orientation aids are not sufficient for a city navigation scenario. Additionally, the driving experience of the bicycle is different from the Segway, e.g. engine noise, standing pose, etc., the proper vibro-tactile patterns need to be found out.

3   Design and Prototype

There are several benefits from using AR display in navigation. The route information is immersed into the real world. It's unnecessary for the driver to mentally project the route from the 2D map into the environment. The driving performance therefore can be improved [12]. Moreover, the video-see-through display does not block the driver's view. When the driver glances at the display, he is not detached from the traffic. In addition, by using AR display extra information can be overlaid in another layer, which would be useful for scenarios like a city tour guide.

To avoid the influence of the ambient noise, we propose using the vibro-tactile feedback instead of using the audio feedback for turning instructions, which is similar to a shoulder-tapping system [15]. The turning instruction is delivered to the driver via the actuators mounted on the corresponding grip of the Segway. Different vibro-patterns are used to represent distance and direction hints.

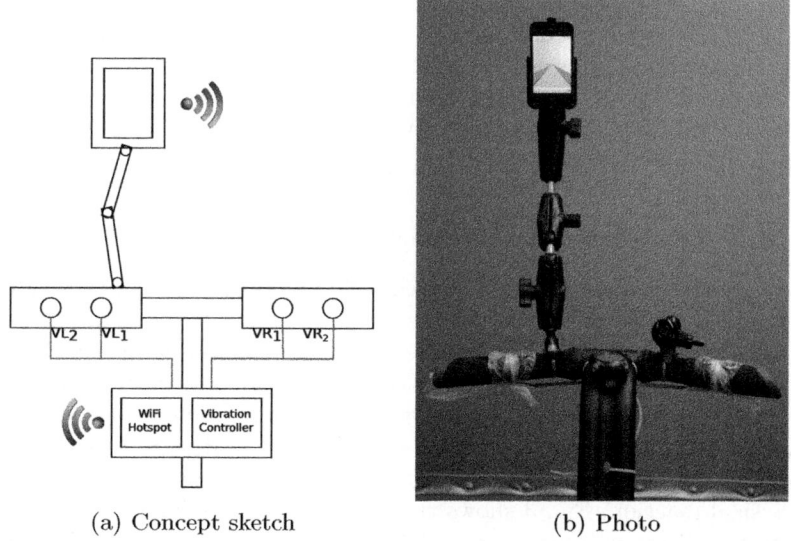

(a) Concept sketch   (b) Photo

Fig. 2. System configuration on the Segway handlebar. The mobile device displays the AR-View and sends turning instructions to the vibration controller via WLAN. Then the controller triggers the corresponding vibro-patterns.

We have implemented a prototype of our navigation system on the iOS platform. An iPhone4 is mounted on the Segway handlebar by adjustable arms. The height of the display is adjusted to the driver's eye level. Since we use the integrated camera of iPhone4, to have a better perspective view of the camera input, the back-facing camera needs to point to the heading direction. In the beginning of our design, we considered using different display devices, e.g. Head Mounted Display (HMD). But so far it has not been allowed by the traffic regulations to wear such an equipment while driving in the street, so we did not use the HMD in the current prototype.

On each grip we attach two vibrators [1] which are controlled by an Arduino Uno prototype board. The iPhone4 sends turning signals to Arduino via a stackable Wi-Fi module, see Fig. 2(a), 2(b). To absorb the shock from the Segway, we put a piece of sponge between the vibrator and the grip. For a better receiving of vibration signals, we compared the tactile perception on palm and finger tips, and found out the finger tips were more sensitive. Therefore, we attach the vibrators to the position of the grip under finger tips.

3.1 Navigation Graphical Interface

In the AR interface, we have a video layer and a graphical layer, see Fig 1(b). The user selects the starting point and the destination from a standard map view. Then a corresponding route is fetched from google map, which is a set of waypoints indicating geolocations (latitude, longitude and elevation). From these geolocations, a 3D representation of the route is created and rendered in the graphical layer. The color of the route is adjusted to increase the contrast. Furthermore the transparency of the route polygons is adjusted to avoid occluding on-ground traffic signs. To reduce the route complexity to the driver, only a certain range of the route is displayed. Additionally, when the user gets close to the next turning point, an arrow pointing to the correct turning direction will show as a turn-by-turn visual hint. When the driver goes to a wrong direction or reaches the destination a corresponding sign will appear.

3.2 Turning Instruction Feedback

We provide two turning instruction feedback, audio and vibro-tactile. The driver can choose the feedback type. Here we only explain the design of the vibro-patterns. Erp [8] suggested magnitude, frequency, temporal and location as primary parameters of tactile information coding. We can adjust the vibration temporal patterns and location patterns, while the frequency and magnitude are not applicable with the actuators we have used. The design of patterns should not conflict with the traditional navigation information and could be mapped to the physical reaction. Fig. 3 shows the 5 vibro-patterns. The temporal patterns indicate the distance information. Discrete pulses (felt less intensive) mean an event in distance. While a continuous vibration (felt more intensive) represents an event is very close. The location patterns describe the direction information. The vibration on the left (or right) grip means turning to that direction. The vibration on both sides corresponds to the destination instructions. A vibration interleaved on left-right grips for multiple times indicates a wrong heading direction.

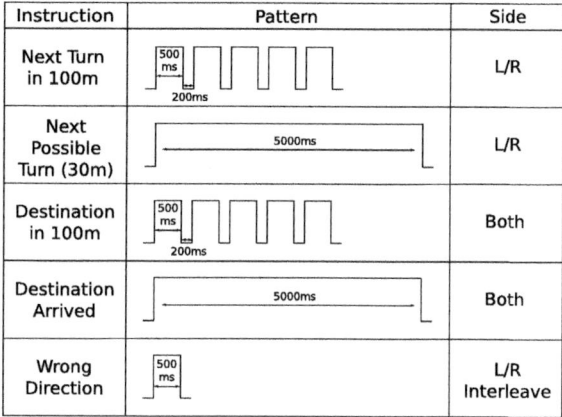

Fig. 3. Vibration patterns of navigation instructions

In our initial studies, we compared continuous versus discrete vibrations, as proposed by [5], where the number of pulses indicated the distance (1: Turn-now, 2: Near, 3: Far and 4: Very-far). The users felt that the pulse counting even required more concentration on the tactile channel while driving the Segway, which was not preferred by users. Especially due to the Segway speed is much slower than the car speed, it is unnecessary to give an instruction beyond 100 meters, which takes 18 seconds in 20km/h speed. In our user study, we found the 2 level distance instructions are sufficient. The 100m instruction informed users to slow down and search for a street junction. The 30m instruction can be interpreted as "turn at the next possible turning point" and it was triggered 5 seconds before the turning point. Users had enough time to show the turning gesture (pointing the direction with the corresponding arm) and tilt the handle-bar. Their comments indicated that the vibro-patterns were intuitive and easy to remember, even though the vibro-patterns were only introduced to them very shortly.

4   Setup and Experiments

4.1   Study 1: Driving Test in Real Traffic

Design. The first study is a driving test in real traffic. The goal is to test users' subjective workload of different navigation methods in the real environment. The test area is around the campus and the road condition is good for driving the Segway. Three navigation conditions were compared:

Fig. 4. Part of the test area and route samples (Google Map, http://maps.google.de/)

- **MA**: A TVN using Map plus Audio instructions [2]
- **ARA**: AR navigation interface plus Audio instructions
- **ART**: AR navigation interface plus vibro-tactile instructions

A commercially available in-vehicle navigator was used for comparison, which features a 2D map navigation interface (see Fig. 1(a)) and audio turning instructions. This navigator is widely used (more than 10 thousand downloads) and well accepted (rated 4.5 out of 5). Therefore it has the basic features of a TVN and fulfills our comparison requirements. All navigation conditions run on an iPhone mounted on the Segway. The iPhone speaker volume and the screen brightness are adjusted to maximum.

A within-subject-design is used, and each participant has to drive the Segway along 3 routes using different conditions respectively. The order of the conditions are counterbalanced for different participants. To avoid learning effects from the routes, we select them from different areas. Each route partly goes along a main street which has relatively dense traffic. The length of test routes varies from 2.1km to 2.5km and they contain 11 to 13 turning points, two samples are shown in Fig. 4.

Procedure. In the beginning of the test, a Segway driving tutorial was given by the experimenter (E) on a parking lot, including driving basics, traffic rules of the Segway driving and a 1km trial in real traffic. After that, the real test started. E first introduced and demonstrated the navigation interface to the participant (P). Then E set the destination in the navigation system so that P did not know his destination in advance. P had to drive to the target following the navigation information, while E followed P by bike. When a destination was successfully reached, P had to answer a standard NASA-TLX questionnaire [11] to evaluate the subjective work load of that task. Further comments and problems encountered during the test drive was recorded as voice memos. The same procedure repeated 3 times using 3 conditions separately. P further rated the weights of the 6 aspects of NASA TLX. At the end, a post-test questionnaire was filled out. The questions are listed in Fig. 6. Overall each user test took about 80 to 90 minutes.

Samples. The studies were conducted within two weeks. The wind speed varied from 5 to 15 km/h. 9 participants took part in this study: 2 females and 7 males, all students from the university, aged from 26 to 34. All participants had valid driver licences for the Segway and had normal or corrected eyesight. Most of them had none or very little on road Segway driving experience before, see Fig. 6.

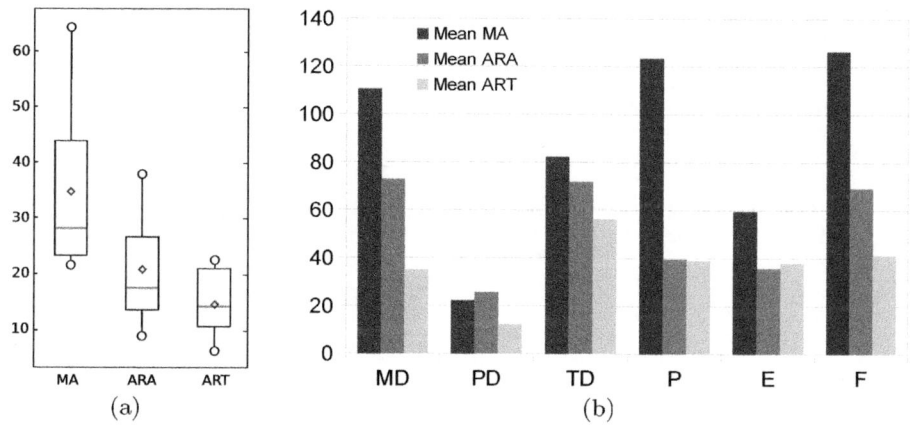

Fig. 5. NASA-TLX subjective workload rating. The left figure shows the overall workload rating (min-[1st quartile-median-3rd quartile]-max). Mean values are marked by blue diamond signs. The right figure presents the weighted rating of Mental Demand (MD), Physical Demand (PD), Temporal Demand (TD), Effort (E), Performance (P) and Frustration (F) under different navigation conditions.

Results. *NASA-TLX*: Users' average rating were 34.9, 20.9 and 14.7 for MA, ARA and ART respectively, see Fig. 5(a). We used a one-way ANOVA to examine the effect of different navigation methods on users' subjective workload. We found a significant effect on the workload ($F_{2,24} = 8.114, p < 0.005$). Post-hoc comparisons indicated that participants had significantly less workload in ARA than MA ($p = 0.032$), as well in ART than MA ($p = 0.001$). But there were no difference between ARA and ART ($p > 0.05$). Comparing the 6 aspects of the NASA-TLX workload separately, see Fig. 5(b), the Mental Demand of ART was significantly lower than MA (mean value 35 and 110, $p = 0.032$). We also found significant difference in Performance among MA, ARA and ART (mean value 123.3, 39.4, and 38.9, $p < 0.01$). Users thought they performed better in ARA than MA ($p < 0.01$), and in ART than MA ($p < 0.01$), while there was

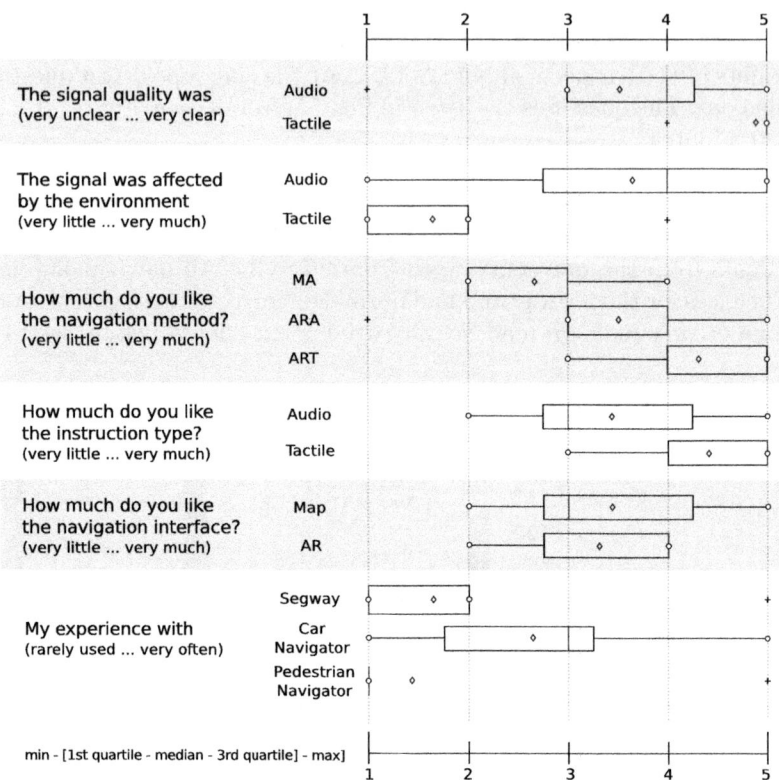

Fig. 6. Results of post-test questionnaire. Mean values are marked by blue diamond signs. Outliers are marked by black cross signs.

no significant difference in performance between ARA and ART. Moreover, the frustration level of ART was significantly lower than MA (mean value 41.1 and 126.1, $p = 0.023$). *Notification Perception*: Users were asked if they can perceive the instructions clearly (the signal quality question in Fig. 6). Mean values were 3.56 and 4.89 for Audio and Tactile respectively. A significant difference was found ($p = 0.0065$). From Fig. 6 we can see that the perception of the audio feedback was affected by different environments a lot, while the tactile feedback was more robust against environment changes.

Environment Influence: We asked users about the influence of the environment to the feedback signal, i.e. ambient noises to the audio quality and the Segway vibration to the vibro-patterns, see Fig. 6. Mean values were 3.67 and 1.67 for Audio and Tactile respectively. Obviously the tactile feedback was much less affected by the environment than the audio feedback.

Preference Statements: Users were asked to rate their preference about different navigation conditions. The mean values were 2.67, 3.44 and 4.33 for MA, ARA and ART separately, see Fig. 6. By performing a one-way ANOVA, we found significant difference ($F_{2,24} = 8.244, p < 0.005$). Post-hoc comparisons showed that ARA is more preferred by the participants ($p = 0.043$) than MA. Users also preferred ART to MA ($p = 0.001$). However, there was no significant preference difference between ARA and ART ($p > 0.05$). The users were also asked to rate their preference of general audio feedback (combining their audio experience in MA and ARA) over tactile feedback. The mean values were 3.4 (audio) and 4.4 (tactile). By pairwise t-test, we found the participants significantly preferred the tactile over the audio feedback ($p = 0.040$). Comparing the interface preference, the mean values were 3.4 (2D Map) and 3.3 (AR). No significant interface preference was found ($p > 0.05$).

Discussion. According to the results of the NASA-TLX rating and the preference, MA caused more subjective workload and was less preferred than AR group by users. From users' comments and our observation during the test, we found several reasons for that.

Environment Awareness: In condition MA, the environment was easily ignored when the user focused on the map interface, because it did not present real environment information. In the experiment, we observed that 2 participants violated traffic rules due to this reason, see Figure 7(a). Starting from a street without bicycle lane, they drove on the automobile lane. After a turning point at a junction, they looked at the map interface to check the route. In the meanwhile, they didn't notice there was a bicycle lane and still stayed on the automobile lane. After a while when they refocused on the driving, they realized the traffic violation and switched to the bicycle lane. On the contrary, in AR mode no traffic violation was observed, because users could see the real environment from the camera input and therefore always drove on the correct lane.

Timing of Notifications: When there were continuous short route segments, MA designed for car navigation delivered future navigation instructions in one notification to prevent missing turning points. For example, "in 50 meters turn left, then in 60 meters turn right, then immediately you reach your destination". It makes sense for car drivers but not for the Segway, because usually a car moves faster and needs more maneuver space than a Segway. Even for a Segway moving in the maximum speed (20 km/h), a distance of 50 meters still takes 9 seconds which means the Segway driver has more time to react than the car driver. To preload extra route information requires extra processing and memorizing for users and therefore increases the mental demanding. The correct timing of notification should always consider the current moving speed of the vehicle and the distance to the next turning point.

Orientation Update: The heading update in MA doesn't use orientation sensors, like a digital compass. The heading direction is calculated by the latest location updates. For example, when the user changes the orientation of the Segway, the displayed map was not aligned to the new heading direction immediately, until a new location update arrived, which could be a delay of several seconds. Since MA is originally designed for the automobile navigation and cars can only move along the road, it is reasonable to update heading in such a way. However, it is different for Segway driving, because the Segway can move much

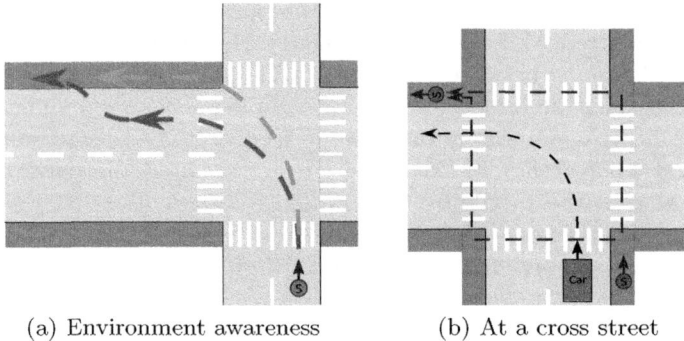

(a) Environment awareness   (b) At a cross street

Fig. 7. Left: The user lost environment awareness when focused on map interface. The red line denotes his/her actual trace. The green indicates the correct driving. Right: At the turning point of a cross street, the Segway has more degrees of freedom than a car, either along the edges or diagonal (if the bicycle way is not available).

more agile, e.g. rotating 180 degrees in place. In addition, there are more possibilities for the Segway driver at a turning point of a junction, i.e. going along the diagonal or edges, see Fig. 7(b). It is necessary to update the instant heading in the Segway navigation interface. In our user study, we found the heading update of MA was confusing to the users. This situation was even worse when there was strong ambient noise or relatively heavy traffic around, which was very normal at a junction of a main street. Due to these facts, the turning instruction played near the turning point was very likely to be missed partly. The user had to check the map for a correct turning directions. We observed that 5 users halted or slowed down to check the map in such situation, and then either went to a wrong direction or kept turning around hesitatingly. Unlike MA, in AR navigation interface the route forward direction was indicated by the 3D route and a turning instruction arrow, which pointed the way to the user directly in the real world. The users commented that it was intuitive and they can verify the forward direction by just one glance.

  Vibro-tactile patterns: From the post-test results, using our vibro-tactile configuration, the tactile feedback was significantly clearer than audio feedback in real traffic environment and less affected by the environment. Before the user study, some users doubted the vibro-patterns would be hard to be distinguished from the Segway vibration due to the bumpy road. But after the test drive, they commented that although parts of the route was bumpy which caused vibrations of the handlebar, the vibro-tactile patterns' intensity was very different from that. They can perceive the signal clearly without any problem. The driving experience in ART was more relaxed, since users did not worry about missing instructions due to ambient noises. The encoding of the vibro-patterns were commented by users as well. Compared to an initial version of vibro-patterns, the current patterns were considered intuitive, as described in Sec. 3.2. The temporal-location encoding made the patterns easy to remember. In addition, two users expressed that the tactile feedback was more user friendly than the audio feedback. While they were waiting at the traffic lights with some pedestrians, a navigation instruction was played aloud. That attracted the passerby attention immediately, which was very embarrassing to the users. Moreover, because of strong sun light and screen reflection, sometimes the mobile display was hardly visible outdoors. In such case visual and auditory navigation aids were both affected by the environment, but users can still rely on the tactile feedback.

Although the tactile feedback was well accepted, we found a potential drawback of our current configuration. The designed vibration amplitude of the vibrator is limited [1], which means we better contact it with bare hands. If textile is used in between, the signal perception could become ambiguous. For example, in cold weather people usually wear gloves outdoors. The solution to such situation could be that we utilize a stronger motor or sew the motor inside gloves [18].

2D Map Preference: Although the 2D Map interface is more abstract and misses environment awareness, it can provide an overview of the area, from which users can preload upcoming turns and verify the route by checking the surrounding street network. In the AR interface, due to the perspective view, only the routes inside the viewing frustum were presented to users. The same issue was also found in previous works [12]. In our user study, some users commented that it was enough for them to know the next turning point. Preloading extra turning information was considered to be more mental demanding to them. While some other users, especially those who got used to the 2D Map interface of TVN, preferred to have more information for the route verification. This result was also reflected in the interface preference rating, see Fig. 6.

4.2   Study 2: Lane Switching Test in Artificial Environment

Design. The second study is a Lane Switching Test (LST). The goal is to evaluate the impact of audio and tactile notification to the driving performance. LST is inspired by the Lane Change Test (LCT) [11], which evaluates the influence of the secondary task (e.g. visual, cognitive, etc.) to the primary task, car driving, in a controlled experiment. The influence is reflected by the driving performance, including sign perception, reaction, maneuver, and lane keeping. Since LCT is conducted in a simulator, the trace can be recorded and compared to an ideal maneuvering trace. The average deviation will be the performance indicator. However, since the ambient noise and the road condition could change the perception result from the indoor study, we want to measure the signal perception and users' reaction in the outdoor driving condition. Limited by the GPS accuracy and update rate, to trace a Segway movement sufficiently accurate in outdoor environment is not practical. Therefore we only measure the signal perception and reaction, which gives us the interval of reaction time. The primary task for a user is to drive the Segway, and the secondary task is to switch lanes when an instruction is perceived. If users can react faster in one condition, it means more space to maneuver in real traffic and less safety risk, e.g. assuming the Segway is moving in maximum speed 20km/h, every 100ms delay of reaction results in 0.6m further displacement.

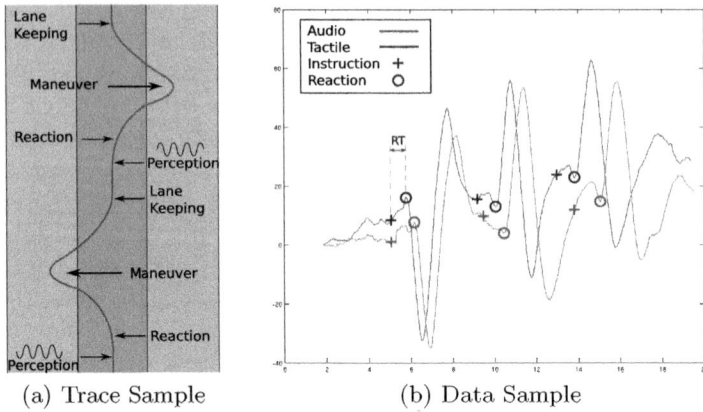

(a) Trace Sample   (b) Data Sample

Fig. 8. Left: Segway trace example in LST. Right: A sample of gyroscope data in LST. Here we plot Audio and Tactile results together for comparison. The lane switching signal is marked by cross signs, which indicates the time point when the instruction is played. The time points of reaction are marked by circles. RT for Reaction Time.

We conduct the study on a long straight road (about 150m) of a parking lot. Three lanes, left, middle, and right are defined along this road. The within subjects design is used. Each participant needs to do this test under audio and tactile conditions separately. He/She starts from the middle lane at one end of the road and drives the Segway to the other end in the speed of about 15 to 20km/h. The experimenter sends switching signals to the iPhone mounted on the Segway via wireless connection. When the iPhone receives the signal, depending on the test mode, it either plays the audio instruction ("left" or "right" speech) or triggers the vibration (a pulse of 1 second length on the left or right grip) via a Wi-Fi connection (less than 10ms latency). When the participant receives a switching instruction, he/she has to switch to the corresponding lane and then returns back to the the middle lane immediately (to ensure that the participant does not know the upcoming instruction), see Fig. 8(a). No visual information is used in this test. We measure the driver's reaction time from the time point when the notification is played to the time point the handlebar is tilted (detected by the gyroscope of iPhone4). The data is collected by the mounted iPhone4, see Fig. 8(b).

Procedure and Samples. In the beginning, the experimenter (E) explained the procedure and demoed the correct maneuver. The participant (P) had several trials and then the real test started. Every P made 2 round trips using audio or tactile instruction respectively (the order was balanced). In each round trip E triggered 8 to 10 instructions depending on the Segway speed. Directions, left and right, were equally selected in a random order. 10 participants took part in this study: 2 females and 8 males, aged from 26 to 35, all students from the university.

Results. In this study, all participants perceived and reacted to instructions correctly. The environment influence from the test location was very little. The mean reaction time were 1220.5ms and 891.2ms for Audio and Tactile respectively, see Fig. 9(a), 9(b). They were significantly different ($p < 0.0001$). The result indicated that by using tactile feedback instead of audio feedback Segway drivers can respond faster to instructions by 27% (in average 330ms faster). Assuming the Segway speed is 20km/h, 330ms delay corresponds to almost 2 meters further displacement.

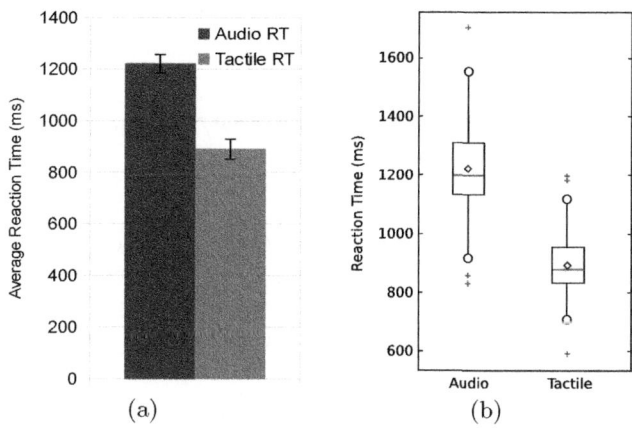

Fig. 9. Left: Average reaction time of audio and tactile feedback in LST (with 95% confidence interval). Right: Reaction time distribution. Mean values marked by blue diamond signs.

5   Conclusion

In the beginning of this study, we presented two hypotheses. We now review them in light of our results.

5.1   The Utility of Navigation Interfaces

"Compared with the 2D-Map navigation interface in TVN, AR interface can reduce users' subjective workload. "

Our user study demonstrated that participants experienced less cognitive workload in AR navigation interface (ARA and ART) than 2D Map navigation interface (MA). From our observation and users' comments, it was because MA was originally designed for in-vehicle navigation which was not suitable for the Segway. First, the driving of the Segway is different from the automobile: it is more agile than a car, and the maximum speed is limited to 20 km/h. Second, AR interface directly augments the environment with navigational instructions, which is intuitive to users. Third, the map interface detaches the user from the environment, which can result in safety risks. However, users' preference and comments indicated that the map interface can provide an overview of the route information and is helpful for preloading the upcoming turning points, especially for the users who are used to the 2D map based navigator. The design of the Segway navigation interface in the future should combine the features of map and AR modes, e.g. the screen displays the map interface when it is far from the next turning point, and replaces the interface by AR view when approaching the turning point. When designing a Segway navigation system, due to its unique features (agile movement and limited speed), the notification timing should take the current speed into account. While the heading update should utilize the orientation sensor.

5.2   The Effectiveness of Navigation Instructions

"The vibro-tactile turning instructions can be perceived by drivers clearly, and it improves their driving performance. "

Indicated in the post-test results, users perceived vibro-tactile instruction very clear in real traffic. The tactile signal was robust to environment changes. The proposed vibro-patterns were intuitive to use and preferred by users. The driving performance was significantly improved when using tactile instructions than using auditory instructions.

5.3   Design Implications and Future Research

Design vibro-patterns: In this study, we prototyped vibro-patterns for Segway navigation. It was demonstrated that the tactile feedback was superior to audio feedback for Segway drivers. Information encoded in vibration can be perceived faster, and is robust to the listening conditions. Therefore it has high potential to be used in other scenarios of the Segway. For example in noisy environment like airports, or higher temporally demanding tasks like security patrols or first aids.

In our study, to keep the mental demanding low we limited the number of patterns. Since the Segway is widely used in city touring, airport, security patrol, etc., various scenarios benefit from more information delivered to users than direction and distance, e.g. announcing Point Of Interest around the user. It would be worthwhile to investigate how such information can be encoded into a vibro-tactile patterns while keeping the complexity low. Or how other tactile displays can work for the Segway. One possible solution is to attach vibro-motors to the user's helmet and deliver directional information of POI, like the concept of the vibro waist belt [5].

Design AR navigation Interface: The current AR route visualization does not consider the object visibility in the scene, i.e. the route that should be occluded by a facade looks like being in front of the building. The occlusion is very important for the user to have the correct perception of depth, which makes the distance estimation easier and makes the AR layer more realistic. One possible direction is to render a 3D city model into the depth buffer as occluders. Furthermore, to improve environment awareness and reduce the violation to traffic rules, computer vision techniques could be used to detect lanes and highlight the correct lane on the AR display.

Design Segway user study: Since there was no on-road user study for Segway navigation before, we have some experience from the experiment to share. First, test areas and routes should be carefully selected. The test areas should have similar traffic pressure and the route complexity should be comparable to each other. Second, the driving security has the first priority. Some streets with heavy traffic should be avoided. During an experiment, the experimenter should follow the participant as an observer and also warn him/her about potential security risks (only if necessary). Third, if a participant has little experience with the Segway before, the tutorial has to be given thoroughly, covering different driving situations and including an on-road trial. Furthermore, since the on-road test depends on the weather condition, it is important to keep comparable weather conditions for all participants, e.g. temperature, wind, etc. In addition, the frequency of the user study is limited by the battery capacity of the Segway and other devices, which should be considered when scheduling experiments.

Alternative navigation display: The current mobile screen is hardly visible under strong sunlight. For AR perspective view, the pose of the display is also limited. The mobile mounting setup is fixed and does not adapt to the current pose of the Segway. To improve the viewability and comfort, other display modalities should be investigated. For example, a mobile laser projector can be used as an alternative display to project instructions (vector graphics) on the ground in front of the Segway.

Extension to bicycle: In this study we focused on the Segway use case. The current AR-Tactile navigation system can be deployed to a bicycle. Due to different driving experience, some adaptations should be implemented. For example, since the bicycle rider can hold the grips in different way, the design space should be explored, e.g. vibrators could be integrated into the helmet or the bicycle seat ([6,7]).

Acknowledgments. This work was supported by NRW State within the B-IT Research School. The authors would like to thank Chat Wacharamanotham for his valuable comments during the experiments.

References

1. Lilypad Vibe Board, http://www.sparkfun.com/products/8468
2. Skobbler, http://www.skobbler.net/
3. Wikitude Drive, http://www.wikitude.org/en/drive
4. Aleccia, J.: Segway scooters can lead to serious injuries, experts warn. Website (2010), http://goo.gl/r2QRL
5. Boll, S., Asif, A., Heuten, W.: Feel your route: A tactile display for car navigation. IEEE Pervasive Computing 10(3), 35–42 (2011)

6. De Vries, S.C., Van Erp, J.B.F., Kiefer, R.J.: Direction coding using a tactile chair. Applied Ergonomics 40(3), 477–484 (2009), http://linkinghub.elsevier.com/retrieve/pii/S0003687008001531

7. Van Erp, J.B.F.: Vibro-tactile information presentation in automobiles, University of Birmingham, pp. 99–104 (2001)

8. Van Erp, J.B.F.: Guidelines for the use of vibro-tactile displays in human computer interaction. Human Factors, 18–22 (2002)

9. Jensen, B.S., Skov, M.B., Thiruravichandran, N.: Studying driver attention and behaviour for three configurations of gps navigation in real traffic driving. In: Proceedings of the 28th International Conference on Human Factors in Computing Systems, CHI 2010, pp. 1271–1280. ACM, New York (2010), http://doi.acm.org/10.1145/1753326.1753517

10. Kern, D., Marshall, P., Hornecker, E., Rogers, Y., Schmidt, A.: Enhancing Navigation Information with Tactile Output Embedded into the Steering Wheel. In: Tokuda, H., Beigl, M., Friday, A., Brush, A.J.B., Tobe, Y. (eds.) Pervasive 2009. LNCS, vol. 5538, pp. 42–58. Springer, Heidelberg (2009), http://dx.doi.org/10.1007/978-3-642-01516-8_5

11. Mattes, S.: The lane change task as a tool for driver distraction evaluation (2003)

12. Medenica, Z., Kun, A.L., Paek, T., Palinko, O.: Augmented reality vs. street views: A driving simulator study comparing two emerging navigation aids. In: Mobile HCI 2011 (2011)

13. Pielot, M., Poppinga, B., Boll, S.: Pocketnavigator: vibro-tactile waypoint navigation for everyday mobile devices. In: Proceedings of the 12th International Conference on Human Computer Interaction with Mobile Devices and Services, Mobile-HCI 2010, pp. 423–426. ACM, New York (2010), http://doi.acm.org/10.1145/1851600.1851696

14. Poppinga, B., Pielot, M., Boll, S.: Tacticycle: a tactile display for supporting tourists on a bicycle trip, vol. 41. ACM (2009), http://portal.acm.org/citation.cfm?id=1613911

15. Ross, D.A., Blasch, B.B.: Wearable interfaces for orientation and wayfinding. In: Proceedings of the Fourth International ACM Conference on Assistive Technologies, Assets 2000, pp. 193–200. ACM, New York (2000), http://doi.acm.org/10.1145/354324.354380

16. Schmidt-Belz, B., Laamanen, H., Poslad, S., Zipf, A.: Location-based mobile tourist services: first user experiences. In: Conference for Information and Communication Technologies in Travel & Tourism, pp. 115–123

17. Srikulwong, M., O'Neill, E.: A comparative study of tactile representation techniques for landmarks on a wearable device. In: Proceedings of the 2011 Annual Conference on Human Factors in Computing Systems, CHI 2011, pp. 2029–2038. ACM, New York (2011), http://doi.acm.org/10.1145/1978942.1979236

18. Ueda, J.: Wearable device that vibrates fingertip could improve one's sense of touch (August 4, 2011), http://www.physorg.com/news/2011-08-wearable-device-vibrates-fingertip.html

19. Wickens, C.D.: Processing Resources in Attention. Academic Press (1984)

Route Guidance Modality for Elder Driver Navigation

SeungJun Kim[1], Jin-Hyuk Hong[1], Kevin A. Li[2], Jodi Forlizzi[1], and Anind K. Dey[1]

[1] Human-Computer Interaction Institute, School of Computer Science,
Carnegie Mellon University, Pittsburgh, PA 15213, USA
[2] AT & T Research, Labs, Florham Park, NJ 07932, USA
{sjunikim,forlizzi,anind}@cs.cmu.edu,
kevinli@research.att.com, hjinh7@gmail.com

Abstract. Differences in perceptual and cognitive abilities between the young and elderly have implications for in-car tasks. As a primary example, although in-car navigation systems enhance situational awareness, this comes at the cost of increasing visual distraction and cognitive load. To address these shortcomings, this paper explores the efficacy of multi-modal cues for providing route guidance information. We present the results of a study evaluating the impact of multi-modal feedback on driving performance and cognitive load. We found that the full combination of visual, auditory, and haptic feedback was generally most useful to reduce way-finding errors. However, our study highlighted a number of differences between elder and younger drivers for their *safer* navigation. Adding more modalities strained the already high workload of elder drivers. In contrast, adding haptic feedback to traditional audio and visual feedback led to more attentive driving by younger drivers. Therefore, for elder drivers, navigation systems need to be personalized to enhance the benefit of auditory feedback without increasing the number of sensory feedbacks. For younger drivers, it is necessary to incorporate new non-visual feedback to minimize distractions caused by visual feedback. We demonstrate these results through task performance-based measures, subjective workload measures and through objective workload measures that use psycho-physiological responses of participants to predict a driver's cognitive load in near real-time.

Keywords: Elderly driver, Car navigation, Cognitive load, Divided attention, Haptics, Psycho-physiological measurement.

1 Introduction

As our society ages, the number of drivers over the age of 65 is rapidly growing. However, the cognitive effects of aging can force them to relinquish control of their cars. Unfortunately, quality of life is acutely linked with the ability to maintain independence in mobility [1, 29]. Thus, reduced mobility combined with the need for mobility independence has substantial negative impact on an individual as well as their family, who often takes on the burden of care [24].

Decay in vision, hearing, and general mobility collectively reduce the performance of elderly drivers (*e.g.*, [10]). Age-related decreases in spatial cognition ability leads to challenges for elderly individuals in accurately forming a mental representation of

J. Kay et al. (Eds.): Pervasive 2012, LNCS 7319, pp. 179–196, 2012.

a spatial environment and efficiently navigating such environments. For example, it has been found that older adults have difficulty in understanding 'you-are-here' maps, which are used to plan simpler driving routes, even though they may increase driving time [30]. In an on-road driving assessment [15], older adults forgot to check blind spots and made errors when asked to report road marking and traffic signs as they drove. In addition, it has been found that older adults are affected more when taking their eyes off of the road, and thus do not use secondary displays in cars as commonly as younger drivers do [18, 20]. These secondary displays, such as in-car navigation systems, typically enhance drivers' situation awareness, at the cost of increased visual attention and cognitive load. These shortcomings are harder for elderly drivers to overcome; technologies such as GPS systems are often considered too difficult for older drivers to use effectively as a driving aid [20].

We are interested in improving the driving performance of elderly drivers. The relationship between workload and performance is complex. Performance can be affected by workload being too high or too low [27], resulting in a saturation of cognitive capability, the loss of situational awareness or a reduced sense of alertness. Multiple resource theory proposes that the cognitive burden from information overload can be reduced by utilizing multiple modalities to present information [33]. This allows users to process information in parallel rather than sequentially [4].

This paper examines how the usage of multi-modal route guidance cues can lead to safer driving by studying the impact of different combinations of modalities on driving performance for elder and younger drivers.

1.1   Study Overview

The focus of this paper is an investigation of the most effective combinations of feedback modalities for younger and elder drivers' navigation. We compare driver performance for four different combinations of sensory feedback: 1) *visual plus auditory*, 2) *visual plus haptic*, 3) *auditory plus haptic*, and 4) *visual plus auditory plus haptic*.

Based on previous studies [18], we hypothesized that elder drivers will exhibit lower driving performance than younger drivers, independent of modality combination. Informed by multiple resource theory, we also hypothesized that different combinations of multi-modal feedback would reduce the workload required to process navigation information, and that this would be observed through differences in driving performance and cognitive load. To evaluate these combinations, we implemented a driving simulation test-bed with auditory and visual feedback. We also instrumented a steering wheel with vibrotactile feedback. Thirty-three participants (17 elderly) performed a series of tasks using our simulation with each of the feedback combinations described above. We measured driving performance as well as subjective and objective measures of task workload to compare the effectiveness of the different feedback combinations. We define *effectiveness* as providing route guidance without decreasing task performance or increasing cognitive load: a more *effective* guidance system should result in *safer* driving.

We make two contributions. First, we evaluated the effectiveness and safety benefits of different combinations of multi-modal navigation cues for elder and younger drivers. Second, our mixed-methods assessment approach based on task performance, divided attention and induced workload allowed us to evaluate models for predicting cognitive load based on psycho-physiological responses of the two age groups in real time.

We begin our paper with a discussion of impoverished attention in driving environments and the benefits of using multiple attention resources. We then describe the test-bed we developed for our study to evaluate four multi-modal route guidance combinations. We describe the results of our study, where we found that the *visual plus auditory plus haptic* condition generally led to improved way-finding performance with higher driver satisfaction. Surprisingly, we found that for elder drivers, *auditory plus haptic* was safer than using all three modalities. These results highlighted the need to be sensitive to the already heavier workload for older drivers. We also found that for elders, auditory feedback was indispensible, while for our younger drivers, the addition of haptic feedback to the typical combination (*i.e.*, *visual plus auditory*) was effective for safer driving. We conclude with a discussion of our results and implications for designing multi-modal route guidance systems.

2   Background Work

In this section, we discuss related work on performance and attention in driving, the effect of using multiple modalities in interfaces, and on the objective measurement of cognitive load.

Impoverished-Attention in a Driving Environment. The split attention effect while driving stems from the cognitive load from secondary tasks. Impact of these tasks has been assessed through measurement of eyes-off-the-road occurrence, driver reaction time, and accuracy within a dual-task paradigm (*e.g.*, [7], [13], [21]). Artificial tasks such as short term memory tests are often employed as secondary in-vehicle tasks during a primary simulated driving task, to assess the impact of the secondary tasks on driving performance, using, for example, eye-gaze data. Similar approaches have been used to evaluate the effects of heterogeneous secondary tasks (*e.g.*, mobile phone use *vs.* eating in car) [7, 13, 28], and different dashboard and navigation displays [18, 19].

GPS route guidance systems are a canonical secondary information source in the car, and can both positively and negatively impact workload. They enhance drivers' situational awareness while causing drivers to take their eyes off the road. As observed in prior work [18], the cost and benefits of such systems depend on a driver's cognitive capabilities.

Multiple Attention Resources. Human attention is finite, however we can enhance one's mental processing capability leveraging multiple cognitive channels. From the Multiple Resource Theory [33], we know that information services that use multiple channels can facilitate perception of information more effectively than single-modal services. In learning, it has been shown that learners can accommodate more new information when it is presented using auditory and visual channels [22]. Most conventional GPS systems use both, which should improve drivers' ability to process navigation information over using either channel alone.

Even though such an approach is useful, existing studies of in-car information services have focused on single modalities (*e.g.*, [14], [31]). Even fewer have focused on elderly drivers and their cognitive workload, even though multi-modal approaches for in-vehicle secondary information systems could be especially beneficial in reducing attention demands for this population. For younger adults, the effect of multi-modality and the use of tactile feedback are advantageous for navigating, particularly when used as a back-up or confirmation of information available from other modalities [17]. Thus, we focus our efforts on studying multi-modal feedback during navigation tasks, using assessments based on performance and cognitive load, especially with respect to elderly drivers.

Cognitive Load Assessment. Performance-based methods are frequently used to assess experimental conditions in dual-task settings. In driving situations, these methods examine the ways that a driver's responses deteriorate (*e.g.*, lag in reaction time or increase in errors) when using finite cognitive resources to perform two or more tasks. This objective approach has been demonstrated to have a strong link with cognitive load [3]. However, recent work has shown that driver response may be less sensitive to subtle differences in cognitive load [9]. Different combinations of modality feedback may not impact performance in a measurable way, so we also focus on measures of cognitive load.

Subjective rating-based methods such as the NASA TLX [11] or Likert-scales use participants' own judgment of their efforts. This approach is applied *post-hoc*, is non-intrusive, and is a reliable indicator of users' preferences for particular test conditions [3]. However, even when users struggle to complete a task in a timely fashion, they may self-report the task as having a low workload, if they believe they did not make any errors [25]. This calls for a more objective measure of workload.

Psycho-physiological response analysis can provide such a measure. Some believe that this approach can more sensitively assess cognitive load over a continuous time frame [3], allowing for detection of changes in cognitive load even when no deterioration in task performance is demonstrated. We also note that psycho-physiological measures can be applied across a variety of stimuli modalities, and with different numbers of stimuli [32]. This approach also supports assessment for tasks like navigation that leverage major cognitive processes such as perception, memory and reasoning [2]. An advantage of physiological responses is that they do not require an overt response by the operator, while at the same time, most cognitive tasks do not require overt behavior. While this approach is promising, it has yet to be validated with a driving task such as we are proposing in this paper.

Finally, the frequency and length of eye fixations is usually correlated with changes in workload (*e.g.*, [6]). However, the sum of these measures could linearly increase in cases where task duration is prolonged due to an individual's abilities or the difficulty of a given task. Therefore, the proportion of these measure's totals or overall task durations have been used to provide more meaningful results.

Accordingly, our study uses measures of task performance, and subjective and objective ratings of cognitive load, induced by different navigation feedback mechanisms, to determine which are most appropriate for younger and elder drivers. We additionally validate whether psycho-physiological responses can be used in assessment in such situations.

3   Experimental Design

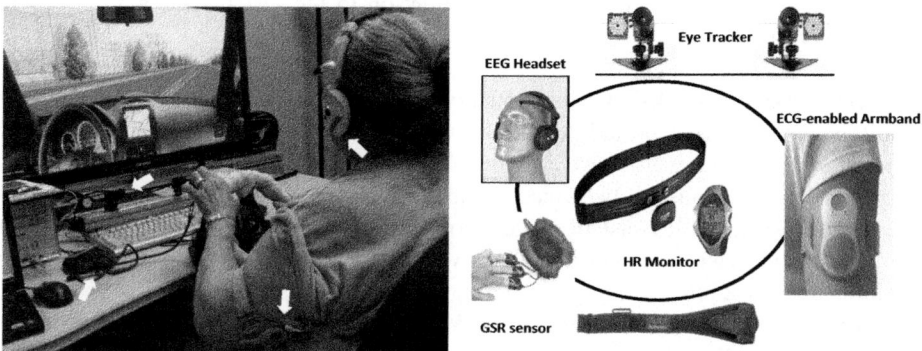

Fig. 1. Our experimental test-bed includes a three-dimensional driving simulator with a wheel joystick set, contactless gaze tracker, and multiple psycho-physiological sensors

3.1   Test-Bed Implementation

We implemented a three dimensional driving simulator to conduct our experiment. In the simulator, drivers are given specific routes to navigate. Geospatial information from Google Maps for Pittsburgh is graphically rendered in this simulator on a 58-inch widescreen LCD HDTV (screen size: 1.290m × 0.723m, resolution 1280 × 1024). Participants can navigate through the simulated cities using a virtual wheel and two foot pedals (see Fig. 1). We automatically record simulator state, driver input from the virtual wheel and foot pedals and psycho-physiological responses for later analysis of driving performance.

Each navigation route is 3.36km long and includes 12 intersections: 4 right turns, 4 left turns and 4 which drivers pass straight through. During each driving condition, participants encounter 12 light signals, 3 stop signs, 5 pedestrians (such as a person pushing a baby carriage) crossing the road from right to left and 5 other pedestrians (such as a man wearing a business suit, holding a suitcase) crossing the road from left to right, whom they are expected to avoid. In the case of missed turns, a U-turn must be made to get back on the route again. Route guidance information is provided using three different types of sensory feedback as follows (see Fig. 2.).

Visual Feedback (V). We implemented a 2D bird's-eye-view map display mode (on-screen size: 12cm × 12cm, see Fig. 2.), commonly employed in GPS navigation systems and usually installed on the lower-right side of a driver's head. The map display is synchronized with car movement in real-time and the suggested route is highlighted. It supports both global awareness (*i.e.*, a driver's understanding of nearby road networks) and local guidance for use as navigation aids. However, given the nature of this sensory feedback, drivers need to consistently monitor the device (increasing eyes-off-the-road time) in order to determine where they are supposed to turn. Earlier work found that elder drivers had greater difficulty in using systems with only visual feedback [18]. We hypothesize that drivers using multi-modal navigation systems that incorporate visual feedback will be able to leverage an alternative feedback modality, and only selectively pay attention to the visual feedback, improving overall performance.

Auditory Feedback (A). We implemented three kinds of voice commands: two for route guidance: 'turn left' and 'turn right', and one for driving instructions in case of missed turns: 'wrong way, make a U-turn' (Fig. 2.). In the case of no missed turns during a driving session, twelve voice commands prompt route guidance information, designed to occur at a constant distance of 45m in front of every intersection where drivers should make turn decisions (45m was determined empirically as early enough to initiate turns at intersections considering typical driving speed, while not so early as to forget the provided turn information). When using this sensory feedback, drivers do not have to take their eyes off the road to obtain route guidance information, however they may have to be careful not to miss or forget the provided information since this feedback supports only local guidance (*i.e.*, the information is not persistent) and is triggered at a specific moment for each intersection. We hypothesize that auditory feedback will be the easiest and most comfortable modality for elder drivers.

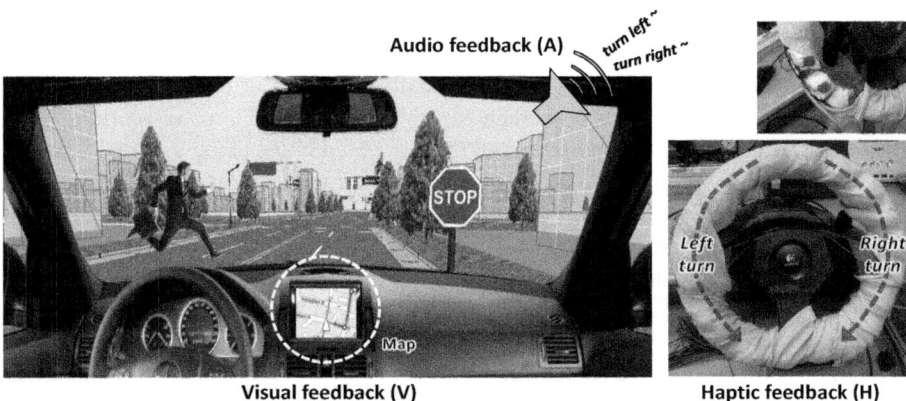

Fig. 2. Traffic events, including pedestrians, lights, and stop signs are incorporated into the driving simulation test-bed. Route guidance information is provided using three different types of sensory feedback: visual feedback ('V'), auditory feedback ('A'), and haptic feedback ('H'). Haptic wheel that triggered turn right cues with clockwise vibrations and turn left cues with counterclockwise vibrations (bottom right). Vibration motors mounted on steering wheel, padded with memory foam (top right).

Haptic Feedback (H). We developed an enhanced prototype of a vibrotactile steering wheel that provides haptic feedback, as shown in Fig. 2 (right). It provides a confusion-free vibrotactile localization with the use of memory foam (*e.g.*, unresolved issue in other settings such as [14]) and a higher resolution by using a larger number of actuators (*e.g.*, more than six epicenters employed in [17]). We installed twenty vibration motors onto the front face of the wheel. In initial pilot studies we found that vibrations generated from one motor would get transferred all along the core of the wheel, making it difficult to determine which particular motor had been turned on. To localize the vibrations, each vibration motor was padded with memory foam, solving the problem (See Fig. 2.). We used an Arduino Mega 2560 to control 20 motors embedded in the steering wheel to produce vibration patterns.

For right-turn information, the wheel creates a clockwise vibration from the one o'clock to five o'clock positions of the wheel, while for left-turn information it provides a counterclockwise vibration from eleven o'clock to seven o'clock. We activated and deactivated vibration motors appropriately to generate these different directions. By triggering spatially separated vibrotactile motors, we hoped to elicit *sensory saltation* [8] whereby users would perceive a direction of motion. Each vibration sequence was repeated 8 times to ensure the driver would not miss the cue. All participants responded that there was no confusion about the turn direction cue provided by the wheel. Cues were triggered at a constant distance (45m) from the turn.

3.2   Pilot Study

We conducted two stages of a pilot study. In the first stage, we focused on validating each type of sensory feedback, especially the usability of the vibrotactile wheel and auditory voice-commands that we developed for this study. In particular, we validated the vibrotactile localization and representations for effective turn cues, additional auditory cues for the case of missed turns, and the service timings of vibrotactile and auditory cues. Four pilot subjects evaluated a number of different versions of cue representations, and based on their feedback, we iterated on the design of the auditory and haptic cues.

The second stage of the study was used to decide which combinations of feedback modalities to explore in the actual study, as well as to re-validate our cue design. Seven pilot subjects, including the four subjects from the first stage of the study were asked to perform a virtual driving task using all possible combinations of the three modalities: *visual only, auditory only, haptic only, visual plus auditory, visual plus haptic, auditory plus haptic,* and *visual plus auditory plus haptic.* After all the tests, we collected pilot participants' responses for three aspects (preference, cognitive load, and performance) through Likert-scale questions as well as the NASA-TLX assessment after each test. We found that in almost all cases, the multi-modal conditions outperformed the single-modal conditions, in terms of preference, cognitive load and performance. There was only one exception: *visual only* was tied for the third most preferred condition, with *auditory plus haptic,* ranking ahead of *visual plus haptic.* Based on these results, we chose to focus on the multi-modal conditions in our main study.

3.3   Participants in the Main Experiment

We recruited 33 study participants: 16 younger participants (age M=25.4, SD=5.46, age range: 19-36, gender: female 31% and male 69%); 17 older participants, over the age of 65, with normal or corrected-to-normal vision and hearing (age M=73.8, SD=7.48, age range: 65-91, gender: female 65% and male 35%). Participants were recruited through lifelong learning institutes at two local universities, a local center for behavioral decision research, and through bulletin board ads placed around the university campus and local apartments. Participants were compensated with $15 (US), with an additional $5 for parking as necessary.

3.4   Task, Test Conditions, and Procedure

Participants were asked to wear six sensor devices during their driving tasks and were asked to execute all driving tasks in front of two cameras installed at the bottom of the simulation screen in order to capture gaze tracking (see Fig. 1). Participants were shown how to use our test-bed, and how to respond to each of the traffic events, driving rules and regulations. Participants then performed one iteration of practice driving with each feedback modality. Users had no trouble interpreting any of the directional cues. To ensure participants felt the vibrotactile cues, we instructed them to hold the steering wheel with both hands at all times.

Each participant then performed virtual driving tasks using the 4 multi-modal combinations of route guidance feedback: 1) *visual plus auditory feedback* (V+A), 2) *visual plus haptic feedback* (V+H), 3) *auditory plus haptic feedback* (A+H), and 4) *all three forms of feedback* (V+A+H). Order of presentation was counter-balanced using a Latin square method.

After each condition, participants filled out a questionnaire including the NASA-TLX assessment. After all four tests, they filled out a post-questionnaire where we collected demographics, information about driving experience, and their comparative evaluations of the four multi-modal conditions.

3.5   Measurement

Measure 1: Task Performance. For driving and navigation task performance measures, in this paper we used the following metrics: *driving time*, *lateral lane deviation* (distance between the center of the right-hand lane and a car's current position), *the number of missed turns*, *traffic signal violations*, *stop sign violations*, and *the number of incidents that placed pedestrians in danger*, which indicates moments when the car intersected with pedestrians.

Measure 2: Divided Attention. As a measure for divided attention, we measured eye gaze movement and extracted the coordinates where a subject's gaze intersected with the screen. In this study, we focused on metrics related to eyes-off-the-road issues, as follows: *eyes-off-the-road time*, which indicates how long a participant's gaze remained on the secondary display or off the road (*e.g.*, rear-view mirror, stereo, dashboard); *eyes-off-the-road frequency*, which indicates how many times gaze is drawn to the secondary display; *eyes-off-the-road time at a glance*, which indicates the average length of a single glance on the secondary display (*i.e.*, equals eyes-off-the-road time / eyes-off-the-road frequency); *eyes-off-the-road percent*, which indicates the proportion of the eyes-off-the-road duration in comparison to the duration of driving time; *gaze movement distance*, which indicates the distance in which a participant's gaze travels over the screen during a driving task; *gaze movement distance per 1-minute driving*, which indicates the distance over which a participant's gaze travels over the screen per minute. Given different individual driving times, in this paper we focused our analysis on three metrics: eyes-off-the-road time at a glance, eyes-off-the-road percent, and gaze movement distance per 1-minute driving.

Measure 3: Subjective Ratings. After each driving condition, we subjectively measured workload by having participants use the NASA-TLX workload assessment tool. This is a multi-dimensional rating procedure that derives an overall workload score based on a weighted average of ratings on six subscales: *Mental Demand, Physical Demand, Temporal Demand, Own Performance, Effort* and *Frustration*. After completing all driving sessions, participants were asked to rate the most annoying and most useful modality condition, and to rate their agreement with the following statements: 1) Preference - "*I would use the following navigation mode.*", 2) Cognitive load - "*The following mode was easy for me to use.*", and 3) Performance - "*I drove well using the following mode.*" They responded using a 6-point Likert scale: *disagree strongly (score: 1) - disagree moderately (2) - disagree slightly (3) - agree slightly (4) - agree moderately (5) - agree strongly (6).*

Measure 4: Psycho-physiological Responses. We measured participants' psycho-physiological responses using six sensor devices: a contactless eye tracker (SmartEye 5.6), an ECG-enabled armband (SenseWear Pro3), a wireless EEG headset (NeuroSky mindset kit), a wireless HR monitor belt (Polar RS800CX HR monitor), another wireless physiological monitor belt (BioHarness^{TM} BT) and a GSR (galvanic skin response) finger sensor (LightStone biofeedback sensors). These devices measure and record information about pupil size, blink rate, GSR, heat flux (rate of heat transfer on the skin), heart rate and heart rate variability, inter-beat (RR) interval, ECG (electrocardiography, electrical activity of the heart over time) and EEG (electroencephalography, electrical activity of the brain). The value of these psycho-physiological signals in assessing cognitive load have been demonstrated in [9].

4   Results

For the task performance, eye tracking, and NASA-TLX assessment measures, we performed one-way repeated measures ANOVA analysis (route guidance modality as a within-subject factor and age group as a between-subjects factor) and the Bonferroni *post-hoc* test. For the analysis of Likert-scale rating data, Friedman tests and a Wilocoxon Signed Rank *post-hoc* test were conducted.

4.1   Elder Drivers' Navigation

As hypothesized, elderly drivers exhibited significantly lower task performance and higher task workload than younger drivers across all conditions (see Fig. 3).

Specifically, elders took 1.7 times longer to complete the driving tasks ($F_{1,27}=23.6$, $p<.001$), had 2.6 times more missed turns ($F_{1,27}=4.81$, $p=.037$), and reported 1.3 times higher task workload using the NASA TLX assessment ($F_{1,27}=4.31$, $p=.047$). There were no significant differences in eye-off-the-road measures between age groups. The only exception to these navigation measures was that elder drivers obeyed stop signs significantly better than younger drivers ($F_{1,27}=7.04$, $p=.013$).

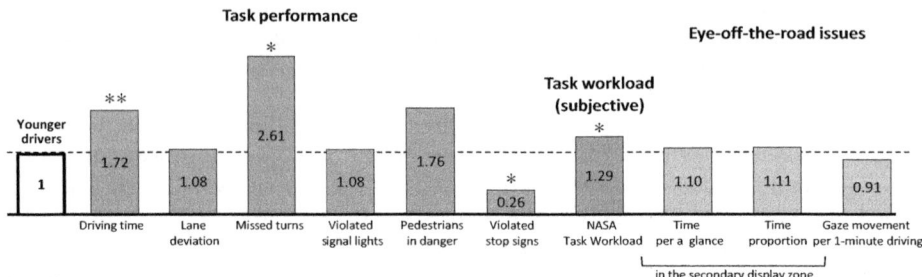

Fig. 3. When driving using route guidance systems, elder drivers exhibited worse task performance, and higher task workload, compared to younger drivers. All the measured values from the younger group were set as *1* (*the left-most bar*). The numbers in each bar represent the proportions of the measured values from elder group to the values from younger group. For example, elder drivers missed *2.61* times more numbers of turns at intersections than younger drivers. * *p<.05.* **p<.001.*

4.2   Effects of Route Guidance Modalities

In our analysis, we treat *visual plus auditory* to be the baseline condition, as it is what is found in most conventional GPS systems. Route guidance modalities significantly impact eye-off-the-road issues across all participants (eye-off-the-road time per glance: $F_{3,81}=23.9$, *p<.001*, eye-off-the-road time proportion: $F_{3,81}=33.3$, *p<.001*); however they did not have much impact on navigation performance (*i.e.*, mean differences in the number of missed turns, $F_{3,81}=0.605$, *p=.614*). In particular, when using *auditory plus haptic* feedback (A+H), participants' eye gazes dwelled off the road almost 0.2 seconds less per glance independent of age group (*p<.001*), and eye-off-the-road time proportion (= total eye-off-the-road time / total driving time) was also significantly reduced (elder drivers: 4% less, *p=.009*, younger drivers: 9% less, *p<.001*- differences, not ratio, between the proportion measures), than when using the baseline condition. The significant reductions in eye-off-the-road issues by the use of 'A+H feedback' were consistently found within each age group and also in the post-hoc comparisons with other modalities (*i.e.*, A+H *vs.* either V+A, V+H, or V+A+H).

Interestingly, we found that younger drivers' eye-off-the-road metrics associated with visual feedback were reduced when using haptic feedback. When younger drivers used V+A+H, eye-off-the-road time proportion was significantly lower (by 3.1%, *p=.048*), than when using the baseline condition V+A; no such phenomenon was shown for the elder group (see Fig. 4). In order of impact, this eye-related issue differed significantly as follows: V+A (greatest issue) ≥ V+H ≥ V+A+H > A+H (least issue). We further note that this result is due to the impact of visual feedback, rather than auditory feedback. When using haptic feedback instead of visual feedback (A+H rather V+A), younger drivers' eye-off-the-road time proportion was also significantly reduced (*p<.001*). In addition, there were no significant eye-off-the-road issues when adding audio feedback (V+A+H *vs.* V+H), nor when replacing audio feedback with haptic feedback (V+A *vs.* V+H).

These results indicate that the degree of drivers' engagement with a particular feedback modality differs by age group and by the combinations of feedback used; in other words, there are significant differences in cognitive engagement with different route guidance modalities for the two age groups. Service providers should take this into account and consider the adoption of a novel modality into conventional GPS systems based on the expected user population.

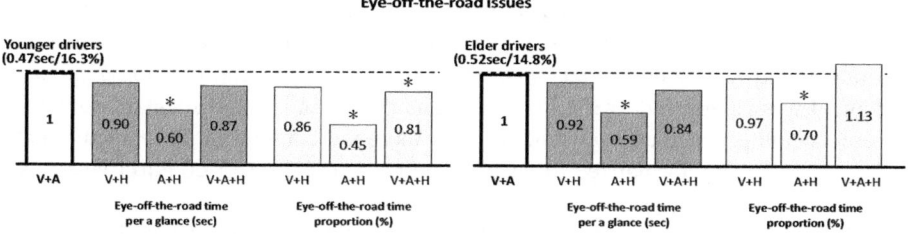

Fig. 4. Route guidance modalities have a significant impact on eye-off-the-road issues within each age group (*$p<0.05$). The numbers in each bar graph represent the proportions of the measured values when using each navigation mode to the measured values when using the baseline mode, *V+A* (*the left-most bars* for each age group). For example, the first seven bars for younger group (*left*) show that younger drivers' *eye-off-the-road time proportion (%)* was significantly lower when using *A+H* or *V+A+H* than when using the baseline (*V+A*), *0.45* factor and *0.81* factor, respectively. The next seven bars for elder group (*right*) show that elder drivers exhibited such significant reduction only when using *A+H*.

4.3   Modality Differences between Age Groups

From participants' self-reports of preference, performance and load, we found that elder drivers relied on auditory feedback, while younger drivers relied on visual feedback. Elder drivers significantly disliked and had difficulty using the 'V+H'-based route guidance (with no auditory feedback) even though when using this modality their driving and navigation performance was not worse and their eye-off-the-road issues were not greater, compared to those from the other modalities (*e.g.*, V+A+H *vs.* V+H - Likert preference: Z=-3.02, p=.003; Likert cognitive load: Z=-2.66, p=.008; Likert performance: Z=-2.75, p=.006). In contrast, younger drivers disliked the most, had the most difficulty using, and thought they performed the worst when using the 'A+H'-based route guidance (with no visual feedback), even though the effects were not always significant. In particular, in all three aspects (preference, cognitive load, and performance) younger drivers rated the A+H modality as significantly worse than the baseline modality, V+A (Likert preference: Z=-3.13, p=.002; Likert cognitive load: Z=-2.36, p=.018; Likert performance: Z=-2.38, p=.017).

We saw consistent results in our summative questions about sensory feedback. 71% of elder drivers thought the auditory modality was the most useful and 59% thought the visual modality was the most annoying. In contrast, 63% of younger drivers thought the visual modality was most useful and 50% of them thought the auditory modality was most annoying. Both groups ranked haptic feedback between auditory and visual feedback.

4.4   Psycho-physiological Task Workload

For each age group, we examined the psycho-physiological assessment of drivers' task workloads (high, medium, and low, labeled from the NASA-TLX task workload) induced by the four multi-modal route guidance conditions, and built a model that measures the task workload based on these psycho-physiological measurements. Participants who experienced a measurement problem (*e.g.*, no eye gaze tracking data for a significant amount of driving time) were excluded from the analysis, leaving 12 younger and 11 elder participants. Data from each psycho-physiological sensory channel was segmented every 3 seconds, and the mean (μ) and standard deviation (σ) were calculated for each segment. All told, there were a total of 59 extracted features. The features were normalized for each participant, and discretized into five states.

Table 1. Classification accuracies and high-ranked physiological features for each of age group. Task workload classes were determined based on the NASA-TLX results.

	Younger group	Elder group
Bayesian Networks	82.3%	76.2%
Naïve Bayes	53.3%	51.0%
Neural Networks	64.2%	58.4%
High-ranked features	GSR (μ), heat flux (μ) BR.Amp (μ, σ) EEG $\beta_2,\gamma_1(\mu)$, pupil size (μ)	heat flux (μ), BR (μ) blink (σ, μ), HR (μ) GSR (μ)

We used three machine learning techniques 1) Bayesian Networks[1], 2) the Naïve Bayes[1] classifier, and 3) neural networks, to build two models, each of which estimates the task workload based on the psycho-physiological features and the NASA TLX results (ground truth) for one of the age groups. The performance of the models was evaluated using five-fold cross validation, where the data were randomly divided into five parts with four parts used for training and one part for testing. We report the average performance from repeating this process five times.

Table 1 shows the prediction performance of the models for each age group. Among the three techniques, Bayesian networks had the best performance, with accuracies of 82% and 76% for the younger and the elder groups, respectively. With all 3 techniques, younger drivers were modeled better than elder drivers. In terms of features, the psycho-physiological features that were most predictive of load, differed between the two age groups, although both GSR (μ) and heat flux (μ) were highly ranked for both groups. For example, eye-blink had higher information gain for the elder group, while EEG features had higher information gain for the younger group.

When analyzing individual prediction results, we found that the prediction rates are quite high, which indicates the feasibility of applying our psycho-physiological

---

[1] We implemented the Bayesian Networks and the Naïve Bayes classifiers based on the SMILE reasoning engine for graphical probabilistic models contributed to the community by the Decision Systems Laboratory, University of Pittsburgh (http://dsl.sis.pitt.edu). In particular, for the Bayesian Networks, we first learned the structure with the K2 algorithm and then applied the EM algorithm to learn the parameters.

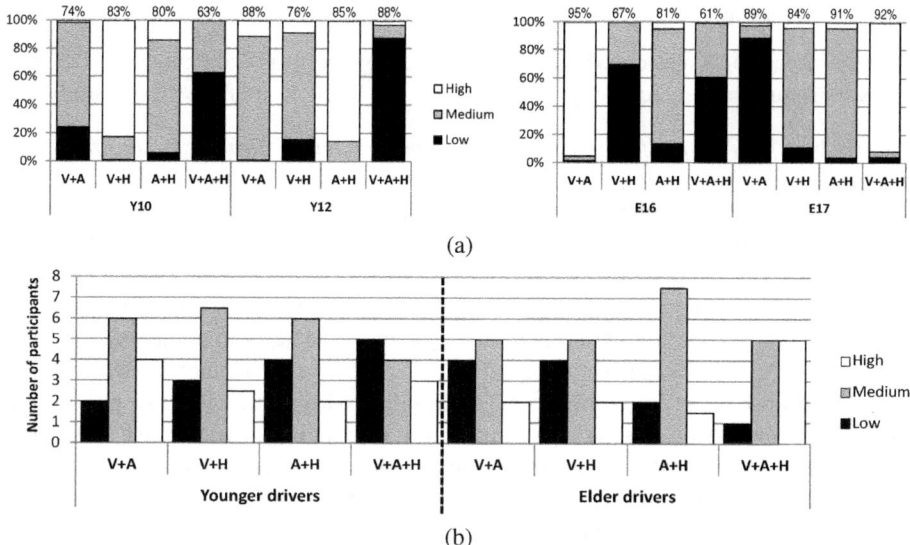

(a)

(b)

Fig. 5. Psycho-physiological assessment: (a) Two participant examples from each age group (each bar shows the ratio of classified samples during the driving with the corresponding navigation feedback modality. For example, *83%* of *Y10*'s samples indicated *V+H* condition induced *high* task workload.), (b) Across all participants divided by age group.

approach for assessing task workload in driving tasks. Fig. 5(a) shows the results for 4 of our participants, in which the prediction of task workload is correctly assessed except for one case. S16 identified V+A+H as having *medium* workload (through the NASA-TLX assessment), but our Bayesian network model classified the workload as *low* based on his psycho-physiological measurements. (Note that in this instance, almost 40% of the driving sensor samples were classified as representing *medium* workload, meaning that our psycho-physiological assessment is very capable, despite the incorrect assessment). Our proposed psycho-physiological assessment approach also allows us to rank the navigation feedback modality for each participant, *e.g.*, the ranking of Y10 is {V+A+H, V+A, A+H, V+H} while the ranking of E17 is {V+A, V+H, A+H, V+A+H}. In addition, this approach allows for an assessment of workload every 3 seconds while driving (as opposed to the one-time, post hoc NASA TLX), allowing it to be extended and applied to a real-time monitoring system. Fig. 5(b) shows the ranking of the modalities across all participants based on the psycho-physiological approach. There were differences between the two age groups, with many younger drivers expressing lower task workload than elder drivers with V+A+H but higher task workload with V+A. Also, individual differences were found in ranking the four navigation feedback modalities, *e.g.*, 5 younger participants had low workload with V+A+H but 3 other younger participants had high workload with this combination. These results, while useful, suggest future work to personalize the psycho-physiological assessment of task workload.

4.5   Discussion

Several important issues emerged from our study of multi-modal navigation feedback, and we discuss those here, along with a discussion of the limitations of our study.

Elderly benefit from multi-modal feedback, but have more difficulty using navigation systems
Older drivers made a higher number of secondary task errors and experienced a higher task workload, compared to younger drivers. However, our study also revealed that the existence of visual feedback did not cause drivers much trouble in managing their visual attention. This result implies that multi-modal services can support elderly drivers in their interaction with navigation systems, especially in managing their visual attention, without negatively impacting their driving performance. Older drivers were able to use other modalities to navigate safely. However, when using these other forms of feedback, their workload remained higher and their secondary task performance was still lower than that of the younger drivers. Older drivers still experience greater workload than younger drivers, even when using multi-modal services. Although the reluctance of elder drivers to use navigation systems can be reduced through the provision of multi-modal services, they may still face greater difficulties than younger drivers in using route guidance information. Therefore, developers of systems for elder drivers may need to focus more on reducing drivers' cognitive burden than on resolving effects of divided attention.

Different combinations of feedback worked best for elder and younger drivers
It is clear from the results in Table 2 that different combinations of feedback worked best for younger and elder drivers. In terms of subjective and objective workload reduction and safe driving, the combination of all modalities worked best for younger drivers, which was predicted by multiple resource theory. It also had them driving the slowest and the fewest instances of taking their eyes off the road (except for the non-visual multi-modal condition). It is quite interesting that although younger drivers preferred the conventional feedback of *visual plus auditory*, this combination ranked lowest overall. Incorporating haptic feedback appears to be the most important for younger drivers, with the three combinations including haptic feedback were best.

Younger drivers stated that visual feedback was the most useful and auditory feedback was the most annoying. Despite this preference for visual feedback, it did not improve their task performance and did create issues of divided attention.

For elder drivers, the results were more mixed. The non-visual multi-modal combination, *auditory plus haptic*, was the best in terms of task performance and divided attention. It did not rank particularly high on the workload measures, although it did induce high cognitive load in the fewest number of drivers. In stark contrast to the younger drivers, the combination of all modalities ranked lowest over all measures, although both this combination and *visual plus haptic* ranked lower than the other combinations. It is also noteworthy that, similar to the younger drivers, the most preferred combination ranked lowest over all measures. For elder drivers, including auditory feedback was the most useful, with *auditory plus haptic* and *visual plus auditory* performing the best.

Table 2. Comparison of the multi-modal conditions for each of our measures, for both age groups. A (conventional): V+A, B: V+H, C: A+H, D: V+A+H. A sign of inequality indicates which condition was better for safer navigation (except for driving time). For example, *C>A* in elder drivers' *lane deviation* means that elder drivers made smaller lane deviation with *C* than *A*.

		Younger	Elder
Subjective Reporting	Stated preferences (Likert)	A>D>B>C	D>A>C>B
	NASA-TLX	D>B>C>A	B>A>C>D
Task Performance	Missed turns	D>B=C=A	C=D=A>B
	Violated regulations	D>C>B>A	A>C>B>D
	Lane deviation	D>B>A>C	C>A>D>B
	Driving Time (faster to slower)	A>C>B=D	B>C>A>D
Eye Gaze	Off-time at a glance	C>D>B>A	C>D>B>A
	Off-time percent	C>D>B>A	C>B>A>D
	Move per 1-min driving	A>C=B>D	C>D>A>B
Physiological	As focusing on the 'Low's in Fig.5	D>C>B>A	A=B>C>D
	As focusing on the 'High's in Fig.5	C>B>D>A	C>A=B>D

Elder drivers stated that visual feedback was most annoying, and this is consistent with past work [15]. This could indicate why elder drivers rated *visual plus haptic* as being significantly less preferable for them despite there being no deterioration in performance or divided attention. This may not be due to the existence of visual feedback, as *auditory plus haptic* was not rated highly either (Table 2). In terms of multi-modal feedback, this may not imply that elder drivers are reluctant to use visual feedback, but instead, that they prefer to have auditory feedback included. As the overall results for elders were mixed, so are the recommendations for improved navigation systems. It may be that navigation systems need to be customized according to the cognitive and perceptual abilities of a particular elder. Their needs or preferences must be taken into account as well; our results would recommend a different navigation system if one wanted safer navigation *vs.* higher satisfaction.

How to incorporate haptic feedback in navigation systems
Our results indicate that a vibrotactile steering wheel can be used as a navigation aid for reducing eyes-off-the-road issues, but not for reducing task performance errors. To incorporate haptic feedback in navigation systems for elder drivers, it could be used as a replacement for visual feedback since older drivers significantly rely on auditory feedback. For younger drivers, haptic feedback should be added to conventional systems, as the combination of all modalities resulted in more attentive driving.

Workload can be estimated in near real-time
Another issue we explored was psycho-physiological task workload assessment. Our results showed that workload models for each age group were able to predict the task workload of individual drivers with quite high accuracies during driving tasks which include dependence on multi-modal navigation systems. This psycho-physiological approach allows for workload assessment every three seconds while driving, making it a promising approach for a near real-time workload monitoring system. This approach has great potential applicability in the design of intelligent route guidance systems. As seen in the learning domain [27], loads which are either too high or too

low can lead to low task performance. If this phenomenon also exists in the driving domain (*e.g.*, suffering from too noisy traffic), our route guidance system may be able to provide services with relatively lower noise through use of visual or haptic feedback without auditory feedback. If drivers' workload is too low (*e.g.*, if driving on the highway becomes monotonous), in-vehicle information systems may be used to provide more detailed information to help maintain attentive driving (*e.g.*, preventing drivers from becoming drowsy).

Limitations. We acknowledge the potential shortcomings of our study here. First, this study was conducted in a custom-built driving simulator in a lab setting. To replicate this study in a real environment, more experimentation is needed to understand the set of sensory distractors. A challenging issue will be in conducting field research with elderly subjects (*e.g.*, ethical issues such as losing decision-making capacity during the course of a study [12]). The video game-like task implemented in this study may have resulted in differences in virtual driving abilities between two age groups, since younger drivers may have had more exposure to video games. There may be potential gender differences in the driving task, since males may play more driving games than females. Other differences may be caused by the difference between local and non-local residents in knowing a route, in years of driving or frequency of computer usage.

While we didn't technically control for the experience in using simulated driving, we found little effect of the age factor. We provided sufficient practice time for both age groups, with no use of any test modalities as well as in all of the test modalities. Our simulated driving task using no test modalities showed no variation between age groups in the task performance and the divided attention measures; the only exception was the driving time (*i.e.*, slower driving of the elderly). All elderly participants had more than 30 years of driving experience; this factor did not result in worse virtual-driving. In this study, we included only the age factor in the analysis and balanced our populations only by this factor. We focused our analysis on the evaluation of route guidance modalities within each of age groups rather than the comparison of age groups within each of driving condition. We used other demographic factors collected as a criterion to filter out additional participants.

Lastly, in the current stage of this study we did not use the standard lane-change test [15, 22] to regulate the use of fixed driving speed condition or extra road signs that can stimulate extra cognitive load or attention management. Use of this standard test would allow others to replicate our results more easily.

5   Conclusions

We conducted a study exploring the modalities used to provide route guidance feedback for drivers. Our study revealed that 'multi-modal' route guidance systems can enhance older drivers' visual attention management. However, these drivers still experienced higher task workloads and exhibited lower navigation performance than younger drivers for such in-vehicle dual-tasks.

We learned that the combination of modalities should be designed differently for older drivers than for younger drivers. For younger drivers, *visual plus auditory plus haptic* was generally the best in terms of improved task performance and reduced induced workload. When designing a navigation system for this population, haptic feedback should be included, as it improved performance across almost all measures. For elder drivers, while the results were more mixed, *auditory plus haptic* was the best. Due to these mixed results, a customized solution may be necessary depending on their needs to be safer or more satisfied. Auditory feedback should be included in any route guidance system for elder drivers.

Our results indicate the importance of understanding differences in cognitive engagement with different route guidance modalities across age groups. To address this issue, we demonstrated that our psycho-physiological response-based assessment is a highly-accurate approach for predicting drivers' cognitive workloads when driving with navigation systems. We leave the personalization of predictive models and the personalization of route navigation systems to future work.

Acknowledgments. This work was generously funded by General Motors, the National Science Foundation and Quality of Life Engineering Research Center (EEEC-540865). We would also like to thank Eija Haapalainen for her efforts with the modeling of cognitive load using psycho-physiological signals.

References

1. Ball, K., Owsley, C.: Increasing mobility and reducing accidents of older drivers. In: Schaie, K.W., Pietrucha, M. (eds.) Mobility and Transportation in the Elderly, pp. 213–250. Springer, New York (2000)
2. Beatty, J.: Task evoked pupillary responses, processing load, and the structure of processing resources. Psychological Bulletin 91, 276–292 (1982)
3. Cegarra, J., Chevalier, A.: The use of tholos software for combining measures of mental workload: Toward theoretical and methodological improvements. Behavior Research Methods 40(4), 988–1000 (2008)
4. Chandler, P., Sweller, J.: The split-attention effect as a factor in the design of instruction. British Journal of Educational Psychology 62(2), 233–246 (1992)
5. Collia, D., Sharp, J., Giesbrecht, L.: The 2001 national household travel survey: A look into the travel patterns of older Americans. Journal of Safety Research 34, 461–470 (2003)
6. De Waard, D.: The measurement of drivers' mental workload. PhD Thesis, University of Groningen (1996)
7. Dingus, T.A., Klauer, S.G.: The relative risks of secondary task induced driver distraction. Society of Automotive Engineers, Technical Paper Series 2008-21-0001 (2008)
8. Geldard, F.A.: Sensory Saltation: Metastability in the Perceptual World. Lawrence Erlbaum Associates, Hillsdale (1975)
9. Haapalainen, E., Kim, S., Forlizzi, J., Dey, A.: Psycho-physiological Measures for assessing Cognitive Load. In: Proc. Ubicomp 2010, pp. 301–310 (2010)
10. Hakamies-Blomqvist, L., Siren, A., Davidse, R.: Older drivers - a review. VTI rapport 497A, Swedish National Road and Transport Research Institute (2004)
11. Hart, S.G., Staveland, L.E.: Development of NASA-TLX (Task Load Index): results of empirical and theoretical research. In: Hancock, P.A., Meshkati, N. (eds.) Human Mental Workload, pp. 139–183. Amsterdam, North-Holland (1988)
12. High, D.M., Doole, M.M.: Ethical and legal issues in conducting research involving elderly subjects. Behav. Sci. Law. 13(3), 319–335 (1995)
13. Horberry, T., Anderson, J., Regan, M.A., Triggs, T.J., Brown, J.: Driver distraction: The effects of concurrent in-vehicle tasks, road environment complexity and age on driving performance. Accident Analysis & Prevention 38, 185 (2006)

14. Hwang, S., Ryu, J.: The Haptic steering Wheel: Vibro-tactile based navigation for the driving environment. In: IEEE Intl' Conf. PERCOM Workshops, pp. 660–665 (2010)

15. International Organization For Standardization. ISO-26022: Road Vehicles – Ergonomic Aspects of Transport Information and Control Systems -Simulated Lane Change Test to Assess in-Vehicle Secondary Task Demand. International Standard. Geneve (2010)

16. Kay, L., Bundy, A., Clemson, L., Jolly, N.: Validity and reliability of the on-road driving assessment with senior drivers. Accid. Anal. Prev. 40, 751–759 (2008)

17. Kern, D., Marshall, P., Hornecker, E., Rogers, Y., Schmidt, A.: Enhancing Navigation Information with Tactile Output Embedded into the Steering Wheel. In: Tokuda, H., Beigl, M., Friday, A., Brush, A.J.B., Tobe, Y. (eds.) Pervasive 2009. LNCS, vol. 5538, pp. 42–58. Springer, Heidelberg (2009)

18. Kim, S., Dey, A.K.: Simulated augmented reality windshield display as a cognitive mapping aid for elder driver navigation. In: Proc. CHI 2009, pp. 133–142 (2009)

19. Kim, S., Dey, A.K., Lee, J., Forlizzi, J.: Usability of car dashboard displays for elder drivers. In: Proc. CHI 2011, pp. 493–502 (2011)

20. Kostyniuk, L., Streff, F., Eby, D.: The older driver and navigation assistance systems. The University of Michigan Transportation Research Institute, Final report UMTRI-97-47 (1997)

21. Lengenfelder, J., Schultheis, M.T., Ali-Shihabi, T., Mourant, R., DeLuca, J.: Divided Attention and Driving: A Pilot Study Using Virtual Reality Technology. Journal of Head Trauma Rehabilitation 17(1), 26–37 (2002)

22. Mattes, S., Hallén, A.: Surrogate Distraction Measurement Techniques: The Lane Change Test. In: Regan, M.A., Lee, J.D., Young, K.L. (eds.) Driver Distraction: Theory, Effects, and Mitigation, p. 107. CRC Press (2008)

23. Mayer, R.E.: Multimedia Learning, 2nd edn. Cambridge University Press (2009)

24. McCarthy, D.P.: Elder drivers and technology. In: Mann, W.C. (ed.) Smart Technology for Aging, Disability and Independence, pp. 247–283. John Wiley & Sons, N.J. (2005)

25. Mital, A., Govindaraju, M.: Is it possible to have a single measure for all work? International Journal of Industrial Engineering Theory 6, 190–195 (1999)

26. Mourant, R.R., Tsai, F.-J., Al-Shihabi, T., Jaeger, B.K.: Measuring Divided Attention Capability of Young and Older Drivers. TRR Journal 1779, 40–45 (2001)

27. Nachreiner, F.: Standards for ergonomics principles relating to the design of work systems and to mental workload. Applied Ergonomics 26(4), 259–263 (1995)

28. Strayer, D.L., Drews, F.A., Crouch, D.J.: A comparison of the cell phone driver and the drunk driver. Hum. Factors 48, 381–391 (2006)

29. Suen, S.L., Sen, L.: Mobility Options for Seniors. In: Transportation in an Aging Society: A Decade of Experience, pp. 97–113. Transportation Research Board (2004)

30. Eby, D.W., Trombley, D.A., Molnar, L.J., Shope, J.T.: The assessment of older drivers capabilities: A review of the literature. UMTRI-98-24 (1998)

31. Van Erp, J.B.F., Van Veen, H.A.H.C.: Vibro-Tactile Information Presentation in Automobiles. In: Eurohaptics 2001 Conference. University of Birmingham, Birmingham (2001)

32. Veltman, J.A., Gaillard, A.W.K.: Physiological indices of workload in a simulated flight task. Biological Psychology 42, 323–342 (1998)

33. Wickens, C.D.: Processing resources in attention. In: Parasuraman, R., Davies, R. (eds.) Varieties of Attention, pp. 63–101. Academic Press, New York (1984)

34. Yeh, Y., Wickens, C.D.: Dissociation of performance and subjective measures of workload. Human Factors 30(1), 111–120 (1988)

Interactive Environment-Aware Handheld Projectors for Pervasive Computing Spaces

David Molyneaux[1,2], Shahram Izadi[1], David Kim[1,3], Otmar Hilliges[1], Steve Hodges[1], Xiang Cao[1], Alex Butler[1], and Hans Gellersen[2]

[1] Microsoft Research, Cambridge, UK
{davmo,shahrami,bdavidk,otmarh,shodges,xiangc,dab}@microsoft.com
[2] School of Computing and Communications, Lancaster University, UK
hwg@comp.lancs.ac.uk
[3] School of Computer Science, Newcastle University, UK

Abstract. This paper presents two novel handheld projector systems for indoor pervasive computing spaces. These projection-based devices are "aware" of their environment in ways not demonstrated previously. They offer both *spatial awareness*, where the system infers location and orientation of the device in 3D space, and *geometry awareness*, where the system constructs the 3D structure of the world around it, which can encompass the user as well as other physical objects, such as furniture and walls. Previous work in this area has predominantly focused on infrastructure-based spatial-aware handheld projection and interaction. Our prototypes offer greater levels of environment awareness, but achieve this using two opposing approaches; the first *infrastructure-based* and the other *infrastructure-less* sensing. We highlight a series of interactions including direct touch, as well as in-air gestures, which leverage the shadow of the user for interaction. We describe the technical challenges in realizing these novel systems; and compare them directly by quantifying their location tracking and input sensing capabilities.

Keywords: Handheld projection, geometry and spatial awareness, interaction.

1 Introduction

There are many interpretations of Weiser's early vision of Pervasive and Ubiquitous Computing [25]. One notion is of the 'smart' space, typically instrumented rooms with embedded sensors (such as cameras or ultrasonic sensors) that are used to infer the activities and interactions occurring within [2,12,17,21,29]. One critical question for these types of spaces is how to enable *user interaction* beyond the traditional forms of desktop computing. Many examples have been explored in the literature including the use of large displays, tabletops, mobile phones, or fixed and steerable projection [2,7,12,15,19,20,28]. As pico-projector technology matures and begins to appear within phones and digital cameras, an interesting and under-explored design space is the use of handheld projection to augment such spaces.

This paper presents two novel systems that enable handheld projectors to be used for interaction within such spaces. Unlike prior work [1,3,4,7,8,19,21,23,24,26,27], our systems provide both a high degree of *spatial awareness*, where the device can

J. Kay et al. (Eds.): Pervasive 2012, LNCS 7319, pp. 197–215, 2012.
© Springer-Verlag Berlin Heidelberg 2012

sense its location and orientation in 3D space, and *geometry awareness*, where the system can construct the 3D structure of the world around it, both encompassing the user as well as physical objects, such as furniture and walls. Previous work has mostly focused on infrastructure-based spatial-aware handheld projection and interaction.

Our prototypes take two opposing approaches in realizing both spatial and geometry awareness. The first system embeds some of the sensing into the environment. A novel *infrastructure-based* system uses four ceiling-mounted Kinect cameras to both track the 3D location of the handheld projector but also reconstruct the geometry of an entire room. The projector is coupled with an onboard infrared (IR) camera and Inertial Measurement Unit (IMU), which additionally enables finer sensing of user's hands and the orientation of the device. This creates a system with both spatial and geometry-awareness, which allows novel types of interaction, including shadow and physics-enabled virtual interactions. Existing mobile projection systems often use an off-the-shelf tracking solution such as a Vicon motion capture system [3,4], which only provides 3D pose, but no geometry sensing.

Our second system takes an *infrastructure-less* sensing approach providing whole-room geometry and spatial awareness through a handheld device that combines a pico-projector with a Kinect depth camera. A Simultaneous Localization And Mapping (SLAM) system [10], is used to estimate the 6 Degrees-Of-Freedom (DOF) pose of the device, and at the same time create a detailed reconstruction of the scene.

Although the systems share similar goals they have their unique tradeoffs. In this paper we describe each system in detail, as we feel each informs the design space for handheld projection for pervasive smart spaces. We demonstrate the novel interactive scenarios that each system can enable. Our contributions are summarized as follows:

- A novel infrastructure-based handheld projector system, which combines 6DOF tracking with detailed geometry-awareness of the environment.
- A novel infrastructure-less handheld projector system, which affords a high degree of environment sensing by using a new SLAM system [10].
- Novel interaction techniques based on hand gestures in front of the projector.
- Quantitative experiments comparing tracking accuracy in respect to location and orientation, and evaluating touch accuracy for geometry-aware interactions.

2   Related Work

There is a great deal of research in the area of smart spaces including systems based on cameras and other situated sensors [2,12]. To help scope the related work we focus on infrastructure and infrastructure-free projector-camera systems.

Cao et al. [3,4] used a high-end commercial motion capture system to enable full 6DOF tracking of a handheld projector and stylus. This *infrastructure-based* approach provides interaction techniques for both single and multiple projectors. In particular, the system includes full 6DOF spatial awareness. However, scene geometry is not sensed directly. Instead the user interactively defines multiple planar surfaces in the environment. This calibration allows the projection to be pre-distorted so that the image appears correct on a planar surface, even when the projector is held at an oblique angle. A "flashlight" metaphor [24] allows virtual content to appear anchored in the real world, with content being revealed when 'illuminated' by the projector.

Other researchers have taken a different perspective and explored *infrastructure-free* sensing. Common approaches couple a camera with the mobile projector for onboard sensing - Beardsley et al. [1] and Raskar et al. [18,19] used calibrated projector-camera systems to detect fiducial markers attached to walls which are used to recover the camera pose, allowing the projection of perspective-corrected graphics. Similarly Willis et al. [27] created a projector-camera system that simultaneously projected an invisible IR fiducial alongside the regular visible light image, allowing two devices to sense when their projections nearby, enabling new multi-projector interactions.

Other infrastructure-free systems use an onboard camera to detect gesture and touch input from the user. For example, SixthSense [14] detects finger gestures in the air by using colored markers worn on the fingers, and Hotaru [23] allows touch input on the projection surface by attaching an LED marker to the finger.

Other systems use other onboard sensors (rather than a camera) to detect the orientation and motion of the handheld projector, thereby supporting limited spatially-aware interaction. For example MotionBeam [26] uses an IMU to control the behavior and perspective of a projected game character.

In addition to the work presented so far which focuses on *spatially aware* systems, we are interested in increasing the sensing fidelity of such projectors by enabling *geometry awareness*, i.e. detecting the geometric structure of physical objects around the projector, including walls, tabletops as well as the user (e.g. their hands and body).

One category of systems looks at geometry awareness in the context of a single instrumented space. Examples have explored the use of steerable projectors and cameras to track and project content anywhere within the space [7,15,20]. More recently, LightSpace [29] looks at *static* projection but more fine-grained sensing permitted by Kinect, exploring on surface and in-air interactions across a wall and tabletop surface. A logical progression of this approach is to support 360-degree whole room sensing, as proposed in our infrastructure-based approach in this paper.

Other systems have explored geometry awareness in the context of mobile projection. The RFIG system [19] can be used to detect objects in the environment in addition to walls. This allows the system to be used to augment objects with planar surfaces with overlaid digital content. Omnitouch [8] is a wearable short throw Kinect camera coupled with pico-projector, enabling touch interactions on planar objects in the field-of-view of the camera. The system has no spatial awareness and geometry awareness is limited to the raw Kinect data and constrained to planar surfaces only.

Another area looks at mobile cameras to sense the geometry and camera pose simultaneously [6,10]. These SLAM systems appeal as they offer a completely infrastructure-free approach, and are becoming popular with the rise of the Kinect. [10] uses a Kinect to perform dense SLAM, and demonstrates many new interaction scenarios and his system forms the basis of our second prototype.

Prior work has explored either spatially or geometry aware projection in the context of infrastructure-based or infrastructure-free systems. However, the combination of the two has been underexplored, and it is unclear what the tradeoffs of taking an infrastructure or infrastructure-free approach are. In contrast, we aim to tackle the fundamental technical challenge of supporting both spatial and geometry sensing to augment physical spaces with interactive projection. We do this by describing two novel prototypes which take two different approaches to environment sensing. We describe the tradeoffs of each by exploring the interaction space each enables, and evaluating sensing fidelity comparatively.

3   Prototype 1: RoomProjector

RoomProjector uses multiple fixed Kinect cameras to generate a coarse representation of the surfaces in an environment, and track objects and people that inhabit the space. This provides spatial-awareness similar to the Vicon motion capture systems used in [3,4], but goes beyond previous handheld projector systems in terms of the geometry-awareness it affords.

3.1   Infrastructure-Based Sensing

Instead of using traditional diffuse IR illumination coupled with high-speed IR camera tracking of retro-reflective markers (such as in the Vicon motion capture system used in [3]), our infrastructure-based approach relies on multiple fixed Kinect depth-sensing cameras.

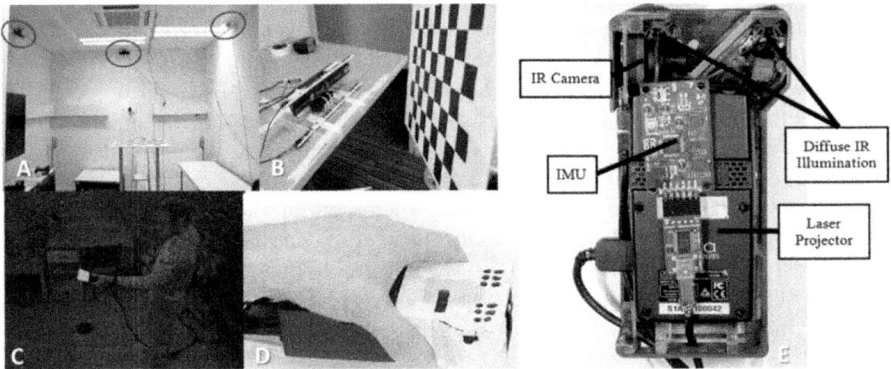

Fig. 1. A) Room infrastructure, highlighting three of four ceiling-mounted Kinect cameras. B) Intrinsic calibration of the IR Kinect camera using a checkerboard pattern illuminated with diffuse IR. D) For location sensing the projector is covered with IR reflective tape. C) This enables easy identification in the Kinect IR images. When visible to multiple Kinect cameras, the 3D location of the projector can be determined. E) Projector hardware main components.

The RoomProjector prototype uses four regular Kinect cameras mounted on the ceiling (2.75m high) at the mid-point of each wall in a rectangular room (4x3m) and angled down at 45° (see Fig. 1.A). To sense the whole room simultaneously, the depth maps from each independent camera are registered by performing standard camera calibration [9]. Here the intrinsic optical parameters are recovered (see Fig. 1B) and the extrinsic 6DOF pose of each Kinect is determined using a large printed checkerboard, which defines a shared world origin (see Figure 1A).

3.2   Geometry Reconstruction

A GPU-based computer vision processing pipeline (shown in Figure 2) is used to transform the raw depth data from the Kinect sensors into surface meshes representing the coarse geometrical structure of the room as follows: A reference background frame is captured per camera, by averaging a number of depth map samples when the room is empty. This data is re-projected using the camera calibration matrices as a single fused point cloud. A background mesh is generated without users in the room, using an offline Poisson surface reconstruction [11]. When users enter the scene the reference background frame is used to extract the foreground. This data is smoothed using an edge preserving bilateral filter. Normals and a polygon mesh are computed. This technique processes 640x480 pixels from each camera in real-time (at 30FPS – the framerate of the Kinect).

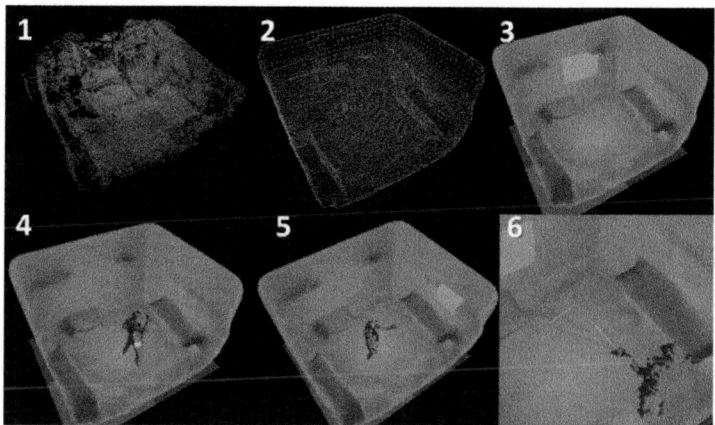

Fig. 2. The vision pipeline: 1) Aligned point-clouds from each camera. 2) Meshed representation (wireframe) using Poisson Surface Reconstruction. 3) Fully shaded mesh. 4) Foreground segmentation (Note: color of foreground object is composed of different colors representing each camera). 5 and 6) Tracked projector with frustum and projection rendered.

3.3   Projector Tracking

In order to track the 3D location of the handheld projector within the space, we cover it with retro-reflective tape and leverage the fact that the Kinect's structured light pattern will appear much brighter in the 2D Kinect IR image when reflected off the projector. This allows the projector to be located within the 2D IR image, as pixels will have very high intensity values (see Figure 1C). Depth measurements are still reported in these locations of the depth map.

Triangulation of the object's position in 3D space is performed by first binarising each image from the four cameras with a threshold, performing closing and dilation morphology operations to first remove noise then join regions, then extracting the largest connected component. As the 3D location of each of the pixels associated with the largest connected components can be obtained from the depth map, we can project rays from the camera center through each of these 3D points for each camera and calculate intersections. We store all ray intersection locations and use the center of mass of this 3D point cloud for the location of the projector. A Kalman filter is subsequently used to increase robustness to multi-camera occlusions (which can otherwise cause brief loss of tracking) and reduce jitter.

This Kinect-based infrastructure provides the projector system with a coarse surface representation of the entire room geometry, as well as its absolute location (3DOF) within the space. To sense the orientation of the device, and of course provide projection output, we designed a prototype handheld device (see Fig.1E) , coupled with our Kinect-based sensing infrastructure. This uses an Aaxatech L1 Laser pico-projector with 800x600 pixel resolution. A Microstrain 3DM-GX3 IMU is mounted on the projector, generating device orientation estimates at a rate of 500Hz.

3.4   Environment-Aware Projected Content

With the 3D orientation data from the IMU and the 3D position tracked from the Kinect-based infrastructure, we can now determine the 6DOF pose of the projector within our virtual reconstruction (see Figures 2 and 3).

The addition of coarse surface geometry of the room, allows the system to determine which prominent physical surface the user is pointing at with the projector (e.g. table, floor or wall). Virtual digital content, such as 2D images, can be associated with any surface of the reconstructed room mesh by simply projective texturing onto the 3D model. Once the 3D model is textured with this virtual content, the projector can be used to reveal the content, when the device points directly at that region of the reconstructed 3D model.

This allows a flashlight-like metaphor as in [3,4,24] to be implemented very easily with our system as shown in Figure 3. However, this carries the additional benefit that the given that the surface geometry is known, the projected content can be automatically corrected to account for off-axis projection (in contrast to existing systems which require a specific manual calibration step e.g. [3,4]).

3.5   Freehand Shadow Interactions

Beyond associating content within the environment using a geometry-aware flashlight metaphor, the RoomProjector also allows for novel freehand user interactions. It does this with a novel fusion of onboard and infrastructure-based sensing. Two 950nm IR LEDs (which do not interfere with the 830nm wavelength of the Kinect) are mounted in the projector case either side of the projection aperture (see Figure 1E). A monochrome IDS UI-1226-LE camera with 752x480 pixel resolution, 60Hz frame rate and 60° wide-angle lens is used for sensing objects in front of the device. The optical axes of the projector and camera are coaxial – an IR hot-mirror, mounted directly in front of the projector lens and angled at 45° redirects IR light from the scene sideways into the camera. Mounting the projector and IR camera coaxially allows the projector-camera relationship to be represented with a one-off projective homography calibration to account for small offsets and scaling without the need for full 3D pose recovery of the projector relative to the camera.

This IR camera senses the presence of hands of the user interacting in front of the device. This allows us to support novel forms of interaction for a handheld projector by reacting to different gestures made in front of it. Of course, when a user places their hand in front of the device to gesture, a real *shadow* is naturally cast onto the projection. The coaxial nature of the optics means that 2D camera image (which detects nearby IR reflective objects such as hands) exactly maps the shadow that will be cast onto the 2D projected image.

Using this technique it is possible to create shadow-based interactions which effectively enable indirect interaction with projected content at a distance. We illustrate this concept in Figure 3A and B where we show how the virtual shadow can be used to perform physics-based interactions such as controlling virtual balls, which respond to collisions with the shadows as if they were real.

In this technique we first segment the hand from the background using a Gaussian blur, binary threshold and closing morphological operations to close holes. The resulting binary mask image is then down-sampled, and for each foreground pixel a static rigid body is created in a 2D physics simulation. These rigid bodies interact with the other dynamic objects, such as the virtual spheres in the physics simulation.

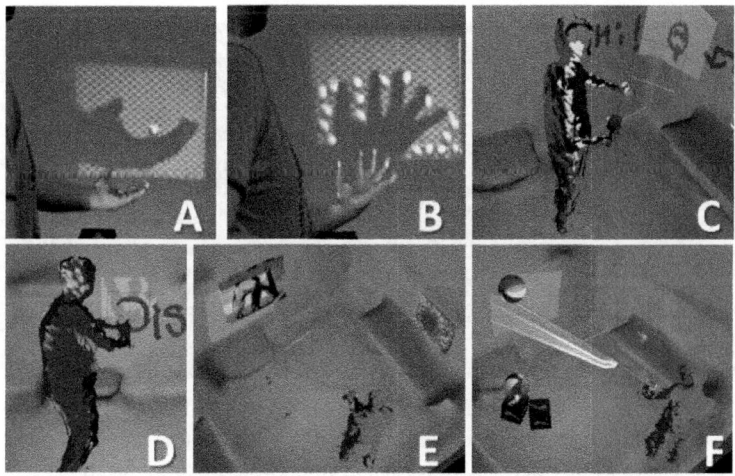

Fig. 3. Spatially and geometry-based shadow interactions: A and B) User interacts with virtual physics-enabled objects using a real shadow. C) Sensing projector pose, user's hands, and a flashlight metaphor to enable writing and painting using the real shadow. D) Painting in midair. E) Flashlight metaphor implemented by texturing the 3D model and revealing through the projector. Note: projection is automatically corrected for the surface. F) Debug output showing how physics interactions are enabled within the space through rods raycast onto the 3D model.

While the use of shadows have been discussed in other related work [5,13,16,30] by leveraging physics, projection onto the hands and fingertip tracking, we demonstrate a number of simple yet compelling techniques that further capture the natural affordances of real-world shadows for interaction.

3.6   Shadow Menus and Fingertip Gestures

A natural extension to the physics enabled shadow interaction metaphor is to combine simple finger-based gestures. One compelling example is shown in Figure 4E. When the user holds their hand directly in front of the projector menu items are associated with each finger and displayed onto the wall above the fingertips. The user then touches their palm with the fingertip, in a manner akin to placing the associated menu item in the palm of the hand, to activate the particular menu item. Active menu items are rendered on the palm to provide visible feedback of selection.

Figure 4F and G shows one final example of a shadow technique for interacting with a large document using the projector. Here a thumb and forefinger gesture activates and deactivates fingertip-based annotation.

To implement these techniques, once the hand is segmented, fingertips are detected by first tracing the contour around the hand, and then using a peak-and-valley algorithm to label candidate pixels [21] as shown in Figure 4A-D. Connected component analysis provides 2D coordinates for each fingertip, and these are tracked over time using a Kalman filter. A simple gesture recognizer allows the motion of and distance and angles between fingertips or other state (such as a finger disappearing from view) to trigger commands.

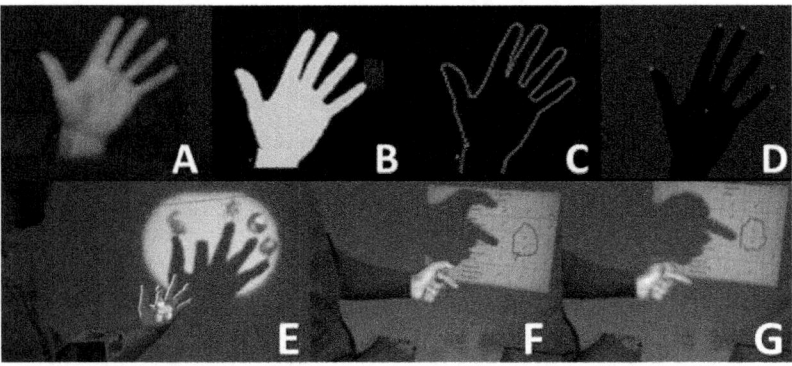

Fig. 4. Fingertip sensing using onboard IR camera: A) raw diffuse IR image captured by onboard camera. B) image corrected and binarized. C) the contour of the hand is traced. D) fingertips are sensed using peak-and-valley algorithm. These fingertip locations can be used for a shadow menu (E) or finger-based shadow gestures for document interaction (F and G).

3.7   Spatially-Aware Shadows

So far these shadow interactions are conducted in the coordinate space of the camera, rather than the global (or room) coordinate space. To enable these interactions to coexist with environment-aware features, which require the Kinect-based infrastructure, we fuse the data from the onboard camera and the infrastructure. For certain 2D interactions, for example, using the shadow to draw on the projection screen as shown in Figure 4F and G, as the 3D pose of the projector is known, the 2D fingertip location sensed using the IR camera can be raycast onto the surface mesh of the room. This allows us to sense exactly within the room where a shadow is being projected. For example, a continuous stream of point sprite "ink" can be created and rendered at the raycast 3D location as shown in Figure 3C. These annotations remain fixed in the real world, allowing the flashlight metaphor to extend the interaction space beyond the frustum of the projector.

The shadow-based physics interactions can therefore be extended to support more detailed 3D interactions. Instead of using a 2D physics simulation and creating rigid bodies to interact with 2D objects, we use the technique highlighted in [29]. Here a Sobel filter is run on the IR handheld camera image. Any valid pixels on the contour of the hand will have a rigid, ray-like box object created from the projector center to a 3D location (determined by raycasting the 2D pixel coordinate into the 3D scene and testing for a 3D intersection with the room mesh). This enables the user to perform basic interactions with 3D virtual objects, as these rigid boxes exert a collision force whenever they intersect another virtual object. Hence, we can pick virtual objects up, hold them, or push them around merely using this shadow, as shown in Figure 3F.

For other interactions, the true 3D location of the hand is required, localized by taking the segmented foreground and using a machine learning-based classifier for identifying the user's hands [22]. We make use of the onboard camera image, but now combine this with the hand classifier which uses the depth data from the room cameras to coarsely provide an estimated location of the hand in front of the projector, as well as a bounding box or sphere around the hand position. This allows us to either map fingertip estimates from the onboard camera onto the bounding region of the sensed hand. Or alternatively map recognized gestures in the camera image, such as a pinch gesture, with the 3D location of the hand, as shown in Figure 3C and D.

3.8   Complementing Shadow Interaction with Shadow Projection

A problem that exists when rendering 3D objects in the room is that we can only render these using a 2D projection onto available surfaces. Sometimes this projection looks reasonable, whereas other times it is unclear how the 2D projection should appear. This is particularly the case when the 3D object is in mid-air, away from the surface being projected onto but still in the field of view of the projector.

Here we begin to explore the possibilities for better user feedback of arbitrary virtual 3D objects, not by rendering them, but instead rendering the shadows of the object [16]. This effect is demonstrated in Figure 5, where the projector is pointed towards a virtual 3D object, a Piñata dangling in mid-air in the room. Moving the projector around this object casts different shadows onto the surface behind, and therefore gives the user a sense of the object's geometry and 3D location without needing to render the full, shaded object – which given that it is in the middle of the room would appear incorrect when projected on a wall.

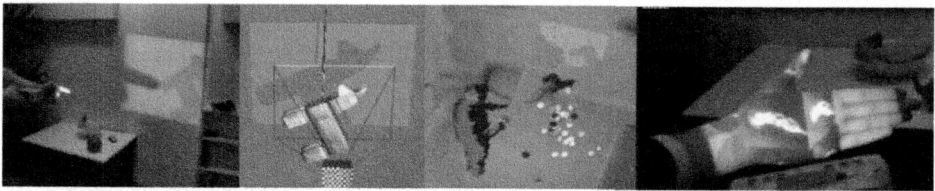

Fig. 5. From left: Revealing a virtual 3D object by viewing its virtual shadow rendered onto the projected display. This shadow can interact with the real shadow generated by the user's hands. Revealing the hidden scene by projecting an augmented reality view onto the hand.

The concepts for revealing 3D objects through their shadows nicely compliment the idea of real interactive shadows, and it is possible to combine the two concepts. In Figure 5 left, we show how the virtual shadow of the object can be knocked side-to-side by the real shadow being cast by the user's hands into the projection. A simple yet effective extension to this technique, inherently supported with the RoomProjector, is for the user to place their hands in front of the projector to reveal a full rendering of a 3D object being rendered as a shadow. The hand therefore becomes a kind of viewport or window into the virtual world, as shown in Figure 5 (far right).

3.9   Beyond Infrastructure

In addition to interactions based on the IR image from the handheld unit, the room-based infrastructure delivers some unique ways of enabling wider-scale, room-based interaction. In this sense, the small sensing window of projector is overcome, and user interaction is enabled throughout the entire room. The mesh representation of surfaces in the room may be used to control interactions with virtual objects. The use of multiple Kinect cameras minimizes the sensing (and hence interaction) dead space that would otherwise occur due to occlusions with a single mobile camera. Sensing the environment and distinguishing foreground objects such as the user in the room enables a wide variety of scenarios not possible with previous systems [3,4,29].

The main limitation to the room infrastructure is *coarseness*. Due to the distance between the cameras and objects and surfaces, only prominent surfaces can be recovered from the scene. The hybrid tracking of the projector can occasionally be noisy due to issues of camera occlusions or ferrous objects interfering with the IMU. This coarseness is evaluated later, but led to our second infrastructure-free prototype.

4   Prototype 2: SLAMProjector

The RoomProjector system introduced a variety of interaction possibilities. Our second prototype embeds a projector with a mobile Kinect camera, and uses a system capable of building a model of the environment in real-time and simultaneously tracking the location of the device within this reconstructed model [10]. SLAM systems which support this functionality are common in the AR and robotics communities [6,10] and typically use a single camera to reconstruct small scenes and augment them with virtual content in real time.

Our SLAMProjector system uses depth data only for tracking, as opposed to RGB; useful when working with pico-projectors with low brightness and dim room lighting.

4.1   Infrastructure-Free Flashlight and Enhanced Geometry-Awareness

The SLAMProjector prototype measures 140x65x53mm and contains the same Laser projector, together with elements of an off-the-shelf Kinect camera: the RGB and IR cameras and the IR emitter, which all connect to a single PCB, as seen in Fig. 6 (top).

The SLAM system tracks the 6DOF pose of the Kinect device, and simultaneously creates a high-quality 3D model of the scene (for details see [10]). Unlike the RoomProjector, we have to calibrate the full intrinsic and extrinsic parameters of the projector and cameras in this system using a known checkerboard calibration pattern.

The flashlight metaphor can be used to accurately re-render content in exactly the same location without the need for any infrastructure, unlike our previous system and the work of others [2,3,14,15]. These digital textures can be warped correctly onto planar objects, but given the 6DOF pose of the device, it is possible to render 2D textures onto a surface with any arbitrary geometry using projective texturing, as highlighted in Figure 6 (bottom left).

Perhaps the most unique feature of our system is the ability to quickly acquire and update an accurate 3D model of a dynamic scene in real-time, and in this sense the SLAMProjector is far more geometry-aware than our earlier prototype.

Fig. 6. Top: SLAMProjector hardware. The main components from left-to-right are the IR emitter, RGB camera, IR camera and projector. Bottom left: Warping projected content onto arbitrary shaped surfaces in real-time. Bottom center: A real-world object is scanned using the SLAMProjector and the 3D segmented object pasted onto a nearby wall. Bottom right: particles interact with the scene and are rendered in real-time using a flashlight metaphor.

This 3D model can be re-rendered back using the projector to both act as feedback to the user of the underlying SLAM system (e.g. to show the extent and quality of the reconstruction), but also as a mechanism for coupling interaction with output. Figure 6 (bottom center) shows how users can touch any object to automatically segment a high quality model from the plane. Once these segmented objects are acquired multiple virtual copies can be generated in any arbitrary location. In this example, the user pastes a 3D scan of a model human torso onto the wall.

4.2   SLAMProjector Interactions

We believe that the ability to couple projector output to user interactions such as those in [10] can be compelling. For example, in Figure 7 we show how a user can paint on any surface (see [10]). Adding the direct output of the projector makes this more natural and gives the user direct feedback. Similarly, in Figure 6 where the particles fall onto and into arbitrary surfaces, the projection gives them a more fluid feeling.

However, this scenario is different to the painting example, in that we typically paint onto surfaces, whereas 3D particles can exist anywhere within free space. As highlighted in our previous RoomProjector prototype, such 3D renderings cannot be handled using a 2D projection effectively. So while the SLAMProjector may have the greatest 3D capabilities, at times the fidelity of the input cannot be mapped naturally to the fidelity of the output – the projection itself.

One of the interesting possibilities that can be explored with the SLAMProjector is the transition from direct multi-touch interaction to the indirect interactions outlined in the previous sections. Multi-touch is an intuitive way of interacting with objects up close and within easy reach, but in a larger room indirect shadow interactions may be preferred. In the example shown in Figure 7 (right), the 3D model is used to calculate the distance between the device (hence the user) and projection. If this is below a threshold (typically 1-1.2m), the user can interact directly using multi-touch gestures. As the device is moved further away the interaction automatically switches to indirect interaction. Here, we demonstrate how this implicit mode switch can be used to switch between shadow touch for activating a virtual button, to direct touch, simply by moving the projector closer. Labels on the buttons also update to reflect the mode.

Fig. 7. Left and Center Left: Painting on any surfaces as in [10] but with coupled output. Center Right: Virtual buttons are triggered by touch if the projector is close to the surface (implying the user can reach the surface) or (Right) by shadow if the user is at a distance.

5   System Evaluation

We have shown two very different prototypes for augmenting indoor pervasive computing spaces using interactive, environment-aware handheld projectors, each enabling different interaction possibilities. So far we have qualitatively introduced and discussed the two systems based on their sensing capabilities and highlighted the interaction techniques enabled by each system's unique capabilities.

Both systems rely on information about their 3D pose and geometry of the environment in order to correctly display spatially registered graphics. Both systems also depend on sensing human input for interaction. In this section we detail initial findings from a number of experiments we conducted to evaluate tracking and input accuracy. Tracking accuracy is of great importance in terms of user experience, especially for the kind of spatial interactions described – even small error in pose noticeably reduces visual quality when renderings are not aligned with the real world. Likewise, input accuracy directly impacts user experience – a system that does not respond correctly to input will clearly be frustrating to use.

5.1   Tracking Accuracy

The first experiment compares tracking accuracy of each system. We use an 8 camera Vicon motion capture system as ground truth. A test scene is constructed on a circular tabletop in the center of the room and a gantry fitted to the table with a tiltable projector mount attached. A controlled circular motion around the tabletop can be performed repeatedly for both systems. We alter the mouting height and angle of the projector relative to horizontal to simulate realistic positions and orientations.

5.2   Procedure

Each projector was moved around the tabletop at walking speed once at each of the three mounting heights above the ground – 0.6m, 1.1m and 1.6m – and at each of the tilt angles of 0°, 22.5°, 40° and 45°, resulting in 12 total revolutions around the tabletop. The table contains various small objects (e.g. a book, a toy car) in arbitrary locations on the table. Once placed, these objects remain static for all the experiments. Figure 8 shows the experimental setup and projectors with Vicon markers attached. For both prototypes we compute a calibration matrix to align the respective world origins with the Vicon coordinate system. We synchronize pose and orientation streams from all three systems, which are sampled at 30Hz (the Kinect update rate).

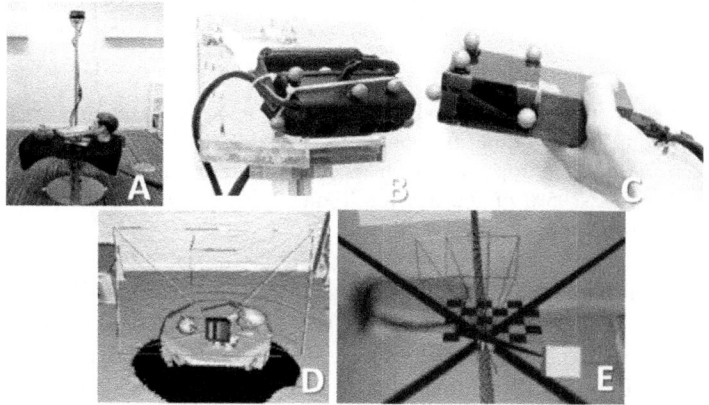

Fig. 8. A) Experimental setup showing test scene and gantry. B) SLAMProjector with Vicon markers. C) RoomProjector with Vicon markers. E) RoomProjector exhibits good positional accuracy but rotation is erroneous (grey frustum is rotation as reported by our prototype, red is ground truth). D) SLAM Projector provides better rotation estimates but can drift over time.

5.3   Results

Figure 9(a-c) summarize result from this initial experiment. For the RoomProjector we can see that the error in position is relatively low along all three axes with a Mean error of 30.9mm, SD=7.6 in 3D location. In contrast the orientation error is relatively high with a combined Mean error of 8.9°, SD=3.8. However, when this error is decomposed into the rotations about individual axes it becomes apparent that the yaw error dominates (M=8.3°,SD=3.9). This can be explained by magnetic distortions in the room. Yaw is measured by the IMU's magnetometer while pitch and roll are from the 3-axis accelerometer. To quantify how significant this effect was, we performed a one-off full magnetic 3D calibration by measuring the yaw error when the projector was lying horizontally and aligned with the room yaw origin using a 3D grid at 0.5m intervals throughout the whole room, then re-performed the experiment. As seen in Figure 9 (c), applying the nearest neighbor calibration to the projector orientation during the experiment almost halves the yaw error (M=4.2°, SD=3.6), however, unless continually updated, this method of calibration only works well for static environments as any ferrous objects moved inside the room will introduce new error.

In contrast, the SLAM system provides comparable but slightly worse positional accuracy (M=34.0mm, SD=17.2 vs. M=30.9mm). A paired t-test reveals that the difference is not statistically significant (p>0.05). However, the SLAM system does provide better rotational accuracy (M=2.2°, SD=1.3 vs. M=8.9° Mean orientation error), and here a paired t-test shows statistical significance (p<0.05).

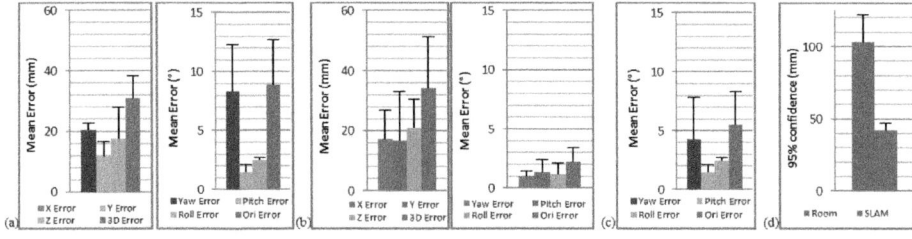

Fig. 9. Mean error, relative to ground truth, split into location and rotation error in each dimension and combined error for (a) RoomProjector and (b) SLAMProjector system. (c) Mean orientation error of RoomProjector, 3D magnetic calibration applied, (d) Button diameter required to encompass 95% of touches for Room Projector and SLAM Projector over all participants and targets. Error bars show SD.

When compared qualitatively, despite higher latency, the SLAMProjector provides much tighter visual integration of real-world and projected graphics. Due to the projective nature of the projector systems, the large Mean orientation error in the RoomProjector is one explanation, as a few degrees error results in visually more significant offsets the further away the projection surface is. This makes orientation error very noticeable when the graphics need to be tightly coupled with a physical surface. In contrast, 3D location error is visually much less apparent, with small lateral shifts appearing as just a minor offset from the true projection position.

It is interesting that the location accuracy of the RoomProjector is very good – making this system an interesting candidate in scenarios that only require 3D position, or using this tracking method in combination with a better source of rotation data than an IMU. However, in practice the room is currently limited to only track one object as there is no easy way to distinguish between multiple retro-reflective objects e.g. fiducial markers would have to be significantly larger than the projector to be detected over typical working distances of 2-6m. One possible solution would be to correlate movement seen in the IR cameras with motion sensed by the IMU, as shown in [15].

The tracking in the RoomProjector system is also stateless, i.e., each frame a new location is computed without considering the previous frames. However, the SLAM system tracks off the model it is building, hence pose error incorporated in the model is cumulative and 3D location can potentially begin to drift over time. Typically this occurs when the majority of the frame is taken up by only one or two planar surfaces, (e.g. walls), but more experiments are necessary to fully quantify this issue.

5.4   Touch Accuracy

One of the compelling possibilities of geometry-aware projector systems is to enable multi-touch interaction on arbitrary surfaces. Both our systems provide touch input but at very different levels of fidelity. To quantify these capabilities and differences we conduct a second experiment investigating touch accuracy across our two systems.

For the SLAM system we use the touch detection technique in [10]. This technique robustly detects and tracks multiple fingertips based on the distance to reconstructed surfaces. For the RoomProjector we detect touch by initially looking at a 3D estimate of the user's hand (as in [22]). This position is noisy and centered on the hand rather than individual fingers. We refine this 3D position by combining it with the onboard IR camera. This projects detected fingertip positions into the 3D scene by ray-casting through the projector center until the finger disappears (close to the surface it has the same illumination brightness as the surface and hence cannot be segmented). We decide whether a finger touches a target based on the intersection of the last detected ray with reconstructed surfaces. We compare the distance along the ray to the intersection point with the distance of the users hand measured by the Kinect cameras.

5.4.1   Procedure
Ten virtual targets are positioned on physical surfaces in the room; 7 targets were planar (3 vertical, 4 horizontal) and 3 non-planar in various orientations (e.g a large beach ball, or life-size head model as shown in Figure 8A). These positions are fixed and defined in world coordinates. The actual target is projected onto the real world, similar to buttons or other UI elements in a real world application. We place physical markers at target locations, enabling participants to easily find the sparsely distributed targets in the room. To isolate touch accuracy from tracking error we use the 6DOF pose from the Vicon system for both systems, and detect touch with the projector.

8 users (5 male, 3 female) between the ages of 24 and 43 years were recruited to perform this target acquisition task. Each participant performed 3 blocks of 10 target acquisition rounds, where each button was shown until a click was recorded. The presentation order of conditions was counter-balanced. Presentation order of targets was sequential as we measure accuracy, not task completion time, hence motor memory and other learning effects play less of a role. Participants were asked to be as accurate as possible with their touches.

5.4.2   Results and Discussion
The participants produced 240 clicks, on the 10 surfaces. Our results represent the real-world performance of our system and hence the cumulative error of system and

user. This error can be decomposed into 3 sources – error in the calibration between the projector and camera system, error in finger detection location (the dominant source of error), and user error when clicking targets. Over all users and targets the SLAMProjector performed significantly better than the RoomProjector (Mean 3D Error=33.8mm, SD=5.5, versus M=75.9mm, SD=19.0). Figure 9(d) shows the button diameter which consistently encompasses 95% of user clicks.

When comparing the results for SLAMProjector with [8], at first glance, our 95% results appear worse than even their far distance condition. However, the far results reported in [8] are for shoulder to arm's length distances (average ~40-60cm), which is closer than typical SLAMProjector sensing distances, which average 70-100cm due both to the minimum sensing distance for Kinect and also as the SLAMProjector is held in the opposite hand. Hence we believe our results for SLAMProjector are consistent with an extrapolation of those from [8], but with the additional benefit of fully non-planar touch detection.

6   Discussion

To explore the sensing fidelity of each system and consequently the interaction fidelity, we have performed two experiments quantifying tracking and input accuracy. As shown in Table 1, when comparing our systems with the state of the art we achieve better fidelity of sensing for both spatial and geometry awareness and touch sensing with SLAMProjector comparable to the current state of the art [8] for touch, but also offering the addition of non-planar multi-touch and spatial awareness.

Table 1. Comparison of the portable projector systems in related work

	Spatial-aware	Geometry-aware	User Input
RoomProjector (infrastructure, high computation, non-mobile)	6DOF, 31mm,9° mean 3D pose accuracy from infrastructure	- planar and non-planar - background capture step - coarse surfaces	- whole body - hand gestures and fingertip recognition (@50cm dist. max)
SLAMProjector (infrastructure-less, high computation, mobile)	6DOF, 34mm,2° mean 3D pose accuracy, stand-alone	- planar and non-planar - no user in the loop - fine surfaces	- hand gestures at arm's length - finger touch 41.7mm button dia. for 95% detection at 0.7-1m - 3D sensing
Cao et al. [3,4] (infrastructure, medium computation, non-mobile)	6DOF -high accuracy from infrastructure	- multiple planar surfaces - requires user in the loop for surface definition	- physical button - device motion
Harrison et al. [8] (infrastructure-less, low computation, mobile)	None	- planar surfaces at < 1m distance	- finger touch detection, 31-38.5mm button dia. for 95% detection at arm's length (far)
Raskar et al.[18,19] (infrastructure, medium computation, mobile)	6DOF from fiducial markers or active tags and tilt sensing	- single planar object surface from active tag or fiducial tagged surface	- physical button - device motion
Mistry et al. [14] (infrastructure-less, low computation, mobile)	None	None	- hand gestures and fingers with coloured caps only

It is interesting to compare the RoomProjector to the others as there are similarities to Cao and Raskar's work [3,4,18,19]; both supporting 6DOF tracking. While Cao's Vicon system offers more accurate tracking, the study showed our system still provides relatively accurate location data, hence is useful in scenarios where a more expensive and intrusive tracking system cannot be used or where orientation is less important. Furthermore, Kinect enables the coarse geometry of the room to be sensed "for free". This added fidelity enables richer interactions such as automatic geometry distortion correction, whole body interactions with physics, shadow interaction with 3D objects, and more accurate registration between virtual and physical.

The final SLAMProjector prototype is the most advanced in terms of sensing fidelity, and also removes the need for infrastructure. It provides stand-alone tracking comparable with RoomProjector, yet provides far higher geometry awareness than the RoomProjector or any of the related work. In terms of gestural input, the user's hands can be segmented and used for both multi-touch and indirect shadow interaction.

However, this does not simply mean that infrastructure-based systems should be replaced by the SLAMProjector. One unique capability that RoomProjector offers (which is not exploited by other infrastructure based approaches) is the ability for this system to sense beyond the frustum of the projector-camera system. Here, the system can coarsely sense humans within the whole space and allow for whole body interactions. For mobile systems, it is rare to be able to capture the entire user while using the system to track and map. Another issue with the SLAM system when used for shadow interaction is that if the user is occluding a large part of the Kinect depth image this can degrade the tracking quality of the projector. Drift can also occur on rapid movement or when pointed at a mostly planar scenes with little varying depth.

There is, however, another important issue that surfaced, and that is the fidelity mismatch between the 2D projected and 3D sensing. The painting examples work perfectly when painting directly onto a surface, with the ink appearing immediately in place. However, when painting in 3D the output fidelity clearly cannot match the sensing. Hence two interesting avenues emerge in terms of future interaction research, firstly, exploring how to leverage other feedback mechanisms to reveal 3D scenes using inherently 2D output. Shadows and revealing the world through the user's hands are two, but there are certainly others. The second is technical, exploring the use of technologies to overcome the limitations of 2D projection, coupling input fidelity more closely with output. Here mobile stereo projection, or video see-through devices with projection are interesting routes for exploration, as are more traditional forms of AR, such as optical see-through HMD or head mounted projection.

7   Conclusion

In this paper we presented two prototype environment-aware handheld projector systems for augmenting indoor pervasive computing spaces and providing users with interactive interfaces anywhere within a room. Both systems have interesting design characteristics and interaction possibilities. RoomProjector is more infrastructure heavy than SLAMProjector. However, both offer unique possibilities and are novel systems in their own right. We introduced novel gesture-based interactions with mobile projectors through a variety of hand gestures in front of the projector. These include shadow-based interactions that utilize both real and virtual shadows as well as the use of hands for an AR view of content in 3D space.

We believe that handheld projection will become increasingly well-established over the coming years, as work relating to the various underlying technologies matures. We hope that some of the techniques and experiences we have reported in this paper will inform the future direction of this work.

References

1. Beardsley, P., Baar, J.V., Raskar, R., Forlines, C.: Interaction using a handheld projector. IEEE Computer Graphics and Applications 25(1), 39–43 (2005)
2. Brumitt, B., Meyers, B., Krumm, J., Kern, A., Shafer, S.: EasyLiving: Technologies for Intelligent Environments. In: Thomas, P., Gellersen, H.-W. (eds.) HUC 2000. LNCS, vol. 1927, pp. 12–27. Springer, Heidelberg (2000)
3. Cao, X., Balakrishnan, R.: Interacting with dynamically defined information spaces using a handheld projector and pen. In: Proc. of ACM UIST 2006, pp. 225–234 (2006)
4. Cao, X., Forlines, C., Balakrishnan, R.: Multi-user interaction using handheld projectors. In: Proc. ACM UIST 2007, pp. 43–52 (2007)
5. Cowan, L., Li, K.: ShadowPuppets: collocated interaction with mobile projector phones using hand shadows. In: Proc: ACM CHI 2011, pp. 2707–2716 (2011)
6. Du, H., et al.: Interactive 3D modeling of indoor environments with a consumer depth camera. In: Proc. Ubiquitous Computing (UbiComp 2011), pp. 75–84. ACM (2011)
7. Ehnes, J., Hirota, K., Hirose, M.: Projected augmentation - AR using rotatable video projectors. In: Proc: 3rd IEEE and ACM ISMAR, pp. 26–35 (2004)
8. Harrison, C., Benko, H., Wilson, A.D.: OmniTouch: Wearable Multitouch Interaction Everywhere. In: Proc. ACM UIST 2011 (2011)
9. Hartley, R., Zisserman, A.: Multiple View Geometry in Computer Vision. Cambridge University Press (2003)
10. Izadi, S., Kim, D., Hilliges, O., Molyneaux, D., et al.: KinectFusion: RealTime Interactions with Dynamic 3D Surface Reconstructions. In: Proc. ACM UIST 2011 (2011)
11. Kazhdan, M., Bolitho, M., Hoppe, H.: Poisson surface reconstruction. In: Proc. Geometry Processing (SGP 2006), Switzerland, pp. 61–70 (2006)
12. Kidd, C.D., et al.: The Aware Home: A Living Laboratory for Ubiquitous Computing Research. In: Yuan, F., Hartkopf, V. (eds.) CoBuild 1999. LNCS, vol. 1670, pp. 191–198. Springer, Heidelberg (1999)
13. Krueger, M.: Artificial Reality 2. Addison-Wesley Professional (1991)
14. Mistry, P., Maes, P., Chang, L.: WUW - Wear Ur World - A Wearable Gestural Interface. In: ACM CHI 2009 Extended Abstracts (2009)
15. Molyneaux, D., Gellersen, H., Kortuem, G., Schiele, B.: Cooperative Augmentation of Smart Objects with Projector-Camera Systems. In: Krumm, J., Abowd, G.D., Seneviratne, A., Strang, T. (eds.) UbiComp 2007. LNCS, vol. 4717, pp. 501–518. Springer, Heidelberg (2007)
16. Naemura, T., Nitta, T., Mimura, A., Harashima, H.: Virtual Shadows- Enhanced Interaction in Mixed Reality Environment. In: IEEE VR 2002, p. 293 (2002)
17. Raskar, R., et al.: The office of the future: a unified approach to image-based modeling and spatially immersive displays. In: Proc. SIGGRAPH 1998, pp. 179–188 (1998)
18. Raskar, R., VanBaar, J., Beardsley, P., et al.: iLamps: geometrically aware and self-configuring projectors. ACM Trans. Graph. 22(3), 809–818 (2003)
19. Raskar, R., et al.: RFIG Lamps: interacting with a self-describing world via photosensing wireless tags and projectors. ACM ToG 23(3), 406–415

20. Pinhanez, C.: The Everywhere Displays Projector: A Device to Create Ubiquitous Graphical Interfaces. In: Abowd, G.D., Brumitt, B., Shafer, S. (eds.) UbiComp 2001. LNCS, vol. 2201, pp. 315–331. Springer, Heidelberg (2001)
21. Sato, Y., et al.: Fast tracking of hands and fingertips in infrared images for augmented desk interface. In: Proc: AFGR. IEEE (2000)
22. Shotton, J., et al.: Real-time human pose recognition in parts from single depth images. In: Proc. CVPR 2011, pp. 1297–1304 (2011)
23. Sugimoto, M., Miyahara, K., Inoue, H., Tsunesada, Y.: *Hotaru*: Intuitive Manipulation Techniques for Projected Displays of Mobile Devices. In: Costabile, M.F., Paternó, F. (eds.) INTERACT 2005. LNCS, vol. 3585, pp. 57–68. Springer, Heidelberg (2005)
24. Teller, S., Chen, J., Balakrishnan, H.: Pervasive pose-aware applications and Infrastructure. IEEE CG&A 23(4), 14–18 (2003)
25. Weiser, M.: The Computer for the Twenty-First Century. Scientific American 265(3), 94–100 (1991)
26. Willis, K.D.D., Poupyrev, I., Shiratori, T.: Motionbeam: Character interaction with handheld projectors. In: Proc: ACM CHI 2011, pp. 1031–1040 (2011)
27. Willis, K.D.D., Poupyrev, I., et al.: SideBySide: ad-hoc multi-user interaction with handheld projectors. In: Proc. ACM UIST 2011, pp. 431–440 (2011)
28. Wilson, A., Izadi, D., Hilliges, O., et al.: Bringing physics to the surface. In: Proc: ACM UIST 2008, pp. 67–76 (2008)
29. Wilson, A., Benko, H.: Combining multiple depth cameras and projectors for interactions on, above and between surfaces. In: Proc: ACM UIST 2010, pp. 273–282 (2010)
30. Xu, H., Iwai, D., Hiura, S., Sato, K.: User Interface by Virtual Shadow Projection. In: Proc: SICE-ICASE, pp. 4817–4818 (2006)

.NET Gadgeteer: A Platform for Custom Devices

Nicolas Villar[1], James Scott[1], Steve Hodges[1], Kerry Hammil[1], and Colin Miller[2]

[1] Microsoft Research
[2] Microsoft Corporation
{nvillar,jws,shodges,khammil,colinmil}@microsoft.com

Abstract. .NET Gadgeteer is a new platform conceived to make it easier to design and build custom electronic devices and systems for a range of ubiquitous and mobile computing scenarios. It consists of three main elements: solder-less modular electronic hardware; object-oriented managed software libraries accessed using a high-level programming language and established development environment; and 3D design and construction tools designed to facilitate a great deal of control over the form factor of the resulting electronic devices. Each of these elements is designed to be accessible to a wide range of people with varying backgrounds and levels of experience and at the same time provide enough flexibility to allow experts to build relatively sophisticated devices and complex systems in less time than they are used to. In this paper we describe the .NET Gadgeteer system in detail for the first time, explaining a number of key design decisions and reporting on its use by new users and experts alike.

1 Introduction

Over the past decade there have been a great many examples in the pervasive and ubiquitous computing research communities where the creation of a new type of digital device has led to valuable research insights. These include mobile battery-powered devices such as SenseCam [18] and Ambient Wood probes [28], situated and augmented displays like the Prayer Companion [11] and Augurscope [29], and distributed systems like the Local Barometer [12] and telepresence proxies [20]. In each of these cases, custom hardware and software in a custom form factor were critical to building devices that could be evaluated in realistic settings.

Of course, developing custom devices from scratch requires a considerable investment of time, money and expertise. Anything which can be done to minimize these requirements, thereby accelerating the process and increasing the scope for exploring a wider design space, is very valuable. A large range of tools and platforms introducing many innovative concepts in this regard have become established over the past few years. For example Phidgets [14] makes it easy to put together new combinations of sensors and actuators in conjunction with a PC, which is valuable in applications with generous size, cost and power consumption requirements. For more constrained applications with basic requirements in terms of processing and I/O bandwidth, platforms like Arduino [1] are an ideal choice. For space-critical and battery-powered distributed sensing applications a range of Mote-like devices [17] are a good option. We review these existing approaches and others in detail in the following section.

J. Kay et al. (Eds.): Pervasive 2012, LNCS 7319, pp. 216–233, 2012.

Despite the many qualities existing platforms bring collectively, we envisage an integrated platform for the creation of custom devices which simultaneously provides:

- **flexibility** over device **form factor** as well as the **hardware and software**;
- **accessibility** to new users and **extensibility** of the platform;
- **versatility** to scale up to **sophisticated standalone devices** and **complex systems**.

This paper describes in detail for the first time the platform we have created to this end, which we call Microsoft .NET Gadgeteer (abbreviated as Gadgeteer hereafter). By combining the above elements we seek to extend the reach and the sophistication of existing tools. Our research contribution is a platform which enables ourselves and others to more effectively explore and iterate new research concepts and design ideas.

We start this paper with an overview of the large body of related work, which includes both research papers and commercial products. Following this we present an example Gadgeteer device implementation which grounds the subsequent three sections – these detail many of the design decisions we took as the Gadgeteer system developed from a research concept to an open-source project with commercially available components. Although many of these decisions are tightly bound together, we have broadly split them into aspects relating to the electronic hardware, the software experience, and mechanical design and we present them in that order. Finally we report on the various ways in which we have evaluated and applied our platform.

2   Related Work

There is a great deal of previous work in the broad domain of tools to support the design and creation of electronic devices, both in the form of research papers and commercial products. To help set our work in this context, we focus the discussion around the broad areas which we identified above as key properties.

2.1   Accessibility

We believe that the accessibility of a tool is generally an important factor in its adoption. In the embedded development space one system with a particularly low barrier for entry is littleBits, which consists of tiny circuit boards with simple functional elements which snap together magnetically [6]. This results in a system requiring no soldering, wiring or programming. Of course, the 'pre-programmed' nature of the system coupled with the relatively simple functionality embodied in each module limits the scope of what can be built, but the system is great for basic 'hardware sketching'. Like littleBits, with the Lego® Mindstorms system [20] it is quick and easy to assemble and re-configure electronic systems from the 8 different input and output modules available but in this case there is the added flexibility of a central controller unit, programmed using a visual programming language which makes it easy for researchers and kids alike to use.

Arduino [1], targeted at designers, supports a range of embedded development circuit boards and also leverages an accessible programming environment [4]. Devices are programmed using a derivative of the Wiring language and an integrated development environment (IDE) derived from the Processing IDE. The language is a simplified version of C, which, together with the IDE provides a minimalist and beginner-friendly programming experience. This accessibility has resulted in widespread online documentation in the form of a myriad of design ideas and tutorials, which has in turn made it even easier for others to pick up the platform and extend their knowledge of it. The mBed programmable microcontroller platform [3] is similar in many ways to Arduino, but one key difference is the online IDE, which is particularly accessible because it can be used via a web browser without installing any software.

Like Arduino, the d.tools system [16] was also conceived to support designers with little or no programming experience to prototype functional devices. The d.tools authoring environment provides a visual programming interface, intended to more closely resemble a storyboarding process than a traditional textual programming activity.

Both the MetaCricket toolkit [24], and more recently the xTel platform [35] employ a virtual machine running on an embedded microcontroller, together with a set of high-level libraries to access and program against sensors and actuators, as a mechanism to lower the complexity of programming embedded hardware.

Inspired by littleBits and Mindstorms, in Gadgeteer,we employed a modular hardware design as a way to lower the barrier to entry for users with little hardware experience (see Section 4). Like Arduino, we opted for a textual programming environment with simplified API and built-in helper libraries to aid beginners (see Section 5). We also developed a system of drivers, which allows the underlying implementation of individual hardware modules to be abstracted for beginners.

2.2   Versatility

Another important attribute of a platform is versatility – the ability to use the same platform in different ways. Of course, this is often at odds with accessibility, because the factors which make a platform easy to use often also limit its ability to address complex tasks. However, as others have pointed out [26], the combination of "low threshold" accessibility with the versatility of a "high ceiling" is a valuable goal. A common versatility feature for hardware toolkits is support for integrating additional electronic components. For example, many Arduino boards share a standardized layout of stackable connectors, which provide access to a number of digital, analog and communication interfaces on the processor. Arduino can be augmented either by wiring custom electronics to these connectors, or by using a *shield* – a pre-made extension board. Many hundreds of different shields exist [2], and popular ones include functionality such as Ethernet, GPS and motor control.

A similar approach of baseboards and stackable add-on modules has been used in a number of other embedded platforms, including Gumstix [15], Smart-Its [13] and Berkeley Motes [17]. Another related system is the Bug Labs BUG platform [8], which includes slots into which a small range of hardware peripherals can be attached. However, all these platforms tend to be limited in the number of additional modules which can be connected. For example, the BUGbase unit supports just 2-4 modules and with Arduino complex shields will use up much of the I/O functionality exposed by the connectors, so in many cases only one shield can be used at a time. In some cases – depending on the number and selection of I/O used by different shields – it is possible to stack and use a number of shields together, but it is not possible to independently chose a range of shields and assume they will all work together.

More recently, the Grove [10] and TinkerKit products [33] have introduced Arduino shields into which a number of hardware modules can be connected. These provide a way to extend Arduino hardware without the need for soldering, for peripheral modules based on a small set of common electrical protocols.

The Gadgeteer design includes a novel and practical system of *sockets* as a way to extend the basic processing unit with additional hardware modules (see Section 4.1). In particular, the use of sockets and multiple *socket types* maximizes the utilization of different processors' I/O capabilities, supports many different combinations of hardware modules and provides a way for different hardware modules to be developed independently of each other while ensuring compatibility between them.

2.3   Flexibility of Form Factor

In our experience, the form factor of a device – its size, shape and finish – is becoming increasingly important, especially when a prototype is to be deployed in a user-facing scenario. A variety of established CAD tools may be used in conjunction with a growing number of 3D printing 'direct digital manufacturing' techniques, thereby enabling experts such as industrial designers to turn their concepts into real artefacts. In recent years, online tools and services have started to appear – both in terms of 3D design tools such as the TinkerCAD 3D designer [33] and 3D printing services like Shapeways [32]. We have also started to see applications which greatly simplify the process of 3D design for certain form factors such as MagicBox [23].

Of course, in order to get the most from a custom enclosure, it is important to have control over the form factor of the electronic assembly it contains. As described above, many Arduino implementations are based on a circuit board which supports a number of plug-in shields – resulting in a very specific form factor for the assembled electronics, with little flexibility to readily change this. However, many derivatives and third-party variants of Arduino have been developed to support applications with space constraints or specific form-factor requirements. These include the LilyPad Arduino [7] for wearable computing; the Fio Arduino [9], intended for wireless applications and including a Bluetooth chipset and a rechargeable battery, and the Seeeduino Film [31], which uses a flexible circuit in place of a rigid PCB.

One approach to supporting flexibility in the form factor of a given device taken by a number of systems is the use of cables to connect physically discrete peripheral modules to a central processing unit. The Phidgets [14] toolkit, for example, supports a collection of sensors and actuators that connect to a PC either directly via USB, or via a USB interface board. d.tools [16] takes a similar approach, allowing the components which comprise the interface of a prototype system to be readily embedded into objects. In the Switcharoo system [4] this approach is taken even further by enabling simple controls to be added to foamcore prototypes in such a way that an RFID reader can detect interaction with them and this information was used in the Macromedia

Director authoring environment. The Calder toolkit [21] built upon this work by further untethering the user interface elements of the prototype from the desktop.

Of course, in the above cases a PC of some kind is required, although with the latest integration technologies such a device can be very compact, e.g. the Phidgets single board computer. In the case of LEGO Mindstorms, the controller 'brick' can more easily be integrated into a device and flexibly connected with sensors and motors via cables, although the platform is mainly aimed at robotics applications where the appearance of the resulting construction is less important than its physical configuration.

One of the most refined platforms in terms of the appearance of the resulting devices is the Bug Labs system [8]. BUG modules and the BUGbase are supplied in enclosures which give prototypes a professional appearance. Unfortunately, there is no control over the physical configuration of a completed prototype, other than which module is connected to which socket, so the result is more of a configurable device rather than a free-form prototype.

With Gadgeteer, compact scale of the electronics and connectors, together with the use of flexible ribbon cables to connect hardware modules provides considerable freedom in the design of devices with varied form-factors. We believe that the integration with CAD and rapid manufacturing technologies, see Section 6.2, is also novel.

2.4   Complex Devices and Systems That Are Easy to Build

As outlined in the introduction, our ultimate aim is to enable researchers to build sophisticated devices and systems which empower them to take their work in new directions. We feel that accessibility, versatility and flexibility are key elements in this, and a platform which combines elements of all these is likely to go a long way towards our goal.

In the remainder of this paper we present the .NET Gadgeteer platform. It shares many characteristics with the work discussed above, but we have strived in particular to supplement hardware and software design elements with a high level of control over form-factor. We have also emphasized the extensibility of Gadgeteer along with the power of the underlying software tools. We believe that this unique combination is valuable in supporting the rapid creation of sophisticated standalone devices and complex systems.

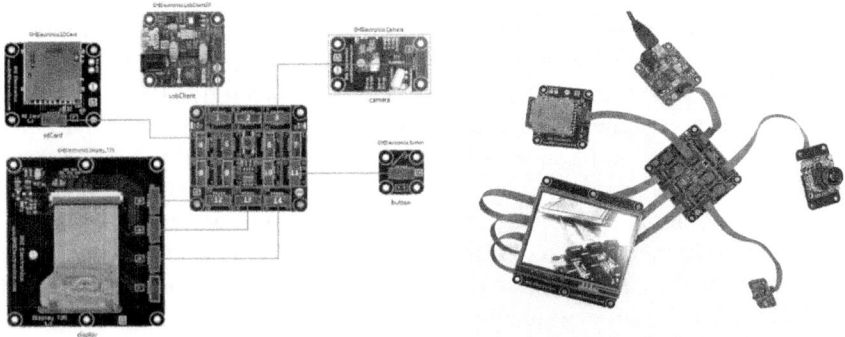

Fig. 1. Designer view (left) and assembled electronics (right) for digital camera example

3   An Example Gadgeteer Device: A Digital Camera

Before presenting details of the design and implementation of Gadgeteer, we illustrate the end user experience for a device which is relatively simple to build using the platform – a digital stills camera. To accomplish this, a Gadgeteer *mainboard* is combined with five *modules:* camera, push button, display, SD card and a USB client module for powering and programming the device. Having created a new Gadgeteer project in Visual Studio, which brings up the Designer view (Fig. 1 left), representations of the hardware modules listed above are dragged and dropped into place. The Designer suggests how to connect modules to compatible mainboard sockets, and the real hardware is then connected accordingly using 7 cables, Fig. 1 right (in this case the display module requires 3 cables).

```
void ProgramStarted()
{
    // Associate events with event-handling methods
    button.ButtonPressed += new Button.ButtonEventHandler(button_ButtonPressed);
    camera.PictureCaptured += new Camera.PictureCapturedEventHandler(camera_PictureCaptured);
}

void button_ButtonPressed(Button sender, Button.ButtonState state)
{
    camera.TakePicture();
}

void camera_PictureCaptured(Camera sender, GT.Picture picture)
{
    // Show the picture on the display
    display.SimpleGraphics.DisplayImage(picture, 0, 0);

    // Save the picture to the SD card
    sdCard.GetStorageDevice().WriteFile("picture.bmp", picture.PictureData);
}
```

Fig. 2. Code listing for digital camera example

Fig. 3. 3D model of case (left) and realized device (right)

To implement the software logic for the digital camera, two *event handlers* for the button.ButtonPressed and camera.PictureCaptured events are required, and need to be populated with one and two lines of code respectively (Fig. 2). The device can then immediately be tested. A solid modeling package can readily be used to create a simple casing based on a "jigsaw box" template, automatically using 3D models of the electronic components as reference geometry to quickly create holes suitable for mounting the modules, exposing the camera lens and so on (Fig. 3). The physical enclosure can be created from a sheet of acrylic or plywood using a laser cutter and the whole thing can be assembled within an hour or so.

4   Modular Electronics

In the example above, we already introduced the notion that .NET Gadgeteer devices are based on a mainboard, to which a number of peripheral modules can be connected. The mainboard includes a processor, memory and a number of physically identical 10-pin sockets. Each module provides certain functionality, such as sensing, actuation, display or communications ability. In this way, designs based on new combinations of electronic components may be rapidly prototyped and iterated upon.

4.1   Socket Types

Key to the design of Gadgeteer is that each mainboard socket supports one or more *socket types*. This is an important concept which we arrived at after some experimentation. Although the sockets are physically identical, which means that only one type of cable is required, each socket can be associated with one more multiple *socket types*, which determine its electrical configuration. We define socket types for many of the common embedded interface standards such as UART serial communications, I2C, SPI, general-purpose digital input and output (GPIO), PWM output, analog input/output, USB host, USB client, an LCD controller interface, and others. The full specification is online at http://gadgeteer.codeplex.com/

We chose to support a range of interface standards instead of using a single bus type for two related reasons. Firstly, embedded processors typically have hardware support for many of these standards. Secondly, many existing peripheral electronic components already support one (or more) of these standards, but the standard differs from one component to the next. For example, a temperature sensor might have I2C support, while a small OLED display might support SPI. Thus, by supporting many different socket types we enable a wide range of Gadgeteer modules to be built simply with existing components, without requiring an additional processor to perform protocol translation "glue". This promotes extensibility and versatility as it is easy to build new types of module, and easy to create mainboards based on new processors by simply mapping the pins/functions available on that mainboard to a set of sockets. We expect the set of socket types to increase gradually as new embedded interface standards achieve prevalence.

A key aspect of our implementation is that mainboard sockets can support multiple types. To give a simplified example, the socket type specification for type **A** is as follows: Pins 1, 2 and 10 are connected to the +3.3V, +5V and Ground lines respectively, which is standard across all socket types; in addition pins 3, 4 and 5 are analog inputs (AIN). Furthermore, pins 3, 4 and 6 double as general-purpose input/outputs

(GPIOs). The definition for socket type **I** specifies that pins 8 and 9 are the dedicated I2C data (SDA) and clock (SCL) lines, and that pins 3 and 6 are GPIOs.

A socket on a mainboard can therefore support both socket type A and socket type I at the same time. The table below shows the actual pin-out and the image to the right shows how the physical connector would be labeled. The number 10 is a unique numerical identifier for that socket on the mainboard. Note that some combinations of socket types are not possible due to clashes between pin allocations.

Pin 1	Pin 2	Pin 3	Pin 4	Pin 5	Pin 6	Pin 7	Pin 8	Pin 9	Pin 10
+3.3V	+5.0V	AIN / GPIO	AIN / GPIO	AIN	GPIO		SDA	SCL	GND

Most modules need just a single socket to connect to a mainboard, although they can use several if necessary. For example, LCD display modules need three sockets due to the large number of signals needed to drive them. To help determine electrical compatibility, modules are labeled with the compatible socket types. For example, a sensor module that needs an I2C connection to the mainboard would be labeled with the letter I.

Early on in the design of Gadgeteer, we settled on the use of a common type of connector across the range of different interface standards we support. This is different to many earlier systems, such as Calder [21] but we believe it has two important advantages: firstly, it prevents complication when two or more different interface types are combined on the same physical connector as described above, and secondly it means that only one type of cable is necessary. It is important to note that we have carefully specified the socket types so that connecting incompatible socket types together does not cause the hardware to fail permanently. Thus, while such misconnection is one of the more common errors made when using Gadgeteer, it has temporary effects only. The Designer view (Fig. 1) automatically checks that the connections are compatible, so debugging such misconnections involves double-checking that the physical hardware matches the Designer view.

4.2   Mainboard Examples

We have designed the Gadgeteer socket types to be independent of the underlying processor, enabling a range of different mainboards to be built. The main requirement for the processor is simply enough speed and memory (RAM and flash) to support the .NET Micro Framework coupled with the .NET Gadgeteer core libraries detailed in the next section. We built two prototype mainboards with different processors in-house to demonstrate the processor-independent nature of the platform. The first is based on GHI Electronics' EMX processor module with a 72MHz ARM 7 CPU, 4.5MB Flash and 16MB RAM. It has 14 sockets with 35 socket type letters between them. The second is based on Device Solutions' Nano processor module which includes a 200MHz ARM 9 processor with 8MB Flash and 8MB RAM, with 10 sockets. Commercial retailers have since made their own retail versions based on the same two processors, as well as a third based on a 240MHz ARM 9 processor. See Fig. 4.

Fig. 4. Example Gadgeteer mainboards, the smallest of which is 37mm x 57mm

4.3   Module Examples

At present over 40 .NET Gadgeteer-compatible modules are either in development or available for public release from retail manufacturers (Fig. 5). A few examples are:

- A **button+LED** module using socket type X (3 GPIOs, 1 interruptable). The button is wired to a digital interrupt input while the LED is wired to a digital output; there is no processing onboard.
- An **accelerometer** based on the Bosch BMA180 sensor (with no additional processing elements) which uses socket type I (I2C interface).
- A 320x240 **LCD display** module using socket types R, G and B.   Mainboards can typically gang these socket types up with type Y (GPIO), so, for "headless" devices not using an LCD, the mainboard sockets are still useful.

Fig. 5. Gadgeteer compatible modules include displays of various sizes & resolutions, a variety of sensors, actuators, user controls, storage and communications modules, plus power supplies

4.4   Supplying Power

Every Gadgeteer socket type provides access to common 5V and 3.3V power buses and ground through three dedicated pins. Modules are typically powered from these pins, but it is the responsibility of the user to ensure that exactly one module is *providing* power. Suitable modules are colored red. The most often used red module provides USB Client functionality, and can be powered from the USB port of a PC or from a mains adapter. Other red modules that have been prototyped support a range of Li-ion rechargeable batteries and a USB serial connection (see Fig. 5 bottom left).

5   Object-Oriented Software Architecture

Gadgeteer software is written in C# using Visual Studio (or the free version Visual C# 2010 Express), and uses the .NET Micro Framework (NETMF) platform for the underlying runtime support. This combination delivers a fully-featured development environment, with code auto-completion, in-line help, and the ability to debug code "live" with breakpoints and stepped execution, using "managed" C# code (i.e. strongly typed, object oriented and memory safe code).

On top of NETMF, we provide a set of software libraries known as GadgeteerCore, also written in C#, and a Designer plug-in for Visual Studio. These provide a framework which enables end user code to be abstracted away from particular mainboards and supports a wide and extensible range of modules, while allowing mainboard and module designers to provide device-driver-like supporting code for their hardware.

GadgeteerCore's API is event-driven rather than using a "while(true)" loop common in many microcontroller scenarios. This promotes versatility by more easily supporting complex behaviors where multiple simultaneous control loops are occurring. End user code starts with the ProgramStarted() method called at startup, in which event handlers or timers are set up, as shown in Fig. 2.

5.1   Supporting Development of Module and Mainboard Drivers

One of the key elements of Gadgeteer is that mainboard and module hardware must come with software "drivers". This simplifies the end user experience; an end user of a camera module is not exposed to the underlying protocols by which the camera is controlled, but instead uses a Camera object with an API such as TakePicture() method and PictureCaptured event.

However, places an additional burden on hardware developers who may not have much experience with C# or NETMF. We therefore tried to make this as simple as possible through providing templates for modules and mainboards. Each consists of:

- A readme.txt with instructions on how to customize the other files
- A GadgeteerHardware.XML file, which instructs the Designer on how to show the module/mainboard to the end user and on socket compatibility issues
- A C# software file containing an example driver to be customized
- A WiX-based utility (http://wix.sourceforge.net/) which automatically produces an "MSI" installer for distributing drivers to users as part of the compilation process.

5.2   Module Examples

Revisiting the three example modules from Section 4.3:

The **button+LED** module comprises very simple hardware, but the software provides a surprisingly rich API. In addition to using the button and LED as two separate devices, another mode of use is where the button and LED together become a "toggle" where a button press automatically toggles the LED and the user's code can handle toggle-on and toggle-off events.

The **accelerometer** module hides the I2C interface details (e.g. the device address) and provide a high level API including a property for the high-acceleration detection threshold, an Acceleration class used to return typed 3D acceleration values, and the ability to ask for continuous measurements (at a configurable time interval) – these are implemented using a timer internal to the module software, but the end user simply sets up an event handler which is periodically called with the current Acceleration.

The **LCD display** module driver derives from an abstract class DisplayModule in GadgeteerCore. The abstract class provides APIs for end users for outputting to the display using either a windowing toolkit (WPF) or simple bitmap operations. Therefore, the module driver itself simply has to specify the implementation details of how to get bitmaps onto that particular display type (e.g. sending the bitmap to the processor's built-in LCD controller, or sending the bitmap over SPI).

6   Flexibility of Form Factor

As commented earlier, in many situations the form factor of a device is as important as the functionality it embodies. This is particularly true in research contexts, where enabling user evaluation of a new device or concept with a realistic prototype may be critical. For this reason, Gadgeteer has been designed from the outset to be both compact and to support a wide variety of form factors. Features enabling a number of mechanical construction approaches and the latest rapid fabrication processes have been included in Gadgeteer in a way which we believe sets it apart from most of the previous work described in Section 2.

6.1   Flexibility in the Mounting of Modules

The most obvious mechanical feature of Gadgeteer is the use of ribbon cables instead of rigid PCB-mounted headers or single wires. This permits components to be mounted arbitrarily with respect to one another while using a minimal number of cables. Furthermore, high-density ribbon cables of multiple lengths terminated with IDC connectors are used to reduce the space required. Compared to the industry standard 2.54mm pitch interconnect, Gadgeteer's 1.27mm pitch connectors require around 25% of the footprint and under half the height.

The mounting holes are another key element of all mainboards and modules. We use a standard 3.2mm diameter hole size which is compatible with both metric M3 and imperial 4-40 machine screws. We maintain a keep-out area around the screw hole which allows the use of mounting pillars which are large enough to incorporate off-the-shelf threaded inserts. The mounting holes are on a fixed 5mm pitch grid which means they can be readily attached to a perforated baseplate. To this end we have designed a push-fit plastic pillar. This pillar is end-stackable, thereby allowing modules to be stacked on top of each other if required.

6.2   Full 3D CAD Integration for More Sophisticated Physical Design

We have created detailed 3D CAD models of each mainboard and module. When modeling an enclosure for a particular device, these may be imported into the CAD tool and used as reference geometry to ensure that mounting holes, apertures and other features align as required. In many CAD packages it is also possible to check for potential interference between adjacent elements of an assembly before a design is realized. We have used this technique with both 3D-printed and laser-cut enclosures.

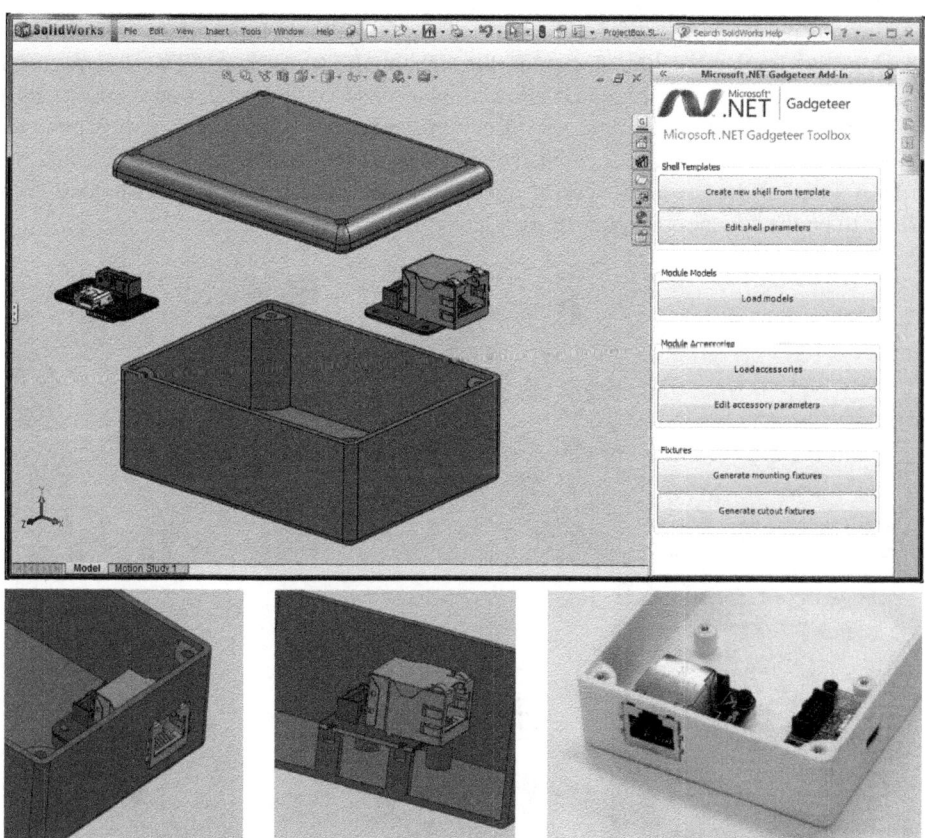

Fig. 6. The Gadgeteer SolidWorks add-in allows users to create simple custom enclosures based on templates and import 3D CAD models of mainboards and modules (top). The add-in also supports automatic creation of the appropriate mounting bushes and apertures (bottom left, middle), allowing the hardware to fit neatly in the 3D printed custom enclosure (bottom right).

We have also developed a plug-in utility for the SolidWorks parametric 3D CAD package which allows a user to specify which mounting holes and apertures are to be used for each module in order that they are automatically incorporated in the design, see Fig. 6. This has proven invaluable because it not only automates the generation of such features, but it results in their automatic re-generation whenever elements of the design are altered – for example, if a particular module is moved the associated mounting bushes will automatically move to follow. Our plug-in currently supports both laser-cutting and 3D printing enclosure fabrication; the user selects between these to control the type of mounting bush feature generated – either a clearance hole for a plastic pillar to be screwed in place or an extruded bush for a threaded insert.

7   Examples of Gadgeteer in Use

At various points during the development of the Gadgeteer platform, we validated our design and implementation decisions through public workshops. These introduced newcomers to the technology and allowed us to observe and reflect on its utility as a prototyping tool. In this section we reflect on the lessons learned during this process. We have also used Gadgeteer extensively to support our own research projects and we report some of these experiences, using them as a vehicle to highlight what we consider to be the salient properties of the platform.

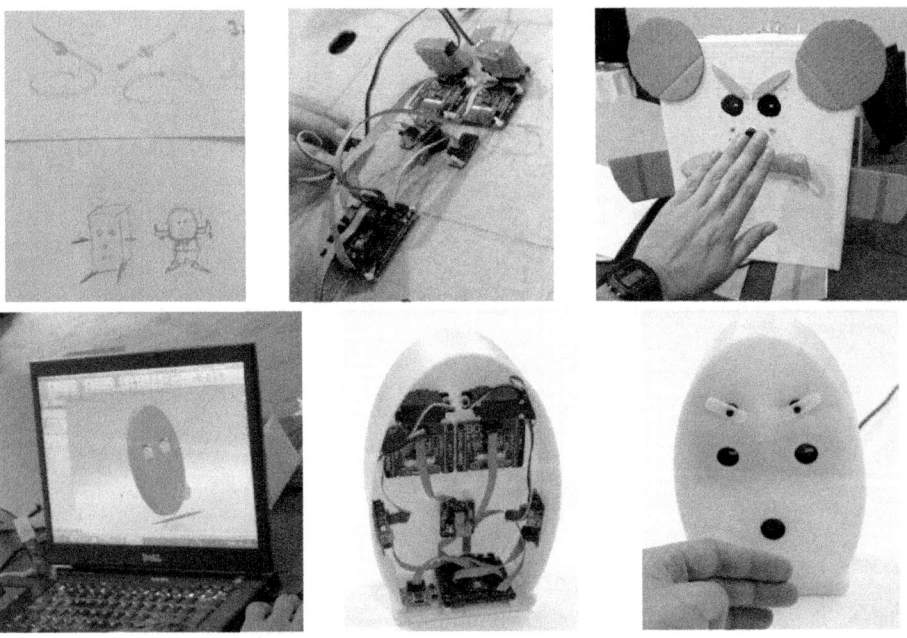

Fig. 7. A day's worth of prototyping – from sketch (top left) to finished device (bottom right), via cardboard prototype and custom 3D-printed enclosure design. The team that created this toy bear had not used C# or SolidWorks extensively before the workshop.

7.1   Accessibility to New Users

We organized a Gadgeteer workshop as part of the TEI'11 conference, which attracts a large number of participants that regularly build custom devices. The workshop hosted 18 participants of varied backgrounds and skill sets, ranging from interaction design to computer science. We asked participants to form into groups of 3 or 4 members, so that each group had members with programming and design / 3D CAD modeling experience. (NB they had not necessarily used C# or SolidWorks.) The morning was focused on introducing participants to the hardware and software concepts and the SolidWorks CAD support. Participants were then guided through the process of building a simple device – a digital camera, which included a display, shutter button and an additional component of their choosing. The rest of the day was spent in freeform ideation and creation of novel prototypes. Groups were given simple prototyping materials for mounting the hardware modules such as cardboard, tape and plastic screws.

All groups managed to create functional prototypes by the end of the day. One group created a remote control car, complete with a Zigbee wireless controller and animated light effects. Another group created a tool for color-blind people, which would display the name of the primary color of an object held up to its sensor. A third group created an interactive toy bear, featuring a friendly expression which would turn fierce when approached (see Fig. 7). Two of the groups used the 3D CAD tools 'in anger' to design robust enclosures for their prototypes. The results were rendered using a 3D printer during the course of the following 24 hours, allowing the assembled and fully-functional prototype to be showcased at the conference's main demo session, which took place 48 hours after the workshop.

7.2 Hi-fidelity Custom Devices to Support Studies in the Wild

During the development of Gadgeteer, we have used the platform several times in collaborative research projects. In [26] we contributed to a project examining the role of audio clips as "sonic mementos," which could be captured and subsequently re-experienced by families in a similar way to physical mementos of a holiday. The technical artifact that facilitated this research was a device that looked like an old transistor radio, but was actually a highly custom system for browsing and playing digital audio files, shown in Fig. 8. The device was made by repurposing a genuine radio using Gadgeteer components. The custom design of the device was central to the research questions being addressed, and the ability deploy the self-contained prototype with participants in their homes was fundamental to the research methodology.

In a second collaboration [19], Gadgeteer was used to develop a smart shopping-trolley accessory: a battery-powered device which was clipped to the handle of the trolley to reveal information about products that were identified using a built-in bar-code scanner. This project provided an opportunity to illustrate the value of a high-fidelity, standalone and self-contained device built with Gadgeteer. The resulting device (Fig. 8) includes the barcode scanner, LED display, battery power supply, data logging capabilities, as well as a database of product barcodes that allows it to be used in a real supermarket. The device was iteratively designed and rapidly manufactured over a period of two weeks. Experimental subjects were able to use the device without help from the researchers, who were instead able to focus on observing the interaction and decision-making process. In this sense, we believe that Gadgeteer can help custom research devices such as this 'disappear,' and allow the researcher's energy to focus on the research itself, rather than on managing the technology.

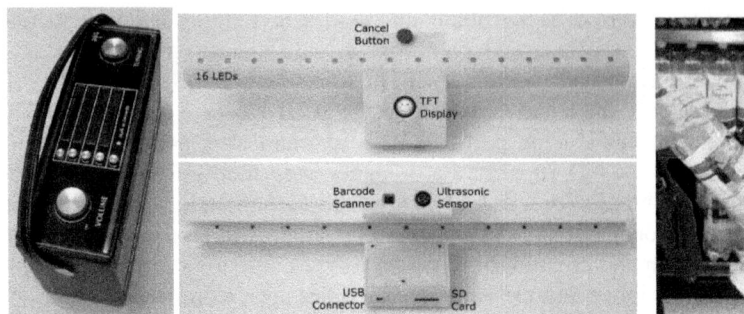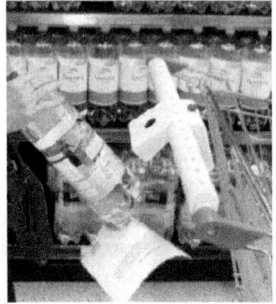

Fig. 8. Two example custom devices built with Gadgeteer to support research deployments: the Family Memory Radio (left) and the Lambent Shopping Trolley handle (middle, right)

7.3   Iterative Design of More Complex Systems

In previously published work [30] we used Gadgeteer to both iteratively prototype and batch produce a number of custom embedded interactive devices which make up a distributed system. In this case, the research programme called for an embedded device that was capable of: sensing the temperature and humidity of the environment; detecting user movement in front of the device; measuring the ambient light levels in the room; presenting a basic user interface; logging data locally, and synchronizing and communicating over a wireless mesh network. As is often the case, there were a number of commercial products that approximated the requirements, but nothing off-the-shelf that fitted the bill exactly.

Using Gadgeteer, we were able to rapidly and iteratively design a solution. Fig. 9 shows four different prototypes, built over a period of four days. The first prototype was a rough 'hardware sketch,' built using laser-cut cardboard and used primarily to evaluate the use of a passive infrared sensor to detect user motion. The subsequent prototypes were rendered in plastic using a 3D printer. In a classic demonstration of the value of iterative prototyping, each prototype taught us something valuable, and we were able to feed the lessons into the next iteration. One key aspect was the positioning of the temperature sensor: in the first two examples, the temperature sensor is built into the enclosure, and is only exposed to the outside via a small slit on the front of the case. We quickly found that heat generated by the power supply and the processor was affecting the sensor readings. In the third prototype, the sensor was moved outside of the enclosure. This was found to be still too close to the source of heat, so in the final prototype it was mounted on an external 'arm,' which successfully solved the issue. Other changes included the introduction of a rotary encoder to support user input (between prototypes 2 and 3), the repositioning of the rotary encoder from the top to the side of the device, and the repositioning of the light level sensor from the front to the top of the device. These choices were all affected by functional and usability reasons. This strengthens our conviction that having freedom in the physical form-factor and external design of a device can be as important as having control over its hardware configuration and software it executes.

In order to carry out the research reported in [30], we needed around 40 "copies" of this custom device. We considered designing a custom circuit board and enclosure for this, but decided against it when we estimated the cost of such an effort compared with the material costs of using Gadgeteer components and additional 3D printed enclosures. The latter turned out to be far more cost-effective even before we considered the possibility of re-using the Gadgeteer modules at the end of the project.

Fig. 9. Iterative prototypes of a custom-built device from initial cardboard prototype (left) through to final design (right) which was used in the batch-production of 40 units

8   Conclusions and Future Work

This paper presented the .NET Gadgeteer system, an integrated platform to support the development of custom devices such as those often used in pervasive and ubiquitous computing research. Our work was motivated by our perception that there was scope to enhance existing tools and approaches and we have described the opportunities we saw in this regard and how our chosen solutions unfolded as the Gadgeteer platform developed. We hope that our experiences will inform future research in this area and encourage others to help us refine and enhance the extensible platform we have created. Although we haven't conducted a formal evaluation of Gadgeteer in use or a direct comparison with other tools, we also hope that we have demonstrated the value of Gadgeteer by way of examples presented in this paper, and we encourage others to evaluate it and potentially adopt it in their research. To this end we have made the .NET Gadgeteer software freely available for download at http://gadgeteer.codeplex.com/ under an Apache 2.0 open source licence and we have been working with various manufacturers to create an ecosystem of mainboards and modules which are available to buy – see http://netmf.com/gadgeteer for more details.

We are continuing to develop many different elements of Gadgeteer. We are exploring the possibility of supporting languages other than C# and use of an in-browser IDE to extend accessibility of the tool. We are developing an advanced networking library which allows integration of Gadgeteer prototypes with phone-, desktop- and cloud-based applications. And we want to provide even more accessible 3D design tools which integrate tightly with on-line fabrication services to make this aspect of the platform accessible to those who don't have traditional 3D CAD training and direct access to laser cutters and 3D printers.

Whilst our motivation for developing the .NET Gadgeteer platform was to expedite the process of turning design ideas in the pervasive and ubiquitous computing space into working prototypes, we have also received a great deal of interest from both educators and hobbyists. In the case of education, Gadgeteer appeals because it enables students – whether at high school or university level – to build and program tangible devices using modern programming paradigms and tools, thereby exciting them to learn eminently transferrable computer science skills. We have already started some initial pilot studies in high schools in the UK and US to get experience with Gadgeteer in this domain. In the case of hobbyists the attraction appears to be the simple ability to build sophisticated gadgets with little previous experience remarkably quickly. We are working with several manufacturers to look for opportunities to reduce the cost of Gadgeteer components, in particular the entry cost for a mainboard and minimal set of modules. We believe this will be important to extend accessibility of the platform into schools and for hobbyists.

References

1. Arduino, `http://arduino.cc/`
2. Arduino Sheilds, `http://shieldlist.org/`
3. The ARM MBed, `http://mbed.org/`
4. Avrahami, D., Hudson, S.E.: Forming interactivity: a tool for rapid prototyping of physical interactive products. In: Proceedings of the 4th Conference on Designing Interactive Systems: Processes, Practices, Methods, and Techniques (DIS 2002), pp. 141–146 (2002)
5. Banzi, M.: Getting Started with Arduino. O'Reilly (2008) ISBN: 978-0-596-15551-3
6. Bdeir, A.: Electronics as material: littleBits. In: Proceedings of the 3rd International Conference on Tangible and Embedded Interaction (TEI 2009), pp. 397–400 (2009)
7. Buechley, L., Eisenberg, M., Catchen, J., Crockett, A.: The LilyPad Arduino: Using Computational Textiles to Investigate Engagement, Aesthetics, and Diversity in Computer Science Education. In: CHI 2008, pp. 423–432 (2008)
8. Bug Labs, `http://www.buglabs.net/`
9. Funnel Arduino, `http://funnel.cc/`
10. Grove System, `http://www.seeedstudio.com/wiki/GROVE_System`
11. Gaver, W., Blythe, M., Boucher, A., Jarvis, N., Bowers, J., Wright, P.: The prayer companion: openness and specificity, materiality and spirituality. In: Proceedings CHI 2010, pp. 2055–2064 (2010)
12. Gaver, W., Boucher, A., Law, A., Pennington, S., Bowers, J., Beaver, J., Humble, J., Kerridge, T., Villar, N., Wilkie, A.: Threshold devices: looking out from the home. In: CHI 2008, pp. 1429–1438 (2008)
13. Gellersen, H., Kortuem, G., Beigl, M., Schmidt, A.: Physical Prototyping With Smart-Its. IEEE Pervasive Computing 3(3), 74–82 (2004)
14. Greenberg, S., Fitchett, C.: Phidgets: easy development of physical interfaces through physical widgets. In: Proceedings of the 14th Annual ACM Symposium on User Interface Software and Technology (UIST 2001), pp. 209–218 (2001)
15. Gumstix, `http://www.gumstix.com/`

16. Hartmann, B., Klemmer, S.R., Bernstein, M., Abdulla, L., Burr, B., Robinson-Mosher, A., Gee, J.: Reflective physical prototyping through integrated design, test, and analysis. In: Proceedings of UIST 2006 (October 2006)

17. Hill, J., Szewczyk, R., Woo, A., Hollar, S., Culler, D., Pister, K.: System architecture directions for network sensors. In: ASPLOS 2000 (2000)

18. Hodges, S., Williams, L., Berry, E., Izadi, S., Srinivasan, J., Butler, A., Smyth, G., Kapur, N., Wood, K.: SenseCam: A Retrospective Memory Aid. In: Dourish, P., Friday, A. (eds.) UbiComp 2006. LNCS, vol. 4206, pp. 177–193. Springer, Heidelberg (2006)

19. Kalnikaité, V., Rogers, Y., Bird, J., Villar, N., Bachour, K., Payne, S., Todd, P.M., Schöning, J., Krüger, A., Kreitmayer, S.: How to Nudge In Situ: Designing Lambent Devices to Deliver Salience Information in Supermarkets. In: Proceedings of UbiComp 2011 (2011)

20. Kuzuoka, H., Greenberg, S.: Mediating awareness and communication through digital but physical surrogates. In: CHI 1999 Extended Abstracts, pp. 11–12 (1999)

21. Lee, J.C., Avrahami, D., Hudson, S.E., Forlizzi, J., Dietz, P.H., Leigh, D.: The Calder toolkit: wired and wireless components for rapidly prototyping interactive devices. In: Proceedings of DIS 2004, pp. 167–175 (2004)

22. LEGO Mindstorms, http://mindstorms.lego.com

23. Magic Box, http://magic-box.org/

24. Martin, F., Mikhak, B., Silverman, D.: MetaCricket: a designer's kit for making computational devices. IBM Syst. J. 39(3-4), 795–815 (2000)

25. The Microsoft. NET Micro Framework, http://netmf.com/

26. Myers, B.A., Hudson, S.E., Pausch, R.: Past, Present and Future of User Interface Software Tools. ACM Transactions on Computer Human Interaction 7(1), 3–28 (2000)

27. Petrelli, D., Villar, N., Kalnikaite, V., Dib, L., Whittaker, S.: FM radio: family interplay with sonic mementos. In: Proceedings of CHI 2010 (2010)

28. Rogers, Y., Price, S., Fitzpatrick, G., Fleck, R., Harris, E., Smith, H., Randell, C., Muller, H., O'Malley, C., Stanton, D., Thompson, M., Weal, M.: Ambient wood: designing new forms of digital augmentation for learning outdoors. In: Proceedings of the 2004 Conference on Interaction Design and Children: Building a Community, IDC 2004 (2004)

29. Schnädelbach, H., Koleva, B., Flintham, M., Fraser, M., Izadi, S., Chandler, P., Foster, M., Benford, S., Greenhalgh, C., Rodden, T.: The Augurscope: a mixed reality interface for outdoors. In: Proceedings of CHI 2002, pp. 9–16 (2002)

30. Scott, J., Bernheim Brush, A.J., Krumm, J., Meyers, B., Hazas, M., Hodges, S., Villar, N.: PreHeat: Controlling Home Heating Using Occupancy Prediction. In: Proceedings of UbiComp 2011. ACM (September 2011)

31. Seeeduino Film, http://www.seeedstudio.com/wiki/index.php?title=Seeeduino_Film

32. Shapeways, http://shapeways.com

33. Tinkercad, http://tinkercad.com/

34. TinkerKit, http://store.arduino.cc/eu/index.php?main_page=index&cPath=16

35. Tokuhisa, S., et al.: xTel: A Development Environment to Support Rapid Prototyping of Ubiquitous Content. In: TEI 2009, Cambridge, UK (February 2009)

Recognizing Handheld Electrical Device Usage with Hand-Worn Coil of Wire

Takuya Maekawa[1], Yasue Kishino[2], Yutaka Yanagisawa[2], and Yasushi Sakurai[2]

[1] Graduate School of Information Science and Technology, Osaka University
takuya.maekawa@acm.org
[2] NTT Communication Science Laboratories
surname.name@lab.ntt.co.jp

Abstract. This paper describes the development of a new finger-ring shaped sensor device with a coil of wire for recognizing the use of handheld electrical devices such as digital cameras, cellphones, electric toothbrushes, and hair dryers by sensing time-varying magnetic fields emitted by the devices. Recently, sensing the usage of home electrical devices has emerged as a promising area for activity recognition studies because we can estimate high-level daily activities by recognizing the use of electrical devices that exist ubiquitously in our daily lives. A feature of our approach is that we can recognize the use of electrical devices that are not connected to the home infrastructure without the need to equip them with sensors. We evaluated the performance of our approach by using sensor data obtained from real houses. We also investigated the portability of training data between different users.

Keywords: Activity sensing, Electrical devices, Wearable sensors.

1   Introduction

Problems closely related to our daily lives such as the aging of society and adult diseases have become serious in modern society. Therefore, such pervasive computing applications as supporting the care of the elderly, fitness monitoring, and lifelogging are attracting attention [1,2] and various technologies have been studied to realize these applications. In particular, human activity recognition using sensors is one of the most important tasks in relation to the pervasive computing applications. Two main approaches are used for activity recognition studies: environment augmentation and wearable sensing. Many environment augmentation approaches use ubiquitous sensors such as RFID tags and/or switch sensors installed in the environment [3,4,5]. The wearable sensing approach attempts to recognize a user's activities by employing such sensors as body-worn accelerometers to capture characteristic body movements and postures adopted for certain activities [6,7,8,9]. On the other hand, sensing the usage of home electrical devices has recently emerged as a promising area for activity recognition because we live surrounded by large numbers of electrical devices, and frequently use them when we perform daily activities. Therefore, we can estimate high-level daily activities by recognizing the use of electrical devices. For example, when

J. Kay et al. (Eds.): Pervasive 2012, LNCS 7319, pp. 234–252, 2012.

we detect that a user is using a hair dryer, we can know that she is drying her hair. Environment augmentation and wearable sensing approaches have been employed to recognize the use of electrical devices. Some studies employ ubiquitous sensor nodes attached to each electrical device to detect its use [10,5]. However, this distributed sensing approach requires large numbers of sensor nodes for electrical devices. Therefore, its deployment and maintenance costs, e.g., battery replacement costs, are high. Several studies have attempted to monitor the use of electrical devices with small numbers of sensors. For example, the system proposed in [11] employs a single central sensor to monitor the total electrical load of a home's power meter and then separates the individual loads of electrical devices in the home with statistical signal processing methods. Also, the systems proposed in [12,13] recognize the use of electrical devices by monitoring noise on the home infrastructure (home electrical systems).

The above systems focus on electrical devices connected to home electrical systems via outlets. On the other hand, we attempt to recognize the use of portable electrical devices such as digital cameras, cellphones, electric shavers, video game players, and music players with the wearable sensor approach. Our previous work [14] also focuses on portable electrical devices and employs Hall effect magnetic sensors [15] attached to a user's hands to monitor the magnetic fields emitted by the permanent magnets and relatively large motors incorporated in portable electrical devices. However, the system requires multiple Hall effect sensors (four or more sensors) attached to different parts of the hands to achieve high recognition accuracies. (See section 2 for more detail.) By contrast, in this paper, we describe our attempt to capture the magnetic fields emitted by sources different from those described in [14] and attempt to achieve high recognition accuracies with a single sensor on the hand. In detail, we try to develop a new hand-worn sensor device with a coil that can capture (sense) small time-varying magnetic fields emitted by, for example, electrical circuits, motors, boost converters, and conductive wires, included in portable electrical devices. Then, we extract the characteristic frequencies of the magnetic fields emitted by electrical devices and recognize which electrical device the wearer is using with machine learning techniques. Note that, because wearing several sensors places large burdens on a user in her daily life, sensing with small numbers of sensors is important. Here, we focus on the wearable sensor approach because it allows us to sense users' activities in both indoor and outdoor environments. Portable electrical equipment such as digital cameras and cellphones are frequently used out of doors. Also, with the wearable sensor approach, we can recognize the use of electrical devices that are not connected to the home's electrical systems. In addition, the approach does not require any sensors installed in the user's environment, e.g., ubiquitous sensors attached to each electrical device.

In the rest of this paper, we first introduce work related to detecting the use of electrical devices. Then, we describe the design of our prototype sensor device and show example sensor data obtained from the device when a wearer performs several activities (the use of electrical devices). After that, we introduce a machine learning-based method that identifies which electrical device a wearer is using. In the evaluation, we test user-dependent and user-independent recognition models. In the first case, we evaluate the recognition accuracies of test data obtained from a user at her house by using recognition models trained with sensor data obtained from the same user also at her house. In the second case, we evaluate the recognition accuracies of test data obtained from a user at her house by using recognition models trained with sensor data obtained from other users at their houses. That is, we investigate the portability of training data between different users when the users employ the same model of electrical device in their houses. The contributions of this paper are that we propose and develop a new hand-worn device with a single sensor for recognizing the use of electrical devices that does not place large burdens on the wearer. We also investigate the recognition performance using sensor data obtained from three real houses. To our knowledge, this is the first study that recognizes the use of portable electrical devices with a hand-worn coil.

2   Related Work

As mentioned in section 1, environment augmentation and wearable sensing approaches are used to detect/recognize the use of electrical devices. Some studies employ distributed ubiquitous sensors attached to each electrical device [5,10]. For example, [5] uses wireless sensor nodes that monitor the state changes of daily objects including electrical devices. The system proposed in [10] employs magnetic or light sensors attached to each electrical device to detect its use and estimate its energy consumption. While these approaches can achieve fine-grained measurements of electrical events, their deployment and maintenance costs, e.g., costs related to battery replacement, are very large. Several studies monitor the use of electrical devices with sensor nodes shaped like a power strip [16,17]. For example, the sensor node developed in [17] has electrical outlets and supplies electrical devices connected to the outlets with electrical power. The sensor node also monitors electrical current drawn from each outlet. Unlike the above distributed sensing approach, several studies attempt to detect the use of electrical devices with a single or small numbers of sensors that monitor home electrical systems. The system proposed in [11] uses a single central sensor that monitors current and voltage signals in a home's power meter. With statistical signal processing approaches, the system attempts to recognize the use of whole-house electrical devices using only sensor data from the power meter. Also, several studies recognize the use of electrical devices with the infrastructure mediated sensing approach [12,13]. The systems proposed in [12,13] monitor the electrical noise on the house power-line infrastructure. The systems detect the unique noise signature emitted by each electrical device and identify which electrical device is being used.

   While the above environment augmentation approaches focus on electrical devices connected to home electrical systems, we concentrate on handheld electrical devices and employ the wearable sensing approach. The system proposed in [14] also concentrates on handheld electrical devices and employs a wearable sensor device. The study uses Hall effect magnetic sensors on finger-rings to capture the magnetic fields emitted by magnetic components such as permanent magnets and motors incorporated in portable electrical devices. A Hall effect sensor outputs a voltage in proportion to the magnetic flux density that penetrates its element. Because a Hall effect sensor is also affected by the earth's magnetism, sensor data from the sensor on a finger ring change according to the orientation of the wearer. Therefore, the system employs two or more Hall effect sensors attached to the same hand and attempts to cancel out the effect of the earth's magnetism by using data from the sensors. However, wearing several sensors places large burdens on a user in her daily life. Also, the system proposed in [14] mainly focuses on magnetic components such as permanent magnets and motors that emit strong magnetic fields comparable to the earth's magnetism. On the other hand, we attempt to capture small time-varying magnetic fields emitted by components such as electrical circuits, motors, and conductive wires incorporated in portable electrical devices by using a new single magnetic sensor device that is not affected by the earth's magnetism. Also, because the system proposed in [14] mainly uses static magnetic fields emitted by permanent magnets, (calibrated) sensor data values from the hand-worn sensors are simply used as features for recognizing electrical device usage. By contrast, we focus on time-varying magnetic fields emitted by an electrical device, and so we employ the characteristic frequencies of the device's magnetic fields, which can be robust features because the number of features is larger. (See section 4 for more detail.) Note that we consider that the system proposed in [14] and our system are complementary rather than competing techniques because several simple portable electrical devices such as flashlights do not emit time-varying magnetic fields but only static magnetic fields. Moreover, we consider that, by combining our method with the environment augmentation approaches that focus on electrical devices connected to home electrical systems, we can recognize the use of both portable and stationary electrical devices in both indoor and outdoor environments.

Also, the system proposed in [18] uses the human body as an antenna to capture electromagnetic noise from home electrical infrastructures and electrical devices. The study attempts to recognize gestures by employing the electromagnetic noise.

3 Prototype Sensor Device

3.1 Design

As mentioned in sections 1 and 2, we want to capture time-varying magnetic fields emitted by portable electrical devices. To achieve this, we focus on a coil of wire. The electromotive force will be induced in a coil of wire when the magnetic flux through the coil changes in accordance with Faraday's law of induction $V = -N\frac{d\Phi}{dt}$, where V is the electromotive force in volts, N is the number of turns of wire, and $\frac{d\Phi}{dt}$ is the change in the magnetic flux through the coil given in webers. Therefore, with a coil of wire, we can easily convert the time-varying magnetic fields into time-series voltage values, which correspond to sensor data.

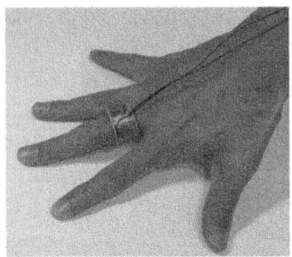 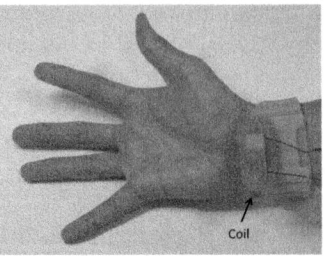

Finger-ring shaped device   Bracelet shaped device

Fig. 1. Our prototype finger-ring and bracelet shaped sensor devices

Here, because we assume a wearable sensor device, the magnetic flux from the earth's magnetism that penetrates the sensor (coil) changes when the wearer changes her orientation. However, we consider that the effect of the orientation change is small because the sensor outputs only the amount of change in the flux. In section 3.2, we show example data obtained from our sensor device.

Here, because the magnetic fields attenuate greatly with distance from the source, we should attach the sensor to or near the wearer's hand so that it is close to the electrical devices she is holding. To achieve transparent activity sensing in daily lives, we should embed the sensor in an item such as a finger ring, bracelet, or wristwatch that are worn on or close to the hand in the wearer's daily lives. Our approach, which employs a coil of wire, is particularly suitable for developing a finger-ring shaped sensor device because we can easily implement such a device simply by winding a conductive wire around a finger ring. Fig. 1 shows our prototype finger-ring and bracelet shaped sensor devices. We made the finger-ring device simply by winding a wire around a plastic shank. We made the bracelet shaped device simply by attaching a coil to a silicon wrist band. Because they are prototypes, each coil of wire in Fig. 1 is connected to a sensor board. The sensor board samples sensor data (voltage values) at about 2000 Hz, amplifies the sensor data, and then sends them to a host PC via a USB cable.

3.2   Sensor Data

Here we show example sensor data obtained from our prototype devices. The upper graph in Fig. 2 shows a sensor data sequence obtained from our finger-ring shaped sensor device on the wearer's right middle finger when he used a hair dryer and then used an electric toothbrush. The x-axis indicates time and the y-axis indicates the magnetic sensor data value. The lower part of Fig. 2 shows a frequency spectrogram computed from the time-series sensor data. As shown in the spectrogram, the peak frequencies related to hair dryer use and toothbrush use are different. Note that we can see constant noise in the sensor data that was caused by the amplifier on the sensor board. Also, our finger-ring device may be affected by noise from the human body.

Fig. 3 shows sensor data sequences obtained from our finger-ring device on the middle finger when the wearer used a digital camera, a cellphone, and a

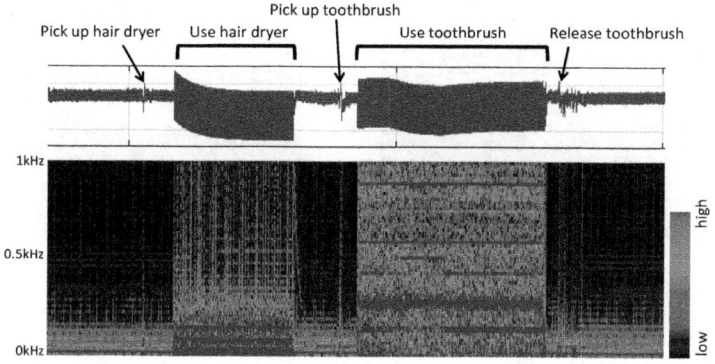

Fig. 2. Example sensor data obtained from our finger-ring device worn on the right middle finger when the wearer used a hair dryer and an electric toothbrush

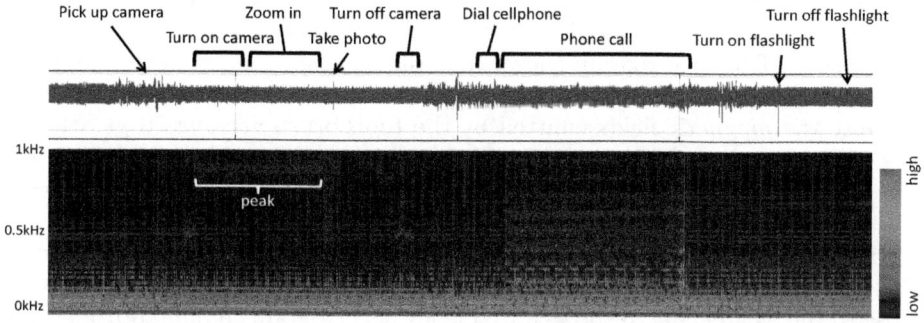

Fig. 3. Example sensor data obtained from our finger-ring device on the right middle finger when the wearer used a digital camera, a cellphone, and a flashlight

flashlight in this order. Fig. 3 also shows a frequency spectrogram computed from the sensor data. We can see a characteristic peak frequency when the motor for the zoom function in the camera was working ('turn on camera' and 'zoom in' in Fig. 3). However, even when the camera was ON, we could not find any characteristic peaks when the motor was not working. With the cellphone, we could not find any characteristic peaks when the wearer was dialing. However, there were characteristic peaks when the wearer was talking on the phone. This may be caused by an oscillator in the phone. With the flashlight, although we could find transient noise in the sensor data when the wearer turned it on, the duration of the change (noise) was very short. Also, we could not find any characteristic peaks while the flashlight was ON. We consider that it is difficult for our device to detect the use of such simple electrical devices as flashlights. Of course, our device has a limit of detecting magnetic field. Our device could not detect the use of electrical devices with very weak magnetic field, e.g., several cellphones and TV remote controls. On the other hand, Fig. 4 shows a

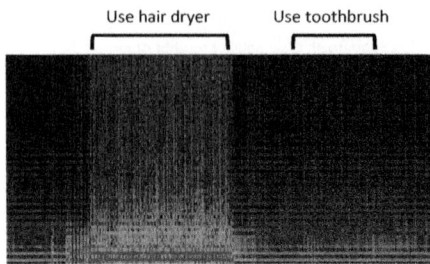

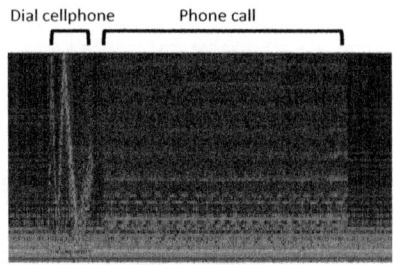

Fig. 4. Example spectrogram computed from sensor data obtained from our bracelet device on the right wrist when the wearer used a hair dryer and an electric toothbrush

Fig. 5. Example spectrogram computed from sensor data obtained from our finger-ring device on the right middle finger when the wearer used a cellphone in front of an induction heater

frequency spectrogram computed from sensor data obtained from our bracelet shaped sensor device when the wearer used a hair dryer and then used an electric toothbrush. The spectrogram shows that the bracelet shaped device could not sense any magnetic flux changes when the wearer used the toothbrush. This is because the magnetic fields emitted by the toothbrush attenuated greatly, and the coil on the bracelet, which was far from the toothbrush, could not capture the magnetic fields. We consider that it is difficult for the bracelet device to capture magnetic fields emitted by handheld devices.

Here we investigate the effects on our device of external factors present in our daily life environment. Our device may be affected by strong magnetic sources close to the wearer. Fig. 5 shows a frequency spectrogram computed from sensor data obtained from our finger-ring device when the wearer used a cellphone while he was using his left hand to stir a pot on an induction heater, which is one of the strongest magnetic sources in home. The heater had an effect when the wearer was dialing because the phone was in front of his body and close to the heater (about 15-20 cm) at the time. However, the heater had no effect during phone calls because the phone was held to his ear and was far from the heater (about 40-50 cm). The sensor data seem to be very similar to those in Fig. 3. Fig. 6 shows frequency spectrograms computed from sensor data obtained from our finger-ring device when the wearer used a cellphone close to a large LCD TV. Although we could find noises caused by the TV across the entire frequency band when the wearer used the cellphone in contact with the TV (0 cm), there was little or no effect from the TV when the wearer was at a reasonable distance from it. As shown in the above examples, our device is not affected by strong magnetic components as long as it is not extremely close to them because the magnetic fields attenuate greatly according to distance. The effects of strong magnetic sources around the wearer are small except in certain extreme cases. Fig. 7 shows frequency spectrograms computed from sensor data obtained from our finger-ring device on the right middle fingers of two wearers when they were not using any electrical devices. The sensor data in Fig. 7 (a) and

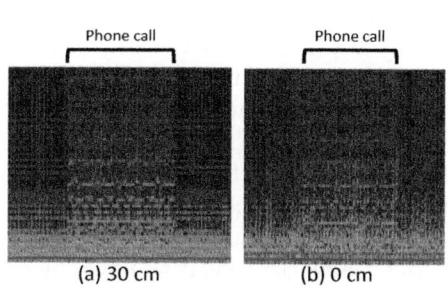

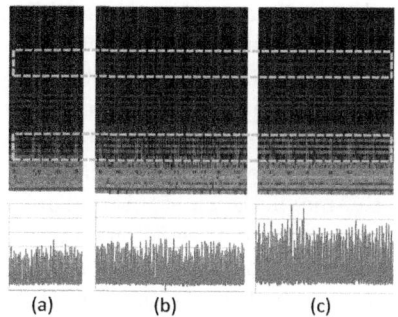

Fig. 6. Example spectrograms computed from sensor data obtained from our finger-ring device on the right middle finger when the wearer used a cellphone 30 and 0 cm from an LCD TV

Fig. 7. Example spectrograms computed from sensor data obtained from different two wearers. (a) Wearer A at place 1, (b) wearer B at place 1, and (c) wearer A at place 2.

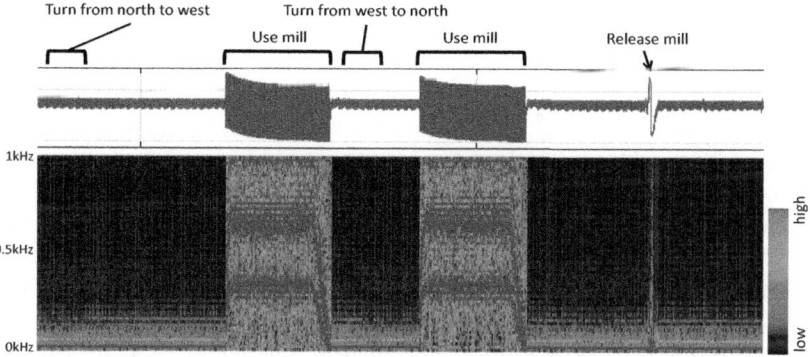

Fig. 8. Example sensor data obtained from our finger-ring device on the right middle finger when the wearer used a mill facing in different directions

(b) were obtained from different wearers at the same place. Even though these data were obtained at the same place, the frequency characteristics indicated by the rectangles in Fig. 7 were somewhat different. The lower portion of Fig. 7 shows the energy computed when we focus only on frequencies indicated by the lower rectangle, and we can also find differences in the energy. The sensor data in Fig. 7 (a) and (c) were obtained from the same wearer at different places. The frequency characteristics were also somewhat different. From these data, we consider that our sensor device is slightly affected by both environmental magnetic noise in each house and noise from the human body (finger). These small noises constantly affect sensor data obtained from our device.

In section 2, we mentioned that when the wearer changes her orientation, the magnetic flux from the earth's magnetism that penetrates the sensor (coil) also changes. Fig. 8 shows a sensor data sequence obtained when our finger-ring device was being worn on the right middle finger and the wearer used an electric pepper mill while facing west and north. Fig. 8 also shows a frequency spectrogram computed from the sensor data. Sensor data obtained when the wearer used the mill while facing in different directions look like very similar. This is because our device does not capture static magnetic fields but only time-varying magnetic fields. Even when the wearer is facing north or east, the magnetic flux density from the earth's magnetism is stable and our device is not affected by the earth's magnetism. Moreover, there were no changes in the sensor data when the wearer changed her orientation. This may be because the device outputs only the amount of change in the magnetic flux. We consider that the earth's magnetism has little effect on our device.

4   Recognition Method

By using sensor data obtained from our prototype device, we attempt to identify which electrical device the wearer is using. We first extract features from sensor data and then recognize the extracted feature vector sequence by employing the hidden Markov model (HMM). We describe our method in detail below.

4.1   Feature Extraction

We obtain time-series sensor data from our sensor device, and we compute a feature vector for each sliding time window. We extract features based on the FFT components of 128 sample time windows. In section 3.2, we mentioned that the magnetic fields emitted by each electrical device have characteristic frequencies. Therefore, we simply use the FFT component values as features. In addition, we use the variance and energy, which can capture the intensity of sensor data changes, computed in each window as features. The energy feature is calculated by summing the magnitudes of the squared discrete FFT components. The DC component of the FFT is excluded from this summation. For normalization, the sum was divided by the window length. As above, we construct a 66 (64+1+1) dimensional feature vector from each window.

4.2   Classification Methodology

With the above procedure, we obtain a feature vector sequence. We classify each feature vector in an appropriate class (electrical device) by employing supervised machine learning techniques. That is, we model each class by using labeled training data (feature vector sequences) in advance. After that, we recognize test data with the learned models. Note that a label includes information about the class label of its related electrical device and the start and end times of its use. We prepare a model for each electrical device by using a left-to-right HMM where the values of the observed variables correspond to extracted feature vectors, and we represent its output distributions by using Gaussian mixture densities. We also prepare an HMM that corresponds to a situation that the wearer does not use any electrical devices. In our implementation, we use four-state HMMs with four Gaussian mixtures in each state. We employ the Baum-Welch algorithm [19] to estimate the HMM parameters. When we recognize test data (feature vector sequence) using the learned HMMs, we use the Viterbi algorithm to find the most probable state sequence in/across the HMMs [19]. From the state sequence, we can know into which HMM (electrical device) a feature vector at time t is classified.

4.3   Adapting User-Independent Models

When we want to recognize an end user's electrical device usage, it is very costly for the end user to prepare labeled training data by herself. Therefore, in section 5, we try to recognize the end user's electrical device usage (test data) with user-independent models, which are trained on labeled sensor data from other users. In section 3.2, we mentioned that noises in houses and from the human bodies (fingers) constantly affect the sensor data obtained from our device. The features of the noises depend on each house and finger. To reduce the effects of the noises, we adapt the user-independent models to the end user by employing techniques usually employed in speech recognition studies. In detail, we employ maximum-likelihood linear regression (MLLR) adaptation [20] to compute the linear transformation of the mean parameters of the Gaussian mixtures in the user-independent models (HMMs). That is, we shift the output distributions of the models by using the test data so that each state in the HMMs is more likely to generate test data. A new estimation of the adapted mean $\hat{\mu}$ is given by $\hat{\mu} = A\mu + b = W\xi$, where μ is the initial mean, A is a $k \times k$ transformation matrix, where k is the number of dimensions of the feature vector, b is a bias vector, W is a $k \times (k+1)$ transformation matrix that is decomposed into $W = [b \ A]$, and ξ is the extended mean vector $\xi = [1 \ \mu_1 \ \mu_2 \cdots \mu_k]^T$. Therefore, we estimate the W that reduces the mismatch between the user-independent models and the test data by using the EM technique. We then try to adapt the user-independent models to the user by employing the estimated linear transformation.

5   Evaluation: Core Experiment

In this evaluation, we collect sensor data from three residents (participants A, B, and C) in their own houses and investigate the recognition performance by employing user-dependent models. That is, we learn recognition models by using training data obtained from a participant and then recognize test data from the same participant by using the models. We also investigate the portability of the training data by using user-independent models. That is, we recognize test data from a participant with recognition models trained on sensor data obtained from other participants in their houses. With the user-independent models, an end user need not prepare training data herself. In addition, we adapt the user-independent models to each participant to create user-adapted models by using unlabeled test data obtained from the participant. Then, we recognize the test data using the adapted models of the participant.

Table 1. Electrical devices used in our experiment

	Devices		Devices
A	digital camera	H	mill
B	digital camcorder	I	induction heater
C	hair dryer	J	blender
D	electric toothbrush	K	CD player
E	handheld vacuum cleaner	L	laptop PC
F	electric screwdriver	M	game console
G	electric shaver	N	toy (car)

Table 2. Recognition accuracies (overall F-measure) in percentages for each participant with user-dependent models

Finger	Participant	Accuracy (%)
middle	A	83.7
	B	75.6
	C	84.0
ring	A	78.1
	B	81.8
	C	75.5

5.1 Data Set

The most natural data would be acquired from the normal daily lives of the participants. However, obtaining sufficient samples of such data is costly because researchers must observe their normal daily lives. We collect sensor data by using a semi-naturalistic collection protocol [6] that permits greater variability in participant behavior than laboratory data. In the protocol, participants perform a random sequence of activities (use of electrical devices) following instructions on a worksheet. The participants are relatively free as regards how they perform each activity because the instructions on the the worksheet are not very strict, e.g., "vacuum the room" and "listen to an arbitrary track from a CD." During the experimental period, each participant completed data collection sessions that included a random sequence of use of the electrical devices listed in Table 1. A participant wore our device on his right middle or ring finger since people commonly wear rings on these fingers, and completed twelve sessions wearing our device on each hand. The device was connected via cables to a laptop carried in a backpack. To annotate the collected sensor data, each participant also wore a head-mounted camera that captured the region in front of her body.

We selected the devices in Table 1 from common portable electrical devices used in our daily lives that include components which may emit time-varying magnetic fields, e.g., motors, radio communication modules, and coils. The device list also includes an induction heater, which emits strong magnetic fields. We prepared three sets of electrical devices and gave each participant one set. Because we wanted to investigate training data portability, we included the same models of electrical devices in the three sets. For example, when a participant brushes his teeth, he uses the same electric toothbrush model that the other participants use. The electrical devices used in the experiment were located in their appropriate places in each house. For example, an electric toothbrush and shaver were placed on a washstand. Also, with respect to devices that are usually used in various places such as digital cameras and camcorders, we instructed the participants to use the devices at various locations both in and outside the house. We explain the use of several electrical devices in Table 1 in detail. With the 'digital camera,' because our device can capture the magnetic fields from the

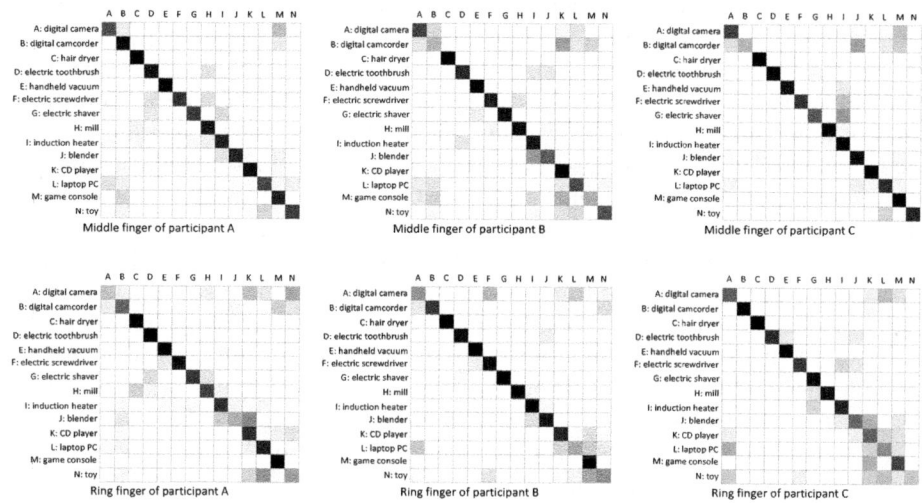

Fig. 9. Visual confusion matrices of the three participants when we use user-dependent models

camera only when its motor is running as mentioned in section 3.2, we regard that 'digital camera' use relates only to when the participant turns it on and employs its zoom function. The 'CD player' used in our experiment is portable and has buttons for operating it on its body, and each participant used the player while holding it. With 'laptop PC,' we instructed the participants to find Yahoo! News with Google and read a news article on the web site. The 'game console' used in our experiment was Sony PlayStation Portable. The 'toy (car)' used in our experiment has a remote control that is connected to the car by a cable, and each participant controlled the car using the remote control.

5.2 Results: User-Dependent Models

To evaluate the user-dependent models, we conducted a 'leave-one-session-out' cross validation. That is, we tested one session obtained from our device worn on a participant's finger by using models trained on other sessions obtained from our device worn on the same finger of the same participant. To evaluate the performance of our method, we used F-measure ($\frac{2 \cdot precision \cdot recall}{precision + recall}$) calculated based on the results for the estimated class at each time slice. Table 2 shows the recognition performance for each participant and for each finger. We achieved high accuracies of about 80% in each house. While the accuracies for the two fingers were not very different, the accuracies for the middle finger (81.1% on average) were slightly better than those for the ring finger (78.5% on average).

Fig. 9 shows the confusion matrices of the three participants. In these results, the recognition accuracies related to electrical devices that include strong magnetic sources (e.g. motors) such as a hair dryer, toothbrush, and and shaver were very high. However, the recognition accuracies related to electrical devices that do not emit strong magnetic fields such as a digital camera and a toy were sometimes poor. Because the remote control of the toy does not include strong magnetic sources such as motors but only several buttons and conductive wires, it was difficult for our device to capture the magnetic fields in some cases depending on the way the remote control was held. Also, the recognition accuracies related to 'laptop PC' were sometimes poor. The laptop PC includes several components that emit strong magnetic fields such as a CPU and an HDD. However, because these components are distributed throughout the PC, our device was sometimes unable to capture the magnetic fields depending on the hand positions on the PC. Also, the accuracies for the blender were poor in some cases. We used a fixed type blender in our study. When the participants used the blender, they pushed the start button without holding onto the blender. Because relation between the blender and the hand position was not fixed, sensor data obtained from the device worn on the hand were slightly different each time the blender was used. By contrast, the recognition accuracies were high for electrical devices that the user held in her hand. The recognition accuracies were also particularly high for handheld electrical devices that emit strong time-varying magnetic fields. This may be because the sensor data features obtained from such devices are not altered by small changes in the way the devices are held.

5.3   Results: User-Independent Models

To evaluate the user-independent models, we conducted a 'leave-one-participant-out' cross validation. That is, we tested sensor data obtained from our device worn on one participant's finger by using models trained with labeled sensor data obtained from our device worn on the same finger of remaining participants. To increase the quantity of training data, we collected sensor data (12-session data) from three additional participants in our home-like experimental environment. That is, we tested sensor data from one participant by using models trained with the sensor data of the other five participants. Note that sensor data from the additional three participants were not used as test data. We tested the sensor data from participants A, B, and C obtained in section 5.1. Here, we used HMMs with four Gaussian mixtures in each state when we constructed the user-dependent models. In this evaluation, we tested larger numbers of Gaussian mixtures in each state because we needed to capture electrical device usage performed by many participants. Fig. 10 shows the transitions of the accuracies when we increased the number of Gaussian mixtures. (Fig. 10 also includes the results for the user-dependent models.) In many cases, a larger number of mixtures provides better results when we used the user-independent models. When the number of mixtures was 128, the average accuracies for the three participants for the middle and ring fingers were 82.2% and 80.3%, respectively. Surprisingly, these results were superior to those of the user-dependent models (81.1% and 78.5% when the number of mixtures was 4). This may be because the user-independent models could capture the various ways that the electrical devices were used by the other five participants. Each user-dependent model for an electrical device was trained based on just 12 occasions of device use. On the other hand, each

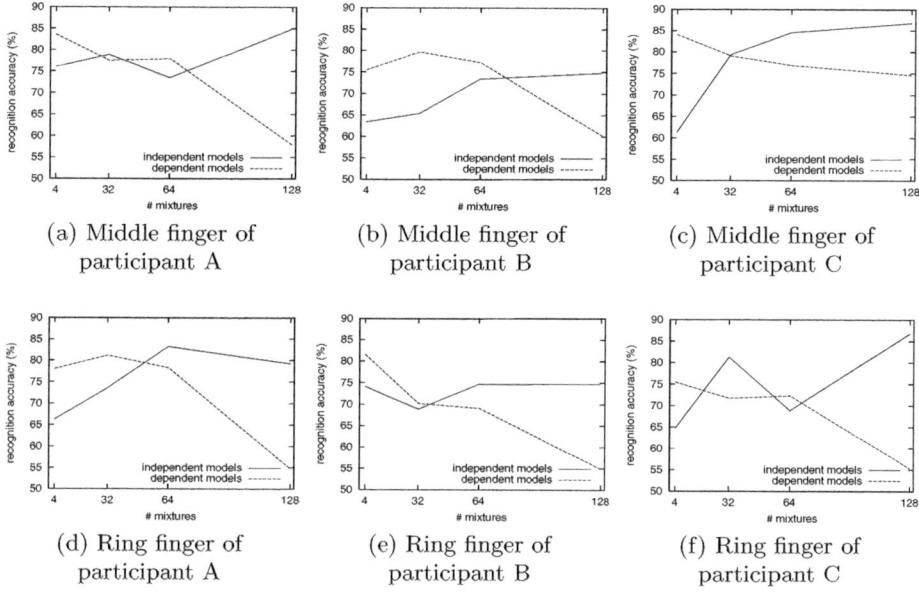

Fig. 10. Transitions of the recognition accuracies when we increase the number of Gaussian mixtures in each state

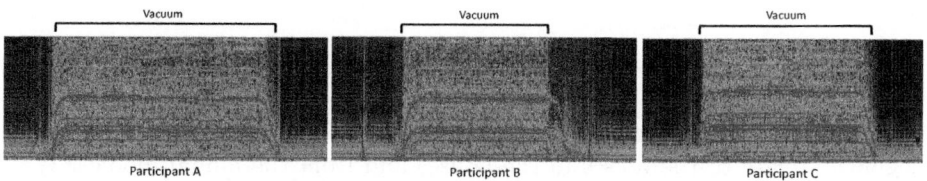

Fig. 11. Spectrograms computed from sensor data obtained from our finger-ring device worn on the right middle finger when the participants used handheld vacuum cleaners

user-independent model was trained with 60 occasions of device use. As a result, we could recognize a participant's electrical device usage with high accuracy without labeled training data from the participant.

However, the recognition accuracies for participant B were relatively poorer than those for other participants when we used the user-independent models. We consider there to be three main factors that interrupt the sharing of training data among users (participants): (1) The features of the environmental magnetic noise in each house may be different. (2) Our finger-ring device can be affected by noise from the human body (finger) because the magnetic flux densities may be slightly affected by magnetic and diamagnetic materials in the finger. Thus, the features of the noise obtained from each participant's finger may be different. (3) The ways of using (holding) electrical devices may depend on each participant, and so the features of sensor data obtained from each participant may be different. Fig. 11 shows examples of spectrograms computed from sensor data obtained

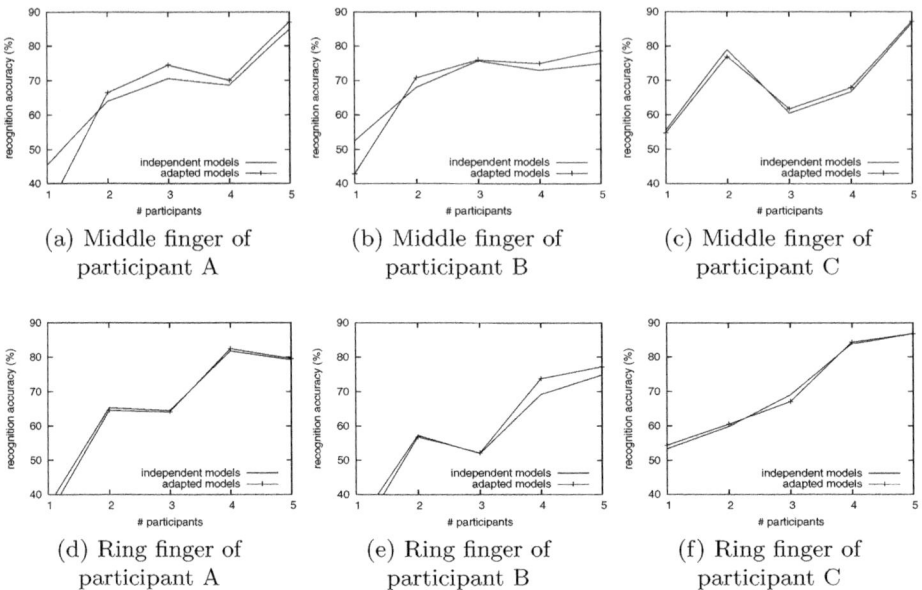

Fig. 12. Transitions of the recognition accuracies when we increase the number of participants whose sensor data are used as training data. We used 128 mixtures in each state.

from our device worn on the middle fingers of participants A, B, and C when they used handheld vacuum cleaners. We first focus on sensor data segments where the participants did not use the cleaner. The features of the sensor data segments relate to the noises in the houses and from the human bodies. While these frequency characteristics were similar, the spectrogram for participant B seems to include small noises over the entire frequency band. (This may be caused by a power transmission tower near participant B's house.) We consider that the noises degrade the recognition accuracies for participant B. On the other hand, the peak frequencies of participant C when he was vacuuming are very different from those of participants A and B. This may be because participant C held the vacuum differently from participants A and B. However, if the user-independent models were trained with sensor data that included the use of the vacuum by other participants that was similar to that of participant C, the models may successfully recognize the use of the vacuum by participant C. Generally, a larger quantity of training data means a better learned model that captures various types of electrical device usage. In fact, the recognition accuracies related to participant C's vacuum usage were good. (81.1% and 85.2% for the middle and ring fingers when the number of mixtures was 128).

Here we investigate the number of participants whose sensor data are used as training data. Fig. 12 shows transitions of the accuracies when we increased the number of participants whose sensor data are used as training data. For example, when the number is two, we train the models by using sensor data from

Table 3. Electrical devices used in our second experiment

	Devices		Devices		Devices		Devices
A	hair dryer 1	F	electric shaver 2	K	handheld vacuum cleaner 2	P	blender
B	hair dryer 2	G	electric shaver 3	L	electric toothbrush 1	Q	CD player 1
C	induction heater 1	H	electric screwdriver 1	M	electric toothbrush 2	R	CD player 2
D	induction heater 2	I	electric screwdriver 2	N	electric toothbrush 3	S	cellphone 1
E	electric shaver 1	J	handheld vacuum cleaner 1	O	mill	T	cellphone 2

two randomly selected participants. Basically, the recognition accuracies improve as the number of participants shows increases. As described above, employing sensor data obtained from many participants enables us to capture various types of electrical device usage. Fig. 12 also includes the recognition accuracies we obtained when we used the user-adapted models described in section 4.3. In many cases, the accuracies with the adapted models were slightly better than those with the independent models. When # participants was five, the average accuracies were 84.4% and 81.3% for the middle and ring fingers, respectively. These results were superior to those of the user-independent models (82.2% and 80.3%). The adaptation techniques improved the recognition accuracies by about 1 to 2% by employing unlabeled sensor data of the participant. In particular, the improvements related to participant B were significant (3.8% and 2.4%). As described above, the accuracies for participant B were poorer than those for other participants because of the effects of the noises in the house and/or from the human body. We consider that the adaptation techniques reduced the effects of these noises.

6   Evaluation: Scalability of Our Approach

In this evaluation, we investigate the scalability of our approach. We collect sensor data from a set of many electrical devices that includes the same or similar types of devices, and recognize the data by using user-dependent models.

6.1   Data Set

We collected sensor data in our home-like environment. A participant completed data collection sessions that included a random sequence of use of the electrical devices listed in Table 3. The participant wore our device on his right middle or ring finger, and completed twelve sessions wearing our device on each hand. The set of electrical devices listed in Table 3 includes several similar devices, e.g., three electric shavers, two CD players. Note that these devices are different products. For example, the three toothbrushes used in the experiment were developed by different manufacturers.

6.2   Results

With the data set, we could also achieve 81.5% for the middle finger and 82.6% for the ring finger even when we employed similar electrical devices. Fig. 13

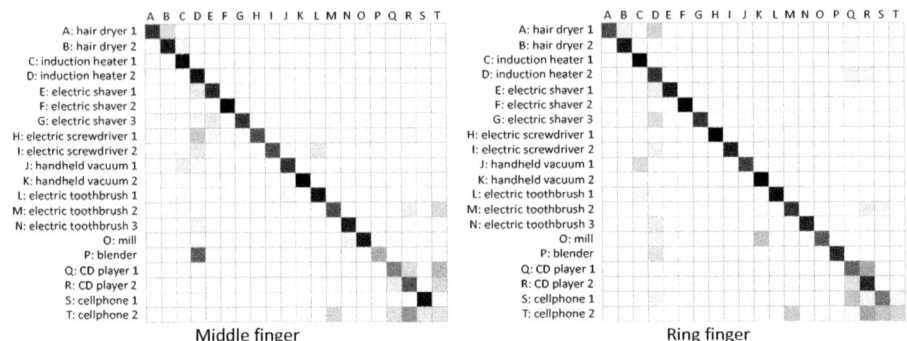

Fig. 13. Visual confusion matrices for sensor data obtained in our home-like environment

shows confusion matrices for the two fingers. As shown in the matrices, the recognition accuracies were very high for electrical devices that emit relatively strong time-varying magnetic fields (from A to P). In many cases, the accuracies as regards these devices were almost perfect. For example, toothbrushes 1 and 3 have similar architectures (rotating-oscillating toothbrushes). However, as shown in Fig. 13, we could distinguish between toothbrushes 1 and 3. We consider that the features used in our approach (FFT components extracted from sensor data) have sufficient expressive power even when we want to distinguish similar devices. However, as shown in Fig. 13, it was difficult to distinguish between CD players 1 and 2. While these players are different products, they were developed by the same manufacturer. These players may include the same or similar magnetic components. The accuracies related to cellphone 2 were also poor. This may be because the intensities of the magnetic fields emitted by the phone were not large. Our device sometimes captured only very small magnetic fields from the phone according to the way the phone was held. Therefore, our recognition method mistakenly classified the use of the cellphone as the use of other electrical devices that emit small magnetic fields, i.e., CD players and a different cellphone.

7   Conclusion

In this paper, we described the development of a finger-ring shaped sensor device by employing a coil of wire for recognizing the use of portable electrical devices. With the device, we captured time-varying magnetic fields emitted by electrical circuits, motors, conductive wires, etc. included in the electrical devices. In the evaluation, we were able to recognize a participant's portable electrical device usage with very high accuracy with training data obtained in her real house. Also, we investigated the portability of training data between different participants. That is, we recognized a participant's sensor data by using models trained with many other participants' labeled sensor data, and confirmed that the models achieved higher accuracies than the models trained with the participant's labeled data. In addition, we reduced the effect of magnetic noises in houses and from the human bodies by using adaptation techniques. As part of our future work, we plan to employ these adaptation techniques according to user's location obtained by a GPS sensor attached to the user. In our current implementation, we simply estimate a single transformation for the adaptation for each user. We also plan to increase sensitivity of our device by increasing the number of turns of wire and/or reducing noise in sensor data that is caused by the amplifier.

References

1. Mynatt, E., Rowan, J., Craighill, S., Jacobs, A.: Digital family portraits: Supporting peace of mind for extended family members. In: CHI 2001, pp. 333–340 (2001)
2. Maekawa, T., Yanagisawa, Y., Kishino, Y., Kamei, K., Sakurai, Y., Okadome, T.: Object-blog system for environment-generated content. IEEE Pervasive Computing 7(4), 20–27 (2008)
3. van Kasteren, T., Noulas, A., Englebienne, G., Kröse, B.: Accurate activity recognition in a home setting. In: Ubicomp 2008, pp. 1–9 (2008)
4. Philipose, M., Fishkin, K., Perkowitz, M.: Inferring activities from interactions with objects. IEEE Pervasive Computing 3(4), 50–57 (2004)
5. Tapia, E.M., Intille, S.S., Larson, K.: Activity Recognition in the Home Using Simple and Ubiquitous Sensors. In: Ferscha, A., Mattern, F. (eds.) PERVASIVE 2004. LNCS, vol. 3001, pp. 158–175. Springer, Heidelberg (2004)
6. Bao, L., Intille, S.S.: Activity Recognition from User-Annotated Acceleration Data. In: Ferscha, A., Mattern, F. (eds.) PERVASIVE 2004. LNCS, vol. 3001, pp. 1–17. Springer, Heidelberg (2004)
7. Lester, J., Choudhury, T., Borriello, G.: A Practical Approach to Recognizing Physical Activities. In: Fishkin, K.P., Schiele, B., Nixon, P., Quigley, A. (eds.) PERVASIVE 2006. LNCS, vol. 3968, pp. 1–16. Springer, Heidelberg (2006)
8. Maekawa, T., Yanagisawa, Y., Kishino, Y., Ishiguro, K., Kamei, K., Sakurai, Y., Okadome, T.: Object-Based Activity Recognition with Heterogeneous Sensors on Wrist. In: Floréen, P., Krüger, A., Spasojevic, M. (eds.) Pervasive 2010. LNCS, vol. 6030, pp. 246–264. Springer, Heidelberg (2010)
9. Maekawa, T., Watanabe, S.: Unsupervised activity recognition with user's physical characteristics data. In: Int'l Symp. on Wearable Computers, pp. 89–96 (2011)
10. Kim, Y., Schmid, T., Charbiwala, Z., Srivastava, M.: ViridiScope: design and implementation of a fine grained power monitoring system for homes. In: Ubicomp 2009, pp. 245–254 (2009)
11. Hart, G.: Nonintrusive appliance load monitoring. Proceedings of the IEEE 80(12), 1870–1891 (1992)
12. Patel, S.N., Robertson, T., Kientz, J.A., Reynolds, M.S., Abowd, G.D.: At the Flick of a Switch: Detecting and Classifying Unique Electrical Events on the Residential Power Line (Nominated for the Best Paper Award). In: Krumm, J., Abowd, G.D., Seneviratne, A., Strang, T. (eds.) UbiComp 2007. LNCS, vol. 4717, pp. 271–288. Springer, Heidelberg (2007)
13. Gupta, S., Reynolds, M., Patel, S.: ElectriSense: Single-point sensing using EMI for electrical event detection and classification in the home. In: Ubicomp 2010, pp. 139–148 (2010)

14. Maekawa, T., Kishino, Y., Sakurai, Y., Suyama, T.: Recognizing the Use of Portable Electrical Devices with Hand-Worn Magnetic Sensors. In: Lyons, K., Hightower, J., Huang, E.M. (eds.) Pervasive 2011. LNCS, vol. 6696, pp. 276–293. Springer, Heidelberg (2011)
15. Lenz, J.: A review of magnetic sensors. Proceedings of the IEEE 78(6), 973–989 (1990)
16. Lifton, J., Feldmeier, M., Ono, Y., Lewis, C., Paradiso, J.: A platform for ubiquitous sensor deployment in occupational and domestic environments. In: IPSN 2007, pp. 119–127 (2007)
17. Jiang, X., Dawson-Haggerty, S., Dutta, P., Culler, D.: Design and implementation of a high-fidelity ac metering network. In: IPSN 2009, pp. 253–264 (2009)
18. Cohn, G., Morris, D., Patel, S.N., Tan, D.S.: Your noise is my command: sensing gestures using the body as an antenna. In: CHI 2011, pp. 791–800 (2011)
19. Rabiner, L.: A tutorial on hidden Markov models and selected applications in speech recognition. Proceedings of the IEEE 77(2), 257–286 (1989)
20. Leggetter, C., Woodland, P.: Maximum likelihood linear regression for speaker adaptation of continuous density hidden Markov models. Computer Speech & Language 9(2), 171–185 (1995)

Self-calibration of RFID Reader Probabilities in a Smart Real-Time Factory

Bilal Hameed, Farhan Rashid, Frank Dürr, and Kurt Rothermel

IPVS - Universitaet Stuttgart
Universitaetsstrasse 38, 70569
Stuttgart, Germany
{bilal.hameed,farhan.rashid,frank.duerr,
kurt.rothermelg}@ipvs.uni-stuttgart.de
http://www.ipvs.uni-stuttgart.de/

Abstract. RFID technology is now widely used to identify, locate, track and monitor physical objects. However, the use of RFID technology in modern manufacturing has been limited because of the unreliability of RFID devices. In addition to this, where it is used, the technology is mostly deployed to be a substitute for manual inventory management. In this paper we present the Smart Factory, a modern factory infrastructure capable of monitoring each and every product part that moves across the factory during the entire production process. In order to overcome the reliability issues in RFID devices, we have built up a probabilistic model to assign probabilities to the RFID readers and to the product part detections. We also present a probability self-calibration algorithm that automatically adapts the probabilities of RFID readers to better reflect their performance at current instance of time.

Keywords: RFID, Self-Configuration, Middleware, and Smart Factory.

1 Introduction

Modern factories are increasingly producing customized products according to the customer's preferences. Building highly customized products is a challenging endeavour but is nevertheless pursued to retain customer loyalty and satisfaction. In variant production, the production process remains the same; however the product parts moving through the assembly lines vary, which results in different variants of the same products being produced. In such a scenario, minor deviations in time or order of product parts could result in incorrect final products. Several major manufacturers including automakers such as BMW, Porsche, and Daimler are now producing build-to order cars, where a customer's order triggers the manufacturing of an individual car variant. Porsche currently offers its customers 10^7 variants to chose from [1].

In order to ensure correct, optimized, and error free assembly processes, manufacturers try to monitor their production processes in real time. Porsche for example, uses a set of error prevention techniques during the assembly process.

J. Kay et al. (Eds.): Pervasive 2012, LNCS 7319, pp. 253–270, 2012.

Barcode technology is used to prevent errors during assembly. Once a semi-assembled car reaches an assembly point, the bar code attached to the car is read to figure out what needs to be done with the car. However, barcode technology has a lot of limitations, such as extensive human interaction and line of sight readings which are also limited to single reads at a time.

Due to the limitations posed by barcode technology manufacturers are now switching over to RFID based systems. RFID provides features such as contactless and non-line of sight identification, multiple tag reads, seamless interfacing with higher level processing devices (PCs) etc., that are essential for real-time production monitoring. Due to these advantages, Ford [2], BMW and Vauxhall [3][4] have deployed RFID based systems, whereby they place a programmed RFID tag on a vehicle skid. During each production step, the tag is read to determine what needs to be done and the updates are automatically written to the tag. This results in eliminating paper work and the associated human errors.

An hindrance to RFID deployment in manufacturing environments, where precision is of utmost importance, is the inherent unreliability of the technology. RFID readers have an accuracy of 80-90% [5], which is further affected by metal objects, interference of multiple readers, or the presence of multiple tags. The accuracy of an RFID reader drops to 70% in case it tries to detect five or more tags [6],[7],[8]. Besides missing out on detecting RFID tags, RFID readers can detect objects incorrectly, overshoot and detect objects passing through neighbouring production lines, and can have duplicate readings.

In order to resolve these reliability issues, we proposed an RFID based framework [9] that used multiple RFID readers deployed on the production lines to monitor product parts and product part sequences. The basic idea of the approach was to detect product parts reliably using unreliable RFID readers. We also developed a probabilistic sequence detection algorithm that assigns probabilities to the detection of product parts and their associated sequences. Redundancies in the deployment of RFID readers were exploited to increase the confidence in the detected sequences.

However, our initial approach assumed that RFID readers would have fixed probabilities of correct readings which are known a-priori. This does not reflect reality, since the accuracy of an RFID reader can change over time or can differ from the very beginning depending upon the installation settings. In fact, our evaluations in this paper showed that even two readers of the same model had different probabilities. In order to overcome this issue, we propose an efficient and scalable self-calibration algorithm in this paper that dynamically updates the probabilities of RFID readers. This ensures that the probabilities of RFID readers reflect the current conditions at all times, and hence the detections of a faulty reader has a minimalistic effect on the overall performance of the real-time monitoring of production parts. We have conducted simulations to evaluate the probability self-calibration algorithm under different settings. The evaluations show that our algorithm is able to estimate the probabilities of physical readers with an accuracy of more than 90% even for physical readers having an accuracy as low as 70%.

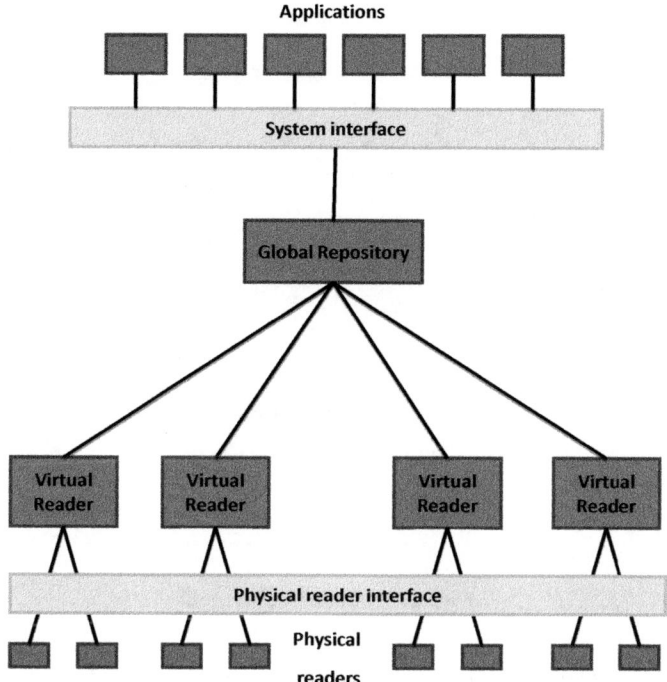

Fig. 1. System Model

The rest of the paper is structured as follows. The system model is discussed in Section 2. In Section 3 we formally discuss the problem that we want to solve. Section 4 presents the probability self-calibration algorithm. Section 5 discusses the evaluations, followed by a review of related work in Section 6. Finally, we conclude the paper with a short summary in Section 7.

2   System Model

Our system model (Figure 1) consists of a global repository, several virtual readers and a large number of physical RFID readers. Figure 2 shows a sample deployment of the system components. These components are described below:

Physical Readers: Physical RFID readers, denoted as prs, are deployed on the production lines. Each product part is tagged with an RFID tag, and as these product parts move across the production lines, they are continuously tracked by the prs. A pr can read several RFID tags within its sensing range.

A *read event* e by a pr is defined as $e = (pp, pr, t)$; where t represents the time at which pp was detected by pr. $(t_i < t_j)$ implies that t_i occurred before t_j. $(pr_i \sqsubset pr_j)$ implies that pr_i is deployed before pr_j on the production line i.e. product parts will first be read by pr_i and then by pr_j.

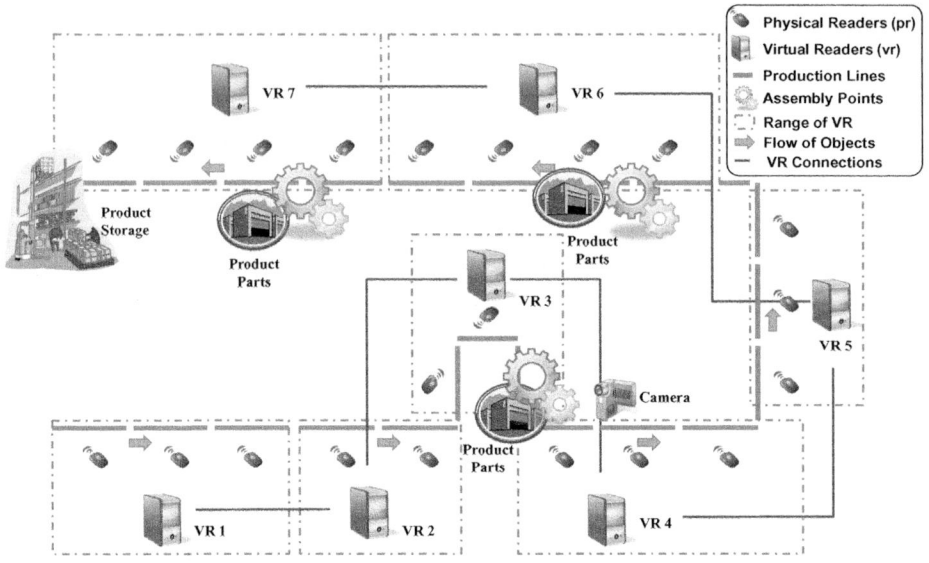

Fig. 2. System Deployment

A *product part order ppo* ($pp_i < pp_j$) implies that pp_i is directly ahead of pp_j on the production line such that there exists no $pp_k : (pp_i < pp_k < pp_j)$. *Non-unique product part orders* are product part orders of the form ($pp_i < pp_j$) and ($pp_i < pp_k$), which implies that pp_i is directly ahead of both pp_j and pp_k. Since product parts move in a sequential order on the production lines, non-unique product part orders cannot exist in reality. However, they can arise as a result of different inconsistent readings (see RFID Reader Errors 3.1).

Virtual Readers: Virtual readers, denoted as *vrs*, represent an abstraction of physical readers. Each *pr* is connected to exactly one *vr*. The manufacturing plant is divided into topological regions, depicted by range of *vr* in Figure 2. These regions are strictly non-overlapping. Every region is associated with exactly one *vr* such that the *vr* can process the raw events generated by the *prs* in that region. In production environments, since the topology of the manufacturing plant does not change very often, the *pr* to *vr* mapping can be done during system initialization. *vrs* are connected with one another such that each *vr* receives information from its predecessor vr_{i-1} and sends information to its successor vr_{i+1}. The *vrs* are responsible for detecting different failures which are detailed in the RFID reader errors (Section 3.1). In addition to this, the *vrs* also compute and continuously re-configure the probabilities of RFID readers.

Each *vr* also has access to two global variables, planned product part order $PPO_{planned}$ and actual product part order PPO_{actual}. $PPO_{planned}$ contains the list of all product parts and the order in which they are suppose to move on the production line. This product part order is planned during production planning, which is discussed in Section 5.1. In the beginning the PPO_{actual} contains the same product part order as $PPO_{planned}$, however over time PPO_{actual} reflects the actual product part order during production.

Global Repository: The repository has knowledge of the entire factory layout, production modules, the locations of the physical readers prs, virtual readers vrs, and the assembly points. The repository does not perform any computations. In fact, it provides other components with the above mentioned information that is necessary for processing data.

3   Problem Statement

In this section we outline the problems that we want to solve. We will also discuss the final goal of our algorithm.

3.1   RFID Reader Errors

In this section we will go through the different errors that affect the reliable operations of the RFID devices. RFID reader errors result from the operations of RFID devices and can be broadly divided into four distinct categories; duplicate reads, false reads, missed reads, and out of order reads.

   Duplicate Reads occur when a pr reads the same pp multiple times. A duplicate read is a read event $e_{duplicate} = (pp_i, pr_i, t_j) \mid \exists \ e = (pp_i, pr_i, t_i)$, where $(t_i < t_j)$.

   False Reads occur when a pr reads a product part incorrectly or overshoots and reads other product parts that are not on the production line, but may come within the sensing range of the pr. Let $PP_{pl} = \{pp_a, pp_b \ldots, pp_n\}$ be a set of all product parts that are supposed to pass through a particular production line. Then a false read is defined as a read event $e_{false} = (pp_o, pr_i, t_j) \mid pp_o \notin PP_{pl}$.

   Out of Order Reads occur due to the read range of the prs, similar to false reads. An out of order read occurs when a pr detects product parts in the order $(pp_j < pp_i)$, when the actual product part order on the production line was $(pp_i < pp_j)$.

   Missed Reads occur as a result of unreliability of prs. Some of the common causes of missed readings include metallic interference and batch tag reads. Let $DPL_{vr} = \{pp_a, pp_b \ldots, pp_n\}$ be a set of all detected product parts at a vr and $DPL_{pri} = \{pp_a, pp_b \ldots, pp_m\}$ be a set of detected product parts by pr_i. Then the complement of DPL_{vr} w.r.t DPL_{pri} ($DPL_{vr} \backslash DPL_{pri} = \{x : x \in DPL \mid x \notin DPL_{pri}\}$) gives us the set of missed readings $DPL_{pri_{missed}}$ of pr_i. The cardinality of set $DPL_{pri_{missed}}$ gives the total number of missed reads of pr_i.

   The goal of our system is to eliminate RFID based sensing errors in order to have an accurate model of the physical world. To achieve this goal, we use a probabilistic model which is discussed below:

   Every pr has an associated probability $p(pr_{actual})$, which reflects the supposed accuracy of the pr, and an estimated probability $p(pr_{estimated})$, which contains the probability of the pr as estimated by our algorithm (Section 4.3). The *probability of read event* $p(e)$ is the probability with which pp was correctly detected by pr. For any read event e, $p(e) = p(pr_{estimated})$. The *probability of a product part order $p(ppo)$* is the probability with which a *ppo* matches reality.

In reality, the probability of a *pr* depends on various *pr* properties and its deployed environment. For instance, $p(pr_{actual})$ is influenced by the type of the reader, the orientation of the reader's antenna and the RFID tag that is being read, and so on. Therefore, each reader has an individual probability which is hard to know a-priori. Our goal is to develop a self-calibrating system that estimates and adapts $p(pr_{estimated})$ during production monitoring.

3.2   Environmental Errors

Environmental errors are deviations from $PPO_{planned}$ as a result of environmental factors such as human intervention, and mechanical failures etc., which result in a physical change on the production line. These deviations result in changed reads, which have to be distinguished from erroneous reads.

Changed Reads are correct readings that are categorized as RFID errors 3.1 by the system. Changes can occur due to product part removal such as $(pp_i < pp_j < pp_k)$ getting changed to $(pp_i < pp_k)$, product part insertion such as $(pp_i < pp_j)$ getting changed to $(pp_i < pp_m < pp_j)$ or change in product part order such as $(pp_i < pp_j)$ getting changed to $(pp_j < pp_i)$. The net effect of all three types of changes is a change in the *ppo*. In variant production, product parts need to move through production lines in pre-defined order to get correctly assembled with their corresponding parts. Changes in *ppo* would result in inconsistent final products and hence are not desirable.

The goal of detecting environmental errors is to detect inconsistencies between physical world and the production plan. Detection of RFID errors is required to accurately detect environmental errors since an inaccurate model of the physical world would make it impossible to make correct assumptions about inconsistencies between the physical world and the production plan. It is worth noting that the effect of a physical change and an RFID error might at first look similar w.r.t the detected read event. For instance, an out of order read may initially look similar to a physical change of product part order. Therefore, we need algorithms to distinguish between RFID and environmental errors.

4   Self-calibration of RFID Reader Probabilities

In this section we present concepts for the self-calibration of physical reader probabilities. First we provide an overview of our approach (Section 4.1). Then we discuss the detection of possible product part orders (Section 4.2). After that we describe the actual probability calibration algorithm (Section 4.3) and in the end we explain the process of change detection (Section 4.4).

4.1   Overview

In this section we will give a brief overview of our approach. The basic steps of our algorithm follows:

1. Detect possible product part orders *ppos*. The outcome of this step are multiple possible *ppos* which are stored in possible product part order list PPPO, which contains all the possible *ppos* deduced by our system.
2. For each *ppo*, calculate $p(ppo)$ which is a probability for *ppo* being the correct order. $p(ppo)$ is calculated from the probabilities of associated read events that participated in the detection of *ppo*.
3. Determine the most probable product part order ppo_{mp} amongst the different conflicting *ppos* in PPPO. If there are two conflicting *ppos*, ppo_i ($pp_i < pp_j$) and ppo_j ($pp_j < pp_i$) with $p(ppo_i)$ being 0.9 and $p(ppo_j)$ being 0.81. ppo_i will be considered as the ppo_{mp}. We assume that ppo_{mp} reflects reality, which is a reasonable assumption if many redundant readings have been considered.
4. Calibrate the probability of individual reader by finding out how many correct and false readings it has made by comparing its read events with ppo_{mp}. In order to distinguish between correct and incorrect readings, we consider different possible errors(false, out of order, and missed readings)

In the next Subsection 4.2 , we first describe the details of the detection of possible product part orders and the most probable product part order (Steps 1-3). Then we describe the reader calibration algorithm in Section 4.3

4.2 Detection of Possible Product Part Orders

Detection of a *ppo* is carried out by applying the following rules:

1. Rule 1: If *pr* detects pp_i at time t_i and then detects pp_j at a later time t_{i+k}, then ($pp_i < pp_j$).
2. Rule 2: If pr_i is deployed before pr_j on the production line i.e. ($pr_i \sqsubset pr_j$), then pp_i detected by pr_j at time t_i is ahead of pp_j detected by pr_i at a later time t_{i+k}, i.e. ($pp_i < pp_j$).

Each vr_i maintains a detected parts list DPL_{pr_i} for each pr_i, which is a list that contains all the product parts detected by pr_i. Whenever a read event $e_i = (pp_i, pr_i, t_i)$ is detected by a pr_i, pp_i is placed in the respective DPL_{pr_i}. The pp_i is also added to the DPL_{vr_i}, which contains all the parts detected at a vr_i. Each *pp* in the DPL_{vr_i} also has an *age*, which shows how recently the *pp* was detected. For every read event of a *pp*, we try to determine the *ppo* of the product part with the previously detected parts using the rules discussed above. Once a *ppo* is deduced, it is added to PPPO. Every *ppo* in PPPO is associated with its respective probability, an event list that contains the read events that led to the deduction of the *ppo* and the age of the *ppo*, which shows how recently the *ppo* was deduced.

If the newly detected *pp* is already present in the DPL_{vr_i}, the age of the *pp* is refreshed. Similarly if the deduced *ppo* is already present in the PPPO, the age of *ppo* is refreshed. In addition to this the events that led to this recent deduction of the *ppo* are added to the event list of the *ppo*, and the probability of the *ppo* is re-computed (cf: Algorithm 1).

Algorithm 1. Probabilistic Product Part Order Detection Algorithm
---

1: Let $e_i = (pp_i, pr_i, t_i)$ be a read event detected at vr_i

2: $DPL_{vr_i} \leftarrow pp_i$;

3: $DPL_{pr_i} \leftarrow pr_i$;

4: **if** $(pp_i ==$ newly detected part) **then**

5:    Detect product part order ppo using product part order detection rules

6:    **if** $(ppo$ deduced) **then**

7:       computeProbability(ppo);

8:       PPPO $\leftarrow ppo$;

9: **else** // pp_i has been detected previously

10:    $DPL_{vr_i}[pp_i] \leftarrow e_i$;

11:    $DPL_{pr_i}[pp_i] \leftarrow e_i$;

12:    refresh age of pp_i;

13:    **for all** $ppo \in$ PPPO that contains pp_i **do**

14:       refresh ppo.age;

15:       computeProbability(ppo);

The probability of a product part order ($o_1 < o_2$) is computed as:

$$p(ppo) = (1 - [(1 - p(ne_{pp_1})) + (1 - p(ne_{pp_2})) - (1 - p(ne_{pp_1} + ne_{pp_2}))];$$

where ne_{pp_1} is the number of read events for pp_1, $p(ne_{pp_1})$ is the probability for these read events to be correct, ne_{pp_2} is the number of read events for pp_2, and $p(ne_{pp_2})$ is the probability for ne_{pp_2} to be correct. The rationale behind this formula is that we can derive an order if at least two read events are correct. If that is the case, then these two(or more) events will reflect the correct order. From a false reading, nothing can be derived since multiple false readings can reflect an arbitrary order. Thus, only if, either all read events for pp_1 are incorrect $(1 - p(ne_{pp_1}))$ or all read events for pp_2 are incorrect $(1 - p(ne_{pp_2}))$, we cannot derive a product part order. In order to not count the incorrect read events twice, we subtract $(1 - p(ne_{pp_1} + ne_{pp_2}))$. This gives us the probability of no correct reading for ($pp_1 < pp_2$). Subtracting this probability from 1 gives us the probability of all the cases where at least one correct reading for pp_1 and at least one correct reading for pp_2 is included in the set of readings.

Due to the possibility of false readings, we might get two conflicting $ppos$ ($pp_i < pp_j$) and ($pp_j < pp_i$) for product parts pp_i and pp_j. For each of these $ppos$ we also get a probability according to the above formula. We assume that the ppo with the higher probability is the actual product part order. The set of ppo_{mp} are used in the next step to calibrate the reader probabilities.

4.3   Self-calibration of RFID Readers

The estimated probability $p(pr_{estimated})$ of a pr is computed as:

$$p(pr_{estimated}) = (productparts - errors)/productparts;$$

where $productparts$ is the total number of pps that passed through pr on the production line, and $errors$ is the sum of all errors of pr, i.e., $errors = $ n(missed

---

Algorithm 2. Probability Self-Calibration Algorithm

1: Let $e_i = (pp_i, pr_i, t_i)$ be a read event detected at vr_i

2: $DPL_{vr_i} = pp_i$
3: $DPL_{pr_i} = pr_i$

4: **if** $pp_i \in PP_{pl}$ **then** // pp_i not a false read
5:     **if** $((pp_{i-1} < pp_i) \in$ PPPO $AND(pp_{i-1} < pp_i).probability > (pp_{i-1} < any)AND(pp_{i-1} < pp_i).probability > (any < pp_i))$ **then**
6:         pp_i not an out-of-order read
7:         **for all** $pr_n \in vr_i$ where n=0 to i-1 **do**
8:             **if** $\neg pp_i \in DPL_{pr_n}$ **then** // pr_n missed to detect pp_i
9:                 $MPL_{pr_n} = pp_i$
10:                 **trigger** estimateProbability(pr_n)
11:     **else** // pp_i is Out-of-Order Read
12:         $OOPL_{pr_i} = (pp_{i-1} < pp_i)$
13:         **trigger** estimateProbability(pr_i)
14: **else** // pp_i not in PP_{pl}
15:     **if** $((pp_{i-1} < pp_i)$ is most probable $ppo \in$ PPPO) **then**
16:         **for all** $pr_n \in vr_i$ where n=0 to i-1 **do**
17:             **if** $(pp_{i-1} < pp_i) \in FPL_{pr_n}$ **then**
18:                 remove pp_i from FPL_{pr_n}
19:                 **trigger** estimateProbability(pr_n)
20:     **else** // pp_i is a false read
21:         $FPL_{pr_i} = (pp_{i-1} < pp_i)$;
22:         remove pp_i from DPL_{vr_i};
23:         **trigger** estimateProbability(pr_i)

24: **if** $((pp_{i-1} < pp_i).probability < ppo_{conflicting}.probability)$ **then**
25:     **trigger** ChangeEvent (PPPO, vr_{i-1}, $ppo_{conflicting}$)

26:   **procedure** estimateProbability(pr_i) **do**
27:     $productparts = n(DPL_{pr_i}) + n(MPL_{pr_i})$
28:     $errors_{pr_i} = n(MPL_{pr_i}) + n(FPL_{pr_i}) + n(OOPL_{pr_i})$
29:     $p(pr_i estimated) = \frac{productparts - errors_{pr_i}}{productparts}$

---

reads) + n(false reads) + n(out of order reads) (cf: Algorithm 2 line 26-29). $p(pr_{estimated})$ is re-computed whenever a part is detected or is categorized as a false, missed or out of order read.

We do not consider duplicate readings since a duplicate does not carry additional information. We filter out duplicate readings in a pre-processing step by aggregating directly succeeding read events of a pp by a pr into one read event for the pp. Furthermore, we do not have to distinguish between the different types of errors in this formula, as we have already explained that we can only make a statement about the order of two product parts if at least two read events are correct. An incorrect event cannot be used to determine the true order since any kind of error (false, out of order, missed reads) will invalidate the ppo.

False Reading Detection: Whenever a read event $e_i = (pp_i, pr_i, t_i)$ is detected by a pr_i, we compare pp_i with PP_{pl}, which is a list that contains all the pps that are planned to pass through this production line to determine if pp_i was supposed to pass through this line. If pp_i is not a part of PP_{pl} we compare the ppo ($pp_{i-1} < pp_i$) detected at pr_i with PPPO. In case ppo ($pp_{i-1} < pp_i$) is not ppo_{mp} in PPPO i.e. there exists other $ppos$ that contradict ppo and have a higher

---

Algorithm 3. Change Detection Event

1:    **upon event** ChangeEvent(PPPO, vr_{i+1}, $ppo_{conflicting}$) **do**
2:     **for all** $pr_n \in vr_i$ **do**
3:      **for all** $ppo \in FPL_{pr_n}$ **do**
4:       **if** $(ppo == ppo_{conflicting})$ **then**
5:        remove $ppo_{conflicting}$ from FPL_{pr_n}
6:        **trigger** estimateProbability(pr_n)
7:      **for all** $ppo \in OOPL_{pr_n}$ **do**
8:       **if** $(ppo == ppo_{conflicting})$ **then**
9:        remove $ppo_{conflicting}$ from $OOPL_{pr_n}$
10:        **trigger** estimateProbability(pr_n)
11:      **for all** $ppo \in MPL_{pr_n}$ **do**
12:       **if** $(ppo == ppo_{conflicting})$ **then**
13:        remove $ppo_{conflicting}$ from MPL_{pr_n}
14:        **trigger** estimateProbability(pr_n)

---

probability, pp_i is categorized as a false read. ppo $(pp_{i-1} < pp_i)$ is inserted into the FPL_{pr_i}, which is a list that contains all the falsely detected ppos by pr_i. After adding the ppo to the FPL_{pr_i}, $p(pr_{estimated})$ of pr_i is recalculated (cf: Algorithm 2 line 14-23).

Out of Order Reading Detection: Once we have determined that pp_i is not a false read, we try to figure out if pr_i has detected pp_i in the correct order. In order to determine this we compare ppo $(pp_{i-1} < pp_i)$ with PPPO. If ppo $(pp_{i-1} < pp_i)$ is found to have a higher probability then any ppo having pp_{i-1} as the first part in the sequence or pp_i as the later part in the sequence, then $(pp_{i-1} < pp_i)$ is not an out-of-order read. However, if $(pp_{i-1} < pp_i)$ is either not present in PPPO or is a ppo with a lower probability as compared to its conflicting ppo we insert it into out of order parts list $OOPL_{pr_i}$, which contains all the ppos that were deduced as a result of out of order reads by pr_i. The $p(pr_{estimated})$ for pr_i is also recalculated at this time (cf: Algorithm 2 line 5-13).

Missed Reading Detection: Once we have eliminated the possibility of pp_i to be a false positive (false read, out of order read), we try to determine if there exist some prs that missed out on detecting pp_i. This is done by comparing pp_i with DPL_{pr} of the prs that are deployed before pr_i to find out if they have also detected pp_i. If pp_i is not already present in a particular prs detected parts list (say DPL_{pr_h}), it is placed in the missed parts list MPL_{pr_h}, which is a list that contains all the product parts that pr_h failed to detect. The $p(pr_{estimated})$ for pr_h is also recalculated (cf: Algorithm 2 line 8-10).

4.4   Change Detection

As pointed out before, the basic problem in detecting physical changes in the order of product parts is to distinguish between RFID errors and actual physical changes. In this subsection, we will analyse different classes of physical changes to see which ones are actually critical, and how they can be distinguished from RFID errors.

If a product part pp_i is removed from the production line at a specific point, the prs deployed prior to this point will not be able to report this change. However, the prs deployed ahead of the point of change would be able to detect this change, which will be reflected by the non-detection of pp_i. vr_i will not penalize the probability of any of the prs for missing to detect this part. This is because vr_i only finds out if pr_i has missed out on detecting pp_i if pp_i is later detected by pr_j, where $(pr_i \sqsubset pr_j)$ (cf: Section 4.3).

If on the other hand ppo is changed or a new pp has been inserted onto the production line, this change will soon be reflected in the PPPO of vr_{i+1}. Initially, physical change cannot be distinguished from RFID errors. Therefore, our strategy is to wait for enough redundant readings before we make a definite statement about the actual product part order. Moreover, old readings (readings before the physical change) will age out since we apply an aging mechanism to readings. This increases the probability of the current state over time.

As an example, consider that the current product part order is $(pp_1 < pp_2 < pp_3)$ with $(pp_1 < pp_2)$ having a probability of 0.9 and $(pp_2 < pp_3)$ also has a probability of 0.9. However, if this ppo gets changed to $(pp_1 < pp_3)$ as a result of removal of pp_2 from the production line. Since prs would no longer be able to detect pp_2, its age out along with all the $ppos$ in which it is participating. Whenever a pp is detected by a pr its age is set to 1. This age is then decreased by an aging unit, every time a pr on the production line fails to detect it. However, if after being missed out by two prs, the third pr detects the pp, its age is again refreshed to 1. Once a pp is aged out, all the $ppos$ in which that pp was participating are also aged out. Eventually the probability of $(pp_1 < pp_3)$ would become greater than the probability $(pp_1 < pp_2)$ and $(pp_2 < pp_3)$, since the two $ppos$ in which pp_2 was participating will be aged out. Whenever the probabilities of conflicting $ppos$ interchange, we trigger a change event which is also sent to the predecessor vr_{i-1} of this vr_i (cf: Algorithm 2 line 24-25).

Once a changed event is received/detected at a vr_i, the vr_i compares the $ppo_{conflicting}$ with the FPL_{pr}, $OOPL_{pr}$ and MPL_{pr} of all of its prs to find and remove $ppo_{conflicting}$ from these lists. The $p(pr_{estimated})$ of all prs that had $ppo_{conflicting}$ in their lists is also recomputed (cf: Algorithm 3).

5   Evaluations

The evaluations section consists of a pre-study conducted in the Smart Factory (Section 5.1) and simulations (Section 5.2). The purpose of the pre-study was to benchmark the accuracy of RFID readers under different conditions. The Smart Factory pre-study shows that we need a system to calibrate the RFID reader probabilities since it is impossible to have a a perfect world in which RFID readers are able to detect all product parts with 100% accuracy. The simulations then demonstrate the effectiveness of the self-calibration algorithm.

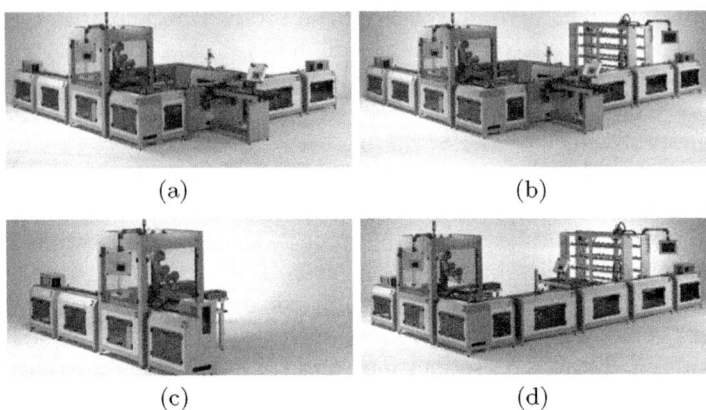

(a)   (b)

(c)   (d)

Fig. 3. Smart Factory Deployment Topologies

5.1   Pre-study: Smart Factory

The Smart Factory [10], [24] is a modern factory infrastructure that is established for conducting research on manufacturing processes using real products and production lines. The Smart Factory has several modules which can be configured into various topologies. Figure 3 shows the various deployment topologies of the Smart Factory. The Smart Factory modules are of two types, active modules such as the robotic arm or the assembly points on which some activity takes place and inactive modules such as the production lines and the storage area. The production process involves product planning and product assembly. Production planning involves plans for the type of products that would be built, the parts that would belong to each product and so on. Planning for a single type of product is a simplified process, however, with variant production, this process becomes quiet extensive.

The Smart Factory produces a stationary box that has three parts: a large cup, a small cup and a thermometer or a hydrometer. Each of these three parts has several different variants such as a large cup without hole, a large cup with hole, a large cup with stripes, etc. The Smart Factory can produce around two dozen product variants. Figure 4 shows four different product variants of the Smart Factory. The product parts are assembled on a baseplate, which in turn is mounted on a tray that moves on the production line. The baseplate has three sockets (placeholders) for the parts, and every part can be placed on any of the three sockets on the baseplate. The assembly of a new part on the baseplate is carried out at the assembly point. When the baseplate reaches the assembly point it stops, a worker places a new part on the plate and updates the terminal which enables the baseplate to move again.

We configured the Smart Factory and deployed nine passive modules (production lines) and three active modules (assembly points) to build our production environment. The factory was configured to mimic the system deployment diagram (Figure 2) presented in Section 2. We deployed three *vrs* and six *prs*. The

(a)   (b)   (c)   (d)

Fig. 4. Smart Factory Product Variants

vrs were Lenovo T61 laptops with 4GB RAM, 100GB harddisk and 2.50 GHz Intel Core 2 Duo processors, whereas the *prs* were Volaré UHF USB readers [26].

We placed RFID tags on each and every part and then studied the effects of tag placement, multiple tag reads, tag orientation, RFID reader power, and reader inference on the accuracy of RFID readers. The metrics that we evaluated are more or less standard metrics to measure the performance of RFID readers [12]. Our studies showed that the accuracy of RFID readers changes with a change in the parameters. As an example the accuracy of the readers decreased if the distance between the reader and the assembly line was increased, or if the reader power was decreased and so on. In addition to this our studies revealed that two RFID readers from the same manufacturer does not have the same accuracy under perfectly similar conditions. The pre-study therefore further highlighted the need to calibrate the RFID reader probabilities.

5.2   Simulation Results

In this section, we discuss the performance of the probability self-calibration algorithm under simulated settings. We decided to evaluate our algorithm in a simulated setting because a simulation environment provides the possibility to evaluate a large scenario. Furthermore, we also wanted to test our algorithm in a controlled setting, whereby we could control/set the ground truths, such as the probabilities of *prs*. The simulations were performed using PeerSim [25], a large scale distributed P2P discrete event simulator. All simulations were performed with 8,000 *prs* distributed across 1,000 nodes (*vrs*), except where otherwise specified.

A cycle in our simulations is the time taken by a *pp* to move from one *pr* to the next one. So after every cycle a new *pp* part is introduced on the production line, while the previous ones move ahead by one *pr*. We start calculating $p(pr_{estimated})$ after 50 cycles so that we have enough redundant readings to make a reasonable estimate. $p(pr_{estimated})$ is then continuously re-calculated every 5 cycles. To evaluate the performance of our algorithm we calculate the *accuracy* with which we are able to determine the estimated probability of each *pr*:

$$accuracy = (1 - |p(pr_{estimated}) - p(pr_{actual})|/p(pr_{actual})) * 100$$

The main performance metric is the time (in cycles) it takes for the algorithm to estimate the probabilities of all *prs* with a high reliability.

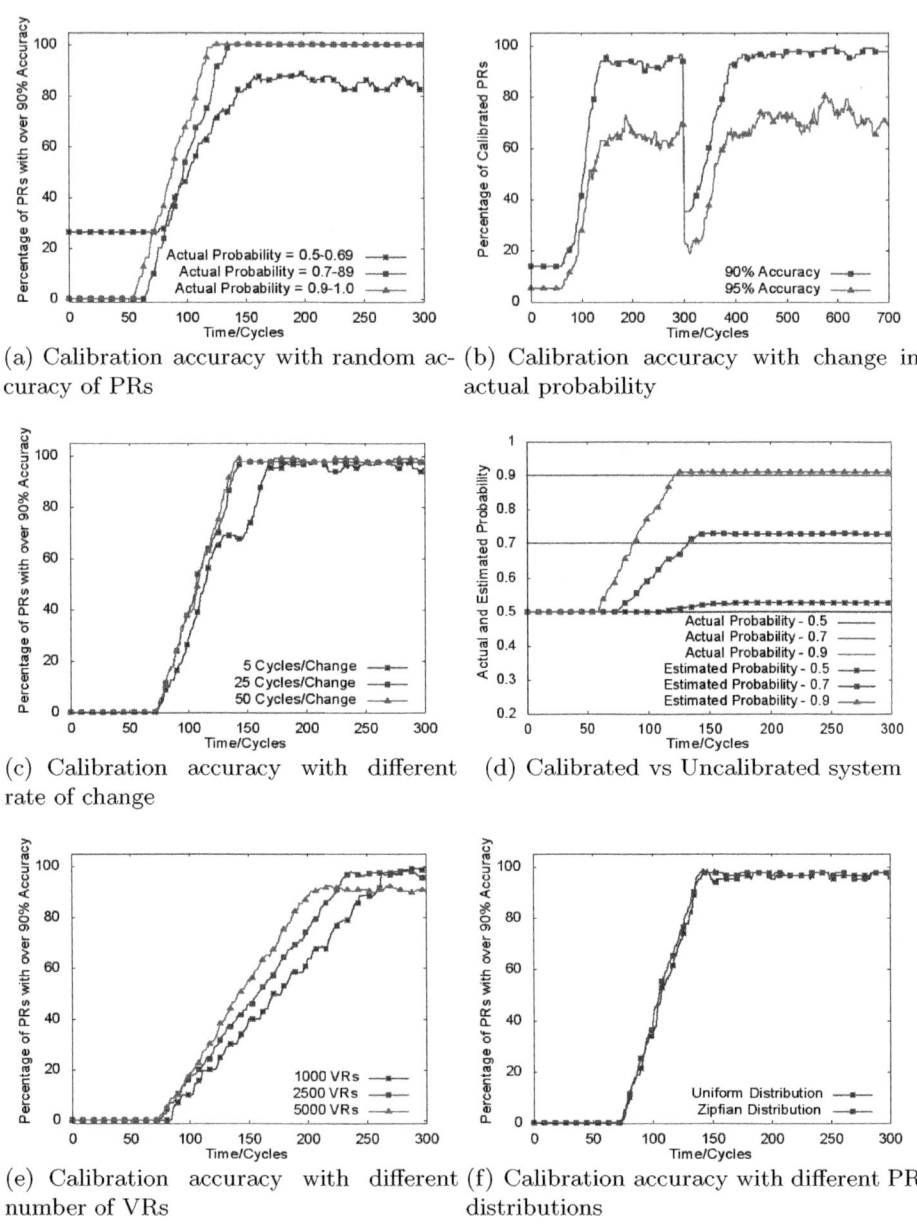

(a) Calibration accuracy with random accuracy of PRs

(b) Calibration accuracy with change in actual probability

(c) Calibration accuracy with different rate of change

(d) Calibrated vs Uncalibrated system

(e) Calibration accuracy with different number of VRs

(f) Calibration accuracy with different PR distributions

Fig. 5. Simulation Results

Effect of Actual Probability of Physical Readers: In this scenario we evaluate the effect of different actual probabilities of *prs* on the performance of the self-calibration algorithm. *Prs* are distributed uniformly among the *vrs*. The rate of induced physical changes is 50 cycle per change and the simulation is run for 300 cycles. The results (Figure 5(a)) show that the higher the actual probability of prs, the less time it takes to calibrate the estimated probability with a relatively high accuracy. This is obvious since it is much harder to estimate the actual probabilities of prs if there are only a few accurate readings.

Effect of Change in Actual Probability of Physical Readers: In this scenario we evaluated the time it takes for the algorithm to calibrate the estimated probabilities, when the actual probabilities of the prs gets changed. Initially we assigned a random actual probability to each pr in the range of 0.5-0.9. Then the accuracy of all prs is abruptly changed. The new actual probabilities also lie within the range of 0.5-0.9. The evaluation runs for 700 cycles, and the changes were induced at the 300th cycle. Figure 5(b) shows the percentage of all prs having an accuracy of over 90% and 95% over the time . After the change is induced at cycle 300, the accuracy of estimated probability drops significantly. However the system becomes stable once again after approximately 100 cycles.

Effect of Rate of Physical Changes: In this evaluation we observed the effect on the performance of self-calibration algorithm under varying rates of physical changes. The actual probability of prs is fixed to 0.7 and they are distributed uniformly among the vrs. The algorithm's performance was tested under three different change rates 50, 25, and 5 cycle/change. Figure 5(c) shows the percentage of prs which have accuracy of over 90% over the time. The results are almost same for 50 cycle/change and 25 cycle/change as can be seen in Figure 5(c), but for the scenario in which we were inducing a change every 5 cycles the calibration time increases along with a decrease in the accuracy of estimated probability. However, once the system reaches a stable state, the rate of change does not have much effect on accuracy of estimated probabilities.

Calibrated vs Uncalibrated System: In this scenario we observed the difference between a system in which pr probabilities are calibrated vs one which does not perform calibrations. We took three sets of readings by setting the actual probabilities of prs to 0.5, 0.7, and 0.9. We then set the estimated probability of all physical readers to 0.5. Figure 5(d) shows how the estimated probability changes over time. In an uncalibrated system since the estimated probability does not change, the error between the actual probability and the estimated probability will never reduce. It is obvious from the results that the error between actual and estimated probabilities in this uncalibrated system could at best by 0 and at worst be 0.4. In normal scenarios, the error will depend on the difference between the configured probabilities for readers and their actual probabilities. However, the error in our system once the algorithm calibrates the estimated probabilities is never greater than 0.05.

Effect of Number of Virtual Readers: In this scenario we observed the effect of the number of vrs on the performance of the self-calibration algorithm. The actual probabilities of prs were fixed to 0.7 for this experiment and prs were distributed uniformly among all vrs. The number of vrs used were 1000, 2500 and 5000. The simulation was run for 300 cycles, with a physical change in the ppo induced every 50 cycles. Figure 5(e) shows the percentage of prs which have accuracy of over 90% over time. It is clear from Figure 5(e) that calibration time is reduced with increase in the number of vrs, but this also increases the error in the probability estimations. The calibration time is reduced because each vr has lesser number of prs and hence a small data sample, which enables the vr to estimate the probabilities quickly. But now since each vr has a smaller data sample, the estimation accuracy suffers.

Effect of Distribution of Physical Readers: In this scenario we observed the effect of pr distribution on the performance of the self-calibration algorithm. The actual probability of prs was set to 0.7 and the simulation was run for 300 cycles with changes induced at every 50th cycle. The prs were distributed amongst the vrs using uniform and zipfian distribution. In zipfian distribution we set $\alpha = 1.0$. This ensured that 80% of the prs are distributed across half of the vrs, whereas the remaining 20% of the prs are distributed across the remaining half of the vrs. Figure 5(f) shows the results of this evaluation. It is obvious from the results that the distribution of prs has no effect on the accuracy of the calibration process.

6   Related Work

The initial research effort in RFID based middleware systems was focused towards developing solutions to handle large amounts of data. Later works also touched upon aspects of object tracking and querying. Savant [11] aims to handle large amount of RFID data in a hierarchical manner by creating a tree of subsystems. High Fan-in System [13] also uses a tree based scheme to handle data and queries. WinRFID [6] on the other hand uses web services for efficient querying and deployment of information. RFID readers are implemented as a service and users could query different readers to access their collected data. RFIDStack [14] tries to reduce data flooding by using publish-subscribe paradigm to route RFID data only to the corresponding and desired locations.

De et al [17] have extended the Savant architecture to use RFID devices for object tracking. Similarly, MAX [18] tries to track object locations by employing a tree like structure, which has a static base station connection with several substations. SCOUT [19] tries to ensure that objects could be tracked scalably on mobile devices. However, none of the systems mentioned above addresses unreliability of RFID readers.

Several techniques have been proposed in order to increase the reliability of RFID readings. Vogt [20] has proposed a method to efficiently and reliably identify a set of RFID tags when the number of the tags are unknown in advance. Vogt uses a time division frame-based approach to detect multiple tags at the same time. Similarly Kodialam et al [21] have also come up with collision based an probabilistic algorithms to estimate the set of tags present at a location. Lehtonen et al [22] have also worked on detecting RFID tags, but there work is focused on detecting cloned tags to identify counterfeit products in the supply chain. Rahmati et al [23] conducted experiments to determine the reliability of RFID tags and the factors that affect their reliabilities.

RF2ID [5] is a complementary work that aims to enhance the reliability of the inherently unreliable RFID infrastructure by exploiting the paths inherent in the movement of objects. However, RF2ID primarily deals with ensuring that all the objects that passed through a certain point have been accounted for. Such a system is useful in logistics and warehousing scenarios, where the concern is accurate tracking and localization of objects [15], [16]. In a factory environment we are additionally burdened with ensuring that the parts move through the production lines in a proper order. Proper ordering of parts in turn can only be ensured if we have a high degree of confidence in RFID detections.

7   Summary and Future Work

In this paper, we have presented concepts for the reliable monitoring of product parts in production with unreliable RFID sensors. Based on a probabilistic model, we have presented algorithms for self-calibration of RFID readers to reflect the probability of real errors. The basic idea of this approach is to exploit redundant readings to get an accurate model, which is then used for calibration.

The evaluations of our probability self-calibration algorithm shows that it reacts robustly to induced changes as it was able to calibrate itself to a stable state with an accuracy of greater than 90% even in the presence of changes induced after every 5 cycle. The evaluations further showed that the algorithm was more accurate if the prs are clustered together within a small number of vrs, since that scenario provides each vr with a significantly larger RFID dataset to calibrate the probabilities. The evaluations also revealed the obvious fact that accuracy of probability self-calibration algorithm is dependent on pr accuracy.

In the future, we would like to extend this work to detect complex manufacturing events from raw RFID readings.

Acknowledgment. The authors would like to thank the anonymous reviewers for their valuable comments and suggestions. This research was supported by GSaME (Graduate School for Advanced Manufacturing Engineering). http://www.gsame.uni-stuttgart.de

References

1. Khodawandi, D.: Principal of Porsche Consulting, Manufacturing (2011)
2. Johnson, D.: WebMon: RFID tags improve tracking, quality on Ford line in Mexico. Engineering 49(11), 16 (2002)
3. Brewer, A., Landers, T.: Radio Frequency Identification: A Survey and Assessment of the Technology. Technical Report, University of Arkansas, Department of Industrial Engineering (1997)
4. Zhekun, L., Gadh, R., Prabhu, B.S.: Applications of RFID technology and smart parts in manufacturing. In: Proceedings of DETC 2004: ASME 2004 Design Engineering Technical Conference and Computers and Information in Engineering Conference, Salt Lake City, Texas (2004)
5. Ahmed, N., Kumar, R., French, R.S., Ramachandaran, U.: RF2ID: A reliable middleware framework for RFID deployment. In: Proceedings of IEEE IPDPS. IEEE Computer Society Press (2007)

6. Prabhu, B.S., Su, X., Ramamurthy, H., Chu, C.-C., Gadh, R.: WinRFID – A Middleware for the enablement of Radio Frequency Identification (RFID) based Applications. In: Mobile, Wireless and Sensor Networks Technology, Applications and Future. John Wiley and Sons, Inc. (2005)
7. The Basics of RFID Technology, http://www.rfidjournal.com/article/articleview/1337/1/129/
8. Hassan, T., Chatterjee, S.: A Taxonomy for RFID. In: HICSS 2006: Proc. of the Intl. Conf. on System Sciences. IEEE Computer Society (2006)
9. Hameed, B., Khan, I., Durr, F., Rothermel, K.: An RFID Based Consistency Management Framework for Production Monitoring In a Smart Real-Time Factory. In: Proceedings of 2010 Internet of Things Conference, Tokyo- Japan (Best Paper Award) (2010)
10. Lucke, D., Constantinescu, C., Westkamper, E.: Smart factory - a step towards the next generation of manufacturing. In: Manufacturing Systems and Technologies for the New Frontier. Springer (2008)
11. Oat Systems and MIT Auto-ID Center: The Savant. Technical Manual (2002)
12. Li, T., Wang, D.: Experimental studying measurement metrics of RFID system performance. In: ASID 2009 Proc. of the 3rd International Conference on Anti-Counterfeiting, Security, and Identification in Communication (2009)
13. Franklin, M.J., Jeffery, S.R., Krishnamurthy, S., Reiss, F.: Design Considerations for High Fan-in Systems: The HiFi Approach. In: CIDR (2005)
14. Floerkemeier, C., Lampe, M.: RFID middleware design: addressing application requirements and RFID constraints. In: sOc-EUSAI 2005: Proc. of the 2005 Joint Conf. on Smart Objects and Ambient Intelligence (2005)
15. Weinstein, R.: RFID: A Technical Overview and Its Application to the Enterprise. IT Professional 7(3) (2005)
16. McCarren Airport RFID System Takes Off, http://www.rfidjournal.com/article/view/1949/1/1
17. De, P., Basu, K., Das, S.K.: An Ubiquitous Architectural Framework and Protocol for Object Tracking Using RFID Tags. In: Proc. of the Intl. Conf. on Mobile and Ubiquitous Systems: Networking and Services (2004)
18. Yap, K.-K., Srinivasan, V., Motani, M.: MAX: human-centric search of the physical world. In: Sensys (2005)
19. Kumar, S., Alaettinoglu, C., Estrin, D.: SCalable Object-tracking through Unattended Techniques (SCOUT). In: Proc. of the Intl. Conf. on Network Protocols, ICNP (2000)
20. Vogt, H.: Efficient Object Identification with Passive RFID Tags. In: Mattern, F., Naghshineh, M. (eds.) PERVASIVE 2002. LNCS, vol. 2414, p. 98. Springer, Heidelberg (2002)
21. Kodialam, M., Nandagopal, T.: Fast and Reliable Estimation Schemes in RFID Systems. In: Proceedings of MobiCom (2006)
22. Lehtonen, M., Michahelles, F., Fleisch, E.: How to detect cloned tags in a reliable way from incomplete RFID traces. In: IEEE International Conference on RFID (2009)
23. Rahmati, A., Zhong, L., Hiltunen, M., Jana, R.: Reliability Techniques for RFID-Based Object Tracking Applications. In: Dependable Systems and Networks (2007)
24. Lernfabrik video, http://www.youtube.com/watch?v=hyetywtayVI
25. PeerSim: A Peer-to-Peer Simulator, http://peersim.sourceforge.net/
26. Volare RFID readers, http://www.kenetics-group.com/data/Volare/Volare%20UHF-USB.pdf

AWESOM: Automatic Discrete Partitioning of Indoor Spaces for WiFi Fingerprinting

Teemu Pulkkinen and Petteri Nurmi

Helsinki Institute for Information Technology HIIT
Department of Computer Science, P.O. Box 68,
FI-00014 University of Helsinki, Finland
{teemu.pulkkinen,petteri.nurmi}@cs.helsinki.fi

Abstract. WiFi fingerprinting is currently one of the most popular techniques for indoor localization as it provides reasonable positioning accuracy while at the same time being able to exploit existing wireless infrastructure. To facilitate calibration efforts and to overcome fluctuations in location measurements, many indoor WiFi positioning systems utilize a discrete partitioning, e.g., a grid or a topological map, of the space where the positioning is being deployed. A major limitation of this approach, however, is that instead of considering spatial similarities in the signal environment, the partitioning is typically based on an uniform division of the space or topological constraints (e.g., rooms and walls). This can significantly decrease positioning accuracy when the signal environment is not sufficiently stable across all partitions. Moreover, current solutions provide no support for identifying partitions that are not compatible with the current wireless deployment. To overcome these limitations, we propose AWESOM (Activations Weighted by the Euclidean-distance using Self-Organizing Maps), a novel measure for automatically creating a discrete partitioning of the space where the WiFi positioning is being deployed. In addition to enabling automatic construction of a discrete partitioning, AWESOM provides a measure for evaluating the goodness of a given partitioning for a particular access point deployment. AWESOM also enables identifying partitions where additional access points should be deployed. We demonstrate the usefulness of AWESOM using data collected from two large scale deployments of a proprietary wireless positioning system in a hypermarket environment.

1   Introduction

WiFi fingerprinting is currently one of the most popular and widespread solutions to indoor positioning. Contrary to other indoor positioning techniques, such as infrared [1], ultrasound [2] or powerline positioning [3], laptops, PDAs, smartphones and other off-the-shelf devices readily support collecting wireless access point measurements, which makes it possible to enable positioning on these devices without need for specialized hardware. Moreover, WiFi fingerprinting is

J. Kay et al. (Eds.): Pervasive 2012, LNCS 7319, pp. 271–288, 2012.

capable of providing reasonable positioning accuracy while at the same being able to exploit existing wireless infrastructure.

Systems for WiFi fingerprinting operate on measurements that consist of signal strengths of wireless access points at different locations [4,5]. During a *calibration* phase, signal strength measurements are collected at various locations in the environment. These measurements are then used to construct a *radio map* that captures variations in signal strengths at different locations. Once the radio map has been constructed, the position of a wireless client can be determined by comparing the observed signal strengths of the client against the radio map.

To obtain high level of positioning accuracy, WiFi fingerprinting systems require that calibration measurements are collected densely from the environment where the positioning is being deployed [6,7]. As the collection of calibration measurements is work and time intensive, this approach clearly is infeasible for large-scale deployments. To improve the feasibility of the calibration effort, a popular alternative is to use a discrete partitioning, e.g., a grid or a topological map, of the space where the positioning is being deployed. The use of a discrete partitioning facilitates calibration efforts since collected signal measurements can be associated with a grid cell instead of a specific point in the environment [8]. Moreover, the partitioning helps to balance between position accuracy and the size of the radio map that is needed for positioning [9,10].

In existing fingerprinting systems, the discrete partitioning is typically based on an uniform division of the space (e.g., a grid) [9] or topological constraints (e.g., rooms, walls or other obstacles) [10]. A major limitation with this approach, however, is that the resulting partitioning is not necessarily compatible with the signal environment of the deployment. This can significantly decrease positioning accuracy, particularly when the spatial variations in the signal environment are not sufficiently stable across all partitions. Moreover, current fingerprinting solutions provide no support for identifying partitions that are not compatible with the current wireless deployment. To overcome these limitations, we have developed AWESOM (Activations Weighted by the Euclidean-distance using Self-Organizing Maps), a novel measure for automatically creating a discrete partitioning of indoor spaces. AWESOM relies on self-organizing maps to construct a topological mapping of the signal environment. The compatibility between the partitioning and the signal environment can then be evaluated by comparing the real-world proximity of the locations where measurements were collected with the proximity of the corresponding signal measurements in the topological map. In addition to enabling the automatic creation of a discrete partitioning, AWESOM enables evaluating the suitability of a particular partitioning for a given access point deployment, as well as identifying areas where positioning accuracy can be improved with additional access points. Furthermore, the topological map constructed by AWESOM enables associating measurements with different parts of the partitioning in a semi-automatic manner, thus significantly reducing re-calibration efforts.

AWESOM has been born from the inherent difficulties of deploying WiFi fingerprinting in large-scale indoor spaces. Existing tools, such as Ekahau site survey[1], only provide information about the coverage of access points at different locations. Good coverage of access points does not automatically translate into good positioning accuracy and consequently careful design of the wireless infrastructure is needed. However, previously tools for supporting the access point deployment process have been lacking. AWESOM fills this gap and significantly facilitates the deployment of WiFi fingerprinting systems in large-scale environments. To demonstrate the benefits of AWESOM, we consider location measurements collected from two large-scale deployments of a proprietary WiFi positioning system in a retail environment.

2   Related Research

WiFi fingerprinting was first introduced as part of the RADAR system [6]. The radio map that RADAR uses consists of average signal strengths of access points at various locations. To determine the position of a client, the current measurement is compared against the entries in the radio map and the position of the client is estimated as the (weighted) average of the k-best matching measurements. The RADAR system is an example of a system that uses a so-called *deterministic* estimation method as it considers signal measurements as scalar values. Deterministic methods have also been widely applied for GSM localization. For example, Varshavsky et al. [11] use deterministic fingerprinting for indoor GSM localization within multistory buildings, whereas Chen et al. [12] use deterministic fingerprinting for metropolitan scale GSM positioning.

Instead of representing signal measurements as scalars, *probabilistic* methods consider signal measurements as samples from a random variable and represent variations in the observed signal values using probability distributions. To estimate the position of the client, Bayesian inference is used to compute the posterior distribution of the client's location given the most recent signal measurements [13]. Existing systems for probabilistic fingerprinting differ mainly in (i) how they model the probabilities of observing a particular signal measurement; and (ii) whether they track the position of the client over time.

The NIBBLE system was one of the first approaches to probabilistic fingerprinting [14]. In NIBBLE, observed signal strengths are mapped into one of four discrete values (none, low, medium or high) and together with a binary noise variable these values are given as an input to a Bayesian network that infers the most likely location from a discrete set of choices. Roos et al. [15] work directly on the signal values and compare representing fingerprints as signal strength histograms versus kernel density functions. The evaluation of the methods indicated that both methods improve on deterministic fingerprinting with the histogram method providing slightly better positioning accuracy. In the LOCADIO system position estimation is based on signal strength histograms and temporal tracking [16]. The tracking is implemented using a two-state hidden Markov model which utilizes a movement classifier that infers whether the user is stationary or

---

[1] www.ekahau.com

moving. Ladd et al. [17] and Hightower et al. [18] implemented tracking using particle filters instead of hidden Markov models.

An alternative to signal strength histograms is to use a discrete partitioning of the space where the positioning is deployed. Haeberlen et al. [10] propose a system where a grid-based partitioning is used. Location measurements collected within the same grid are aggregated using Gaussian distributions, and the location of the client can then be estimated by evaluating the cumulative distribution function (CDF) of the resulting Gaussian given the current signal strength measurement. Nurmi et al. [9] propose a variation of this approach for on-device GSM positioning. Instead of using the CDF, locations are estimated by computing the likelihood of each location given the current signal measurement and feeding this as an input to a particle filter that tracks the position of the client over time. Other variations include utilizing a hierarchical sensor model that combines fingerprinting with a signal propagation model [19], and modeling temporal correlations between successive signals collected at the same location using an auto-correlation model [7].

Also other techniques for reducing calibration efforts have been proposed. Instead of using of a discrete partitioning, Krumm and Platt [8] propose reducing the number of locations where calibration measurements are collected. Values for other locations are then derived using interpolation. A variation of this approach was proposed by Chai and Yang [20,21] who use unlabeled traces from other users to support the interpolation process. Instead of requiring calibration efforts from expert personnel, a number of approaches have proposed shifting the calibration effort to users of the positioning system [22,23,24]. As an example, Park et al. [24] use a Voronoi diagram-based method for identifying areas with high positioning uncertainty. Whenever a user of the system is within an area with high spatial uncertainty or an area where position estimates are unstable, the system prompts the user to collect more wireless measurements. While these systems can significantly reduce calibration efforts, their main limitation is the lack of support for reducing the size of the radio map that is needed for positioning. Moreover, it is unclear how well the used measures for interpolating and comparing measurements translate from office and campus environments to commercial spaces, such as airports or retail spaces, where the number of people and sources of interference contain significant dynamic variation over time.

From a methodological point of view, AWESOM is related to approaches that use non-linear projection techniques for mapping wireless environments. Koo and Cha [25] used multidimensional scaling (MDS) to locate access points in an unsupervised way. However, instead of focusing on fingerprinting, the authors focused on enabling triangulation based positioning, which has coarser positioning accuracy than fingerprinting-based positioning. Pulkkinen et al. [26] use the Isomap algorithm to transform WiFi fingerprints from a high-dimensional manifold into a two-dimensional representation. By labeling some of the fingerprints with ground-truth coordinates, the authors are able to correlate the mapping with matching geographical coordinates through least squares regression. This procedure can be interpreted as a non-linear interpolation technique where, instead of interpolating signal strength values, location coordinates for measurements are interpolated from a small set of anchor points based on the proximity of signal measurements in the non-linear manifold. Similarly to the other interpolation techniques, a limitation of this approach is that it is unable to reduce the size of the radio map that is needed for positioning. Moreover, as we discuss in Sec. 3.1, self-organizing maps provide an efficient and iterative way to measure fingerprint similarity compared to Isomap and other non-linear manifold techniques.

3   Methodology

WiFi fingerprinting builds on the premise that spatial variations in the signal environment are sufficiently strong for distinguishing between different locations. Building on this premise, AWESOM uses self-organizing maps to construct a similarity map that captures correlations in the signal environment across different locations. Fingerprints that are similar will have similar neuronal activation patterns in the constructed similarity map (see Sec. 3.1). By correlating these activation patterns across different locations, AWESOM is able to identify areas that should be merged into the same partition (see Sec. 3.2). In addition to supporting the creation of a discrete partitioning, AWESOM provides a fitness measure that enables assessing the goodness of particular access point deployment for a given partitioning (see Sec. 3.3). As we demonstrate in the experiments section, the fitness measure provides an intuitive and effective way of detecting areas that would benefit from the deployment of additional access points. In summary, AWESOM provides two contributions:

1. A measure for evaluating the similarity of fingerprints across different locations, and a principled methodology for creating a discrete partitioning that reflects the spatial characteristics of the signal environment.
2. A fitness measure that enables (i) evaluating the compatibility of a particular discrete partitioning for a given access point deployment; and (ii) suggesting locations for deploying additional wireless access points.

3.1   Self-organizing Maps

Self-organizing maps (SOMs) are a non-linear projection technique that creates a (typically two-dimensional) similarity diagram from high-dimensional input signals [27]. A self-organizing map consists of a set of *neurons*, which are connected to the input signals through a set of *weights*. In our case the input signals consist of WiFi fingerprints collected from different locations, and the weights determine how the fingerprint measurements are mapped into neurons. Let k denote the number of access points that can be observed in a given environment, we use $\mathbf{x} = (x_1, \ldots, x_k)$ to denote the input signals and $\mathbf{w_j} = (w_{j1}, \ldots, w_{jk})$ to denote the weight vector of neuron j.

Let N denote the number of fingerprints that have been collected in the calibration phase and let $M \leq N$ denote the number of distinct locations where the measurements have been collected. To initialize the self-organizing map, we first create a two-dimensional map with M neurons. Alternatively, neurons could be placed at an uniform distance from each other. To initialize the weights of the neurons, we use principal component analysis (PCA) to project the calibration measurements onto a M dimensional subspace. The eigenvectors of this subspace are then used as the initial weight vectors. While the weights could also be initialized with random values, we use PCA for the initialization as it speeds up the convergence of the weights when the SOM is being trained.

To train the self-organizing map, the fingerprint measurements are iteratively given as input to the SOM. For each measurement $\mathbf{x}$, we identify the best-matching neuron i^* by evaluating the inner product of the input signal and the weight vector, i.e., $i^* = \arg\max_j \mathbf{w_j x}$. Once the best-matching neuron has been identified, the weights of all neurons are updated using an iterative update equation. Specifically, the new weight of neuron j is calculated as follows:

$$\mathbf{w_j}(t+1) = \mathbf{w_j}(t) + \eta(t) H_{i^*,j}(t) \left(\mathbf{x} - \mathbf{w_j}(t) \right), \tag{1}$$

where t is the number of measurements that have been considered, $\eta(t)$ is a learning rate parameter that varies over time and $H_{i^*,j}$ is a neighborhood function, or kernel, centered around the best-matching neuron i^*. A common choice for the neighborhood function is to use a Gaussian kernel, i.e.,

$$H_{i^*,j} = \exp\left(-\frac{d_{i^*,j}}{2\eta(t)^2} \right). \tag{2}$$

Here $d_{i^*,j}$ is the Euclidean distance between neurons i^* and j in the lattice defined by the self-organizing map. A common choice for the learning rate parameter, on the other hand, is an exponential decay function:

$$\eta(t) = \eta(0) \exp\left(-\frac{t}{\beta} \right). \tag{3}$$

Here $\eta(0)$ and β are constants that control the rate of decay. In the experiments we have used the default initialization values $\eta(0) = 0.1$ and $\beta = 1000$ for these parameters. We chose an iteration threshold of 100 times the number of neurons in the network. The algorithm was allowed to run until this number of iterations was reached, or until η reached a floating point underflow.

In terms of runtime performance, training the SOM typically takes few minutes. The runtime depends on the number of neurons in the network, the size of the dataset (fingerprints and the number access points). For example, running the SOM on our second test environment required around 170 seconds (3090 55-dimensional fingerprints, 10300 iterations and 103 neurons) on an off-the-shelf laptop.

3.2   Creating a Discrete Partitioning

To apply the self-organizing map for creating a discrete partitioning of the space where positioning is deployed, we need a measure for assessing the (dis)similarity of fingerprints in the signal space. Our method for measuring similarity builds on the observation that measurements that are closely related to each other should result in similar activation patterns across the self-organizing map. This idea can be applied in practice by creating a ranking of the neurons for each of the input signals. The ranking is formed by calculating the activation value $\mathbf{w_j x}$ of each neuron for a given input signal $\mathbf{x}$, and sorting the neurons in descending order of activation value. Given a pair of signals $(\mathbf{x}, \mathbf{y})$, we compare the activation patterns of the signals using the rank-correlation between the two ordered lists of neurons. As a measure of rank correlation, we use the Kendall τ coefficient, which compares the number of pairs for which the ranks agree with the number of pairs for which the ranks disagree.

Due to the fluctuating nature of WiFi signals, the spatial distribution of fingerprint measurements often contains multiple modes that are at different locations. In case of the SOM, this behavior can cause fingerprints to have similar activation patterns even when they are not geographically co-located. Consequently, if we rely exclusively on the correlation coefficients when creating a partitioning of the space, distant locations could be merged together into the same partition. To overcome this effect, we create a discrete partitioning of the space using spatial clustering on the combination of rank correlation coefficients and locations of the fingerprint measurements. This ensures that the resulting partitioning is compatible both with the signal environment and with geographical proximity. To enable efficient clustering, we use a density-based clustering algorithm that simultaneously compares the proximity of two points in the physical space and the signal space. Measurements from different locations are merged into the same partitioning whenever they are sufficiently close to each other in both spaces. The algorithm that we use for clustering is an extension of the DJCluster algorithm proposed by Zhou et al. [28]. The clustering operates by identifying, for each point x, all points y that are within distance d_ϵ of each other in the physical space. To ensure that the resulting partitioning is compatible with obstacles present in the physical space, as our distance measure we use the Euclidean distance of the shortest path between the two locations. In our implementation, these distances are precomputed. Once the locations that are located within close proximity of each other have been identified, we further prune the set of points by eliminating points that are not sufficiently close in the signal space.

We evaluate proximity in the signal space using a significance test on the rank-correlation coefficients $\tau_{x,y}$ of the activation patterns. We consider two points to be co-located whenever their correlation exceeds the value $\tau^* = 0.64$, which corresponds to a significance level of 0.01 in a one-tailed significance test[2]. Measurements that satisfy both the spatial and signal environment similarity constraints are merged together into the same partition and partitions that share common points are progressively merged to form larger areas. The locations of the measurements that are clustered together can then be used to determine the

---

[2] Calculated using a normal approximation where we have assumed the number of measurements to be equivalent to ten which was selected to ensure the effect size of the significant correlations is sufficiently high.

different partitions of the space, e.g., using Voronoi diagrams or by calculating bounding boxes based on the locations of the corresponding measurements. In the experiments we follow the latter approach.

3.3   Evaluating Compatibility of a Discrete Partitioning

In addition to supporting the creation of a discrete partitioning of space, AWE-SOM can be used to evaluate the compatibility of a particular division of space for a given wireless environment. This process relies on a so-called fitness measure, which calculates a score that reflects the suitability of the signal environment in different areas of the discrete partitioning. As we demonstrate in the experiments section, the resulting scores can also be used to help in designing where to deploy additional wireless access point.

The fitness measure that we consider is based on the observation that regions of the partitioning that have poor coverage tend to result in activation patterns with high spatial variability. In other words, measurements from these regions tend to share activation patterns with other regions of the partitioning, including those that are not geographically co-located. To define a measure that scores regions of the partitioning based on their fit with the wireless infrastructure, we consider how well correlations between activation patterns reflect proximity in physical space. Specifically, for a given region g, we identify all regions z that have a significant correlation with g. As a measure significance we consider the same threshold $\tau^* = 0.64$ that is used as part of the creation of a discrete partitioning; see the previous section. Let G denote the set of regions with a significant correlation, i.e., $G = \{z : \tau_{g,z} \geq 0.64\}$, we define the fitness $F(g)$ of region g as the average distance between g and the regions in set G, i.e.,

$$F(g) = \sum_{z \in G} \frac{d(g, z)}{\#G} \tag{4}$$

where $d(g, z)$ denotes the distance between regions g and z, and $\#G$ denotes the number of elements in the set G. Similarly to the previous section, as the distance measure we use the (precomputed) Euclidean distance of the shortest path connecting two regions. This measure was selected to ensure the fitness metric takes into account also topological constraints (e.g., walls and other obstacles in the environment). As we demonstrate in the experiments section, the resulting fitness scores can also be used to detect areas with poor coverage and placing access points close to these locations can improve accuracy of wireless fingerprinting systems.

4   Description of Environments

To demonstrate the usefulness of AWESOM, we consider data collected from two large-scale deployments of a proprietary positioning system. Both deployments

Table 1. Dataset statistics

Dataset	#Fingerprints	#Grid cells	#AP	RSS Range
Environment 1	8700	290	32	55
Environment 2 - HTC	3090	103	42	61
Environment 2 - Samsung	3090	103	55	61

have been performed in a retail environment where the number of people and the sources of interference vary significantly in the course of the day. The positioning system that we have used to collect measurements relies on a grid-based partitioning of the space where the positioning is being deployed. Consequently the measurements considered in our experiments are related to specific grid cells. However, the grid partitioning used in our first environment uses a relatively small grid size, which enables simulating a situation where the measurements are collected at equally spaced locations instead of specific grid cells. The datasets that were used in the experiments are summarized in Table 1.

4.1   Environment 1: German Supermarket

As our first test environment we consider two sections (≈ 15 m $\times 45$ m and ≈ 27 m $\times 52$ m) of a supermarket in Saarbrücken-Güdingen, Germany. The layout of the area that we consider in the evaluation was divided manually into grid cells based on so-called shelf meters so that each aisle is divided into 9 grid cells, each one shelf meter long. Grid cells were also included at both ends of an aisle. Accordingly, each aisle in the first section contains 11 grid cells. The second section followed the same scheme where applicable, with grid cells of varying sizes covering areas without defined shelves. The area that we consider contains in total 290 grid cells. The grid structure used in the experiments is shown in Fig. 1 together with the locations of the deployed access points. We recorded fingerprint measurements from this environment using a *Samsung Google Nexus S* smartphone which was running Android version 2.34 ("Gingerbread"). For each grid cell, we collected 30 signal strength fingerprints at a sampling rate of approximately 1Hz.

4.2   Environment 2: Finnish Supermarket

As our second test environment we consider a large grocery store (≈ 128 m $\times 59$ m) in Helsinki, Finland that belongs to a major national chain of supermarkets. We manually divided the store layout into 103 grid cells so that each of the 14 aisles in the supermarket was divided into three cells and that there were grid cells located at both ends of an aisle. The cells at the ends of the aisles were placed so that they neighbored the last cells of two consecutive aisles. The remaining areas of the supermarket were divided into grid cells by covering areas with similar product categories using a single grid cell; see Fig. 2 for the grid

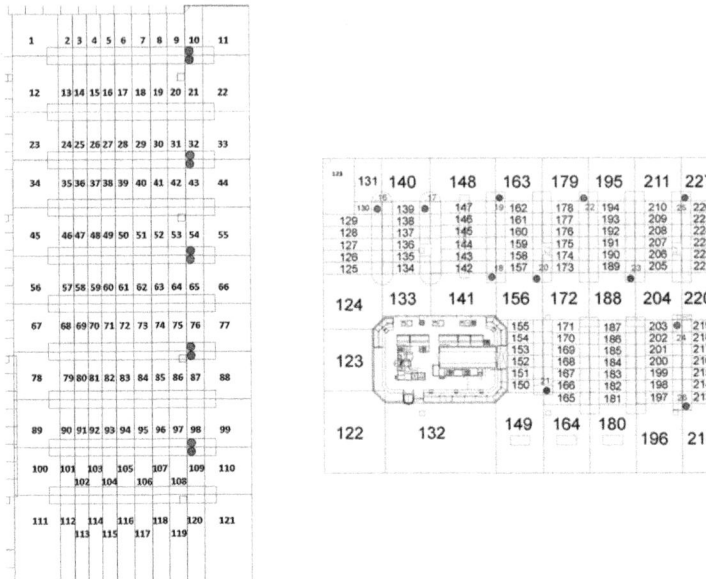

Fig. 1. The grid structure of the retail environment that was used in the experiments in Saarbrücken-Güdingen. The dots on the map correspond to the locations of the wireless access points that had been deployed in the environment, and their colors represent the different wireless channels to which they were tuned. The cell at the bottom-right in the grid on the left is physically adjacent to the cell at the top-left in the grid on the right in the retail space.

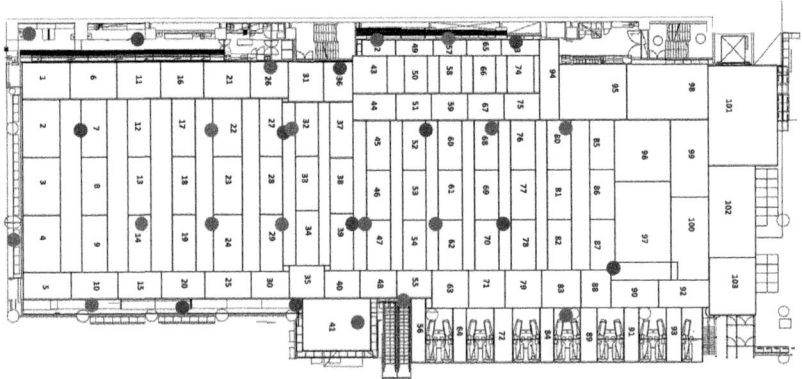

Fig. 2. The grid structure of the retail environment that was used in the experiments in Helsinki. The dots on the map indicate the locations of the wireless access points that had been deployed to the environment, with colors corresponding to the different wireless channels used

structure that was used. This grid structure was originally designed to facilitate management of product location information, and as part of our previous work we have used this grid structure to develop navigation support [29,30] and location-based advertisements for the retail environment.

To enable positioning within the supermarket, we installed 29 wireless access points at different locations inside the store; see Fig. 2 for the locations of the access points. In addition to these access points, signals from up to 26 additional access points that belonged to other networks could be observed within the supermarket. The large number of visible access points is due to the supermarket being located at the ground floor of a mall. Consequently, measurements from other shops and the supermarkets own production network could be observed.

We collected measurements using two devices: an *HTC Hero* smartphone and a *Samsung NC10* notebook. At the time of data collection, the HTC Hero was running Android 1.5 ("Cupcake") and the collection was implemented using native Java and Android libraries. The notebook was running Ubuntu 10.04 and we used python code that interfaced with the pyiw library to collect measurements. The notebook had an Atheros AR5007EG Wireless network adapter. Both devices were used in their original wireless interface configurations during data collection. For the purposes of evaluation, we used both devices to record 30 signal strength fingerprints from each grid cell using a recording frequency of 2Hz. The fingerprints were stored as vectors consisting of MAC-address and signal strength pairs. No processing steps were performed on the measurements before the training and estimation phases. All measurements were recorded by standing roughly in the center of the designated grid cell facing the entrance of the store. During the data collection the store was moderately crowded. We refer to these two datasets as HTC and Samsung respectively; see Table 1.

5   Results

In the following we present results from applying AWESOM to signal fingerprints gathered from the two supermarket deployments described in the previous section. The evaluation focuses on the capability of AWESOM to support two tasks: (1) creating a discrete partitioning of space; and (2) facilitating access point deployment.

5.1   Creating Discrete Partitioning

To justify the use of rank-correlation coefficients for measuring similarity between fingerprint measurements, as the first step of evaluation we demonstrate that the rank-correlation coefficients $\tau_{x,y}$, which measure similarities in neuronal activation patterns between two fingerprint measurements (see Sec. 3.2), provide an intuitive measure of the spatial variation in signal characteristics. To demonstrate this, Fig. 3 illustrates the variation in the values of the rank-correlation coefficient as a function of physical distance. From the figure we can observe that the correlation measure has a significant dependence on physical proximity. As the spacing of grid cells is sparser in the second test environment, the resulting correlation coefficient plot decreases more rapidly than in the corresponding plot

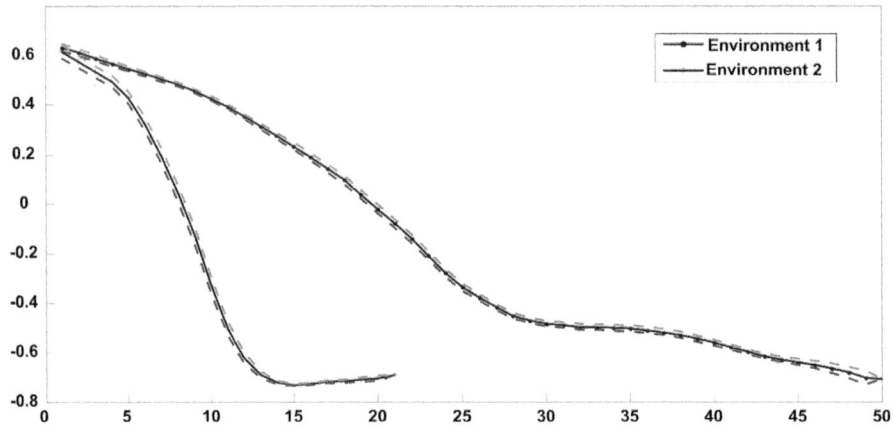

Fig. 3. Correlation of neuronal activation patterns as a function of distance. The values on the x-axis correspond to distance in grid cells and the values on the y-axis correspond to the average correlation calculated across all cells. The dashed lines indicate the confidence interval of the resulting values.

of the first test environment. When translating the distances in grid cells into meters, these results suggest that the correlation values can be significant up to a distance of approximately 10 meters, i.e., a distance of $3 - 4$ grid cells in the second test environment.

As the next step of evaluation we consider the capability of AWESOM to extract a meaningful discrete partitioning from fingerprint measurements. To conduct this experiments, we used the spatial clustering approach described in Sec. 3.2 to construct a grid representation for the two test environments. With the first environment we used a threshold of 5 meters (i.e., we set $d_\epsilon = 5m$) for identifying measurements that are co-located in the physical space, whereas for the second environment we set d_ϵ equal to 10 meters. The difference in proximity threshold is due to different spacing of the grid cells where fingerprints are collected between the two environments. To simulate measurements that are collected at continuous locations, we ignore the presence of obstacles, i.e., we consider the direct Euclidean distance between grid cells instead of the shortest path connecting them. Experiments for the second environment were conducted using the Samsung dataset; see Table 1.

The partitioning resulting for the first test environment is shown in Fig. 4, whereas the partitioning resulting for the second environment is shown in Fig. 5. As the figures indicate, the two partitionings have mainly merged adjacent locations together. More crucially, the partitionings do not suffer from the multimodal nature of signal variations that rank-correlation coefficients alone could suggest. The results of the first environment also illustrate that physical proximity does not dominate the partitioning as, e.g., grid cells $112 - 120$ are allocated individual partitions despite being only approximately one meter apart in the physical space. As this area is located adjacent to an open space, the spatial

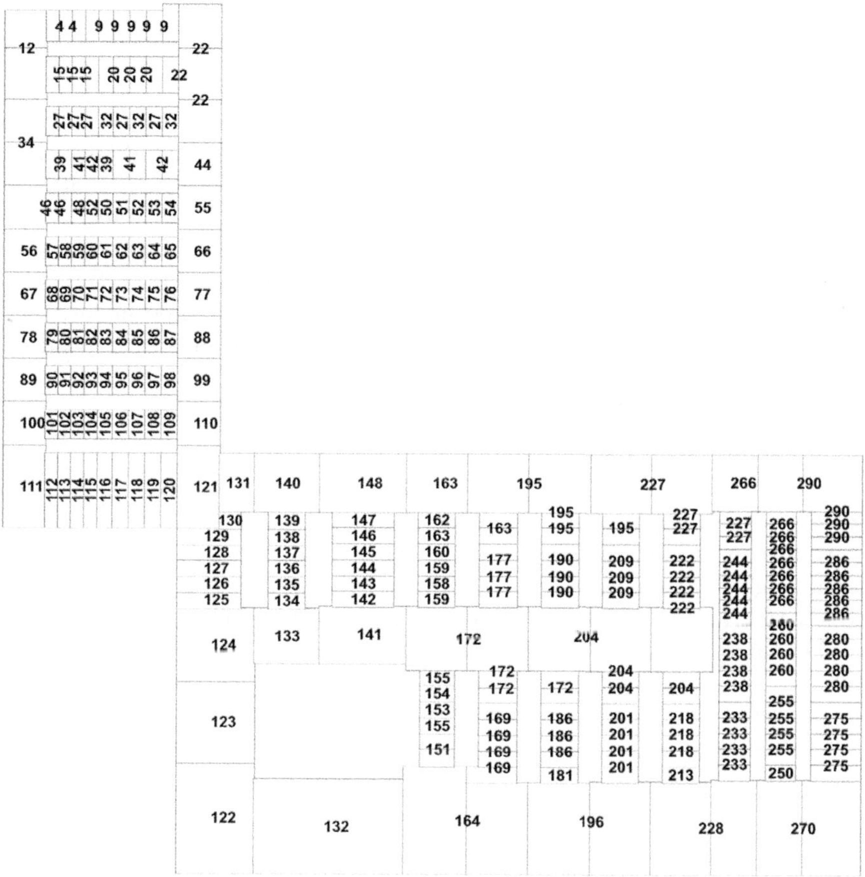

Fig. 4. The generated grid structure of the first retail environment. Numbers indicate cluster indexes.

Fig. 5. The generated grid structure of the retail environment in the second retail environment. Numbers indicate cluster indexes.

variation in the signal environment is high. It is thus likely that these cells correlated highly with cells from a separate part of the store, but this tendency was curbed by the Euclidean distance constraint.

As part of the experiments, we also evaluated how AWESOM affects positioning performance. These experiments were conducted using the SAMSUNG dataset as training data and the HTC dataset for testing; see Table 1. The results of this experiment indicate that AWESOM has negligible effect on positioning accuracy (slight improvement in median accuracy, but slight decrease in 95 percentile error) while at the same time providing significant improvements in the runtime performance of the positioning system. Specifically, in the experiment, the use of AWESOM for creating a partitioning reduced the runtime of the positioning engine by approximately 60%.

5.2   Access Point Deployment

As the final step of the evaluation we demonstrate the possibility to use AWE-SOM for determining areas where to install additional wireless access points. These experiments were conducted using the measurements from the second test environment. To conduct the experiment, we first selected two access points that were located far from each other. Measurements from these two access points were then used to train and test a WiFi fingerprinting system, and from the test results we calculated the resulting median and 95 percentile positioning accuracy of the system. As the positioning system we used a proprietary WiFi positioning system that provides accuracy comparable to or better than state-of-the-art indoor WiFi positioning systems such as Horus [7].

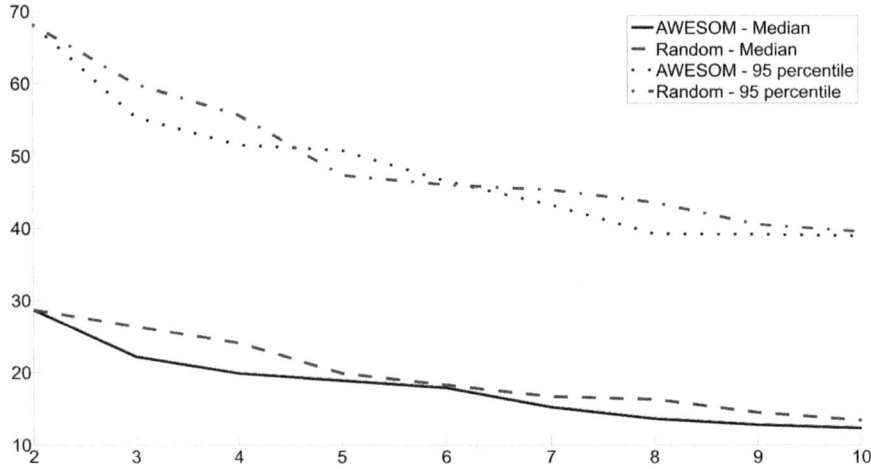

Fig. 6. Comparison between AWESOM and random approach to access point deployment. The values on the x-axis correspond to the number of access points that had been deployed, whereas the values on the y-axis correspond to the accuracy of the positioning system. As a measure of accurate we have considered the Euclidean distance between two locations.

Once the accuracy of the system had been evaluated we used the fitness measure described in Sec. 3.3 to identify the region g with the highest fitness score $F(g)$. We then located the access point that was closest to this partition, and measurements from this access point were included in the training and testing sets. The modified sets were then used to re-evaluate positioning accuracy. This procedure was continued iteratively until a total of 10 access points were included in the environment. As part of the experiment we also compared AWESOM against a random access point selection metric which added a randomly selected access point from those that were not yet considered.

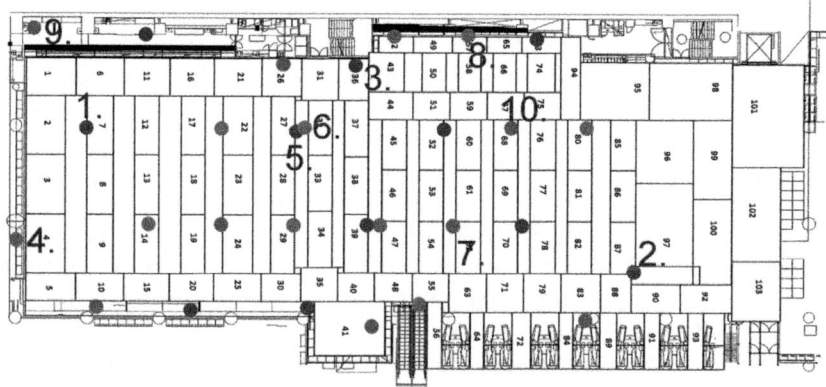

Fig. 7. The order in which AWESOM suggested access points should be added (from 2. onwards). The colors correspond to the different wireless channels used.

The positioning accuracy resulting from the two access point selection strategies (AWESOM and random) is illustrated in Fig. 6. As the figure indicates, AWESOM consistently outperforms the random strategy and leads to rapid improvements in positioning accuracy. Fig. 7, on the other hand, illustrates the order in which AWESOM includes access points as part of the deployment. The figure indicates a consistent and intuitive pattern of including access points, thus demonstrating the potential of using AWESOM for optimizing wireless access point deployments.

6   Conclusions and Discussion

In this paper we described AWESOM, a method for facilitating large-scale deployments of wireless fingerprinting systems. AWESOM combines self-organizing maps, a rank correlation measure that considers neuronal activation patterns, spatial clustering and a weighted Euclidean centroid technique into a framework that provides a principled way to create a discrete partitioning of a space in a way that is both compatible with the signal environments and reflects the spatial topology of the environment. As demonstrated in experiments conducted using data collected from two large-scale deployments of a proprietary fingerprinting system, AWESOM is able to construct partitionings that balance the influence of spatial similarities, i.e., geographical co-location, with similarities of signal space characteristics. In addition, we demonstrated that AWESOM lends itself well to a fitness measure that can be used to evaluate the suitability of a particular division of space or to suggest improvements in the wireless infrastructure in terms of access point placement. A comparison against a random access point selection method demonstrated that AWESOM can indeed identify access point locations that are beneficial for improving location accuracy.

The work in this paper focused on the use of self-organizing maps, although alternative non-linear techniques, e.g., Isomap [31] or Laplacian Eigenmaps [32], could also be used for projecting the signal strength measurements. These methods provide some advantages over self-organizing maps, for example, they are able to recover more complicated relationships between the input signals than what the self-organizing map is capable of capturing. The Isomap algorithm can handle gaps in the non-linear manifold and only needs one parameter to run, performing most of the work in an unsupervised fashion. In comparison, self-organizing maps force the relationship on a predefined topology. A key advantage of the self-organizing map compared to other non-linear projection techniques, however, is that it automatically creates a classifier from the input data. Furthermore, SOM supports iterative usage, whereas other non-linear projection techniques rely on eigenvalue decomposition techniques which necessitate reconfiguring the entire mapping whenever new input signals become available. The results in this paper also demonstrate that SOMs provide an intuitive way of measuring (dis)similarity between fingerprint signals. As part of our future work we plan to explore the use of other non-linear projection techniques for supporting fingerprinting systems.

Acknowledgments. This work was supported by EIT ICT Labs. The work was also supported in part by the ICT program of the European Community, under the PASCAL2 network of excellence, ICT-216886-PASCAL2. The publication only reflects the authors' views. The authors are grateful to K-Citymarket Ruoholahti in Helsinki, Finland, and Globus in Güdingen, Germany for providing environments for deploying and testing the positioning. The authors would like to thank Gerrit Kahl, Markus Löchtefeld, Antonio Krüger and other members of the DFKI Intelligent Retail Laboratory for support with the deployment of the positioning engine. The authors also would like to thank Sourav Bhattacharya and Patrik Floréen for comments on the work.

References

1. Ward, A., Jones, A., Hopper, A.: A new location technique for the active office. IEEE Personal Communications 4(5), 42–47 (1997)
2. Priyantha, N.B., Chakraborty, A., Balakrishnan, H.: The cricket location-support system. In: Proceedings of the International Conference on Mobile Computing and Networking (Mobicom), pp. 32–43 (2000)

3. Patel, S.N., Truong, K.N., Abowd, G.D.: PowerLine Positioning: A Practical Sub-Room-Level Indoor Location System for Domestic Use. In: Dourish, P., Friday, A. (eds.) UbiComp 2006. LNCS, vol. 4206, pp. 441–458. Springer, Heidelberg (2006)
4. Kjærgaard, M.B.: A Taxonomy for Radio Location Fingerprinting. In: Hightower, J., Schiele, B., Strang, T. (eds.) LoCA 2007. LNCS, vol. 4718, pp. 139–156. Springer, Heidelberg (2007)
5. Varshavsky, A., Patel, S.: Location in ubiquitous computing. In: Krumm, J. (ed.) Ubiquitous Computing Fundamentals, pp. 285–320. Chapman and Hall/CRC (2010)
6. Bahl, P., Padmanabhan, V.N.: RADAR: An In-Building RF-Based User Location and Tracking System. In: Proceedings of the 19th Conference on Computer Communications (INFOCOM), vol. 2, pp. 775–784. IEEE Computer Society (2000)
7. Youssef, M., Agrawala, A.: The Horus location determination system. Wireless Networks 14, 357–374 (2008)
8. Krumm, J., Platt, J.: Minimizing calibration effort for an indoor 802.11 device location measurement system. MSR-TR-2003-82, Microsoft Research, Seattle, WA (2003)
9. Nurmi, P., Bhattacharya, S., Kukkonen, J.: A grid-based algorithm for on-device GSM positioning. In: Proceedings of the 12th International Conference on Ubiquitous Computing (UbiComp), pp. 227–236 (2010)
10. Haeberlen, A., Flannery, E., Ladd, A.M., Rudys, A., Wallach, D.S., Kavraki, L.E.: Practical robust localization over large-scale 802.11 wireless networks. In: Proceedings of the 10th Annual International Conference on Mobile Computing and Networking (MobiCom), pp. 70–84. ACM (2004)
11. Varshavsky, A., de Lara, E., Hightower, J., LaMarca, A., Otsason, V.: GSM indoor localization. Pervasive and Mobile Computing 3, 698–720 (2007)
12. Chen, M.Y., Sohn, T., Chmelev, D., Haehnel, D., Hightower, J., Hughes, J., LaMarca, A., Potter, F., Smith, I., Varshavsky, A.: Practical Metropolitan-Scale Positioning for GSM Phones. In: Dourish, P., Friday, A. (eds.) UbiComp 2006. LNCS, vol. 4206, pp. 225–242. Springer, Heidelberg (2006)
13. Honkavirta, V., Perälä, T., Löytty, S.A., Piché, R.: A comparative survey of WLAN location fingerprinting methods. In: Proceedings of the 6th Workshop on Positioning, Navigation and Communication (WPNC), pp. 243–251. IEEE (2009)
14. Castro, P., Chiu, P., Kremenek, T., Muntz, R.: A Probabilistic Room Location Service for Wireless Networked Environments. In: Abowd, G.D., Brumitt, B., Shafer, S. (eds.) UbiComp 2001. LNCS, vol. 2201, pp. 18–34. Springer, Heidelberg (2001)
15. Roos, T., Myllymäki, P., Tirri, H., Misikangas, P., Sievänen, J.: A probabilistic approach to WLAN user location estimation. International Journal of Wireless Information Networks 9(3), 155–164 (2002)
16. Krumm, J., Horvitz, E.: LOCADIO: Inferring motion and location from Wi-Fi signal strengths. In: Proceedings of the 1st International Conference on Mobile and Ubiquitous Systems (Mobiquitous), pp. 4–14. IEEE (2004)
17. Ladd, A.M., Bekris, K.E., Rudys, A., Kavraki, L.E., Wallach, D.S.: Robotics-based location sensing using wireless ethernet. Wireless Networks 11, 189–204 (2005)
18. Hightower, J., Borriello, G.: Particle Filters for Location Estimation in Ubiquitous Computing: A Case Study. In: Davies, N., Mynatt, E.D., Siio, I. (eds.) UbiComp 2004. LNCS, vol. 3205, pp. 88–106. Springer, Heidelberg (2004)

19. Letchner, J., Fox, D., LaMarca, A.: Large-scale localization from wireless signal strength. In: Veloso, M.M., Kambhampati, S. (eds.) Proceedings, the Twentieth National Conference on Artificial Intelligence and the Seventeenth Innovative Applications of Artificial Intelligence Conference (AAAI/IAAI), pp. 15–20. AAAI Press (2005)

20. Chai, X., Yang, Q.: Reducing the calibration effort for location estimation using unlabeled samples. In: 3rd IEEE International Conference on Pervasive Computing and Communications (PerCom), pp. 95–104. IEEE (2005)

21. Chai, X., Yang, Q.: Reducing the calibration effort for probabilistic indoor location estimation. IEEE Transactions on Mobile Computing 6(6), 649–662 (2007)

22. Bolliger, P.: Redpin - adaptive, zero-configuration indoor localization through user collaboration. In: Proceedings of the first ACM International Workshop on Mobile Entity Localization and Tracking in GPS-less Environments (MELT), pp. 55–60. ACM (2008)

23. Barry, A., Fisher, B., Chang, M.L.: A Long-Duration Study of User-Trained 802.11 Localization. In: Fuller, R., Koutsoukos, X.D. (eds.) MELT 2009. LNCS, vol. 5801, pp. 197–212. Springer, Heidelberg (2009)

24. Park, J., Charrow, B., Curtis, D., Battat, J., Minkov, E., Hicks, J., Teller, S.J., Ledlie, J.: Growing an organic indoor location system. In: Proceedings of the 8th International Conference on Mobile Systems, Applications, and Services (MobiSys 2010), pp. 271–284 (2010)

25. Koo, J., Cha, H.: Autonomous Construction of a WiFi Access Point Map Using Multidimensional Scaling. In: Lyons, K., Hightower, J., Huang, E.M. (eds.) Pervasive 2011. LNCS, vol. 6696, pp. 115–132. Springer, Heidelberg (2011)

26. Pulkkinen, T., Roos, T., Myllymäki, P.: Semi-supervised Learning for WLAN Positioning. In: Honkela, T., Duch, W., Girolami, W., Kaski, S. (eds.) ICANN 2011, Part I. LNCS, vol. 6791, pp. 355–362. Springer, Heidelberg (2011)

27. Haykin, S.: Neural Networks: A Comprehensive Foundation. Prentice Hall (1998)

28. Zhou, C., Frankowski, D., Ludford, P., Shekhar, S., Terveen, L.: Discovering personally meaningful places: An interactive clustering approach. ACM Transactions on Information Systems 25(3), 12 (2007)

29. Bhattacharya, S., Pulkkinen, T., Nurmi, P., Salovaara, A.: Monstre: A mobile navigation system for retail environments. In: International Workshop on Smart Mobile Applications (SmartApps) (2011)

30. Nurmi, P., Salovaara, A., Bhattacharya, S., Pulkkinen, T., Kahl, G.: Influence of landmark-based navigation instructions on user attention in indoor smart spaces. In: Proceedings of the 15th International Conference on Intelligent User Interfaces (IUI), pp. 96–105. ACM Press (2011)

31. Tenenbaum, J.B., de Silva, V., Langford, J.C.: A global geometric framework for nonlinear dimensionality reduction. Science 290(5500), 2319–2323 (2000)

32. Belkin, M., Niyogi, P.: Laplacian eigenmaps for dimensionality reduction and data representation. Neural Computation 15(6), 1373–1396 (2003)

Indoor Pedestrian Navigation Based on Hybrid Route Planning and Location Modeling

Kari Rye Schougaard[1], Kaj Grønbæk[1], and Tejs Scharling[2]

[1] Department of Computer Science, University of Aarhus, Denmark
{kari,kgronbak}@cs.au.dk
[2] Alexandra Institute, Aarhus, Denmark
tejs.scharling@alexandra.dk

Abstract. This paper introduces methods and services called PerPosNav for development of custom indoor pedestrian navigation applications to be deployed on a variety of platforms. PerPosNav is built on top of the PerPos positioning middleware [8] that fusions GPS, WiFi and inertial tracking into indoor positioning with high accuracy in many types of buildings. The challenges of indoor navigation are discussed and the PerPosNav services are introduced. PerPosNav combines symbolic and geometry based modeling of buildings, and in turn combines graph-based and geometric route computation. The paper argues why these hybrid approaches are necessary to handle the challenges of indoor pedestrian navigation. Furthermore, a fluent navigation is maintained via route tracking and navigation services that generate instructions based on how the user moves in relation to the prescribed route. The viability of PerPosNav has been proven by implementation of support for multiple modes of pedestrian indoor navigation: 1) augmented signs, 2) map based navigation on smartphones, 3) auditory navigation on smartphones solely via earbuds, and 4) augmented reality navigation. Experiences from the use of the PerPosNav services are discussed and compared to other indoor pedestrian navigation approaches.

1 Introduction

Today car navigation systems (www.tomtom.com, www.garmin.com, www.motorola.com/motonav, www.magellangps.com, etc.) have become widespread for route planning and navigation on roads. These systems use GPS for positioning and they utilize digitized roadmaps as graph-based location models [3] With the emergence of smartphones with built-in GPS, similar route planning and navigation has also become available for pedestrians, e.g., in cities via services like maps.google.com or maps.bing.com. Outdoor pedestrian navigation on smartphones is typically handled similar to car navigation, i.e., utilizing GPS and the same graph-based location model (road map), but emancipating from the constraints put on the roads when assuming the user travel by car. This implies that, e.g., walking is allowed in opposite directions on one-way roads, walking may utilize paths through streets that are dead ends for car traffic, etc.

J. Kay et al. (Eds.): Pervasive 2012, LNCS 7319, pp. 289–306, 2012.

For ideal pedestrian navigation, though, the typical roadmap based navigation is insufficient, since pedestrians have a much higher degree of freedom in their movement, for instance in open squares and other places with no explicit road layouts. Pedestrians may also freely move in and out of buildings such as shopping malls, hospitals, convention centers, office buildings, airports, parking lots, etc. where continued navigation support is needed.

The most widespread smartphone navigation services deal with location models and route planning similarly to their car navigation counterparts. In cases where the maps contain squares and other areas without roads, these areas are usually modeled using "virtual paths" that, e.g., connect two roads on opposite sides of the square or that follow the edges of a square between ingoing/outgoing roads. For instance, if you are standing in the middle of Piazza san Pietro in Rome and ask maps.google.com on your smartphone for directions, then your starting point jumps to an arbitrary point on the edge of the square and you are directed on a detour following the periphery of the square, instead of just directing you in the right direction across the square from the beginning. Your navigation starts from this arbitrary point instead of your actual location, since the "virtual paths" cannot cover all positions on open areas. we propose to use a hybrid route planning approach where routes on the graph of roads and "virtual paths" are supplemented with use of the geometric properties of such squares and areas when computing shortest paths.

1.1   Challenges Inherent in Indoor Pedestrian Navigation

When moving to *indoor* pedestrian navigation we face several new challenges including how to achieve reliable positioning. For outdoor navigation it is commonplace to rely on GPS for positioning, while for navigating indoors we cannot trust GPS alone due to fading and reflected satellite signals [16]. Thus we need to supplement with other kinds of positioning such as WiFi-based positioning, dead reckoning, and RFID based positioning. Except for dead reckoning, indoor positioning technologies require infrastructure that is not ubiquitously available. This means that a general-purpose navigation system must be able to integrate with different kinds of positioning technologies. Most of the literature on indoor pedestrian navigation [11], [12], [18], [21] put the main focus on how to obtain reliable and accurate positions by means of UWB, dead reckoning, WiFi positioning etc., whereas less effort is put into providing a well-structured and efficient navigation functionality, or efficient navigation interfaces. The PerPos [8] platform provides cloud services that, e.g., take care of providing the most accurate position possible, given the positioning hardware and the building conditions, as well as offering location model and route planning services. Here we introduce route tracking and navigation services for the PerPos platform.

Assuming we can achieve indoor positions from the PerPos middleware, we need to model "virtual paths" for indoor environments. However, this approach also comes up short in the indoor case: many buildings have large atriums, squares, open office spaces, open shopping areas, etc., where there are no natural paths and there may be blockings by furniture and interior installations. We claim that for pedestrian navigation a hybrid approach to location modeling, and route planning, is needed. In PerPosNav routes are computed by a hybrid approach: 1) a graph specifically defined for pedestrian navigation, termed Navigation Graph, is used to compute the part of the routes that go through areas covered by the graph; 2) for other areas, the geometric structure of the location is used to find the shortest possible route across the open space. This solves the problem that routes on a Navigation Graph are restricted to positions on the graph, which we saw above for navigation from the Piazza san Pietro.

For indoor navigation, obtaining a proper location model based on some existing building model often presents an issue. Building models or more precisely models of the space within a building, which are often termed location models, are not commonly available. It is expensive to model a building only for the sake of providing navigation. Fortunately, many countries start to require by government regulations that newly constructed public buildings should to be defined in an architectural 3D digital model. PerPosNav provides support for semi-automatic conversion of an architectural model into a useful location model for navigation.

Another challenge for pedestrian navigation is the nature of pedestrian movement. Because of the lower speed of travel compared to navigation in vehicles, there is a larger uncertainty about the tracked target's position relative to the speed of its travel. Furthermore, pedestrians are not confined to rigid movements or bound to travel on well-defined paths, but can move freely, stop suddenly, turn on the spot, step to the side, etc. This implies, that the pedestrian navigation system must make do with less information regarding the target's position and travel direction than when navigating a car, which keeps to roads with a speed, which under normal traffic conditions at least is fairly easy to predict. The PerPosNav Route Tracking Service supports giving instructions also when the user comes to a halt or turns around, by taking into consideration historical tracking of the users' movements.

Finally, many of the existing pedestrian navigation systems are landmark based [26] [7]. However, it is cumbersome and will introduce an extra cost to the navigation application to annotate large amounts of buildings with landmark information. Especially, when the building utilization and decoration change frequently, thus requiring frequent modifications of landmarks to avoid erroneous landmark-based navigation. To address this challenge, we present a novel form of auditory navigation, where the navigation instructions are based solely on the geometry of traversed and near-by locations. No annotation of the location model with landmark information is therefore necessary. By using geometric information of the building structure more meaningful navigation instructions than the length of the next route segment and angle of turn can be given.

1.2   From Positioning Challenges to Navigation Challenges

The primary focus of the literature on indoor pedestrian navigation is on the positioning methods [11], [12], [18], [21]. These papers, although talking about navigation, are more about achieving accurate positions indoor by means of dead reckoning, Wi-Fi, Particle filters and similar approaches. A secondary focus is on geo-annotation where "landmark" information relevant for giving navigation instruction, e.g., to disabled people, is stored as annotations on the location model [4], [30]. A final focus is on the user interface [1], [22], here the focus is primarily on visual navigation, e.g., in AR with arrows and paths layered on top of video streams of the real world.

Thus we see a gap in the area of supporting computation of route plans and tracking the users during navigation to provide ongoing relevant navigation instructions. The PerPosNav approach combines some of the above foci and focuses on providing fundamental location model and route computation support for efficient navigation provided to users in several different modes (visual, auditory, environment based, augmented reality), depending on the needs of the users in a domain.

2   The PerPos Platform - Support for Positioning and Navigation

The PerPos Platform [8] provides a range of services relevant for applications based on positioning. See Figure 1 for an overview. The figure illustrates how data flows from the sensors through the PerPos Middleware and PerPosNav to the applications, while the services can depend on functionality from other PerPos services, which are not part of the main flow of data.

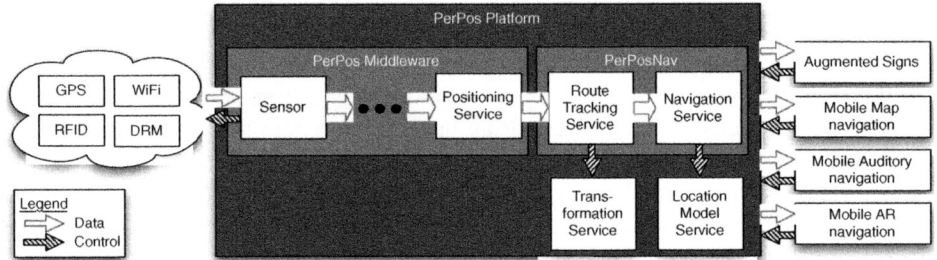

Fig. 1. Overview of the relevant parts of the PerPos Platform

2.1   Diverse Positioning Technologies and Positioning Middleware

Positioning technologies range over GPS, signals strength from cell-towers, RFID, Bluetooth, WiFi, and dead reckoning, to mention only the most widespread. Moreover, different communication protocols and data formats exist for different devices of the same type. Positioning middleware aims to shield application developers from the heterogeneity of positioning technologies, and to provide computed positioning and related functionalities high accuracy [5], [14], [20], [25], [27]. Furthermore, the Positioning Middleware often provides statistical methods for improving positioning in navigation and other tracking applications [14], [20], [25], [27], [29].

The indoor navigation projects being described in Section 1.2 have been developed specifically for and tested with one or a few specific positioning technologies. This makes sense, because even though a positioning middleware can provide positioning using different technologies in the same manner, it cannot altogether abstract from important quality parameters. E.g., the accuracy, precision, and frequency of positions varies. However, by handling some of the issues coming with the quality variance for navigation systems in a service for tracking on a route (presented in Section 3.1), our navigation systems can be used with different types of positioning.

2.2   Location Model Service

When referring to a location in a building, coordinates do not make much sense. Often, the distance between two things given by a coordinate system is of less importance than being in the same room. E.g., I am interested in being in the same room as the projector I wish to use, rather than the distance being only 2 meters, the latter could as well mean it is attached to the ceiling right underneath the floor. To provide such context information, we need modeling of the locations in the building.

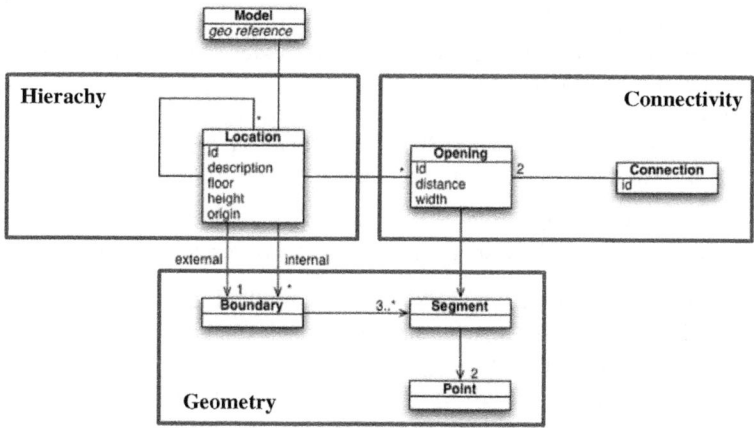

Fig. 2. UML diagram for the PerPos location model

There are two main approaches for modeling indoor environments: building models (used in the GIS and architecture communities, and standardized in, e.g., IFC) model the concrete structures of the building in a geometric representation, whereas location models model the "hollow parts" of the building, the rooms etc., in a symbolic model, which possibly also models the connections between the rooms and the geometric structure of the hollow spaces. Like other second-generation location models ([25], [31]), PerPos features a hybrid location model, which combines a hierarchical structure, a connection structure, and a geometric structure (See Figure 2). Moreover, the PerPos location model supports specification of a Navigation Graph.

- **Hierarchical Structure.** The PerPos location model has a symbolic hierarchy: a tree. A node in the tree represents a building, a floor, or a room. The child relation models containment. This allows for efficient replies to containment queries. For simplicity, we use a tree rather than a lattice. Crosscutting sets of locations: wings, departments, shoe shops, etc. are defined by using annotations.
- **Connection Structure.** The connectivity between rooms is represented in a graph structure. Each node represents a room and an edge between the nodes represents a physical opening between the corresponding rooms. The edge contains information of the geometric extent of the opening between the rooms.
- **Navigation Graph.** The PerPos Location Model supports optional specification of a Navigation Graph. A number of points, where a choice must be made when navigating, termed Decision Points, are defined for the location model. Decision

points are connected to each other by routes, which are composed of segments. The Navigation Graph is additional to the Connection Structure Graph, and is used to specify the network of "virtual paths", that should be used when navigating visitors through the building. Specification of a Navigation Graph allows you to express in the location model that a certain part of a location is a walking area, or that the main connection through a building is the hallway and not a series of connected offices.

- **Location Geometry.** The geometric extent of the building structures is represented in 3 dimensions. The geometric specification allows mapping of positions given in any of the most common coordinate reference systems to locations in the location model. The location model specifies its local coordinate reference system (CRS), in terms of a rotation matrix that defines it relative to a global CRS. Our transformation service can now translate positions given in the most common CRSs to the CRS of the location model. Specification of the geometric extent of locations allows for better visualizations.

A hybrid location model, as the PerPos location model (Figure 2), supports all of the most common application requests for functionality as described by [3]:

- Position queries: the answer can be given as symbolic locations or as coordinates.
- Nearest neighbor queries: this in turn requires a distance function, preferably a distance along a traversable path.
- Range queries: requires a definition of geographic areas and ability to answer which ones among a set of objects of interest are contained in a specified area.
- Visualization: model and route visualization can be a representation of a concrete part of a building or a more abstract representation as for example a visualization of a graph that represents the building.

Both containment and connectivity between rooms and a representation of the geometrical structures of rooms is needed to answer all of these questions satisfactorily. Becker and Dürr [3], furthermore, list navigation support as a requirement. They sum up the demands on the location model originating from navigation as being able to generate a route, and being able to model weights and attributes on connections. In order to support various navigation types, we strengthen the requirements as follows:

- Support for specification of a Navigation Graph in the building, to encode information of, e.g., main connections between parts of a building and of walking areas or routes in large rooms.
- Support for route generation that takes the possibility of free movement in locations into account, i.e. allows navigation outside of a Navigation Graph.

In the following sections we explain how our route generation service, navigation service and navigation modes depend on the dual hybrid approach: both symbolic and geometric functionality in the hybrid location model and both Navigation Graph and free movement, which makes up the hybrid route generation service.

As examples and proofs of concept of the PerPos Location Model, we have modeled a mall, a hospital, and two office complexes: a set of university buildings and a software company site. We can generate location models from a partial set of IFC XML. The use of these models is illustrated in the experiences section.

2.3   Route Generation Service

Operating on its location model PerPos features several graph searching algorithms based on some form of Dijkstra's algorithm [10]. For navigation purposes we use a route obtained from a Visibility Graph [13] (similar to the Corner graph of [26]). For each room obstructions of the direct route between the entry and exit are taken into account, e.g., in concave rooms or rooms containing other building elements. Visibility graph routes enable navigation to any position in the building by the shortest route.

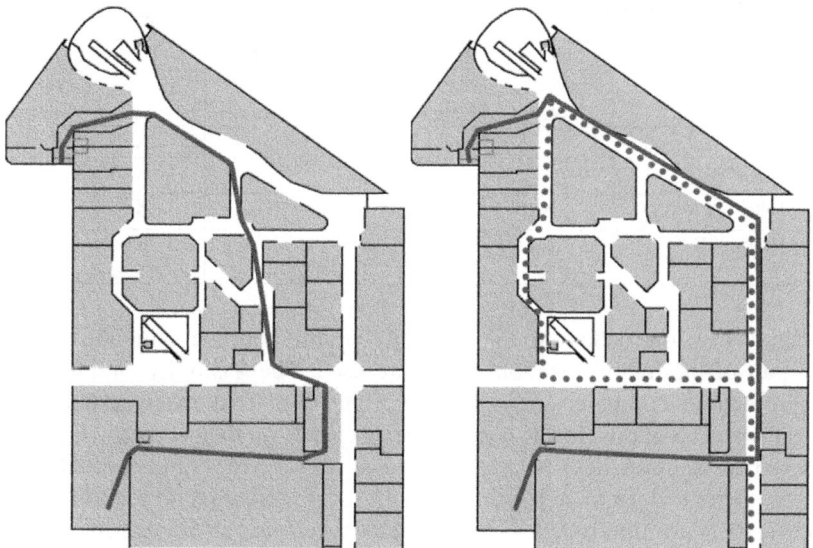

Fig. 3. A visibility-graph route in a mall (left side) and a hybrid route (right side), first and last parts are generated from a visibility graph and the two straight line parts in the middle are retrieved from a navigation graph (dotted)

An example of output from the route generation service is available in Figure 3, left. The route traverses a very complex room: the walking area of a mall, which is defined as one location in the location model.

As stated above, it is possible to specify a Navigation Graph for a location model [6] [7] [26]. For ease of use, PerPos provides functionality for generating routes between Decision Points. The Route Generation Service then uses the Navigation Graph for making routes. Figure 3, right illustrates a hybrid route composed of first a Visibility Graph route, then a Navigation Graph route and last a Visibility Graph route again. This is very useful, when you want to ensure that routes do not go through certain areas: e.g., certain wards in a hospital have restricted access, or should not be used as passage; likewise routes in office buildings and malls should in most circumstances not pass through meeting rooms, offices, auditoriums, or shops. In Figure 3, the main hallways of a mall are preferred for navigation. The hybrid route generation consists of this combination of Navigation Graph and Visibility Graphs routes.

3   PerPosNav – Unified Support for Multiple Navigation Modes

We synthesize a hybrid location model supporting symbolic locations and geometry, with a hybrid route generation, combining shortest routes derived automatically from the location model with routes from a designed route network. In the following we will argue that the dual hybrid approach is needed to satisfy the demands posed by our navigation modes, which are detailed in Section 4.

Table 1. Overview of location model functionality used by navigation modes

		PerPos Location Model Functionality			PerPosNav	
		Visibility Graph	Navigation Graph	Geometry of location	Tracking Service	Navigation Service
Nav. Modes	Augmented Signs		X		X	X
	Mobile Map	X	X	X	X	X
	Mobile Auditory	X		X	X	X
	Mobile AR	X	X	X	X	X

When navigation modes use the Visibility Graph, both the symbolic and the geometric part of the hybrid location model are used. The Visibility Graph depends on the representation of connections between symbolic locations when searching for routes between locations. Inside a location, it depends on the geometric representation to ensure that the route does not cut off corners in concave rooms. A Visibility Graph could be generated from a purely geometric representation of building elements. However, the algorithm runs faster when the entire space is divided into parts where entry and exit points are given. In the Mobile Map mode, we judge that it would be confusing for the user and not satisfactory to show routes that cut off corners in concave rooms or pass through internal building structures. Moreover, symbols for locations are needed, for example, when choosing a destination. We therefore conclude that to support a range of navigation modes that includes showing a route on a map, the geometric representation is indispensable. One could make do without the symbolic connection structure, but symbolic identification of locations is necessary.

Turning to hybrid route generation, the strong argument for the Navigation Graph is absence of a digital location model. It takes considerably less time to construct a Navigation Graph than to model the whole building. In some cases, a mode of navigation that does not need a full location model is desirable, e.g., Augmented Signs. Furthermore, in public buildings with many visitors, it is often paramount that navigation users are not directed through certain parts of the building, but follow intended connections. Nonetheless, it is also desirable that navigation is possible in buildings or in parts of buildings, where a digital model is available, but the owners do not want to create and maintain a Navigation Graph. For example, this could be the case when most users are habitual users that do not need navigation. We conclude that there is a demand for both automatically generated and specifically designed navigation routes. A versatile Navigation platform should support both.

3.1   Route Tracking Service

The Route Tracking Service tracks a user on a route. The route is the suggested and anticipated route of the user. The positioning functionality of the PerPos Platform delivers the position of the tracked user. If a position is within a threshold distance of the route the user is considered *on route*. The service then projects the position to the closest segment of the route, or as second choice to the closest segment of a Navigation Graph. Snapping the position to the most likely position on the anticipated route is similar to techniques used by satellite navigation systems for vehicles. A variant of this technique is used in [6] [7], but few navigation papers discuss how they manage the tracking. The threshold distance can be adjusted according to the accuracy of different positioning techniques, e.g., based on the accuracy estimation delivered by the PerPos Platform. This allows a navigation application to be deployed with different positioning technologies, without modifying the navigation application specific code.

The service keeps track of relevant parts of the tracking history. Specifically it remembers at which Decision Point the user was last observed. The service summarizes the current state of the user in one of the following Route Tracking States

- At a Decision Point - possibly knowing which Decision Point the user came from.
- Moving between two Decision Points – possibly knowing the direction.
- Just left a Decision Point or Not on the Route

The state also includes additional information like the projected position, ids of Decision Points, etc. This knowledge of the user's Route Tracking State is necessary and sufficient to generate intelligible navigation instructions, also when the user is not following the expected route, when the positioning system for some reason is currently not delivering positions, etc. Knowledge of the history of the user's placement at Decision Points can be used in the navigation application specific parts to reason about the navigation instructions the user has previously received.

3.2   Tailorable Navigation Service

The Navigation Service collects navigation information to forward to the navigation mode specific generation of navigation instructions. It extends the Route Tracking state with the following Navigation State information that does not mention the tracking explicitly, but captures most of the information in navigation related terms:

- On route – possibly knowing the user's direction
- Leaving or entering the route
- Off route, at the destination or disappeared

The Navigation Service determines when to re-calculate a route and when to start a navigation session for this route. It also incorporates information of the position of the user's last visited and expected next Decision Point. Both functionalities contains points for extension or can be replaced by navigation mode specific variants. However, most of the variation between navigation modes lies in how the navigation state is presented for the user.

4   Navigation Modes – Supported by PerPosNav

The navigation service generates a navigation state based on a tracking state and provides callback points for specialized types of navigation. Four modes of navigation have been implemented as a part of PerPosNav. Despite their differences they are all based on functionality in the PerPos platform especially the PerPosNav services. Even though they differ in using the Navigation Graph or the Visibility Graph to define routes, they all use the route tracking service to obtain information of whether the users are on route or not, and where they are on the route.

A challenge for indoor pedestrian navigation is that often both position and direction information is inaccurate in comparison to the travel speed [9]. When accurate position and direction information is available, a navigation instruction such as an arrow can be given, but when position or direction information is uncertain, more information must be given in order for the user to correctly relate the navigation instructions to the environments [9].

The sign based solution operates with a certain position (at the sign) and navigation information in the form of arrows can be given. In the mobile solutions there is more uncertainty attached to the position and direction. Our solution is to provide more information: either maps or navigation information that relates to the geometry of the locations. This enables the users to make up for positioning errors. Our augmented reality navigation has only been used in early prototype tests. Our experience was that position and direction information were not sufficiently accurate to base instructions solely on direction arrows. Many navigation instruction arrows were therefore not helpful for the navigation task. This experience lies in line with [7] and [15]. They augment photos of landmarks with navigation information in the form of arrows, and either need to improve the position information by analyzing the camera angle to avoid misleading navigation instructions [15] or used in advance prepared pictures and superimposed arrows [7].

4.1   Augmented Signs Navigation

The central idea in augmented stationary signs for personalized navigation is that, when the user approaches the sign, the navigation instructions for the user are displayed on the sign [26] [9]. Signs are placed at Decision Points in the building. The sign should provide enough information to navigate to the next Decision Point.

In our implementation navigation instructions are shown on sign displays at Decision Points in the physical buildings in terms of arrows assigned with the relevant user's ID communicating the direction to take in the Decision Point. Based on the generated route, navigation instructions are produced for designated Decision Points. Navigation possibilities for a Decision Point are encoded by determining the possibilities for turning left, turning right, going straight etc. The direction of the arrow on the sign display is calculated on basis of the position of the display and the position of the next Decision Point for the user. The user's next Decision Point is available from the attached navigation state. The text direction for the user pseudonym written on the arrow is calculated from the last Decision Point visited by the user. This information is also made available by the default implementation of the Navigation Service.

Privacy is an issue for Augmented Signs. Other bystanders should not be able to determine who is going where. In our implementation, privacy is partly handled by using pseudonyms for the users. Each user is assigned a numeric id and navigation instructions are provided for that pseudonym id.

4.2   Mobile Map Navigation

Pedestrian navigation on the basis of visual clues projected on top of a map is known from GPS navigation services on smartphones such as maps.google.com and maps.bing.com and from research projects also for indoor navigation [2] [7]. The user's position is used to center a map shown to the user. On top of this map, the route is drawn. In our implementation each next navigation instruction is presented in the form of an arrow drawn on top of the map, highlighting the Decision Points where the user gets directions.

The PerPosNav functionality used for mobile map based navigation is the same as for solutions using augmented signs. The same Navigation Graph is used for finding routes and encoding the direction possibilities. However, for the first and last portion of the route, free movement through locations is supported, and the geometry-aware Visibility Graph is used to find a route from the current location of the user to the Navigation Graph, and likewise to go from the Navigation Graph to the destination.

The direction of the navigation arrows are calculated as vector by relating the position of the Decision Point to the position of the end of the next route segment on the map, and align the arrow with this vector.

4.3   Mobile Auditory Navigation

For auditory navigation or text based navigation instructions, there are three obvious options: 1) navigation instructions in terms of the segment length to travel and the angle to turn, 2) using landmarks to explain the route, and 3) using the geometrical structure of the rooms to explain the route. The last of which, we have implemented.

Since the location model includes a geometric description of locations, geometry based auditory navigation instructions can use this information. Thus we generate navigation instructions such as "Turn left down the corridor. Take the second door on the right", "Cross the room", "Go to the other end of the room, and take the last door on your left". The geometrical characteristics of the locations are visually available for the users. In this respect the approach resembles landmark-based navigation.

The navigation instructions are generated as follows: In an off-line phase, the locations in the location model are annotated with room types as listed below. When a user requests navigation, the Route Finding Service generates a Visibility Graph route. Navigation instructions are attached to Decision Points in the route, by considering each of the room types and how the route proceeds through a given room type.

The list of room types is rather short. A short list makes the navigation instructions generated on the basis of the room type recognizable for the user. This means that the user can identify erroneous instructions, e.g., a wide corridor with few exits is mistaken for an oblong room.

- Staircase: staircases between floors and other sloping rooms
- Lift: rooms connected to several floors
- Corridor: Narrow (less than 5 m wide) oblong rooms, with 4 or more doors
- Oblong room: Rooms that are more than twice as long as they are wide
- Rectangular room: Rooms with 4 sides facing each other two and two
- Convex room: Convex rooms and rooms that contain other rooms within them
- Room: Rooms that do not fall in the other categories

The list has been constructed experimentally based on generation of navigation in-structions by hand for routes in two office buildings and a mall.

To construct the navigation instructions, the route is obtained from the Location Model Service, and each segment of the route is considered. For each room the route traverses we calculate information of which doors or openings can be used for enter-ing and exiting the room, their relation to each other, and whether the route goes around corners or around building elements that are in the room. This information is used in generation of the navigation instructions.

For Staircase, Lift and Corridor room types, the type info is used in the instruc-tions, e.g.: "Take the staircase. Go two floors up" or "Turn right down the corridor". The other room types are not used in the navigation instructions. But for corridors and oblong rooms we can use "the other end" as a part of a navigation instruction. It is difficult both for a human and for a machine to generate understandable navigation instructions for complex rooms. For concave rooms we base instructions on following a wall, counting the number of doors passed, and crossing to an opposing wall.

4.4   Mobile Augmented Reality Navigation

The PerPosNav services also supports a Mobile Augmented Reality mode of naviga-tion, similar to those proposed by [22]. In this navigation mode, the user has to hold a smartphone in an upright position pointing the camera in the walking direction. Then the navigation instructions will appear as visual cues (arrows and path lines) rendered on top of the video stream from the camera.

In this mode, we look ahead in the computed route to draw paths and arrows unify-ing Navigation Graph and Visibility Graph parts of the route into a navigation path to be displayed. The Navigation Service State is combined with continuously keeping track of directions of the camera to generate the navigation instructions.

This mode is, however, particularly sensitive to accuracy of both the positioning and compass/dead reckoning sensors' ability to provide a precise camera-direction to render arrows and paths such that they are precisely aligned with the video of the real environment in front of the user. Currently a proof-of-concept prototype has been implemented to verify that the capabilities of our PerPosNav services are sufficient to support this mode. To become practically usable in indoor environments, more robust directionality support needs to be developed in addition to the high accuracy indoor positioning provided by PerPos middleware. This improvement of directionality sup-port is left as an important item of future work.

5   Experiments in Real World Environments

In this section we discuss the experiences from two real world experiments with applications build on PerPosNav.

5.1   Augmented Signs Deployed at a Hospital

Navigation at hospitals has become an increasingly complicated task as hospitals are merged into bigger units or otherwise tend to grow in size. The motivation for the augmented signs experiments was the limitation of traditional signs to overcome the increasing complexity. The experiments were conducted in collaboration with a local Digital Sign company with the need to innovate their current production line of traditional signs. After initial ethnographical user studies (patients only) and a subsequent design phase, a prototype was built, implemented and tested at the local hospital.

If a personalized navigation is to replace traditional sign based way finding at hospitals, it must embrace all patient and visitor groups It was therefore deduced that smart phone based way finding was not an option. Also, a physical integration with the hospital seems to improve patient confidence despite the often stressfull situation they are in. Given these considerations we developed a concept based on digital floor projections (Section 4.1) and combined these with RFID based tracking as illustrated in Figure 4. The Projected images reflect the surroundings of each Decision Point and are configured to overlay the way finding arrows at the correct positions.

In the experiment each patient was handed a small tag to be carried along between two wards in the hospital. Each patient was associated to a number to allow anonymity as argued in section 4.1. For the prototype we used active RFID tags with an average signal range of 15 meters. At each Decision Point a projector and a RFID antenna was set up and we were thus able to sense the presence of a nearby patient/tag. The 15 meters range meant that the same patient would be sensed at several Decision Points at the same time. This was however handled by the probabilistic filtering technique in the underlying PerPos middleware.

The user study was conducted over two days and included 15 patients interviewed by ethnographers. All users found that the overall experience of being guided by the prototype was "good", "easy" or "perfect" and the floor projections as "smart" and "funny". Most of the users found it easy and unproblematic to carry the tags along. A few found the tag a bit confusing, referring to it as "something new".

The conclusion from the experiments is that the positioning middleware and the PerPosNav service gave us the functionality we needed to create the described prototype. We are now investigating cheaper RFID technologies and a more energy efficient projection technology to transform the concept into a commercial product.

5.2   Mobile Map Navigation Used in Shopping Mall and Office Environment

The augmented sign approach has the major drawback that physical installations are needed, which results in installation costs and requires maintenance. In many cases like in shopping applications or facility management tools, we can afford to ignore certain user groups and in contrast to the previous use case move to a smart phone platform. In comparison to the augmented signs the smart phone is both tracking device and user interface. It is thus possible to guide the user at any point of the route. One way to give continuous navigation instructions is to display the user's current position and navigation directions on graphical maps of floor plans as described in section 4.2. The main limitation is the accuracy of the positioning method available.

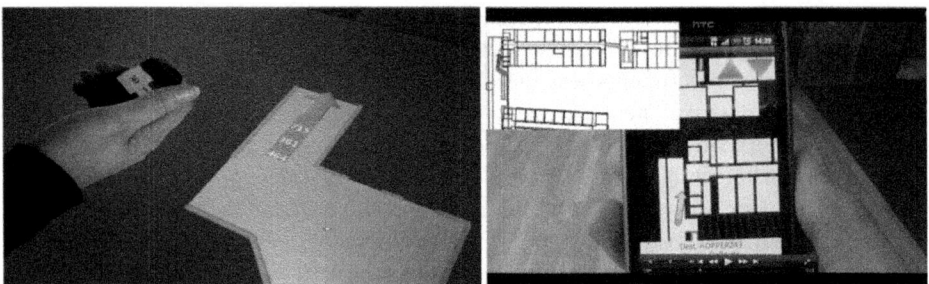

Fig. 4. Augmented signs using tags and floor projection (left) and mobile map (right)

We built a mobile map navigation app for the Android platform. Floor plans were generated from the location model of the environment. The appropriate floor and selection of the floor plan is displayed according to the user's current position, but the user can zoom and pan the map to change between greater level of detail and better overview. The position of the user is calculated by the PerPos middleware using the WiFi, compass and accelerometer sensors on the phone.

We conducted experiments with the app in both a shopping mall and an office building. After the first user feedback we learned that users expect a fairly specific position indication on the map and a fluent movement of this 'indication dot' as the user moves. To avoid that the dot jumps due to imprecise position measurements we instructed the positioning middleware layer only to move the target according to an adaptive pedestrian movement model and only along the proposed route. The new approach gave the needed improvement of user experience and we could implement it without changing the PerPosNav services making it available to all navigation types.

5.3   Summary of Experiments

The two navigation modes evaluated in the experiments are quite different in nature, but draw on the same core functionality of PerPosNav. Tracking and Navigation services monitor movements of each user, and generate the needed control information for producing navigation instructions for the user, Routes between locations are calculated based on building model and navigation graph supporting dynamic creation of new locations. The navigation graph can be modified if needed e.g., in case of blocking of hallways due to reconstruction. Without the combined qualities of PerPosNav, each navigation mode would require extensive development and testing before a solution with the same flexibility could be deployed.

6   Comparison of PerPosNav with Related Work

Two categories of work are related to the work presented here: Platforms for implementations of navigations systems and navigation systems.

Several platforms for location aware applications exist: Trax [17], MiddleWhere [25], The Location Stack [14] and LOC8 [27]. These frameworks or platforms are not designed with a specific intention to support navigation, but aim for generally supporting location aware applications. Trax [17] provides an explicit design to allow different providers of positioning, content, and location based services. MiddleWhere [25] focuses on incorporation of heterogeneous location sensing technologies, and provides a world model for tracking the location and context of interesting objects. The location Stack [14] pioneered the layered approach, which is now structuring several positioning middlewares. LOC8 [27] separates the location model from the sensing model, but uses a cross-layer approach in allowing the context and location information to influence the fusion of sensor data. None of the projects offers specific support for making Navigation Graphs nor offers Route Tracking. However, both functionalities could be built on top of the platforms.

The amount of work in the area of pedestrian navigation is too large to survey here, but we relate our work to examples of the most important approaches. Previous work on navigation systems where different modes share parts of the system, parallel to the shared Route Tracking and Navigation Services in our case, include [2] and [9]. Butz et al [9] present a hybrid navigation system that present navigation instructions both on a 3d screen as a 3D virtual walkthrough and on a palm pilot as graphics. Baus et al [2] work with 3 different screen sizes: large (SmartBoard), mobile (PDA), and a small monitor to clip on glasses. The authors do not discuss in detail how they divide shared and presentation media specific functionality. Nor do they discuss the capabilities of basic parts, e.g., how the route is generated or building information structured.

uNavi [6] [7] navigates users on routes obtained from a custom made Navigation Graph. They provide both maps with a route overlay and landmark based navigation with superimposed navigation arrows on pictures along with a textual description of the route. The landmark-based navigation has been manually prepared for each of the possible options at Decision Points. While manual preparation gives a high quality, it means that navigation instructions need editing when wall colors, shops, etc. change.

Tactile Wayfinder [24] uses a belt with tactile output to convey navigation information. The direction of the next waypoint and the waypoint after that (look ahead) is given by vibrating areas on the belt. The rhythm and intensity of the direction signal allows the user to distinguish between the next and the look-ahead waypoint. A tactile navigation system such as Tactile Wayfinder could be implemented on top of Per-PosNav. The Route Tracking System would help handle situations like when the user leaves the route and a new route should be calculated. Issues like these are not mentioned in [24].

Landmark based pedestrian navigation, with visual aid such as photos augmented with arrows conveying navigation instructions [15] or using, e.g., names of shops or distinctive colors in the environment in navigation instruction text [26], could be added to PerPosNav. The PerPos location model allows annotations of points, locations, and connections such as doors or doorways. Landmark annotations in the form of text or images may be used when generating navigation instructions. Most indoor locations are not well documented by photos annotated with positions and shared in social applications. Pictures to aid navigation would therefore have to be made expressly to support navigation applications, as is done in uNavi [6] [7]. It would be interesting to compare spatial knowledge acquisition and navigation performance when using the geometry of the locations, landmarks and both in navigation instructions.

The idea of egocentric navigation (e.g., giving directions relative to the user), which is central to our auditory navigation system, has also been explored in [23] and [28], as an alternative to allocentric (birds eye view) route finding. Instead of using the simpler approach of finding routes in a Visibility Graph, the above works partition concave rooms into convex sections and use these invisible soft boundaries in their navigation instructions. However, it is not obvious that a user would understand the references to these invisible boundaries. The authors themselves mention that their algorithm needs further work. Furthermore, it seems they have not actually implemented a navigation system on top of their navigation enabling location model.

Generally, the presentations of the mentioned navigation systems do not clearly discuss how situations like the user not following the route or the positioning system temporarily being unavailable are determined and can be properly dealt with. Furthermore, most of these works do not discuss whether and which parts of the navigation functionality can be shared between different modes of navigation, instead of implementing resembling functionality over and over for all modes of navigation.

7   Conclusion and Future Work

This paper presents PerPosNav and four navigation modes: 1) augmented signs, 2) mobile maps, 3) auditory, and 4) augmented reality. We have briefly presented the PerPos platform for positioning and navigation applications. We explain how different kinds of navigation applications may use the location model, and we have argued for the need of a hybrid approach both for representation of locations and for route generation in order to offer rich navigation support. Most existing systems and research prototypes investigate only one kind of navigation.

As a part of the PerPos platform we have created a framework for navigation: PerPosNav. We have split the generation of navigation instructions into a basic functionality for tracking on a route, PerPosNav Route Tracking Service, and a pluggable service for generating navigation instructions, PerPosNav Navigation Service. The route tracking service delivers basic information such as whether the client is on the route, is moving in the right direction, or is leaving the route. This basic part of a navigation application, which is used for example to determine when the user is off route and a new route should be generated, is not elaborated on in most presentations of navigation applications. Furthermore, it is a novel approach to split out this service and share it between several navigation applications. We have tested the feasibility of the four navigation modes, that all use the PerPosNav Route Tracking Service.

Additionally, we presented a novel form of auditory navigation, where the navigation instructions are based solely on the geometry of the locations. No annotation of the location model with landmark information is therefore necessary. By using geometric information of the building structure more meaningful navigation instructions than the length of the next route segment and angle of turn can be given.

The next step is to make more thorough user studies. We are currently making the first study of the use of auditory navigation. We also intend to investigate how the use of different kinds of positioning with varying qualities affects the usability of the different navigation modes. Moreover, it is interesting how well the usage of location geometry as a kind of landmarks (in the auditory mode) supports navigation in comparison to using traditional landmarks.

Acknowledgements. We thank the PerPos group for help in implementing the middleware supporting PerPosNav. In particular we would like to thank Henrik Blunck and the anonymous reviewers for their constructive comments on the paper. We thank for the financial support granted by the Danish National Advanced Technology Foundation under J.nr. 009-2007-2.

References

1. Arikawa, M., Konomi, S., Ohnishi, K.: Navitime: Supporting Pedestrian Navigation in the Real World. IEEE Pervasive Computing 6(3), 21–29 (2007)
2. Baus, J., Krüger, A., Wahlster, W.: A resource-adaptive mobile navigation system. In: IUI 2002, pp. 15–22 (2002)
3. Becker, C., Dürr, F.: On location models for ubiquitous computing. Personal and Ubiquitous Computing 9(1), 20–31 (2005)
4. Beeharee, A., Steed, A.: Minimising Pedestrian Navigational Ambiguities Through Geoannotation and Temporal Tagging. In: Jacko, J.A. (ed.) HCI 2007, Part II. LNCS, vol. 4551, pp. 748–757. Springer, Heidelberg (2007)
5. Bellavista, P., Corradi, A., Giannelli, C.: The PoSIM middleware for translucent and context-aware integrated management of heterogeneous positioning systems. Computer Communications 31(6), 1078–1090 (2008)
6. Bessho, M., Kobayashi, S., Koshizuka, N., Sakamurai, K.: A Pedestrian Navigation System using Multiple Space-Identifying Devices based on a Unique Identifier Framework. In: International Conference on Machine Learning and Cybernetics (2007)
7. Bessho, M., Kobayashi, S., Koshizuka, N., Sakamura, K.: uNavi: Implementation and Deployment of a Place-Based Pedestrian Navigation System. In: COMPSAC 2008, pp. 1254–1259 (2008)
8. Blunck, H., Godsk, T., Grønbæk, K., Kjærgaard, M.B., Jensen, J.L., Scharling, T., Schougaard, K.R., Toftkjær, T.: PerPos: a platform providing cloud services for pervasive positioning. In: COM.Geo (2010)
9. Butz, A., Baus, J., Krüger, A., Lohse, M.: A hybrid indoor navigation system. In: IUI 2001, pp. 25–32 (2001)
10. Dijkstra, E.: A note on two problems in connexion with graphs. Numerical Mathematics (1), 269–271 (1959)
11. Gartner, G., Frank, A., Retscher, G.: Pedestrian Navigation System - in Mixed Indoor/Outdoor Environment – The NAVIO Project. In: Proceedings of the CORP 2004 and Geomultimedia 2004 Symposium, Vienna, Austria, February 24-27, pp. 165–171 (2004)
12. Glanzer, G., Walder, U.: Self-contained indoor pedestrian navigation by means of human motion analysis and magnetic field mapping. In: WPNC 2010, pp. 303–307 (2010)
13. Hershberger, J., Suri, S.: An optimal algorithm for Euclidean shortest paths in the plane. SIAM Journal on Computing 28(6), 2215–2256 (1999)
14. Hightower, J., Brumitt, B., Borriello, G.: The location stack: a layered model for location in ubiquitous computing. In: Proceedings of the 4th IEEE Workshop on Mobile Computing Systems and Applications (2002)

15. Hile, H., Grzeszczuk, R., Liu, A., Vedantham, R., Košecka, J., Borriello, G.: Landmark-Based Pedestrian Navigation with Enhanced Spatial Reasoning. In: Tokuda, H., Beigl, M., Friday, A., Brush, A.J.B., Tobe, Y. (eds.) Pervasive 2009. LNCS, vol. 5538, pp. 59–76. Springer, Heidelberg (2009)

16. Kjærgaard, M.B., Blunck, H., Godsk, T., Toftkjær, T., Christensen, D.L., Grønbæk, K.: Indoor Positioning Using GPS Revisited. In: Floréen, P., Krüger, A., Spasojevic, M. (eds.) Pervasive 2010. LNCS, vol. 6030, pp. 38–56. Springer, Heidelberg (2010)

17. Küpper, A., Treu, G., Linnhoff-Popien, C.: Trax: a device-centric middleware framework for location-based services. IEEE Communications Magazine 44(9), 114–120 (2006)

18. Meng, L., Reichenbacher, T., Zipf, A.: Map-based Mobile Services - Theories, Methods and Implementations, 260 pages. Springer, Heidelberg (2005) ISBN 3-540-23055-6

19. Ladetto, Q., Gabaglio, V., Merminod, B.: International Symposium on Location Based Services for Cellular Users, Locellus (2001)

20. Langdal, J., Schougaard, K.R., Kjærgaard, M.B., Toftkjær, T.: PerPos: A Translucent Positioning Middleware Supporting Adaptation of Internal Positioning Processes. In: Gupta, I., Mascolo, C. (eds.) Middleware 2010. LNCS, vol. 6452, pp. 232–251. Springer, Heidelberg (2010)

21. May, A.J., Ross, R., Bayer, S.H., Tarkiainen, M.J.: Pedestrian navigation aids: information requirements and design implications. Personal Ubiquitous Comput. 7(6), 331–338 (2003)

22. Narzt, W., Pomberger, G., Ferscha, A., Kolb, D., Müller, R., Wieghardt, J., Hörtner, H., Lindinger, C.: Augmented reality navigation systems. Universal Access in the Information Society, vol. 4(3), pp. 177–187. Springer, Heidelberg (2006) ISSN 1615-5289

23. Ohlbach, H.J., Stoffel, E.P.: Versatile Route Descriptions for Pedestrian Guidance in Buildings–Conceptual Model and Systematic Method. In: AGILE 2008 Proc. (2008)

24. Pielot, M., Boll, S.: *Tactile Wayfinder*: Comparison of Tactile Waypoint Navigation with Commercial Pedestrian Navigation Systems. In: Floréen, P., Krüger, A., Spasojevic, M. (eds.) Pervasive 2010. LNCS, vol. 6030, pp. 76–93. Springer, Heidelberg (2010)

25. Ranganathan, A., Al-Muhtadi, J., Chetan, S., Campbell, R., Mickunas, M.D.: MiddleWhere: A Middleware for Location Awareness in Ubiquitous Computing Applications. In: Jacobsen, H.-A. (ed.) Middleware 2004. LNCS, vol. 3231, pp. 397–416. Springer, Heidelberg (2004)

26. Ruppel, P., Gschwandtner, F., Schindhelm, C.K., Linnhoff-Popien, C.: Indoor Navigation on Distributed Stationary Display Systems. In: COMPSAC, vol. (1), pp. 37–44 (2009)

27. Stevenson, G., Ye, J., Dobson, S., Nixon, P.: LOC8: A Location Model and Extensible Framework for Programming with Location. IEEE Pervasive Computing 9(1), 28–37 (2010)

28. Stoffel, E.-P., Lorenz, B., Ohlbach, H.J.: Towards a Semantic Spatial Model for Pedestrian Indoor Navigation. In: Hainaut, J.-L., Rundensteiner, E.A., Kirchberg, M., Bertolotto, M., Brochhausen, M., Chen, Y.-P.P., Cherfi, S.S.-S., Doerr, M., Han, H., Hartmann, S., Parsons, J., Poels, G., Rolland, C., Trujillo, J., Yu, E., Zimányie, E. (eds.) ER Workshops 2007. LNCS, vol. 4802, pp. 328–337. Springer, Heidelberg (2007)

29. Toftkjær, T.: Accurate Positioning of Pedestrians in Mixed Indoor/Outdoor Settings: A Particle Filter Approach to Sensor and Map Fusion. PhD. Dissertation, Aarhus University, Department of Computer Science

30. Völkel, T., Kühn, R., Weber, G.: Mobility Impaired Pedestrians Are Not Cars: Requirements for the Annotation of Geographical Data. In: Miesenberger, K., Klaus, J., Zagler, W.L., Karshmer, A.I. (eds.) ICCHP 2008. LNCS, vol. 5105, pp. 1085–1092. Springer, Heidelberg (2008)

31. Ye, J., Coyle, L., Dobson, S., Nixon, P.: A Unified Semantics Space Model. In: Hightower, J., Schiele, B., Strang, T. (eds.) LoCA 2007. LNCS, vol. 4718, pp. 103–120. Springer, Heidelberg (2007)

Estimating Position Relation between Two Pedestrians Using Mobile Phones

Daisuke Kamisaka[1], Takafumi Watanabe[1], Shigeki Muramatsu[1],
Arei Kobayashi[2], and Hiroyuki Yokoyama[1]

[1] KDDI R&D Laboratories Inc., 2-1-15 Ohara, Fujimino-shi, Saitama 356-8502, Japan
{da-kamisaka,tk-watanabe,mura,yokoyama}@kddilabs.jp
[2] KDDI CORPORATION, 3-10-10 Iidabashi, Chiyoda-ku, Tokyo 102-8640, Japan
ar-kobayashi@kddi.com

Abstract. In a complex indoor environment such as a huge station in an urban area, sometimes the direction and distance relative to another person are more important for pedestrians than their absolute positions, e.g. to search for a lost child. We define this information as the position relation. Our goal is to develop a position relation estimation method on a mobile phone with built-in motion sensors. In literature, methods of cooperative navigation using two pedestrians' positions estimated by pedestrian dead reckoning and a range sensor have been proposed. However, these methods cannot be applied to a mobile phone because pedestrian dead reckoning does not work well when a mobile phone is in a bag, and because there is no range sensor in a phone. In fact, no Bluetooth is reliable as a substitute range sensor. This paper proposes another approach to estimate the position relation of pedestrians. Our method finds the timing when two pedestrians are in close proximity to each other and walk together by using Bluetooth as a proximity sensor and corrects the parameters of position updates dynamically, even if absolute positions are unknown. The algorithm and evaluation results are presented in this paper.

Keywords: relative position, pedestrian dead reckoning, cooperative navigation, indoor positioning, gait analysis, accelerometer, magnetometer, mobile phone.

1   Introduction

Sometimes people are interested in other people's position relative to their own in an indoor environment, for example, to meet a friend in a crowded station, to search for a lost child in a commercial complex, or to grasp directions and distances of team members in fire-fighting operations. Location based services such as Google Latitude [1] do not satisfy these needs. Many indoor positioning techniques focus on finding one's own absolute position. Such people know their own absolute positions, but do not know the whereabouts of the person they are looking for. The information they need is in "which direction" to go and "how far" from where they are. We call this the "position relation."

J. Kay et al. (Eds.): Pervasive 2012, LNCS 7319, pp. 307–324, 2012.
© Springer-Verlag Berlin Heidelberg 2012

Our final goal is to develop a method of estimating the position relation between two pedestrians even in an indoor environment, using mobile phones with built-in motion sensors. When the absolute positions are accurate, the position relation between them is also accurate. However, there is no infallible indoor positioning method. Pedestrian Dead Reckoning (PDR) is a promising technique and has become more practical today because the use of mobile phones with built-in motion sensors (e.g. Android phones and iPhones) has spread widely throughout the world and such devices have become more familiar to individuals. PDR incrementally estimates the current position using motion sensors such as an accelerometer and a magnetometer without any external infrastructures even in an indoor environment, but it also has weaknesses. Two pedestrians' positions are sometimes estimated to be far apart due to accumulative errors even though actually they are walking together. Hybrid positioning techniques that integrate PDR and a range measurement (e.g. laser range finder) between the two pedestrians to improve positioning accuracy have been proposed. If we apply this technique to off-the-shelf mobile phones, there is no other choice but to use Bluetooth as a range sensor. Unfortunately, the distance accuracy of Bluetooth is insufficient as a range sensor. Another problem is that PDR estimates would be unreliable when a mobile phone is not fixed to the pedestrian's body, e.g. in a bag.

To obtain the position relation between two pedestrians, absolute position is a sufficient but unnecessary condition. It can also be gained without accurate absolute positions. Therefore, we changed our perspective and focused on estimating position relations without absolute positions.

We defined the position relation of two persons represented by two metrics: a distance and a relative angle. Figure 1 shows (a) absolute positions and (b) position relation. The relative angle from $\mathbf{p}^A$ to $\mathbf{p}^B$ is a clockwise angle from the heading direction of $\mathbf{p}^A$ to $\mathbf{p}^B$. Absolute positions $\mathbf{p}^{A1}$ and $\mathbf{p}^{A2}$, and $\mathbf{p}^{B1}$ and $\mathbf{p}^{B2}$ are obviously different, whereas their position relations are equally represented by the distance d^{AB} and the relative angle ω^{AB} as shown in (b). In other words, position relation estimation can work even under the condition that absolute position estimation does not work. We propose a simple approach for estimating the position relation. Our method detects timings at which the two pedestrians are walking together and adjusts parameters to transform the difference of positioning errors. It takes no account of whether the azimuth is north or south.

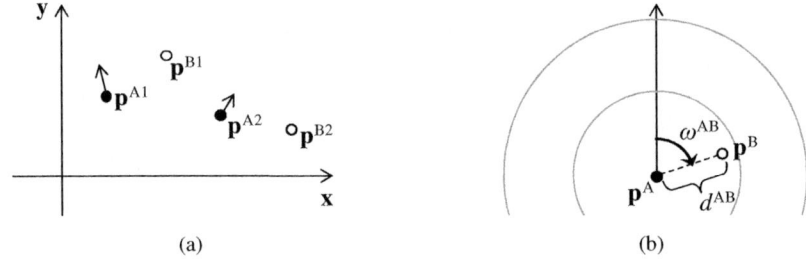

(a)   (b)

Fig. 1. Absolute positions and position relation

2   Related Work

There are two approaches to obtain the position relation: estimating each person's absolute position and directly estimating the position relation without the absolute position.

PDR is a typical positioning method for an indoor environment with no external infrastructures such as a Global Positioning System (GPS) or WiFi [3]. It measures and accumulates movements of the pedestrian relative to the previously determined position to estimate an absolute position. The positioning errors are accumulated [4], and thus errors of position relation between two pedestrians are also accumulated. Various techniques to suppress such errors have been studied. Hybrid positioning integrates multiple positioning methods to improve positioning accuracy. Integrating PDR with absolute positioning such as GPS or WiFi is effective [2, 5, 6, 7]. An Extended Kalman Filter (EKF) is often used because it integrates multiple observed inputs including different uncertainties [11]. Frank et al. proposed an indoor positioning system for pedestrians using PDR and WiFi fingerprinting [5]. Kourogi et al. presented a pedestrian navigation system using PDR, GPS, and radio-frequency identification (RFID) [2]. Both systems require an external infrastructure. Cooperative navigation is also a type of hybrid positioning, but it does not require any external infrastructure. It integrates two pedestrians' positions and the range measurement between them. Strömbäck et al. proposed a cooperative sensor fusion using a foot-mounted inertial measurement unit and ultra-wideband (UWB)-ranging equipment assuming solders etc. [8]. Rui et al. proposed a cooperative positioning system between two autonomous underwater vehicles using acoustic ranging [9].

If we apply those methods to mobile phones, there is no other choice but to use Bluetooth as a range sensor. However, Bluetooth has a great degree of uncertainty because its reception conditions heavily depend on the device, the environment, and the situation due to shadowing, multipath fading and orientation of antenna [10], and its communication distance is limited (up to 100 m, Class 1). Some studies use Bluetooth for ranging or localization. Kotanen et al. presented local positioning with Bluetooth using a radio wave propagation model, but they say that the threshold levels necessary to convert the received signal strength indication (RSSI) value to a received power level are defined quite loosely for positioning purposes [12]. Sheng et al. also proposed a position measurement using Bluetooth by disabling the automatic transmission power control, but it is evaluated under the line-of-sight condition only [13]. Moreover, even if range measurements are accurate, the relative angle is not corrected in principle. EKF is useful and powerful but just a tool for integration, thus if the inputs include widely-distributed errors, EKF cannot extract accurate results.

Due to these issues with estimating absolute positions, we selected another approach. To the best of our knowledge, there are no studies that address the position relation of multiple pedestrians without absolute positions. We used Bluetooth as a proximity sensor and locally adjusted two pedestrians' positioning results when proximity was detected while the two persons were walking.

3   Position Relation Estimation

3.1   Application Scenario and Requirements

We focused on estimating the position relation of two pedestrians (called nodes) who are initially walking together and then apart. We assumed the following application scenario: A couple is shopping in a huge mall (GPS-denied environment). The man and woman have ordinary mobile phones respectively in their trouser pocket and bag (major positions of mobile phones for males and females according to a global survey regarding phone carrying behavior in public spaces [14]). They shop together at first, but then go their separate ways and begin to shop freely at some point. After the man finishes shopping, he wishes to join the woman but is not sure where she is now. Then, he pulls out his mobile phone and starts to search for her using an application launched beforehand. Once it is launched, the application continues tracking the position relation of the persons and displays the relative angle and the distance to the other person from the user.

According to the application scenario above, we defined the following requirements and conditions:

- An ordinary mobile phone with a built-in motion sensor (an accelerometer and a magnetometer) is used.
- No external positioning references (such as GPS and WiFi) are used.
- No extra devices (such as range finder) are used.
- The mobile phone is carried in a trouser pocket or bag.

3.2   Errors of Bluetooth and PDR

1. Errors of Bluetooth

Bluetooth RSSI is not a reliable way of estimating the distance between two nodes but is useful for proximity detection. Figure 2 shows RSSI vs. the distance between two nodes observed by mobile phones in a park. The RSSI value does not mean received power directly and is represented in proportion to the ideal received power range called the Golden Receive Power Range [12]. It depends on devices [15] (this is one of the reasons that distance estimation is difficult).

According to Fig. 2(a), the more distant the two nodes are, the more widely the RSSI distribute. For example, at measured RSSI = -11 (r1), the actual distances are distributed in the 10 m to 120 m range with a standard deviation of 21.6 m. Therefore, it is difficult to use Bluetooth RSSI as a range sensor. However, at RSSI = 0 (r2), the actual distances are concentrated within 10 m and the mean and the standard deviation of the distances remain 1.39 m and 1.36 m, respectively. Therefore, we can identify that two nodes are in proximity when measured RSSI indicates 0 (the maximum). Figure 2(b) shows detailed densities of the actual distance for both RSSI values.

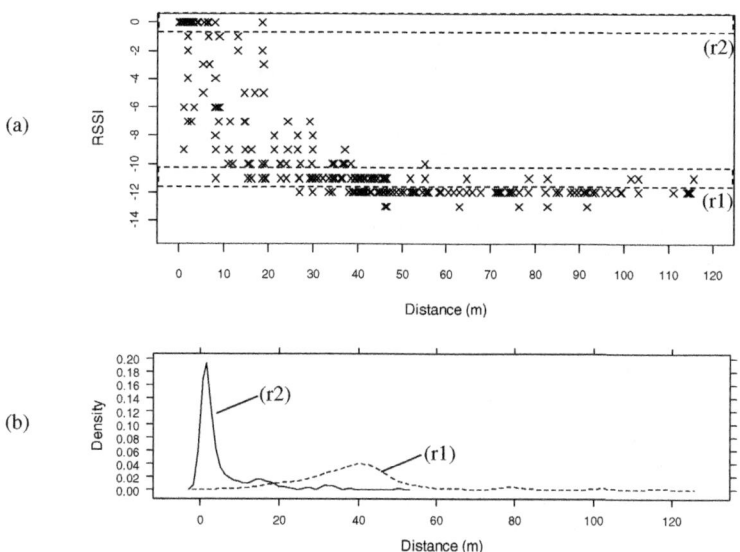

Fig. 2. Distance vs. RSSI and distance distributions ((r1) RSSI = -11, and (r2) RSSI = 0)

2. Errors of PDR

Typical PDR consists of three core techniques: step detection, step length estimation, and heading direction estimation [6, 16, 17]. A previous study reported that the position errors of PDR can be approximated by Gaussian distribution [2]. This is correct as long as the sensor is tightly fixed on the user's body. Otherwise the estimated positions i.e. step length and heading direction sometimes involve bias errors.

Figure 3 shows position errors per one step regarding four typical cases recorded independently. The correct azimuth angle is 0° (i.e. north) and the step length is normalized by the correct length for each step, thus the coordinate (0, 1) is the correct destination from the origin (0, 0). Case (a) is an ideal case that has few errors. In Case (b) the estimated positions are overrun due to biased step lengths. Generally, the step length is maintained at a constant value in one walk as long as he/she walks at a constant speed [19], so the estimation error emerges as a bias error. In Case (c), the estimated directions are offset to the west. This is caused by the orientation offset of the mobile phone with respect to the user's body, or the acceleration component generated by the body movement. Case (d) is the situation in which the sensor is in the bag. It indicates that the lateral axis was taken for the forward axis. There are some PDR methods with sensors not fixed on the pedestrian's body (e.g. pocket [16] and hand [17]) and a technique which could estimate where the mobile phone is [24], but to the best of our knowledge, a PDR method in the case where the sensor is carried in a bag has not yet been studied. Randell et al. evaluated PDR using sensors in a backpack, and reported that it was less accurate [18]. If sensors are in a bag, it is difficult to identify the heading direction in which the user is moving even if the orientation of the sensors is identified. In this case, the resultant estimated direction will be unexpected.

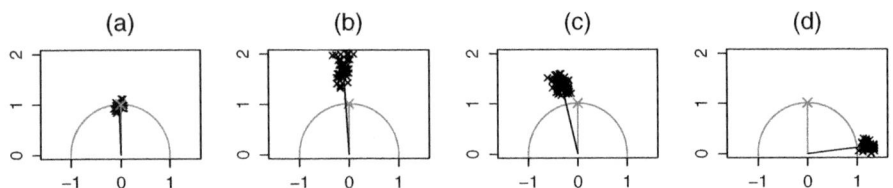

Fig. 3. Errors of directions and step lengths in four cases: (a) ideal case, (b) bias error of step length, (c) bias error of heading direction, and (d) direction estimation failure (bag)

According to these errors, both range measurements using Bluetooth equipped with a mobile phone and PDR when a mobile phone is in a bag are unreliable. Therefore, simply integrating them by existing methods is also ineffective.

However, Bluetooth is usable not as a range sensor, but a proximity sensor. The biased absolute positions cannot be corrected without some additional inputs such as GPS, but position relation can be estimated by integrating two pedestrians' different biased results (e.g. (b) and (d)). The basic idea of our method is to adjust two node's biases so that their movements are equivalent when Bluetooth detects that they are in close proximity to each other.

3.3   Principle

Let $\mathbf{p}_n^A = [x_n^A \ y_n^A]^T$ and $\mathbf{p}_k^B = [x_k^B \ y_k^B]^T$ be local position vectors of two nodes A and B at step n and k, respectively. The position relation between these two nodes, $\mathbf{R}_{n,k}^{AB}$, is represented as $\mathbf{R}_{n,k}^{AB} = (d^{AB}, \omega^{AB})$ as shown in Fig. 4.

The estimated positions of each node include different bias errors of step length and direction. This means that the two nodes are on different local coordinate systems. To obtain the position relation is to estimate the coordinate transform matrix $\mathbf{T}^{AB}$ to integrate these two local coordinate systems. $\mathbf{T}^{AB}$ is a two-by-two matrix containing a scaling factor and a rotation factor. The world coordinate system is not necessary. The principle of our method is to dynamically update $\mathbf{T}^{AB}$ when the two nodes are in close proximity to each other to maintain equivalency of both the local coordinate systems. We defined two states, *Near-field state* and *Far-field state*, based on whether the two nodes are in close proximity to each other, as shown in Fig. 5.

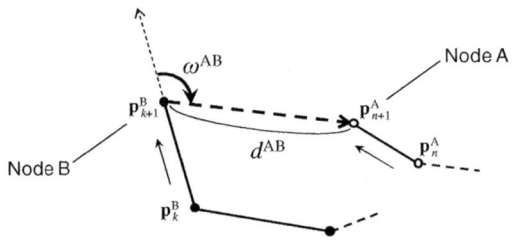

Fig. 4. Position relation

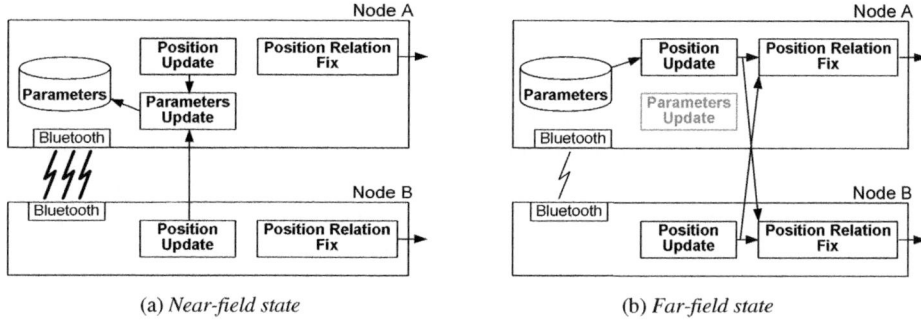

(a) *Near-field state*   (b) *Far-field state*

Fig. 5. System architecture and two states

(a) *Near-field state*: The two nodes are in close proximity to each other. This is the training phase. $\mathbf{T}^{AB}$ is updated using the position changes that the two nodes traveled in this state. The position relation outputs are maintained at a specific constant value because the fact they are in close proximity to each other is apparent to them and estimation is unnecessary.

(b) *Far-field state*: The two nodes are not in such close proximity to each other. This is the standalone phase. The changes of each node's local positions are tracked independently and the position relation between them is updated using the most recent $\mathbf{T}^{AB}$.

The state transition occurs based on Bluetooth RSSI. When a measured RSSI value indicates the maximum constant $RSSI_{max}$, the state is the *Near-field state*, otherwise the *Far-field state*. $RSSI_{max} = 0$ in most devices. We assume that the data between the two nodes are exchanged via Bluetooth if available, or the cellular network.

The three main components of our method, the position update (tracking), the parameters update (adjusting), and the position relation fix are explained in the following subsections.

3.4   Position Update (Tracking)

Position update tracks each node's local position changes used to fix the position relation when in the *Far-field state* and to update the parameter $\mathbf{T}^{AB}$ when in the *Near-field state*. Existing PDR methods can be employed as the position update but it is just an option because an absolute azimuth angle and a common coordinate system shared by the two nodes are not required. The only requirement is tracking the node's position changes locally.

When a new step for each node is detected, each local position is updated as follows:

$$\mathbf{p}_{n+1}^{A} = \mathbf{p}_{n}^{A} + \mathbf{T}_{n+1}^{AB}\mathbf{d}_{n+1}^{A}, \quad \mathbf{p}_{k+1}^{B} = \mathbf{p}_{k}^{B} + \mathbf{d}_{k+1}^{B}$$

$$\mathbf{d}_{n+1}^{A} = \begin{bmatrix} l_{n+1}^{A}\sin\theta_{n+1}^{A} \\ l_{n+1}^{A}\cos\theta_{n+1}^{A} \end{bmatrix}, \quad \mathbf{d}_{k+1}^{B} = \begin{bmatrix} l_{k+1}^{B}\sin\theta_{k+1}^{B} \\ l_{k+1}^{B}\cos\theta_{k+1}^{B} \end{bmatrix} \tag{1}$$

where l^A_{n+1} and l^B_{k+1} are step lengths, θ^A_{n+1} and θ^B_{k+1} are direction angles, $\mathbf{d}^A_{n+1}$ and $\mathbf{d}^B_{k+1}$ are step vectors for A and B, and $\mathbf{T}^{AB}_{n+1}$ is the most recent coordinate transform matrix at this time, respectively. Each θ shows the relative angle from each initial direction, so does not directly indicate an azimuth angle in which the pedestrian is heading. The position update counts steps (increments n and k), and estimates step length l and direction θ, so it mainly consists of three components: step detection, step length estimation and direction estimation. It is performed by each node independently. Note that for simplicity in the notation we do not use the node subscript A and B.

1. Step detection

The number of steps is counted by detecting peaks of the gravitational component of the acceleration measured by an accelerometer. Figure 6 shows the typical time series of the gravitational component of acceleration while the same person is walking. It is calculated by $\mathbf{a}_t \cdot \mathbf{G}$ ('$\cdot$' denotes a dot product operation), where $\mathbf{a}_t$ is a 3-axis acceleration vector measured at time t and $\mathbf{G}$ is a 3-axis gravity vector approximated by the simple mean of acceleration vectors measured within a time sufficiently long to the gait cycle (approximately 0.5 sec) given by $\mathbf{G} = \Sigma_m \mathbf{a}_i$ ($m \geq 2f_s$), where f_s is the sampling rate of the sensor. According to the figure, the peaks are easily counted even if the sensor is in a bag as well as when the sensor is carried at the waist.

2. Step length estimation

The step length at time t is estimated by linear approximation according to the following equation:

$$l_t = r_c c_t + r_h h + b \tag{2}$$

where l_t and c_t are step length and cadence (steps per minute) at time t, h is the height of the pedestrian, and r_c, r_h and b are their coefficients trained by multi-regression analysis, respectively. Some previous studies employed vertical acceleration amplitude into their step length approximation [6, 20]; however, we do not employ such methods because it varies with the carrying positions of a mobile phone. The technique is further discussed in [17].

3. Direction estimation

Direction estimation tracks direction changes of the node. It is obtained by two elements: a base vector fixed to the pedestrian's body, and a frame of reference anchored in the Earth's surface.

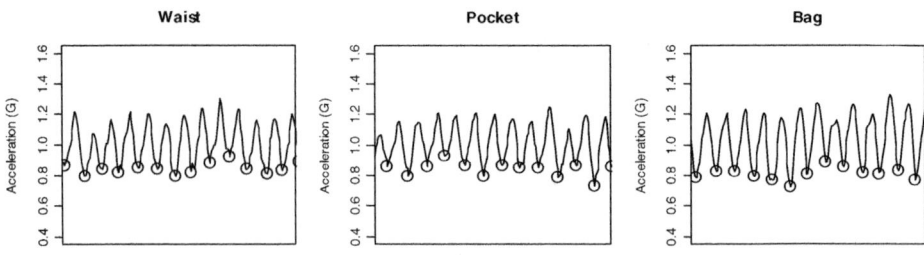

Fig. 6. Gravitational acceleration component and step timings (denoted as '$\circ$')

The only thing the base vector has to do is to indicate a consistent direction with respect to the pedestrian's body (i.e. it does not require indication of the forward direction in which the pedestrian is heading), so an arbitrary vector $\mathbf{B} = [b_x\ b_y\ b_z]^T$ can be used as the base vector.

The frame of reference is a north-and-east coordinate system represented by two orthogonal vectors, the east vector $\mathbf{E} = \mathbf{G} \times \mathbf{M}$ and the north vector $\mathbf{N} = \mathbf{E} \times \mathbf{G}$ ('×' denotes a cross product operation). The magnetic vector $\mathbf{M}$ can be approximated by $\mathbf{M} = \Sigma_m \mathbf{m}_i$ ($m \geq 2f_s$), where $\mathbf{m}$ is a 3-axis magnetic vector measured by a magnetometer.

For simplicity, we define a clockwise angle from vector $\mathbf{a} = [x_a\ y_a]^T$ to $\mathbf{b} = [x_b\ y_b]^T$ as:

$$A(\mathbf{a},\mathbf{b}) = \alpha \arccos\left(\frac{\mathbf{a} \cdot \mathbf{b}}{\|\mathbf{a}\|\|\mathbf{b}\|}\right) + \beta \qquad \left(\alpha, \beta = \begin{cases} 1, & 0 \quad (x_a y_b - x_b y_a < 0) \\ -1, & 2\pi \quad (\text{Otherwise}) \end{cases}\right) \tag{3}$$

The direction angle θ is given by $\theta = A(\mathbf{N}, \mathbf{B}')$, where $\mathbf{B}'$ is the projection of $\mathbf{B}$ on the Earth's surface in the frame of reference given by $\mathbf{B}' = [\mathbf{B} \cdot \mathbf{E}\ \ \mathbf{B} \cdot \mathbf{N}]^T$.

For general PDR methods aiming at estimating absolute positions, $\mathbf{B}'$ must be the heading direction of the pedestrian, but if the mobile phone is not fixed to the body, it becomes extremely difficult because the heading of the mobile phone does not always correspond to the heading of the pedestrian. However, because just for the position relations, the position update is free of the influence of the absolute direction, $\mathbf{B}$ can be an arbitrary constant vector.

3.5 Parameters Update (Adjusting)

Parameters update estimates $\mathbf{T}^{AB}$ for adjusting A's local coordinate system to match that of B's. It contains two parameters, a scaling factor of step length r^{AB} and a clockwise rotation factor φ^{AB}, as follows:

$$\mathbf{T}^{AB} = \begin{bmatrix} r^{AB} \cos\varphi^{AB} & r^{AB} \sin\varphi^{AB} \\ -r^{AB} \sin\varphi^{AB} & r^{AB} \cos\varphi^{AB} \end{bmatrix} \tag{4}$$

The parameters are updated when the following two conditions are satisfied.

- Both nodes continue walking at least N steps.
- Standard deviation of the estimated directions of each node during the *Near-field state* is less than threshold S. This means each node walks almost straight.

The two parameters are updated when in the *Near-field state* so that their movements are equivalent as shown in Fig. 7. When A and B satisfy the condition at step n to $n+i$ and k to $k+j$ respectively ($i \geq N$, $j \geq N$), r^{AB} is set so that the two nodes' straight-line distances traveled in i and j steps are equal, and φ^{AB} is calculated so that the two nodes' mean directions in i and j steps are equal, given by the following equations:

$$r^{AB} = \left\|\mathbf{p}^B_{k+j} - \mathbf{p}^B_k\right\|\left\|\mathbf{p}^A_{n+i} - \mathbf{p}^A_n\right\|^{-1}$$
$$\varphi^{AB} = A\left(\mathbf{p}^A_{n+i} - \mathbf{p}^A_n, \mathbf{p}^B_{k+j} - \mathbf{p}^B_k\right) \tag{5}$$

When the transition from the *Near-field state* to *Far-field state* occurs at time t, $\mathbf{T}^{AB}$ will be rollbacked to that at $t - T_G$ to avoid using $\mathbf{T}^{AB}$ estimated in an unstable moment to which the state is about to transition.

3.6   Position Relation Fix

The position relation output at step n and k is switched based on the state as follows:

$$\mathbf{R}_{n,k}^{AB} = (d^{AB}, \omega^{AB}) = \begin{cases} \left(\left\| \mathbf{p}_{n+1}^{A} - \mathbf{p}_{k+1}^{B} \right\|, \quad A\left(\mathbf{d}_{k+1}^{B}, \mathbf{p}_{n+1}^{A} - \mathbf{p}_{k+1}^{B} \right) \right) & (Far-field\ state) \\ (0, \qquad\qquad N/A) & (Near-field\ state) \end{cases} \quad (6)$$

When in the *Near-field state*, the position relation estimation is unnecessary for the pedestrians because the fact they are in close proximity to each other is apparent to them. As a result, the distance error is reset to a low level (within a distance in which the RSSI value can be maintained at 0).

4   Evaluation and Results

4.1   Experimental Setup

We evaluated our method using sensor data collected while walking. We prepared test courses in an open-sky environment, Shinjuku Gyoen National Garden [21] and Yoyogi Park [22] to eliminate location-dependent magnetic anomalies and evaluate the potential performance of our method under a normal geomagnetic field. The subjects numbered a total of 16 males and females, divided into 8 pairs. Each pair consisted of close friends and they walked the specified route at a natural pace. They could chat freely while walking. Each pair started to walk together from one end of the course, then parted to go different routes, and finally met up again and stopped at

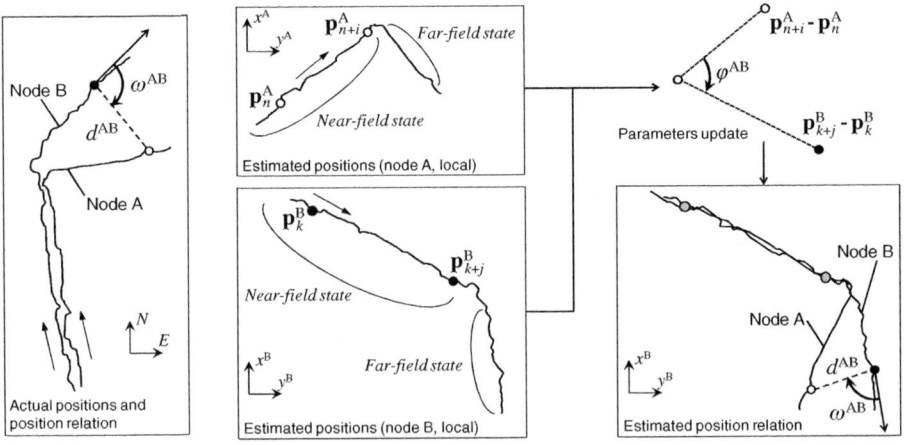

Fig. 7. Parameters update process to calculate the two factors of $\mathbf{T}^{AB}$

another end of the course, two times. The routes were approximately 290-390 m long (depending on each pair). Figure 8 shows an example. The distance between the two nodes is up to approximately 90 m across bushes. In such case, Bluetooth was disconnected. Each subject carried two mobile phones (SOLAR PHONE SH007 [23]): one mobile phone was fixed at his/her waist and the other mobile phone was carried in a trouser pocket (male) or put in a bag (female). The mobile phone records a 3-axis acceleration and magnetism at 32 Hz, and Bluetooth RSSI. The evaluation was performed offline after the data collection experiment was finished. We defined a female subject as A and a male subject as B. The thresholds used are: $N = 10$, $S = 20°$, $T_G = 10$ [sec], respectively. The parameters r_c, r_h, b and h are determined with respect to each subject.

We compared our method with a single position update as a typical PDR for reference and with a typical range-measurement-based method using EKF [9] (called RMB). The single position update updates the positions with no adjustment. Regarding RMB, the estimated position is corrected while Bluetooth is connected, based on $D(RSSI) = d_{max}^{(RSSI/RSSI_{min})}$, where d_{max} is the maximum distance at which the two nodes can keep connected and $RSSI_{min}$ is the RSSI when a distance between the two nodes equals d_{max}. These values were set as: $d_{max} = 70$ [m] and $RSSI_{min} = -13$, respectively. The parameters for EKF were optimized beforehand.

4.2   Summary of the Results

We evaluated the accuracies of the estimated position relation i.e. d^{AB} and ω^{AB}.

Figure 9 shows the mean absolute errors of estimated distances between the two nodes [m]. When the mobile phone was fixed at the waist, the errors remained at a low level regardless of the method. The mean errors were: 31.2 m for PDR, 16.0 m for RMB, and 9.9 m for the proposed method, respectively. When the mobile phones were in a pocket and a bag, the errors of PDR were significantly increased due to direction estimation failure whereas the errors of the other two methods were less increased. The mean errors were: 174.0 m for PDR, 25.4 m for RMB, and 12.9 m for the proposed method, respectively.

Fig. 8. Test course example at Shinjuku Gyoen National Garden

Figure 10 shows the mean absolute errors of relative angles from B to A [deg.]. When the mobile phone was fixed at the waist, the errors of PDR and RMB were sometimes over 60° whereas the errors of the proposed method were less than 35° for all pairs. The mean errors were: 35.6° for PDR, 54.7° for RMB, and 19.1° for the proposed method, respectively. When the mobile phone was not fixed, the errors of PDR were increased the same as the distance error. The errors of RMB exceeded those of PDR. RMB could adjust the distances but could not suppress relative angle errors. The mean errors were: 64.8° for PDR, 70.3° for RMB, and 26.4° for the proposed method, respectively. This shows that our method is capable of recognizing a 6-way relative angle on average even when the mobile phone is not fixed at the waist.

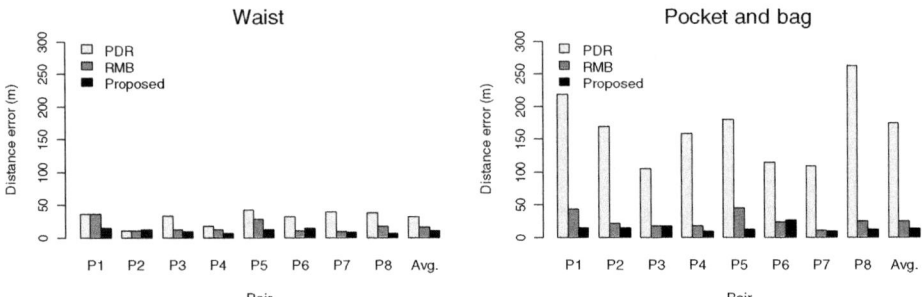

Fig. 9. Mean absolute distance error per pair

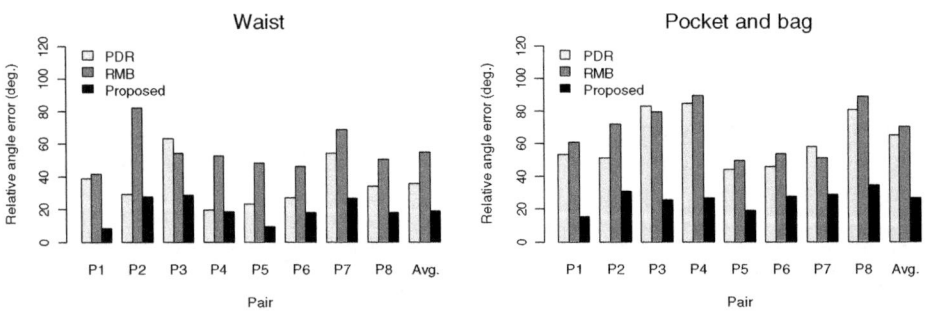

Fig. 10. Mean absolute relative angle error per pair

5   Discussion

5.1   Error Analysis

A radar plot is an effective way of visualizing the position relation from one's perspective to another person. We assume it is a basic application for position relation estimation. Both the distance and the relative angle are important for accurate radar plots. Figures 11 and 12 show examples of radar plots of A's relative positions from B's perspective for waist and pocket/bag, respectively. The point at time t is given by

$[d_t^{AB} \sin\omega_t^{AB} \ d_t^{AB} \cos\omega_t^{AB}]^T$. A symbol in the center (0, 0) stands for B and the top of the figure always corresponds to the forward direction of B.

All of these results indicate homothetic trajectories compared with actual trajectories in spite of the approximate 20° of relative angle errors described above. There are no significant differences between the pairs or the ways of carrying mobile phones. However, there are also several errors categorized into two types: the rotation error and the scaling error. The pair P1 in Fig. 11 and the pair P2 in Fig. 12 are typical examples of scaling error and rotation error, respectively. P6 in Fig. 12 includes both errors. The errors denoted as 'x' are the points when B was at a corner in the course where a slight time difference between actual and estimated data causes significant error.

Now, let us look at the two examples, P1 (waist) and P6 (pocket/bag). Figure 13(a) shows the two nodes' trajectories of P1 estimated by PDR and our method. The PDR's result includes both rotation and scaling errors, whereas our method's result adjusted those errors so that the two nodes can re-join. The shape of the adjusted trajectory is accurate and thus the relative angle is also accurate, but as a result, the entire trajectory is scaled down. The scaling factor r^{AB} used in the *Far-field state* was 0.82. When the distance between the two nodes is represented in a physical unit (i.e. meter), there is still the scaling difference between the local coordinate system shared with the two nodes and the actual world coordinate system remains. The bias error of step lengths of either A or B remains in the resultant estimation errors. In this case, we should adjust B to A, not A to B. Evaluating the reliability of the estimated step lengths online will allow our method to identify which node it is more appropriate to adjust. Step length is estimated using cadence, thus its reliability depends on the reliability of the step detection. The variance of time intervals of the step timings can be used as an index.

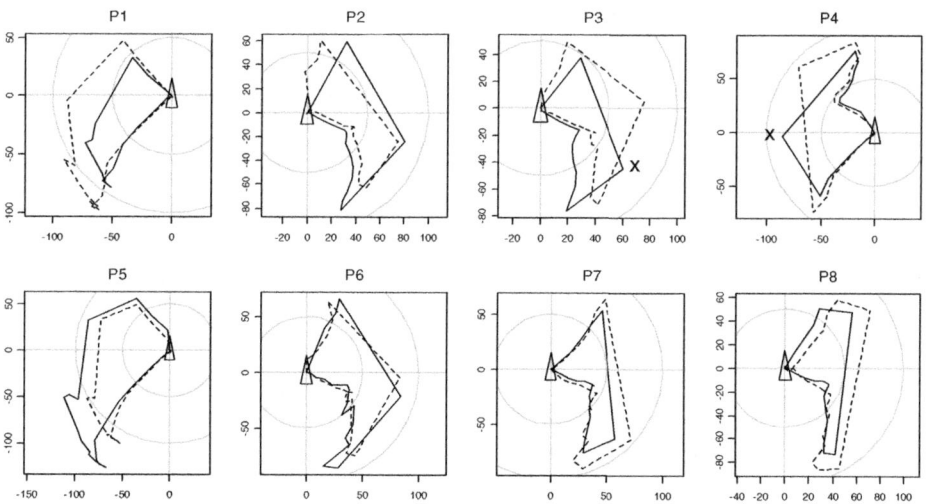

Fig. 11. Radar plot per pair (waist, dashed line: actual, solid line: estimated, unit: [m])

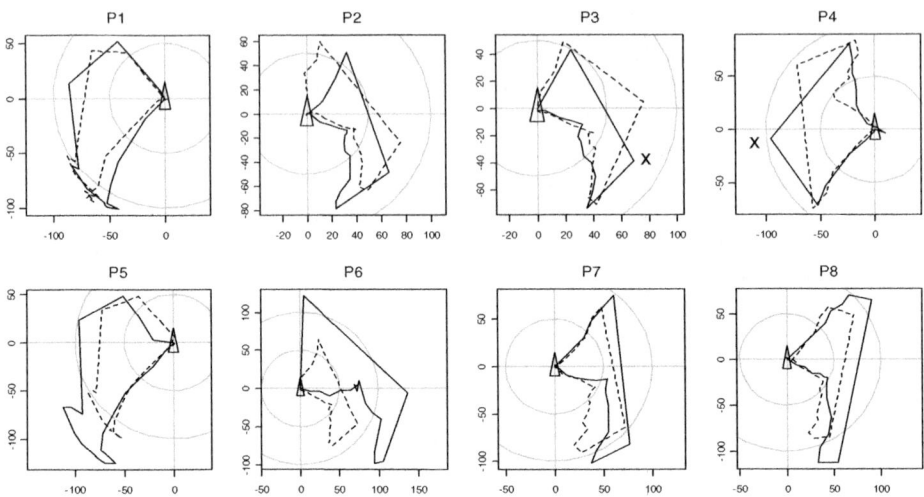

Fig. 12. Radar plot per pair (pocket/bag, dashed line: actual, solid line: estimated, unit: [m])

Figure 13(b) shows the two nodes' trajectories of P6. Our method's result seems to be similar to the actual one, but its scale is too large. There are several reasons for this. For B, the step timings were over-counted in spots due to acceleration disturbances, and thus the cadences were increased incorrectly, then the step lengths were longer than they actually were. As a result, r^{AB} used in the *Far-field state* reached as much as 2.1. This is an obviously invalid value, and therefore should be filtered out by post-processing. The step lengths of A were adjusted, so they were estimated to be walking parallel incorrectly, i.e. caused rotation error.

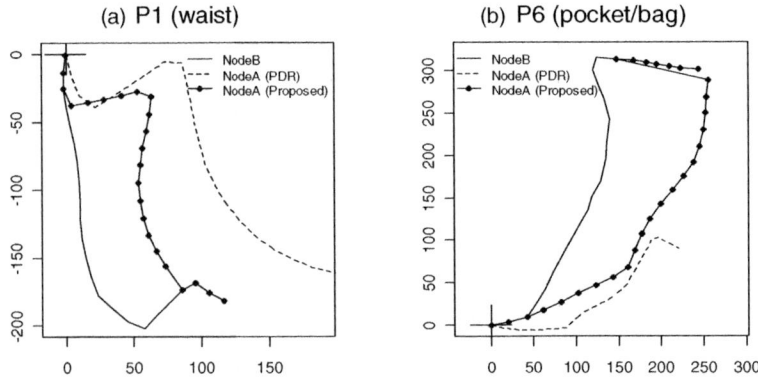

Fig. 13. Estimated local trajectories with the scaling errors ('+' denotes starting position)

5.2   Proposed Method vs. RMB

We compared our method and RMB by the radar plots. Figure 14 shows a typical example of the relative positions estimated by RMB and our method. The numbers in the figure indicate time. In Case (a), regarding RMB, when the time is less than 9, the trajectory was rotated from the actual whereas the distance was almost accurate; however, when the time is over 16, even the distance was shortened and as a result the entire trajectory was distorted. Our method's trajectory maintains its form with a few scaling errors. In Case (b), regarding RMB, the time 5-7 and 14-23 (i.e. within the inner circle), the estimated distances are comparatively correct, but the relative angles are significantly rotated from the actual. When the time is 8-13, the estimated trajectory is bound to the circle of 50 m and cannot come out of that because Bluetooth was connected but the measured RSSI value did not change. In principle, range measurement can only adjust the position on the straight line between the two nodes, thus the relative angle cannot be handled. Moreover, the estimated distance

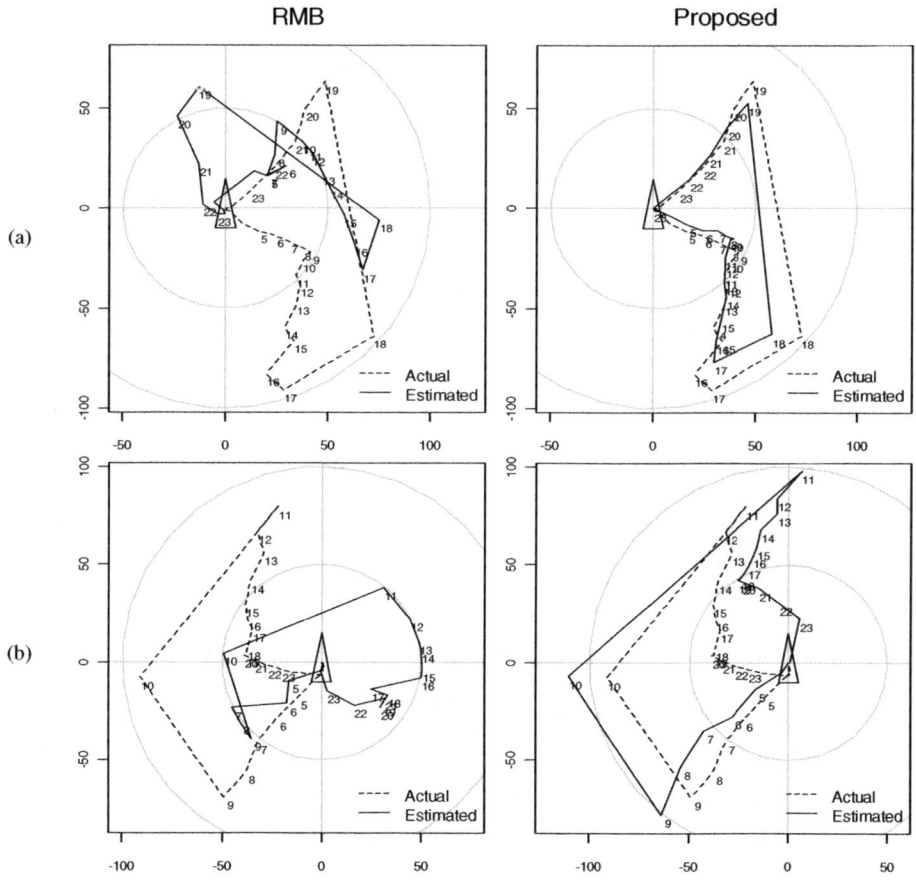

Fig. 14. RMB vs. the proposed method (radar plot, unit: [m])

using Bluetooth becomes more obscure along with the actual distance as discussed in Section 3.2. These two errors are the weak points of RMB. On the contrary, our method showed sufficiently good results to grasp the position relation visually, for both Cases (a) and (b).

5.3   Performance Simulation as a Guide Application

We assumed a navigation system that guides a pedestrian in the correct direction to meet and join another person, as described in Section 3.1. We simulated the time necessary for our method to guide B to reach distant A. To find and meet the other person, the estimated relative angle is more important than the distance because he/she can reach the person as long as the relative angle is correct even if the distance is incorrect, whereas the opposite is not true.

Figure 15 shows the relationship between relative angle error and estimated time necessary for B to reach A (the lower the better). The gray particles and the line plot stand for simulated necessary time, and the plotted points are the real data of each pair. The necessary time is normalized by the necessary time with no error (i.e. theoretical value).

The necessary time t_r for each pair of the mean absolute error μ_e and the standard deviation σ_e given is simulated according to the following procedure. First, (1) A is at rest 500 m away from B. Next, (2) B measures the relative position of A including error normally distributed around μ_e with standard deviation σ_e, then (3) B moves to the measured relative angle with a specified step length 0.7 m, (4) Step (2) and (3) are repeated, and finally (4) if the actual distance between the two nodes becomes less than 5 m, t_r is the number of steps at that time.

PDR and RMB are widely distributed, whereas our method is concentrated in the left side of the figure. To suppress the necessary time to less than 2.0, the relative angle error should remain less than 38°. The mean necessary time for each method is:

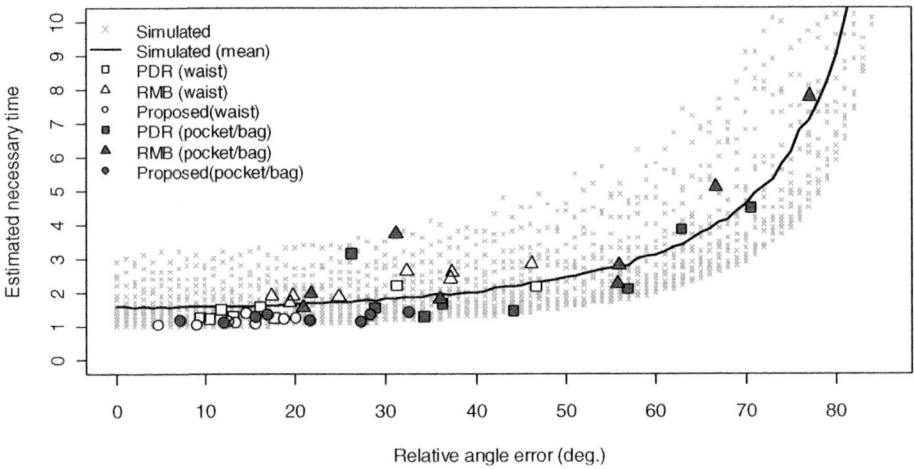

Fig. 15. Necessary time vs. relative angle error

3.2, 3.9, and 1.3 for PDR, RMB, and our method, respectively. In our method, 76.5% indicated less than 1.5, whereas only 44.1% of PDR and 11.8% of RMB were included. These results show that our method is effective for guiding a pedestrian to meet another person.

6   Conclusion

This paper presented the approach to estimate a position relation of two pedestrians in an indoor environment without estimating absolute positions.

The position relation estimation method presented in this paper adjusts the two local coordinate systems dynamically when the two nodes are walking together using Bluetooth as a proximity sensor. The experimental results show that our method is feasible in a real field because it effectively corrects both the relative angle and the distance, which previous methods find difficult to handle, even if the two pedestrians with mobile phones in a bag are far apart. The simulation results show that our method has the potential to guide one person to reach another person with a slight increase in necessary time compared with the theoretical value. Several errors are discussed, which are caused when the scaling factor is calculated using the step lengths with significant error.

The experiments were conducted in an outdoor environment at this time, but in an indoor environment such as a shopping mall, Bluetooth interference or reflections might occur and people would show different behaviors (e.g. more often lingering and much less straight walking). We aim to conduct further experiments in an indoor environment. In such a situation, the z-axis position relation (e.g. floor number) is also required. Recent smart phones equipped with a barometer would be available to track vertical movements. Nodes A and B are static roles at this time, but we plan to employ a dynamic role decision mechanism by evaluating the reliability of position updates of each node. The position updates in the *Far-field state* are a completely standalone process at this time, but we are currently investigating improvements that can be performed even in the *Far-field state*, for example, by detecting an inconsistency between the estimated distance and RSSI (i.e. the estimated distance is too short in spite of the *Far-field state*).

References

1. Google Latitude, http://www.google.com/latitude
2. Kourogi, M., Sakata, N., Okuma, T., Kurata, T.: Indoor/Outdoor Pedestrian Navigation with an Embedded GPS/RFID/Self-contained Sensor System. In: Pan, Z., Cheok, D.A.D., Haller, M., Lau, R., Saito, H., Liang, R. (eds.) ICAT 2006. LNCS, vol. 4282, pp. 1310–1321. Springer, Heidelberg (2006)
3. Mezentsev, O., Lachapelle, G., Collin, J.: Pedestrian Dead Reckoning – A Solution to Navigation in GPS Signal Degraded Areas. Geomatica 59(2), 175–182 (2005)
4. Fischer, C., Gellersen, H.: Location and Navigation Support for Emergency Responders: A Survey. Pervasive Computing, 38–47 (2010)

5. Frank, K., Krach, B., Catterall, N., Robertson, P.: Development and Evaluation of a Combined WLAN & Inertial Indoor Pedestrian Positioning System. ION GNSS (2009)
6. Fang, L., Antsaklis, P.J., Montestruque, L.A., McMickell, M.B., Lemmon, M., Sun, Y., Fang, H., Koutroulis, I., Haenggi, M., Xie, M., Xie, X.: Design of a Wireless Assisted Pedestrian Dead Reckoning System - The NavMote Experience. IEEE Trans. IMS 54, 2342–2358 (2005)
7. Cavallo, F., Sabatini, A.M., Genovese, V.: A step toward GPS/INS personal navigation systems: real-time assessment of gait by foot inertial sensing. In: Intelligent Robots and Systems (IROS) 2005, pp. 1187–1191 (2005)
8. Strömbäck, P., Rantakokko, J., Wirkander, S.-L., Alexandersson, M., Fors, I., Skog, I., Händel, P.: Foot-mounted inertial navigation and cooperative sensor fusion for indoor positioning. In: Proc. ION 2010 (2010)
9. Rui, G., Chitre, M.: Cooperative positioning using range-only measurements between two AUVs. In: Proc. OCEANS 2010. IEEE (2010)
10. Forno, F., Malnati, G., Portelli, G.: Design and Implementation of a Bluetooth ad hoc Network for Indoor Positioning. IEEE Proceedings-Softw. 152, 223–228 (2005)
11. Welch, G., Bishop, G.: An Introduction to the Kalman Filter. Dept. Comput. Sci., Univ. North Carolina, Chapel Hill, Tech. Rep. TR95041 (2000)
12. Kotanen, A., Hannikainen, M., Leppakoski, H., Hamalainen, T.D.: Experiments on Local Positioning with Bluetooth. In: Proc. ITCC 2003, April 28-30, pp. 297–303 (2003)
13. Sheng, Z., Pollard, J.K.: Position Measurement using Bluetooth. IEEE Trans. on Consumer Electronics 52(2), 555–558 (2006)
14. Cui, Y., Chipchase, J., Ichikawa, F.: A Cross Culture Study on Phone Carrying and Physical Personalization. In: Aykin, N. (ed.) HCII 2007. LNCS, vol. 4559, pp. 483–492. Springer, Heidelberg (2007)
15. Bardwell, J.: Converting Signal Strength Percentage to dBm Values. WildPackets White Paper (2002)
16. Steinhoff, U., Schiele, B.: Dead Reckoning from the Pocket - An Experimental Study. In: Proc. PerCom 2010 (2010)
17. Kamisaka, D., Muramatsu, S., Iwamoto, T., Yokoyama, H.: Design and Implementation of Pedestrian Dead Reckoning System on a Mobile Phone. IEICE Trans. ISS E94-D(6) (2011)
18. Randell, C., Djiallis, C., Muller, H.: Personal Position Measurement Using Dead Reckoning. In: Proc. ISWC 2003, pp. 166–173. IEEE Computer Society (2003)
19. Perry, J.: Gait Analysis: Normal and Pathological Function. SLACK Incorporated, Thorofare (1992)
20. Weinberg, H.: Using the ADXL202 in Pedometer and Personal Navigation Applications. APPLICATION NOTE AN-602, Analog Devices, Inc. (2002)
21. Ministry of the Environment Government of Japan: Shinjuku Gyoen National Garden, http://www.env.go.jp/garden/shinjukugyoen/english/index.html
22. Tokyo Metropolitan Park Association: Yoyogi Park, http://www.tokyo-park.or.jp/english/park/detail_03.html#yoyogi
23. SOLAR PHONE SH007, http://www.sharp.co.jp/products/sh007/
24. Harrison, C., Hudson, S.: Lightweight Material Detection for Placement-Aware Mobile Computing. In: Proc. UIST 2008, pp. 279–282 (2008)

Clearing a Crowd: Context-Supported Neighbor Positioning for People-Centric Navigation

Takamasa Higuchi[1], Hirozumi Yamaguchi[1,2], and Teruo Higashino[1,2]

[1] Graduate School of Information Science and Technology, Osaka University, Japan
1-5 Yamadaoka, Suita, Osaka 565-0871 Japan
[2] Japan Science and Technology Agency, CREST
{t-higuti,h-yamagu,higashino}@ist.osaka-u.ac.jp

Abstract. This paper presents a positioning system for "people-centric" navigation, which estimates relative positions of surrounding people to help users to find a target person in a crowd of neighbors. Our system, called PCN, employs pedestrian dead reckoning (PDR) and proximity sensing with Bluetooth only using off-the-shelf mobile phones. Utilizing the feature of "group activity" where people naturally form groups moving similarly and together in exhibitions, parties and so on, PCN corrects deviation of distance and direction in PDR. The group information is also helpful to identify the surrounding people in the navigation. A field experiment in a real exhibition with 20 examinees carrying Google Android phones was conducted to show its effectiveness.

1 Introduction

Let us think of a party place as shown in Fig. 1. Since the place is highly crowded with those present, our view is often obstructed by the surrounding people as Fig. 2. Thus we can hardly find a particular person in such a crowd even if we know that he/she is nearby. Unfortunately, there is few technology that can help us in such situations. Infrastructure-based location systems using ultrasound, infrared or RF usually need a lot of embedded sensors on the walls and dedicated receivers at clients. WiFi-based systems [3,16] are most popular, but accuracy is greatly affected by noise from the other APs. The related indoor positioning methods are surveyed in Section 2. We strongly believe that such navigation should be achieved instantly and easily without relying on special equipment. Use of off-the-shelf devices such as smartphones is a reasonable option, but to mitigate errors due to sensor noise and other environmental factors is a challenge.

This paper presents a positioning system called *PCN* (the acronym of people-centric navigation) that estimates the relative positions of surrounding people to help users to find a specific person in the crowd of neighbors. PCN employs pedestrian dead reckoning (PDR) and proximity sensing with Bluetooth only using off-the-shelf mobile phones. As demonstrated in our preliminary experiment being presented in Section 3, position errors in PDR may grow up to tens of meters, which may seriously degrade the relative position accuracy. To cope with the problem, we focus on *group activity*, a specific feature in crowded situations

J. Kay et al. (Eds.): Pervasive 2012, LNCS 7319, pp. 325–342, 2012.

Fig. 1. A scene of a party   **Fig. 2.** Finding a person in a crowd

like exhibitions and parties. In such situations, people often move together with some others (*i.e.*, "groups"). These groups may be formed by friends, families and colleagues, or even strangers who are just moving toward the same direction. PCN dynamically detects similarity of their activities by gathering mobile phones' acceleration, direction and received signal strength (RSS) of Bluetooth radios, and then corrects deviation of PDR trace by harmonizing with the traces of other group members. The estimated group information is also helpful for enhancing position awareness of the users, which is usually based on recognition of groups like "three people walking ahead" and "five people standing behind".

To quantitatively observe the performance in terms of group recognition precision and relative position accuracy, we have implemented PCN on Google Android phones and conducted a field experiment with 20 examinees in a real exhibition. The result of the experiment has shown that PCN could achieve group estimation accuracy of 94.8% as well as relative position accuracy of 3.51m. Without depending on any additional infrastructure or dedicated devices, PCN has reduced the position error by 31% compared to a conventional approach.

2   Related Work and Contribution

A number of methods have been investigated to estimate location of mobile nodes. Active Bat [8] is an well-known method that employs TDoA (time difference of arrival) of ultrasound and radio signals to measure the distance between clients and multiple anchors. Taking the advantage of accurate range measurement by TDoA, positioning errors are usually within a few centimeters if the anchors are deployed with a few meters spacing. However, the cost for installation and maintenance of such anchors is not negligible. We have proposed a cooperative localization method called "stop-and-go localization" [9] for mobile nodes with TDoA ranging devices, which achieves accurate positioning with much less dependence on infrastructure. However, accurate distance measurement between commercial mobile devices is still a challenge. Although there are some techniques like Beep-Beep [12] that achieves accurate ranging between mobile phones using propagation delay of sound signals, additional effort such as device-dependent tuning and background sound noise elimination is necessary and thus more instant and simpler positioning is preferable. For more cost-efficient positioning, Virtual Compass

[1] employs wireless ad hoc communication via Wi-Fi and Bluetooth to estimate relative distance between mobile nodes based on RSS. However, RSS-based ranging often incurs large error due to multipath or other signal propagation effects.

Pedestrian dead reckoning [13,15] that estimates the trace of pedestrians using accelerometers, digital compasses and gyro sensors has been investigated so far. While most previous PDR methods have assumed dedicated sensor devices attached to human bodies, some methods such as CompAcc [6] have utilized commercial mobile phones. However, due to noise from the sensors, PDR cannot stand alone as demonstrated in the next section.

Utilizing proximity information is a cost effective way to refine the accuracy of estimated traces obtained by PDR or some other ways. We have presented an encounter-based trace estimation method in [7]. NearMe [11] detects proximity of mobile phones by comparing the list of detected Wi-Fi APs and their RSS. Escort [5] combines PDR with proximity sensing via sound beaconing to estimate relative positions, assuming such services that guide users to their friends in unknown places. Our approach is similar with Escort in the sense that we also use PDR and proximity information. However, both of our goal and approach are totally different from Escort since we pursue the estimation accuracy of neighbors' relative positions to identify the friends nearby, while Escort aims at guiding users to friends not in the surrounding crowd but in some unknown or unfamiliar places. Escort relies on image recognition to finally find friends in a crowd, which may incur additional effort by users. Similarly, [10] enhances the quality of PDR by deriving proximity information from Bluetooth visibility of devices. However, the average error is still around 20m, so that the accuracy would not be enough for such mobile social navigation.

Based on the discussion above, our contribution is two-fold. Firstly, we present a novel positioning method to identify nearby friends in a crowd only using off-the-shelf mobile phones. To the best of our knowledge, this is the first approach that copes with this challenge. Considering the feature of people's behavior in exhibitions, parties and so on, we have come up with the idea of detecting "group activity" via sensors and Bluetooth of mobile phones and utilizing it to correct position errors. Secondly, we have implemented our system on Google Android phones, and have conducted an experiment in a real exhibition. Through this experiment, we could show the effectiveness of our approach in the real world.

3   Preliminary Experiments and Basic Idea

The overview of PCN system is shown in Fig. 3. Clients of PCN (*i.e.*, mobile phones) continuously obtain accelerometer and digital compass readings to estimate step counts and direction. They also estimate a vector of each step called *step vector*, using the direction information and stride length. Since the stride length varies between individuals, it is approximated from the body height. The clients also record RSS from the neighboring clients, which is collected through device discovery process of Bluetooth. The step vectors and RSS are transferred to a centralized server called *PCN server* via 3G or Wi-Fi, and the collected RSS is transformed into distance based on a predefined RSS-to-distance function at

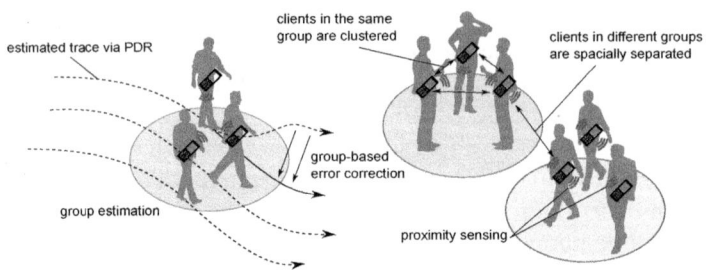

Fig. 3. PCN system overview

server side. Then the PCN server estimates relative positions among users and the results are sent back to the clients to tell the estimated situation.

3.1   Effect of Noise on Proximity and Trace Estimation

As we have stated in the previous sections, step vectors and RSS-based distance contain non-negligible errors. Fig. 4 shows Bluetooth RSS-distance mapping based on real measurement using two Google Android phones (Samsung Nexus S) in our department building receiving a lot of interference from Wi-Fi. We have plotted the measured RSS at each distance (outliers have been eliminated), and indicated their maximum and average values, where error bars show the standard deviations from the average. As shown in previous literature such as [4], we can see that different RSS values were observed at the same distance due to multipath effect, interference and so on. However, we focus on a criterion to characterize this relation based on the maximum RSS values; at 7m or longer distances they never reach -70dBm, while they exceed it at 6m or shorter distances. We utilize this characteristic to detect "proximity" explained later, allowing some inaccuracy around the boundary of two categories.

We have also implemented a simple PDR application on the Android phones to examine the accuracy of step vectors. This application continuously monitors acceleration in the vertical direction to detect steps and the compass readings to estimate the orientation of mobile phones. As shown in Fig. 5, the acceleration in the vertical direction changes synchronously with the user's steps. Therefore we simply count up the number of steps when the acceleration exceeds a threshold where the counting interval is set to 300 milliseconds to prevent double counting. Using this application, we have analyzed the estimated trace of a user walking twice on the boundary of a 5m×10m rectangle region (Fig. 6). On the estimated trace, the true positions of the three different points highlighted by dotted circles are actually the same, and thus we can observe that the position errors grew up to 10.32m after 60m walking. We note that this is the simplest threshold-based PDR where mobile phones are assumed to be held vertically at hands. There are of course more enhanced methods such as [13], and those methods can be used to improve PDR accuracy in PCN since it just uses trace estimation results from PDR. For simplicity of discussion, we assume this simple PDR hereafter.

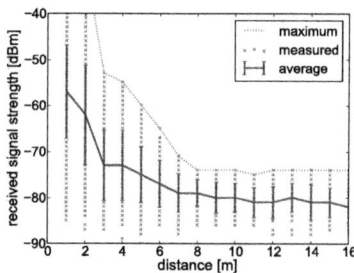

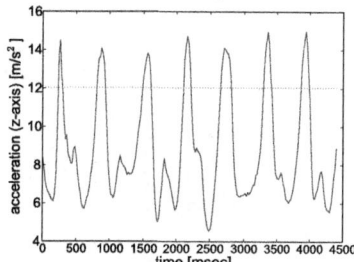

Fig. 4. Distance vs. Bluetooth RSS   **Fig. 5.** Acceleration in vertical direction

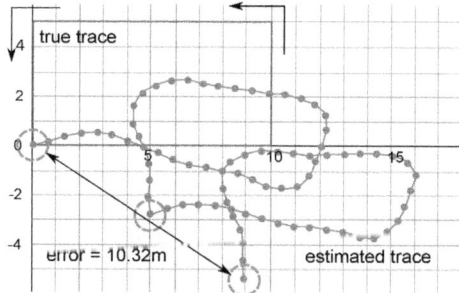

Fig. 6. Trace deviation in PDR   **Fig. 7.** Prototype of PCN client

3.2 Preliminary Experiment for Context-Supported Positioning

In order to calibrate PDR traces, we focus on general observation of human behavior; in crowded situations, the behavior can be categorized into several patterns. For example, in a party, most people stand and talk with each other. They often move around together to join the other groups or to find drinks and foods. To examine similarity of traces in a group, we have conducted the following experiment using the PDR application. We let 15 examinees with Nexus S phones freely form groups and let them walk for 30 minutes in a 10m×10m field where markers were placed with two meters spacing. The examinees also took videos of markers to record true traces as shown in Fig. 8. The obtained traces were broken down into subtraces of 2 sec., and the average direction of each group was derived at each time. Then directions of the subtraces were compared to each group average to examine the deviation of orientation within and without the group. Fig. 9 shows the cumulative distribution of directional deviation from the group average. The deviation was 30 degrees or less for about 80% of subtraces in the same group, while it distributed uniformly for those in different groups.

Assuming that users in the same group have similarity of traces, PCN corrects the estimated traces that are deviated from the "group traces". Since the group information is estimated from the collected acceleration, direction and Bluetooth RSS, we do not need any additional information for the error correction. We

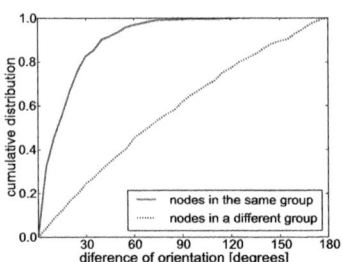

Fig. 8. Preliminary experiment   **Fig. 9.** Deviation of moving directions

define two criteria to recognize groups; nodes (mobile phones) currently in the same group (i) have been close to each other, and (ii) have moved similarly for some duration. Properties (i) and (ii) are called **proximity** and **trace similarity**, respectively. Based on these properties, *group likelihood* is calculated and the most likely grouping is adopted.

The estimation process of PCN is as follows. When the current traces are reported from the clients to the PCN server, deviated directions and positions are calibrated based on the trace similarity and proximity properties, respectively. For this purpose, groups are estimated using the past acceleration, direction and Bluetooth RSS information. After that, the Bluetooth RSS values are utilized to reflect the relative distance among the nodes.

Fig. 7 shows a screenshot from our PCN client on the Android platform. If group estimation is correct, the user can identify the target person in the group of three people behind the group of three people in front of him/her. This context information helps to mitigate the bad effect of position errors in recognizing the target person.

4   System Design

Let S denote the set of PCN clients. PCN server estimates relative positions of these clients using Bluetooth RSS and user traces reported by each client $A_i \in S$. Estimated trace via PDR is obtained as a sequence of 2-dimensional step vectors s_k, each of which represents the displacement by a step. For every τ sec., we define a *movement vector* of each A_i by the total displacement over the last τ sec. We denote the movement vector of A_i at time t by $u_{i,t}$ in the algorithm descriptions below. As well, we let $r_{ij,t}$ denote measured RSS between A_i and $A_j \in S$ at time t.

4.1   Proximity Sensing via Bluetooth Scans

First, we describe the design of proximity sensing. As mentioned above, PCN clients collect Bluetooth RSS from nearby clients via device discovery process, or Bluetooth scan. Since Bluetooth does not have explicit broadcast mechanism, it is the only way to instantly collect peer-to-peer RSS without link management.

Ordinary Android phones basically take more than 10 sec. for each attempt of Bluetooth scans, which imposes a severe limitation on the frequency of the scan attempts. To make matters worse, while the process of a scan, nodes hardly respond to the inquiries from other neighbors because they quickly change their radio frequency meanwhile. Consequently, nodes often miss nearby nodes if they just repeat Bluetooth scans.

Although the scan mechanism of Bluetooth is designed to robustly detect all the devices in the radio range, nearby nodes are relatively free from influence of unexpected signal attenuation, and usually respond more quickly to the inquiries. In proximity sensing, quickly detecting the neighbors in close proximity is more important than ensuring exhaustive detection. For that reason, we decided to interrupt each Bluetooth scan in 5 sec. from the beginning. As a result of preliminary experiment, we confirmed that the success rate of scans between nearby nodes within 5m is degraded by only about 10% by such interruption. In addition, we randomly determine the timing of scans to avoid misdetection caused by simultaneous scan attempts. At each time, nodes start scanning with probability of p_{scan}, or otherwise they sleep for a designated backoff time. In our implementation, we set p_{scan} to 0.5 and randomly pick out backoff time from 2.5 sec. to 7.5 sec. Thus, we achieve reasonable performance in proximity sensing only using Bluetooth.

4.2 Extracting Group Activities

PCN extracts group activities using recent user trails and measured RSS. These data are periodically reported by each client and maintained in the form of fixed length sequences. For each client A_i and time t, let $R_{ij}(t) = \{r_{ij,t}, r_{ij,t-\tau}, \ldots, r_{ij,t-(N-1)\tau}\}$ be the sequence consisting of the last N samplings of RSS from A_j, and $U_i(t) = \{u_{i,t}, u_{i,t-\tau}, \ldots, u_{i,t-(N-1)\tau}\}$ be the sequence of its recent N movement vectors. In this paper, we set the unit time τ to 2.0 sec. and the window size N to 30, respectively.

We characterize similarity of activity (*i.e.*, group) by two measures; (i) **proximity** and (ii) **trace-similarity**. In proximity property, people in the same group are assumed to be continuously close to each other. For each pair $A_i, A_j \in S$ of clients, we quantify this feature by the number of recent Bluetooth scans with RSS that exceeds a threshold Θ_{prox}:

$$n_{ij}(t) = |\{r_{ij,t'} | r_{ij,t'} \in R_{ij}(t), r_{ij,t'} > \Theta_{prox}\}| \qquad (1)$$

where Θ_{prox} is given as a system parameter. In trace-similarity property, the clients in the same group are assumed to have traces that are spatiotemporally similar to each other. To quantify this feature, we extend edit distance on real sequences (EDR)[2], a similarity measure for trajectories which was originally designed for similarity-based retrieval on a trajectory database. For each pair $A_i, A_j \in S$ of clients, we define the edit distance between sequences of their recent movement vectors. In general, edit distance between two sequences A and B is defined by the number of insert, delete, and replace operations that are needed to convert A into B. We regard corresponding movement vectors $\boldsymbol{u}$ and $\boldsymbol{v}$ to be matched if they satisfy the both of following criteria:

$$\big|\ \|\boldsymbol{u}\| - \|\boldsymbol{v}\|\ \big| < \Theta_l, \quad |\arg(\boldsymbol{u}) - \arg(\boldsymbol{v})| < \Theta_\theta \tag{2}$$

where Θ_l and Θ_θ are matching thresholds. Note that we skip the angular criteria if $\boldsymbol{u} = \boldsymbol{0}$ or $\boldsymbol{v} = \boldsymbol{0}$ since we cannot define orientation of the vector in such cases. Let U and V be the sequences of movement vectors, where the length of each sequence is n and m, respectively. We define the edit distance between U and V by the following recursive formula:

$$ED(U,V) = \begin{cases} n \cdot w & \text{if } m = 0 \\ m \cdot w & \text{if } n = 0 \\ \min\{ED(Rest(U), Rest(V)) + c, \\ \qquad ED(Rest(U), V) + w, \\ \qquad ED(U, Rest(V)) + w\} & otherwise \end{cases} \tag{3}$$

where $Rest(U)$ represents a sub-sequence of U without the first element. c is a cost function of a replace operation where $c = 0$ if the first element of U and that of V satisfy the matching criteria, and $c = 1$ otherwise. Insert and delete operations correspond to temporal shifting on user traces. We let w denote the cost of such a shifting operation, and set it to 0.5. There could be a small difference in timing of movements even if A_i and A_j belong to the same group. We intend to mitigate the impact of such temporal variations by imposing a smaller cost value to insert and delete operations.

We define the edit distance $d_{ij}(t)$ between the sequences of recent movement vectors for each client pair A_i and A_j, say $U_i(t)$ and $U_j(t)$, as follows:

$$d_{ij}(t) = ED(U_i(t), U_j(t)) \tag{4}$$

For short, we denote $n_{ij}(t)$ and $d_{ij}(t)$ by just n_{ij} and d_{ij} in the following descriptions. In PCN, clients that satisfy both proximity and trace-similarity each other are regarded as a group. We represent the group relationship between clients A_i and A_j by binary random variable G_{ij}, where $G_{ij} = 1$ if they belong to the same group and $G_{ij} = 0$ otherwise.

Probability distribution of G_{ij} under given measurements of n_{ij} and d_{ij} can be derived by the well-known Bayes' rule:

$$P(G_{ij}|n_{ij}, d_{ij}) = \frac{P(n_{ij}, d_{ij}|G_{ij}) \cdot P(G_{ij})}{\sum_{G_{ij}=0}^{1} P(n_{ij}, d_{ij}|G_{ij}) \cdot P(G_{ij})} \tag{5}$$

For simplicity, we assume that n_{ij} and d_{ij} are independent under given G_{ij}:

$$P(n_{ij}, d_{ij}|G_{ij}) = P(n_{ij}|G_{ij}) \cdot P(d_{ij}|G_{ij}) \tag{6}$$

Here we also assume that there is no prior information about group relationship between A_i and A_j, that is, $P(G_{ij} = 0) = P(G_{ij} = 1) = 0.5$. Under these assumptions, Eq.(5) can be simplified as:

$$P(G_{ij}|n_{ij}, d_{ij}) = \frac{P(n_{ij}|G_{ij}) \cdot P(d_{ij}|G_{ij})}{\sum_{G_{ij}=0}^{1} P(n_{ij}|G_{ij}) \cdot P(d_{ij}|G_{ij})}. \tag{7}$$

Distributions $P(n_{ij}|G_{ij})$ and $P(d_{ij}|G_{ij})$ in Eq. (7) can be obtained by a prior learning, which will be discussed in Section 5.1. To classify clients $A_i \in S$ ($i = 1, 2, \ldots, n$) into activity groups, for each pair of $A_i, A_j \in S$, we first calculate the probability that they belong to the same group based on n_{ij} and d_{ij}. Hereafter let us call the probability $P(G_{ij} = 1|n_{ij}, d_{ij})$ *group likelihood*.

Next, we construct a "grouping graph" as follows. Each client corresponds to a vertex of the graph, and we add an edge between A_i and $A_j \in S$ if and only if group likelihood $P(G_{ij} = 1|n_{ij}, d_{ij}) > \Theta_{group}$, where Θ_{group} is a threshold. In this paper, we set Θ_{group} to 0.5. Finally we regard each connected component on the grouping graph as an activity group.

4.3   Context-Supported Relative Positioning

In this section, we describe the detailed design of our context-supported relative positioning. The estimation is completed through two phases; In the former phase, we correct user traces based on the trace-similarity of activity groups. Bending the trace within the limits of expected PDR error, we alleviate the impact of sensor noise. In the latter phase, we determine the positional relationship of user traces based on RSS with the help of proximity of activity groups. As well as reducing the position error, it is also helpful to enhance the "perceptibility" of the resulting estimated positions.

Modeling PDR Error. To correct user trace, PCN first estimates the expected error in the movement vectors. Assuming that PDR on client A_i has detected m steps during the last τ sec., the movement vector $\boldsymbol{u}_{i,t}$ can be denoted by $\boldsymbol{u}_{i,t} = \sum_{k=1}^{m} \boldsymbol{s}_k$, where $\boldsymbol{s}_k$ is the step vector by the k-th step. PDR error is mainly caused by i) error of step length estimation, ii) error of direction estimation, and iii) misdetection of user steps. Errors caused by i) and ii) occur in every step $\boldsymbol{s}_k$, and accumulated in the movement vector. Expected error of step $\boldsymbol{s}_k$ can be denoted as $\boldsymbol{e}_k = \boldsymbol{e}_{l_k} + \boldsymbol{e}_{\theta_k}$, where $\boldsymbol{e}_{l_k}$ is the error of estimated step length, say l, and $\boldsymbol{e}_{\theta_k}$ is the error caused by directional distortion (Fig. 10(a)). We assume that $\boldsymbol{e}_{l_k}$ is in the same direction as $\boldsymbol{s}_k$ and its length follows Gaussian distribution $\mathcal{N}(0, \sigma_l^2)$. For $\boldsymbol{e}_{\theta_k}$, we assume that direction estimation error $\Delta\theta$ follows Gaussian distribution $\mathcal{N}(0, \sigma_\theta^2)$, and approximate $\boldsymbol{e}_{\theta_k}$ by a vector which is orthogonal to $\boldsymbol{s}_k$ with a length of $l\Delta\theta$. Under this modeling, we can uniquely determine the error distribution of each step $\boldsymbol{s}_k$. We empirically set the model parameter σ_l and σ_θ to 0.5m and 30.0 degrees, respectively.

The error caused by iii) occurs regardless of the number of detected steps in the last τ sec. We denote this basic error by $\boldsymbol{e}_0$ and model it as follows:

$$P(\boldsymbol{e}_0) = \mathcal{N}(\boldsymbol{0}, \sigma_0^2 \boldsymbol{I}) \tag{8}$$

where $\boldsymbol{I}$ is a 2-dimensional unit matrix. We empirically set σ_0 to 1.0m.

Correcting User Traces. Using the constructed step-level error prediction model, we estimate the probability distribution of a movement vector as follows. As mentioned above, PDR error is accumulated in the movement vector step-by-step as shown in Fig. 10 (b). Let $\boldsymbol{u}'_k$ be a partial movement vector composed

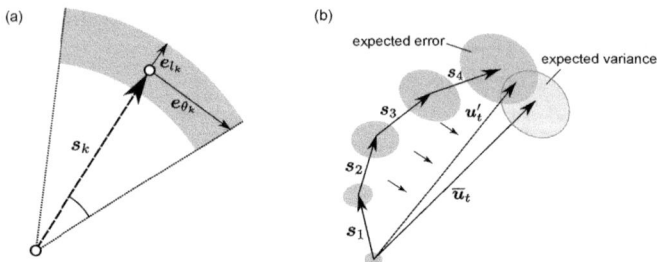

Fig. 10. Correcting user traces: (a) step-level error prediction model of PDR, (b) correcting a movement vector $\boldsymbol{u}_t$ according to the average vector $\overline{\boldsymbol{u}}_t$ of the group.

of $\boldsymbol{s}_1, \boldsymbol{s}_2, \ldots, \boldsymbol{s}_k$. We recursively predict the distribution of $\boldsymbol{u}_{i,t}$ by sequentially deriving the distributions of $\boldsymbol{u}'_k$ $(k = 0, 1, 2, \ldots, m)$, namely $P(\boldsymbol{u}'_k|\boldsymbol{s}_{1:k})$. Since the error caused by misdetection of user steps could occur regardless of the users' movement, we apply the distribution in Eq. (8) as an initial distribution:

$$P(\boldsymbol{u}'_0) = P(\boldsymbol{e}_0). \tag{9}$$

Given the distribution at the $(k-1)$-th step (*i.e.*, $P(\boldsymbol{u}'_{k-1}|\boldsymbol{s}_{1:k-1})$), we can derive the distribution at the next step using the step-level error prediction model. Relationship between $\boldsymbol{u}'_{k-1}$ and $\boldsymbol{u}'_k$ can be represented as follows:

$$\boldsymbol{u}'_k = \boldsymbol{u}'_{k-1} + \boldsymbol{s}_k + \boldsymbol{e}_k \tag{10}$$

where $\boldsymbol{e}_k$ is the error vector included in $\boldsymbol{s}_k$. According to the recursion formula, the updated distribution $P(\boldsymbol{u}'_k|\boldsymbol{s}_{1:k})$ can be derived from the previous distribution $P(\boldsymbol{u}'_{k-1}|\boldsymbol{s}_{1:k-1})$ and step-level error distribution $P(\boldsymbol{e}_k|\boldsymbol{s}_k)$:

$$P(\boldsymbol{u}'_k|\boldsymbol{s}_{1:k}) = \int \left\{ \int P(\boldsymbol{u}'_k|\boldsymbol{s}_k, \boldsymbol{e}_k, \boldsymbol{u}'_{k-1}) \cdot P(\boldsymbol{u}'_{k-1}|\boldsymbol{s}_{1:k-1})d\boldsymbol{u}'_{k-1} \right\} \cdot P(\boldsymbol{e}_k|\boldsymbol{s}_k)d\boldsymbol{e}_k \tag{11}$$

Here, we sample N_p particles $\boldsymbol{u}'^{(j)}_{k-1}$ $(j = 1, 2, \ldots, N_p)$ from the previous distribution $P(\boldsymbol{u}'_{k-1}|\boldsymbol{s}_{1:k-1})$ to represent it by Monte Carlo Approximation:

$$P(\boldsymbol{u}'_{k-1}|\boldsymbol{s}_{1:k-1}) \simeq \frac{1}{N_p} \sum_{j=1}^{N_p} \delta(\boldsymbol{u}'_{k-1} - \boldsymbol{u}'^{(j)}_{k-1}) \tag{12}$$

By this particle-based representation, the updated distribution in Eq. (11) can be transformed into:

$$P(\boldsymbol{u}'_k|\boldsymbol{s}_{1:k}) = \frac{1}{N_p} \sum_{j=1}^{N_p} \left[\int P(\boldsymbol{u}'_k|\boldsymbol{s}_k, \boldsymbol{e}_k, \boldsymbol{u}'^{(j)}_{k-1}) \cdot P(\boldsymbol{e}_k|\boldsymbol{s}_k)d\boldsymbol{e}_k \right]. \tag{13}$$

For each particle $\boldsymbol{u}'^{(j)}_{k-1}$, we sample a single particle $\boldsymbol{e}^{(j)}_k$ from the step-level error distribution $P(\boldsymbol{e}_k|\boldsymbol{s}_k)$ to approximate it as follows:

$$P(\boldsymbol{e}_k|\boldsymbol{s}_k) \simeq \delta(\boldsymbol{e}_k - \boldsymbol{e}^{(j)}_k) \tag{14}$$

Note that we sample an error value *for each of N_p particles* to reasonably approximate the step-level error distribution $P(e_k|s_k)$ overall. By this approximation, Eq. (13) can be transformed into:

$$P(\boldsymbol{u}'_k|\boldsymbol{s}_{1:k}) \simeq \frac{1}{N_p} \sum_{j=1}^{N_p} \left[\int P(\boldsymbol{u}'_k|\boldsymbol{s}_k, \boldsymbol{e}_k, \boldsymbol{u}'^{(j)}_{k-1}) \cdot \delta(\boldsymbol{e}_k - \boldsymbol{e}^{(j)}_k) d\boldsymbol{e}_k \right]$$

$$= \frac{1}{N_p} \sum_{j=1}^{N_p} \left[\delta \left(\boldsymbol{u}'_k - (\boldsymbol{u}'^{(j)}_{k-1} + \boldsymbol{s}_k + \boldsymbol{e}^{(j)}_k) \right) \right] \quad (15)$$

Based on the discussion above, we design the error prediction algorithm as follows. First, we sample N_p particles $\boldsymbol{u}'^{(j)}_0$ ($j = 1, 2, \ldots, N_p$) from $P(\boldsymbol{u}'_0)$ in Eq. (9). Then, for each step $\boldsymbol{s}_k$, we add $\boldsymbol{s}_k$ and $\boldsymbol{e}^{(j)}_k$, which is an error value sampled from $P(\boldsymbol{e}_k|\boldsymbol{s}_k)$, to each particle $\boldsymbol{u}'^{(j)}_k$. After repeating this operation for all the steps $\boldsymbol{s}_k$ in the period of recent τ sec., we can obtain the probability distribution $P(\boldsymbol{u}_{i,t})$ of the movement vector in the form of Monte Carlo representation as $P(\boldsymbol{u}_{i,t}) = P(\boldsymbol{u}'_m|\boldsymbol{s}_{1:m})$. We set N_p to 500 in our experiment in Section 5.

Assuming the trace-similarity in an activity group, we correct the current movement vector to make it approach the average movement vector of the group it belongs to. We achieve reasonable correction by harmonizing the predicted error distribution of PDR and expected distribution given by the assumption of trace-similarity among people in the same activity group. Let $\overline{\boldsymbol{u}}_t$ be the average movement vector of group G which A_i of interest belongs to; $\overline{\boldsymbol{u}}_t = \frac{1}{|G|} \sum_{A_j \in G} \boldsymbol{u}_{j,t}$. The distribution of expected movement vector is modeled based on the preliminary experiment described in Section 3. For each movement vector $\boldsymbol{u}_{i,t}$ and its corresponding group average $\overline{\boldsymbol{u}}_t$, we compare the length and direction of $\boldsymbol{u}_{i,t}$ and $\overline{\boldsymbol{u}}_t$. To model the distribution, we assume that the ratio of $\max\left(\frac{||\boldsymbol{u}_{i,t}||}{||\overline{\boldsymbol{u}}_t||}, \frac{||\overline{\boldsymbol{u}}_t||}{||\boldsymbol{u}_{i,t}||} \right)$ follows a one-sided Gaussian distribution $\mathcal{N}(1.0, \sigma^2_{g_l})$ and $(\arg(\boldsymbol{u}_{i,t}) - \arg(\overline{\boldsymbol{u}}_t))$ follows $\mathcal{N}(0.0, \sigma^2_{g_\theta})$. Based on the result of our preliminary experiment, we set the parameters σ_{g_l} and σ_{g_θ} to be 0.50 and 30.0 degrees, respectively. Since we found that the distribution of $(||\boldsymbol{u}_{i,t}|| - ||\overline{\boldsymbol{u}}_t||)$ varies with the moving speed of users, here we employ the ratio of the norms, which is more robust against the users' movement, in modeling trace-similarity. By multiplying these two distributions, the distribution of expected movement vector under given group average $\overline{\boldsymbol{u}}_t$ can be derived. Weighting each particle $\boldsymbol{u}'^{(j)}_k$ with the distribution $P(\boldsymbol{u}_{i,t}|\overline{\boldsymbol{u}}_t)$, we calculate the expected value of $\boldsymbol{u}_{i,t}$, which is to be the corrected movement vector $\tilde{\boldsymbol{u}}_{i,t}$:

$$\tilde{\boldsymbol{u}}_{i,t} = \sum_{j=1}^{N_p} \boldsymbol{u}^{(j)}_{i,t} \cdot \frac{P(\boldsymbol{u}^{(j)}_{i,t}|\overline{\boldsymbol{u}}_t)}{\sum_{k=1}^{N_p} P(\boldsymbol{u}^{(k)}_{i,t}|\overline{\boldsymbol{u}}_t)}. \quad (16)$$

If either $||\boldsymbol{u}_{i,t}||$ or $||\overline{\boldsymbol{u}}_t||$ is zero, we replace it by a sufficiently small value ($<< 1$) to approximate the corresponding weight. What we essentially do in Eq. (16) is to multiply two different distributions of $\boldsymbol{u}_{i,t}$ together, normalize the product so that it becomes a valid PDF, and compute the mean of the new PDF to derive the corrected movement vector.

Determining Relative Positions. PCN determines relative positions of the clients based on the corrected movement vectors and measured RSS. If some external positioning infrastructure such as Wi-Fi APs is available, we can start the estimation from those approximate user positions; if not, we initially place each client on a virtual coordinate system at random. Then, at every τ sec., we update and refine these positions using the corrected movement vectors and measured RSS. For each client A_i, we first independently update its position by adding the corrected movement vector $\tilde{u}_{i,t}$ to its previous position $p_{i,t-1}$. We use the resulting position $p_{i,t}^{(0)}$ as an initial estimation of A_i's position at time t, and adjust it based on peer-to-peer RSS by the following iterative algorithm.

At each iteration k, we put virtual attracting force $f_{ij,t}^{(k)}$ between all the client pairs A_i, A_j which have observed RSS of more than Θ_{prox} during the last τ sec.:

$$
f_{ij,t}^{(k)} = \begin{cases} \kappa \cdot \max\left(0, \|p_{j,t}^{(k-1)} - p_{i,t}^{(k-1)}\| - d_p\right) \cdot \dfrac{p_{j,t}^{(k-1)} - p_{i,t}^{(k-1)}}{\|p_{j,t}^{(k-1)} - p_{i,t}^{(k-1)}\|} & \text{if } r_{ij,t} > \Theta_{prox} \\ 0 & \text{otherwise} \end{cases}
$$

$$(17)$$

where $p_{i,t}^{(k-1)}$ and $p_{j,t}^{(k-1)}$ are the estimated positions of A_i and A_j in the virtual coordinate system at the previous iteration $k-1$, and κ is an algorithm parameter that characterizes the strength of the force. d_p is the maximum range where RSS of more than Θ_{prox} can be observed ($d_p = 6.0$m in our preliminary experiment).

As discussed in Section 3, the large deviation of measured RSS imposes a limitation to proximity sensing; basically the only information we can obtain from the measured RSS is whether the distance between the nodes are within d_p. To pursue finer-grained positioning, we inspire some heuristics to the position estimation utilizing the assumption of proximity among members of an activity group. For client pairs in the same group, we replace d_p by d_p' ($d_p' < d_p$), where d_p' is also a possible range for the measured RSS. It leads estimated positions of the nodes in the same group to be closer, which is expected to enhance the positioning accuracy in most situations. We set d_p' to 3.0m in this paper.

In psychological science, it is said that human perceives objects in close proximity as a group[14]. Based on this observation, we slightly adjust the node positions to spatially separate each group. This could help users intuitively identify the estimated positions with actual surrounding people. We put this heuristics to the position estimation by adding weak force $f'_{ij,t}^{(k)}$ between each client pairs:

$$
f'_{ij,t}^{(k)} = \begin{cases} \kappa' \cdot \max\left(0, \|p_{j,t}^{(k-1)} - p_{i,t}^{(k-1)}\| - d_{p'}\right) \cdot \dfrac{p_{j,t}^{(k-1)} - p_{i,t}^{(k-1)}}{\|p_{j,t}^{(k-1)} - p_{i,t}^{(k-1)}\|} & \text{if } G_{ij} = 1 \\ -\kappa' \cdot \max\left(0, d_{p'} - \|p_{j,t}^{(k-1)} - p_{i,t}^{(k-1)}\|\right) \cdot \dfrac{p_{j,t}^{(k-1)} - p_{i,t}^{(k-1)}}{\|p_{j,t}^{(k-1)} - p_{i,t}^{(k-1)}\|} & \text{otherwise} \end{cases}
$$

$$(18)$$

where κ' ($\kappa' << \kappa$) is a constant given as an algorithm parameter. Thus, we separate each group by adding attracting force between the pairs in the same group, whereas putting repulsive force to the pairs in different groups. Note that we choose κ' to be much smaller than κ to make the measurement-based attracting force $\boldsymbol{f}_{ij,t}^{(k)}$ takes priority in determining the estimated positions, intending to maintain the consistency with RSS measurements.

Under the assumptions above, we update the "velocity" $\boldsymbol{v}_i^{(k)}$ of each node A_i according to the resultant force affecting to A_i:

$$\boldsymbol{v}_i^{(k)} = \alpha \left(\boldsymbol{v}_i^{(k-1)} + \sum_{A_j \in S \setminus \{A_i\}} \left(\boldsymbol{f}_{ij,t}^{(k)} + \boldsymbol{f'}_{ij,t}^{(k)} \right) \right) \tag{19}$$

where α is a dumping coefficient, which is given as an algorithm parameter. Note that $\boldsymbol{v}_i^{(0)} = (0,0)$ for each client. Then we adjust the position of each client A_i depending on its *velocity*:

$$\boldsymbol{p}_{i,t}^{(k)} = \boldsymbol{p}_{i,t}^{(k-1)} + \boldsymbol{v}_i^{(k)}. \tag{20}$$

We repeat the operations above until the number of iteration k reaches the termination criterion k_{term} or total amount of *velocity* $\|\sum_{A_i \in S} \boldsymbol{v}_i^{(k)}\|$ converges to less than v_{term} to determine estimated positions $\boldsymbol{p}_{i,t}$ at time t.

5   Evaluation

To collect sensor data and RSS logs in real environment, we conducted a field experiment in a public trade fair. As a part of a technical event named Knowledge Capital Trial 2011 (http://www.kmo-jp.com/en/), the trade fair was held at a 27m×40m-sized hall as shown in Fig. 11. Totally 16 industrial companies and universities exhibited their state-of-the-art technology while thousands of visitors went around the booths.

We let 20 students hold Nexus S phones and asked to go around the event place with a group of four people. A sensing application equipped with PDR and proximity sensing was running on each phone to record users' traces and RSS logs. Each group entered the place at the entrance, and then looked around 6-12 booths for about 30 minutes. After that, they left there through the exit shown in Fig.11. Usually they stayed at each booth for 1-5 minutes on average. To collect ground truth data of user traces, we assigned an additional person to each group to plot their true positions on a field map with time stamps, as well as taking their photos at certain time intervals. After conducting such experiment three times, we collected real sensor data and RSS logs which are about 1,800 minutes long in total (90min. logs for 20 examinees). In the following evaluation, we used logs of 2 experiments as a learning dataset to construct group classifier, and the remaining one as a test dataset to examine the performance.

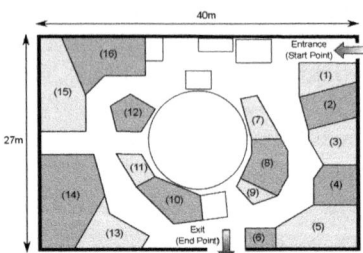

Fig. 11. Floor map

Fig. 12. Field experiment

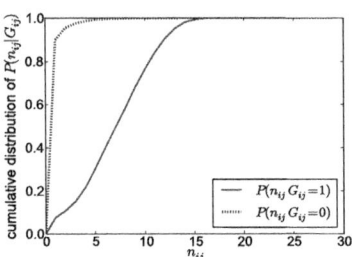

Fig. 13. Distribution of n_{ij}

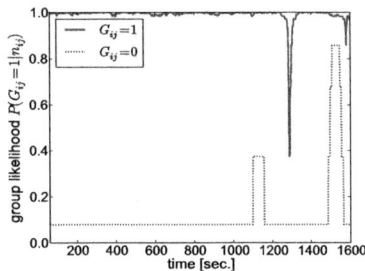

Fig. 14. Group likelihood (proximity)

5.1   Constructing Group Classifier

At first, we modeled proximity and trace-similarity of activity groups based on the learning dataset, and synthesized those models to construct a group classifier.

Proximity Model: Analyzing the learning dataset, we calculated the distribution of n_{ij}, which has been introduced as a proximity measure between two clients in Eq. (1). Fig. 13 shows the distribution in two different cases: one is for the pairs in the same group ($G_{ij} = 1$) and another is for ones in the different groups ($G_{ij} = 0$). As shown in the resulting distribution, $n_{ij} \leq 1$ in more than 90% cases for the pairs in different groups, while $n_{ij} \geq 2$ for as much as 95% for the same group cases. Thus, we can accurately distinguish whether or not a pair of clients belongs to the same group by observing the recent RSS measurements.

To examine the classification capability of the proximity feature, we tried constructing a group classifier only using the proximity model. We picked out RSS logs of three clients, say A_i, A_j, and $A_{j'}$ from the test dataset, where A_i and A_j belong to the same group while $A_{j'}$ is not. After applying the proximity-based group classifier to the pairs (A_i, A_j) and $(A_i, A_{j'})$, we obtained a series of group likelihood. The result is shown in Fig. 14. For the pair (A_i, A_j), the group likelihood is successfully around 1 throughout the experiment. As for $(A_i, A_{j'})$, the likelihood is less than 0.1 almost throughout the experiment. A problem is that the group likelihood of $(A_i, A_{j'})$ rises around $t = 1,100$ sec. and $t = 1,500$ sec. This is because these two groups were going around nearby booths at that time. The trace-similarity model, which will be discussed in the next section, helps to distinguish such nearby groups.

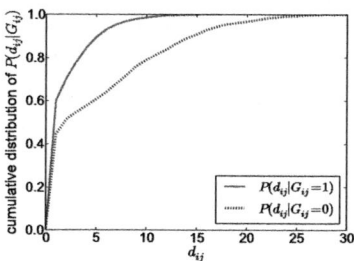

Fig. 15. Distribution of edit distance

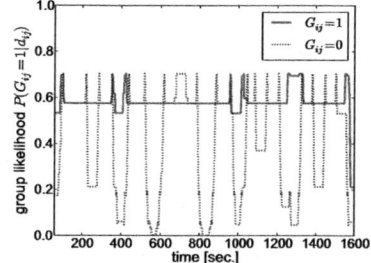

Fig. 16. Group likelihood (edit distance)

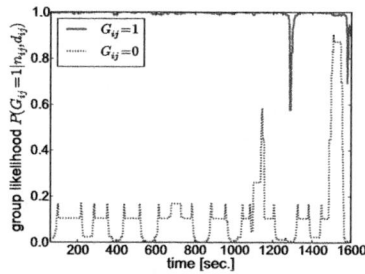

Fig. 17. Group likelihood (synthesized)

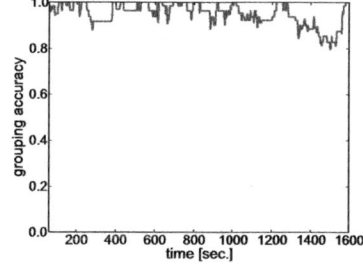

Fig. 18. Accuracy of group estimation

Trace-Similarity Model: We calculated the distribution of d_{ij}, which has been defined as a trace-similarity measure in Eq. (4). The resulting distribution is shown in Fig. 15. Since we conducted this experiment in an exhibition, users spent much time staying at each booth. This leads the distribution of d_{ij} to be biased to zero. However, the probability that $d_{ij} \geq 5$ is around 40% for the clients in the same group while the corresponding probability for the different group cases is no more than 10%. This difference takes an important role in distinguishing nearby activity groups.

We also tried constructing a group classifier only using the trace-similarity model, and then applied the resulting classifier to the traces of pairs (A_i, A_j) and $(A_i, A_{j'})$, which correspond to the previous section. As a result, we obtained a series of group likelihood shown in Fig. 16. When the two clients are both staying at a booth, the group likelihood is relatively high regardless of whether they are in the same group or not. On the other hand, while the nodes travel between the booths, the likelihood in different group cases falls to around zero. The latter feature contributes to separation of nearby groups, as we mentioned above.

Group Classifier: Finally, we synthesize these two models using the Bayes' rule in Eq. (7) to construct a complete group classifier. Fig. 17 shows the group likelihood for pairs (A_i, A_j) and $(A_i, A_{j'})$ based on the resulting group classifier. Recalling the proximity-based group likelihood in Fig. 14, the likelihood of $(A_i, A_{j'})$ unsuccessfully rises when their groups are nearby. In Fig. 17, a failure around $t = 1,100$ sec. is mitigated since the large trace dissimilarity suppressed the group likelihood. Thus, the proximity and trace-similarity models complement each other to achieve better grouping accuracy. Note that if the nearby groups take similar behavior, these groups are regarded as the same group as $t = 1,500$ sec. in Fig. 17. Although this is a wrong estimation, we believe that it rarely affects the performance of PCN since users would also perceive such people as if they were in the same group.

5.2   Results

We evaluated the performance of PCN from three aspects, namely, grouping accuracy, relative positioning error, and perceptibility of the estimated positions.

Grouping Accuracy: Appropriate group classification is a key to enhance positioning performance with our context-supported correction mechanism. We applied the group classifier to all the sensor data and RSS logs in the test dataset to classify those 20 clients into activity groups. Then we evaluated the grouping accuracy by the accuracy rate of *pairwise membership test*: for each pair of nodes, we checked whether they are in the same group or not, and compared them with the actual grouping (5 groups of 4 people). As shown in the temporal change of resulting grouping accuracy in Fig. 18, we successfully achieved accuracy rate of more than 90% over most pieces of time in the experiment, with average grouping accuracy of 94.8% (1.7% false positives and 3.5% false negatives). On the other hand, we can also see that the grouping accuracy temporarily drops around $t = 1,400$ sec. As discussed in Section 5.1, this is because several groups were staying at nearby booths, which leads the group classifier to misinterpret them as a single group. Although expanding the window size N to consider older histories of proximity and trace-similarity is a possible way to distinguish such groups, we should carefully select the parameter since larger N could make it hard to detect time variation of groups (*i.e.*, joining and leaving) immediately.

Relative Positioning Error: To evaluate the efficacy of our context-supported error correction mechanism, we evaluated relative positioning error to nearby nodes which are within 10m from each node A_i of interest. We represent the set of such nearby nodes at time t as $S_i(t) \subseteq S$ and define the average relative position error denoted by $err(t)$ as follows:

$$err(t) = \frac{1}{|S|} \sum_{A_i \in S} \left(\frac{1}{|S_i(t)|} \sum_{A_j \in S_i(t)} ||\boldsymbol{p}_{ji,t} - \tilde{\boldsymbol{p}}_{ji,t}|| \right) \qquad (21)$$

where $\boldsymbol{p}_{ji,t}$ and $\tilde{\boldsymbol{p}}_{ji,t}$ represent the true and estimated positions of A_j at time t from a local view of A_i, respectively.

We applied our context-supported relative positioning algorithm to the test dataset, and evaluated the relative position error every 2 sec. In Fig. 19, we compared the position error with a straightforward method which performs relative positioning using RSS and plain user traces without group-based correction. As a benefit of the context-supported correction mechanism, our method achieved higher positioning accuracy over most pieces of time through the experiment. The average positioning error of our method was 3.51m, which corresponds to improvement of 31.3% compared to the plain approach.

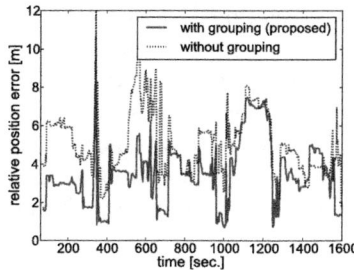

Fig. 19. Relative position error

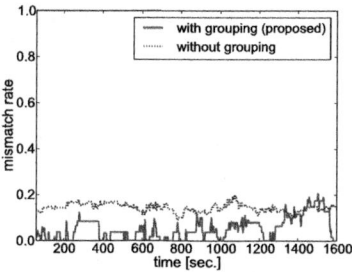

Fig. 20. Mismatch rate between geometrical clusters and activity groups

Perceptibility of the Estimated Positions: Finally, we evaluated our system from a viewpoint of "perceptibility", which is also an important feature in PCN. As mentioned in Section 4.3, human intuitively perceives objects in close proximity as a group[14]. Based on this observation, we applied a clustering algorithm to the estimated positions to find geometrical clusters which would be regarded as a group in human perception. Comparing such geometrical clusters to actual activity groups, we evaluated the perceptibility of the estimated positions.

For geometrical clustering, we used a hierarchical clustering algorithm with the group-average method. It defines inter-cluster distance between two clusters C_1 and C_2 by the following formula:

$$d(C_1, C_2) = \frac{1}{|C_1||C_2|} \sum_{p \in C_1} \sum_{q \in C_2} d(p, q) \tag{22}$$

where $d(p, q)$ is the Euclid distance between estimated positions p and q of two clients, and $|C_1|$ and $|C_2|$ represent the size of C_1 and C_2, respectively. We start the clustering from $|S|$ clusters each of which contains a different client in S. Calculating the inter-cluster distance for all the pairs of clusters, we pick out a pair with the shortest distance to merge them to a single cluster. We repeat this bottom-up clustering process until the shortest distance falls to a threshold. We set this threshold to 1.5m in the evaluations below.

We evaluated the consistency between the resulting geometrical clusters and actual activity groups by failure rate of pairwise membership test. Fig. 20 shows the result compared to the straightforward method without group-based correction. For the compared method, errors in estimated traces make the positional relationship between the clients go wrong, which leads average mismatching rate to be 14.3%. In contrast, our method suppressed such failures to 5.1% owing to the group-based correction. This corresponds to the improvement of 64% and even be close to the average failure rate for true positions of 3.9%.

6   Conclusions

In this paper, we proposed a novel social navigation framework, called PCN, that leads users to their friends in a crowd of neighbors. PCN provides relative positions of surrounding people based on sensor readings and Bluetooth RSS, both of which can be easily obtained via off-the-shelf mobile phones. Through a field experiment in a real trade fair, we demonstrated that PCN improves positioning accuracy by 31% compared to a conventional approach owing to its context-supported error correction mechanism. Furthermore, we showed that the geometrical clusters in the estimated positions are highly consistent with actual activity groups, which would help users to easily identify actual nearby people.

References

1. Banerjee, N., Agarwal, S., Bahl, P., Chandra, R., Wolman, A., Corner, M.: Virtual Compass: Relative Positioning to Sense Mobile Social Interactions. In: Floréen, P., Krüger, A., Spasojevic, M. (eds.) Pervasive 2010. LNCS, vol. 6030, pp. 1–21. Springer, Heidelberg (2010)
2. Chen, L., Özsu, M.T., Oria, V.: Robust and fast similarity search for moving object trajectories. In: Proc. of SIGMOD 2005, pp. 491–502 (2005)
3. Chintalapudi, K., Iyer, A.P., Padmanabhan, V.N.: Indoor localization without the pain. In: Proc. of MobiCom 2010, pp. 173–184 (2010)
4. Chitte, S., Dasgupta, S., Ding, Z.: Distance estimation from received signal strength under log-normal shadowing: Bias and variance. IEEE Signal Processing Letters 16(3), 216–218 (2009)
5. Constandache, I., Bao, X., Azizyan, M., Choudhury, R.R.: Did you see bob?: human localization using mobile phones. In: Proc. of MobiCom 2010, pp. 149–160 (2010)
6. Constandache, I., Choudhury, R.R., Rhee, I.: Towards mobile phone localization without war-driving. In: Proc. of INFOCOM 2010, pp. 1–9 (2010)
7. Fujii, S., Nomura, T., Umedu, T., Yamaguchi, H., Higashino, T.: Real-time trajectory estimation in mobile ad hoc networks. In: Proc. of MSWiM 2009, pp. 163–172 (2009)
8. Harter, A., Hopper, A., Steggles, P., Ward, A., Webster, P.: The anatomy of a context-aware application. In: Proc. of MobiCom 1999, pp. 59–68 (1999)
9. Higuchi, T., Fujii, S., Yamaguchi, H., Higashino, T.: An efficient localization algorithm focusing on stop-and-go behavior of mobile nodes. In: Proc. of PerCom 2011, pp. 205–212 (2011)
10. Kloch, K., Lukowicz, P., Fischer, C.: Collaborative PDR localisation with mobile phones. In: Proc. of ISWC 2011, pp. 37–40 (2011)
11. Krumm, J., Hinckley, K.: The NearMe Wireless Proximity Server. In: Davies, N., Mynatt, E.D., Siio, I. (eds.) UbiComp 2004. LNCS, vol. 3205, pp. 283–300. Springer, Heidelberg (2004)
12. Peng, C., Shen, G., Zhang, Y., Li, Y., Tan, K.: BeepBeep: A high accuracy acoustic ranging system using COTS mobile devices. In: Proc. of SenSys 2007, pp. 1–14 (2007)
13. Steinhoff, U., Schiele, B.: Dead reckoning from the pocket — an experimental study. In: Proc. of PerCom 2010, pp. 162–170 (2010)
14. Wertheimer, M.: Laws of organization in perceptual forms (1938)
15. Woodman, O., Harle, R.: Pedestrian localisation for indoor environments. In: Proc. of UbiComp 2008, pp. 114–123 (2008)
16. Yin, J., Yang, Q., Ni, L.M.: Learning adaptive temporal radio maps for signal-strength-based location estimation. IEEE Transactions on Mobile Computing 7(7), 869–883 (2008)

Paying in Kind for Crowdsourced Work in Developing Regions

Navkar Samdaria[1], Akhil Mathur[2], and Ravin Balakrishnan[1]

[1] University of Toronto, Toronto, Canada – M5S2E4
[2] Bell Labs India, Alcatel-Lucent, Bangalore, India - 560045
{navkar,ravin}@dgp.toronto.edu,
akhil.mathur@alcatel-lucent.com

Abstract. In developing regions, the reach of crowdsourcing services such as Amazon Mechanical Turk (mTurk) has been limited by the lack of adequate payment mechanisms and low visibility amongst the crowd. In this paper, we present a commodity based model for crowdsourcing where crowd workers get paid in kind in the form of a commodity instead of money. Our model makes crowdsourcing services more visible to users in developing regions and also addresses the issue of payment. We conducted two field studies in urban India to evaluate the applicability of our proposed model. Our results show that the commodity based crowdsourcing model reached workers with very different demographics from the typical mTurk workers. We also found that users preferred to receive a commodity instead of money as remuneration.

Keywords: crowdsourcing, mobile phones, humans as pervasive computing resources, commodity exchange model, developing regions, Amazon Mechanical Turk, India.

1   Introduction

Microtasking services such as Amazon Mechanical Turk allow its users to distribute tasks to a large number of crowd workers. The majority of these tasks are those which are difficult for computers, yet simple for humans (for example, surveys, image labelling, audio transcription, and finding specific information on a website). It has been estimated that in the last decade, over 1 million workers have earned $1-2 billion via crowdsourced work allocation [2].

Microtasking platforms hold a particular promise for workers in developing regions like India. They provide workers an opportunity to earn money without being physically co-located with the work provider, and the dollar remuneration when converted to local currency also becomes quite significant [11]. A recent survey of 733 mTurk workers [11] showed that 36% of the respondents were from India. The Indian workers were young (with an average age of 26-28 years), well-educated and had a higher standard of living than the average Indian. In another study with 200 mTurk workers, Khanna et al. [5] report that nearly 80% of respondents had at least a Bachelor's degree, with another 11% currently in college. Interestingly, 92% of the

J. Kay et al. (Eds.): Pervasive 2012, LNCS 7319, pp. 343–360, 2012.

workers had a PC and internet connection in their homes. However, those with a Bachelor's degree or higher constitute only 6% of India's working age population (15-60 years) [13] and home PC penetration in India is estimated at <10% [3]. These statistics suggest that the reach of microtasking services has been limited to the educated elite in developing regions. We believe that there is tremendous untapped potential for microtasking services in developing regions if they are made more pervasive and available to a larger number of workers. We argue that there are three major reasons why microtasking services have not been able to reach more workers in developing regions:

(*i*) *Access*: Most microtasking platforms are hosted on the internet. Internet penetration in developing regions like India is low, as a result of which a large number of potential workers are unable to access microtasking services. On the contrary, penetration of mobile phones in developing regions is very high (64.7% of the population in India as per the latest statistics [14]) which make them a promising platform to address the issue of accessibility of microtasking services.

ii) *Visibility:* The visibility of microtasking services is also quite low in developing regions, and the potential workers are not aware of them. If some of these services can be brought from the digital world into the physical world, it may increase their awareness among the workers.

iii) *Payment:* A major problem impeding the growth of microtasking services in developing regions is the lack of adequate payment mechanisms for the crowd workers. More than 60% [8] of the Indian population do not have a bank account, which makes it difficult for a microtasking service to pay them for their work via the traditional banking system. An obvious solution to this problem is to give the workers some commodity or service in return of the work. However, the choice of the commodity should be such that it is useful for the worker immediately or in the near future. For example, a microtasking service named txteagle [4] provides mobile phone airtime as the commodity in exchange for work. However, one can argue that the workers may not be in the need for mobile airtime every time they do the work, and as subscribers in India are unable to convert airtime to cash payouts, this leads to lower participation in the microtasking service.

The problem of *Access* has been addressed by initiatives like txteagle [4] and MobileWorks [6] which push microtasks to the worker's mobile phone using SMS or the USSD protocol. In this paper, we investigate the applicability of an alternate model of crowdsourcing which address the aforementioned problems of *Visibility* and *Payment* with existing crowdsourcing systems. We propose a model in which workers are presented with the opportunity to do microtasks whenever they feel the need for a commodity, and on completion of the microtasks, they get their desired commodity as remuneration. At a strictly objective level, it is effectively a change in the currency of remuneration, but subjectively we hypothesize that getting a commodity 'for free', particularly at the time when said commodity is to be consumed, is perhaps a better motivator to do the microtasks than simply working for money.

We present two field studies to explore the applicability of our proposed model in real-life scenarios. Results show that our proposed model increases the reach of microtasking services to those user segments which are less likely to join existing microtasking services like mTurk. We also found that users have different motivations to work on microtasks such as "desire to earn", "desire to save", and "desire for commodity". The conventional crowdsourcing models only appeal to their "desire to earn", while our proposed model can fulfill all three desires.

In the next two sections, we describe our crowdsourcing model and give an overview of the related work. Then, we describe evaluations with user populations in urban India and report their results before finally outlining and discussing the key findings.

2   Model Description

Our proposed commodity-centric crowdsourcing model (CCCM) assumes that there is a repository which consists of microtasks contributed by various work-providers. In the conventional crowdsourcing model (for example, mTurk), crowd workers will go to this microtask repository and express a desire to do tasks. The repository will first collect information on the background and qualifications of the workers and then push appropriate tasks to them.

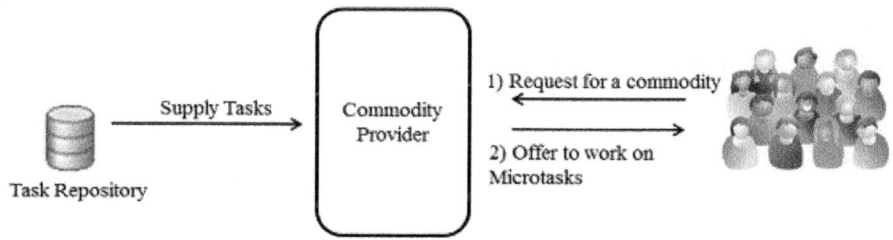

Fig. 1. Overview of Commodity-Centric Crowdsourcing Model

In CCCM (see Fig. 1), the microtasking repository does not interact with the workers directly, but through an intermediary we call a *Commodity Provider*. A Commodity Provider can be any entity which offer a commodity to the worker, and in return ask the workers to perform microtasks. A commodity may comprise of a good or a service. For example, an auto-rickshaw[1] driver can be a Commodity Provider who provides auto-rickshaw service for free or on a discounted price in return for the performance of some microtasks, or the ACM digital portal can be a Commodity Provider which provides scientific articles to a student worker on completion of a microtask. It's important to note that at some level a commodity could be equated to cash, since most tangible goods and services essentially have a monetary value in most societies. Of course, the nature of the commodity might well determine how easily a cash equivalent can be determined; for example, a discount on an auto-rickshaw ride has an obvious cash equivalency. However, we believe that by casting the compensation as a commodity in terms of how it is described and provided, it enables users to not think of it in direct monetary terms and as such might well

---

[1] An auto-rickshaw is a three-wheeled vehicle which is very common for public transport in India. They offer a cheaper alternative to taxis and attract a large number of passengers every day. There are more than 100,000 auto-rickshaws currently operating within the city of Bangalore alone. (http://en.wikipedia.org/wiki/Auto_rickshaw).

ascribe a value to the commodity that they would not typically ascribe to the monetary equivalent. The findings of recent studies from economics literature [17, 18] also highlight the advantage of commodity compensation over its monetary equivalent.

When users (potential crowd workers) approach a Commodity Provider, they are given an option of doing a microtask to get the commodity, or they can choose to pay for the commodity as they would normally do. If they decide to do microtasks, the Commodity Provider fetches tasks from the repository and passes them to the workers. The credit earned by the workers after completing the task is exchanged for the commodity being offered by the Commodity Provider. In case the credit earned is less than the value of the commodity; the workers get a discount on the commodity proportional to the credits earned by them, and they pay the remaining amount in cash. Later, the microtasking service pays money to the Commodity Provider in return of the task credits, along with a small commission for its services.

Because a crowd worker will expect to get instant remuneration for his/her work, this model is better suited to those tasks which can be done in spurts (surveys, image categorization) and do not require a formal verification. For example, crowd workers may not prefer doing an essay writing task which requires quality checks from the task giver, resulting in a delay in remuneration.

While CCCM can be applicable to both physical Commodity Providers like the auto-rickshaw drivers and online Commodity Providers such as the ACM digital portal (for scientific articles), in this paper we are mainly interested in studying the application of CCCM in physical settings in developing regions. We argue that the integration of CCCM with physical Commodity Providers can increase the visibility of microtasking services. The Commodity Provider can leverage the high mobile penetration in developing regions to distribute tasks to the workers on their mobile phones, hence solving the problem of *Access*. CCCM also address the problem of payment mechanism to a great extent: instead of paying all the crowd workers, the microtasking service only has to pay the Commodity Providers which are far fewer in number than the crowd workers.

3   Related Work

Perhaps the closest and most relevant work related to our proposed model is reCAPTCHA [9] which asks a user of a system 'X' to solve image captchas in order to get access to the system X. In the context of our model, the system X is the Commodity Provider and 'access to X' is the commodity for which a user will do the image captcha task. In contrast to reCAPTCHA, we are inclined to explore the applicability of the CCCM model in physical settings in developing regions to solve the problems of *Visibility* and *Payment*.

There has been some interesting work on developing microtasking services that specifically target workers in developing countries. txteagle [4], started in Kenya, is one such service which makes use of standard channels like text, voice, and USSD to distribute and administer tasks to the workers. Sample tasks include software localization, evaluation of search results, categorization of blog sentiments, and market research. Payment to the workers is made in the form of mobile airtime. MobileWorks

[6] is another such service which uses a web-based mobile application to distribute OCR tasks and pays its workers in cash. SamaSource [12] is a non-profit organization seeking to empower workers in developing countries. They recruit and train the workers (women, youth and refugees) to work on microtasks and earn their livelihood. Ushahidi [7] is an open source platform from Kenya, which allows users to crowdsource crisis information through text messaging using a mobile phone, email, and the web.

In addition to these there are more than 50 other companies running online task marketplaces of various kinds [2]. In addition to mTurk, some examples include CrowdFlower, CrowdSifter, CloudCrowd, LiveWork, LogoTournament, CastingWords, and SmartSheet which draw workers from developing countries. All the listed examples are internet based solutions and fail to tackle the issues of *Access* and *Payment*.

Among all the crowdsourcing services mentioned above, txteagle makes use of mobile phones to distribute tasks which makes it more accessible to the workers in developing regions. It pays the workers with mobile airtime to solve the *Payment* problem. However, txteagle's approach is different from our proposed Commodity-Centric Crowdsourcing Model (CCCM) in many ways. At a high level, txteagle follows the mTurk-like model where users would approach the microtasking service, and work on some tasks to get paid. On the contrary, in our model users work only when they need a commodity. CCCM makes sure that there is a need for the commodity before pushing the tasks to the workers whereas in txteagle tasks are pushed irrespective of the need for the commodity. Apart from solving the issue of payment, we conjecture that our model would expand the range of the crowdsourcing workforce by bringing in workers of different demographics.

Finally, there has been work around bringing microtasking services into the physical world. Florian et al. [1] developed a mobile application to facilitate location based crowdsourcing. Other researchers [10, 15, 16] discuss different approaches with sensing devices like smartphones for getting people at some specific location to contribute to microtasks.

4   Evaluation

We explored the effectiveness and applicability of the CCCM model in developing regions via two user evaluations in urban India. The first (primary) study is focused on evaluating the basic premise of the CCCM model with potential target populations, while the second (ancillary) study is a follow-up intended to see if the CCCM model might also apply to those populations who might have previously participated in more conventional mTurk like activities online.

4.1   Study 1

The primary focus of our work is to determine whether or not the CCCM model is viable, and to gauge its potential amongst user populations that currently do not partake in conventional crowdsourcing activities. One example of such a user population are people in the lower- to middle- income demographic in urban Indian cities who have some literacy of technology but do not necessarily use it extensively in their daily lives, and who might be motivated by payment by commodity. We also had to decide as to an appropriate Commodity Provider for this initial validation study. Our main criteria in this regard was to pick a Commodity Provider who came into contact with a broad cross-section of the target user population in their daily regular business activity, and who also could capture the attention of the users for a reasonable period of time. One possible class of Commodity Provider that met this criteria are the drivers of auto-rickshaws, as they tend to cater to a broad population base and, crucially, have a "captive" audience for the duration of the rickshaw ride. As such, we enlisted auto-rickshaw drivers as the Commodity Providers, who offered auto-rickshaw service (i.e. the commodity) for free or on a discounted price and in return they asked the passengers to complete microtasks on mobile phones.

Participants. Three auto-rickshaw drivers from Bangalore, India participated in our first study as commodity providers. Two auto-rickshaw drivers were selected at random and one was selected via a referral. The drivers were male, in the age group of 25-35 years. Their monthly earnings were in the range of Rs. 15,000-20,000 (Rs. 50 = ~ USD 1). None of them were fluent in speaking English, but they could identify common English words such as 'Hello', 'Start', 'Exit', 'Right', 'Left'. Their language of communication was Hindi and Kannada (the local language spoken in Bangalore). All of them were numerically literate with an education level below 10th grade. All of them owned a mobile phone, which was primarily used for dialing and receiving calls.

Methodology. The auto-rickshaw drivers were given a Java enabled mobile phone with a pre-loaded microtasking application (details in the next section). They were instructed to offer their passengers (crowd workers) an opportunity to avail of a discount on the journey fare in return for working on the microtasks. The total amount earned by a passenger was discounted from the journey fare. A discount on the journey fare was given only if the work done by a passenger was worth more than Rs. 5 and the maximum discount a passenger can get cannot exceed the journey fare. For their service as a Commodity Provider in our model, drivers received 20% commission on the work being done by the passenger.

We put flyers in Kannada and English in front of the passenger's seat which provided instructions to the passengers on running the microtasking application. Each auto-rickshaw driver was given a small pocket diary and was asked to maintain a record of the date of the journey, gender of the passenger, approximate age for every passenger, total journey fare, discount offered, and journey duration. Before the study, a researcher trained the drivers on using the application and ensured that they understood the purpose of the application.

We conducted semi-structured interviews with the auto-rickshaw drivers at the end of the day to get their feedback as well as the passengers' reactions towards the microtasking application. The total discount given by the auto-rickshaw drivers on that day was reimbursed to them along with the 20% commission. The dispatch of daily payment was necessary to maintain the trust of drivers in the system. Apart from the commission a fixed compensation of Rs. 500 was given to each driver for participating in the study.

The microtasking application had a data logging feature which recorded the performance of workers on each microtask. At the end of the study, we collected all the logs for analysis.

Microtasking Application. We developed a J2ME application which can be used to work on various microtasks. We deployed our application on a Nokia C2-01 which costs Rs. 4000. The application starts with a welcome screen and prompts the user to choose between two modes: Passenger Mode and Driver Mode. Fig. 2 shows the application in Passenger and Driver Modes.

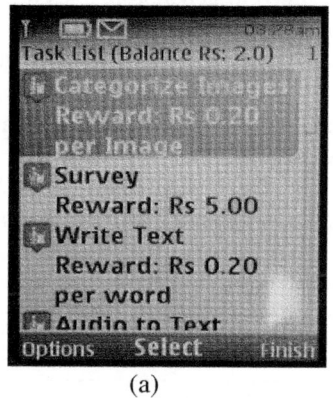
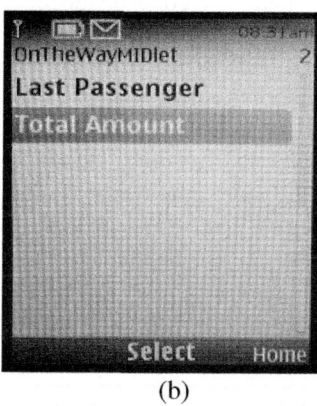

(a)   (b)

Fig. 2. (a) Screenshot of Passenger Mode (b) Screenshot of Driver Mode

Passenger Mode. In the Passenger Mode, users are shown a list of all available microtasks. The order of tasks in the list is chosen randomly at the start of the application so as to avoid any bias caused by the task ordering on user's task preference. Users can work on the tasks of their choice and are allowed to switch between tasks at any point of time. The asterisk key (*) is used to exit the current task and return to the task list. The top of the screen shows the *Balance* i.e. the total discount accumulated by the passenger. 'Balance' is a colloquial word for Credit in the context of mobile phones in India – the use of this word made it easier for both passengers and drivers to understand its use in context of our application.

Driver Mode. In order to reduce the learning curve for the drivers we kept the driver interface very simple with minimal functionality. In this mode, drivers can view:
a) The total Balance for the last passenger
b) The total Balance for all passengers on a day.

Choice of Tasks. We did a survey of all available tasks on mTurk and found four categories of tasks which can be supported by low-end mobile phones with basic text and voice capability:

a) Selection Tasks (ST), which require users to select an answer from a set of options,
b) Data Entry Tasks (DET), which require users to type in data from any source into the application,
c) Transcription Tasks (TT), which require users to convert speech into text, and
d) Language Translation Tasks (LTT), which require users to translate text from one language to another.

In our application, we included at least one task representing each of the four categories except Language Translation Tasks. LTT were deliberately left out because typing in a non-English language is challenging on a low-end mobile phone. Table 1 shows all the available tasks and the rewards associated with them.

The tasks on Image Categorization (IC) were borrowed from mTurk, while handwritten notes of a college student were scanned to generate images for the task IT. For the task AT, we used the audios of numbers (for example, one, two) instead of audios of English words (for example, cat, dog). This was done to ensure that proficiency in the English language does not affect a worker's performance on the task. Lastly, task SV was designed to collect demographic information like age, gender, education level, and monthly income of users. Both IC and IT tasks had 100 images each while 20 audio clips were available in AT. There was only 1 SV task with four questions on user demographics. Fig. 3 shows the design of all the four available tasks.

Table 1. Types of ST, DET and TT tasks supported by our microtasking application

Task	Description	Reward (Rs. 50 = ~ USD 1)	Task Category
Image Categorization (**IC**)	Look at an image and answer YES if it contains a person.	Rs. 0.2 per image	Selection
Image to Text (**IT**)	Type the word shown in the scanned image	Rs. 0.2 per image	Data Entry
Audio to Text (**AT**)	Convert a 5-6 sec audio to text	Rs. 1 per audio	Transcription
Survey (**SV**)	Choose an answer from multiple options.	Rs. 5 for the complete survey	Selection

It is important to note that we did not crawl mTurk or other microtasking services to import their tasks automatically into our application. Instead, we manually chose particular tasks for our application which are suitable for Indian users. For example most of the AT tasks on mTurk have audio in an American accent which might be difficult for Indian users to understand. Therefore, we chose to use numeric audio clips in an Indian accent for our AT tasks. In short, the format and categories of the tasks in our application were similar to the tasks on popular microtasking services like mTurk, but the content of the tasks was tailored to suit the target users.

As mentioned in the model description, the need for instant remuneration makes it difficult to validate the work done by the workers. However, we wanted to ensure that the passengers are doing the work seriously instead of merely guessing or randomly answering the questions in the task. To achieve this, we introduced a "qualification phase" at the beginning of each task which consisted of a few challenges whose answers were already known to us. It should be noted that the users (passengers and driver) are not aware of the qualification phase. During the qualification phase, each user response is verified and reward is credited to users balance only if the answer is correct. If users answer 80% of the challenges correctly, they are allowed to proceed to the remaining task, otherwise they are asked to work on some other task.

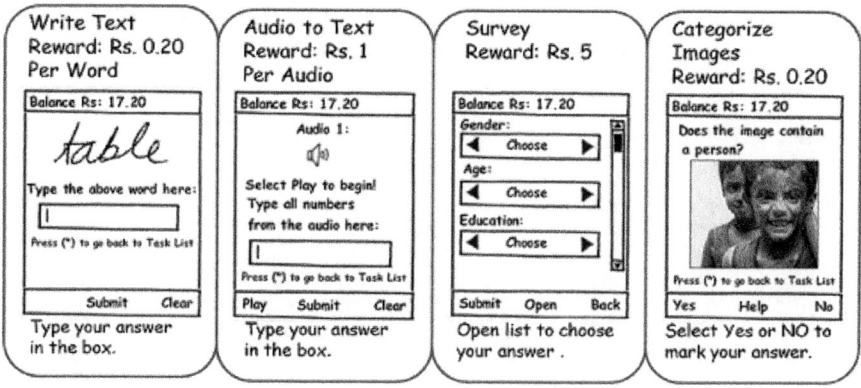

Fig. 3. Tasks available in the microtasking application

Results. The results of our study are promising and suggest that the Commodity Centric Crowdsourcing Model indeed has potential in developing countries. During the two week study, auto-rickshaw drivers offered the phone to 204 passengers for doing the microtasks, out of which 174 (25 female, 149 male) accepted the offer and availed of a discount of value greater than Rs. 5. The total discount availed by 174 passengers altogether was Rs. 4433 ($\mu = 25.4$, $\sigma = 11.9$). On average each passenger worked on ~79 microtasks to complete a total of 13,781 microtasks involving IC, IT and AT tasks. Fig. 4 shows the distribution of discounts among passengers. More than 100 passengers got a discount in the range of Rs. 15-25.

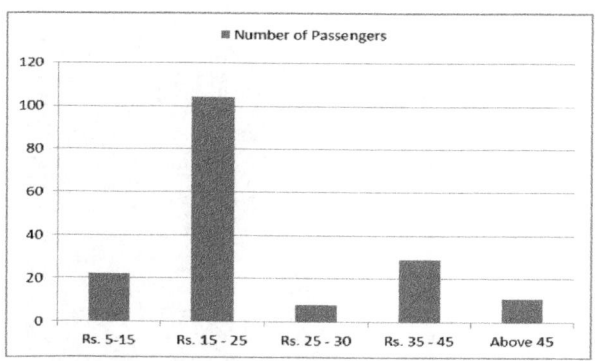

Fig. 4. Distribution of discounts among passengers (Rs. 50 = ~ USD 1)

Average journey fare and journey duration was Rs. 41.2 and 27 minutes respectively, while average time spent on microtasks was 13 minutes. As expected, we observed a strong correlation between journey fare and the discount (Pearson's $r(172) = 0.77$, $p < 0.05$). Fig. 5 shows the results from the survey task. Out of the 174 passengers 71(15 female, 56 male) passengers responded to the survey task (SV). 73% of the respondents had an education level of grade 12 or lower, and more than 50% of the respondents had a monthly income less than Rs. 5000. In contrast, recent mTurk survey of 200 Indian workers reported that nearly 80% of the respondents had at least a bachelor's degree [5]. This result implies that CCCM is capable of reaching segments of workers who typically are not mTurk users.

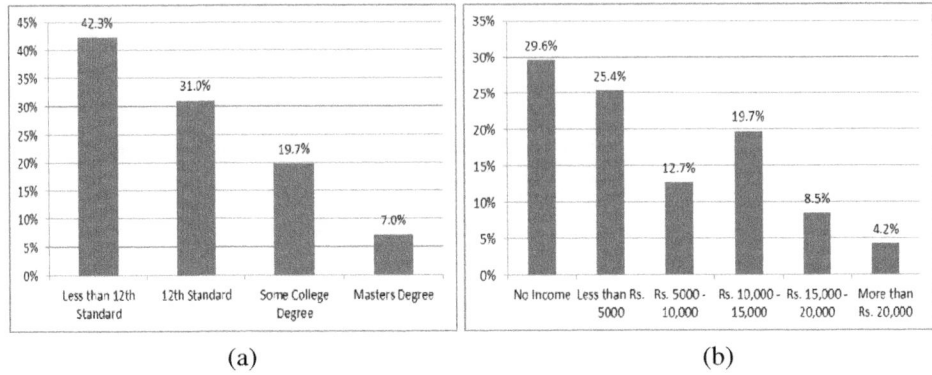

(a)   (b)

Fig. 5. (a) Education level of the survey respondents, (b) Monthly income of the survey respondents

Task Accuracy. The accuracy for both Image Classification (IC) and Image-to-Text (IT) tasks was 91.2% and 92.5% respectively while Audio-to-Text (AT) had an accuracy of 79.65%. One possible explanation for the low accuracy in AT can be the existence of traffic noise in the auto-rickshaw[2] which might have made it difficult for the user to listen to the audio. Fig. 6 shows a user listening to the audio inside an auto-rickshaw.

Fig. 6. A user sitting inside an auto-rickshaw is working on audio transcription and listens to the audio by keeping the phone close to his ears

Task Preference. IC and AT were clearly the favorite among the users with 66% and 64% users attempting to work on each respectively while only 24% users attempted to work on IT task. Majority of the users who started the IC or AT task carried on to

---

[2] An auto rickshaw does not have a door on either side which makes it difficult to avoid the surrounding noise.

finish all the available challenges[3] before moving on to another task. Only 17% of users who started working on IT carried on to finish all the available challenges for IT. The low response to IT is understandable as mobile text entry is relatively difficult and takes more time. Although AT also required users to enter text, we believe that the idea of listening to an audio clip made it more alluring for the users to do the task.

Next we discuss the qualitative findings of our study.

Change in Work Behavior of Auto-Rickshaw Drivers. On the 4th day of the study, two of the auto-rickshaw drivers told us that they prefer to serve those passengers who they thought would be able to work on Microtasks. They would often go and wait near an education institute (for example, colleges, private tuition institutes) hoping to serve a student, even if it required them to travel an extra mile to reach there. Earlier they used to wait outside temples, hospitals, shopping malls; but now they preferred to wait near places where they could find potential workers for the microtasks. Additionally, they started preferring passengers who would travel for shorter distances (30-45 minute drives) so as to reduce the loss of time in case a passenger denies working on the microtasks during the journey.

Selection Bias by Auto-Rickshaw Drivers. Auto-rickshaw drivers would often decide whether to offer a passenger a phone based on his/her age, gender, appearance, boarding point, and his/her familiarity with English. Instead of offering the phone to the passenger right at the start of the journey, the drivers chose to interact with them for a few minutes and gauge their ability to do microtasks. Only when they thought that the passenger might be able to do some tasks, they would offer the phone to him/her.

This result is particularly interesting because it shows that the drivers were using their "human intelligence" to profile the workers. Microtasking services such as mTurk also ask the users for their profile information at sign-up and assign the tasks accordingly. The drivers accomplished the same using their human intelligence.

Motivated Auto-Rickshaw Drivers. Auto-rickshaw drivers were quite excited about the system and wanted to take the full advantage of the earning opportunity presented to them. One of the drivers commented – *"God has given me this golden opportunity to earn some extra money. Now I have to work hard and earn as much [money] as I can."*

Happy Passengers. We interviewed 5 passengers (2 female, 3 male) to get feedback on the system. Three of them were studying in a college, one was doing a job and one was a housewife. All the participants said that they would like to work on these tasks mainly because a) it allows them to get immediate discount on the auto-rickshaw fare, and b) it is a good way to pass time during the journey.

Auto-rickshaw drivers often mentioned that passengers returned a small share of the discount as a gesture of regards (like a tip) towards the driver. This amount varied from Rs 1 to 10. The custom of tipping auto-rickshaw drivers is not at all common in India – the only reason why the passengers gave this tip was because they were happy

---

[3] As mentioned in the description of the microtasking application, the IC and AT tasks had 100 images each, while IT task had 20 audios.

with the discount given by the auto-rickshaw driver. One of the drivers quoted a passenger saying –

"I [passenger] am very happy today; you [driver] have given me a discount, I will also give you some discount."

Passengers Work More When They Are Travelling in a Group. Out of the 174 passengers, 45 passengers were accompanied by one or more people. We observed that multiple passenger trip earned greater discounts than the ones with only single passenger (t(172) = 2.89, p < 0.01). This result was surprising because we were expecting that people travelling in group would spend less time working on tasks as they might be busy talking to each other. We also observed that the passengers travelling in group solved AT with an accuracy of 89.45% which is greater than the overall accuracy of AT (79.65%). Although we do not have any data to explain the cause of this result, we believe that the presence of one more person might have enhanced the ability of the group to hear, interpret and remember the content of the audio, thus resulting in higher accuracy.

Retained Interest of Passengers. We came across 6 cases when a passenger travelled twice in the same auto-rickshaw. The auto-rickshaw drivers reported that while travelling for the second time the passengers immediately asked for the phone. Many of the passengers asked the drivers for their phone number and showed interest in travelling regularly with them.

4.2   Study 2

Results of the first study show that CCCM is capable of reaching segments of workers who typically are not mTurk users, by bringing crowdsourcing tasks to them and by commodity based compensation. This is the key result that bolsters our premise for the CCCM model. As an added exploration, however, we felt it might be useful to see if the model also appeals to a typical mTurk user (e.g. a college student). In essence, in addition to expanding the reach of crowdsourcing tasks to broader populations, as shown in Study 1, we are looking at whether a simple change in compensation from monetary to commodity might make a difference to existing populations who already partake in crowdsourcing activities. While this second study, unlike Study 1, is arguably not as crucial to assessing the validity of the entire CCCM model, it nonetheless will shed some light as to the compensation aspect of the model. Therefore, we designed a comparative user study with college students in urban India to compare their reactions to CCCM as compared to a mTurk-like interface.

Participants. Eighteen undergraduate students (5 female, 13 male) from a engineering college in Gandhinagar (India) participated in the study. Participants were aged between 19-22 years and were enrolled in a Computer Science program. The students were hired through an open call via email and public announcement. All the students lived on the college campus and each participant owned a PC with 24 hour internet connectivity. None of the participants had prior exposure to mTurk or any other microtasking platform.

Methodology. To compare the CCCM model against the conventional mTurk-like crowdsourcing model, we created two different web interfaces. The first interface (I1) was built on the mTurk model where users can login and work on a microtask to earn money. The second interface (I2) was a meal and beverage coupon gallery, where users can do a microtask in return for a food or beverage (i.e. commodity) coupon. Because the students lived on the college campus and bought their daily meals from the college cafeteria, we decided to choose meal and beverage coupons as the commodity of our crowdsourcing model. I2 had coupons for five different varieties of food items valued in the range of Rs. 10-40. In order to get a coupon, users had to complete microtasks of equivalent value. The coupons could only be redeemed at the college cafeteria. We bought coupons from the college cafeteria in advance and gave them to the students on completion of the microtask. In both I1 and I2, the microtasks submitted by the workers were verified and they were informed about its acceptance within 24 hours of the submission.

Table 2 below shows the list of available tasks and the reward associated with each of them. All the tasks and the rewards associated with them were taken from mTurk. The Article Writing (AW) task required the worker to write a 200-300 word article on a given topic. The reward for each topic was different and varied between Rs. 10-40. In Audio Transcription (AT) task, workers had to transcribe English language audios, while the Extract text from images (ETI) task required the workers to extract textual content from an image. All these tasks can be found in abundance on mTurk and they attract large number of workers with varying skill sets.

Table 2. Available tasks in I1 and I2

Task	Description	Reward (Rs. 50 = ~ USD 1)
Article Writing (**AW**)	Write a 200-300 word article	Rs. 10-40
Audio Transcription (**AT**)	Transcribe 10 audio files each 5-7 secs in duration	Rs. 1 per audio
Extract Text from Images (**ETI**)	Identify and extract content from 20 scanned images	Rs. 0.50 per image

We did a within-subject experiment in which participants were randomly divided into two groups. For counterbalancing, one group was subjected to I1 first and I2 later (with a gap of one day in between to verify the tasks submitted for I1) and vice versa for the second group. The study was conducted in a week's time with each group being subjected to I1 and I2 for 3 days. At the end of the study follow-up interviews were conducted with all the participants. For I1, students could collect their cash earnings from the researcher after their tasks were approved. For I2, coupon codes were sent to the users on their mobile phone after the task was approved. Apart from this, each participant was given Rs. 50 for their participation in the study.

Results. Out of the 18 participants, two participants failed to participate in the second half of the study, thus resulting in a total of 16 participants (8 in each group). In I1, participants completed tasks worth Rs. 690 ($\mu = 43.12$, $\sigma = 58.49$) as compared to Rs. 1460 ($\mu = 91.25$, $\sigma = 88.73$) with I2.

Paired t-tests show a trend that users worked and earned more ($t(15) = 2.04$, $p < 0.06$) in I2 (CCCM) than in I1 (mTurk model). Fig. 7 shows distribution of tasks completed in both I1 and I2. Extract Text from Image (ETI) got the highest hits among all the three available tasks. During the exit interviews, participants reported that ETI was the easiest of all three tasks, while Audio transcriptions (AT) and article writing (AW) were both challenging and required more time to complete. Few of the participants reported problems in audio streaming, which might be a reason for the low popularity of AT.

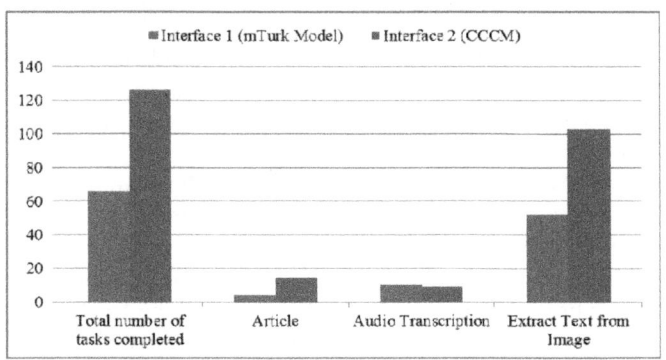

Fig. 7. Number of task completed by users in both I1 and I2

Seven participants out of 16 said they would prefer I2 while 5 participants voted for I1 arguing that once they leave the college campus, the coupons will lose their importance. The remaining 4 participants were neutral because they felt that the amount of work required in both the models is the same. A participant commented that he prefers I2 because it allows him to fulfill his desires and also save money at the same time. Giving an example, he said:

"As a student, I have to spend my money wisely and cannot afford to eat burger often; but this [coupon] gives me opportunity to do so. If I get money instead, I will think of saving the money and may not fulfill my desires".

Therefore, his desire for a commodity (burger) motivated him to do the microtasks. Another user mentioned:

"I eat here (college cafeteria) daily, so these coupons could be used daily. Also it feels good to get something for free."

Overall, we observed three types of motivations for participants to work on microtasks:

M1) Desire to earn - participants thought that the platform helps them earn something, either money or commodity.

M2) Desire to save on daily expenses - participants thought that the platform enables them to save on daily expenses by giving a commodity for free.

M3) Desire for commodity – participants thought that the platform helps them satisfy their longing for the commodity.

The decision to work on I1 is only based on motivation M1 while all M1, M2, M3 come into play when a user is exposed to I2. On basis of these results we argue that our model is capable of attracting users' with varied levels of motivation. Moreover we believe that microtasks, when tied to a commodity, can leverage the existing visibility of the commodity, thereby increasing the overall visibility of microtasking platforms.

5   Discussion

CCCM Increases the Visibility and Reach of Microtasking Services. Out of the 71 passengers who completed the survey task in the first study, more than 73% had an education level of grade 12 or less. In contrast, past surveys with mTurk users in India have reported that a large majority of the users at least had a bachelor degree [5, 11]. This result implies that CCCM has the potential to reach those segments of workers which are less likely to be on mTurk.

We also found that the educated and technology savvy crowd workers in our second study had different motivations to perform microtasks, such as *'desire to earn'*, *'desire to save'*, and *'desire for commodity'*. Services like mTurk only cater to the *'desire to earn'*, thus leaving out a section of crowd workers who may have other motivations. CCCM, however, attracts workers with all three motivations and can therefore increase the adoption of microtasking services even among the educated and technology savvy users.

User Profiling and Task Distribution. We observed that the auto-rickshaw drivers offered the mobile phone to only selected passengers. The selection criterion was based on their perceived understanding of passengers' capability to work. The main factors affecting their choice were – passenger's gender, age, language of communication, dressing, and boarding point of the journey. This result is particularly interesting because it shows that the drivers were using their "human intelligence" to profile the workers. Microtasking services such as mTurk also ask for a worker's profile information at sign-up and assign them the tasks accordingly. The drivers accomplished the same using their "human intelligence" and their perceived understanding of a user's profile.

We believe that the intelligence of the human mediators (commodity providers) can be used to recruit and distribute tasks effectively. For example, in the auto-rickshaw scenario, we can group the microtasks into following user categories: 1) College Student, 2) Housewife, 3) Working Professionals, and 4) Others. Before handing over the phone to the passenger (crowd worker), an auto-rickshaw driver can choose one of these categories based on his perceived profile of the passenger. This will ensure that the microtasks given to a worker are relevant for them. For instance, a task related to food recipes can be pushed to a housewife.

Additionally, relevant tasks can be distributed based on the commodity chosen by a worker. For example, a person seeking to purchase an online scientific article is likely to be capable of performing intellectual tasks like article writing. In future, we will explore these task distribution mechanisms based on human-intelligence and commodity choice.

Choice of Tasks and Commodities in CCCM. One of the characteristics of CCCM is that the commodity provider remunerates the workers right after the microtask is completed. This need for instant remuneration, however, leaves little time for task verification. Secondly, when crowd workers are in need of a commodity, they may not have time work on lengthy microtasks.

Therefore, those tasks, which can be (a) done in spurts and (b) do not require a formal verification, are better suited for this model. For example, tasks involving content verification, categorization, surveys and OCR tasks will be preferred over tasks like essay writing.

The choice of commodities in CCCM should be based on the type of microtasks that we want to get done from the workers. For example, microtasks related to surveys and advertisements would prefer to have new crowd workers every day. Such microtasks would benefit from a commodity such as 'auto-rickshaw fare' (study 1) which is more likely to see new workers every day. Similarly, a microtask which requires data from the same set of workers over a period of time would benefit from commodities like 'cafeteria food coupons' (study 2) as the cafeteria is more likely to see the same set of college students every day.

Human Intermediaries as Pervasive Computing Resources. It is clear that the human intermediaries (commodity providers) have a major role to play in the CCCM model. The auto-rickshaw drivers used their human intelligence to profile the passengers and offered the mobile phone only to those passengers who they perceived as qualified enough to work on the microtasks. They also helped the passengers in resolving any queries about the interface or the tasks.

It is important to devise proper incentives for the Commodity Providers to keep them motivated over time. We offered a 20% commission on the value of the microtasks to the auto-rickshaw drivers and found that they were happy with it. Other incentive mechanisms like fixed monthly salaries for Commodity Providers can also be explored.

Payment to Commodity Providers. CCCM reduces the complexity of payment by the microtasking service. Instead of paying all the crowd workers, a microtasking service only has to pay the Commodity Providers. For our study, we paid the commodity providers (auto-rickshaw drivers) in cash. However, in a real-life system the amount can be transferred into their bank accounts.

If the Commodity Providers do not have a bank account, as was the case with the three auto-rickshaw drivers we recruited, they can be given a commodity relevant to them. For example, the auto-rickshaw drivers require fuel on a daily basis, so a microtasking service can give them fuel credits which can be redeemed at different fuel stations. The microtasking service can then do a banking transaction with the fuel station, which is more likely to have a bank account.

Microtask Distribution in Physical Settings. In a real-world deployment of CCCM in physical settings, distribution of microtasks can happen over SMS as demonstrated by Gupta et al. [19]. When a worker approaches the commodity provider (e.g. auto-rickshaw driver), he/she can send a authorization SMS to the microtask repository along with the cellphone number of the worker. In response, the microtasking repository can push the tasks to the worker's phone directly. After the task completion, a notification about the total earning can be sent to both the worker and the commodity provider.

Apart from reducing the burden on the commodity provider, this approach also helps the microtasking repository to gradually create a profile of the workers based on the type of tasks completed by them. This profile information can later be used to push relevant tasks to the workers.

Limitations of the Model. In our model, the crowd workers do the microtasks for a short period of time which makes it hard for them to become task experts. However, in service like mTurk, workers repeatedly do the same microtasks over a period of time, hence developing an expertise in that microtask.

The need for instant remuneration in our model makes it challenging to use those microtasks (for example, summarizing a paragraph of text) which need verification or quality check from the task provider. The worker would want the commodity instantly and may not want to wait till the verification is complete. We feel that those tasks which can be completed in small spurts are more suitable for this model.

Clearly, our proposed model cannot replace the conventional model of crowdsourcing used by services like mTurk. However, it is an effective way of reaching a much more diverse population of crowd workers who are less likely to join mTurk like services voluntarily.

6   Conclusion and Future Work

We presented a Commodity-Centric Crowdsourcing Model (CCCM) which enables the users to get a commodity of their choice by working on microtasks. Our proposed model address the problems related to low visibility of microtasking services and lack of adequate payment mechanisms in developing regions. We did user evaluation in urban India to understand the applicability of this model in developing regions.

For the first study, we created a prototype application for low-end mobile devices which was used by passengers of auto-rickshaws to work on microtasks. The results show that the passengers were motivated to work on microtasks for a discount on the auto-rickshaw fare. We were also able to reach crowd workers with very different demographics from a typical mTurk user, which proves the ability of CCCM in increasing visibility of microtasking services. Our second study was aimed to collect reaction of a typical mTurk user towards CCCM in comparison to convention crowdsourcing model. Results show that users have different motivations to work on microtasks such as "desire to earn", "desire to save" and "desire for commodity". CCCM caters to all these motivations, while conventional crowdsourcing models only appeal to their "desire to earn". As a result, a higher number of microtasks were done in the study with CCCM as compared to the conventional model.

We discussed the importance of human intermediaries (commodity providers) in user profiling and task distribution, and suggested ways of designing microtasking application leveraging these capabilities of the human intermediaries. We also discussed the limitation of the model which include - (a) it cannot create expert crowd workers, b) the need for instant remuneration limits the kind of tasks that can be used in the model. We do not claim that CCCM will replace the conventional crowdsourcing model. However, we do believe that it can complement the conventional model and help the microtasking services reach a much diverse set of users without worrying about the complexity of paying them with money.

In future, we want to address the issues of user profiling and task distribution and are excited about the idea of using human (Commodity Provider) intelligence for task distribution. We also plan to conduct long term user studies with auto-rickshaw drivers to understand the dynamics of the model over a longer period of time.

Acknowledgements. We thank the reviewers and the shepherd for their valuable comments. We also thank Bill Thies, Khai Truong, Animesh Nandi and Sharad Jaiswal for their continuous assistance. Finally, we are grateful to our participants for their time and effort.

References

1. Alt, F., Shirazi, A.S., Schmidt, A., Kramer, U., Nawax, Z.: Location-based Crowdsourcing: Extending Crowdsourcing to the Real World. In: ACM Nordic Conference on Human Computer Interactions, Reykjavik, IC (October 2010)
2. Frei, B.: Paid Crowdsourcing: Current State & Progress towards Mainstream Business Use. Smartsheet White Paper (September 2009)
3. BCG Report: The Internet's new Billion: Digital Consumers in Brazil, Russia, India, China and Indonesia (September 2010)
4. Eagle, N.: txteagle: Mobile Crowdsourcing. In: Aykin, N. (ed.) IDGD 2009. LNCS, vol. 5623, pp. 447–456. Springer, Heidelberg (2009)
5. Khanna, S., Ratan, S., Davis, J., Thies, W.: Evaluating and Improving the Usability of Mechanical Turk for Low-Income Workers in India. In: Symposium on Computing for Development, DEV (2010)
6. MobileWorks, http://www.mobileworks.com/
7. Okolloh, O.: Ushahidi or 'testimony': Web 2.0 tools for crowdsourcing crisis information. Participatory Learning and Action (59) (2009)
8. Reserve Bank of India: Report on trend and banking in India (October 2009), http://rbidocs.rbi.org.in/rdocs/Publications/PDFs/RTP081110FL.pdf
9. reCAPTCHA, http://www.google.com/recaptcha
10. Reddy, S., Estrin, D., Srivastava, M.: Recruitment Framework for Participatory Sensing Data Collections. In: Floréen, P., Krüger, A., Spasojevic, M. (eds.) Pervasive Computing. LNCS, vol. 6030, pp. 138–155. Springer, Heidelberg (2010)
11. Ross, J., Irani, L., Silberman, M.S., Zaldivar, A., Tomlinson, B.: Who are the crowdworkers?: shifting demographics in mechanical turk. In: CHI 2010, Atlanta, Georgia, USA, April 10-15 (2010)
12. Samasource website, http://www.samasource.org/
13. TeamLease Services. Indian Labour Report 2007: The Youth Unemployability Crisis (2007), http://www.teamlease.com/images/reports/Teamlease_LabourReport_2007.pdf
14. Telecom Regulatory Authority of India (TRAI), http://www.trai.gov.in/Default.asp
15. Willett, W., Aoki, P., Kumar, N., Subramanian, S., Woodruff, A.: Common Sense Community: Scaffolding Mobile Sensing and Analysis for Novice Users. In: Floréen, P., Krüger, A., Spasojevic, M. (eds.) Pervasive Computing. LNCS, vol. 6030, pp. 301–318. Springer, Heidelberg (2010)
16. Yan, T., Kumar, V., Ganesan, D.: Crowdsearch: Exploiting Crowds for Accurate Real-Time Image Search on Mobile Phones. In: ACM Mobisys, San Francisco, CA (2010)
17. Kube, S., Maréchal, M.A., Puppe, C.: The Currency of Reciprocity - Gift-Exchange in the Workplace. Institute of Empirical Research in Economics, University of Zurich (July 2008)
18. Kurosaki, T.: Wages in Kind and Economic Development: Their Impacts on Labor Supply and Food Security of Rural Households in Developing Countries. Institute of Economic Research, Hitotsubashi University (2008)
19. Gupta, A., Thies, W., Cutrell, E., Balakrishnan, R.: mClerk: Enabling Mobile Crowdsourcing in Developing Regions. In: CHI 2012, Austin, Texas, US, May 5-10 (2012)

Tangible and Casual NFC-Enabled Mobile Games

Luis F.G. Sarmenta

Nokia Research Center
955 Page Mill Road, Palo Alto, CA, USA
luis.sarmenta@nokia.com

Abstract. As Near-Field Communication (NFC) becomes a mainstream feature in today's smartphones, it opens up a new range of applications and games. In this paper, we introduce and explore the idea of *tangible and casual NFC games*. First, we show how we can use NFC not just for its conventional use cases of information lookup and exchange, but in novel interaction techniques that offer players the fun of manipulating physical objects as part of the gameplay. Further, we show how using the unique ID present in most NFC tags and cards enables us to create games that can be downloaded and played by users "on impulse" – anytime, anywhere, without the need to distribute application-specific tags or install any infrastructure. To demonstrate these techniques, we present several NFC games we have implemented, including novel variations of popular traditional games and toys. We also present results from a public beta trial showing that users around the world are able to successfully play and enjoy our games using transit cards, ID cards, and other cards they already have.

Keywords: HCI, tangible user interfaces, RFID.

1   Introduction

NFC (Near Field Communication) [13] is a form of RFID (Radio Frequency Identification) technology that permits point-to-point wireless communication over a short distance (i.e., a few cm). Although NFC technology has been available for several years, interest in NFC has undergone a significant revival in the past year as major players in the mobile phone industry, including Google, Nokia, RIM, Samsung, and others, have started including NFC capabilities, not just in experimental phone models, but in their mainstream smartphone platforms and devices [5].

To date, various applications of NFC have been promoted by industry (e.g., [13]) and studied by academia (e.g., [9]). The general public probably associates NFC most often with *payment-related applications* such as payments, ticketing, couponing, etc. [2], but other use cases and applications have also been proposed, including: *information lookup* (e.g., for bus schedules, virtual museum tour guides [1], movies, advertisements, etc.), *service or action initiation* (e.g., SMS requests, registrations or subscriptions, etc.), *location-based applications* (e.g., Foursquare "check-ins" [7], local information lookup), *local peer-to-peer pairing and data exchange* (e.g., Bluetooth pairing, or business card sharing [13]), and *ID or asset tracking*.

J. Kay et al. (Eds.): Pervasive 2012, LNCS 7319, pp. 361–369, 2012.

In this paper, we focus on another application area in which we believe NFC has a strong potential for bringing value: *mobile gaming*.

The idea of using NFC for mobile gaming is not new. Over the years, several games have been demonstrated using NFC or RFID, including *location-based games* (e.g., geocaching, treasure hunts, chasing games, etc. [6]), *collectible card games* (e.g., Mattel's Hyperscan, cited in [11]), *static smart poster-based games* (e.g., quiz games [10]), *dynamic projector-based games* (by DOCOMO Euro-Labs [3,8]), and *peer-to-peer games* (e.g., 2-player games where NFC is used to establish a Bluetooth connection [14], or multi-player games similar to "hot potato", where NFC is used to "pass" a virtual object from one player to another by tapping phones [12]).

Our contribution in this paper is to expand the horizons of NFC-enabled mobile games even further by showing how we can use NFC to create new mobile games that are both *tangible* and *casual*. By **tangible** we mean that our games use NFC as an *interactive* mechanism to offer players the fun of manipulating physical objects as an integral part of the gameplay. This is different from many prior NFC games, which use NFC only momentarily for Bluetooth pairing, or only for ID or information lookup purposes that can also be achieved with visual barcodes [4]. By **casual**, we mean that our games are designed to reach out to the growingly important market segment of gamers who do not seriously plan or budget for their gaming ahead of time. Specifically, our games are designed to be downloadable and playable "on impulse", requiring only an NFC-enabled phone and a few *non*-application-specific NFC tags. This is different from most previous NFC-enabled games, wherein game developers first had to invest money and effort into distributing application-specific tags and/or installing infrastructure (e.g., smart posters or readers in certain locations), *and* users then had to go out-of-the-way to actually play the games (e.g., go to physical stores to buy application-specific cards, or run around town looking for tags to tap). With our games, game developers can simply post new games to the application store. Users can then download these new games any time they feel like it, and immediately start playing them wherever they are, using NFC cards they already have, such as transit cards, ID badges, hotel keys, loyalty cards, and others.

This paper has three main parts. First, we present several new NFC-enabled games that we have developed that are not only interesting in themselves, but also demonstrate new interaction design patterns that can be mixed-and-matched to create many other new games. Next, we describe the techniques we have developed to enable these games to be playable "casually" using NFC tags and cards users already have. Finally, we present results from a public beta trial of our applications.

2   New NFC-Enabled Games and Interaction Design Patterns

2.1   NFC Matching Game

Figure 1 shows our first game, an NFC-enabled variation on the traditional children's matching game. As in the traditional game, players start by laying out a deck of visually identical cards. Here, however, instead of flipping over a card to reveal a picture, players tap or wave a phone over a card to briefly reveal a picture on the phone screen. Any number of players can play by passing around a single phone and taking turns tapping two cards per turn, trying to reveal cards that match. For example, Figs. 1(a) and 1(b) show a player tapping two non-matching cards, while Figs. 1(c) and 1(d) show a later turn where another player taps two matching cards.

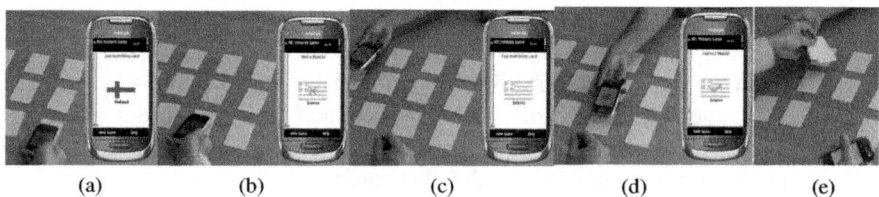

(a)   (b)   (c)   (d)   (e)

Fig. 1. NFC Matching Game

This game demonstrates a basic pattern we call **MAGIC WINDOW**, wherein the game produces the "magical" effect of revealing an unseen virtual object as the user taps or waves the phone over the physical game pieces. It also demonstrates how tangibility enables what we call **MIXED HUMAN-DIGITAL GAMEPLAY**, wherein part of the gameplay is enforced by the human players, rather than by the software. As shown in Fig. 1(e), players can keep score themselves by simply taking the cards *physically* every time they make a match (just as they would in the traditional game).

2.2   NFC Drum Repeat

Figure 2 shows NFC Drum Repeat, a game similar to the classic game Simon. Here, instead of pressing buttons on a toy device, a player taps NFC tags with his phone to play drum sounds. In each round, the phone plays a sequence of drum beats, as shown in Fig. 2(a), and the player then has to repeat this sequence by tapping the corresponding tags in the right sequence, as shown in Fig. 2(b). There are also other modes of play, such as "Reverse" mode, "Free Play" mode, and a mode where the player has to hit the right drum at the right time. We also have a version that allows users to record their own sounds to use in place of the original drum sounds, and another version, shown in Fig. 2(c), that can be played using a real teddy bear with NFC tags embedded in its paws, for a more truly "tangible" experience.

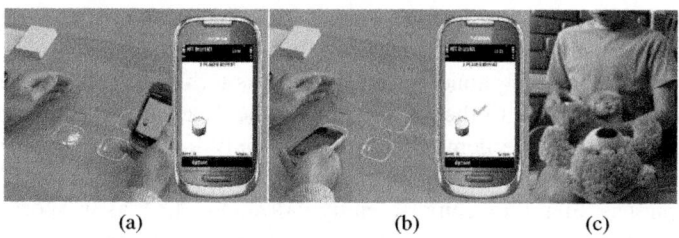

(a)   (b)   (c)

Fig. 2. NFC Drum Repeat game

This game demonstrates two useful patterns that can be used in designing other NFC games: SEQUENCE MATCH, wherein the game challenge involves tapping certain tags in a certain sequence, and the TAG-AS-BUTTON pattern, wherein the tapping of an NFC tag is used as an equivalent to the pressing of a button or key.

2.3   NFC Word Shuffle

Figure 3(a) shows our NFC Word Shuffle game. Here, players physically shuffle a deck of NFC-tagged alphabet cards, and then draw and lay out a subset of them (6 to 16 cards) on a playing surface. They then try to form as many words as possible, within a time limit, by tapping on the alphabet cards.

(a)   (b)

Fig. 3. PARALLEL PLAY in (a) NFC Word Shuffle, and (b) NFC Gem Shuffle

Although it can be played alone, NFC Word Shuffle is most engaging when played with multiple players using their own phones, tapping on the same cards at the same time. This kind of gameplay, which we call PARALLEL PLAY, enables a new kind of engaging user experience that is not possible in a conventional multiplayer mobile game wherein players play only by touching their own phone screens. Since players are playing in the same physical space, they have to think fast, move fast, and avoid bumping into each other as they try to reach the cards they want to use. At the same time, interesting new social effects are possible, as players can see how well the other players are doing, or even "cheat" by watching other players find words.

2.4   NFC Gem Shuffle

Figure 3(b) shows NFC Gem Shuffle, an NFC-enabled game we have developed that is akin to the traditional "battleships" game, and which demonstrates a game pattern we call HIDE-AND-SEEK. In this game, the first player "hides" virtual gems "inside" NFC cards by tapping his phone on different cards (while the player is not looking). He then passes the phone to the second player, the "seeker", who then tries to guess and tap the cards with the gems. If the players only have one NFC-enabled phone, they can share the phone, and play by taking turns as hider and seeker. If both players have NFC phones, then they can also enjoy PARALLEL PLAY as in Word Shuffle. The players would hide gems for each other in the *same* set of cards, and then exchange phones and start seeking for gems *at the same time*, as shown in Fig. 3(b).

2.5   NFC Shakespeare Shuffle and Nursery Rhyme Shuffle

Figure 4 shows our NFC Shakespeare Shuffle game. Here, a player uses 3 to 5 NFC tags. As each tag is tapped, the phone plays (audibly) a fragment of a quote from Shakespeare. The goal of the game is to tap the tags in the correct order to complete the quote, and then to complete as many quotes as possible within a time limit. We also have a variant that uses nursery rhymes from Mother Goose instead.

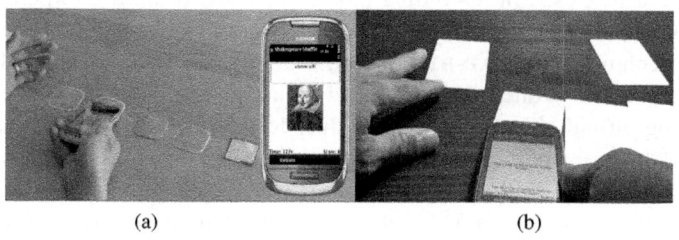

(a)   (b)

Fig. 4. Shakespeare Shuffle

This game applies forms of the MAGIC WINDOW and SEQUENCE MATCH patterns. It also further shows how the tangibility afforded by NFC-based user interfaces creates novel experiences not possible in conventional mobile gaming. For example, in informal trials (with adults and children), we observed that some players naturally discovered that instead of having to remember *where* they heard each quote fragment, they can reposition the tags themselves in *physical* space as they scan through and listen to them (as shown in the example in Fig. 4(b)). Then, after they have gone once through all the tags and put them in their right places, they can easily recompose the whole quote by tapping the (rearranged) tags from left to right.

3   Enabling Casual NFC Gaming

In addition to demonstrating new interaction techniques, our games also demonstrate the novel ability to use read-only *non*-application-specific tags that the user already has for other purposes, and which have not been pre-configured specifically for each game. We are able to achieve this by using the *unique id* (UID) field of each NFC tag. This is a read-only number that is typically: (a) globally unique, and (b) readable in a wide variety of NFC cards people already have, including cards whose main data blocks are secure and unreadable, such as transit cards, hotel keys, credit cards, etc. Specifically, we have developed several techniques that work by building a mapping between the UIDs of the tags used in the game (which represent distinct individual physical objects) and a corresponding virtual object or action in the software space.

In one of our techniques, **MAP-BY-PROMPT**, the application on the phone shows the user a virtual object, and then waits for the user to tap a physical token. The UID from the tapped tag is then mapped to the corresponding virtual object. For example, in NFC Drum Repeat, the game starts with a setup phase wherein the phone tells the user to lay out any 4 NFC tags he may have. The phone then proceeds to display to the user each of the 4 different drums, prompting the user to tap the tag that he wants to use for each drum. From then on, the user can use his 4 tags as the 4 drums in any of the tasks of the game. Note that the "prompt" from the software does not have to be fully automated, but may also be initiated by the user. For example, the software may allow the user to first use the phone's touchscreen to choose a particular virtual item (e.g., a certain kind of drum) before tapping the physical tag that the user wants to map to that item. Aside from NFC Drum Repeat, we use MAP-BY-PROMPT in Gem Shuffle (where it is used in the hiding phase), and Word Shuffle (where it is used to allow the user to create a deck of alphabet cards out of "recycled" NFC cards).

Another technique is **MAP-BY-ORDER**, wherein we add UIDs to the end of a growing list U as the game progresses, and then map the UIDs to virtual objects in a corresponding virtual objects list V, according to their respective positions on the list (i.e., the UID of the first tag tapped during a game is stored as $U[0]$ and mapped to virtual object $V[0]$, while the UID of the next (different) tag tapped is stored as $U[1]$ and mapped to virtual object $V[1]$, etc.). Combined with another technique we call **VIRTUAL SHUFFLE**, wherein we randomize the order of the objects in the virtual objects list V, MAP-BY-ORDER is useful in games like the Matching Game and Shakespeare Shuffle, wherein the gameplay involves randomness and does not require the application logic to know the physical position of the tags. In such games, these techniques allow the games to "just work" *without* requiring a registration step. For example, in Shakespeare Shuffle, a player can simply pull out any 5 NFC cards from his wallet and start playing immediately with the cards. As the player taps the 5 cards (in any order), a different part of the same quote is played back for each card, as if the system somehow "magically" hid content in the cards before even seeing them.

4   Evaluation

In October 2011, we released the NFC Matching Game, Shakespeare Shuffle, and Nursery Rhyme Shuffle for free to the public, first through Nokia's Beta Labs web site, and then more widely through Nokia's application store. (Thanks to Hae-Jin Lee for the visual design of the released versions, not shown here.) Since blank NFC tags were not easily available, our apps told users, "You can use NFC tags you already have, including tap-able transit cards, ID cards, etc." To ensure users' privacy, we did *not* include any data collection or reporting functionality in the games themselves. However, our download and help pages encouraged users to visit Beta Labs to learn more about the games and give feedback. Users who signed in to Beta Labs and clicked on the download or "join the trial" links in our project page were registered as trial members, and sent an email inviting them to complete an online survey.

As of mid-February 2012, we had around 2250 registered trial members on Beta Labs, and had received 47 usable responses (excluding a few responses that looked like "spam"). As shown in Fig. 5(a), we found (somewhat disappointingly, but not unexpectedly) that most of the survey respondents were not able to play the games. The most common reason was simply not having an NFC-enabled phone. (Although the Beta Labs web site had a list of compatible phone models, apparently many users ignored this list.) Among users who had NFC phones, many were unable to find any

NFC tags that worked, or were able to find a few working tags, but not enough to really play with. The left half of Fig. 5(b) shows types of cards from different countries that users said they tried but which did not work. Most of the user reports were not specific, so some of these cards may not have been contactless at all, or may have been using a non-NFC protocol. Notably, however, we see that many users tried playing with their credit cards, but said that these did not work. Some of these cases may have been due to a known limitation in the Nokia JavaME runtime at the time regarding reading "Type 4" NFC smartcards. In our own tests, we also found that some credit cards *do* work, but due to the size and position of the antenna inside the card, users have to position the phone in exactly the right way to read the card.

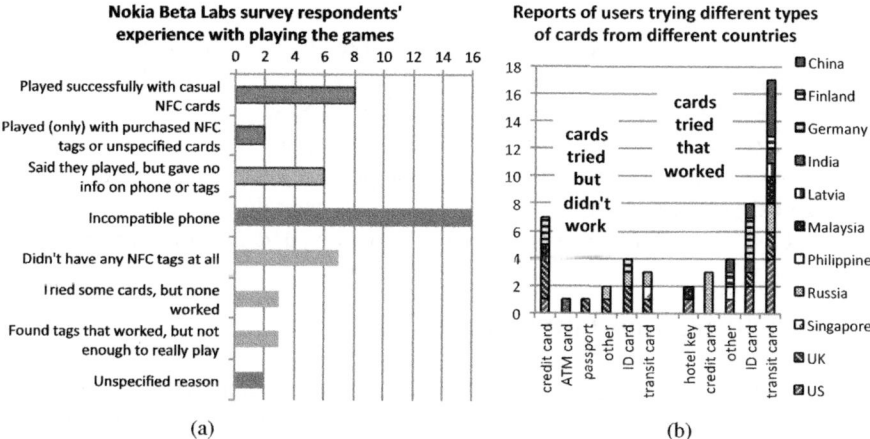

Fig. 5. Users' success in playing the games and finding NFC cards

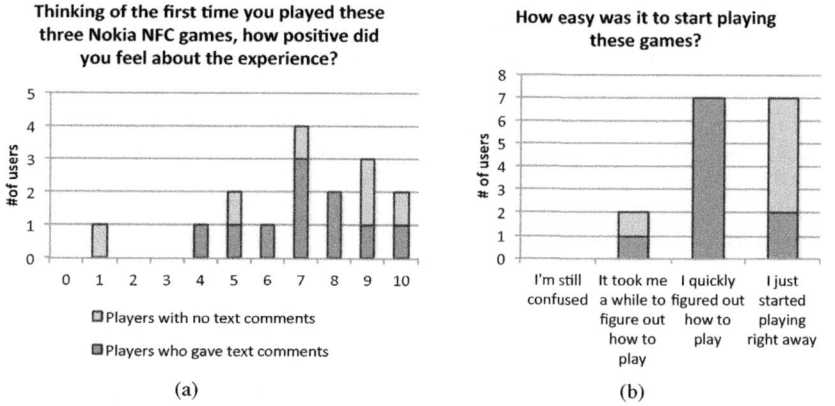

Fig. 6. Survey responses from users who were able to play the games

On a positive note, it is encouraging to see that a good fraction of the users (16 of 47) *were* able to play, and moreover, that most of them were able to do so by using "casual" NFC cards. As shown in the right half of Fig. 5(b), transit cards in several cities around the world worked well with our games. (These cities include Beijing, Boston, Helsinki, Kuala Lumpur, Los Angeles, Moscow, Mumbai, San Francisco, and others.) Several people also reported playing with student or government ID cards, and other cards such as loyalty cards, club membership cards, etc. Some also pooled cards with their friends. Furthermore, as shown in Fig. 6, players generally had a positive experience, and found it easy to start playing the games. Several users were very positive (e.g., "I enjoyed all the games. I will play multiplayer this weekend with my friends," and, "Very nice games especially for children."), while some found the games too simple (e.g., "It's very boring!!"). The general sense we got from users was somewhere in-between (e.g., "I was pretty amazed by the NFC functionality but overall the gameplay is not very interesting," and "They're creative but too simple."). We take these as positive results, since we did not really expect users to be too excited about the simple non-branded content used in our games, but really intended the games to be eye-opening demos of the possibilities of NFC.

In summary, while our trial results show that NFC phones and tags may not yet be as ubiquitous as we would want them to be, the positive results we *did* get from users encourage us, and show that *when* NFC phones and tags *do* become more pervasive, games that use our techniques would be easy to deploy, and easy to learn and enjoy.

5   Conclusion and Future Directions

In this paper, we introduced the idea of tangible and casual NFC games, showed several novel examples, and identified reusable design patterns for even more games. We also showed how, by using UID mapping techniques, we now make it possible to create NFC-based games that users around the world can play using transit cards and other everyday NFC cards, instead of requiring game developers to install smart posters or sell tags. One possibility for further research would be to explore adding a social dimension to this gamification of everyday NFC cards (e.g., like done in [4] for barcodes). It would also be exciting to see our techniques applied toward creating more games, especially *educational games*, wherein the intuitive, tangible, "magical", and face-to-face kind of gameplay that NFC enables can bring much value.

References

1. Blöckner, M., Danti, S., Forrai, J., Broll, G., De Luca, A.: Please Touch the Exhibits! Using NFC-based Interaction for Exploring a Museum. In: Proc. MobileHCI 2009 (2009)
2. Boyd, J.: Here comes the wallet phone. IEEE Spectrum 42(11) (2005)
3. Broll, G., Graebsch, R., Holleis, P., Wagner, M.: Touch to Play – Mobile Gaming with Dynamic, NFC-based Physical User Interfaces. In: Proc. MobileHCI 2010 (2010)
4. Budde, A., Michahelles, F.: Product Empire – Serious play with barcodes. In: Proc. Internet of Things Conference (2010)
5. Clark, M.: A definitive list of NFC Phones. Near Field Communications World (viewed in February 2012), http://www.nfcworld.com/nfc-phones-list/

6. Coulton, P., Rashid, O., Bamford, W.: Experiencing 'Touch' in Mobile Mixed Reality Games. In: Proc. of the 4th Intl. Conf. in Computer Game Design and Technology (2006)
7. Foursquare.com: Experimenting with NFC check-ins for Google I/O (May 9, 2011), http://blog.foursquare.com/2011/05/09/ experimenting-with-nfc-check-ins-for-google-io/
8. Hardy, R., Rukzio, E., Holleis, E., Wagner, M.: Mobile interaction with static and dynamic NFC-based displays. In: Proc. MobileHCI 2010 (2010)
9. Procs. of IEEE International Workshops on Near Field Communication (2009-2011)
10. Leichtenstern, K., Andre, E.: Studying Multi-User Settings for Pervasive Games. In: Proc. MobileHCI 2009 (2009)
11. Martinussen, E.S., Arnall, T.: Designing with RFID. In: Proc. of TEI 2009 (2009)
12. Nandwani, A., Coulton, P., Edwards, R.: NFC Mobile Parlor Games Enabling Direct Player to Player Interaction. In: Proc. 3rd Int'l. Workshop on NFC (2011)
13. Near Field Communication and the NFC Forum: The Keys to Truly Interoperable Communications (October 2007) http://www.nfc-forum.org/resources/ white_papers/nfc_forum_marketing_white_paper.pdf
14. Qt Bluetooth Tennis (2011), http://doc.qt.nokia.com/qtmobility-1.2/bttennis.html

Big Brother Knows Your Friends: On Privacy of Social Communities in Pervasive Networks

Igor Bilogrevic[1], Murtuza Jadliwala[2,*], István Lám[5], Imad Aad[3],
Philip Ginzboorg[4], Valtteri Niemi[4],
Laurent Bindschaedler[1], and Jean-Pierre Hubaux[1]

[1] LCA1, EPFL, Lausanne, Switzerland
[2] EECS Department, Wichita State University, USA
[3] Nokia Research Center, Lausanne, Switzerland
[4] Nokia Research Center, Helsinki, Finland
[5] Faculty of Electrical Engineering and Informatics, BME, Hungary
firstname.lastname@{epfl.ch,wichita.edu,nokia.com}, lam@crysys.hu

Abstract. Wireless network operators increasingly deploy WiFi hotspots and low-power, low-range base stations in order to satisfy users' growing demands for context-aware services and performance. In addition to providing better service, such capillary infrastructure deployment threatens users' privacy with respect to their social ties and communities, as it allows infrastructure owners to infer users' daily social encounters with increasing accuracy, much to the detriment of their privacy. Yet, to date, there are no evaluations of the privacy of communities in pervasive wireless networks. In this paper, we address the important issue of privacy in pervasive communities by experimentally evaluating the accuracy of an adversary-owned set of wireless sniffing stations in reconstructing the communities of mobile users. During a four-month trial, 80 participants carried mobile devices and were eavesdropped on by an adversarial wireless mesh network on a university campus. To the best of our knowledge, this is the first study that focuses on the privacy of communities in a deployed pervasive network and provides important empirical evidence on the accuracy and feasibility of community tracking in such networks.

1 Introduction

Every day, mobile operators collect large amounts of users' data that is mined for commercial and performance goals, such as billing, throughput, coverage and usage statistics. In addition to the explicit information (such as cost, duration, location) that can be derived from the communications, operators and infrastructure owners are able to gain additional knowledge based on the communication and contextual patterns, without any action from the user for this regard [1,2]. Users' home/work locations [1,2], activities [3], interests [4] and social networks [5,6] can be inferred from their location and social interactions, much to the detriment of not only their own privacy, but also to that of their peers.

---

* The co-author was with EPFL when this work was accomplished.

J. Kay et al. (Eds.): Pervasive 2012, LNCS 7319, pp. 370–387, 2012.

More recently, telecom manufacturers have also added support for seamless, low-cost, wireless device-to-device communications, such as Nokia Instant Community [7], AirDrop by Apple [8] and FlashlinQ by Qualcomm [9], thus complementing existing infrastructure-based communications. The possibility of real-time data sharing among devices, without the need for infrastructure, enables people to form localized and short-lived groups or *communities* of users, which can emerge in scenarios where the infrastructure is inadequate, expensive, untrusted or hostile [10,11]. Although still an emerging research subject in the wireless domain [12], pervasive communities and their structured networks of interactions are able to significantly improve the performance of opportunistic networks [13,14], by leveraging on the structural properties and patterns of the evolving user interactions. In the literature, there are several routing and packet-forwarding algorithms [15,16,14] that exploit the underlying evolving social interactions to improve the network performance, mostly based on the frequency of recorded Bluetooth encounters. Similarly, social communities have been studied from the behavioral perspective [5,17,18], in order to analyze people's preferences and group formation characteristics. The undoubted value of friendship networks and social ties to service providers such as Facebook and Twitter has also dramatically increased their monetary value [19], as more and more targeted advertisements and tailored services are being proposed to groups of users with similar attitudes and interests.

In spite of the soaring interest for the analysis and exploitation of pervasive communities in the wireless domain, in regard to privacy very little has been achieved. Privacy of communities and their members is a major concern in regions where the ability to keep such information from being inferred by unscrupulous third-party providers or suppressive governments is critical [10,11]. Furthermore, the increased availability of public WiFi hotspots and the rapid deployment of low-power and low-range cellular base stations (femtocells) [20] makes such inference even more accurate, as more precise user proximity data can be collected, regardless of the kind of upper-layer protocols and applications. The risks of unsolicited user profiling, data censorship, racial discrimination and political repression, based on users' physical proximity derived from short-range communications, are a major concern. Because most of the existing literature on communities in wireless networks has been primarily focused on performance or human behavior, to the best of our knowledge there is no single empirical work that has addressed the issue of the privacy of communities in deployed wireless networks.

In this paper, we address the problem of community privacy by taking a comparative analysis of the exposure of social relationships and encounters in a deployed wireless peer-to-peer (P2P) network. Over a four-month trial (March-June 2011) with 80 participants, we studied and quantified the extent of leakage of private community information by users, by providing empirical evidence about the network or infrastructure owner's accuracy of reconstruction of the social communities of people. Our work is unique in three respects:

- We provide the first privacy analysis of the extent of exposure of community information in a deployed wireless network.
- We experimentally evaluate and compare the wireless sniffing stations owner's accuracy of reconstruction of the social communities of people, based on the observed traffic patterns, with the local proximity and encounter data that is collected by the mobile devices.
- We characterize the evolution of the social interactions among the participants and evaluate the strength of their interactions by implementing three different social interaction measures that take into account the number, the proximity, the recency and aging effects of social relationships in the underlying wireless network.

The remainder of the paper is organized as follows. In Section 2 we introduce and detail the trial framework, its system and network models, whereas in Section 3 we outline the community and privacy analysis. In Section 4 we present the results of the analysis of communities and their privacy *vis-à-vis* the external adversary. We discuss the related work in Section 5. We conclude the paper and suggest ideas for further work in Section 6.

2   Trial Setup

During four months (March-June 2011), we conducted a large-scale trial with 80 participants on the EPFL university campus, in order to collect encounter and proximity data. Similarly to previous data collection campaigns [21,22,23], we programmed and distributed 80 Nokia N900 smartphones to the volunteering participants, sampling a coherent population of master's students and instructors of two classes taught during the spring semester. The participants were asked to carry their device with them as frequently as possible, and they were allowed to use it as their primary phone. The complete description of the goals and methods of the questionnaires and interviews is described in [24]. At the end of the trial, we obtained useful information from 66 devices, amounting to almost ten GBs of collected log data and over 8 million packets captured by the adversarial network. The remaining 14 devices were either not used regularly or did not collect the data properly, hence they were excluded from the analysis.

2.1   Device Configuration

The Nokia devices were configured with both standard infrastructure-based communications, such as cellular and WiFi, as well as with a novel WiFi-based P2P technology, called *Nokia Instant Community* or NIC [7]. Users could connect to both standard Internet services using the WLAN or cellular interface of the device, as well as to an experimental context-aware wireless P2P messaging platform − in order to exchange information with their physical neighbors in a P2P fashion (Fig. 1(a)). Moreover, several campus and course-related applications were developed in order to stimulate and encourage the usage of the devices

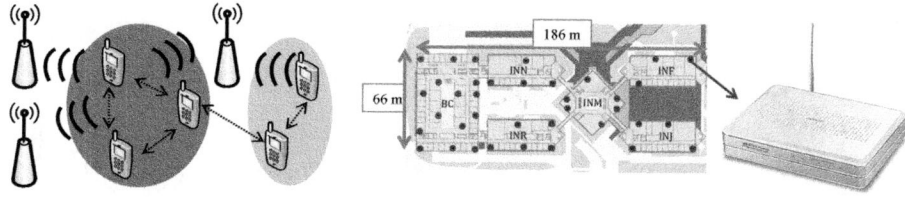

(a) Trial network architecture.   (b) Deployed wireless mesh network of 37 APs controlled by the adversary.

Fig. 1. Trial setup and deployed eavesdropping network controlled by the adversary

throughout the duration of the trial. In order to enhance the context-awareness of the pre-installed applications, the devices were running background services that collected and stored, at regular intervals of [1-30] seconds, information such as the list of neighbors, the associated Received Signal Strength Indicator (RSSI) and the time stamp in the local memory. Whenever a participant connected to the Internet with the device, the new encounter logs were uploaded on a centralized database storing all device logs. To preserve users' anonymity, we removed all personal identifier information (such as the mapping between MAC address - IMEI - participant ID) from the database.

2.2 Adversarial Model and Infrastructure

We emulate a practical adversary who monitors a fixed area using a limited number of wireless sniffing stations. Specifically, the adversary is the owner of a deployed wireless mesh network of 37 APs (Asus WL-500gP APs running Open-WRT Linux) in a specific region of the campus [25], covering one level of six interconnected buildings which have a very high user (student) density (Fig. 1(b)). The coverage area includes the classrooms in which the two classes that the students attended took place. We assume that the adversary passively eavesdrops on the participants' communications, and that he[1] periodically uploads the eavesdropped data to a centralized server, populating a unified log database for each AP.

In order to perform the pervasive community reconstruction attack discussed in the following section, we assume that the adversary collects the 3-tuple (Time stamp, Source MAC, RSSI) from the messages sent by the participants' smartphones. As encryption is sometimes used to protect the confidentiality of network and application-layer data in real networks, we assume that the adversary does not have access to such data. This reinforces the practicality and better embodies real-world limitations that an external adversary might have, being much weaker than the omniscient Dolev-Yao adversary [26]. Moreover, the information collected by the adversary is present in almost all kinds of wireless networks and

---

[1] For conciseness and without loss of generality, we refer to the adversary in the masculine form, although both masculine and feminine forms apply.

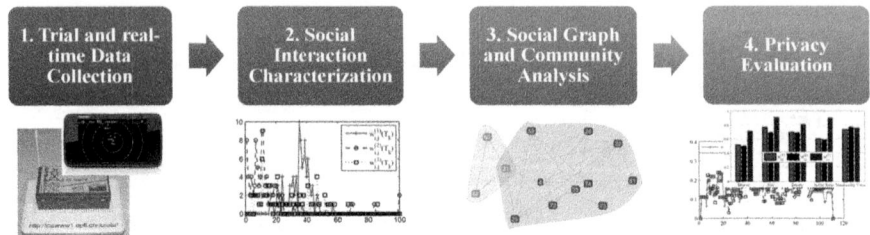

Fig. 2. Flowchart of the pervasive community privacy evaluation process

technologies (such as Bluetooth, WiFi and cellular), which enlarges the applicability and scope of the results. In this work, we assume that the adversary does not have direct access to any information stored on the mobile devices, and that all devices are honest (i.e., not colluding with the adversary). As part of our future work, we will consider a stronger adversary that can collude and gain access to some of the mobile devices as well.

3   Community Analysis

In order to evaluate the extent of community information leakage in our setting, we first need to define the analytical framework that captures the pervasive community information from the collected data. In this section, we introduce some background on communities in wireless networks and describe how we evaluate communities and their privacy in our trial. A flowchart of the entire process is depicted in Fig. 2.

3.1   Background

In society, people tend to organize themselves in social groups or communities, such as family, work colleagues and hobby groups, where members usually have stronger similarity traits with other members than with non-members [27]. From a graph-theoretic perspective, people and their relationships can be represented by an undirected graph $G = (V, E, W)$, where the vertex set V corresponds to people, the edge set E expresses the existence of a relationship between people, and the weight function W quantifies the intensity of such relationship. In their simplest form, communities can then be represented as subgraphs $\{C_i = (V_i, E_i, W_i,)\}_{i=1}^{M}$, where $C_i \subseteq G$ and M is the number of communities C_i.

Several community detection (or clustering) algorithms are present in the literature, and they work on either unweighted/weighted and undirected/directed graphs. Although hierarchical clustering [28] and modularity-based algorithms [29] − surveyed in [27] − have been applied to community detection, most of them lack a fundamental characteristic that is intrinsic to social communities. People are often members of several communities at the same time, such as friends, family members and work colleagues, and most of the aforementioned algorithms assign a single vertex to only one community. In order to allow a vertex to be assigned to multiple (possibly overlapping) communities, Palla *et al.* [30] developed a technique, the *Clique Percolation Method (CPM)*, which allows different communities to share vertices. The idea is that communities are formed by the union of adjacent k-cliques (complete graphs with k vertices), where two k-cliques are adjacent if they share $k - 1$ vertices. Due to the social nature of our trial and the experimental setting, we use the CPM algorithm to detect pervasive communities based on physical proximity and encounter data.

After the pervasive communities have been discovered, several privacy-sensitive statistics can be obtained from the community structure, their overlap and their members. We describe the relevant statistics in Section 3.3.

3.2   Trial Framework

In order to model the collected encounter data using a graph, hereafter we describe the type of information that is used in order to define the existence and intensity of relationships between users.

Trial Data. In our trial, we have two sources of proximity information: (i) the local device logs collected by the mobile devices and containing encounter (list of neighbors, the time stamps and the RSSI values of received packets), and (ii) the adversarial (sniffing) logs containing the headers of the packets sent by the mobile devices, which include the time stamps and RSSI values of received packets at the sniffing stations, as well as the device ID of the sender.

We use these two data sources in order to formulate the "strength" or intensity of the social relationships between users and to define the weights of the edges connecting the respective vertices in the social graph $G = (V, E, W)$. There are two types of proximity information in our network: device-to-device RSSI data (collected on the devices) and device-to-AP RSSI data (collected by the adversary). From the local device logs, we can directly obtain the device-to-device proximity information because the recorded RSSI values on the receiving device depend on the real distance to the sending device. However, this is not exactly the case for the RSSI values recorded by the adversarial network, as they depend on the distance between the sending device and the receiving sniffing station, and not the receiving mobile device. Therefore, the adversary needs to derive the device-to-device proximity information from the device-to-AP RSSI values. Hence, we first need to estimate the position of a device, and then compute the device-to-device proximity information in order to determine the weights between vertices of the social graph.

To this end, we developed a robust localization algorithm based on RSSI trilateration [31], which determines the estimated position of a received packet based on the RSSI at all sniffing stations that received that packet. Using the position estimate, we then compute the distance and RSSI between mobile devices, as described later in this section.

Social Interaction Intensity. We define three distinct weight functions $\{w_{i,j}^{(d)}\}_{d=1}^{3}$ between the vertices $i, j \in V$, taking progressively into account the proximity, the intensity and the aging and recency of the relationships between users. We divide the timeline of the trial into discrete time intervals $\{T_k\}_{k=1}^{N}$, where $N = 120$ days, and for each day T_k we define the weights $w_{i,j}(T_k)^{(d)}$ between users i, j.

The first and simplest weight function is the (shifted, non-negative) average of the RSSI value between a pair of users i, j for each day T_k, defined as

$$w_{i,j}(T_k)^{(1)} = \left(\frac{1}{c_{i,j}(T_k)} \cdot \sum_{q=1}^{c_{i,j}(T_k)} RSSI_{i,j}(T_k, q) \right) - r_{min}$$

where $c_{i,j}(T_k)$ is the sum of the number of packets received by i (and sent by j) and received by j (and sent by i) during the day T_k, $RSSI_{i,j}(T_k, q)$ is the RSSI value of a packet q received by a user i (and sent by j) or received by j (and sent by i) during the day T_k, and r_{min} is the minimum RSSI value that was recorded during the trial. For instance, we fix $r_{min} = -100$ dBm as no RSSI values lower than -100 dBm have been recorded by any device. Apart from the intensity, this weight function does not consider the duration of the encounters (as it normalizes the intensity by the number of packets) between users or any aging or recency effect.

The second weight function takes into account the duration of the encounters through the sum of the (shifted, non-negative) RSSI values between users i, j, for each day T_k. It is defined as

$$w_{i,j}(T_k)^{(2)} = c_{i,j}(T_k) \cdot w_{i,j}(T_k)^{(1)} = \sum_{q=1}^{c_{i,j}(T_k)} (RSSI_{i,j}(T_k, q) - r_{min})$$

As the devices who are in continuous radio contact automatically exchange more context messages than the non-connected devices, this weight function takes into account the duration of the contacts, in addition to their intensity.

As communities of mobile devices are dynamic and evolve over time, the third weight function captures the natural evolution of social relationships between individuals, where past experience, recency and current state determine the intensity of interactions among people [32]. In this way, two users that have spent much time together in the past, but have not met on a given day, would still keep a relationship during that day (which is not the case for $w_{i,j}(T_k)^{(1)}$ and $w_{i,j}(T_k)^{(2)}$), even if its intensity is lower due to the aging effect − thus avoiding strong temporal fluctuations. Inspired by the formulations in [32,33], we define the third weight function as

$$w_{i,j}(T_k)^{(3)} = \mathbf{1}_{c_{i,j}(T_k)>0} \left(\tau \cdot w_{i,j}^{(3)}(T_{k-1}) + (1 - \tau) \cdot \gamma_{i,j}(T_k) \right) \tag{1}$$
$$+ (1 - \mathbf{1}_{c_{i,j}(T_k)>0}) \cdot \left(w_{i,j}^{(3)}(T_{k_e}) \cdot \theta_{i,j}(T_k, T_e) \right)$$

where

$$\gamma_{i,j}(T_k) = \frac{1}{\alpha} \cdot w_{i,j}(T_k)^{(2)}$$

$$\theta_{i,j}(T_k, T_e) = \exp\left(-\frac{\lambda(T_k - T_e)}{1 + \sum_{r=0}^{\min(T_k - T_e, T_e)} m_{i,j}(T_e - r)}\right)$$

$$m_{i,j}(T_k) = \begin{cases} 1 & \text{if } \gamma_{i,j}(T_k) > \beta \\ 0 & \text{otherwise} \end{cases}$$

and $\mathbf{1}_{c_{i,j}>0}$ is the indicator function, $0 \le \tau \le 1$ is the aging coefficient, $\alpha > 0$ is the normalization factor, $0 < \lambda \le 1$ is the temporal decay value, $0 \le T_e \le T_{k-1}$ is the last day before T_k when users i, j exchanged messages, $m_{i,j}(T_k) \in \{0, 1\}$ is the recency factor that indicates whether a meeting took place during T_k or not, and $\beta \ge 0$ is the meeting threshold value. The idea behind the formulation is the following: If users i, j exchanged at least one message on a day T_k, then the weight of their edge is an exponential moving average of the aged weight – accumulated up to the day before (T_{k-1}) – and the recent day's weight; on the contrary, if i, j did not exchange any message on day T_k, the current day's weight is a function of the previously accumulated weight, the frequency of their encounters just before the last encounter and the amount of time between the last time i, j had exchanged messages (T_e) and the current day T_k.

The weight functions can be directly applied to the local-device proximity information, as the available proximity information (time stamps, RSSI values from neighboring devices and their IDs) are sufficient for their computations. However, an intermediate step is required in order to compute the weights by using the external (adversarial) proximity information (time stamps, RSSI values from devices to sniffing APs and device IDs). In the following we show how to use the external proximity information in order to compute the edge weights.

User-Distance Estimation by the Adversary. As the adversary does not have access to device-to-device proximity data, he can decide to only use the estimated positions of a user i in a day T_k, defined as $P_i(T_k) = \{p_i(T_k, 1), \ldots, p_i(T_k, b)\}$, where b is the number of subintervals of a day T_k and $p_i(T_k, z) = (x_i(T_k, z), y_i(T_k, z)) \in \mathbb{R}^2$ is the estimated position of user i in the subinterval z of day T_k. Moreover, because there is a possibility that a user's packet may not be detected in each subinterval z, due to mobility or radio interference, we assume that the last position estimate $p_i(T_k, z_{last})$ of a user i is valid in f subsequent subintervals, if no $\{p_i(T_k, z_{last} + 1), \ldots, p_i(T_k, z_{last} + f)\}$ are available (Fig. 3).

With such information, the adversary computes the edge weights as follows:

(1) $\forall z \in \{1, \ldots, b\}$, compute $p_i(T_k, z)$ for all users i observed on day T_k.
(2) $\forall z \in \{1, \ldots, b\}$, compute the estimated Euclidian distance $d_{i,j}(T_k, z) = \|p_i(T_k, z) - p_j(T_k, z)\|$ between any two users i, j observed on day T_k.

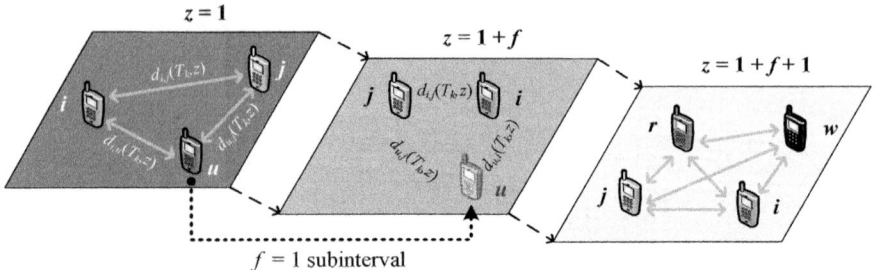

Fig. 3. Users' positions estimates by the adversary. In this example, the adversary has the position estimate of user u at $z = 1$ but not at subsequent subintervals. In this case, u's last position estimate (at $z = 1$) is assumed to be valid in f subsequent subintervals. Here $f = 1$.

(3) $\forall z \in \{1, \ldots, b\}$, compute the estimated RSSI value according to the adapted Haka-Okumura model for indoor radio propagation [34]

$$\widehat{RSSI}_{i,j}(T_k, z)[dBm] = P_t + 20 \log\left(\frac{\lambda}{4\pi}\right) + 10n \log\left(\frac{1}{d_{i,j}(T_k, z)}\right)$$

where $P_t = 20$ [dBm] is the transmission power of the mobile device, $\lambda = 0.125$ [m] is the wavelength, $n = 4.8$ is the path-loss exponent suited for office environments such as the university buildings under observation. The $\widehat{RSSI}_{i,j}(T_k, z)$ value replaces $RSSI_{i,j}(T_k, q)$ in the weight functions $w_{i,j}^{(d)}(T_k)$, where $z \in \{1, \ldots, b\}$.

Weight Distributions. Due to the different features of a social relationship that each weight function models, their numeric values fall in different domains. For example, if $\alpha = 100$, $\beta = 1$, $\lambda = \tau = 0.5$ we have $0 \leq w_{i,j}^{(1)} < r_{min}$, $0 \leq w_{i,j}^{(2)} < 2.5 \cdot 10^5$ and $0 \leq w_{i,j}^{(3)} < 600$. It is therefore necessary to put them on the same scale for the identification of communities, as simply comparing the absolute values of the three weight functions is pointless. Hence, rather than comparing absolute values, we compare the weight distributions relative to the maximum of each weight function for each day T_k. To this end, we select an equal number of bins $I^{(d)}$ for each weight function $w_{i,j}^{(d)}(T_k)$. We then count the number of weight values that fall inside each such bin for all weight types, and we compare the distributions.

Fig. 4(a) and Fig. 4(b) show the relative edge weight distribution for a day T_k, by using the internal (local device) and external (adversarial estimate) input data, respectively. We see that, compared to the adversarial data, the local device data yields more pronounced characteristics for all three weight types and provides a more discriminating information set for the subsequent community detection phase, whereas the external data is less feature-rich due to the presence of uncertainty in the estimates of the proximity between users. This means

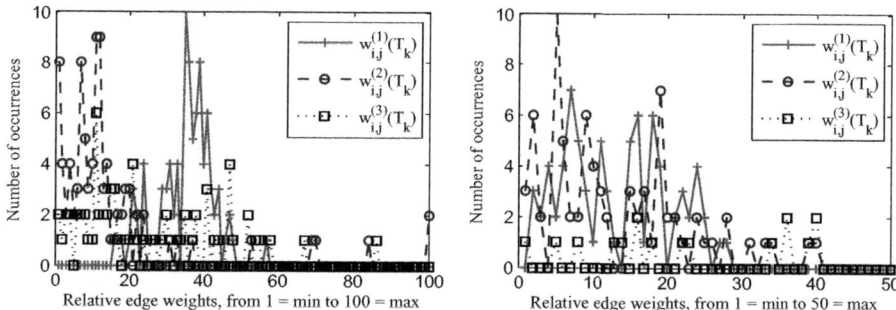

(a) Using internal (local device) input data.

(b) Using external (adversarial estimates) input data.

Fig. 4. Relative edge weight distribution for different input data sets

that the adversary will likely struggle to infer with high accuracy the community characteristics for that day. We quantify such inaccuracies in Section 4.

Next, we describe the method we adopted to evaluate the extent of community information leakage and the related privacy measures.

3.3   Communities and Privacy

Having quantified the social interaction intensity as edge weights between any two trial participants, we now outline the community detection process, the suitable community statistics and privacy measures used to evaluate community privacy in our work.

Community Detection. In its simplest form, the CPM community detection algorithm is defined for undirected and unweighted graphs [32], thus requiring only connectivity between vertices in order to discover communities. However, in order to consider the "strength" of the interactions between vertices, it was extended to work on weighted graphs by the use of a threshold weight w^*. In its weighted version, the CPM algorithm considers the existence of an edge $e_{i,j}$ between two vertices i, j if and only if the weight $w_{i,j}^{(d)} > w^*$. In order to determine the threshold weight w^*, Palla *et al.* propose to choose a value such that "the largest community becomes twice as big as the second largest one"[30], which is below the critical value w^*_{crit} for which a giant connected component arises [35].

In our experiment, we calibrated the $\{w^*_q\}_{q=1}^T$ threshold values on a per-day basis, instead of keeping the same w^* throughout the trial. Because most of the participants followed one specific class that took place on Wednesdays, and the remaining days they might or might not have followed any common classes, we registered high RSSI proximity values on course days and more sparse values on non-course days. Hence, the per-day threshold $\{w^*_q\}_{q=1}^T$ was better suited for such bi-modal proximity patterns.

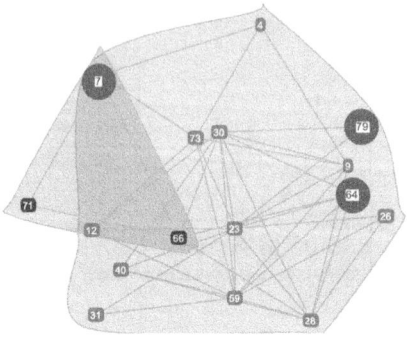   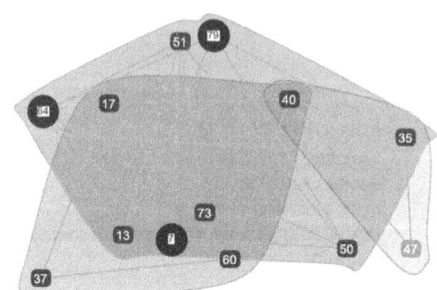

(a) Communities inferred by using inter-   (b) Reconstructed communities by the ad-
nal data.   versary.

Fig. 5. Detected communities on a day T_k based on internal (local device) and external (adversarial estimates) data, respectively. The larger vertices are present in both
community sets.

To illustrate the output of CPM, Fig. 5(a)[2] and 5(b) show an example of
the detected communities on a given day, based on the internal data and the
observations of the adversary respectively. As it can be seen, some communities
detected by the adversary are not present in the internal case; there is however an
overlap between the members (the larger vertices) of the two sets of communities.
We discuss and quantify this difference in Section 4.

Community Statistics. In addition to detecting communities and their members, we compute five privacy-relevant and common community statistics
$\{S_{(i)}(T_k)\}_{i=1}^{5}$ that will be compared in the accuracy evaluation process. In particular, for each day T_k of the trial we compute and compare the following statistics:
S_1 is the community degree (the number of edges shared between two communities), S_2 is the distribution of the community size (the number of members of
each community), S_3 is the community density (proportion of edges out of all
possible edges relative to the sparsest set with $|C_i| - 1$ vertices), S_4 is the ratio
of total out- and in-degree of communities and S_5 is the community membership
value (the number of communities a vertex belongs to). The difference between
the results obtained using the internal and external input data is defined by Eq.
(2) as the ratio between the absolute difference of the observed statistics over
the maximum value

$$\Delta S_i(T_k) = \frac{|S_i^{ext}(T_k) - S_i^{int}(T_k)|}{\max_{\forall T_k} \left(S_i^{ext}(T_k), S_i^{int}(T_k) \right)} \qquad (2)$$

We have $\Delta S_i(T_k) = 0$ when the adversary's statistics is exactly the same as the
statistics obtained using the internal proximity data, and $\Delta S_i(T_k) = 1$ when the

---

[2] The figure is obtained by using the CFinder application developed by the authors
of the CPM algorithm, freely available on www.cfinder.org.

two statistics have the largest discrepancy (or lowest similarity). We define the adversary's accuracy in inferring the community statistics as $1 - \Delta S_i(T_k)$.

Community Privacy. In addition to the differences in statistics $\Delta S_i(T_k)$, it is crucial to assess the similarity of the community composition in order to ascertain in a comprehensive way the privacy leakage of community information. To this end, we compute the well-established Jaccard index measure [36] for community similarity on each day T_k, which is a statistic that computes the similarity between two sample sets (or communities) C_i, C_j, where values close to zero mean that the adversary did not accurately infer the communities and their members, whereas values close to one indicate a very good adversarial accuracy in inferring the same communities. The Jaccard index is defined as

$$J(C_i, C_j, T_k) = \frac{|C_i(T_k) \bigcap C_j(T_k)|}{|C_i(T_k) \bigcup C_j(T_k)|} \tag{3}$$

In order to evaluate the adversary's accuracy of reconstruction of the communities in our pervasive network, we compute the Jaccard index on each day T_k between the communities $C_i(T_k)$, detected using internal device data, versus the reconstructed communities $C_j(T_k)$, detected using the adversarial estimated proximity information. Given $J(C_i, C_j, T_k)$ for each i, j on a day T_k, we define the Jaccard index matrix $JMat(T_k)$, where each element of the matrix is defined as $JMat(T_k)_{i,j} = J(C_i, C_j, T_k)$, i.e., the Jaccard index for all pairs of communities C_i and C_j. Without having access to the internal data, the adversary has no prior knowledge about which community C_i corresponds to which reconstructed community C_j. Therefore, in order to consider the best possible match for any pair of internal/reconstructed communities for each day T_k, we choose the match $(C_i(T_k), C_j(T_k))$ that maximizes $JMat(T_k)_{i,j}$. We then compute the aggregated Jaccard index over all such best matches as

$$JI(T_k) = \text{avg}_{\forall i} \left(\max_{\forall j} (JMat(T_k)_{i,j}) \right) \tag{4}$$

for each day T_k of the trial where there is at least one community detected by using both the internal and adversarial proximity information.

In the next section we quantify the community privacy leakage by computing the accuracy measure $1 - \Delta S_i(T_k)$, and similarity $JI(T_k)$ for each day T_k and weight function $\{w_{i,j}^{(d)}\}_{d=1}^3$, comparing the results obtained using the internal (local device) and external (adversarial) input data respectively.

4   Privacy Evaluation

In this section we provide the experimental evaluation of the privacy of pervasive communities through a comparative analysis of the adversary's accuracy of reconstruction of both community statistics and memberships. First, we evaluate the privacy across the three weight functions $\{w_{i,j}^{(d)}\}_{d=1}^3$ (inter-weight accuracy), by comparing the similarity between communities and the accuracy of

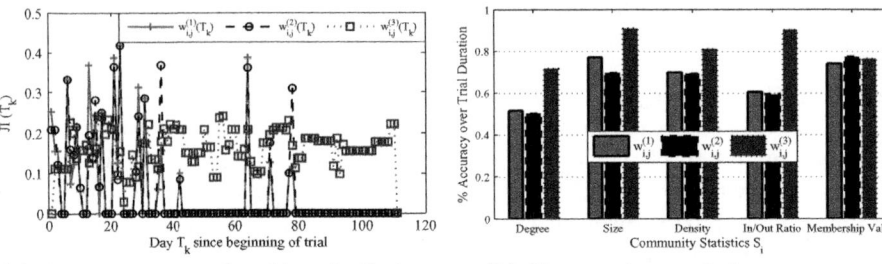

(a) Community memberships similarity.   (b) Community statistics accuracy.

Fig. 6. Adversary's accuracy of reconstruction of the pervasive communities for the three weight functions

their statistics obtained by using the internal (local device) proximity information with the external (adversarial estimates) data collected by the set of wireless sniffing stations. This will allow us to observe the evolution of the accuracy while increasing the sophistication of the weight functions, taking progressively into account several features of human and social behavior such as proximity, intensity, aging and recency of social relationships. Second, we perform an intra-weight comparison for the more realistic weight function $w_{i,j}^{(3)}$, in order to characterize the effect of the aging factor τ on the similarity and accuracy of community reconstruction attained by the adversary.

Fig. 6 and 7 show the adversarial reconstruction similarity and accuracy results with respect to the communities detected using internal data, for the inter-weight and intra-weight scenarios respectively. For Fig. 6(a) and 7(a), a value of $JI(T_k) = 0$ means that on day T_k there were no communities detected either using the internal proximity data or the external one. The complete list of the experimental parameters – selected in order to provide as much information as possible – can be found in the Appendix, which is provided as a supporting file to this document.

4.1   Inter-weight Accuracy

By observing Fig. 6(a), we first notice that the adversary is able to correctly reconstruct communities and identify their members in $20\% - 40\%$ of the cases, compared to the communities detected by using internal proximity data. In general, we observe that there is a significant difference in terms of similarity results between the first two weight functions $w_{i,j}^{(1)}, w_{i,j}^{(2)}$ and the third function $w_{i,j}^{(3)}$. The former two functions are solely based on the observations made on each particular day and independently of what happened in the previous days. Therefore one noticeable characteristic is the increased fluctuations in the similarity from one day to the other, which is a much less visible aspect for the latter weight function. As $w_{i,j}^{(1)}, w_{i,j}^{(2)}$ are very exposed to the periodicity of the course schedule of the participants, the adversary's similarity of reconstruction of the actual communities and their members greatly depends on the amount of data

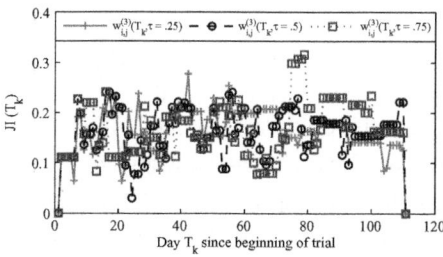 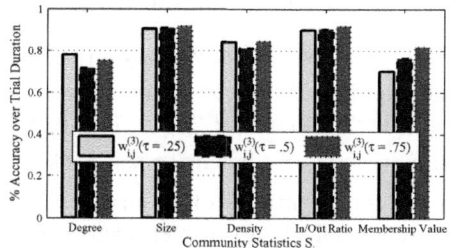

(a) Community memberships similarity.   (b) Community statistics accuracy.

Fig. 7. Adversary's accuracy of reconstruction of the pervasive communities for three different values of the aging factor τ

collected by his wireless mesh network. We notice that for the days when most students attended a particular class, the reconstruction similarity is higher (up to 40%) than for days in which students do not attend classes together. Hence even the two basic weight functions are able to provide a sensible similarity to the adversary when the users' movements are tracked by several sniffing stations simultaneously.

Contrary to $w_{i,j}^{(1)}$ and $w_{i,j}^{(2)}$, $w_{i,j}^{(3)}$ is able to capture more proximity information and allow the CPM algorithm to detect communities on the days in which the other two weight functions were unable to provide a sufficient amount of data. At the same time, however, the peaks of similarity tend to be much lower (25%) compared to the other functions. This suggests that $w_{i,j}^{(3)}$, while being able to produce more community information with scarce data, performs worse in the identification of the members in each community.

Regarding the difference in community statistics, depicted in Fig. 6(b), we observe a better accuracy for $w_{i,j}^{(3)}$ compared to $w_{i,j}^{(1)}$ and $w_{i,j}^{(2)}$. In four out of five community statistics, $w_{i,j}^{(3)}$ has an almost 40% better accuracy compared to the other functions, which indicates that the former function provides better results on a higher structural community level rather than on an lower, individual community member level.

In general, we observe that all three weight functions are better able to produce accurate community statistics (Fig. 6(b)) than to identify the correct community members (Fig. 6(a)). In particular, $w_{i,j}^{(3)}$ shows that it is possible to achieve very accurate community statistics only by relying on externally collected data, thus shrinking the discrepancy between the community statistics based on internal data and adversarial's estimates down to 9%. This result indicates that, by collecting and analyzing radio information passively and without access to the devices themselves, an adversary is able to breach the privacy of community information very successfully, although the more fine-grained identification of members of any given community remains a more challenging task.

4.2 Intra-weight Accuracy

Fig. 7(a) shows the adversary's performance in correctly identifying the communities and their individual members when using $w_{i,j}^{(3)}$ with three different values of the aging factor $\tau = \{.25, .5, .75\}$. According to its definition in Eq. (1), we assign an increasing coefficient to the past accumulated weight information $w_{i,j}^{(3)}(T_{k-1})$ in the computation of the current day's weight function $w_{i,j}^{(3)}(T_k)$. The goal is to study the effect of the "retention" of the intensity from the past on the privacy (or lack thereof) of community information.

One recurring characteristic, present also in the inter-weight comparison, is that the CPM algorithm detects communities in all days of the trial, independently of the amount of information available to the adversary on each particular day, even for a small value of τ. When $\tau = .25$, as expected the similarity fluctuates more when compared to $\tau = .5$, especially at the beginning of the trial.

However, Fig. 7(a) shows that the stabilization of the similarity is not achieved by simply increasing the value of τ from .25 to .75; in fact, for the intermediate value of $\tau = .5$, we notice that the fluctuations are less pronounced than for a smaller or larger value. This suggests that, for relatively small or large values of the aging factor, the similarity achieved by the adversary tends to diverge more frequently from steady values, indicating that a stable value for the aging factor is more likely to be in the middle of the possible values $[0.25, 0.75]$, rather than at any of the extremes. When $\tau = .75$, the adversarial similarity increases sharply as the time passes, especially towards the end of the trial. This is somewhat surprising, as we would expect that by increasing the emphasis on the past – rather than on the current weight information – the similarity would be more stable when going through the trial. This is an interesting aspect to consider in further studies on our community data.

When observing the results on the accuracy of the community statistics, as shown in Fig. 7(b), we notice that, among the three considered values of τ, $\tau = .5$ is the least accurate, compared to smaller or larger values of τ. Moreover, in four out of five statistics, the largest value of $\tau = .75$ produces the best accuracy on average over the trial duration. This suggests that, although not converging towards a stable interval for the accuracy in identifying the communities and their members, putting more emphasis on the past accumulated information does increase (on average) the adversary's accuracy in computing correct community statistics using only passively collected data from fixed WiFi access points.

Overall, the results indicate that although less stable and more accurate at inferring community structures, emphasizing the past yields better accuracy for both community detection, identification of their members and for generic community statistics. This finding in particular is concerning in regard to privacy, as the amount of individual and community data that is collected by external parties might provide very accurate statistics, especially for group and community-targeted services. These results are significant, as they show how the message source ID, contained in almost any kind of radio message, not only is enough to provide accurate social community statistics, but it is also sufficient to successfully infer almost half of the members of such communities.

5   Related Work

The structural properties of short-lived communities in pervasive networks have been recently investigated from the performance [13,14] and routing [15,16,14] perspectives; the authors of [5,17,18] investigated similar issues on the socio-behavioral level while studying people's preferences and group formation characteristics. For instance, it is shown that performance of packet-forwarding algorithms could greatly benefit from the human mobility and sporadic nature of inter-contacts [13], as the different connection frequencies between members of the same community with respect to members of other communities could significantly improve intra-community packet-forwarding while not disrupting inter-community communications. Similarly, [16] shows how forwarding performances similar to state-of-the-art algorithms could be achieved at a sensibly lower resource utilization if structural properties of communities are considered.

With respect to privacy, several works on location privacy address the risk and propose protection mechanisms for users' locations [37,38,39]. These contributions focus mostly on individual mobile users and their current neighbors. However, to the best of our knowledge, there is no prior study on the increasingly important issue of pervasive community privacy and its evaluation on a deployed network. This work constitutes the first building block for analyzing community privacy issues in pervasive networks.

6   Conclusion and Future Work

In this paper, we have addressed the important aspect of community privacy in pervasive networks. We have conducted an experimental analysis of the adversary's accuracy of reconstruction, on one hand, of the communities and their individual members and, on the other hand, of the generic community statistics that are less dependant on the correct identification of individual users inside such communities.

Through a fine-grained characterization of the intensity of social contacts among people, we quantified the accuracy in both community reconstruction and community statistics for the whole duration of the trial, showing that even basic social intensity functions capture very accurately the generic statistics, such as the degree of a community, its size and density of links. However, reconstructing more specific information about the composition of each community and their individual members remains more challenging, even when using a more comprehensive model for characterizing the intensity of social relationships, which considers recency, aging, and contact frequency in addition to proximity and duration. As a result, there is a substantial risk that accurate community information may be easily collected, inferred and misused by external third-parties, much to the detriment of users' community privacy.

Our results provide empirical evidence about the two distinct levels of community information leakage to external observers, who may be able to infer with high accuracy the different social groups and generic communities of people in pervasive networks, while being much less accurate in determining the affiliation of any particular individual to a community. As part of our future work, we intend to pursue the analysis of this dual flow of community information leakage and derive mitigation mechanisms in order to reduce information leakage and the gap between the accuracy of both generic statistics and specific people's affiliations to communities. We also intend to study the adversary's accuracy of classification of the communities and their members based on the type of their relationship, such as friends, classmates, study group and strangers.

References

1. Gruteser, M., Hoh, B.: On the anonymity of periodic location samples. Security in Perv. Comp. (2005)
2. Hoh, B., Gruteser, M., Xiong, H., Alrabady, A.: Enhancing security and privacy in traffic-monitoring systems. IEEE Perv. Comp. 5 (2006)
3. Matsuo, Y., Okazaki, N., Izumi, K., Nakamura, Y., Nishimura, T., Hasida, K.: Inferring Long-term User Property based on Users. In: IJCAI (2007)
4. Noulas, A., Musolesi, M., Pontil, M., Mascolo, C.: Inferring interests from mobility and social interactions. In: NIPS Workshop on Analyzing Netw. and Learning w. Graphs (2009)
5. Crandall, D., Backstrom, L., Cosley, D., Suri, S., Huttenlocher, D., Kleinberg, J.: Inferring social ties from geographic coincidences. Proc. Nat. Academy of Sciences 107 (2010)
6. Mardenfeld, S., Boston, D., Pan, S., Jones, Q., Iamntichi, A., Borcea, C.: Gdc: Group discovery using co-location traces. In: Int. Conf. on Social Comp. (2010)
7. Rhiain: Nokia instant community gets you social,
   http://conversations.nokia.com/2010/05/25/
   nokia-instant-community-gets-you-social/
8. Apple AirDrop, http://www.apple.com/macosx/whats-new/
9. Corson, M., Laroia, R., Li, J., Park, V., Richardson, T., Tsirtsis, G.: Toward Proximity-aware Internetworking. Wireless Communications (2010)
10. Reeves, S.: Internet is double-edged sword in arab revolts (2011),
    http://middle-east-online.com/english/?id=46109
11. Follman, M.: "Bluetoothing" Iran's revolution. Markfollman.com (2010)
12. Zhang, D., Guo, B., Li, B., Yu, Z.: Extracting social and community intelligence from digital footprints: An emerging research area. Ubiq. Intell. and Computing (2010)
13. Hui, P., Chaintreau, A., Scott, J., Gass, R., Crowcroft, J., Diot, C.: Pocket switched networks and human mobility in conference environments. In: ACM SIGCOMM Workshop on DTN (2005)
14. Chaintreau, A., Hui, P., Crowcroft, J., Diot, C., Gass, R., Scott, J.: Impact of human mobility on opportunistic forwarding algorithms. IEEE TMC (2007)
15. Hossmann, T., Spyropoulos, T., Legendre, F.: Know thy neighbor: Towards optimal mapping of contacts to social graphs for dtn routing. In: INFOCOM (2010)
16. Hui, P., Crowcroft, J., Yoneki, E.: Bubble rap: social-based forwarding in delay tolerant networks. IEEE TMC (2010)

17. Eagle, N., Pentland, A., Lazer, D.: Inferring friendship network structure by using mobile phone data. Proc. Nat. Academy of Sciences 106 (2009)
18. González, M., Herrmann, H., Kertész, J., Vicsek, T.: Community structure and ethnic preferences in school friendship networks. Physica A: Statistical Mechanics and its Applications 379 (2007)
19. Business Week: Facebook's value tops amazon.com; trails only google on web, http://www.businessweek.com/news/2011-01-28/ facebook-s-value-tops-amazon-com-trails-only-google-on-web.html
20. Femto Forum, http://femtoforum.org/fem2/pressreleases.php?id=277
21. Gong, N.-W., Laibowitz, M., Paradiso, J.A.: Dynamic Privacy Management in Pervasive Sensor Networks. In: de Ruyter, B., Wichert, R., Keyson, D.V., Markopoulos, P., Streitz, N., Divitini, M., Georgantas, N., Mana Gomez, A. (eds.) AmI 2010. LNCS, vol. 6439, pp. 96–106. Springer, Heidelberg (2010)
22. Henderson, T., Kotz, D., Abyzov, I.: The changing usage of a mature campus-wide wireless network. In: Int. Conf. on Mobile Comp. and Networking (2004)
23. Eagle, N., Pentland, A.: Reality mining: sensing complex social systems. Pers. and Ubiq. Computing 10 (2006)
24. Aad, I., Jadliwala, M., Bilogrevic, I., Niemi, V., Hubaux, J.P., Ginzboorg, P., Leppänen, K.: Nokia Instant Community at EPFL: a real-world large-scale wireless peer-to-peer trial. Technical Report EPFL-REPORT-170421 (2011)
25. Aziala-net, http://icawww1.epfl.ch/aziala/index.html
26. Dolev, D., Yao, A.: On the security of public key protocols. IEEE TIT 29 (1983)
27. Fortunato, S.: Community detection in graphs. Physics Reports 486 (2010)
28. Hastie, T., Tibshirani, R., Friedman, J.: The Elements of Statistical Learning, 2nd edn. (2008)
29. Newman, M.: Fast algorithm for detecting community structure in networks. Physical Review E 69 (2004)
30. Palla, G., Derényi, I., Farkas, I., Vicsek, T.: Uncovering the overlapping community structure of complex networks in nature and society. Nature 435 (2005)
31. Bindschaedler, L., Jadliwala, M., Bilogrevic, I., Aad, I., Ginzboorg, P., Niemi, V., Hubaux, J.P.: Track Me If You Can: On the Effectiveness of Context-based Identifier Changes in Deployed Mobile Networks. In: NDSS (2012)
32. Palla, G., Barabási, A., Vicsek, T.: Quantifying social group evolution. Nature 446 (2007)
33. Xu, K., Yang, G., Li, V., Chan, S.: Detecting dynamic communities in opportunistic networks. In: ICUFN (2009)
34. Bose, A., Foh, C.: A practical path loss model for indoor wifi positioning enhancement. In: Int. Conf. on Inform., Comm. & Signal Proc. (2007)
35. Derényi, I., Palla, G., Vicsek, T.: Clique percolation in random networks. Physical Review Letters 94 (2005)
36. Jaccard, P.: Etude comparative de la distribution florale dans une portion des alpes et du jura (1901)
37. Beresford, A., Stajano, F.: Location privacy in pervasive computing. IEEE Perv. Comp. 2 (2003)
38. Hong, J., Landay, J.: An architecture for privacy-sensitive ubiquitous computing. In: Conf. on Mobile Systems, Applications, and Services (2004)
39. Jadliwala, M., Bilogrevic, I., Hubaux, J.-P.: Optimizing Mixing in Pervasive Networks: A Graph-Theoretic Perspective. In: Atluri, V., Diaz, C. (eds.) ESORICS 2011. LNCS, vol. 6879, pp. 548–567. Springer, Heidelberg (2011)

Map-Aware Position Sharing
for Location Privacy in Non-trusted Systems

Pavel Skvortsov, Frank Dürr, and Kurt Rothermel

Institute of Parallel and Distributed Systems, Universität Stuttgart
{pavel.skvorzov,frank.duerr,
kurt.rothermel}@ipvs.uni-stuttgart.de

Abstract. Many current location-based applications (LBA) such as friend finder services use information about the positions of mobile users. So-called location services (LSs) have been proposed to manage these mobile user positions efficiently. However, managing user positions raises privacy issues, in particular, if the providers of LSs are only partially trusted. Therefore, we presented the concept of private position sharing for partially trusted systems in a previous paper [1]. The basic idea of position sharing is to split the precise user position into a set of position shares of well-defined limited precision and distribute these shares among LSs of different providers.

The main contributions of this paper are two extended position sharing approaches that improve our previous approach in two ways: Firstly, we reduce the predictability of share generation that allows an attacker to gain further information from a sub-set of shares to further increase the position precision. Secondly, we present a position sharing algorithm for constrained movement scenarios whereas the existing approach was tailored to open space environments. However, open space approaches are vulnerable to map-based attacks. Therefore, we present a share generation algorithm that takes map knowledge into account.

Keywords: Location-based service, privacy, obfuscation, sharing, map-awareness.

1 Introduction

Location services (LS) such as Yahoo! Fire Eagle, Google Latitude, InstaMapper, or Trace4Youstoring the positions of mobile users have become an important prerequisite for many advanced location-based applications (LBA). In particular, LS are beneficial if various LBAs have to be provided with the position of the mobile user. For instance, the position of a user could be accessed by several social networks like Facebook and Gowalla, a friend alert service, a location-based advertising service, a traffic congestion service, etc. Obviously, in such scenarios the LS, which usually runs on powerful servers, relieves the mobile device from sending individual positions to each LBA.

However, since user positions are privacy-sensitive information, problems might arise if the LS provider is not fully trusted by the mobile user. This might be the case for various reasons. For instance, the provider might be malicious and misuse data, e.g., selling it to another party. However, even if the provider itself is not malicious, he

J. Kay et al. (Eds.): Pervasive 2012, LNCS 7319, pp. 388–405, 2012.

might simply be unable to protect the data from attacks. As various examples in the past show, even infrastructures that were deemed to be trustworthy were subject to successful attacks, information leaks, loss of data, etc. [2], [3], [4]. With the advent of cloud computing, we are likely to see even more cloud-based location services in the future operated by non-trusted providers. Using these services is certainly attractive from a monetary and technical point of view, however, it requires concepts to reduce privacy risks.

Besides LSs, LBAs might also be only partially trusted by the mobile user. However, LBAs have to be provided with position information of a certain quality to provide the requested functionality. This leads to a situation, where the user might want to trade-off his privacy in terms of the precision of positions provided to LBAs and the quality of service provided by the LBA. For instance, it might be necessary to provide a friend alert service with positions of a precision of 200 m, whereas 1 km precision might be sufficient for Facebook to show location-based status messages. In other words, the user might want to define different *privacy levels* corresponding to different degrees of precision individually for each LBA.

In [1], we proposed the concept of *position sharing* to solve the above privacy issues. The basic idea is that the (trusted) mobile device of the tracked user splits up the precise position information into so-called position shares of limited precision. These shares are distributed among a set of LSs of *different* providers, i.e., each LS only manages position information of strictly limited, well-defined precision. The mobile users provides LBAs with access rights to access a certain number of position shares from different LSs. Using a so-called share fusion algorithm, these shares can be combined to yield a position of a certain precision which is higher than the precision of the single shares stored at the LSs. Fusing all shares restores the precise position. Therefore, different privacy levels can be defined for individual applications by providing the LBA with access rights to a certain number of shares. Besides the possibility to define different privacy levels, this approach has another important advantage: it has a graceful degradation of privacy property since a compromised LS will only reveal information of strictly limited precision. Therefore, it is possible to utilize not fully trusted LSs to store position information and still limit the risk since no single point of failure exists w.r.t. privacy.

In this paper, we are going to improve our previous system further. As a first main contribution, we propose a new share generation algorithm that increases location privacy by reducing the predictability of share generation. Therefore, it becomes harder for an attacker to derive more precise positions than intended from a certain number of shares. Secondly, our first approach only targeted free space environments where users can move without restriction. However, in highly structured areas such as cities this makes it easy for an attacker to restrict and therefore predict positions of high precision. Therefore, as the second main contribution of this paper, we propose a novel *map-aware position sharing approach* that considers movement restrictions given by the physical environment. The basic idea is to adapt the size of obfuscation areas defined by shares based on map information. Therefore, a sufficiently large area of possible positions is retained also under movement restrictions.

The rest of this paper is structured as follows. First, in Section 2 we present our system model, problem statement and formal definition of obfuscation security. In Section 3 we describe the basic position sharing approach and two extended approaches including the new map-aware position sharing. Then in Section 4 we analyze the security of obfuscation provided by the our approach. After that we overview the related work in Section 5. Finally, we conclude the results of our work and give some perspective for the future research.

2   System Model and Problem Statement

In this section, we introduce the different components of our location management system together with the formal notation used in this paper.

Our system consists of three types of components: mobile objects, location servers, and location-based applications (see Figure 1).

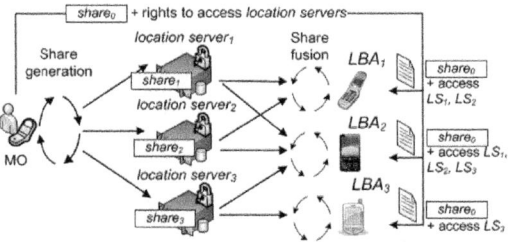

Fig. 1. System model

Mobile objects (MO) are the objects whose positions are managed on location servers and used by location-based applications. MOs correspond to users carrying a mobile device such as a smart phone with a position system like GPS. Using this positioning system, the MO can determine its current position, denoted as p_{user}. For the sake of simplicity, we assume p_{user} to be perfectly precise and accurate. This is a reasonable simplification if we assume that the imprecision introduced by position obfuscation is much greater than the imprecision of the positioning system. However, the algorithms could easily be extended to also consider the intrinsic imprecision of the positioning system.

On the MO, a trustworthy component is located that runs a share generation algorithm. Given a precise position p_{user}, a number of n shares, and a lowest precision ϕ_{min}, the share generation algorithm generates a set of position shares denoted as $S = (s_0, \{s_1, \ldots, s_n\})$:

$$\text{generate}(p_{user}, n, \phi_{min}) = S \tag{1}$$

In more detail, S consists of a so-called master share s_0 which represents a position with lowest precision ϕ_{min}. $s_1, \ldots, s_n$ are called refinement shares. Given s_0 and a set $S_k \subseteq S$ of k refinement shares, a refined position p_k can be calculated using a share fusion algorithm:

$$\text{fuse}(s_0, S_k) = p_k \tag{2}$$

The basic idea is that each refinement share increases the precision by a well-defined value Δ_ϕ. That is, fusing k refinement shares and the master share yields a position p_k of higher precision $\phi_k = \phi_{min} - k\Delta_\phi$, where $\phi_k < \phi_{k-1}$. Fusing all shares reconstructs the precise position p_{user}.

The precision ϕ is represented as a radius, if the obfuscation area is circular. However, later we will see that obfuscation areas do not need to be circular areas. Instead, an obfuscation area can have any shape. Therefore, we additionally measure the precision as the size of the area[1]. Thus, we say that a higher precision corresponds to a smaller radius and a smaller area, while a lower precision corresponds to larger radius and larger area of the obfuscation shape.

After share generation, the MO distributes the shares among a set of location servers (LS), denoted as L, where every LS is operated by a different provider. Formally, share distribution is defined as an injective function that distributes every refinement share to an unique LS:

$$\text{distribute}(\{s_1, \ldots, s_n\}, L) : S \to L \tag{3}$$

The master share is known to everybody — in particular, every location-based application, — for instance, through full replication at every LS and unrestricted access by location-based applications. Hence, every location-based application can track MOs with (at least) a precision of ϕ_{min}. Therefore, ϕ_{min} is usually chosen large, i.e., with a low precision.

Refinement shares are only known to authorized location-based applications (LBA). The MO specifies, which precision each LBA should get. Usually, this decision defines a tradeoff between the quality of service an LBA can provide with a certain precision of information, and the privacy requirements of the MO. The trusted share generation component running on the MO's device determines, how many refinement shares from the set of refinement shares are required for this precision using the above formula for ϕ_k. Then, the MO assigns access rights to refinement shares. Shares and the respective access rights are sent together to the LSs. LSs use common access control mechanisms to deliver refinement shares only to authorized LBAs. LBAs receive the necessary access rights (credentials) together with the relevant LS addresses from the MO.

The injective mapping ensures that each LS only knows exactly one refinement share (plus the master share). Therefore, a compromised LS reveals only one refinement share equivalent to a position of strictly limited precision. The precision available to an attacker increases linear with the number of compromised servers. This ensures the most important property of the approach: graceful degradation of privacy (increase of precision) with the number of compromised shares.

Theoretically, the mapping of shares to LS or the precision increase Δ_ϕ could be adjusted to the individual trustworthiness of the LS, giving more trusted LSs better or more shares. The individual trust value could be defined by a trust management system, for which several concepts have been described in the literature [5]. However, such optimizations are beyond the scope of this paper. Here, we simply assume that every server stores one refinement share per position, and every refinement share has the same precision increase Δ_ϕ.

---

[1] In order to make both precision metrics comparable, it is possible to convert the area of a non-circular obfuscation shape to a radius of a virtual circle with the size of the area.

We also assume that each MO stores a map of the environment. For each location, a map contains a binary Boolean value: true if the MO could be located at this location (e.g., a street, building, etc.); false otherwise (e.g., a lake, agriculture field, etc.). As shown later, this map knowledge is used by the share generation algorithm to generate shares that do not allow for the derivation of position information of higher precision than intended. A simple example of a binary map representation derived from a given map (Figure 2a) is presented in Figure 2b.

Fig. 2. (a) Basic map: roads and squares; (b) Binary representation of the map knowledge

Finally, we assume that share generation is only triggered sporadically rather than with every update of the positioning system. Typically, this is the case when using a "check-in" usage pattern, where the user manually publishes her position sporadically at certain locations. Although the presented algorithms could also work with continuous positions updates, subsequent (close) positions might reveal additional information to an attacker. Such problems arising from continuous updates are beyond the scope of this paper. Instead we assume that a minimum position update interval is ensured that guarantees that succeeding obfuscation shapes of precision ϕ_k do not intersect.

Problem Statement and Obfuscation Security Metrics. The problem is to find a secure share generation algorithm (implementation of function generate(p_{user}, n, ϕ_{min})) such that the following property is fulfilled for the generated shares: Given the master share s_0 and a set S_k of refinement shares, it should not be possible to derive a position with higher precision than the intended precision $\phi_k = \phi_{min} - k\Delta_\phi$. Informally, we say that the generated shares are insecure. Obviously, if this would be possible, the MO could not effectively control the precision of information offered to LBAs by assigning access rights to a certain number (k) of shares corresponding to the intended precision (ϕ_k).

The above statement is very strict considering the fact that an implementation of a share generation algorithm might always lead to a certain degree of insecurity. The best we can do is to design an algorithm that *minimizes* the insecurity of shares as much as possible. Therefore, we introduce metrics, called *obfuscation security metrics*, that quantify the degree of share security. As we will see later, we use probabilistic share generation algorithms. Therefore, our security metrics are also probabilistic metrics expressing the probability that an attacker can reveal a position of a certain precision. We propose two metrics:

Let s_0 and S_k be a master share and a set of refinement shares, and p_k be the area resulting from the fusion of these k shares. Then the obfuscation security metrics $P(\phi_{k,\text{attack}})$ defines the probability that an attacker can refine the MO's position to an area with precision $\phi_{k,\text{attack}}$ where $\phi_{k,\text{attack}} \leq \phi_k$. A perfectly secure set of shares would lead to a probability of 0.0 for every $\phi_{k,\text{attack}} \leq \phi_k$. This metrics gives insight into the absolute precision that an attacker can gain, for instance, an attacker can calculate a position of 500 m precision with 90% probability.

The second obfuscation security metric, $P_{10\%}$, defines the probability that an attacker can pinpoint the MO's position to an area of 10% size of p_k. A perfectly secure set of shares leads to $P_{10\%} = 0.1$. Or in other words: The position of MO is uniformly distributed within the obfuscation area. A non-uniform probability distribution of MO within p_k increases $P_{10\%}$ to values greater than 0.1. This metrics is based on a relative area size compared to p_k. It has to be noted that the choice of using 10% instead of another value is somewhat arbitrary reflecting the case that the attacker can gain a position of much higher precision than intended. We could also use any other relative area size.

3   Position Sharing Approaches

In this section, we present three different position sharing approaches. As basis, we start with a brief description of our basic approach published in [1], called OSPS-ASO (Open Space Position Sharing with Any Share Order). Then, we improved this approach in two ways: Firstly, the share generation of OSPS-ASO is (to a certain degree) predictable, i.e., from k out of n shares information with a higher precision than the intended precision ϕ_{min} $k\Delta_\phi$ can be derived. Therefore, we present an improved share generation algorithm called OSPS-FSO (Open Space Position Sharing with Fixed Share Order), which decreases the predictability of shares. Secondly, OSPS-ASO does not consider map knowledge, which can also be used by an attacker to increase the precision unintentionally. To solve this problem, we present a map-aware share generation algorithm called CSPS (Constrained Space Position Sharing), which considers movement restrictions given by the physical environment.

3.1   Basic Approach: OSPS-ASO

In order to explain how OSPS-ASO implements the concept of position sharing, we first give a detailed definition of shares and explain the share fusion algorithm, before we explain the generation of shares.

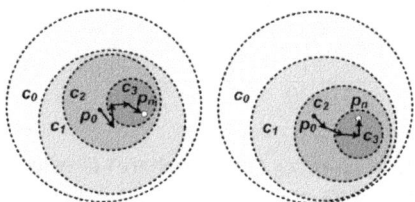

Fig. 3. OSPS-ASO: fusion of the same set of shares in different order

Algorithm 1 shows the share fusion algorithm of OSPS-ASO. With this open space approach, positions are defined as circles with radius (precision) ϕ. The master share s_0 is simply a circle c_0 with radius $r_0 = \phi_{min}$ centered at p_0. Each refinement share defines a shift vector that shifts the center of the previous obfuscation circle. At the same time, the radius is decreased by value Δ_ϕ. The fusion algorithm incrementally shifts the positions of obfuscation circles starting from p_0, and after each shift decreases the radius by Δ_ϕ.

Algorithm 1. OSPS-ASO: fusion of shares

1: **function** $fuse\_k\_shares\_OSPS\_ASO(n, c_0, s_1 \ldots s_k)$
2: $\Delta r \leftarrow r_0/n$
3: $p \leftarrow p_0$
4: $r \leftarrow r_0$
5: **for** $i = 1$ **to** k **do**
6:     $p \leftarrow p + s_i;$
7:     $r \leftarrow r - \Delta r$
8: **return** $c_k = \{p, r\}$

Note that with this approach, shares can be added in any order since the shift operation is a commutative operation (therefore the name "Any Share Order"). As a consequence, the maximal length of shift vectors has to be limited by $\Delta r = r_0/n = \Delta_\phi$. As a result, any refined circle is completely contained in the previous circle. Two examples of share fusion in different orders for $n = 4$ and $k = 3$ given refinement shares are shown in Figure 3.

The algorithm for share generation is shown in Algorithm 2. Input parameters to this algorithm are the precise user position p_{user}, radius $r_0 = \phi_{min}$ of the master share, and the total number of refinement shares n.

Algorithm 2. OSPS-ASO: generation of shares

1: **function** $generate\_n\_shares\_OSPS\_ASO(p_{user}, n, \phi_{min}, \Delta_\phi)$
2: **select randomly** p_0 **such that** $distance(p_0, p_{user}) \leq \phi_{min}$
3: **do**
4:     **for** $i = 1$ **to** $n - 1$ **do**
5:         select rand. s_i with $|s_i| \leq \Delta_\phi$ such that $p_{user} \in c_i$
6: **while** $distance(p_0 + \sum_{i=1}^{n-1} s_i, p_{user}) > \Delta_\phi$
7: $s_n \leftarrow p_{user} - (p_0 + \sum_{i=1}^{n-1} s_i)$
8: **return** $s_0 \ldots s_n$

In the first step, position p_0 of c_0 (master share) is selected such that p_{user} is distributed uniform at random within c_0 (2). Then we calculate $n - 1$ refinement shares. For each of these shares, we choose a random direction and random length within the valid length interval $[0, \Delta_\phi]$ (3-6). The last (nth) refinement share has to connect the end point of the concatenated $n - 1$ refinement shares to p_{user} (7). If the resulting length of the nth vector is smaller than or equal to the length constraint Δ_ϕ, we have found a valid set of refinement shares. Otherwise, we repeat the process, i.e., re-calculate $n-1$ random refinement shares, and try to connect their end point to p_{user} within the given length constraint.

3.2 Extended Approach 1: OSPS-FSO

Next, we are going to present the improved position sharing approach OSPS-FSO that improves the security of calculated shares.

The design goal of OSPS-ASO was to be able to combine shares in any order. Therefore, also a missing share does not prevent share fusion altogether. Also if refinement shares are missing, the remaining shares can still be fused to a position of increased precision where the precision increase linearly depends on the number of missing shares. This increases the robustness of OSPS-ASO w.r.t. failed LSs.

However, as we have shown in [1], the predictability of further shares can be also increased as an attacker knows more and more refinement shares. The obtained precision increases beyond the intended precision, e.g., if the constrained share generation parameters make the resulting vectors correlated. This is due to the length restriction of shift vectors, which ensures that refined obfuscation circles are completely contained within the unrefined circles.

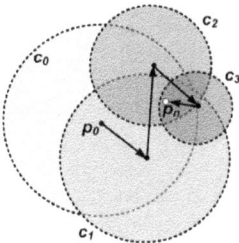

Fig. 4. Fusion of shares in a fixed order without area adjustment

We will show that the security of obfuscation can be substantially increased by combining shares only in fixed order (therefore the name "Fixed Share Order"). Unfortunately, by fixing the share order, the robustness of the scheme w.r.t LS failures of attacks is decreased. However, if the availability of location information is critical, robustness can be achieved by other means such as replication of shares.

Algorithm 3 shows the adapted share fusion algorithm of OSPS-FSO. Similar to OSPS-ASO, each refinement share defines a shift of the center of the previous circle c_{i-1}. The result is again a circle c_i with a different (predefined) radius r_i. However, since the length of the shift is not restricted anymore, c_i might not be completely contained within c_{i-1} (see Figure 4). Instead, the new obfuscated position p_k is defined by the intersection of c_i and the previous obfuscation area. Consequently, p_k might not be a circle anymore but an area defined by the intersection of multiple circles. Only the master share s_0 still must be a circle of radius $r_0 = \phi_{min}$. We denote A_k to be the size

---

Algorithm 3. OSPS-FSO: fusion of shares

1: **function** $fuse\_k\_shares\_OSPS\_FSO(n, c_0, s_1 \ldots s_k, r_1 \ldots r_k)$
2: $\quad A_k \leftarrow c_0$
3: $\quad p \leftarrow p_0$
4: $\quad$**for** $i = 1$ **to** k **do**
5: $\quad\quad p \leftarrow p + s_i$
6: $\quad\quad c_i \leftarrow \{p, r_i\}$
7: $\quad\quad A_k \leftarrow A_k \cap c_i$
8: $\quad$**end for**
9: $\quad$**return** A_k

---

of the area resulting from the intersection of k circles, i.e., the fusion of k refinement shares and the master share:

$$A_k = \text{area}(c_0 \cap c_1 \cap \ldots \cap c_k) = \pi * r_k^2 \tag{4}$$

We say, the obfuscated position p_k has the precision ϕ_k if $A_k = \pi * (\phi_{min} - k\Delta_\phi)^2$. That is, we compare the obfuscation area to a circle covering an area of the same size.

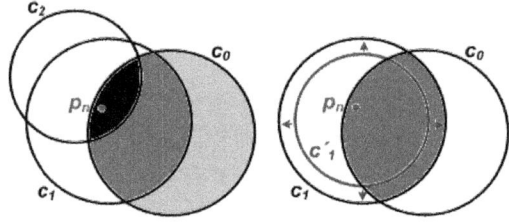

Fig. 5. OSPS-FSO: (a) intersection of 3 circles c_0, c_1, c_2; (b) adjustment of intersection area through radius increase of c_1' to c_1: $A_1 = \text{area}(c_0 \cap c_1) = \text{area}(c_1')$

Moreover, we need another modification to ensure that every additional share increases the precision by a well-defined value Δ_ϕ. We achieve this by an adjustment of the radius r_i of circle c_i such that A_i equals the area of the initial (non-adjusted) circle c_i'. Algorithm 4 shows the share generation algorithm of OSPS-FSO. In lines 8-10, we increase the radius to match the desired size A_k, as it is shown in Figure 5.

However, only increasing the radius is not sufficient for secure share generation, if an attacker knows the share generation algorithm. If we only increase radius r_i without changing the circle center p_i, an attacker can simply reduce the obfuscation area A_i by decreasing the obtained radius r_i down to the initial (non-increased) value of the radius r_i' (see Figure 6a). In order to avoid such an attack, the center of circle c_i must be adjusted so that the original position of c_i' within c_i cannot be found.

Algorithm 5 shows a secure algorithm for increasing r_i by also moving the center p_i. First, for the current p_i we determine the radius r_i which makes the intersection area large enough; we used radius increase $\Delta r = r/20$ (4-6). Then we perform the random shift of p_i, not longer than $r_i - r_i'$ (7-9). After that we check whether the current radius r_i

Algorithm 4. OSPS-FSO: generation of shares

1: **function** $generate\_n\_shares\_OSPS\_FSO(p_{user}, n, \phi_{min}, \Delta_\phi)$
2: **select randomly** p_0 **with** $distance(p_0, p_{user}) \leq \phi_{min}$
3: $A_0 \leftarrow \text{area}(c_0)$
4: **for** $i = 1$ **to** $n - 1$ **do**
5: $\quad r_i \leftarrow \phi_{min} - i * \Delta_\phi$
6: $\quad$ **select rnd.** s_i **with** $p_{user} \in c_i$
7: $\quad A_i \leftarrow \text{area}(c_i)$
8: $\quad$ **while** $\text{area}(\cap_{j=1}^{i}(c_j)) < A_i$ **do**
9: $\quad\quad r_i \leftarrow$ **increase**(r_i)
10: $\quad$ **end while**
11: **end for**
12: $s_n \leftarrow p_{user} - (p_0 + \sum_{i=1}^{n-1} s_i)$
13: **return** $s_0 \dots s_n, r_0 \dots r_n$

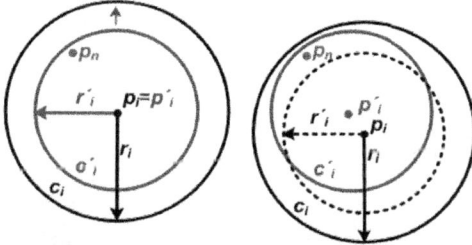

Fig. 6. Adjustment of p_i during radius increase: (a) no adjustment of p_i; (b) randomized adjustment of p_i

Algorithm 5. Radius increase with adjustment of p_i

1: **function** $increase(r_i, p_i, \Delta r, p_n)$
2: $r_i' \leftarrow r_i$
3: $A_i \leftarrow \text{area}(c_i')$
4: **while** $\text{area}(\cap_{j=1}^{i}(c_j)) < A_i$ **do**
5: $\quad r_i \leftarrow r_i + \Delta r$
6: **end while**
7: $x_{shift} \leftarrow$ **get_random_shift**(p_i, r_i', r_i)
8: $y_{shift} \leftarrow$ **get_random_shift**(p_i, r_i', r_i)
9: $p_i \leftarrow$ **shift**$(p_i, x_{shift}, y_{shift})$
10: **if** $\text{area}(\cap_{j=1}^{i}(c_j)) < A_i$ **then**
11: $\quad r_i \leftarrow$ **increase**(r_i)
12: **else**
13: $\quad$ **while** $(\text{area}(\cap_{j=1}^{i}(c_j)) > A_i)$ **and** $(p_n \in c_i)$ **do**
14: $\quad\quad r_i \leftarrow r_i - \Delta r$
15: $\quad$ **end while**
16: $\quad r_i \leftarrow r_i + \Delta r$
17: **end if**
18: **return** p_i, r_i

is satisfying the area condition (10). If the intersection area is again not large enough, we call the function **increase**(r_i, . . .) recursively (11). If the intersection area now exceeds the target value A_i, we decrease the current radius r_i until it achieves the required size (12-16).

In Figure 6b, it is shown that after the adjustment of p_i the target position p_n can be located anywhere within c_i. In other words, an attacker is not able to reduce the obfuscation area A_i just knowing the share generation algorithm.

3.3   Extended Approach 2: CSPS

Although OSPS-FSO as presented in the previous sub-section solves the problem of predictable refinement shares in an open space environment, it is not sufficient for restricted movement scenarios. If an MO cannot or is at least unlikely to move in certain areas such as lakes or agriculture fields, these areas can be subtracted from the obfuscated position p_k calculated by the share generation algorithm of OSPS-FSO. This effectively reduces the size A_k of p_k to a value below the intended precision $\phi_{min} - k\Delta_\phi$ (see Figure 7a).

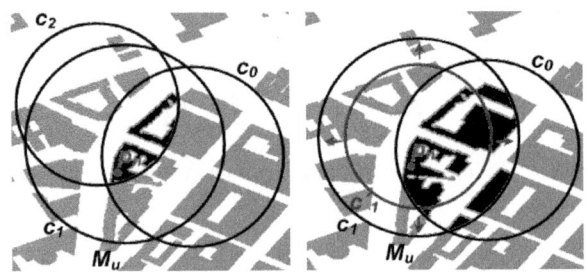

Fig. 7. CSPS: (a) intersection of 3 circles c_0, c_1, c_2 and the map representation M_u; (b) adjustment of intersection area through radius increase of c_1: $A_1 = \text{area}(M_u \cap c_0 \cap c_1) = \text{area}(c'_1)$. The black area depicts the effective obfuscation area where the user can actually be located.

Obviously, this unintended size reduction of p_k is due to the fact that OSPS-FSO does not consider such movement restrictions during share generation. This problem can be solved by considering movement restriction during radius adjustment. As prerequisite, a user-defined map M_u is required which defines possible positions of MO. Depending on the type of MO, M_u might contain general areas such as streets, shops, public places, as well as individual areas such as the user's home and working place. In general, M_u should reflect all movement restrictions that a possible attacker could know. Obviously, if an attacker is aware of additional movement restrictions that were not considered during share generation, he can possibly further reduce the obfuscation area.

Based on M_u, we can now modify the share fusion and share generation algorithm to consider movement restrictions to define our Constraint Space Position Sharing Approach (CSPS). The main idea of the map-aware share generation algorithm of CSPS is to increase in each share generation step i the radius of circle c_i, until the size[2] of $M_u \cap (c_0 \cap \ldots \cap c_i)$ is equal to $\phi_{min} - i\Delta_\phi$ (see Figure 7b). Informally, this means that we increase the intersection area until there are enough locations where the MO can *actually* be located.

Compared to the fusion algorithm of OSPS-FSO (Algorithm 3), only a small change in is required. The obfuscated position is not only defined by the intersection of the circles c_i, but also the intersection with M_u to remove areas where the user cannot be located. Thus, line 2 is modified to: $A_k \leftarrow M_u \cap c_0$.

The map-aware share generation algorithm of CSPS is similar to Algorithm 4, with additional c_0 increase before the main cycle for generating shares $s_1 \ldots s_n$:

---

while area$(M_u \cap c_0) < A_0$ **do**
  $r_0 \leftarrow$ **increase**(r_0)
end while

Also, the condition of line 8 of Algorithm 4 now must include M_u:

---

while area$(M_u \cap \cap_{j=1}^i (c_j)) < A_i$ **do**

---

4 Evaluation of Obfuscation Security

In this section, we evaluate the obfuscation security provided by the share generation algorithm. For a quantitative comparison, we use the metrics introduced in Section 2. First, we introduce our attacker model before we describe the evaluation results.

Attacker Model. On the one hand, attackers include *external attackers* who try to circumvent the access control mechanisms of LSs to get access to as many secret refinement shares as possible. Since preventing such attacks basically requires well-known access control mechanisms, which are not specific to position sharing, we will not consider this kind of attack further in our evaluation.

On the other hand, attackers also include *internal attackers* in form of malicious LS or LBA providers. In general, such internal attackers have access to k out of n shares. In detail, a LS has access to 1 out of n shares, namely, the single share managed by the LS. A compromised LBA has access to the k out of n shares for which it received access rights from the MO. As already described in the beginning, k defines a trade-off between the QoS that can be offered by the LBA due to the limited precision of position information, and the degree of lost privacy should the LBA misuse the position information. Therefore, in our approach adjusting k is the basic means of controlling privacy risks. Therefore, we focus our evaluation on such internal attacks where the attacker knows k out of n shares. We should note that we do not explicitly consider the case of colluding internal attacker, i.e., multiple malicious LS or LBA providers that exchange their shares to increase the number of (compromised) shares. To handle this case, the MO needs to assess the risk that providers collude, which is a different

---

[2] The size of intersection area is calculated through space discretization: we count the number of points covered by the intersection shape and convert this number into the corresponding area value proportionally.

problem of defining suitable trust relations and modeling relations between providers—
for instance, which LS are sharing the same server (cloud) infrastructure operated by
the same third-party provider, or which providers have to reveal their data to the same
legal entity because they fall under the same jurisdiction, etc.

As already mentioned, adjusting k is only then an effective means to control privacy
if the precision of positions derived from these shares are well-defined. If the share
generation algorithm is perfectly secure, an attacker with k compromised shares can
calculate a position with at least the precision $\phi_k = \phi_{min} - k\Delta_\phi$. However, due to a
certain predictability of share generation, he might even increase the precision beyond
that value as already discussed in Section 3. Since we assume that the share generation
algorithm is known to everybody, the attacker can use a *Monte Carlo Simulation* to
simulate the process of share generation and predict further possible refinement shares
from the known shares. To this end, he runs the share generation algorithm many times
to sample the probability distribution of the MO position and analyzes the resulting
position distribution to determine the most likely area where the MO is located in.

To quantify the (undesired) effect of share prediction and the resulting effective security of shares, we use the metrics $P_{10\%}$ and $P(\phi_{k,attack})$ already defined in Section 2.

4.1   Open Space Evaluation (OSPS-ASO vs. OSPS-FSO)

In our first evaluation, we start with the assumption that MOs can move without restrictions in an open space. This evaluation shows the difference between our old approach
OSPS-ASO presented in [1] that fuses the refinement shares in arbitrary order, and the
fixed order fusion approach OSPS-FSO presented in this paper.

As mentioned, in the ideal case each share should increase the precision by exactly
Δ_ϕ. Depending on the predictability of share generation, the attacker can gain a higher
precision $\phi_{k,attack} \leq k\Delta_\phi$ from k (compromised) shares with a certain probability
$P(\phi_{k,attack})$. Figure 8 plots $\phi_{k,attack}$ over k for different probabilities $P(\phi_{k,attack})$
(the total number of refinement shares is $n = 5$; $\phi_{min} = 10000$ m). Figure 8a shows
the results for our old algorithm OSPS-ASO; Figure 8b shows the results of OSPS-FSO
proposed in this paper.

Obviously, with 100% probability (curve $P(\phi_{k,attack}) = 100\%$), the attacker can
derive a precision $\phi_{k,attack} = k\Delta_\phi$ for both algorithms as intended by the position
sharing concept. With lower probability, the attacker can also gain a higher precision
for OSPS-ASO as well as OSPS-FSO, so both algorithms show a certain degree of
predictability. However, we can see that the predictability of OSPS-FSO is significantly
lower (i.e., closer to the ideal curve $P = 100\%$) than for OSPS-ASO. For instance,
with $P(\phi_{k,attack}) = 80\%$ probability and $k = 2$ compromised shares, the effective
precision $\phi_{k,attack} = k$ of OSPS-ASO is 3.91 km and 4.58 km for OSPS-FSO (the
ideal precision increase of a non-predictable share generation algorithm for $k = 2$
would be $\Delta_\phi = 10$ km $- 2 \cdot 2$ km $= 6$ km).

The fact that OSPS-FSO is less predictable than OSPS-ASO is also shown in Figure 9. Here, we consider the metric $P_{10\%}$ introduced above, i.e., the probability that
an attacker can locate the user within an area of 10% size of the actually intended area

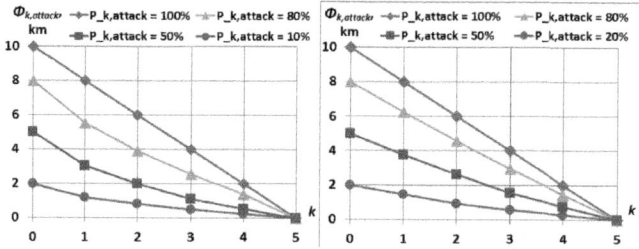

Fig. 8. (a) Precision $\phi_{k,attack}$ corresponding to probability values $P(\phi_{k,attack})$ depending on k for OSPS-ASO; (b) Precision $\phi_{k,attack}$ corresponding to probability values $P(\phi_{k,attack})$ depending on k for OSPS-FSO. $n = 5$; $r_0 = 10$ km; 100 runs of the Monte Carlo method

resulting from the fusion of k shares. That is, instead of considering the absolute value of precision increase as before, we now consider the relative increase in precision. In the ideal case, $P_{10\%}$ should be 10%. This figure plots $P_{10\%}$ for OSPS-ASO and OSPS-FSO over different numbers of compromised shares out of a total number of $n = 5$ refinement shares ($\phi_{min} = 25$ km). Up to $k = 2$, both algorithms nearly lead to the same small increase in precision. However, for larger numbers of compromised shares, OSPS-FSO shows a much lower predictability than OSPS-ASO: for $k > 2$ its value of $P_{10\%}$ is more than 2 times lower.

So, overall we can state that for open space scenarios our new share generation algorithm OSPS-FSO creates shares which significantly more secure than created by OSPS-ASO.

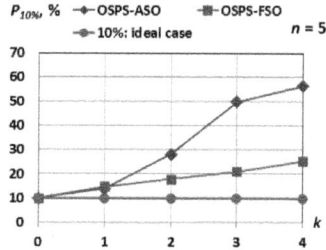

Fig. 9. Comparison of share generation algorithms: probability $P_{10\%}$ to derive an area covering 10% of the obfuscation circle c_k; $n = 5$; $r_0 = 25$ km; 100 runs using Monte Carlo method

4.2 Constrained Space Evaluation (OSPS-FSO vs. CSPS)

In this sub-section, we consider a constrained space movement model where MO only move in certain areas defined by the introduced map M_u. In this evaluation, we compare the proposed (open-space) approach OSPS-FSO, which does not consider any movement constraints, against the proposed map-based approach CSPS, which is aware of the movement constraints defined by M_u.

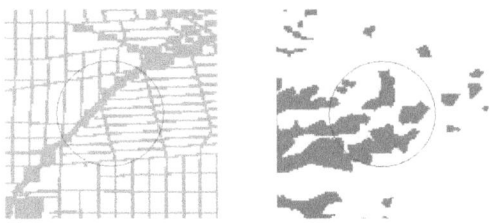

Fig. 10. (a) Map M_{LA}: roads and squares of Los Angeles City; (b) Map M_{BW}: forests of Baden Württemberg

Obviously, the difference between OSPS-FSO and CSPS depends on the concrete map. If the map does not define any constraints, OSPS-FSO and CSPS will behave similarly. If there are many constraints, we expect a bigger difference between both algorithms. Therefore, we used two real maps for our evaluation. The first map (M_{LA}) defines streets and places in a part of Los Angeles (see Figure 10a). The second map (M_{BW}) defines coarser movement constraints in a part of the state of Baden Württemberg (Germany), where the MO can move everywhere except for forests (see Figure 10b).

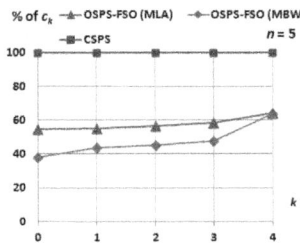

Fig. 11. Relative effective area size; 100 runs of the Monte Carlo method

In order to compare OSPS-FSO and CSPS, we compare the sizes of the obfuscation areas calculated by OSPS-FSO and CSPS after the intersection with the map M_u. CSPS adjusts the obfuscation area A_k such that the intersection area $A_k \cap M_u$ always has the desired obfuscation area size $\pi \cdot (\phi_{min} - k\Delta_\phi)^2$. In contrast, OSPS-FSO does not consider the map, which reduces the effective obfuscation area size where the MO can actually be located. Obviously, a smaller effective obfuscation area size is less secure. Therefore, as performance metric we calculate the *relative effective area size* of OSPS-FSO compared to the desired obfuscation area size $\pi \cdot (\phi_{min} - k\Delta_\phi)^2$. Since CSPS adjusts the obfuscation area such that the effective size is equal to $\pi \cdot (\phi_{min} - k\Delta_\phi)^2$, it always has a relative size of 100%.

Figure 11 shows the relative effective area sizes for the two maps over different numbers of shares (k) known by the attacker. Each figure depicts the results for different total numbers (n) of shares. The curve labeled "OSPS-FSO (MLA)" depicts the results of OSPS-FSO for map M_{LA}; "OSPS-FSO (MBW)" depicts the results for map M_{BW}.

First, we can observer that the coarse-grained map M_{BW} has a stronger effect on the effective area size since it constraints larger areas where the MO cannot be located. Moreover, we see that the relative effective area size increases for larger k. The reason for this is that usually smaller obfuscation areas (higher numbers k of refinement shares) tend to overlap more with regions where the user can actually be located. For instance, an area of only a few 10 meters will have almost 100% overlap with a building or street where the user can be located.

Comparing our map-aware approach CSPS and the open-space approach OSPS, we see that CSPS leads to a relative improvement of the effective obfuscation area size between about 40% and 60% for the two maps. Therefore, we can conclude that considering map knowledge is essential to guarantee the security of obfuscation. By considering map knowledge, CSPS guarantees that the effective obfuscation area size is equal to the desired area size for k shares.

5 Related Work

There are many different techniques to preserve the privacy of user locations while using LBS. They can be classified into methods based on access control, cryptographic encryption, k-anonymity, and spatial obfuscation ([6], [7], [8]).

The application of *access control* (e.g., [9]) using privacy policies allows users to define which LBAs are authorized to access the user's private location information. However, privacy policies do not provide ultimate (technical) guarantees against the misuse of user's data by LBS.

The classic method of *encryption* applied to the user's position information has a general drawback: no geometric operations over the encrypted data are possible at the LS, or only at a very high cost.

k-anonymity based methods (e.g., [10]) are managing the user position so that it cannot be distinguished from $k - 1$ positions of other users. This is achieved by adding a trusted anonymizer to the system, which manages the interaction between users and LBS. The anonymizer updates the exact user position by a set of k user positions (k-cluster). The common problem of k-anonymity based approaches is that they require total trust in a third party that operates the anonymizer. Also, the needed cluster of k users is not always available, especially clusters which satisfy additional constraining parameters such as area size and position diversity.

Spatial *obfuscation* (e.g., [11]) secures the user position by sending coarsened location information to the LBS. There is no need for a trusted third party, but on the other hand the problem of trading-off between precision and privacy raises. By selecting a large obfuscation area a user makes it impossible to query his position with acceptable precision, while a fine-granular location information provides only a low privacy level.

Our position sharing approach presented in [1] removes this shortcoming of obfuscation approaches. It uses spatial obfuscation as a basic mechanism and allows for a gradual refinement of the user position's precision by collecting data shares from different providers. The idea of decomposing a user's position information into shares has been also applied by Marias et al. [12]. The proposed method based on *secret sharing* solves the problem of limited trust to providers, but provides no gradual refinement of precision: only the complete set of shares gives the target position, while the absence of even a single share results in the absence of position information of any precision.

The problem of map-awareness regarding obfuscation techniques is a relatively rare topic, although it affects significantly the spatial obfuscation approaches. The *PROBE* approach proposed by Damiani et al. [13] considers map features with pre-defined probability values assigned to them. The distribution of probability of a user to be located within the given region is also assumed to be known a-priori. Moreover, a personalized model of privacy sensitivity for various map features is presented. The algorithm expands the obfuscation cells over the discrete space step-by-step. The resulting obfuscation region can have any shape, but the approach lacks some flexibility due to the enforced cell-based space representation.

The *landscape-aware obfuscation* of Ardagna et al. [14] provides a defense against Bayesian inference based on the prior probability density over the given area. This work presents the theoretical background for map-awareness. Also Ardagna et al. present the idea of adjusting the radius of obfuscation disk in order to preserve the user's privacy affected by the landscape knowledge. In our work, we adopt the similar principle to the position sharing approach.

6   Summary

In this paper, we have presented a new position sharing approach for managing obfuscated user positions on a set of untrusted location services (LSs). The basic idea of position sharing is to split the precise user position into a set of imprecise position shares and distribute these shares among LSs of different providers. Location-based applications (LBA) can query these shares from the LSs and fuse them to a position of well-defined precision depending on the number of shares they got access rights for from the tracked user. Since each LS only stores a single share of well-defined precision, a compromised LS will not reveal the precise user position but rather a position of strictly limited precision (graceful degradation of privacy).

We have presented enhanced share generation algorithms and fusion algorithms that further improve our basic position sharing approach presented in [1]. Firstly, we reduced the predictability of share generation that allows an attacker to gain further information from a set of compromised shares to further increase the position precision. Secondly, we presented a position sharing algorithm for constrained movement scenarios. Since typically users are likely to be located in areas like streets, buildings, etc. rather than areas like lakes or agriculture fields, open space approaches such as [1] are vulnerable to map-based attacks. Therefore, we presented a share generation algorithm that takes map knowledge into account.

Possible future research directions include the following. CSPS could be modified to additionally provide k-anonymity guarantees by adjusting the obfuscation area until it covers k other users. Moreover, the current approach is targeted at "position check-in" scenarios where the user only sporadically updates his position rather than continuously sending position updates. In future work we plan to design position sharing approaches that also support such continuous tracking scenarios. Finally, it would be interesting to also consider individual trust-levels of different location service providers. For instance, we could store more shares or shares of higher precision on LSs that are more trustworthy than others.

References

1. Dürr, F., Skvortsov, P., Rothermel, K.: Position sharing for location privacy in non-trusted systems. In: PerCom 2011, Seattle, USA, pp. 189–196 (March 2011)
2. Privacy Rights Clearinghouse: Privacy rights clearinghouse (June 2011), http://www.privacyrights.org/data-breach
3. Mokbel, M.F.: Privacy in location-based services: State-of-the-art and research directions. In: MDM 2007, Mannheim, Germany (May 2007)
4. Pedreschi, D., Bonchi, F., Turini, F., Verykios, V.S., Atzori, M., Malin, B., Moelans, B., Saygin, Y.: Privacy protection: Regulations and technologies, opportunities and threats. In: Mobility, Data Mining and Privacy, pp. 101–119 (2008)
5. Gutscher, A.: A Trust Model for an Open, Decentralized Reputation System. In: IFIPTM 2007 (August 2007)
6. Riboni, D., Pareschi, L., Bettini, C.: Privacy in Georeferenced Context-Aware Services: A Survey. In: Bettini, C., Jajodia, S., Samarati, P., Wang, X.S. (eds.) Privacy in Location-Based Applications. LNCS, vol. 5599, pp. 151–172. Springer, Heidelberg (2009)
7. Krumm, J.: A survey of computational location privacy. Personal and Ubiquitous Computing 13(6), 391–399 (2009)
8. Solanas, A., Domingo-Ferrer, J., Martínez-Ballesté, A.: Location privacy in location-based services: Beyond ttp-based schemes. In: Proceedings of the 1st International Workshop on Privacy in Location-Based Applications (PiLBA), Malaga, Spain (October 2008)
9. Hauser, C., Kabatnik, M.: Towards privacy support in a global location service. In: WATM/EUNICE 2001 (September 2001)
10. Kalnis, P., Ghinita, G., Mouratidis, K., Papadias, D.: Preventing location-based identity inference in anonymous spatial queries. IEEE Transactions on Knowledge and Data Engineering 19(12), 1719–1733 (2007)
11. Ardagna, C.A., Cremonini, M., Damiani, E., De Capitani di Vimercati, S., Samarati, P.: Location Privacy Protection Through Obfuscation-Based Techniques. In: Barker, S., Ahn, G.-J. (eds.) Data and Applications Security 2007. LNCS, vol. 4602, pp. 47–60. Springer, Heidelberg (2007)
12. Marias, G.F., Delakouridis, C., Kazatzopoulos, L., Georgiadis, P.: Location privacy through secret sharing techniques. In: WOWMOM 2005. IEEE Computer Society (June 2005)
13. Damiani, M.L., Bertino, E., Silvestri, C.: Protecting location privacy against spatial inferences: the probe approach. In: SIGSPATIAL ACM GIS 2009 Intl. Workshop on Security and Privacy in GIS and LBS, SPRINGL 2009. ACM, New York (2009)
14. Ardagna, C.A., Cremonini, M., Gianini, G.: Landscape-aware location-privacy protection in location-based services. Journal of System Architecture (JSA) 55 (April 2009)

Sense and Sensibility in a Pervasive World

Christos Efstratiou[1], Ilias Leontiadis[1], Marco Picone[1,2], Kiran K. Rachuri[1],
Cecilia Mascolo[1], and Jon Crowcroft[1]

[1] Computer Laboratory, University of Cambridge, Cambridge, UK
[2] Department of Information Engineering, University of Parma, Italy

Abstract. The increasing popularity of location based social services such as
Facebook Places, Foursquare and Google Latitude, solicits a new trend in fusing social networking with real-world sensing. The availability of a wide range
of sensing technologies in our everyday environment presents an opportunity to
further enrich social networking systems with fine-grained real-world sensing.
However, the introduction of passive sensing into a social networking application disrupts the traditional, user-initiated input to social services, raising both
privacy and acceptability concerns. In this work we present an empirical study of
the introduction of a sensor-driven social sharing application within the working
environment of a research institution. Our study is based on a real deployment of
a system that involves location tracking, conversation monitoring, and interaction
with physical objects. By utilizing surveys, interviews and experience sampling
techniques, we report on our findings regarding privacy and user experience issues, and significant factors that can affect acceptability of such services by the
users. Our results suggest that such systems deliver significant value in the form
of self reflection and comparison with others, while privacy concerns are raised
primarily by the limited control over the way individuals are projected to their
peers.

1 Introduction

Social networks are becoming part of our lives, as an increasing percentage of Internet users interact with them on a daily basis. The interaction with social networks is
steadily moving beyond the typical desktop environment, with a significant number of
users interacting with such services through their mobile devices. At the same time the
wide availability of location sensing on smart-phones and the increasing popularity of
location based social services such as FourSquare, Gowalla and Google Latitude, are
introducing a new trend in *fusing social networking with real-world sensing.*

Recently, a number of experimental systems exploit the sensing capabilities of mobile phones in order to further enrich user experience. For example, in CenceMe [1]
a range of the phone's sensing modalities (such as accelerometers, microphone, light,
location) are used in order to detect user activities and upload this information to various social networks like Facebook, Twitter and MySpace. Similarly, in CitySense [2]
crowd-sourced sensed information is used to analyze human behavior so as to produce a
live map of city-wide social activities. Although there is real value in detecting a range
of contextual information through mobile phone sensing, the limited battery life and
the fixed types of sensing modalities available on mobile phones, impose restrictions

J. Kay et al. (Eds.): Pervasive 2012, LNCS 7319, pp. 406–424, 2012.
© Springer-Verlag Berlin Heidelberg 2012

on the type and the accuracy of sensing that can be employed. In certain environments however, such as public buildings [3], the presence of static sensors embedded in the environment can offer significantly more accurate detection of similar types of events, or even *new sensing capabilities* not available on a mobile device. For instance, automated RFID based access doors, nowadays installed in several working environments, can detect the arrival of a person at their workplace more accurately and without expending the battery life of the user's mobile device. Furthermore, a coffee machine augmented with embedded sensing capabilities, is able to detect the fact that the user is having a coffee, an activity that may not easily be detected through a mobile phone.

The increasing availability of sensing technologies within our everyday environment, along with the vision of augmented physical objects with embedded intelligence [4], are creating a fertile opportunity for the design of a new class of social sensing services. We envisage a scenario where static sensors, as well as sensing offered by individual mobile devices can enhance the experience offered by social networking services. Apart from the technical difficulties of designing such an integrated social sensing architecture, there are usability challenges and privacy concerns that arise when users live and interact within an environment where sensed information can be shared with other people. Embedded sensing is inherently passive, performed without the explicit decision of the user. Moreover, the physical device that is collecting information is typically not owned by the user that is being sensed. Both of these characteristics are expected to generate significant privacy concerns. An important challenge in deploying such services is to strike a balance between the value that users are getting out of such service and the level of privacy that they are expected to relinquish. In this work we attempt to investigate significant factors that can affect both the perception of value and concerns about privacy, in sensor-enhanced social sharing services deployed in the working environment of a research institution.

We conducted an empirical study based on a real deployment of such service installed in a research institution in the United Kingdom. The service relied on location sensing, conversation detection, and interaction with physical object in the target working environment. Users were allowed access to real-time high-level social interaction information along with game-like comparisons of different activities, between colleagues in the institution. A two weeks study, involving 21 participants, was aimed at investigating parameters that influence the perceived value that users find in such system, and factors that affect their concern about privacy in that particular environment. Using a combination of surveys, experience sampling techniques, and interviews we are reporting on the significant findings of this study.

2 Motivation

The wide availability of sensing technologies in our everyday environment, presents an opportunity for passive real-world sensing of human activities and social interactions. From as early as 1992 the design of the Active Badge [5] system was motivated by the need for location based services in business environments. Multiple sensor networks embedded in our physical environments, as well as sensing offered by individual devices (mobile phones, augmented physical objects) can be fused in order to allow the

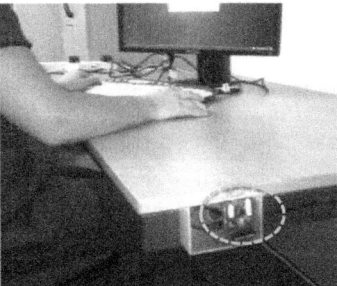

Fig. 1. Infrastructure deployment: Sensor nodes attached to coffee machines and desks, and mobile phones used for localization and information visualization

monitoring and sharing of our social interactions and everyday activities (Figure 1). The significant value that users can extract from such systems, is best illustrated when considering social spaces where multiple people interact on a daily basis. Shared social sensing in the working environment can foster a new application domain for social networking. Users can have the opportunity to monitor their personal behavioral patterns [6] and share it with their colleagues. Game-like features, where colleagues can see who is the most social or most chatty person in their working environment, can potentially enhance personal reflection and motivate social cohesion and efficient collaboration [7]. However, activity sensing in the working environment is typically faced with suspicion and concerns about privacy and surveillance [8]. Although there are valid concerns about employing such technologies in the workplace, it is our belief that most of these concerns are driven by the fact that sensed information collected in such environment is accessible only to the upper management for performance monitoring purposes. A challenging issue is to discover the extent by which a transparent shared social sensing infrastructure can mitigate privacy concerns and deliver significant value to the users.

Motivated by these issues, we conducted an empirical study that involved the deployment of a sensor-enhanced social sharing service. The service offered a flat structure where all users could see information about the location of colleagues and their social interactions, as well as value-added features such as personal statistics (who they interact with the most, how many coffees they had), and "social games" where they were compared with their colleagues according to their social patterns. The aim of the study was to investigate parameters that can affect the acceptability of such services, from privacy concerns and perceived value, to usability issues.

3   Requirements Capturing

The aim of the requirements capturing process was to identify the sensing modalities that are necessary for capturing social interactions in the workplace, and the users' expectation from such service. By conducting a survey of systems that have been deployed in working environments, such as [9,10], we identified that important modalities include: (i) location tracking, (ii) co-location sensing, and (iii) conversation detection.

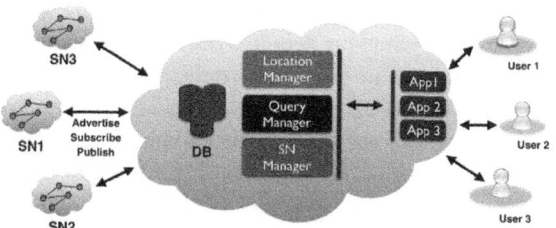

Fig. 2. System Architecture

We decided to further enrich the sensed information with detection of interaction with physical objects.

A group discussion and consultation with potential users of the system was used to discover important functionality that should be offered by such service. A group of 10 potential users was consulted in this process. The users commented both in terms of functionality and usability. The key points that came out of these discussions were: (i) preference towards diffusing sensing in the environment rather than relying on mobile devices, to make the system less intrusive, (ii) an interest in offering a visualized "personal log" about their daily activities in the workspace, (iii) added-value services could include social "games" where people can compete with others on different aspects of their social behavior, (e.g. how much they talk to others, or how much time they spent working at their desk), and (iv) an interest for detecting social gatherings (e.g., meetings, group lunch breaks) that are currently taking place in the building. We designed and deployed our system based on these requirements.

4   System Design and Deployment

The primary objective is to deploy a system that is able to deliver high level social events to users in real-time by employing multiple sensing technologies that are distributed in the users' working environment. The overall system consists of a social event detection system, a range of deployed sensing technologies, and web-based applications that allow users to interact with the service (Figure 2).

4.1   Social Event Detection System

We implemented a system that offers an abstraction interface between the physical sensor networks and the social sensing events that applications are interested in (Figure 2). This system acts as a reconfigurable sensor fusion engine, that combines low-level information from one or more sensor networks to generate composite high-level social activity events. For example, information from bluetooth scanning and sensors embedded on a coffee machine can be combined to detect when a user is having a coffee, while microphones and location tracking can be combined to infer when two people are having a conversation.

More specifically, in our implementation the running applications can specify an interest to a certain event by subscribing to one of the high-level social events that the system supports (e.g., find users in a room, detect conversations, detect a meeting). The *Query Manager* is then responsible for decomposing these high-level subscriptions into the low-level sensing events that are required to detect them. Sensor networks can register and offer their services to the system via a web service API (Figure 2). Each network registration includes the type of the offered sensing and the geographic area that the network covers. This latter piece of information is required to identify when a user is within an area covered by the specific sensor network. The registered sensor networks communicate with the deployed service (either directly or via a broker) through a publish/subscribe communication interface. The subscriptions define interests for certain events in a particular geographic area that is populated by users. The resulting low-level events that are collected from the registered sensor networks are stored in an SQL database inside the service. As most events depend on the physical location of the users, the *Location Manager* is responsible for dynamically adapting the area of interest for these subscriptions as people move about. In essence, the service maintains a sensing space around each user, collecting relevant sensing events from their environment.

The *Query Manager* is also responsible for notifying the application when low-level events can satisfy a high-level subscription. In this case high-level events of the form $\{user\_id, time\_stamp, location, activity\_type, activity\_details\}$ are generated and stored at the database. Applications are then able to further aggregate and visualize these events to the users.

4.2 Sensor Deployment

The deployed system consisted of the following sensing modalities: a localization infrastructure, a conversation sensing infrastructure, a network of sensors attached to physical objects and specifically to desks in offices and coffee machines in communal areas.

Bluetooth Indoor Localization: To monitor the location of the participants, a number of static bluetooth devices were deployed as anchor points covering 12 offices, and 5 communal areas such as a common room, kitchens and coffee rooms. The localization service relied on an Android mobile phone application installed on the participants' phones that could discover their location through bluetooth scanning. Using the RSSI value of the responses received by the anchors, the application could localize users with an accuracy of a few meters. Users that did not have a personal Android phone were offered one for the duration of the study. Overall, the deployment included 11 Samsung Galaxy S, 7 HTC Desire and 3 HTC G2 phones.

Speech Recognition: 17 Nokia 6210 phones were installed inside each room (as static sensors) to detect whether a conversation was taking place. The voice recognition is based on the Hidden Markov ToolKit (HTK) which can deliver over 90% accuracy in conversation detection [9]. Two Gaussian Mixture Models representing speech and silence models are trained under similar background conditions. Immediately after processing, all voice samples were erased from the system.

Sensors: A range of physical objects were augmented with sensors that could detect interactions with the users. Specifically, 21 Imote-2 sensor nodes were attached on the participants' desks. The sensors were used to detect when users were spending time

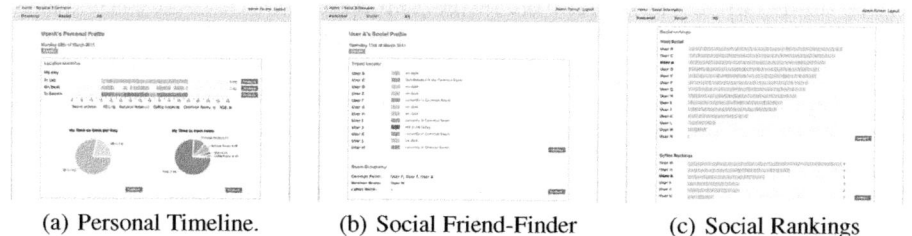

(a) Personal Timeline.   (b) Social Friend-Finder   (c) Social Rankings

Fig. 3. Some of the Web-Based Applications. User names have been anonymized.

at their desk by detecting vibration patters using the 3-axis accelerometers. Furthermore, additional sensors were attached to coffee machines in communal kitchens, as many users during the requirements capturing phase indicated that they would consider interesting to detect coffee breaks. All sensor nodes were deployed as a wireless sensor network, utilizing a tree-based collection routing protocol that could deliver sensed events to the system.

4.3   Web Interface

A web based interface was developed to allow users to view personal information, and social interactions as they were recorded by the sensing service. The users could access the application from their desktop or their mobile phone if needed. The information that the application could deliver can be divided into three main categories: (i) *personal*, showing all social activities of an individual as it was captured from the system, (ii) *social*, allowing the user to see aggregate information related to other people in the working environment, (iii) *all*, where user's could see detailed information about all users in the system.

Personal Information. The personal page of the web application, allowed participants to see all the details that the system was capturing about their social activity. The information included:

– The location of the user in room-level granularity, over time.
– The time period the user was present in their working environment (when they came and left the building).
– The exact time periods the user spent working at their desk.
– The interactions the user had with others based on co-location sensing.
– The amount of time they spent with others in conversations.
– The number of coffee breaks they had during the day.

The page uses a range of visualization techniques to present such information to the user. Timeline graphs allowed users to see how their activities progressed during the day. This visualization was implemented to satisfy the requirement expressed by some users, to be able to see a log of their activities during the day. Furthermore, aggregated information, such as average daily and weekly time at work, on desk, etc. were presented in the form of pie-charts, while bar-charts were used to identify the people they were socializing with most frequently. A snapshot of the personal web page can be seen in Figure 3.a.

Social Information. The social page of the web application, allowed participants to see information related to the social activity of people participating in the study. The section offered two types of information: (i) Real-time details about people's location and about their current activity, such as if they are at their desk, or if they are having a coffee; (ii) Social rankings where users were compared on different aspects of their social activity.

The real-time information were offered mostly for utilitarian purposes, as users had identified such tools as useful added-value services. The social rankings were implemented in order to introduce a *gaming* concept into the system. These include ranking: (i) according to the time each person spends working at their desk, (ii) how much time people spend with other colleagues (*most social*), (iii) who is the highest consumer of coffee, (iv) who is spending most time chatting with colleagues. Their purpose is to allow the participants to compare certain social activities with each other, creating a social gaming experience similar to the features found in services like FourSquare. An example is shown in Figure 3.c.

All Information. This section allowed open access to the details of all people participating in the study. A user could see the time-lines of all participants including the time they came and leave work, the time spent working at their desk, the rooms they visited during the day, etc. Essentially this section gave the user the opportunity to examine detailed information about all other participants, effectively giving complete transparency over the information collected about all people involved in the study.

The different features supported by the application were mainly derived by the requirements that the users expressed during the consultation phase. However, the presented information were organized in increasing levels of detail that user's can have access too, with a clear awareness on our behalf, that these differences might lead to different levels of privacy concern.

5   User Study

Using the social sensing system that was described, we conducted a two weeks user study with 21 participants within a research institution. The target environment was selected for two main reasons. Firstly, reflecting on the adoption process of on-line social networks such as Facebook, we consider educational and research institutions as the most probable environments to be early adopters of such services. Secondly, technological research institutions, are either already instrumented with a range of sensing technologies, or have the capacity to easily introduce such technologies in their environment. The main research questions that we tried to address were:

1. Is there enough value for users so that social sensing in working environments can be considered a typical application, beyond the context of short-term sociological studies?
2. How does visibility of sensed information affect acceptability and privacy concerns?
3. Are there feasible techniques to mitigate privacy concerns without harming the perceived value offered by the system?

In the context of this study we consider acceptability as a function of two main factors: (i) the value that users find in a given service, (ii) the concerns in terms of privacy that they have by the introductions of such service.

5.1 Methodology

The overall methodology that we employed in this study can be broken down into the following steps:

- *Recruiting:* A process of selecting participants with the aim of maintaining a balance in demographics (age and sex) and their job role in the institution.
- *Preliminary Survey:* Participants were asked to fill in a questionnaire that allowed us to capture their experience in social networking systems, and their initial attitude towards the system they were asked to use.
- *Empirical Study:* During the period that participants were interacting with the system, we introduced an interactive feedback tool where participants could indicate their concerns in terms of privacy and usefulness of the system.
- *Interviews:* After the completion of the empirical study, semi-structured interviews with all participants allowed us to capture both experiences and attitudes towards the system.

The following sections describe in detail each of these stages.

5.2 Recruiting Users

In selecting participants we used stratified sampling with snowball sampling within each stratum. During the recruiting process we identified three primary groups of users that represent three main roles of workers in that environment. The three groups were:

- *Research students:* Typically, have flexible working patterns. Their working progress is usually supervised by research and academic staff.
- *Researchers & academics:* More structured working patterns compared to students.
- *Administrative staff:* Strict working patterns, working environment that may be more similar to a corporate working environment.

As we had no prior knowledge about the expected variability within each group, in the recruiting process we tried to have a relatively balanced representation of all three groups. We decided to use snowball sampling within the groups in order to recruit participants that had some form of social relationship with each other. We eventually recruited 21 participants, after discarding a number of users that volunteered, in order to maintain a balanced representation across categories. The group of participants include 8 students, 7 researchers & academics, and 6 administrative staff. Furthermore, the user sample was balanced in terms of gender (with 10 female and 11 male participants), and age with 11 participants in the age group 18-35, and 10 participants in 36-65 group.

Before a user decided to join the study, they were briefed individually, given a description of the sensing technologies that has to be put in place, how data will be collected and who will be able to see sensed data about them. It was explained that they could opt-out and ask the system to cease collecting data at any time during the study. Each participant was compensated with a £5 gift card.

Table 1. Preliminary survey results (a) and system traces results during the study (b)

	Usefulness	Privacy	Risk
Facebook	4.94 (1.06)	4.86 (1.36)	4.38 (1.36)
Twitter	4.92 (1.61)	4.77 (2.13)	4.46 (1.90)
LBS	5.25 (1.16)	6.13 (1.36)	4.36 (1.60)
Track location	4.42 (1.66)	5.00 (1.73)	3.85 (1.52)
Track activities	4.14 (1.46)	5.09 (1.48)	4.14 (1.15)
Track social interactions	4.23 (1.55)	4.71 (1.38)	3.90 (1.04)

(a) Survey Ratings. Scale 1 - 7. Usefulness: 7 extremely useful, Privacy: 7 extremely concerned, Risk: 7 benefit outweighs risk

Days Run	14
Participants	21
Website Visits	2,809
Times Feedback given	743
Low Level Events	408,455
High Level Events	25,431
Conversations Detected	3,380
Meetings Detected	1,058
User Locations Tracked	1,940
Coffee Breaks	384
Desk Activity	9,969

(b) Summary of system traces results during the study

5.3 Preliminary Survey

Before allowing the participants to interact with the system, a short survey was conducted in order to capture some background information about the user group. The main aim was to record their experience with other social networking services and their attitude towards them. The survey consisted of 33 closed questions. 18 questions were related to the users' attitude towards different technologies in terms of usefulness, privacy concerns and risk, formatted in a 7 point Likert scale.

Social Networks: 76% (16) of our participants use Facebook. In fact, 58% (12) of them visit Facebook at least once a day but only 33% of them post information at least once a week. More than half (62%) of the participants are Twitter users, however, this value drops significantly when considering participants of higher age groups (only 1 of the 5 participants aged over 45 use Twitter). Considering location based services like Google Latitude, Gowalla and Foursquare, 38% of the participants reported that they are users of such services, with *no one* from the higher age groups (more than 45). In terms of usefulness, as seen at Table 1(a), participants consider location based services more useful than Facebook and Twitter and yet, at the same time they raise more privacy concerns.

Expectation for the upcoming study: During the recruitment phase of this study, and in particular during the briefing phase, certain participants expressed concerns about their privacy when they would be using the system. We thought it would be useful to capture these concerns before the participants were exposed to the system. We extended the preliminary survey with a set of questions that would allow the users to offer their view about the system, before they actually use it. The questions were presented as hypothetical scenarios where particular sensing technologies are introduced. For example, we asked: "Assume that you are working in an environment where a sensing technology is able to track your location and the location of your colleagues. Consider that such information can become available to you". The participants were asked to comment about their concerns about privacy, usefulness and risk. After analyzing the responses, we identified that users were quite neutral about the usefulness of such services (average 4.2), and moderately concerned about privacy (average 4.9) (Table 1(a)).

5.4 Empirical Study

The twenty one participants were allowed to interact with the system for a period of 2 weeks. 6 of the participants, that form a very close social group, were selected for a focused study on how information visibility can affect privacy concerns and value. Specifically, the 6 participants were only allowed to see information within their close social group. The remaining 15 participants could see information about all other users in the system. The two groups will be referred as "Closed access" and "Open access" groups respectively in the rest of the paper.

After collecting the participants' background information, we commenced the 2-week study. Each participant was given an android phone that had to carry at all times. Furthermore, each user was supplied with a private login and password to access the website. The participants could access the website as often as they wanted, however they were advised to do it at least twice per day. During the study we had 2,809 visits in total from the 21 users (about 10 pages views per day per person) as shown in Table 1(b).

On the website, a "feedback" button was added next to each block of displayed information (an example can be found in Figure 3). When this button was clicked, a form allowed the participants to rate and comment on the usefulness and the privacy concerns of the displayed information. The feedback mechanism was used as a form of experience sampling. It allowed us to observe any possible changes in the participants' attitude during the study. The users were encouraged to use these buttons whenever they felt it was appropriate to offer their opinion. During the study, feedback was given 743 times (Table 1(b)).

The actual running of the study was broken into three stages. At each stage users were allowed access to more functionality and potentially more privacy sensitive information. For the first three days, the users were only given access to their own personal information. This stage allows the participants some time in order to familiarize themselves with what is collected, without inducing significant privacy concerns. At the end of the third day, the "Social" section was enabled allowing users to directly compare themselves with others. The "All" tab was enabled during the last three days of the study. As that tab was allowing access to potentially more sensitive information, we did not want to trigger serious privacy concerns early in the study. The participants were informed by e-mail when more functionality was becoming available to them.

After the study, for each user we collected the results from the questionnaire, the website feedback, and the observed behavior of the users (e.g., how many times they logged in, how much time the were at work, etc). The collected data was used in preparation for the interviews that were conducted. This dataset allowed us to structure the interviews according to the information we had about each individual participant.

5.5 Interviews

The interviews consisted of 31 questions, including 6 closed questions where participants were asked to give markings on a 7-point Liker scale. The interview questions covered the following subjects: (i) overall experience, (ii) perceived value, (iii) privacy concerns, (iv) social impact. Each interview lasted approximately 45 minutes. The interviews were audio recorded and then transcribed into text. The analysis used an open coding scheme that allowed us to discover common themes across participants. In the following section the participants are referred with code names P1 - P21.

6   Results

The analysis of our results builds upon privacy regulation theory developed by social psychologist Irwin Altman [11]. Altman understands privacy to be a dialectic and dynamic boundary regulation process. According to his work privacy is a dynamic response to circumstances rather than a static enforcement of rules; and it is defined by a set of tensions between competing needs. Privacy as a continuous negotiation process is trying to balance the needs of individuals to retain information as private, while explicitly disclosing or publicizing information as means of declaring allegiance or even of differentiating ourselves from others. In [12] Palen and Dourish explore how Altman's theory is applied in the design of novel interactive technologies. According to Palen and Dourish technology plays a disruptive role in this boundary control process. We see the deployment of passive social sensing technologies as such a disruptive technology. In our experimental study our primary aim was to explore the main tensions between competing needs that can affect the specification of privacy boundaries. The presence of passive social sensing allows participants to gain visibility to other's social behavior while exposing their social life to public view. In our analysis we aim to explore the users' experiences that reveal these contradicting needs.

6.1   Demand for Information

During the interviews when participants were asked to explain their experience with the system, it became clear that there was a distinction between practical use and "fun". Practical uses were referred for example to ways were the system helped participants to discover where their colleagues are: P3 mentioned using the service to find out when their close collaborators are in the lab, to meet them. The term "fun" was mainly used in the context of monitoring others' social behavior. P14: *"I liked the ranking games. It was an interesting stimuli. For example chattiness and social encounters. In that sense it was a bit more intriguing and playful."*

Fun: Checking "Others".   The participants were asked to comment on the type of information they most commonly viewed through the web application. 57% of the participants mentioned that they were mostly interested in data from specific individuals. Throughout the interviews comments from the "open access" group, indicated an interest on people that they *did not* have close social ties with: P7: *"I preferred checking on people that I didn't know. Stalking strangers can help you build new bonds in the lab".* Similar comments were also given by P12 and P14.

Motivated by these findings we decided to investigate further this trend. Using the co-location data that were collected by the sensing infrastructure we constructed a social graph of the "open access" group (Figure 4). The thickness of the graphs edges reflect the amount of time the participants spent together during the study, and therefore the social bond between participants. We then mapped on top of the social graph, the interest the participants identified when discussing interest on social behavior. As it

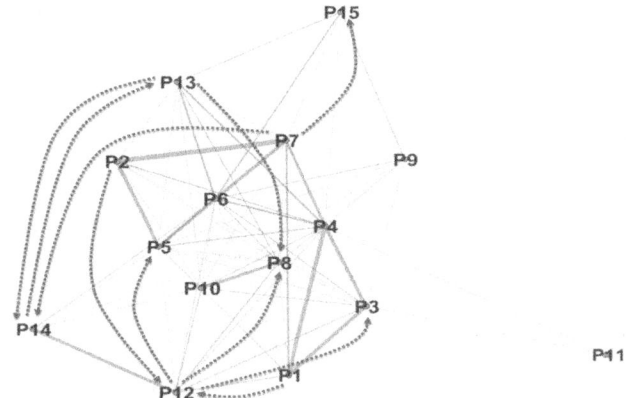

Fig. 4. Social Network and interest between participants (dotted arrows)

became apparent the participants showed a clear interest in people *outside* their close social circle. However, people in the workplace are never complete strangers. P13 mentioned that he was observing P14: *"It was interesting to watch the ranking of people. Especially [P14]. We are both writing our thesis and it was interesting to see who is the hardest worker"*. However, according to the social networking data, the two participants are not close contacts (and they are not currently friends on Facebook). P7 is quite clear on his intentions when monitoring social behavior in the work place: *"Knowing the time people spend with others is very important information as this can help people collaborate and spread ideas. [...] You can find important persons, persons that can influence a lot of others."*

Practical: Helps Me Do My Job. The significance of monitoring "others" is revealing when considering the results from the "closed group". The comments from the close access group were overwhelmingly related to the practical uses of the system. P17: *"There might be some use of the desk sensor for people with special needs... monitoring how long you are on your desk and need to have a break"*. P16: *"It was quicker to pop into the reception for me instead of using the system. If it was large scale it would have been useful as we would know if people are in, so as to reach them"*. The social networking graph showed that the particular group spent significant amounts of time together. In fact, the particular group had a tendency to have the same coffee breaks and lunch breaks and spend them together. Practically, there were not a lot of information that the system could reveal that they didn't already know. Interestingly, when asked to rate the usefulness of the system, the closed group gave significantly lower markings than the open group: 92% of the open group found the system useful versus 60% of the closed group.

Me vs "Others". In addition to practical uses and social monitoring, all participants commented on the value of using such system for self monitoring. The fact that environmental sensing is inherently passive (users do not need to remember to "checkin"), gives people a more objective view on the activities they perform. Participants made comments on their behavior that they didn't expect. P10 commented that although he

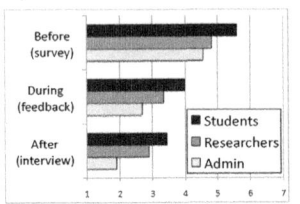

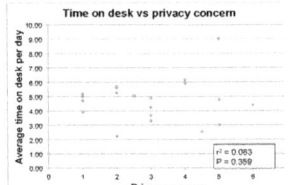

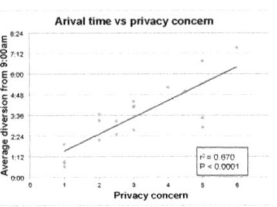

(a) Privacy concern changes during the study.

(b) Correlation between privacy concern and time spent on their desk.

(c) Correlation between privacy concern and time of arrival to work.

Fig. 5. Results

was cutting down on coffee, he could see that over time he didn't actually make much progress. P6 mentioned that she was spending too much time socializing compared to others, while P14 had the opposite comment; not socializing that much. In most personal comments, the comparison was with the general trend they observed with other people. Typically personal monitoring is commonly contrasted with the social behavior of others, not necessarily from within their close social circle.

Relating to the actual system functionality, both personal observation and social behavior, were mostly concerned with general trends in people's behavior, while practical value derived from the system was mainly attributed to the real-time aspects of the system. However, the differences between the open and the closed group, reveal that acceptability of such systems is highly depended on opportunities to monitor social behavior of people beyond their close social ties. Also some of the comments indicated an interest for general behavioral trends of certain role groups in the workplace: e.g. what is the social pattern of research students on writing-up, what is the social pattern of researchers within the lab.

6.2   Privacy Concerns

Overall the exposure of the participants to the system reduced their privacy concern about the system. Figure 5(a), shows the average trend in privacy concern before, during and after the study (scale 1-7 where 7 is extremely concerned). The average level of concern dropped from 5 as recorded in the preliminary survey, to 2.93 during the interviews after the study. During the interviews most participants made comments like: "... I didn't feel more concerned about privacy, but it made me more aware about it". The distinction between *concerned* and *aware* can potentially be interpreted as a tendency of the participants to self-censor their activities knowing that they are being monitored. Although when asked explicitly only 14% of the participants said that they changed their behavior due to the system that was put in place.

How Others See Me.   The actual comments that participants made about privacy varied according to the different types of information that is captured. During the recruitment phase, many participants expressed concerns about privacy regarding the conversation detection system that was put in place, although it was made clear that no actual audio recording would be involved. Surprisingly, at the end of the study, none of the participants expressed any strong concerns about the conversation detection sensing. The most controversial piece of information that was captured was actually the desk occupancy sensing. During the interviews those readings in particular were directly associated by the participants with work performance. P2 mentioned *"When the desk sensor says that I am not on my desk, it does not mean that I don't work"*, while P11 mentioned *"... often I work from home, so the desk sensor did not mean much in my case"*. P10 gives a better explanation on what is the actual concern *"if the statistics do not represent me the way I would like to be represented then there is a problem. Then I will be concerned"*. In fact, most participants claimed that they would not like to be shown in rankings unless they are in a high position. It is clear that the primary concern expressed by most participants is the lack of boundary control over the input in the system. Some participants when discussing possible changes they would like to see in the system, they suggest mechanism that could in fact mitigate such problems. P12 and P8 suggest the possibility of adding comments on social data collected by the system: *"it would be nice if we can add a comment on the data explaining why I am away [...] And this can also provide some information about context."*

Real Behavior vs Perception. Motivated by the fact that one of the primary concerns was about the implications that sensor data made about work performance, we analyzed their markings in terms of privacy with respect to their working patterns. As during the interviews the actual time that participants spent on their desk was proven to be a controversial issue, we decided to estimate the correlation between their desk time and the marking in terms of privacy, however the analysis showed no correlation (Fig. 5(b)). Digging further, we tried to find other factors that are related to the picture of a "good worker". Figure 5(c) illustrates a comparison between the time people arrive in the morning (the time distance from 9:00 am) and privacy concerns. The results identify a strong correlation of the two values. Interestingly these results show that although privacy concern can be related to arrival time, the complains were mostly about the desk sensor readings. We attempt to explain the contradiction between the reported concern during interviews and the results from the data analysis, by considering the prior knowledge that users may have about particular pieces of information. Arrival time does appear to be a privacy concern, but is never expressed as it is typically already known to the participants' colleagues. On the other hand, desk sensing appears to be controversial irrespective of the actual readings, as this is a new piece of information that becomes public.

Unanticipated Usage. Privacy issues can also be exacerbated by unanticipated uses of the system. A case of a controversial use of the system occurred during the study. Participant P12, who had a significantly different working pattern than others, mentioned an experience she had during the study: she was confronted by another participant about her messing with his stuff, because the system recorded activity at his desk when she was the only person in the lab. As expected, P12 gave the highest mark on privacy concern for the system.

The privacy concerns expressed during the interview were significantly lower for the "closed access" group. As expected the fact that data is shared only with close contacts reduced the participants worries. However, when members of the open access group were asked to suggest ways of mitigating privacy concerns they went beyond simply controlling who has access to their sensed information. Most participants concentrated on the input boundary, and how data stream can be switched on/off on demand. Many participants acknowledged that either delivering false or ambiguous information would reduce the usefulness of the system.

6.3   Interacting with the System

As part of the study a number of minor results were produced:

Usability.   The use of mobile phones for indoor localization proved to be a poor choice in terms of usability. A significant number of participants complained about the requirement to carry their phone all the time. Such concerns were expressed primarily by female participants explaining that they do not usually wear clothes with pockets. Anecdotally we witnessed some participants carrying the phone in their hand during the study. In contrast, participants made positive comments on the limited intrusiveness of passive sensing: P16 brought as an example the desk sensor saying *"I liked the fact that it worked without having to carry anything"*. P11 suggested a system where all the functionality is encapsulated in a single device: *"Something I can put on my desk and make everything work"*.

Data Capture.   The participants were asked to mark on a 7-point Likert scale, how much of their social life in the workplace was captured by the fusion of the deployed sensor networks. The results was a rather high 5.18. Although many participants mentioned that the combination of the deployed technologies was enough to capture most aspects of their social behavior, their experience was hampered by the limited scale of the deployment. If more areas were instrumented and more people participated, the rating would have been higher. Participants P3, P5 and P7 said that it would have been preferable if the context of social interactions were captured by the infrastructure (e.g, detecting if a conversation is work related or not).

Interactivity.   Finally, participants, primarily from the students and researchers groups, expressed a desire for more interaction with the system. Participants P4, P7, P8 and P9 argued that they would like to have notifications pushed to the mobile device when an important social activity is detected by the deployed sensors. For instance, P4 asked to be notified when members of his group are having a lunch-break or a meeting. Others mentioned that they would like be able to actuate devices: for example to put their phone in silent mode when in a meeting, or to automatically switch off lights when the last person exits a room. These results further indicate that there is a need for additional applications that can be built on top of our framework that further exploit the collected information.

7   Discussion

Following the completion of the study we were in a position to identify key factors that could affect the balance between perceived value and privacy intrusion in a social network that relies on passive environmental sensing.

The introduction of environmental sensing into a social networking application disrupts the traditional, user-initiated input to social services. With respect to research question 1, the key factor that affects the perceived value of the system is primarily related to self monitoring and comparison with others. Although the public sharing of information is the major factor that affects privacy concern (as contrasted by the low privacy markings by the "closed access" group), at the same time it is one of the factors that added more value to the experience of the participants. Sharing information with others did not necessarily mean complete strangers, but rather colleagues that participants had only limited knowledge about their social behavior. To a significant extent the value was mainly extracted by comparing "others" with themselves. At the same time participants expect different levels of functionality for practical purposes, namely real-time, accurate sensor readings, while social behavior is mainly related to either aggregates, or generic trends for given groups of colleagues. Regarding research question 2, the primary causes of privacy concern relates to the lack of control over the input stream, as an inherent aspect of passive sensing, and the limited control over the possible interpretation of the sensed information by others.

In addressing research question 3, these observations allow us to identify possible system design approaches that have the potential of improving acceptability of such systems. We consider two main categories of data recipients within the system: close social circle, and organization. For the close social circle the delivery of accurate real-time information is a service that can support the practical aspects of the system. As this group is considered more trusted by the participants privacy concerns are typically more relaxed. For the organization circle, it is important to maintain a certain level of visibility in order not to diminish the value derived from "checking on others", or comparing attitudes with general trends. One of the key factors that affect the attitude of users towards the system, is the perceived *objectivity*. Continuous passive sensing means that people do not have the opportunity to either construct an image for their social networking audience or control the details of what is revealed. Potential techniques for mitigating this aspect can include typical obfuscation mechanisms, although the uniform obfuscation of all information could reduce the perceived value. Through the study it became clear that people are happy to share aspects of their lives that show a positive side of their social behavior. At the same time participants show an interest to compare themselves with the general trends of people similar to them. Applying these findings to the event distribution framework, could include the delivery of more accurate information for positive social situations, while data obfuscation and aggregation could be applied to deliver general statistics for the whole population for comparative reasons.

One obvious level of control that many participants requested, is a global "on/off" switch to control the collection of data from the infrastructure. Furthermore, the request for people to access personal data before being released was also hinted by the participants by requesting the ability to add comments to pieces of information. Possible techniques that could be used include delayed data delivery, in combination with learning techniques that can detect unexpected behavior. Delaying the stream of potentially sensitive events for a period of time, allows the implementation of mechanisms for tagging or deleting the information before it is publicized. However, the possibility of allowing users to delete or alter information bears the risk of reducing trust to the system and the validity of the reported data. The successful introduction of such mechanisms should only be considered with the appropriate modifications to the UI where, for example, deleted or altered information is clearly marked.

The results of this study can only be considered within the context of the target environment where it was executed. A research institution is typically more relaxed compared to other working environments and this had a significant impact limiting the concerns people had about the use of such technology for surveillance purposes. Furthermore, the target country where the study was executed implies a specific cultural and political context that affects the participants acceptability. We consider this study as an early probe that will lead to long-term deployments of such systems in a wider range of business environments as part of our future work.

8 Related Work

User studies in sensor enabled social networking have been primarily concerned with Location Based Services (LBS). Early work in the Reno system [13] considers the involvement of the user in disclosing location to their friends. In [14], the authors investigate how and why people use LBS, concluding that main reason that LBS are popular is that they provide both elements of fun and added value to the user. Other studies in the field of social networks show similar findings [15,16]. We contribute to these findings by understanding the value that users find in using sensor-rich social services in the context of a working environment.

In terms of privacy, similar to our findings in [14] the authors concluded that users had few privacy concerns when using an LBS system. This is contrary to previous works [17,18] where it has been found that privacy implications can be a barrier on the adoption of such services. In [17] the type of information that users were willing to share with certain people was further examined. Finally, in [18] the authors found significant differences in privacy settings depending on whether this is for a given purpose (e.g., work related) or just socially-driven. In [13] Mancini et al. explores the implications of location disclosure between family members and concludes that closer bonds can increase privacy concerns. Our work builds on this literature by providing an understanding of privacy implications in a more challenging environment where sensors are embedded in the environment. This is significantly different to LBS as such sensing is inherently passive, performed without the explicit consent of the user.

Finally, apart from location based services, there are novel mobile phone applications where a variety of sensors is used to detect social interactions. In CenceMe [1] the user's mobile phone sensors (accelerometers, light, location, etc) are used to detect a range of social activities. In SoundSense [19], the microphone is used to classify people's social activities where as in emotionSense [9] the user's conversations and emotional status can be detected. In Sensible Organizations [10] wearable sensing devices were used to capture location information, conversation detection, and peoples' co-location to be used for posterior analysis. Findings of such analysis include whether a user carries a disease, the user's financial status, productivity, or even her political preferences. Clearly these applications are valuable to the researchers and the application developers but there is no indication about whether they are useful to the end users.

In this work we fill this gap by understanding the value and the privacy concerns from the monitored user's point of view.

9 Conclusions

Passive sensing can be considered an objective recorder of human behavior, as sensing is not initiated by the user and therefore does not suffer from selective reporting. This fact makes it a significant value multiplier for social networking services as users can observe the real behavior of their colleagues; while at the same time raises significant privacy concerns as users loose control over what is reported about their behavior. Our empirical study of the introduction of a sensor-driven social sharing application within a research institution illustrates the contradicting trends that affect acceptability of such services. Users find value in comparing their behavior with others, typically not from within their close social circle, while privacy concerns are raised when the system shares behavior that is considered less favorable by the participants. In our future work we intend to explore the feasibility of applying techniques to protect users' privacy while maintaining the value of such services.

Acknowledgments. We would like to acknowledge the support of the EPSRC through project FRESNEL EP/G069557/1, and the Gates Cambridge Trust.

References

1. Miluzzo, E., Lane, N.D., Fodor, K., Peterson, R., Lu, H., Musolesi, M., Eisenman, S.B., Zheng, X., Campbell, A.T.: Sensing meets mobile social networks: the design, implementation and evaluation of the cenceme application. In: SenSys 2008, pp. 337–350. ACM, New York (2008)
2. Murty, R., Mainland, G., Rose, I., Chowdhury, A.R., Gosain, A., Bers, J., Welsh, M.: Citysense: An urban-scale wireless sensor network and testbed. In: 2008 IEEE International Conference on Technologies for Homeland Security (May 2008)
3. Wood, A., Virone, G., Doan, T., Cao, Q., Selavo, L., Wu, Y., Fang, L., He, Z., Lin, S., Stankovic, J.: ALARM-NET: Wireless sensor networks for assisted-living and residential monitoring. University of Virginia Computer Science Department Technical Report (2006)
4. Kortuem, G., Kawsar, F., Fitton, D., Sundramoorthy, V.: Smart objects as building blocks for the internet of things. IEEE Internet Computing 14(1), 44–51 (2010)
5. Want, R., Hopper, A., Falcao, V., Gibbons, J.: The active badge location system. ACM Transactions on Information Systems 10(1) (1992)
6. Li, I., Day, A., Forlizzi, J.: Understanding my data, myself: Supporting self-reflection with ubicomp technologies. In: Proceedings of Ubicomp 2011, Beijing, China, pp. 405–414 (2011)
7. Wu, L., Waber, B., Aral, S., Brynjolfsson, E., Pentland, A.: Mining Face-to-Face Interaction Networks Using Sociometric Badges: Predicting Productivity in an IT Configuration Task. In: SSRN 2008 (2008)
8. Sewell, G.: The discipline of teams: The control of team-based industrial work through electronic and peer surveillance. Administrative Science Quarterly 43(2) (June 1998)
9. Rachuri, K.K., Musolesi, M., Mascolo, C., Rentfrow, P.J., Longworth, C., Aucinas, A.: EmotionSense: a mobile phones based adaptive platform for experimental social psychology research. In: Ubicomp 2010, pp. 281–290. ACM, New York (2010)

10. Olguín, D.O., Waber, B.N., Kim, T., Mohan, A., Ara, K., Pentland, A.: Sensible organizations: technology and methodology for automatically measuring organizational behavior. Trans. Sys. Man Cyber. Part B 39, 43–55 (2009)
11. Altman, I.: Privacy regulation: Culturally universal or culturally specific? Journal of Social Issues 33(3), 66–84 (1977)
12. Palen, L., Dourish, P.: Unpacking "privacy" for a networked world. In: Proceedings of CHI 2003, Fort Lauderdale, FL, USA (2003)
13. Mancini, C., Rogers, Y., Thomas, K., Joinson, A., Price, B., Bandara, A., Jedrzejczyk, L., Nuseibeh, B.: In the best families: tracking and relationship. In: Proceedings of ACM CHI 2011, Vancouver, Canada (2011)
14. Lindqvist, J., Cranshaw, J., Wiese, J., Hong, J., Zimmerman, J.: I'm the mayor of my house. In: CHI 2011. IEEE, Vancouver (2011)
15. Ames, M.: Why we tag: motivations for annotation in mobile and online media. In: CHI 2007: Proceedings of the SIGCHI Conference, pp. 971–980. ACM Press (2007)
16. Lampe, C., Velasquez, A., Ozkaya, E.: Motivations to participate in online communities. In: Computer Human Interaction, pp. 1927–1936 (2010)
17. Lederer, S., Mankoff, J., Dey, A.K.: Who wants to know what when? privacy preference determinants in ubiquitous computing. In: CHI 2003 Extended Abstracts on Human Factors in Computing Systems, CHIEA 2003, pp. 724–725. ACM, New York (2003)
18. Tang, K.P., Lin, J., Hong, J.I., Siewiorek, D.P., Sadeh, N.: Rethinking location sharing: exploring the implications of social-driven vs. purpose-driven location sharing. In: Proceedings of the 12th ACM International Conference on Ubiquitous Computing, Ubicomp 2010, pp. 85–94. ACM, New York (2010)
19. Lu, H., Pan, W., Lane, N.D., Choudhury, T., Campbell, A.T.: Soundsense: scalable sound sensing for people-centric applications on mobile phones. In: MobiSys 2009, pp. 165–178. ACM, New York (2009)

From School Food to Skate Parks in a Few Clicks: Using Public Displays to Bootstrap Civic Engagement of the Young

Simo Hosio, Vassilis Kostakos, Hannu Kukka, Marko Jurmu,
Jukka Riekki, and Timo Ojala

Department of Computer Science and Engineering, University of Oulu, Finland
firstname.lastname@ee.oulu.fi

Abstract. We present Ubinion, a service that utilizes large public interactive displays to enable young people to give personalized feedback on municipal issues to local youth workers. It also facilitates discussion and sharing the feedback online using modern social networking services. We present the motivation and rationale behind Ubinion and analyze the results from three large-scale user trials conducted in authentic settings. The evaluation shows that young users are positive about adopting Ubinion, and that they quickly appropriated its use to provide feedback outside the intended scope of the system, but still reflecting their concerns. We argue that Ubinion's design as a fun and informal tool is appropriate for its purpose, and discuss the versatility of public interactive displays as a municipal feedback medium and as content sources for online communities in general.

Keywords: Social computing, urban computing, public spaces, public displays, social networking, civic engagement, information interfaces.

1 Introduction

In this paper we investigate the role of a proliferating pervasive technology, interactive public displays, to allow for collective, semi-anonymous initiation and enhancing of an online community. We utilize these displays in collecting feedback and opinions on topical issues from young users, specifically from pre-teens (<13 y/o), teens (13-17 y/o), and young adults (>17 y/o) and for relaying this feedback online for discussion and access. We regard public interactive displays, deployed in pivotal city locations, as a potential tool for reaching out to the urban youth otherwise often unreachable by social workers. Our focus is on the youth that do not actively participate in municipal youth activities or, indeed, are not even aware of such activities. As many young people are interested in latest gadgetry and games, we see potential in approaching them with playful interfaces and applications that are social and fun to use on high-end, interactive displays.

We have developed a prototype service called Ubinion that runs on interactive displays. The aim of the prototype is to foster engagement of the young in topical municipal issues, and to empower the youth to have their voice heard through such new pervasive technology. The prototype allows the Youth Affairs Department

J. Kay et al. (Eds.): Pervasive 2012, LNCS 7319, pp. 425–442, 2012.

(later: YAD) of Oulu to initiate a topic of discussion, and for the young to respond by giving feedback or comments through interactive public displays. These responses take the form of photographs, with annotated thought bubbles (Figure 1) or protest signs, and end up in Ubinion's online presence in a popular online social networking service (later: SNS), thus aiming to create an online community, initially populated by the semi-anonymous young and their submitted content. To follow-up the feedback, users and youth workers can view and take part in the discussion online. As SNSs are an integral part of teenagers' lives these days, we believe they are efficient tools for fostering discussion about topical municipal issues of interest to the young. Further, as the Oulu officials already have an online presence in SNSs, Ubinion enables increasing interaction between the young and city officials.

In this paper we make three key contributions:

- We develop a novel public service for fostering communication between young citizens and youth officials in a fun and entertaining way.
- We demonstrate how public interactive displays can be used in a many-to-one fashion to facilitate creation of a content-rich community presence in a social networking service.
- We identify how young users appropriate this new communication channel via extensive field trials conducted in authentic settings.

Our contributions are essential for cities or organizations wishing to engage the young in conversation about topical interests using such pervasive technologies. In addition to demonstrating how public displays can be used hand-in-hand with SNSs (here: Facebook and Twitter) to create a content-rich community presence, we also identify the ways in which young users are willing to appropriate this technology to voice their own concerns.

Fig. 1. Sample feedback submitted via Ubinion prototype. Left: "Faster decisions, please." Right: "You are using the City's money wrong, e.g. a new parking lot. No funding cuts to schools!!!"

2   Related Work

Previous research has shown that citizen participation is positive for individuals, institutions [1], as well as for the broader society [2]. While citizens are being increasingly encouraged to take on more active roles [3], citizen participation can only be fostered on the basis of reciprocal trust between people and institutions [4-7]. It has been argued that citizen participation can be viewed from the perspective of benefits to be gained and costs to be borne. Benefits include not only material advantages but also psychological and social ones: satisfaction [8], sense of belonging, and social status rewards [9].

Building on these previous findings, we identified two key requirements for Ubinion. First, the process of giving feedback should be fun and engaging, thus offering satisfaction to those providing feedback. Second, we decided to use SNSs as an intermediary transparent mechanism for building trust between the youth and the institution that is dealing with this feedback (in our case the local youth workers), as well as for intrinsic social status rewards.

2.1 Public Displays

While little previous work has considered using public displays for civic engagement, research on applications utilizing public displays has been steadily gaining momentum, focusing on issues such as user interface design, navigation, awareness, and artistic creativity. Our system draws features from several types of services on public displays: Ubinion is primarily a social application that encourages young people to collectively create something meaningful, yet personalized, on public displays.

Müller et al. [10] reported findings from two prototypes on public displays, *News Displays* and *Reminder Displays*, deployed in a university setting and providing users topical news and situated, contextual reminders. They provided a straightforward mechanism for submitting new information chunks and highlighted the importance of updated content available for viewers, reported also in [11]. Further, they emphasized the recognition of content sources, individuals who have continuous needs for publishing content, for providing fresh content to a system. In our work, we demonstrate how to provide new content by turning casual bystanders into content sources through playfulness, participation, and sociality.

A large networked display installation in the wild, *e-Campus* [12], explored various means of injecting content into their system. They focused in supporting large user population and gathering lessons for future deployments of similar purpose. These include content-related issues, such as the well-known phrase "Content is king", referring to the importance of high-quality content, and the expenses associated with acquiring good content. Further, they highlight maintenance tasks, such as being able to see what the users of applications see. We take advice from these lessons in our work by designing our system to encourage its users to generate socially meaningful, relevant content for themselves and for their peers in SNSs, thus guaranteeing near-perfect uptime and content monitoring capabilities.

The *AutoSpeakerID* and *Ticket2Talk* [13] prototypes augmented an academic conference with information about its participants, enhancing their awareness about each other. *Instant Places* [14] allows users to draw content from Flickr or post simple messages using their Bluetooth device name as the commanding interface. These, like many other deployments, draw pre-generated content from existing sources. In contrast, our focus is on on-the-spot creation of content by our users, supplemented with the ability for follow-up interaction and discussion via popular SNSs.

2.2   Encouraging Use

A key challenge we faced with our system is to encourage social use: build the system so that groups of people can use it simultaneously. This requirement is grounded on the fact that while getting feedback from an individual young person is challenging due to social barriers such as shyness, getting feedback and ideas from a group is seen as far easier. By working together, groups are able to overcome common problems, thanks to team efforts [15]. Therefore a key requirement we identified was to base the functionality on a live camera stream that is able to capture a group of people at the same time.

Previous research [16], [11] has shown that the 'mirror' metaphor is an efficient way of enticing users to approach a display, and become active participants, thus combating display blindness [17], a common problem related to public displays in the wild. The interactive displays deployed in Oulu already include an application that allows users to take a snapshot using integrated cameras, augment the image with a textual message, and send it to friends through e-mail or share it on Facebook. The application has attracted considerable use throughout its deployment [11], and we have observed groups of up to 20 teenagers posing in front of the displays at the same time for long periods of time, taking snapshot after snapshot, trying to capture the perfect moment. As this interaction method has proven effective in capturing attention and enticing people to use a public display in groups, we utilized a similar method in the Ubinion prototype.

3   Ubinion

Ubinion was designed to allow users to interact collaboratively and playfully using large interactive displays in urban space to create content and, at the same time, leave feedback about municipal issues to the local YAD. In addition, it enables follow-up discussion, commenting, and sharing generated content online using SNSs. The system is aimed at the local youth, and the YAD has been involved in all stages of design and evaluation of Ubinion.

Our design process involved a design session with representatives of the YAD to gain a better understanding of their operations and needs. The session took place at the university campus and lasted for two hours. Four local youth workers took part in the session, which was documented with notes, and a questionnaire was delivered to the participants after the session to collect further data. In this case, the youth workers are domain experts in the field, and involving them from the very beginning is a crucial aspect in building a successful prototype [18].

In addition, focus group sessions and informal semi-structured interviews were conducted with young people, to capture their understanding of civic involvement and their perceptions of YAD and its operations. Their use of SNSs was also explored. These sessions were organized in cafeterias favored by the young in downtown Oulu, where we discussed with groups of teenagers and interviewed them on a one-to-one basis as well. In addition, we deployed online questionnaires answered by the youth.

3.1   Existing Practices, Design Requirements, and Guidelines

Our research indicated that YAD currently uses paper-based feedback forms, distributed and collected after specific events for the young. They also use a generic on-line feedback form, and they utilize an online nationwide initiative service. The main tool for reaching young people is still face-to-face conversations in selected schools and youth centers. Interestingly, social media, which our data and interviews showed to be a very integral part of communication practices of today's young, is not efficiently used to reach the young. Despite the seemingly multiple ways of collecting feedback, the youth workers expressed difficulties in reaching as many young people as they would want to, while the youth appeared somewhat uninterested and especially uninformed in YAD's approach and ways of reaching out.

Another finding was that existing feedback and information channels were inadequate in many aspects, and novel solutions were required to keep up with the contemporary communication practices of young people. While the need for an upgrade of existing practices was clearly recognized, YAD officials did not have a clear idea or the required skills on how to exploit new technologies.

In addition, we collected feedback about the possibility of a public display service, since they have previously been successfully used to collect topical opinions and votes e.g. in a campus-setting for students [19]. We inquired about the kinds of benefits that YAD and the youth would see in using such public interactive displays for engaging with the young. The feedback we received was that such a system should aim to reach the young who do not participate actively in official events. The opinion of both the YAD and the youth was that using the latest technology to increase the visibility of informational content is necessary to systematically reach out to the young. In general, the possibility to engage in municipal issues directly from public displays was seen as a fascinating avenue to explore. Moreover, the young felt uncomfortable to visit the premises of YAD in person, as they claimed it added "pressure" to giving feedback. As one of the interviewed youths put it: *"With some other solutions, we can take our time giving the opinions, and don't have to fear that we have to [commit] in realizing the idea."* Thus, the young felt they would benefit from a more anonymous and flexible mechanism of participation.

Finally, our findings showed that YAD considered television, movies, radio broadcasting, and traditional roadside advertising as far too expensive, while social media was seen as a potentially functional communication tool regardless of the target group and the type of activity planned ("mainstream" / "underground"). E-mail and Twitter were not thought to reach the young very efficiently. Despite the recent digital takeover, face-to-face conversations and traditional meetings at youth houses and schools were mentioned as highly important activities. Thus, YAD considered the role of digital and social media as increasingly important and supportive, but definitely not dominant as of yet. On the other hand, our data from talking to youth suggest that they regularly engage in interactions via social media, and they claim to get to know about new events and ideas almost solely through Facebook. It appears that social networking services are channels used heavily by the youth. Our interviews also showed that Facebook is used among the young for discussions around a variety of topics, and not only for status updates and ephemeral sharing. Thus, Facebook could be suited for discussions around concerns of the young.

Of the 13-year olds (the "official" minimum age required to open an account in Facebook), only one out of twenty was reported to not have an account, just to "be different" and for a "matter of principle". One slightly alarming finding during the interviews was that many of the local young start to use Facebook at the early age of eight. *"Either they create the accounts in secret by themselves, or their parents create the accounts for them"*, summarized one of the focus groups we interviewed. This suggests that the age limits of Facebook are not being enforced.

Our key requirements formulated from analyzing previous work as well as through our interactions with YAD and the youth can be summarized as follows:

- **Exploit public displays:** The use of public displays is often highly social by nature [20], and inherently supporting sociality increases the adoption of an application on public interactive displays [11]. They also contribute to a "cutting-edge" image that is attractive to youth. Furthermore, the "honeypot" effect [21] can be exploited to encourage their use.
- **Design for playfulness:** Interactions and interfaces on public displays need to be simple and effortless to use [20]. A public application needs to efficiently attract and motivate its users to engage with it [21, 22]. Previous research has shown that the 'mirror' metaphor [16], [11] is an efficient way of enticing users to approach a display, and become active participants, thus combating display blindness [17]. Also, taking a group photo using an embedded webcam effectively invites multiple users to create content in a social and fun way [11], thus lowering the barrier of interacting with a public display [22]. Collaborative use also combats the feeling of social awkwardness associated with interactions on public displays [21].
- **Use social media:** Social media can be used as a public ground to establish common trust between the youth and YAD institutions [4-7]. In addition, social media services can help manage content creation, storing, and delivery, which are key challenges in pervasive systems [12].

3.2   The Ubinion Prototype

Ubinion allows users to take a snapshot with a web camera embedded in the public display, add comments to an augmented graphical element in the picture, and upload the picture with given comments to a photo album in Ubinion's Facebook page, while the text comments are also replicated to its Twitter feed. Thus, Ubinion integrates two powerful, yet inherently different, online social networking services.

Ubinion consists of three separate parts. The user interface on *public displays* serves as the first entry point to Ubinion; the *Twitter* feed, being simple and easy to browse, allows youth workers and system moderators to rapidly skim the submitted feedback, and to only pick valid ideas and comments; the *Facebook* page, where taken pictures with given comments are uploaded, allows for sharing, commenting and discussing the ideas. The latter enables "liking" suggestions and comments, acting as a ranking mechanism, and offers convenient community-driven moderation as well as admin capabilities for the youth officials to oversee what is happening with the application. Finally, it serves the need for a more relaxed and casual conversation often happening around the less serious comments and photos.

Ubinion's public display UI provides only a few buttons to facilitate rapid and fluid interaction. Users move between screens by touching buttons shaped as large glowing arrows, and the final comment input is performed using a virtual qwerty-style keyboard. The graphical elements, speech bubble and protest sign, can be moved via dragging on the screen. Ubinion aims to be "fun", as using such interfaces can be a liberating experience [23], and make users feel comfortable to leave feedback. Previous research has also shown that while users tend not to perceive playful applications as useful or important prior to using such displays, data collected from actual long term usage shows that the opposite is, in fact, the case [24]. Ubinion's user interface can be seen in Figure 2. Ubinion strives to engage users by embracing the creativity of users [22] by allowing the creation of personalized content. Further, by utilizing a webcam feed, Ubinion makes users real parts of the application and produced content, which has been proven to be an effective way of catching attention [16].

Fig. 2. Ubinion's user interface on public displays. From left: initial instruction screen, example opinions and feedback, webcam image and choice between "speech bubble" or "protest sign" as the augmenting element, and a screen with virtual keyboard to enter text in the chosen graphical element and a submit button.

4   Field Trials

We ran three field trials to evaluate Ubinion in realistic contexts. Each trial was a focused study in a selected event. In two of the three field trials, Ubinion ran on 57" displays already located at the venues. To encourage users in exploring the social networking features of Ubinion, we also provided all-in-one 23" touchscreen PCs and made them available to users.

After consulting the YAD, we chose to ask the following question on Ubinion's first page, and urge the youth to provide feedback: *"What is wrong? Are you annoyed? How could we develop Oulu?"*.

4.1   Data Collection

We collected data by unobtrusively observing users, having at least two researchers present in each trial, and by an online questionnaire. Users had the choice of using extra computers on site to answer the questionnaire after using the prototype, or answering it later online. The form was made public via an easy to remember address: www.ubinion.com. As an incentive to answering the questionnaire, we raffled movie tickets for a local cinema. With the questionnaire we sought to uncover issues related to the usability and user acceptance of Ubinion, and to explore the perception of value of this kind of feedback channel and the actual feedback they submit. The questionnaire featured demographic questions, an adapted version of a standard SUS (System Usability Scale) questionnaire [25] to assess the usability of Ubinion, and questions regarding respondents' expectations regarding their feedback and experience regarding interactions with the YAD.

During the three deployments, we received 262 Ubinion entries, and 195 completed questionnaires (88 male). Of the questionnaire respondents, 70 were pre-teens (<13 y/o), 31 teens (13-17 y/o), and 94 young adults (>17 y/o), with an average age of 15.9 (SD: 5.3). Of the respondents, 152 currently lived in Oulu (67 male, average age 15.5, SD: 4.5).

4.2   Field Trials

The *first* field trial was conducted during a holiday event featuring mostly sporty activities like skateboarding, bouncy castles, and BMX cycling. The event lasted for two days, and was aimed at a pre-teen and teen audience. In order to engage as many visitors as possible, we placed Ubinion next to the main entrance to the exhibition space, a practice suggested in [10]. As the event mainly attracts a younger demographic, our goal with this trial was to attract a mainly pre-teen audience. Among the 88 questionnaire respondents from this trial, there were 69 pre-teens, 13 teens and 6 young adults. (MEAN age: 12.7 years, SD: 5.8 years).

The *second* field trial was organized during a full-day event at the University main campus for students from local senior high schools, aiming to promote and deliver information about different study possibilities available at the university. The event attracts over 4000 students, mostly young adults, each year. Ubinion was situated in one of the main hallways of the university. The selected space is an intersection of several busy walkways, and already houses one of the large interactive displays deployed in Oulu, making deployment easy as we did not have to transport a display from elsewhere. The motivation to have a field trial during this event was to capture a mostly young adult demographic. From this trial, we gathered 94 questionnaire responses from 1 pre-teen, 7 teens, and 86 young adults (MEAN age: 19 years, SD: 2.6 years).

The *third* field trial was organized at a local high school during a school day. We wanted to evaluate the effect of changing from a public fair setting to a more mundane environment where students were attending their normal everyday schedules and not participating in a special event, as was the case with the two previous trials. We also wanted to capture a teenage audience, as the two previous trials had focused mostly on pre-teens and young adults. This trial differed from the two previous ones, as we gathered results only during two lunch breaks and two normal breaks, lasting around two hours in total. Due to logistical difficulties, we had to deploy Ubinion on a 23" touch screen PC, placed in a lobby next to the school cafeteria to make it as visible as possible. This trial resulted in 13 respondents, 0 pre-teens, 11 teens, and 2 young adults (MEAN age: 15.3 years, SD: 1.8 years).

Following the three field studies and our analysis of the results, an interview session with Oulu YAD took place. The interview was organized at the premises of the YAD and included three youth officials both from City and from YAD who commented and evaluated the data collected by Ubinion.

5   Results

We analyzed the 262 entries (opinions) created by users of Ubinion during the three field trials. Two researchers individually examined the submitted entries, and concluded that the feedback can be grouped in four categories: public services, sports, education, and other.

The "public services" category contains 33% of all submitted entries. A few trends can be seen in these entries, namely comments for and against current topics in the local media, such as a new and expensive parking lot that was be built in Oulu. In addition we received comments about public transport, which was seen far too expensive and insufficient for the needs of the young. Further, the situation where the trial was held had an impact on many of these comments. There were several comments about and concrete improvement suggestions for the youth event (first trial) and for the university event (second trial). Generally comments like "Cheaper bus tickets", "We don't want the new parking lot", and "This <event> is really nice" were given in this category.

The sports category contains 13% of the comments. The trend here was to request more sports facilities or events for a certain sport. The most popular requests were to build more skate parks or renovate old ones, obviously due to the nature of the youth event during the first trial. However, more traditional sports got mentions as well, such as swimming and gymnastics. Even though the majority of sports related comments were requesting for something more, some of the existing sports facilities in Oulu got positive feedback and comments from the young. "More BMX parks!", "Build roofing to the skate park in <location>", or "The artificial lawn at <location> is great!" are typical examples of entries in this category.

The education category was the least popular with 6% of all submitted comments. Clearly the most discussed topic here was school food, which was often regarded as being of low quality. However, more severe topics such as bullying among the young and classroom sizes were mentioned as well. Comments such as "School food sucks", "Big classroom sizes are depressing", and "It would be nice to have more sports classes in senior-high school" were given in this category.

The category "Other" contained 47% of comments. In this category we grouped general greetings, random strings, smileys, and other comments that were clearly input just to test the technology, to have an entry submitted, or just to have some fun toying with the prototype. Comments such as "omg lol XD", "yebou", or "save the walruses" are examples of comments in this category.

In total 139 (53%) of the 262 entries were given by groups, consisting of 2 to 12 persons in them, 119 by single persons, and 4 without anyone particularly appearing in the photo. Further analysis revealed that group size did not significantly affect the topic of the given feedback. However, gender did: a Pearson's chi-square test showed that males (males and groups of only males) gave significantly more feedback relating to "sports" than females (females and groups of only females) ($x^2(3$, N=245) = 11.07, p<.05). Figure 3 illustrates the category breakdown per gender.

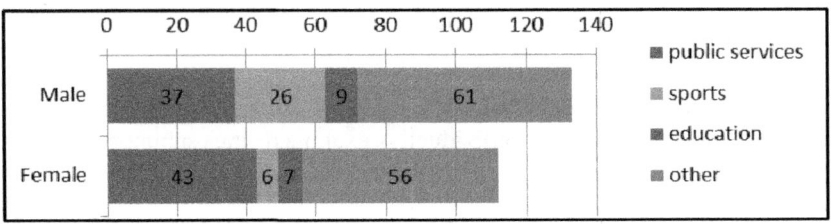

Fig. 3. Feedback collected by Ubinion grouped by topic and gender

5.1   Responses to the Questionnaire

Based on the 195 questionnaire responses, the respondents felt relatively comfortable using Ubinion (4.0 on a 5-point scale, SD=1.0), while they also reported that they perceived the system to be "fun" to use (4.1, SD=1.1). Pre-teens were generally more positive in their responses in this regard. In relation to the social use of the system, the participants mostly agreed that they preferred using the system in a group rather than alone (4.0, SD=1.2), with teens and young adults agreeing slightly more. Overall, respondents were positive about the system (3.9, SD=1.1).

The results also showed that the respondents were not entirely convinced that their feedback was of value to the city officials (3.4, SD=1.1). Especially young adults had doubts about this (3.1, SD=1.1). Analyzing this further, a Pearson's chi-square test was used to examine the relation between users' previous experience in participating in youth activities and believing that the feedback has value to the city officials. The relation was significant ($x^2(8$, N=190) = 17.83, p<.05), showing that participants with no prior experience in youth activities felt their feedback was less valuable.

5.2   Facebook Activity

The Facebook component of Ubinion ran independently and throughout the three trials. We continued collecting data from the Facebook component 6 weeks after the third trial completed, thus bringing the total data-collection period to 5 months. During this time Ubinion's Facebook page received 53 likes and 16 comments. Wall posts, i.e. Ubinion entries, were viewed 991 times, and particularly the gallery section with all of the entries was accessed 122 times. Of the handful of comments made on Facebook, most merely attributed the young themselves or identified their friends in the photos. The most active age group visiting Ubinion on Facebook was 13-17 with 36% of all visits, followed by 27% by 25-34 y/o, and 23.4% by 18-14 y/o. This data was gathered directly from Facebook's page analytics.

5.3   Feedback from the YAD

During a feedback session, youth workers were asked to give insight on Ubinion and its use from the perspective of city officials. Overall, the feedback we received from the youth workers was positive. Facebook was perceived as an increasingly important part of their communication strategy, and a valuable tool in reaching the young. Furthermore, the administration interface provided by Facebook is easy and effortless to use for monitoring and participating in discussions. A shortcoming was the requirement for a person to 'like' the Facebook page prior to being able to participate in the discussion. Also, the youth workers had concerns about using Facebook as the only end point for the content, as they previously had problems with accounts being suddenly banned. However, the pros were seen to greatly overweigh the cons, and Facebook was concluded as a highly suitable solution for the YAD.

The Twitter feed was preferred over Ubinion's Facebook page for the simple task of following the text-based feedback stream. Twitter streams are less cluttered than a Facebook page, and thus it was deemed more suitable for this purpose.

The feedback submitted through Ubinion was seen as valuable but broad, since the youth workers concluded that the feedback was too cluttered in the scope of their purposes. Entries given through Ubinion often contained ideas or opinions on issues that are outside their jurisdiction and would require higher levels of the Oulu administration to address, such as building new sports halls or skate parks. However, it is to be noted that this feedback is valuable as it still reflects the wishes and concerns of the young, and should just be forwarded to different municipal stakeholders.

Overall, the youth officials reacted positively to the results. Based on this meeting, future enhancements were suggested, including an interface for changing the sample pictures and texts in Ubinion's public user interface. A further improvement would be to store the content also on private servers to counter the possibility of getting an account banned in Facebook and losing all the generated data.

6   Discussion

Our results and observations suggest that Ubinion was perceived positively by all age groups in the study, and slightly as more fun to use by pre-teens and teens. The used technology may be a factor in these results, as the youngest age groups are not as accustomed to gadgets and high-end technologies as older ones, making the use of Ubinion exciting and more fun for them. This can be leveraged in reaching the youngest demographics: by building applications with fluid, playful user interfaces and using novel technology, such as large interactive displays with cameras, it is possible to appeal to the young demographics.

However, youth workers were surprised by the fact that we found that less than one third of young adults felt that their feedback had any significant value. Prior participation in youth activities correlated directly with the perceived value of the feedback given, indicating that people more familiar with official youth activities also trust youth workers more. Utilizing applications that connect the young, youth workers, and urban locations where the young can socially use the applications together might be a step towards a more flexible ecosystem, where the young are more aware and willing to engage openly in topical municipal issues. For example in our three trials we reached 130 respondents, 66.7% of all questionnaire respondents, who did not know of any other channels of giving feedback to their local youth affairs department. This as itself is already a contribution to local youth work, and was highly appreciated by the YAD.

Furthermore, we found that respondents preferred giving feedback collaboratively with friends. Utilizing Facebook for discussion and sharing the feedback was seen in a very positive light by especially pre-teens, and interestingly 100% of them were found to already use SNSs. It is worth noting, however, that the youths' positive comments in using Facebook as a discussion mechanism were not reflected in their actual behavior: Facebook, as we discuss later, was mostly used for browsing and voting, but not for discussion.

Finally, our interviews revealed interesting facts about the age of the youngest Facebook users, who were quoted to be as young as eight years old, supporting the findings in [26]. As Facebook officially restricts users below the age of 13, we can only note that this is indeed not the case in real life.

6.1 Effects of Social Settings

The social and physical situation where a trial was conducted affected users' behavior. During the first trial, we noticed Ubinion often being used as a playful gadget instead of a serious feedback medium towards youth workers. Users did not always pay attention to the core idea behind the service when they found out that they could take a photo and upload it to Facebook. This functionality alone worked as sufficient incentive to motivate action, and pre-teens often spent long times playing with Ubinion, taking photos and fooling around with friends in front of the embedded web camera. Some groups, especially of girls, took their photos several times before being satisfied with the result, while boys mostly enjoyed performing various tricks and poses in front of the camera but eventually being satisfied with a single snapshot. This is noteworthy, as the fair also offered a plethora of other activities that we initially thought to attract youngsters away from our prototype. Ubinion was clearly seen as one of the various attractions offered in the fair, thus being a natural addition and a good fit to this environment.

The atmosphere at the university setting in the second trial was more "adult", and users paid more attention to, and questioned the purpose of, the deployment. They spent more time thinking about their feedback, and did not engage in such joyous, playful interactions with the camera nearly as much as users in the first trial. Nevertheless, group-use of Ubinion was preferred here as well. We hypothesize that while pre-teens are still in a playful stage of development, i.e. not afraid to be seen playing in public, high school seniors are much more self-aware, and are not willing to risk looking 'silly' in front of their peers.

In the third setting, a local school, users acted in a slightly more distant and indifferent way towards the prototype installation. Engaging with Ubinion seemed to be socially more embarrassing in this context than in the previous two trials. In this environment, teachers were supervising the breaks and all users were surrounded with close friends with whom they meet daily. We believe this might have caused potential users to completely avoid any chances of being seen as uncool in front of them by using such a technology probe, and secondly to just ignore the prototype in order to leave the "teacher's territory" and leave the premises to spend time outside. A limiting factor in interpreting this environment is the change in the used hardware setup: whereas the other trials featured 57" HD screens, here we only had 23" screens. Perhaps seeing themselves through a camera feed on a larger display would have mitigated some of the social awkwardness, similarly to the other two trials.

These findings highlight the importance of understanding the social context in the deployment of any ubiquitous computing application. We suggest environments where it is socially acceptable to engage playfully as most suited for these kinds of applications that aim to gather feedback through play and sociality. The overarching trend here is that with young people, contexts that are public in nature, such as fairs and exhibitions, are more suitable for these kinds of interactions than more private environments, such as a school.

By deploying novel interactive displays in places where the young already spend their free-time, and by making civic engagement on them fun at the same time, it is possible to reach young who are otherwise not reachable, and to significantly enhance the interaction possibilities between youth workers and the young. Further, as interactive touch screen-based public displays still are novel artifacts in public spaces, they arguably attract more attention than, say, having a similar prototype running on a laptop computer.

6.2   Playful Interaction

Civic engagement can often be seen as a "serious" task. Using playful interfaces that encourage having fun and socializing together with friends can help in lowering the barrier to participation in municipal issues. We were successful in gathering large amounts of feedback using playful elements. Especially among pre-teens, an important factor in the popularity of Ubinion was the aspiration to catch the "perfect pose", clearly a joyful effort towards which pre-teenagers were willing to sacrifice significant amounts of their time, regardless of other attractions close by. Verifying this, some photos taken in the first trial had up to 12 pre-teens posing to the camera. Succeeding in this, groups proceeded to give their feedback or comments. The user interface of Ubinion aims to be fun, as such interfaces can offer a liberating experience [23] and perhaps aid us by making users feel comfortable to leave natural feedback through Ubinion.

Having the deployment in the right spot and offering a possibility to create something in a fun and playful way helps reaching young who might be hard to reach otherwise. Getting any feedback from these people is seen as challenging by the youth workers, and our prototype was perceived as a valuable addition to their toolbox in engaging these less-active youngsters.

Furthermore, the live feed from an integrated camera proved to be a highly efficient way of fostering interest in the public display. We also noticed a very strong honeypot-effect when Ubinion's webcam view was visible. This agrees with Schönböck's findings on making users parts of the display for embracing user engagement [16]. We often witnessed groups of people trying to play and position themselves in the background of pictures being taken by other people. This led to occasional rushes by many interested users to the display. However, once the rush was over, there would again be a more silent period of usage. This is a phenomenon exploitable on public displays. By using interfaces that are easy to learn by just watching someone go and use them, as suggested in [21], people can return any time and start using the application without feeling of embarrassment caused by the uncertainty on how to use it.

It is interesting to point out that while Ubinion was playful and engaged groups and individuals alike, we did not find any substantial difference in the kinds of comments individuals vs. groups gave. This suggests that while our system was successful in attracting users in groups, we did not find any evidence that the group dynamics altered the topics or quality of posts. On the contrary, we found that gender did have a significant effect, as we observed that male individuals or groups of males were significantly more likely to discuss sports.

6.3   Public Displays for Online Communities

It has been suggested that public displays can aid the perception of unity of community knowledge and interests, and that the ability for everyone in the community to contribute to and access online content relating to the community's interests is important [27]. Further, pairing displays with new applications has strong implications on usability, service providing, and participatory democracy [28]. Utilizing interactive public displays with SNSs to foster communities allows not only for these, but also for easy content creation, moderation, and storing, characteristics that can be considered crucial for long-term maintenance of a system [12].

In our interviews, the young expressed a need for anonymity when giving feedback and suggestions to local youth workers, mainly in order to avoid any possible extra workload. Using Ubinion on public displays, they can voice out their concerns and ideas to youth workers semi-anonymously and are not face-to-face responsible for their feedback. They are rather given a possibility to participate personally and devote further to the topic by utilizing the Facebook community that they helped to build, thus enabling also non-anonymous participation.

We argue that public displays can be a good match in especially bootstrapping an online community. They offer a highly public medium that is constantly accessible by everyone and allow for in-situ creation of socially relevant content for their users, a powerful way to engage people to use an application [11]. Content quality and context relevancy in general can be problematic when deploying social applications, causing significant management overhead [12]. By utilizing multiple interactive public displays equipped with modern embedded cameras and touch screens, it is possible to acquire large amounts of high quality, context relevant, personal content to use as building blocks for applications, or indeed in this case, an online community of the young. These user-generated photos can subsequently be used to gain an understanding and support the recording of a "living history" of a community [29], adding value to this approach.

We argue that Ubinion is a step towards utilizing public displays for bootstrapping and supporting online communities. It leverages the appropriate affordances, playfulness, rapid content creation, and sociality, for its target demography, the young, to encourage contribution in creating a community. This community, Ubinion's online presence, is followed and moderated by the local youth authorities. It reflects the concerns and wishes of the young and can act as a mediator between local youth officers and the young.

6.4   Feedback Mechanisms

In addition to feedback actionable by YAD, we observed that the youth decided to comment on issues that they worry about, but are not necessarily of interest to the YAD. Issues such as building new stadiums and parks, for instance, suggest that the youth appropriated this channel of communication as a way to voice their concerns in general, not just in relation to the YAD. Given the context of our trials, we argue that this behavior emerged quite organically, and suggests that Ubinion's public display component was successful in more broadly engaging the youth, who were ready to express their opinions using this medium. Here lies our main contribution: while the service might not evoke opinions to the questions it sets, it efficiently probes the mindset and opinion of the otherwise unreachable urban young.

Beyond the valuable concerns that were voiced via Ubinion, we found that 47% of all feedback consisted of general greetings and random texts typed just for fun or to play with technology. Perhaps unsurprisingly, we attribute this behavior to people's need for self-expression and exposure in their appropriation of communication technology [30]. This frequent behavior also transferred online, in the context of Ubinion's Facebook page. The results suggest that many participants did visit the page to see the photos and comments given there, and to "Like" particular messages. Visitors were quite happy to vote and contribute in this way, but were uneasy about explicitly adding comments.

We believe our study demonstrated a sharp difference between people's use of an online community medium (Facebook) where they are most likely to read and just click to "vote", as opposed to the public display component of Ubinion where users were much happier to interact and invest time and effort into creating content (regardless of being "serious" or "playful"). This is an encouraging finding, suggesting that bringing Ubinion out of the online world and into the community was a successful way to engage users more actively.

6.5   Limitations

We acknowledge that the conducted field trials have certain limitations. First, we cannot rule out the novelty effect in our trials, suggesting that the introduction of novel technology and software in itself contributed to the frequency of usage of

Ubinion in the field trials. Also, the trial settings were explicitly chosen to reach a lot of young users from different demographic groups. Results derived from such popular one-off events are not directly comparable to those of a long-term installation in mundane environments, which we understand is a necessity for a credible evaluation of scalability and generalization of such a system. However, as we deployed Ubinion in three different settings and collected rich data using various different unobtrusive methods, we believe that our results are a valid starting point for discussing the aspects of deploying such a system in public spaces.

A second limitation of our work is that the Facebook component of Ubinion saw very little meaningful postings from users. The few comments received via Facebook were of ephemeral nature [31] and aimed to publicize one's self and friends by identifying people in photographs and thereby sharing the photographs in one's own "stream" on Facebook. The lack of active contributing users is akin to lurking, a behavior that was not unexpected as it is commonly observed in online communities [32, 33]. We believe the relatively low number of comments was due to the high number of off-topic entries and the loss of anonymity and feeling of commitment that occur when posting non-anonymously online [33]. To encourage insightful and lengthier discussions, a public feedback system such as Ubinion needs to better motivate its users to contribute relevant and meaningful entries that entice conversation and perhaps persuade lurkers to contribute. Despite this, non-contributing members are still valuable to the community, and their participation can have far-reaching, positive consequences [33]. For example, in Ubinion's case the high amount of lurking contributes to raising general awareness about everyday issues of the young.

7   Conclusion

We presented Ubinion, a system that combines public interactive displays with online social networking services to enable the youth to voice their opinions and demonstrated how to use these technologies hand-in-hand to bootstrap a content-rich community presence in a modern SNS, Facebook. We argue that public interactive displays, as a public and social medium, can be leveraged in acquiring high quality, context relevant content, a common problem in pervasive systems. Through a series of public trials in authentic settings we show that our system can be effective in collecting feedback from the youth, a segment of the population perceived as challenging to reach by youth workers.

Our system utilized the "mirror-metaphor" and leveraged the honey-pot effect in order to raise interest and adopt a playful character. Our prototype was designed in collaboration with local youth workers and was perceived positively by our test users. Particularly the public display component of our system intended to voice initial concerns was successful, while the Facebook aspect meant to provide a mechanism for follow-up discussions did not gain traction. We found that the youth decided to use Ubinion to voice their broader concerns, not just concerns that relate to youth officials: effectively, it prompted the youth to voice concerns of an adult manner.

Ubinion was proven effective to reach out for the young that would not otherwise engage in any activity with the Youth Affairs Department of Oulu.

Our work suggests that applications with fun, playful interfaces, deployed where it is socially acceptable to interact with them, can be used to collect feedback from otherwise passive and disconnected users. We plan to deploy Ubinion on several interactive displays in Oulu and cooperate with local youth workers, who have already committed to take Ubinion as part of their communication processes with the young, to investigate how it performs over a longer period.

Acknowledgements. This work was supported by Microsoft Research through its PhD Scholarship Programme. The financial support of the Finnish Funding Agency for Technology and Innovation, the European Regional Development Fund, the City of Oulu, and the UBI (UrBan Interactions) consortium is gratefully acknowledged.

References

1. Montero, M.: Introducción a la psicologia comunitaria. Paidos, Buenos Aires (2004)
2. Clary, E.G., Snyder, M.: Community involvement: Opportunities and challenger in socializing adults to participate in society. Journal of Social Issue 3, 581–592 (2002)
3. Bendapuni, N., Leone, R.P.: Psychological Implications of Customer Participation in Co-Production. The Journal of Marketing 67(1), 14–28 (2003)
4. Alford, J.R.: We're all in this together: The decline of trust in Government, 1958–1996. In: Hibbing, J.R., Theiss-Morse, E. (eds.) What is it about Government that Americans dislike?, pp. 28–46. Cambridge University Press, Cambridge (2001)
5. Huseby, B.M.: Government performance and political support: A study of how evaluations of economic performance, social policy and environmental protection influence the popular assessments of the political system. Department for Sociology and Political Science, Trondheim (2000)
6. Orren, G.: Fall from grace: The public's loss of faith in government. In: Nye, J.S., Zelikow, P.D., King, D.C. (eds.) Why People Don't Trust Government, pp. 77–107. Harvard University Press, Cambridge (1997)
7. Uslaner, E.M., Brown, M.: Inequality, trust, and civic engagement. American Politics Research 33, 868–894 (2005)
8. Hirschmann, A.O.: Shifting involvements: Private interest and public action. Princeton University Press, Princeton (1982)
9. Kelly, C., Breinlinger, S.: The social psychology of collective action: Identity, injustice and gender. Taylor & Francis, London (1996)
10. Müller, J., Paczkowski, O., Krüger, A.: Situated Public News and Reminder Displays. In: Schiele, B., Dey, A.K., Gellersen, H., de Ruyter, B., Tscheligi, M., Wichert, R., Aarts, E., Buchmann, A. (eds.) AmI 2007. LNCS, vol. 4794, pp. 248–265. Springer, Heidelberg (2007)
11. Hosio, S., Kukka, H., Jurmu, M., Ojala, T., Riekki, J.: Enhancing Interactive Public Displays with Social Networking Services. In: 9th International Conference on Mobile and Ubiquitous Multimedia, Article 23 (2010)
12. Storz, O., Friday, A., Davies, N., Finney, J., Sas, C., Sheridan, J.: Public Ubiquitous Computing Systems: Lessons from the e-Campus Display Deployments. IEEE Pervasive Computing 5(3), 40–47 (2006)
13. McCarthy, J.F., McDonald, D.W., Soroczak, S., Nguyen, D.H., Rashid, A.M.: Augmenting the social space of an academic conference. In: CSCW 2004, pp. 39–48 (2004)

14. Jose, R., Otero, N., Izadi, S., Harper, R.: Instant Places: Using Bluetooth for Situated Interaction in Public Displays. IEEE Pervasive Computing 7(4), 52–57 (2008)
15. Ardito, C., Costabile, M.F., Lanzilotti, R.: Gameplay on a multitouch screen to foster learning about historical sites. In: AVI 2010, pp. 75–78 (2010)
16. Schönböck, J., König, F., Kotsis, G., Gruber, D., Zaim, E., Schmidt, A.: MirrorBoard – An Interactive Billboard. In: Mensch und Computer, pp. 207–216 (2008)
17. Müller, J., Wilmsmann, D., Exeler, J., Buzeck, M., Schmidt, A., Jay, T., Krüger, A.: Display Blindness: The Effect of Expectations on Attention towards Digital Signage. In: Tokuda, H., Beigl, M., Friday, A., Brush, A.J.B., Tobe, Y. (eds.) Pervasive 2009. LNCS, vol. 5538, pp. 1–8. Springer, Heidelberg (2009)
18. Sharp, R., Rehman, K.: The 2005 UbiApp Workshop: What Makes Good Application-Led Research? IEEE Pervasive Computing 4(3), 80–82 (2005)
19. Day, N., Sas, C., Dix, A., Toma, M., Bevan, C., Clare, D.: Breaking the Campus Bubble: Informed, Engaged, Connected. In: BCS-HCI 2007, pp. 133–136 (2007)
20. Peltonen, P., Kurvinen, E., Salovaara, A., Jacucci, G., Ilmonen, T., Evans, J., Oulasvirta, A., Saarikko, P.: It's Mine, Don't Touch!: Interactions at a Large Multi-Touch Display in a City Centre. In: CHI 2008, pp. 1285–1294 (2008)
21. Brignull, H., Rogers, Y.: Enticing People to Interact with Large Public Displays in Public Spaces. In: INTERACT 2003, pp. 17–24 (2003)
22. Agamanolis, S.: Designing displays for Human Connectedness. In: Workshop on Public, Community and Situated Displays at CSCW 2002 (2002)
23. Shneiderman, B.: Designing for Fun: How Can We Design User Interfaces to Be More Fun? Interactions 11(5), 48–50 (2004)
24. Kukka, H., Kostakos, V., Ojala, T., Ylipulli, J., Suopajärvi, T., Jurmu, M., Hosio, S.: This Is Not Classified: Everyday Information Seeking and Encountering in Smart Urban Spaces. Personal and Ubiquitous Computing (2012), online first
25. Bangor, A., Kortum, P., Miller, J.: An empirical evaluation of the system usability scale. International Journal of Human-Computer Interaction 24(6), 574–594 (2008)
26. Boyd, D., Hargittai, E., Schultz, J., Palfrey, J.: Why parents help their children lie to Facebook about age: Unintended consequences of the 'Children's Online Privacy Protection Act'. First Monday 16(11) (2011)
27. Redhead, F., Brereton, M.: A qualitative analysis of local community communications. In: Proc. Australia conference on Computer-Human Interaction: Design: Activities, Artefacts and Environments, OZCHI 2006, pp. 361–364 (2006)
28. Schuler, D.: Community networks: building a new participatory medium. Commun. ACM 37(1), 38–51 (1994)
29. Taylor, N., Cheverst, K., Fitton, D., Race, N.K.P., Rouncefield, M., Graham, C.: Probing communities: study of a village photo display. In: OZCHI 2007, pp. 17–24 (2007)
30. Harper, R.: Texture: Human expression in the age of communication overload. MIT Press (2011)
31. Reynolds, B., Venkatanathan, J., Gonçalves, J., Kostakos, V.: Sharing Ephemeral Information in Online Social Networks: Privacy Perceptions and Behaviours. In: Campos, P., Graham, N., Jorge, J., Nunes, N., Palanque, P., Winckler, M. (eds.) INTERACT 2011, Part III. LNCS, vol. 6948, pp. 204–215. Springer, Heidelberg (2011)
32. Wasko, M.M., Far, S.: Why should I share? Examining social capital and knowledge contribution in electronic networks of practice. MIS Quarterly 29(1), 35–57 (2005)
33. Nonnecke, B., Preece, J.: Lurker demographics: counting the silent. In: CHI 2000, pp. 73–80 (2000)

Increasing Brand Attractiveness and Sales through Social Media Comments on Public Displays – Evidence from a Field Experiment in the Retail Industry

Erica Dubach Spiegler, Christian Hildebrand, and Florian Michahelles

ETH Zurich, Zurich, Switzerland
{edubach,fmichahelles}@ethz.ch
University of St. Gallen, St. Gallen, Switzerland
christian.hildebrand@unisg.ch

Abstract. Retailers and brands are just starting to utilize online social media to support their businesses. Simultaneously, public displays are becoming ubiquitous in public places, raising the question about how these two technologies could be used together to attract new and existing customers as well as strengthen the relationship toward a focal brand. Accordingly, in a field experiment we displayed brand- and product-related comments from the social network Facebook as pervasive advertising in small-space retail stores, known as kiosks. From interviews conducted with real customers during the experiment and the corresponding analysis of sales data we could conclude three findings. Showing social media comments resulted in (1) customers perceiving brands as more innovative and attractive, (2) a measurable, positive effect on sales on both the brand and the product in question and (3) customers wanting to see the comments of others, but not their own, creating a give-and-take paradox for using public displays to show social media comments.

Keywords: Public Displays, Digital Signage, Pervasive Advertising, Social Media, Social Networks, Field Experiment, Mixed Methods, Retail Industry.

1 Introduction

Public displays – sometimes referred to as digital signage and "digital out-of-home media" (DOOH) – are becoming increasingly common thanks to technological advances and rapidly declining costs [11]. Accordingly, global spending on digital displays has shown strong growth, with sales of $6.47 billion in 2010, which is projected to expand by 16.9% in 2011[1]. Not surprisingly, retailers are showing interest in business-relevant, consumer-facing applications which have the potential to change customers' interaction with retailers and their in-store experiences, giving public displays a prominent place in retail. However, despite these activities and the research interest in using public displays for advertising, it is estimated that DOOH advertising in general has not reached its full potential, largely because of the

---

[1] PQ Media http://www.pqmedia.com/about-press-20091110-dooh2009.html

J. Kay et al. (Eds.): Pervasive 2012, LNCS 7319, pp. 443–460, 2012.
© Springer-Verlag Berlin Heidelberg 2012

difficulty in measuring the return on investment [25]. To quantify the gap: while people on average spend 27% of their time exposed to outdoor advertising, this form of advertising in 2008 only comprised 5% of US media spending [13]. Thus, it is of a fundamental practical as well as theoretical importance to better understand underlying drivers of successful public display advertising strategies and their economic effects in terms of sales.

The field experiment described in this paper was conducted to better understand the effects of social media (SM)-based advertising on customers' attitudes and sales and as such, it was conducted in small-space retail stores (kiosks), where brand-related SM comments were shown on public displays. The newness of this pervasive advertising application prompted an explorative approach in which interviews were used to understand customer attitudes toward using SM comments on public displays, as well as a quantitative analysis of sales data to show how these attitudes might affect sales. The collaboration with the kiosks and the quantitative analysis of the field experiment are described as a case study in "Social Networks in Pervasive Advertising and Shopping" [7]. This paper provides further depth by adding the analysis of customer interviews and the insights gained from understanding the customer's paradoxical attitudes towards SM and public displays.

Interviews conducted during the experiment provided insight into customer opinions and the corresponding analysis of sales data showed the effect on sales, resulting in three findings: (1) SM comments resulted in customers perceiving brands as more innovative and attractive. (2) The subsequent analysis of the sales data shows that displaying SM comments in stores have a measurable, positive effect on sales on both the brand and the product in question. In addition to these findings of practical importance, the paper advances the theoretical discussion by presenting evidence that (3) customers want to see the comments of others, but not their own, creating a give-and-take paradox for using public displays to show SM comments.

2   Related Work and Development of Hypotheses

Pervasive Advertising [17] enables the kind of serendipity common on TV, radio and print, with the added benefit of enabling new ad types [26] such as user-generated comments. Public displays in particular allows for a broad range of content from generic advertisements to ones that are responsive [18] or interactive [9, 16]. Since advertising in general is proven to increase shareholder value through increased sales [34], pervasive advertising research is being conducted to understand how to extend traditional advertising into the domain of pervasive computing. Based on previous findings which have shown the positive influence on the brand due to increased interactivity with the brand on Facebook and customer engagement [36], we expect a positive influence of using Facebook on public displays on a brand's perceived innovativeness.

H1: The more positive a customer's attitude toward Facebook on public displays, the higher the brand's innovativeness will be perceived.

Furthermore, SM provides retailers access to a new type of word of mouth, which is a recognized force in retail [29,1,5] and has the appeal of precisely directing messages to a targeted audience. SM represents the natural technological platform for marketing based on a structured set of social relationships among admirers of a brand, i.e. a brand community [28]. Additionally, SM allows companies to listen to the opinions, wishes and complaints of their customers, as many consumers want constant connectivity, ideally in every facet of their lives [3]. Different consumer brands and retail stores are handling this opportunity and these challenges in different ways, some with spectacular success, (e.g. Nutella allowing its 6.8M Fans to send each other virtual Nutella gifts). As a result, we predict that brands will be perceived as more innovative when companies enable Facebook comments of friends on public displays.

H2: The higher customers' attitude toward seeing Facebook comments of their friends on public displays, the higher the brand's perceived innovativeness.

Research based on prototypes applied in user studies has investigated embedding brands into the natural living environment and context of people [33, 4], inferring a customer's activities for more targeted advertising [21], influencing their shopping behavior by means of persuasive strategies [27] etc. Public displays in retail stores can cater to this, thus satisfying both customer demand and taking advantage of sharing SM user comments in the sales environment to increase sales.

Past research considerably advanced our understanding of how and why consumers may engage in brand communities. However, research has also shown that privacy concerns are rising and may inhibit content production on the individual level [19], though users may nevertheless wish to consume the produced content on the social networking sites [12]. The moderating influence of the previously noted privacy concerns on the one hand and consumers tendency to enjoy seeing the content of others on the other hand, is expected to be positively related toward the brand's innovativeness. Thus, we predict:

H3a: The higher customers' attitude toward Facebook on public displays and attitude toward seeing their own Facebook comments on public displays, the higher the brand's perceived innovativeness.

H3b: The higher customers' attitude toward seeing Facebook on public displays and attitude toward seeing Facebook comments of their friends on public displays, the higher the brand's perceived innovativeness.

From the marketers' perspective, there are many strategic and operational benefits of cultivating brand communities. Brand-community participation results in a positive effect on consumers' attitude and attachment to the brand and the company [14].

From the consumers' perspective, users are interested in receiving brand announcements on their profile page, they feel they are a part of the brand communities they joined, accept friendship requests of the brand pages and value friends' opinion about a brand [23].

Past research findings explain how pervasive technologies may increase a customer's perception of a brand as being highly innovative. However, a test if this perception can also be transformed into an increase in global attractiveness and preference for the brand is still needed. Thus, we predict:

H4a: The higher customers' attitude toward Facebook on public displays and attitude toward seeing their own Facebook comments, the lower the brand's perceived attractiveness.

H4b: The higher a customers' attitude toward seeing Facebook comments of their friends and the higher the perceived innovativeness of the brand, the higher the brand's attractiveness.

Figure 1 summarizes our research model to explain the influence of attitudes towards SM on the perception of the brand's innovativeness and the mediating role of brand innovativeness on overall brand attractiveness.

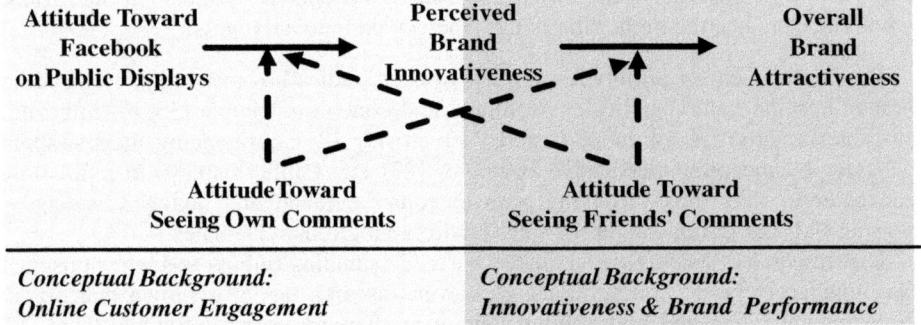

Fig. 1. Overview of Research Model

Past research considerably advanced our understanding of how using SM for brand marketing enables companies to build and maintain close relationships with consumers [20]. However, it is far less understood how consumers' attitude toward SM sites may directly influence their perception of a company active on SM in general, nor is the influence on important business variables such as sales understood. The direct link between the previously introduced developments in the area of pervasive advertising and their effect on either attitude-oriented constructs – such as the perceived innovativeness or attractiveness of a company or directly measurable effects in terms of sales – is still missing [30]. Thus, we finally test if these attitude-oriented effects transform into an increase in sales. In particular, we predict that presenting company-specific content in contrast to a control condition of unrelated content will affect sales volume of the company positively. Furthermore, based on previous work in the area of consumer behavior [32] and our previous discussion on positive influence of customer engagement on innovativeness and brand attractiveness, we expect that (1) product-specific, in contrast to brand-specific information are associated with an increase in sales, as well as (2) SM comments, in contrast to traditional advertising, are associated with an increase in sales, due to the more personal nature of SM in comparison to traditional advertising. Finally, based on previous work in pervasive advertising [17], we predict a higher sales volume for sales locations at public transport meeting places because of the higher frequency of visitors making quick purchases.

H5: Using company-specific content on public displays leads to higher sales volume than random, company-unspecific content.

H6: Product-related content on public displays yields higher sales volume than brand-related content.

H7: SM comments on public displays yield higher sales volume than traditional advertising.

H8: Kiosks located in public transport areas and using public displays yield higher sales volumes than kiosks in standard shopping malls or airport kiosks using public displays.

3   Context of the Study

We conducted a field experiment in partnership with Valora Retail, which operates around 1000 small-space stores, known as kiosks. Sales show high frequency at small volumes of convenience products such as news, sweets, tobacco and lottery: together, kiosks serve 850'000 customers per day, who buy an average of 1.7 articles. These kiosks often function as meeting points and social hubs in the areas they are located in.

In an effort to increase sales and gain third-party advertising revenues, the retailer was conducting a public display experiment involving a total of 50 kiosk locations. Of those, 16 contained suitably large, 40" screens, which we could use for displaying SM comments (see Figure 1) in the field experiment. In addition, the team gained management support to use a kiosk private label brand, the "ok.-" line of products, which allowed for greater control than would have been possible with a national or global brand. Finally, a Facebook "Brand Page" was set up for the ok.- brand in March 2010, 9 weeks ahead of the field experiment. This brand page served as the source for the SM comments shown on the public display. As long as the comments did not violate the company policy (e.g. profanity, obscenities, etc.), we collected the comments by taking the three most recent posts at 8pm each day, regardless of whether the sentiment towards the brand was positive or negative (see also [23]).

Experimental Setup of Field Experiment. The field experiment covered 16 kiosks all over German-speaking Switzerland, located in airports, hubs of public transport, inside shopping centers and rural areas. To experimentally test the effects of SM comments on public displays, the content shown was systematically manipulated (see below).

These 16 kiosks were all equipped with a 40" screen, which featured a standardized layout determined by the retailer: an upper bar with time and date, a lower bar with news headlines and a side bar with infotainment such as weather and horoscopes. The design was part of the retailer's public display experiments and could not be changed for our field experiment. The experimental content was shown in stores for 5 weeks from 5th of May to the 8th of June 2010, so that every one of the five experimental conditions was run for one week. The shown content was visible for 15 seconds within a two-minute loop. Figure 2 above shows an example of the public display placed within the kiosk environment.

Experimental Conditions. We systematically varied the content shown on the public displays. In particular, five different types of content were displayed on the public displays: in the first condition, we varied product- vs. brand-specific content. Secondly, we either presented traditional advertising vs. SM comments harvested the previous day from the ok.- Facebook fan page. Specifically, the three newest comments were collected every evening at 8 pm, including the author's first name and the initial of their last name. In addition, we had one control condition in which no manipulated content was shown. Thus, this resulted in the following conditions shown on the public display: (1) traditional advertisement of the *ok,-* brand, (2) traditional advertisement of the lead product (*ok,-* Energy Drink), (3) SM comments from the *ok,-* Facebook Brand page, (4) SM comments from *ok,-* Facebook Brand page (*ok,-* Energy Drink) and finally, (5) control condition (content unrelated to the *ok,-* brand).

Overall, this produced a final 2 (product vs. brand) x 2 (traditional advertising vs. social network comments) experimental design, and in addition, every kiosk was treated with a control condition where no experimental manipulations were shown. Every kiosk was randomly assigned to one of the five conditions lasting for one week each. Choosing which content to show in which location and choosing the timing was based on a completely randomized experimental design to minimize the impact of the different influences that come from the "natural" setting of this field study [16].

Fig. 2. Social media comments for an energy drink on public display in a kiosk

4   Analysis I: Customer Interviews

During the time of the field experiment, we conducted customer interviews in parallel to measuring sales data. While the cash register sales data was central to evaluating the economic impact of public display advertising on sales, the customer interviews were conducted to better understand the general attitude toward public display advertising, as well as the attitude toward SM and Facebook and the influence on general brand attractiveness. Thus, we present the customer interviews first, and will then provide additional evidence based on quantitative sales data in the next section, Analysis II.

4.1   Mixed Method Approach and Qualitative Interview Data

Interviews. To explore customers' opinions regarding comments from SM on public displays, semi-structured guided interviews were conducted in kiosks showing SM comments on public displays. This method was chosen to account for the newness of the topic, hence the use of mostly open questions instead of a standardized questionnaire.

The interview questions were based on a questionnaire containing 20 questions which allowed yes / no answers with comments, except for two open questions noted below. Customers were first asked if they had noticed the display and whether they had seen the SM comments. In an open question, they were fist asked what they thought about showing SM comments on public displays in general. The next question asked if SM comments on public displays influenced their perception of the company (the comments received were coded for innovativeness of the company). Customers were also asked if this increased the attractiveness of the advertised brand, and the likelihood of purchasing products of this brand. Two questions aimed to determine whether customers would like to see their own comments displayed, and the comments of their friends, though this was hypothetical since no interviewee indicated that they recognized the people whose SM comments were being used on the public display. Since SM comments expressing both positive and negative attitudes towards the brand were shown during the field experiment, an open question asked customers for their opinion of seeing both types of comments. The final set of questions established demographic information, including Facebook usage.

A total of 131 interviews were conducted by approaching every customer in the kiosk after they had concluded a purchase. The answers were recorded on pre-printed questionnaires, which were later transcribed. The interviews were conducted at different times of the day, over the course of 10 days from 30 June to 9 July 2010, at 10 different and randomly chosen kiosk locations, in all of which SM comments were being shown on a public display.

Measurement and Coding Scheme. In a first step, the responses to the interview questions were entered and transcribed. Initial analyses revealed strong differences between participants' answers (e.g., strong rejection of SM vs. strong positive attitude toward SM comments on public displays). To capture these different nuances in customers' answers, for example comments about privacy, a five point Likert scale was set up to capture differences between comments and to analyze the general tendencies and relationships between variables. A five point Likert scale was used to measure (1) customers' general attitude toward displaying SM comments on public displays, (2) their attitude toward imagining seeing their own comments, (3) their attitude toward imagining seeing comments of others and (4) the perceived innovativeness of the brand and the brand's attractiveness. The scale was set up so that two independent coders assigned values between -2 for a strong negative attitude to +2 for a strong positive attitude with a neutral point at zero. To test the reliability of the scales, we conducted interrater reliability tests which are based on the degree of agreement among the two independent raters [31], supporting the quality and substantial degree of consensus with all values above .70 ($M_{Cohen's\ Kappa}$=.814, $M_{Intraclass\ Correlation}$=.875 (Min=.70, Max=.95)). Consumers' use of Facebook was measured by the number of Facebook use per day and consumers use of Facebook on mobile devices was measured by a binary variable (use vs. no use). Consumers' age was measured by discrete variable with six categories (see results section below in further detail). The SM comments themselves were not further analyzed for content, sentiment or attitude, though the interviews did capture customers' opinion of seeing both negative and positive comments.

4.2   Interview Results

Consumer Perceptions of Brand Innovativeness. In this first analysis, we were particularly interested in two questions: (1) consumers' perception of the brands innovativeness, as dependent on their attitude toward displaying Facebook comments on public displays in a retail store, and (2) their attitude toward imagining seeing their own comments, especially in comparison to their attitude toward imagining seeing the comments of others (e.g., friends and acquaintances) on public displays. In addition, four control variables were analyzed: consumers' age, being a fan of the *ok,-* brand's Facebook brand site, intensity of Facebook use per day and use of Facebook Mobile. Table 1 summarizes our results based on a multivariate linear regression model.

Table 1. Results of Multivariate Linear Regression: Drivers to Explain Brand's Perceived Innovativeness

	Estimate	SE	t-Value	p-Value
Constant	.033	.134	.243	.808
Attitude Toward Facebook on PD (FBPD)	.174	.088	1.988*	.049
Attitude Seeing Friends' Comments (FC)	.109	.052	2.116*	.037
Attitude Seeing Own Comments (OC)	.039	.047	.832	.407
FBPD × FC	-.113	.084	-1.349	.180
FBPD × OC	.717	.199	3.6***	<.001
Facebook Mobile Use (MOB)	-.343	.158	-2.165*	.032
Facebook Use (in Hours / Day) (FB)	-.023	.022	-1.043	.299
MOB × FB	.063	.030	2.086*	.039
Age	.009	.030	.291	.771
Fan of Facebook Brand Site	.111	.242	.459	.647
F-Value	4.455***			
R^2	.28			

***p<.001, ** p<.01, *p<.05

As expected, we found a positive and significant influence of consumers' attitude toward displaying Facebook comments on public display (FBPD) in a retail store as well as consumers intention to see the comments of their friends (FC) on the perceived innovativeness of the company ($\text{Beta}_{\text{FBPD}}$=.17, t(119)=1.988, p<.05; Beta_{FC}=.11, t(119)=2.116, p<.05), supporting hypotheses 1 and 2.

While consumers' attitude toward seeing own comments (OC) had no significant influence on perceived innovativeness alone (Beta_{OC}=.04, t(119)=.832, p>.40), we found the predicted interaction between consumers' intention to see their own comments and the general attitude toward integrating Facebook on public displays ($\text{Beta}_{\text{FBPD}\times\text{OC}}$=.72, t(119)=3.600, p<.001), in support of hypothesis 3a and failing to support hypothesis 3b. Figure 3 illustrates the steeper regression slope compared to the simple main effect without controlling for consumers' intention to see one's own comments. Thus, we may already hypothesize that consumers' intention to see their own comments in contrast to seeing others may have different effects on subsequent evaluations of retail stores. This is analyzed in detail in the next section.

Finally, our analyses also revealed a significant interaction between consumers' use of Facebook Mobile (MOB) and intensity of Facebook use (FB) in a positive direction ($\text{Beta}_{\text{MOB}\times\text{FB}}$=.06, t(119)=2.086, p<.05). This result reveals that intense Facebook or Mobile applications use alone does not drive consumers' perception of a company's innovativeness, but rather the interaction of the two variables. Since the main effect of mobile use is significant but negative, this is an example of a disordinal interaction, i.e. mobile use needs to be interpreted in combination with the interaction of Facebook usage [2].

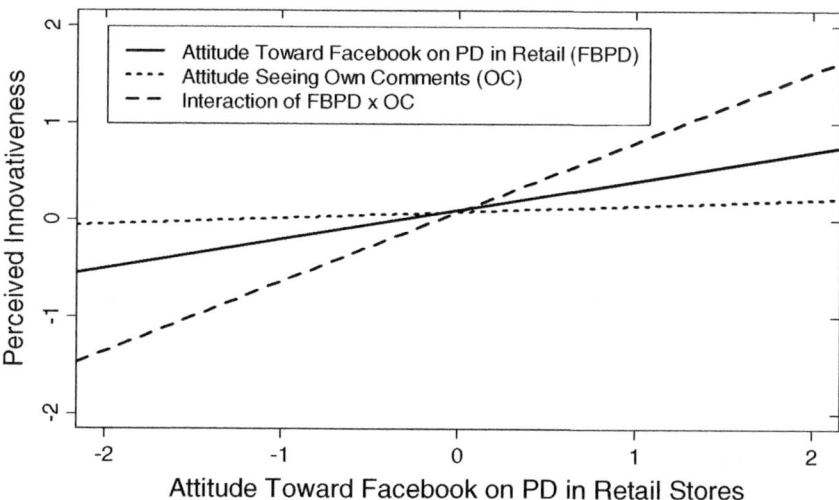

Fig. 3. Illustration of interaction between attitude toward Facebook and attitude to see own comments on public displays on the company's perceived innovativeness

Overall, these initial results have shown that consumers build a strong link between a company's activity on Facebook brand sites and their intention to see their own comments on public displays on the perceived innovativeness of the brand.

Interestingly, the influence of consumers' intention to see the comments of other users was not dependent on this interaction and may have more general implications than the dependencies to see one's own comments. However, (1) it is not clear how innovativeness is further related to the overall attractiveness of the focal brand and (2) how the tension between varying attitudes in seeing one's own compared to friends' comments is moderating this relationship. This detailed analysis will be part of the next section.

Influence on Overall Brand Attractiveness. As we have shown above, a consumer's attitude toward the integration of Facebook in a retail store is positively related to the perceived innovativeness of the company. Now we will expand our analyses by assessing the mediating role of innovativeness on brand attractiveness and the moderating role of consumers' attitude toward seeing own comments, as well as seeing friends' comments on public displays. To test our previous hypotheses, we conducted a moderated mediation analysis [24]. Thus, we use a mediation model which simultaneously estimates the influence of the two moderators (seeing own comments and seeing friends' comments). This model has the advantage over testing every specified hypothesis independently (e.g. with linear models or ANOVAs) by reducing the risk of an otherwise increasing type II error of statistical testing.

Since the effects in the mediator model remain equal compared to our previous analyses (interaction of attitude toward Facebook and attitude toward seeing own comments on perceived innovativeness of the brand ($Beta_{FBPD \times OC}$=.58, $t(125)$=3.616, $p<.001$)), it will now be important to evaluate how a brand's attractiveness is affected.

Our analysis revealed a strong main effect of consumers' attitude toward integrating Facebook on public displays on overall attractiveness of the brand ($Beta_{FBPD}$=.60, $t(123)$=9.612, $p<.001$), as well as a marginal positive effect of watching the comments of others ($Beta_{FC}$=.07, $t(123)$=1.891, p=.06). While the latter influence of watching others significantly interacts with perceived innovativeness of the brand to increase the attractiveness of a focal brand ($Beta_{INNO \times FC}$=.17, $t(123)$=2.062, $p<.05$), the influence of consumers' attitude toward seeing their own comments is as predicted, i.e. we find empirical support that although the possibility to see one's own comments was positively related to the brand's innovativeness (see results of the previous section), the main effect, as well as the interaction with the attitude toward integrating Facebook, is significantly negatively related to the attractiveness of a brand ($Beta_{FBPD \times OC}$=-.25, $t(123)$=1.988, $p<.05$).

Thus, we find support for H4 (a and b) and our prediction that disclosing personal information in a public domain, such as public displays in a retail store, may have negative consequences regarding the overall attractiveness of a brand. In contrast, expecting to see others is strongly positively related to the attractiveness of the brand.

This contradiction is of major importance, since the inherent value of integrating SM into public displays is strongly dependent on the content of its users – however, if privacy concerns hold individuals back from adding content, while expecting others to do so, the irony and paradox of handling both competing preferences at the individual level may inhibit harnessing the full potential of pervasive advertising with public displays.

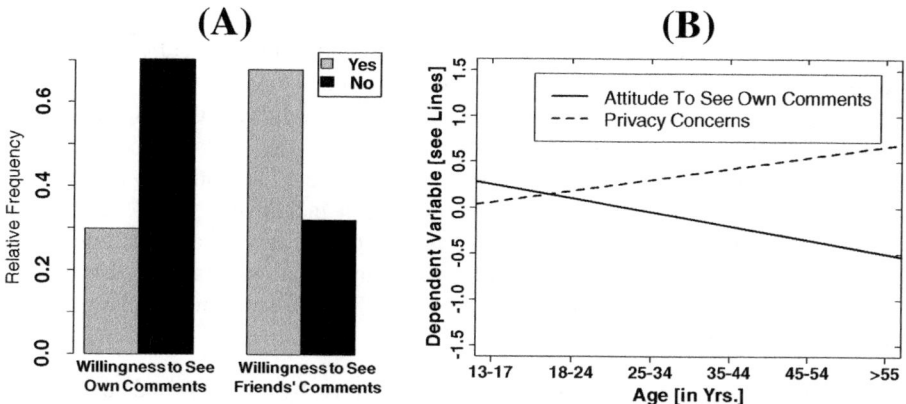

Fig. 4. (A) proportion of consumers' willing to see their own vs. seeing comments of other users; (B) influence of consumers' age on privacy concerns and attitude to see own comments

To further explore this pattern of results, we analyzed the proportion of attitudes toward seeing one's own comments compared to seeing the comments of others by aggregating the data into either general positive or general negative attitude (see Figure 3) and found that both categories are highly statistically different (χ^2(1,N=131)=18.493, p<.001). Moreover, additional analyses revealed that a strong demographic influence underlies this effect: the older consumers are, the less likely they are to want to see their own comments (Beta$_{Age}$=-.15, t(129)=3.909, p<.001) and the higher is their perception of privacy issues (Beta$_{Age}$=.12, t(129)=2.466, p<.05).

Overall, we find that this inherent contradiction of handling consumer preferences to watch the SM content of others, while promoting content production at the individual level, may be one of the key challenges in the early phase of adoption and market diffusion of business models for SM on public displays.

Since the interviews clearly demonstrate that seeing others' SM comments on public displays has a positive effect on customers' overall perception of the attractiveness of the brand, the next question is to determine whether this translates to an increase in sales. For this, we analyzed the sales data gathered during the field experiment, as described above.

5   Analysis II: Sales Data

In the course of the field experiment, sales data was gathered for one of the company's new private label products: a type of energy drink. The data was analyzed to test hypotheses 5 to 8 and to determine the effects on sales of displaying SM comments of the company's new energy drink on public displays. This section details the field experiment conducted and results obtained. Complementary to the previous interview results regarding the more general customer attitudes toward the brand in relation to SM comments on public displays, this section will reveal particular evidence of how customers' buying behavior is influenced by these SM comments on public displays.

5.1   Methodology

Measurement. Sales data from each kiosk participating in the field experiment was transmitted to the retailers' central business intelligence system every night. From there, the retailer provided sales data for all the private label products. This allowed testing the effects of the experiment, which targeted the private label brand as a whole, and also the top-seller energy drink in particular. The data also covered the 5 months leading up to the experiment and provided insight into the development of sales prior to the field experiment. This historical data showed an emerging (rising) trend over time and was used to adjust the experiment data to eliminate this trend and only measure the experimental effect based on the conducted manipulations during the experimental phase.

Statistical Model. In order to test our previous hypotheses and experimental conditions on sales, we applied a repeated measures linear mixed model (LMM) [22]. LMM's provide us with additional flexibility in model specification and allows us to account for inherent store-to-store variation and store heterogeneity within our field experiment as well as to model repeated effects on single stores over time. The respective error terms are assumed to be independent between different stores. Since all stores can be assumed to be randomly selected from a larger population, we specified the respective store as a random effect within our model, since we are not interested in specific effects of single stores but rather the hypothesized effects of our experimental manipulations. Additionally, since we have repeated measurements of single stores over time with high likelihood of correlation with each other (sales volume in one week is not independent of sales volume in the following week), we fitted several LMM's with varying covariance structure as a general procedure for model selection [15]. The general idea is to find the most parsimonious model specification that fits the correlated time series of sales data well. Therefore we started with a simple first-order autoregressive covariance structure (i.e., constant covariance between two measures and increasing the exponent of the covariance parameter with increased time steps) and expanded the model complexity systematically by applying an autoregressive moving-average, a toeplitz-based covariance matrix as well as a more complex unstructured covariance matrix [see 15 for detailed information on how these covariance matrices are specified]. As a general procedure to choose the optimal model specification, we conducted likelihood-ratio (LR) tests between all nested model's [8]. Overall, the best fitting model was based on the unstructured covariance matrix and outweighs its higher number of to be estimated parameters (e.g., testing unconstrained (UN) vs. autoregressive (AR) model with a chi-square distributed LR test of $-2LL_{UN}=842.25$ vs. $-2LL_{AR}=890.66$, $\chi^2(1,13)=48.41$, p<.001).

5.2   Experimental Results

To enable showing SM comments, companies must conduct substantial investments in public displays, as well as investments in organization and infrastructure. Thus, it is important to test for measurable effects in terms of sales volume and to quantify them. Table 2 summarizes the results of the LMM.

As predicted and in support of H5, showing particular and domain related content is positively related to higher sales volume than unspecific random content: the experimental variation of the panel content yielded a significant positive main effect on sales in contrast to the control condition where only random and unspecific content was displayed ($F(1,91)=4.12$, $p<.05$).

Furthermore, presenting specific product information in contrast to brand specific content yielded the expected main effect ($F(1,601)=9.628$, $p<.01$), suggesting that product related content reveals stronger and more behavioral stimulating and compulsive effects than brand presentations, supporting H6.

Table 2. Parameter estimates of fixed effects from repeated measures LMM

	Estimate	SE	t-Value	p-Value
Experimental Condition[1]	24.5	12.06	2.03	.045
Brand Presentation[2]	-33.88	10.89	-3.11	.002
Traditional Advertising[3]	30.69	10.51	2.92	.004
Brand ✕ Traditional Advertising	9.74	15.42	0.63	.528
Small Kiosk Type[4]	-40.43	8.63	-4.68	<.001
Sales Location[5] = Public Transport	26.62	8.21	3.24	<.001
Sales Location[5] = Local Retail	21.04	15.95	1.32	.187
Sales Location[5] = Shopping Mall	-1.57	17	-0.09	.926
Urban Area[6]	0.88	14.58	0.06	.952

[1] Reference Category = Control Condition   [4] Reference Category = Large Kiosk Type

[2] Reference Category = Product Presentation   [5] Reference Category = Airport Location

[3] Reference Category = Facebook Messages   [6] Reference Category = Non-Urban Area

Contrary to what we expected, we found a strong main effect of traditional advertising in contrast to SM comments ($F(1,357) = 28.641$, $p<.01$), thus failing to support H7. Building on previous work on information processing [32], this finding has to be reflected with regard to the general nature of a kiosk: consumers tend to selectively process given information at the point-of-sale due to consumers' time constraints. This means that retailers have to choose public display strategies that allow for very fast information processing with low cognitive involvement. Actively reading SM comments requires cognitive capacity as well as motivation to process textual stimuli, whereas easy to process visual cues of classical advertising are not dependent on this assumption and probably leading to this advantage of traditional advertising at the point of sale. Analyzing the control variables showed a significant effect for the respective sales area ($F(3,1411)=5.267$, $p<.01$), and follow up contrasts revealed that this effect was attributed to the difference between airport and public transport locations ($M_{Airport - PublicTransport}=-26.62$, $SE=8.21$, $p<.01$), supporting hypothesis 8. This suggests that retailers should strongly account for location specific effects that are dependent on the general target audience: while airport area stores are probably more frequented by international consumers that aren't familiar with a specific national brand, and possibly the language of the SM comments, this effect is reversed for locations with a high local awareness, like local public transport areas or shopping centers.

However, there was no significant effect for the degree of urbanity ($F(1,774)=.004$, n.s.) which underlines that the general effect of SM comments on public displays is not dependent on highly urban in contrast to non-urban areas. Note that although airport locations are usually in more urban areas, the general effect between urban and less urban places is less crucial – thus, retailers promoting national brands should focus more on installations on the right target location regarding the sales place, rather than distinguishing between urban and less urban places.

6   Discussion

Overall, the interviews conducted showed that customers attitude towards SM comments on public displays affect the perceived innovativeness of the brand, which in turn increases the overall brand attractiveness. Within these effects though lies the paradox of customers wanting to see comments written by friends on the one hand, while not wanting to see their own comments on the other. Regardless of this, displaying SM comments on public displays is positively associated with sales.

Perception of Brand Innovativeness and Attractiveness. The interviews showed that customers perceive the brand to be innovative due to the SM comments shown on public displays. The perceived innovativeness held true in general for customers who liked seeing SM comments of other people.

In addition to the perception of innovativeness of the brand, customers responded that the SM comments on public displays increased the attractiveness of the brand being shown.

Effect on Sales. The sales data analyzed clearly showed an increase in sales for both product-related SM comments as well as brand-related SM comments, though the product-related SM comments performed slightly better than general brand-related SM comments. However, for both, traditional advertising had a stronger effect still, probably due to the more cognitive as well as time consuming processing of the text-based SM messages in contrast to visual stimuli of classical advertising.

Furthermore, the analysis of our control variables revealed that the prevailing store circumstances are highly relevant for deriving effective retail strategies: while significant sales effects can be revealed by SM comments on public displays in local transportation areas, this effect is reversed for locations that are frequented by more international consumers.

Give-and-Take Paradox. Both qualitative and quantitative analyses point to the positive effects of using SM comments on public displays. However, while expecting to see SM comments of other customers is strongly positively related to the attractiveness of the focal brand, the data also provides support that customers feel that disclosing their own personal information on public displays in a retail store may have negative consequences on the overall attractiveness of a brand. Additionally, customers expressed concerns over privacy which need to be taken into account.

For the retailer, this paradox poses a problem in implementing a pervasive advertising strategy that relies on SM comments provided by customers. Since the medium is of major importance to advertisers, several advertisers have taken the intermediary step of repositioning their content to make it look similar to SM comments from customers in an effort to gain greater consumer acceptance [10]. However, this harbors the risk that the brand might be perceived as insincere, which violates WOM principles. Also, having the company generating content might be a time-consuming effort, since research suggests that due to the customized nature of using content from SM, the timeliness of the content is crucial in order to be meaningful, since delays might invalidate the context [6].

Implications. Our results significantly enrich our understanding of the efficiency as well as the effectiveness of pervasive advertising strategies that rely on SM comments on public displays. Our interviews and field experiment revealed new insights regarding the effectiveness of pervasive computing applications on public displays. Both data from the interviews, as well as the analysis of sales data showed that the integration of social SM on public displays results in measureable effects in terms of brand awareness, willingness to purchase and ultimately on sales.

For the sales data, this was true especially for product-specific SM comments and less so for general brand-related comments. As traditional advertising content still trumped SM comments in this context of busy small-space shops selling low-involvement products, we conclude that the use of SM comments needs to be carefully evaluated. The context of customers ability to process textual stimuli in a shopping environment needs to be considered, possibly resulting in mixing traditional advertising with SM content.

Importantly, customers' paradox attitudes towards wanting to see the comments of others, but without showing their own needs to be taken into account, especially in view of the documented privacy concerns.

Limitations. Though we applied a very careful, fully randomized and balanced experimental design and to have controlled for external variability, ongoing local promotions, as well as external events, might have had relevant, spurious and hard to quantify effects for our respective kiosks. Ideally, the loop of our experimental variations should have been longer to be extensively processed by customers. In addition, we had a sample of 16 kiosks – highly unequal in terms of location, sales volume and so forth. Although our statistical model is ideal and state-of-the-art to account for such variability, future work could attempt to gain access to a larger sample size.

Most importantly the experimental setup of the public display at the point-of-sale and the basic screen layout were constrained by the retailer. Since we were working within an existing experiment of our industry partner, the recommended factors for placement of the public display, the content mix or format [16], could not be implemented. Any future experiment would need to attempt to control these factors.

7   Conclusions

Three main findings are presented that support the use of SM comments in pervasive advertising: (1) Showing SM comments on public displays increases customers' perception of the innovativeness and the attractiveness of the brand. (2) The effect on sales is positive – especially for SM comments relating to a specific product over a brand – though traditional advertising still has a stronger effect. Finally, (3) a give-and-take paradox exists in which customers' are influenced by whether they see SM comments from other people, which affects their opinions positively, versus a conflicted opinions when their own comments are shown. This, together with privacy concerns, poses a challenge for retailers.

Pervasive advertising researchers should consider developing systems that not only embrace customers fluent in the use of SM users but also to those who are not, in order to increase the positive perception of retail brands. Clearly, pervasive advertising research should focus more on local contexts and target groups, in order to more effectively exploit context-related SM content. The give-and-take paradox identified in this field experiment poses the challenge of designing a system that protects identities while still allowing friends to recognize each other on the screen.

Showing comments from SM on public displays improves the perception of innovativeness and the attractiveness of a brand, and – especially if they are product-related vs. brand-related – enhances sales. However, classical advertising still has general advantages due to a lower cognitive load regarding the route of information processing. This leads to our recommendation that a mix of the two advertising strategies should be based on careful analysis of the shopping environment and target group.

Future studies should assess how consumers' privacy concerns can be addressed effectively and examine additional forces that may also moderate the stated give-and-take paradox (e.g., different consumer segments with a stronger tendency to disclose personal information and explicitly gaining value by posting their own comments). Furthermore, an extension on other product categories can help to better understand possible differences between high- vs. low-involvement products. Network based metrics could be applied to expand pervasive technologies toward identifying social hubs in the intersection of real- and online social networks. Finally, the effect on consumers' buying behavior due to semantic differences (e.g. negative vs. positive comments, specific vs. abstract, etc.) in SM comments could be analyzed.

References

1. Agarwal, R., Gupta, A.K., Kraut, R.: The Interplay between digital and social networks. Information Systems Research 19(3), 243–252 (2008)
2. Aiken, L.S., West, S.G.: Multiple regression: Testing and interpreting interactions. Sage, Newbury Park (1991)
3. Arel, S.: The Emergence of Social Media in Digital Signage (accessed July 2011), http://www.ucview.com/pdf/ UCView_Social-Media-in-Digital-Signage.pdf

4. Bauer, C., Spiekermann, S.: Conceptualizing Context for Pervasive Advertising. In: Müller, J., Alt, F., Michelis, D. (eds.) Pervasive Advertising. Springer (2011)

5. Chevalier, J.A., Mayzlin, D.: The Effect of Word of Mouth on Sales: Online Book Reviews. Journal of Marketing Research (2006)

6. Di Ferdinando, A., Rosi, A., Lent, R., Manzalini, A., Zambonelli, F.: MyAds: A system for adaptive pervasive advertisements. Pervasive and Mobile Computing 5 (2009)

7. Dubach Spiegler, E., Michahelles, F., Hildebrand, C.: Social Networks in Pervasive Advertising and Shopping. In: Müller, J., Alt, F., Michelis, D. (eds.) Pervasive Advertising. Springer (2011)

8. Fitzmaurice, G.M., Laird, N.M., Ware, J.H.: Applied Longitudinal Analysis. Hoboken (2004)

9. Hardy, R., Rukzio, E., Holleis, P., Wagner, M.: Mobile Interaction with Static and Dynamic NFC-based Displays. In: Mobile HCI (2010)

10. Jarrett, K.: Interactivity is Evil! A critical investigation of Web 2.0. First Monday 13 (2008)

11. Kuikkaniemi, K., Giulio, J., Turpeinen, M., Hoggan, E., Müller, J.: From Space to Stage: How Interactive Screens Will Change Urban life. IEEE Computer 44(6), 40–47 (2011)

12. Lampe, C., Ellison, N., Steinfeld, E.: Changes in use and perception of facebook. In: ACM Conference on Computer Supported Cooperative Work (2008)

13. Li, K., Edgecliffe-Johnson, A.: Clear Channel Outdoor Fights Back. Financial Times (2010)

14. McAlexander, J., Schouten, J., Koenig, H.: Building Brand Community. Journal of Marketing 66, 38–54 (2002)

15. McCulloch, C.E., Searle, S.R.: Generalized, Linear, and Mixed Models. John Wiley and Sons (2000)

16. Michelis, D., Send, H.: Engaging Passers-by with Interactive Screens. In: 2nd Workshop on Pervasive Advertising, Lübeck, Germany (2009)

17. Müller, J., Alt, F., Michelis, D.(eds.): Pervasive Advertising. Springer Human–Computer Interaction (September 2011)

18. Müller, J., Exeler, J., Buzeck, M., Krüger, A.: ReflectiveSigns: Digital Signs That Adapt to Audience Attention. In: Tokuda, H., Beigl, M., Friday, A., Brush, A.J.B., Tobe, Y. (eds.) Pervasive 2009. LNCS, vol. 5538, pp. 17–24. Springer, Heidelberg (2009)

19. Nosko, A., Wood, E., Molema, S.: All about me: Disclosure in online social networking profiles: The case of FACEBOOK. Computers in Human Behavior 26(3) (2010)

20. Palmer, A., Koenig-Lewis, N.: An experiential, social network-based approach to direct marketing. Direct Marketing: An International Journal 3(3), 162–176 (2009)

21. Partridge, K., Begole, B.: Activity-based Advertising. In: Müller, J., Alt, F., Michelis, D. (eds.) Pervasive Advertising. Springer (2011)

22. Pinheiro, J., Bates, D.: Mixed-Effects Models in S and S-PLUS. Springer, New York (2000)

23. Pletikosa, I., Michahelles, F.: Understanding Social Media Marketing: A Case Study on Topics, Categories and Sentiment on a Facebook Brand Page. In: 15th MindTrek Conference, Helsinki (2011)

24. Preacher, K.J., Rucker, D.D., Hayes, A.F.: Addressing Moderated Mediation Hypotheses: Theory, Methods, and Prescriptions. Multivariate Behavioral Research 42(1), 185–227 (2007)

25. Quercia, D., Di Lorenzo, G., Calabrese, F., Ratti, C.: Mobile Phones and Outdoor advertising: Measurable advertising. IEEE Pervasive Computing (2011)

26. Ranganathan, A., Campbell, R.: Advertising in a pervasive computing environment. In: 2nd International Workshop on Mobile Commerce, Atlanta, USA, September 28 (2002)
27. Reitberger, W., Meschtscherjakov, A., Mirlacher, T., Tscheligi, M.: Ambient Persuasion in the Shopping Context. In: Müller, J., Alt, F., Michelis, D. (eds.) Pervasive Advertising. Springer (2011)
28. Schau, H., Muñiz, A., Arnould, E.: How Brand Community Practices Create Value. Journal of Marketing 73, 30–51 (2009)
29. Shankar, V., Venkatesh, A., Hofacker, C., Naik, P.: Mobile Marketing in the Retailing Environment: Current Insights and Future Research Avenues. Journal of Interactive Marketing 24(2) (2010)
30. Strohbach, M., Martin, M.: Toward a Platform for Pervasive Display Applications in Retail Environments. IEEE Pervasive Computing 10(2), 19–27 (2011)
31. Tinsley, H., Weiss, D.J.: Interrater reliability and agreement. In: Tinsley, H.E.A., Brown, S.D. (eds.) Handbook of Applied Multivariate Statistics and Mathematical Modeling, pp. 95–124. Academic Press, San Diego (2000)
32. Trusov, M., Bucklin, R.E., Koen, P.: Effects of Word-of-Mouth Versus Traditional Marketing. Journal of Marketing 73(5), 90 (2009)
33. van Waart, P., Mulder, I., de BontMüller, C.: Meaningful Advertising. In: Müller, J., Alt, F., Michelis, D. (eds.) Pervasive Advertising. Springer (2011)
34. Vakratsas, D., Ambler, T.: How Advertising Works: What Do We Really Know? Journal of Marketing 63 (1999)
35. Vargo, S., Lusch, F.: Evolving to a New Dominant Logic for Marketing. Journal of Marketing 68 (2004)
36. Verhoef, P., Reinartz, W., Krafft, M.: Customer Engagement as a New Perspective in Customer Management. Journal of Service Research 13(3), 247–252 (2010)
37. Zhu, F., Zhang, X.: Impact of Online Consumer Reviews on Sales: The Moderating Role of Product and Consumer Characteristics. Journal of Marketing 74 (2010)

Automatic Description of Context-Altering Services through Observational Learning[*]

Katharina Rasch[1], Fei Li[2], Sanjin Sehic[2],
Rassul Ayani[1], and Schahram Dustdar[2]

[1] KTH Royal Institute of Technology
School of Information and Communication Technology
Stockholm, Sweden
{krasch,ayani}@kth.se
[2] Distributed Systems Group,
Vienna University of Technology, Austria
A-1040 Wien, Argentinierstrasse 8/184-1
lastname@infosys.tuwien.ac.at

Abstract. Understanding the effect of pervasive services on user context is critical to many context-aware applications. Detailed descriptions of context-altering services are necessary, and manually adapting them to the local environment is a tedious and error-prone process. We present a method for automatically providing service descriptions by observing and learning from the behavior of a service with respect to its environment. By applying machine learning techniques on the observed behavior, our algorithms produce high quality localized service descriptions. In a series of experiments we show that our approach, which can be easily plugged into existing architectures, facilitates context-awareness without the need for manually added service descriptions.

1 Introduction

Context covers all aspects of the current situation of a user, for example user location, current time, physical properties (e.g. temperature, humidity) or medical data (e.g. heart rate and blood pressure). Often the services offered by pervasive devices are what we call *context-altering*, i.e. executing them changes the user context in some way. For instance, an air conditioner service influences the indoor temperature, and switching on a stereo changes the noise level around the user. In our prototype smart home we found that of the 30 available services, over 90% are context altering.

Context-altering services can be described with a context-dependent precondition and effect. The precondition describes the situations under which the service can be executed; the effect of the service describes the context changes that are typically induced when executing the service. Knowledge of the preconditions and effects of context-altering services allows the system to react to

---

[*] This work is supported by EU FP7 STREP Project SM4ALL (Smart hoMes for ALL), under Grant No. 224332.

J. Kay et al. (Eds.): Pervasive 2012, LNCS 7319, pp. 461–477, 2012.

undesired user situations. For example, the system may use the knowledge of user preferences regarding indoor temperature, humidity et cetera to regulate these properties using the available pervasive devices. This view has been taken up in [10]: based on the current user situation, the system automatically composes and executes the services that are necessary to change the context according to the user requests. In [13] we propose a proactive service discovery approach that continuously recommends the currently most interesting services based on user preferences.

Generally the service descriptions should be as detailed as possible, to allow the system to select the best fitting action in any given situation. However, the service descriptions can not be provided a priori by the device manufacturer, since they are highly dependent on the local environment. For instance, opening a window on a cold day will change the readings of the nearby temperature sensors; however, information about which sensors are nearby is not available to the manufacturer, and may even be situation-dependent. For this reason, service descriptions have to be manually fitted to the environment, such that they reflect the interdependencies between the installed devices and sensors. The descriptions must also be updated whenever new sensors and devices are added to the system. However, the manual description of services is tedious and error-prone, hindering non-expert users to adopt the technology [15]. Having to rely instead on technicians to install new devices is not acceptable for most users.

We propose in this paper a method for automatically learning the capabilities of context-altering services without the need for manual input by users or technicians. The idea is to observe the behavior of the service with respect to its environment. Clustering and classification are then applied to the observed data to find typical patterns of preconditions and effects. The proposed approach produces localized service descriptions that reflect the setup of the environment and support situation-dependent effects. Using our approach, new pervasive devices can simply be plugged into an existing installation without manual configuration. Instead the system will automatically recognize the capabilities of the new services and can use them, for example, in service recommendation and composition.

Our contributions in this paper are threefold: we *(1)* extend a formal model for context and context-altering services [13,16] (Section 2), *(2)* present novel algorithms for automatically learning service capabilities from the service behavior using clustering and classification (Section 3) and *(3)* propose an architecture for integrating capability learning in pervasive systems (Section 4). The capability learning is evaluated in a series of experiments in Section 5. The paper finishes with an inspection of the related work and our conclusions.

2   Preliminaries

Before we can proceed with describing our approach for learning service capabilities, it is first necessary to formalize the notions of context and context-aware services.

Context. In [13,16] we present a context model that formalizes the connection between context and context-altering services. The Hyperspace Analogue to Context (HAC) models context as a multidimensional space, where each dimension denotes a type of context and describes the data type (nominal or numeric) and range of the context information. All dimensions together span the multi-dimensional space of all possible context descriptions. The current context of a user can be described as a point in the context space, for example the context point $c = \langle d_{location} = kitchen, d_{curtains} = closed, d_{temp} = 25 \rangle$ describes that the user is currently in the kitchen where curtains are closed and the temperature is 25 °C. If the user moves to the bedroom, then a context change $\Delta c = \langle d_{location} = bedroom \rangle$ can be observed.

We consider the internal status of a device a part of context, since it plays an intrinsic role for describing the user situation. For example, assume that the user is waking up in the morning in a dark room. The different actions the system can take to move the user into a more comfortable awake situation depend on the internal status of the devices in the room; only if the curtains are closed at the moment, opening them is a viable option for increasing the brightness in the room, otherwise the installed lamps must be used.

Context-Altering Services. The idea of a service with context-dependent preconditions and effects is similar to the world-altering services described in [17]; though since we model the surroundings of a service as context, we prefer the more unassuming term *context-altering* for these services. The precondition of a service can be used to filter out unavailable services – only if the current user context fulfills the condition, then this service is a possible execution choice. The service effect describes how the execution of the service changes the user context, and is important for identifying if a service can change an undesired user situation to a more comfortable one.

This service definition does however not consider that many services in pervasive environments can have situation-dependent side effects. For instance, opening the window if it is cold outside will quite likely decrease the indoor temperature; analogously if it is hot outside, the indoor temperature will increase. Service side effects capture how outside factors, for example seasonal changes, influence service capabilities. Knowledge about service side effects can help identify alternatives for broken or undesired services, e.g. opening the window if it is cool outside could be an energy-efficient alternative to using the air conditioner. Definition 1 extends the previous notion of context-aware services [13] with service side effects.

Definition 1 (Context-altering service). *A context-altering service is situated in HAC and is described with:*

- s^{pre}, *the main precondition of the service; when* $c \in s^{pre}$ *then* s *is a possible execution choice.*
- s^{eff}, *the main effect of the service; executing* s *will change* c *according to* s^{eff}.

- s^{side}, the set of side effects of the service. In $s^{side} = \{(s^{spre_0} \to s^{seff_0}), \ldots, (s^{spre_m} \to s^{seff_m})\}$ each pair $(s^{spre_i} \to s^{seff_i})$ with $0 \leq i \leq m$ describes one side effect of the service. If $c \in s^{pre}$ and $c \in s^{spre_i}$, then executing s will change c according to s^{eff} and s^{seff_i}.

Consider an example service s for opening a window: due to mechanical restrictions, the window can only be opened if the curtains in front of it are also open, and opening the window changes not only the internal status of the device, but may also have effects on the room temperature. Service precondition and effect are straightforward to describe: $s^{pre} = \langle D_{window} = closed, D_{curtain} = open \rangle$ and $s^{eff} = \langle D_{window} = open \rangle$.

Each side effect of a service is paired with an additional precondition that describes the context situation under which the side effect occurs. The actual effect of s is then a combination of the service's main effect and all side effects that can be fulfilled. The window service may have a side effect with $s^{spre_0} = \langle D_{tempIn} = [19 - 22], D_{tempOut} = [22 - 30] \rangle$ and $s^{seff_0} = \langle D_{tempIn} = [22 - 30] \rangle$, describing that opening the window on a warm day will increase the indoor temperature. Several such side effects for varying outdoor temperatures may be described for this service.

The distinction between main preconditions/effects and side effects highlights the importance of the former for service discovery and composition. First main preconditions have to be checked to see whether a service is available in a given situation. Only if this is the case, then side effects can provide useful additional knowledge.

3   Learning Service Capabilities

Knowledge of service capabilities allows a pervasive system to react to undesired context situations by executing or recommending services that can change the context to a more comfortable one. However service capabilities can often not be provided directly by device manufacturers. Only those parts of service preconditions and effects that concern a device's internal status can be described a priori. More expressive capabilities depend on the other devices and sensors installed in the pervasive environment, and are localized in several ways:

Preconditions. Inter-dependencies between several devices, often of mechanical nature. For example, curtain in front of window or small hallway were only one of the adjacent doors can be open at a time.

Effects. Depends on installed sensors. For example, heater or lamp cause changes in nearby temperature and light sensors. Several such sensors may be available, with different readings depending on their distance from the device.

Requiring either a technician or an experienced user whenever a new device is added to the system is simply not practical. Instead we propose to automatically learn capabilities by observing a service's behavior. The observations are collected in the service's execution history, and machine learning techniques are applied to find precondition and effect patterns. The effect of a service can be identified by finding the context changes that commonly occur after its execution. Similarly the preconditions of a service are those conditions under which the service is commonly invoked. We start in the following by describing the service execution history, and how it can be obtained. Afterwards we present three algorithms for learning a service's precondition, effect, and side effects, respectively.

3.1   Service Execution History

Definition 2 formalizes the notion of a service's execution history: for every execution of a service, the context prior to the execution and the observed context change after the execution are recorded.

Definition 2 (Execution history). *The execution history H_s of a service s after k executions of s is a set $H_s = \{(c_0 \to \Delta c_0), \ldots, (c_{k-1} \to \Delta c_{k-1})\}$. In H_s each pair $c_i \to \Delta c_i$ with $0 \leq i < k$ records the current context c_i before the $i{-}th$ execution of s and the context change Δc_i observed after the i-th execution of s.*

The set $H_s^{pre} = \{c_0, \ldots, c_{k-1}\}$ is called the precondition history and the set $H_s^{eff} = \{\Delta c_0, \ldots, \Delta c_{k-1}\}$ the effect history of s. As a simple example consider Table 1, documenting seven executions of a service s for opening window blinds.

The left hand side (a) of the table shows in seven rows the context c_i before each of the executions i. There is no connection between rows, i.e. other services may have been executed and changed c between two executions of s. The context is described using five different dimensions, including numeric and nominal dimensions. It stands out that the window blinds are always closed before the execution of s, whereas all other context dimensions vary. This observation indicates that $d_{blinds} = closed$ is a precondition of opening the blinds.

Table 1. Sample execution history

(a) Context before execution

	Temp	Light out	Blinds	Light in	TV
c_0	22	bright	closed	dark	off
c_1	21	dark	closed	dark	on
c_2	22	dark	closed	bright	off
c_3	20	bright	closed	dark	on
c_4	22	dark	closed	bright	on
c_5	22	bright	closed	dark	off
c_6	22	bright	closed	dark	off

(b) Changes after execution

	Blinds	Light in	TV
Δc_0	open	bright	-
Δc_1	open	-	off
Δc_2	open	-	-
Δc_3	open	bright	-
Δc_4	open	-	-
Δc_5	open	bright	-
Δc_6	open	bright	-

The right hand side (b) of Table 1 shows in corresponding rows the context changes Δc_i observed after the $i{-}th$ execution of s. One clear difference between (a) and (b) is that in the former all five dimensions are used for describing c_i, but in the latter only a subset of dimensions is used for Δc_i and many values are missing. This is because c_i describes the full context of the environment, containing values for each available context dimension. On the contrary, Δc_i contains information only about those dimensions whose value changed after the execution.

In the effect history (b) it stands out again that for each execution a context change is observed on the "Blinds" dimension, indicating that $d_{blinds} = open$ is an effect of opening the blinds. Context changes on the "Light in" dimension are only sometimes observed, hinting that $d_{lightIn} = bright$ could be a possible side effect of s. And indeed, when reviewing the precondition history (a), it can be seen that this effect always occurs if $d_{lightOut} = bright$ and $d_{lightIn} = dark$, i.e. a side effect of s is: if it is dark inside and bright outside, then opening the window blinds will result in it being bright inside. The single change on the "TV" dimension on the other hand must be regarded as an error as long as no further observations occur. Such an observation error can happen, for example, if the TV was turned off at the same time as the blinds were opened and the context change for the TV service was erroneously attributed to the blinds service.

Recording the Execution History. A major challenge with recording the execution history is to determine the optimal time for sampling context changes. The optimal *sampling time* is very much dependent on the context type that is being observed. Turning on a light is typically fast and a change in luminosity can be observed after a few seconds. However it may take 10 minutes or longer until significant temperature differences can be observed after turning on the heating. No a priori information is available about the latency of context changes.

A solution to this problem is to record all context changes after a service execution up to a very long sampling time. However, the longer the sampling time is, the higher is also the probability that other services are executed during this time and that the context changes caused by multiple services are overlapping. The optimal sampling time is thus a trade-off between missing important context changes and observing irrelevant changes. We will show later that our algorithms are strong enough to be able to deal with irrelevant context changes, thereby allowing the use of long sampling times which can avoid the problem of high-latency dimensions.

3.2   Learning Main Effects

The main effects of a service are constituted by those context changes which commonly occur when the service is executed. The changes may not necessarily occur in all service executions, since due to e.g. network errors some changes may be missing from the effect history. Therefore we consider a context change to be part of the main effect of a service, if it occurs in at least $\lfloor \vartheta_e * k \rfloor$ of all k service executions. For instance a ϑ_e of 0.9 ignores occasional missing context changes, while at the same time filtering out any unrelated context changes from simultaneously executed services.

Algorithm 1 for learning service main effects takes as input the effect history and the number of service executions, with a global constant ϑ_e. Starting from an empty service effect, for all dimensions that occur in at least one Δc_i of the history (Line 2-3) do: If d_i is nominal, find the most occurring nominal value v. If v occurs in enough service executions then set dimension i in the main effect to v (Line 4-8). If d_i is numeric, an outlier detection [4] must first be performed to remove all values that deviate markedly from the rest of the values on d_i. Such outlier values can occur if the simultaneous execution of other services also resulted in context changes on d_i. If after outlier removal enough values remain, then set dimension i in the main effect to the interval from the minimum value to the maximum value on d_i (Line 9-14).

Algorithm 1. Learning service main effects

1: **procedure** LEARNMAINEFFECTS(H_s^{eff},k)
2:     $s^{eff} = \langle \rangle$
3:     **for** $\forall d_i \in D(H_s^{eff})$ **do**
4:         **if** d_i is nominal **then**
5:             $v = maxOccur(H_s^{eff}, d_i)$
6:             **if** $count(H_s^{eff}|d_i = v) \geq \lfloor \vartheta_e * k \rfloor$ **then**
7:                 $s_i^{eff} = v$
8:             **end if**
9:         **else**
10:            $H_s'^{eff} = removeOutliers(H_s^{eff}, d_i)$
11:            **if** $count(H_s'^{eff}|d_i\ not\ missing) \geq \lfloor \vartheta_e * k \rfloor$ **then**
12:                $s_i^{eff} = [min(H_s'^{eff}, d_i), max(H_s'^{eff}, d_i)]$
13:            **end if**
14:        **end if**
15:    **end for**
16:    **return** s^{eff}
17: **end procedure**

3.3   Learning Main Preconditions

The main preconditions of a service are those context conditions that commonly hold when the service is executed. Analogously to the main effects, we say that a context point is a precondition of a service, if it holds for at least $\lfloor \vartheta_p * k \rfloor$ of all k service executions. Typically we set also $\vartheta_p = 0.9$. Algorithm 2 for learning preconditions proceeds similarly to learning main effects by looking at all dimensions occurring in the precondition history (Line 3). Nominal dimensions are handled analogously to Algorithm 1 (Line 4-5).

For numeric dimensions an additional step is performed to avoid too wide dimension intervals. Take for example a service for switching on a light which has been executed under varying conditions of the outside temperature $tOut$, such that the found interval is $s_{tOut}^{eff} = [-20, 50]$. This result has little informative value as a service precondition, since it merely describes that the service can be executed under any conditions for $tOut$. As preconditions we instead want specific conditions described by a restricted value interval. Let $min(H^{pre}, d_i)$ be the global minimal value and $max(H^{eff}, d_i)$ the global maximal value on d_i in the precondition histories of any service. Then an interval on d_i is only considered a service precondition if it considerably restricts the dimension according to a parameter τ (Line 7-9). For example if $\tau = 0.5$, then only those intervals are considered that restrict the dimension to maximal half of its global size.

Algorithm 2. Learning service main preconditions

1: **procedure** LEARNMAINPRECONDITIONS(H_s^{pre},k)
2:     $s^{pre} = \langle \rangle$
3:     **for** $\forall d_i \in D(H_s^{pre})$ **do**
4:         **if** d_i is nominal **then**
5:             ▷ proceed analogously to LearnMainEffects
6:         **else**
7:             **if** $\frac{max(H_s^{pre}, d_i) - min(H_s^{pre}, d_i)}{max(H^{pre}, d_i) - min(H^{pre}, d_i)} < \tau$ **then**
8:                 $s_i^{pre} = [min(H_s^{pre}, d_i), max(H_s^{pre}, d_i)]$
9:             **end if**
10:         **end if**
11:     **end for**
12:     **return** s^{pre}
13: **end procedure**

A final post-processing step must be performed after the preconditions of all services have been learned. It may be that the context contains static dimensions, which never or rarely change during the whole execution history, e.g. the internal status of an unused device. These dimensions provide little informative value as preconditions and thus should be excluded. If a dimension is static, then references to it will be contained in the preconditions of a majority of services. Therefore it needs to be checked for each dimension $d_i \in D(H^{pre})$, whether more than φ service preconditions contain the same value or value interval for d_i. If this is the case, then d_i is removed from the preconditions of all services.

3.4   Learning Side Effects

Side effects of a service are any additional precondition and effect pairs that can be found in the execution history. For the blinds service in Table 1, one could, for example, see the pair "If $d_{lightOut} = bright \wedge d_{lightIn} = dark$, then $d_{lightIn} = bright$". To be considered a side effect, a precondition and effect pair should be contained in at least $\lfloor \vartheta_s * k \rfloor$ and at most $\lfloor \vartheta_e * k \rfloor$ executions. Setting ϑ_s to a very small value increases the risk that context changes from parallel service executions are found to be side effects. A high ϑ_s on the other hand means that very rare side effects can not be found. For discovery and composition the correctness of service descriptions is essential, therefore we typically set $\vartheta_s = 0.1$, i.e. only side effects occurring in at least 10% of service executions are considered.

As a preprocessing step it is necessary to remove from the history those dimensions which were already used in main preconditions and effects respectively or were found to be static. For preconditions, if $s_0^{pre} = v_1$, then there can be no side effect precondition $s_0^{spre} = v_2$, since side effects only occur if s^{pre} and s^{spre} hold at the same time, which is not possible in this case. Therefore for the precondition history $H_s'^{pre} = H_s^{pre} - D(s^{pre}) - D_{static}$. Analogously for the effect history $H_s'^{eff} = H_s^{eff} - D(s^{eff})$. Additionally, numerical dimensions are discretized to improve the quality of the learning result.

Finding Candidate Effects. It is much easier to find re-occurring patterns in the effect history than in the precondition history, since the former typically contains less data dimension. A pattern can also be called a cluster, denoted as a pair (D, O), where D is the set of dimensions and O the set of indexes of the objects forming this cluster. For the example data in Table 1b, a cluster would be found with $D = \{d_{lightIn}\}$ and $O = \{0, 3, 5, 6\}$. The minimum number of objects in such a cluster must be $minSupport = \lfloor \vartheta_s * k \rfloor$ for a service with k executions. For finding clusters we apply the DBSCAN clustering algorithm [6] and obtain a set of candidate effect clusters A_s, which will be the input to the next step.

Finding Matching Preconditions. Candidate clusters found do not necessarily describe actual service side effects. It can also happen that artificial clusters are found, which contain noise objects from simultaneous service executions, such as the TV effect seen in one execution of the example blind service. We consider a candidate cluster to describe a service side effect if a precondition can be found such that: if and only if the precondition is fulfilled, the side effect happens.

This requirement is very similar to the classification rules found by classification algorithms. Classification is a supervised data mining technique which is applied to an already classified set of training data to find rules for classifying unclassified data. By setting for each c_i in $H_s'^{pre}$ an additional class to indicate whether the item i is contained in the candidate cluster $a \in A_s$ or not, we can apply classification learning to $H_s'^{pre}$ in order to find any rules (i.e. preconditions) for this class (i.e. effect).

Algorithm 3 for side effects learning takes as input the precondition and the effect history of a service, with the main precondition and effect dimensions already removed, plus the number of service executions. In Line 3 effect clustering using DBSCAN is performed, producing a list of candidate clusters. For each of those candidate clusters each item c_i in the precondition history is annotated with a class `cluster` if i is contained in the cluster and a class `nocluster+i` otherwise (Line 5-9). A different class for each non-cluster item is used, since we want to avoid finding rules for $class = $ `nocluster`.

We have found that the PART classification rule learner [7] achieves good results on our context data. The result of running PART on the annotated $H_s'^{pre}$

Algorithm 3. Learning service side effects

```
 1: procedure LEARNSIDEEFFECTS(H_s'^{pre}, H_s'^{eff}, k)
 2:     s^{side} = ∅
 3:     A = cluster(H'^{eff}, ⌊ϑ_s * k⌋)
 4:     for ∀a = (D, O) ∈ A do
 5:         for ∀c_i ∈ H'^{pre} do
 6:             if  i ∈ O then classes[i] = cluster
 7:             else classes[i] = nocluster+i
 8:             end if
 9:         end for
10:         r = best(PART(H'^{pre}, classes) | r.class = cluster)
11:         if  (r.correct)/(r.correct+r.incorrect) > β then
12:             s^{side} = s^{side} ∪ (toScope(r) → toScope(a))
13:         end if
14:     end for
15:     return s^{side}
16: end procedure
```

---

is a set of rules where each rule r is described by its condition, class and accuracy in terms of correct and incorrect classifications. We are only interested in the one rule r with $r.class =$ cluster with the highest number of correct classifications (Line 10). If this rule also has a low number of incorrect classifications according to a parameter β, then we can consider the pair $(r \rightarrow a)$ a side effect of the service (Line 11). Typically we set $\beta = 0.9$.

In Line 12 a function *toScope* is called, which converts rules and clusters to context scopes. For converting a cluster starting from an empty scope s^{seff} do for each dimension $d_i \in D$: if d_i is nominal, find the cluster value v that all items contained in the cluster take on d_i and set $s_i^{seff} = v$. If d_i is numeric, find the minimum value v_{min} and the maximum value v_{max} for all cluster items on d_i and set $s_i^{seff} = [v_{min}, v_{max}]$. Rules consist of a conjunction of $d_i = v$ (for nominal d_i) and $d_i = [v_{min}, v_{max}]$ (for numeric d_i), so converting a rule to a s^{spre} is straightforward.

4   System Architecture

We have implemented capability learning for the use in a smart home prototype. The software architecture of the smart home was deployed during the SM4All project [5]. Only the introduction of a dedicated *Capability learning* component and small changes in the user interface were needed to add automatic service capability learning to the existing pervasive architecture, as shown in Figure 1.

The pervasive environment, depicted in the lower part of the figure, contains the devices and sensors using Universal plug and play (UPnP [9]) and Konnex (KNX [1]) technologies. In order to be usable for our approach, devices and sensors must make their internal status and sensed data available to the system. UPnP directly fulfills this requirement; a device's internal status and sensed data

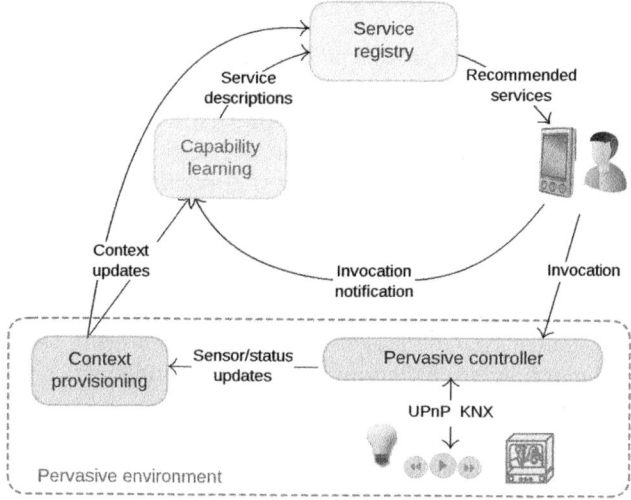

Fig. 1. System architecture

is published using the GENA (General Event Notification Architecture) framework. KNX on the other hand provides only the communication infrastructure to send control signals to devices and does not fulfill any of the requirements. To enable the use of KNX devices in the smart home, the *Pervasive controller* maintains and publishes the status of all installed KNX devices.

Context information from the various sources is collected and processed by the *Context provisioning* component. It is realized using the COPAL (COntext Provisioning for ALl) framework [14], a complex context processing system which produces formatted context events. The context information is used by the *Service Registry* to automatically generate service recommendations based on the current user context and preferences. In the original setup, the *Service registry* uses manually defined service descriptions for generating recommendations.

We have added the *Capability capturing* component, which implements the learning approach presented in this paper. The component is informed by the user client about which services were executed and listens to context change events to build the execution histories of the installed services. It then performs the capability learning, and sends any found service description to the *Service registry*, which can than be used for service recommendation.

5   Experiments and Results

This section reports the results of number of experiments which we carried out in the prototype smart home and through simulation using synthetic data.

5.1   Experiments in the Smart Home Prototype

Experimental Setup. The prototype is owned by Fondazione Santa Lucia[1] and is situated in Rome, Italy. The two bedroom flat is equipped with 13 pervasive devices and 7 sensors. The prototype is aimed mainly at users with physical disabilities, resulting in a strong focus on services for home control. Services are available for controlling doors, windows, curtains, lamps, an automatic bed and media devices. We found that of the 30 installed services, 28 are context-altering. Only two software services used for gathering input from the user are information-providing services [17]. The latency of context changes differs greatly between the devices. Turning on one of the lamps is fast, with a reaction time of about 30 milliseconds. In contrast, when raising or lowering the bed it takes 21 seconds until the action is finished and the device publishes an updated internal status.

Since the prototype is built into a research facility without any access to the outside world, it was not possible to observe any side effects from outside factors such as day/night changes. Most of the services have thus rather simple capabilities referencing only one dimension. Only two service preconditions make use of more than one dimension: the window curtain in the living room can only be closed if the window is closed, and vice versa the window can only be opened if the curtain is open.

For the experiment we set the sampling time to 25 seconds, to ensure that even the context changes from the slowest device were observed and used for capability learning. The parameters of the learning algorithms were set as follows: $\vartheta_e = 0.9$, $\vartheta_p = 0.9$, $\vartheta_s = 0.1$, $\tau = 0.5$, $\varphi = 0.3$, $\beta = 0.9$.

Metrics. In order to check the correctness of the learned capabilities, we first manually described all services, and compared the automatically learned descriptions with the manually provided ones. The number of executions that are necessary until the capabilities are learned correctly serves as a metric for evaluating how quickly the system learns.

Results. We started executing services in the home sequentially, i.e. with at least 25 seconds between each service execution. We found that under these circumstances the system learns the correct service capabilities with on average about 13 executions per service. Using these automatically generated descriptions, service recommendation worked just as well as with manually provided service descriptions. Due to a limited access to the prototype and the time-consuming nature of the experiments, we were only able to run this first experiment in the physical smart home. For further evaluating the system, we ran the following experiments in a simulation, using the same setup as the actual prototype, including devices, sensors and device latencies.

In real-world scenarios it is quite unrealistic that all services are executed sequentially. In order to evaluate how the learning approaches can deal with

---

[1] http://www.hsantalucia.it/

overlapping executions of several services, we gradually decreased the average time between service executions.

The services were executed in a random fashion, and each experiment was run for 10 replications. Table 2 lists the learning results for execution intervals ranging from 30 seconds (i.e sequential execution) to 1 second. In the latter case, 24 other services are executed during the sampling time of one service, creating heavily overlapping context changes. The number of necessary executions until the system correctly learns the capabilities are very stable for the 30, 10 and 5 seconds execution intervals. Only for the somewhat unrealistic case of the user continuously executing a service every second, does the number of necessary execution increase slightly.

Table 2. Number of necessary executions in prototype system

Average time between executions (in s)	30	10	5	1
Average necessary executions per service	13.1	13.8	14.4	20.8
(Standard deviation)	1.8	2.0	1.5	3.5
Worst case necessary executions	21	25	26.2	47.9

Table 2 also lists the worst case of necessary executions until the system correctly learns the capabilities. In these cases typically the effect was learned correctly, however the preconditions were temporarily too strict, e.g. the precondition for switching on the bedroom lamp correctly referenced the status of the lamp, but also required that the TV should be off. This behavior can be avoided by increasing the minimum support necessary for starting the learning process. The higher the minimum support, the longer it takes until all service descriptions are learned. With a lower minimum support, service descriptions are learned faster but may, in rare cases, be temporarily too strict. This system parameter can be easily tweaked by the user to achieve a preferred behavior.

5.2   Experiments Using Synthetic Data

Experimental Setup. The aim of the following experiments is to evaluate capability learning in a pervasive environment with a higher number of services and dimensions, plus more complicated preconditions, effects and side effects, as compared to the smaller-scale prototype system. The simulation environment creates to this end 70 dimensions in a mix of 50% nominal and 50% numeric dimensions. The dimension latencies are Gaussian distributed, with $\mu = \sigma^2 = 1$, i.e. most dimension values change between 1 or 2 seconds after service execution. 50 different services are created, each having main preconditions and effects, plus up to two two side effects. For creating a service effect, first up to three dimensions are randomly drawn from the set of all generated context dimensions, and a random value or value interval is selected for each of them and set as a service effect. Generation of main precondition as well as side effects and their preconditions is performed analogously.

The execution of services is simulated, with the time between two service executions drawn from an exponential distribution with $\mu = executionInterval$. All context changes up to the preset *samplingTime* are recorded. The same parameters as in the prototype experiments were used for the learning algorithms. All of the experiments were performed on a desktop PC with an Intel Core 2 Duo CPU with 3 GHz and 4 GB RAM running Linux, and were run for 25 replications.

Metrics. The results of capability learning and the actual service capabilities are compared using the standard metrics of precision, recall and F1-score. Recall measures which percentage of the service capabilities of interest were found by the learning algorithm. Precision measures which percentage of the learned service capabilities of interest are actual capabilities. The F1-score is the harmonic mean of precision and recall, i.e. $F1 = 2 * (precision * recall)/(precision + recall)$.

Results. The first experiment tests, how well the capability learning algorithm works depending on the number of executions per service. To test the algorithm without any simultaneous service executions, we set $samplingTime = 10$ and $executionInterval = 20$.

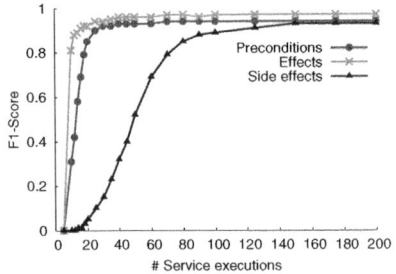 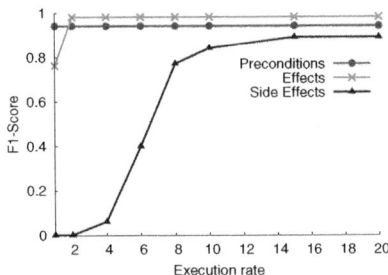

Fig. 2. Accuracy vs execution number   **Fig. 3.** Accuracy vs execution rate

It can be seen in Figure 2 that main preconditions and effects of a service stabilize very quickly with very high accuracy; after 25 executions of each service both precondition and effect learning achieve $F1 > 0.95$ (with 0.01 standard deviation). The learning of service effects stabilized slightly faster, which is not surprising since only a few context dimensions have to be mined, compared to all 70 dimensions for learning preconditions. The accuracy of side effects stabilizes much slower, since they only occur for some service executions, so more executions are necessary before side effects can be reliably mined. The accuracy strongly increases between 20 and 80 executions per service and stabilizes to $F1 > 0.9$ at around 125 executions (with 0.02 standard deviation).

Next we stress tested the algorithm with overlapping service executions. We set the number of executions per service to 100, keep $samplingTime = 10$ and vary the *executionInterval*. For example for *executionInterval* = 1, service executions will happen on average every second, so for each of its executions a service will sample the context changes induced by itself and 9 other services. It can be seen in Figure 3 that the results for main preconditions and effects are very stable even for small execution intervals. The side effect accuracy is stable for two parallel service executions, but degrades for small execution intervals because context changes from overlapping executions are identified as side effects.

Finally we evaluated how well the algorithm can deal with a wide spread of dimension latencies by using a *samplingTime* = 50 and gradually increasing the variance of the generated latencies $1 \leq \sigma^2 \leq 40$. We found that the accuracy of the service capabilities is stable over the whole range of dimension latencies. In terms of algorithm runtime we found that capabilities can be learned in less than 2 seconds per service, for *executionInterval* = 1 and 100 executions per service.

The experimental results show that our approach is able to reliably and quickly learn service main preconditions and effects even under very stressed conditions. Side effect learning is most reliable under normal, more relaxed conditions where individual services are executed mostly sequentially.

6   Related Work

Compared to the number of proposed service description and annotation languages, research on automatic or semi-automatic service annotation is sparse. Patil et al. were among the first to point out the problems of manual annotation [15]. They present the METEOR-S web service annotation framework, which graphically assists the user in annotating web service descriptions. METEOR-S uses linguistic and structural matching between a service's functional description and candidate ontologies to identify the most fitting concepts for describing a service semantically and suggests them to the user during the annotation process. ASSAM is a similar tool by Heß et al., with the difference that ASSAM employs machine-learning techniques to identify fitting concepts by learning from already annotated services [8].

Bowers et al. exploit the additional knowledge contained in scientific workflows for annotation purposes [2]. Scientific workflow systems aim to integrate pre-processing of data, statistical, or data mining processes on the data and post-processing and visualization of the results. An actor in such a workflow is any component (e.g. shell script, web service) that performs work on the data. Actors are annotated with information about the process they perform for facilitating automatic composition of such workflows. Bowers et al. propose to automatically infer missing annotations based on the connections between actors, e.g. if it is known that an actor produces descriptions of genes, then it can be inferred that any other actor that takes the descriptions as input performs work on such descriptions. A similar approach is taken in [11] for finding annotations for inputs and outputs of web services in a service workflow.

A number of works propose to execute services in order to learn about their functionalities. Lerman at al. use machine learning techniques to identify potential input data types for a service [12] and validate them by executing the service with sample data and observing whether the output is satisfying or erroneous. Carman at al. aim to find out how the functionality of a service can be described in terms of other, already annotated services [3]. The target service and varying combinations of existing services are executed using the same input data, and the similarity of the output data is checked until a satisfying combination is found.

Our work distinguishes itself substantially from the described approaches. Previous works concentrate on finding descriptions for service category and input and output data types. As far as we know, no work has been published concerning the automatic description of context-altering services, which are common in pervasive environments. Additionally, all other approaches rely on specific information which may itself be hard to provide; typically either high-quality functional service descriptions and ontologies or partially annotated services and workflows are needed. In contrast, our approach relies solely on observing the environment. Only the data published by devices and sensors is needed, which is a functionality already built into popular technologies such as UPnP.

7   Conclusions and Future Work

In this paper we have presented a novel solution for automatically describing context-altering services through observational learning. Based on a formal model of context called HAC we have described a set of algorithms for learning service capabilities by mining on a service's past behavior. We have shown how service capability learning can be added to existing pervasive architectures. Experimental results, both in a smart home system and using simulation, demonstrate that our algorithms are able to reliably and efficiently identify service capabilities under varying conditions. Our approach is therefore a step towards plug and play context-awareness in pervasive environments.

In the future we want to extend our approach with more complicated relations between preconditions and effect that are currently not supported by our model, such as for example "If it is cooler outside than inside, then opening the window will make it cooler inside". It would also be interesting to study how service parameters, e.g. the setting of the air conditioner, influence service capabilities.

References

1. KNX standard (Version 1.1). Konnex Association Brussels (2004)
2. Bowers, S., Ludäscher, B.: Towards Automatic Generation of Semantic Types in Scientific Workflows. In: Dean, M., Guo, Y., Jun, W., Kaschek, R., Krishnaswamy, S., Pan, Z., Sheng, Q.Z. (eds.) WISE 2005 Workshops. LNCS, vol. 3807, pp. 207–216. Springer, Heidelberg (2005)
3. Carman, M.J., Knoblock, C.A.: Learning semantic descriptions of web information sources. In: Proceedings of the 20th International Joint Conference on Artifical Intelligence, pp. 2695–2700. Morgan Kaufmann Publishers Inc., San Francisco (2007)
4. Chandola, V., Banerjee, A., Kumar, V.: Anomaly detection: A survey. ACM Comput. Surv. 41, 15:1–15:58 (2009)

5. Ciccio, C.D., Mecella, M., Caruso, M., Forte, V., Iacomussi, E., Rasch, K., Querzoni, L., Santucci, G., Tino, G.: The homes of tomorrow: service composition and advanced user interfaces. ICST Transactions on Ambient Systems 11(10-12) (2011)

6. Ester, M., Kriegel, H.P., Sander, J., Xu, X.: A density-based algorithm for discovering clusters in large spatial databases with noise. In: Proceedings of the 2nd International Conference on Knowledge Discovery and Data Mining, pp. 226–231. AAAI Press (1996)

7. Frank, E., Witten, I.H.: Generating accurate rule sets without global optimization. In: Proceedings of the Fifteenth International Conference on Machine Learning, pp. 144–151. Morgan Kaufmann Publishers Inc., San Francisco (1998)

8. Heß, A., Johnston, E., Kushmerick, N.: ASSAM: A Tool for Semi-automatically Annotating Semantic Web Services. In: McIlraith, S.A., Plexousakis, D., van Harmelen, F. (eds.) ISWC 2004. LNCS, vol. 3298, pp. 320–334. Springer, Heidelberg (2004)

9. ISO 29341-1:2008: Part 1: UPnP Device Architecture Version 1.0. International Organization for Standardization, Geneva, Switzerland

10. Kaldeli, E., Warriach, E.U., Bresser, J., Lazovik, A., Aiello, M.: Interoperation, composition and simulation of services at home. In: Eigth International Conference on Service Oriented Computing, pp. 167–181 (2010)

11. Khalid, B., Embury, S.M., Paton, N.W., Stevens, R., Goble, C.A.: Automatic annotation of web services based on workflow definitions. ACM Trans. Web 2, 11:1–11:34 (2008)

12. Lerman, K., Plangprasopchok, A., Knoblock, C.A.: Automatically labeling the inputs and outputs of web services. In: Proceedings of the 21st National Conference on Artificial Intelligence, vol. 2, pp. 1363–1368. AAAI Press (2006)

13. Li, F., Rasch, K., Truong, H.L., Ayani, R., Dustdar, S.: Proactive service discovery in pervasive environments. In: Proceedings of the 7th International Conference on Pervasive Services, pp. 126–133 (2010)

14. Li, F., Sehic, S., Dustdar, S.: Copal: An adaptive approach to context provisioning. In: 2010 IEEE 6th International Conference on Wireless and Mobile Computing, Networking and Communications (WiMob), pp. 286–293 (2010)

15. Patil, A.A., Oundhakar, S.A., Sheth, A.P., Verma, K.: METEOR-S web service annotation framework. In: Proceedings of the 13th International Conference on World Wide Web, WWW 2004, pp. 553–562. ACM, New York (2004)

16. Rasch, K., Li, F., Sehic, S., Ayani, R., Dustdar, S.: Context-driven personalized service discovery in pervasive environments. World Wide Web 14(4), 295–319 (2011)

17. Wu, D., Parsia, B., Sirin, E., Hendler, J., Nau, D.: Automating DAML-S Web Services Composition Using SHOP2. In: Fensel, D., Sycara, K., Mylopoulos, J. (eds.) ISWC 2003. LNCS, vol. 2870, pp. 195–210. Springer, Heidelberg (2003)

Author Index